SERIES EDITORS
Stewart R. Clegg &
Ralph Stablein

Editors
Nathalie Drouin
Ralf Müller
Shankar Sankaran

Novel Approaches to Organizational Project Management Research

Translational and Transformational

ADVANCES IN ORGANIZATION STUDIES

Copenhagen Business School Press
Universitetsforlaget

Novel Approaches to Organizational Project Management Research
Translational and Transformational

Editorial Matter & Selection © Nathalie Drouin, Ralf Müller, Shankar Sankaran & Copenhagen Business School Press, 2013
Individual Chapters © Individual Contributors & Copenhagen Business School Press, 2013

ISBN 978-82-15-02239-0 (Norway)
ISBN 978-87-630-0249-3 (Rest of the world)

ISSN 1566-1075

Series Editors: Stewart R. Clegg & Ralph Stablein
Typeset: Narayana Press
Cover design by Klahr | Graphic Design
Printed in Denmark by Narayana Press, Gylling

Distribution:
Scandinavia except for Norway
DBK Logistic Services, Mimersvej 4
DK-4600 Koege, Denmark
Tel: +45 3269 7788, fax: +45 3269 7789
Email: cbspress@cbs.dk, www.cbspress.dk

Norway
Universitetsforlaget AS
Postboks 508
NO-0105 Oslo, Norway
Tel: +47 2414 7500, fax: +47 2414 7501
Email: post@universitetsforlaget.no, www.universitetsforlaget.no

North America
International Specialized Book Services
920 NE 58th Ave., Suite 300
Portland, OR 97213, USA
Tel: +1 800 944 6190, fax: -1 503 280 8832
Email: isbs@isbs.com, www.isbs.com

Rest of the World
Gazelle Book Services,
White Cross Mills, Hightown,
Lancaster, Lancashire, LA1 4XS,
United Kingdom
Tel: +44 (0) 1524 68765, fax: +44 (0) 1524 63232
Email: sales@gazellebooks.co.uk, www.gazellebookservices.co.uk

Advances in Organization Studies

Series Editors

Stewart R. Clegg
Professor, University of Technology, Sydney, Australia

Ralph Stablein
Professor, University of Otago, New Zealand

The series *Advances in Organization Studies* is a channel for cutting edge theoretical and empirical works of high quality that contributes to the field of organizational studies. The series welcomes thought-provoking ideas, new perspectives and neglected topics from researchers within a wide range of disciplines and geographical locations.

www.organizationstudies.org

Dedicated to our children

Estelle D. Bourgeois and Albert D. Bourgeois
Jonas Müller
Charu Shankar and Ganesh Shankar

–Nathalie Drouin
–Ralf Müller
–Shankar Sankaran

Table of Contents

Our Thanks 8

Notes on the Contributors 9

Foreword 17
    Stewart Clegg

Introduction 19
    Ralf Müller, Shankar Sankaran and Nathalie Drouin

SECTION 1 31
Philosophical Underpinnings of OPM Research
    Ralf Müller, Shankar Sankaran and Nathalie Drouin

Chapter 1 33
Paradigms and Perspectives in Organizational Project Management
Research: Implications for Knowledge-Creation
    Robert Chia

Chapter 2 56
"A" Discourse on the Non-method
    Christophe Bredillet

Chapter 3 95
Thinking in Slow Motion about Project Management
    Jonathan Whitty

Chapter 4 117
Pluralistic and Processual Understandings of Projects and Project
Organizing: Towards Theories of Project Temporality
    Jonas Söderlund

Chapter 5 136
A Model of the Dynamics in Theory Development

Ralf Müller and Jingting Shao

SECTION 2 162
Creative and Innovative Contemporary Approaches

Shankar Sankaran, Ralf Müller and Nathalie Drouin

Chapter 6 164
Actor-Network Theory, Activity Theory and Action Research and their Application in Project Management Research

Michael Er, Julien Pollack and Shankar Sankaran

Chapter 7 199
Simulations for Project Management Research

Elyssebeth Leigh

Chapter 8 220
System Dynamics for Project Management Research

Kim van Oorschot

Chapter 9 237
The Design of Research Programs: Example from a PMO Research Program

Monique Aubry

SECTION 3 266
Learning Across Disciplines

Nathalie Drouin, Ralf Müller and Shankar Sankaran

Chapter 10 268
Power and Politics in Construction Projects

Stewart Clegg and Kristian Kreiner

Chapter 11 294
Application of Behavioural Science and Cognitive Mapping in Project Management Research

Hemanta Doloi

Chapter 12 320
A Natural Sciences Comparative to Develop New Insights for Project Management Research: Genotyping and Phenotyping

Robert Joslin and Ralf Müller

Chapter 13 348
Translational Approaches: Applying Strategic Management Theories to OPM Research

Catherine P. Killen, Kam Jugdev, Nathalie Drouin and Yvan Petit

SECTION 4 381
Upcoming Approaches in OPM Research

Nathalie Drouin, Ralf Müller and Shankar Sankaran

Chapter 14 383
Mixed Methods Research Design: Well Beyond the Notion of Triangulation

Roslyn Cameron and Shankar Sankaran

Chapter 15 402
The Triple Helix of Project Management Research: Theory Development, Qualitative Understanding and Quantitative Corroboration

Serghei Floricel, Marc Banik and Sorin Piperca

Chapter 16 430
Project, Project Theories, and Project Research: A New Understanding of Theory, Practice, and Education for Project Management

Pierre-Luc Lalonde and Mario Bourgault

Chapter 17 452
Pluralist Project Research: Drawing on Critical Systems Thinking to Manage Research Across Paradigms

Julien Pollack

Conclusion 472
Nathalie Drouin, Ralf Müller and Shankar Sankaran

Our Thanks

A book with more than twenty authors from across the world could not have been put together in a year's time without prompt and timely assistance from several people who provided excellent support to the editors throughout this effort.

We start with Professor Stewart Clegg, who agreed to have this book included in the Advances in Organization Studies published by Copenhagen Business School Press soon after we sounded him out about our idea a year ago.

We would like to thank Associate Professor Jens Aaris Thisted, Peer Review Co-ordinator of CBS Press, for agreeing to take on the book during our meeting with him at the EGOS Conference in Helsinki in July 2012 and for his considered advice on the chapters sent for his review.

The energy and enthusiasm embedded in the 'smilies' that Hanne Thorninger Ipsen, Manuscript Editor of CBS Press, sent us through her emails kept us going. She really kept the ball rolling once the chapters had been accepted to take it to the finishing line.

We would like to thank Claire Annals who patiently copyedited the book.
The team at CBS Press has worked hard to get this book out on schedule as we were determined to release it at the 11th IRNOP (The International Research Network on Organizing by Projects) conference in Oslo, Norway.

The editors would like to thank Dr. Gita Sankaran, who helped us when we wanted an experienced proofreader and copyeditor to review what we had written to support the chapters.

We would like to express our gratitude to the prominent scholars from around the world who have endorsed this book.

Last but not the least, we would like to thank all the authors for also helping us by taking prompt action when we asked them to do so and sending us encouraging messages from time to time.

Notes on the Contributors

Monique Aubry, PhD, is a Professor and Director of Project Management Programs at the School of Management, Université du Québec à Montréal (ESG UQAM). Her principal research interest bears on organizing for projects and organizational design, more specifically on Project Management Offices (PMO). She received the 2012 IPMA Research Award for her research on PMOs along with Brian Hobbs and Ralf Müller. The results of her work have been published in major project academic journals and presented at several international conferences, both research and professional. She is a member of the Project Management Research Chair (www.pmchair.uqam.ca) at ESG UQAM. She is member of the Standards Member Advisory Group and the Research Informed Standards Steering committee of the Project Management Institute. She is department editor of *Organizational Side of Project Management and Management of Organizational Projects* for Project Management Journal.

Marc Banik, PhD (Urbana-Champaign), is a Professor of Bio-Industry Management at the École des sciences de la gestion at the Université du Québec à Montréal (ESG UQAM). His teaching and research focus on intellectual property management, R&D management and regulation of health care products. He is a member of the Centre interuniversitaire de recherche sur la science et la technologie (CIRST) at UQAM and teaches principles of management and technology transfer.

Mario Bourgault, PhD, PMP, is a full Professor at École Polytechnique, Montreal, Canada. He has conducted over a decade of research in the field of innovation and project management. Mario has held the Canada Research Chair in Technology Project Management since 2004. He also heads the École Polytechnique Graduate Program in Project Management. His work has been published in a number of journals, including *Project Management Journal, International Journal of Project Management, R&D Management*, and *International Journal of Managing Projects in Business*. In addition to his academic credentials, Mario spent several years in the field working as a professional engineer, and he maintains close ties with the industry by participating in various research projects and acting as an expert consultant.

Christophe Bredillet, PhD (ESC Lille), is a Professor and the Director of the Queensland University of Technology, Australia's Project Management Academy and specializes in the fields of Portfolio, Programme & Project Management (P3M). From 1992 to 2010, Christophe was the Dean of Postgraduate Programmes & Studies, and Professor, Head of School 'Strategic Management & P3M' at ESC Lille. In 2001 he launched a series of International 3PM Weeks hosted by ESC Lille, followed by the first EDEN doctoral seminar in Project Management in 2008. Christophe's main interests and research activities are in the field of Philosophy of Science and Practice in P3M, including principles and theories of P3M, dynamics of evolution of the P3M field, bodies of knowledge, standards, observation of P3M practices and their link with Governance and Performance at organizational, team and individual levels. Christophe was the Executive Editor of the *Project Management Journal* from 2004 to 2012.

Roslyn Cameron, PhD, FAHRI, is a Senior Lecturer and Head of Discipline of Human Resource Management at the School of Business and Law at Central Queensland University, Australia. She is Co-Convenor of the Mixed Methods Research Special Interest Group of the Australian and New Zealand Academy of Management (ANZAM) and a founding Board member of the Prior Learning International Research Centre (PLIRC). Her areas of research interest include skilled migration, workforce development, labour mobility, vocational education and training (VET), recognition of prior learning (RPL) and mixed-methods research. She has received over $1.09 million (AUD) of research funding and has over 70 publications. She has worked on a series of workforce development projects for the Australian rail industry including: Skilled migration; attraction and image; skills recognition and coaching and mentoring. She has contributed chapters to edited books in relation to the use of mixed methods in DBA theses, VET, career development, management disciplines and skills recognition.

Robert Chia, PhD (Lancaster), is Research Professor of Management at the Adam Smith Business School, University of Glasgow. He has authored/edited five books including *Strategy without Design* and *Philosophy and Organization Theory* and published extensively in the top international management journals including the *Academy of Management Journal, Organization Science, Organization Studies, Human Relations, Journal of Management Studies, British Journal of Management, Journal of Management Inquiry* and *Long Range Planning*. His research interests include: The application of process thinking to human actions, decisions and organization; the logic of practice in strategy-making; east-west philosophies/wisdom and their implications for the conduct of business; and the purpose of management education in relation to the university/ industry nexus. Prior to entering academia Robert worked for 16 years in Aircraft Maintenance Engineering and held senior positions in Manufacturing Management and Human Resource Management.

Stewart Clegg, PhD (Bradford), BSc Hons (Aston), is Professor and Research Director of CMOS (Centre for Management and Organisation Studies) at the University of Technology Sydney, Australia. He is one of the most published and cited authors in the top-tier journals in the Organization Studies field. Because the central focus of his theoretical work has always been on power relations he has been able to write on many diverse and ubiquitous topics – because power relations are everywhere!

He is the principal author of two textbooks: *Management & Organizations: An Introduction to Theory and Practice* and *Strategy: Theory and Practice*. He is the chief editor of the *Handbook of Organization Studies, Handbook of Power* and *Handbook of Macro-Organizational Behaviour*. His latest publications are *The Virtues of Leadership: Contemporary Challenges for Global Managers* as principal author and a set of 'Major Works' on *Power and Organizations and Political Power and Organizations'*, jointly edited with Mark Haugaard.

Hemanta Doloi, PhD, is a Senior Lecturer specializing in the Construction Management program at the University of Melbourne, Australia. Hemanta's major research interest is on Life Cycle Project Management and this new methodology has been extended significantly based on the concepts such as process modeling, strategic project management and decision theory over the last few years. He has published over 100 scholarly articles in both international journals and conferences. Hemanta is a sole author of the book *Life Cycle Project Management – A Systems-based Approach to Managing Complex Projects* published in 2008. In 2012 Hemanta was awarded the 'Infinite Value Award in Research and Teaching' by the Australian Institute of Quantity Surveyors (AIQS) and he is widely consulted in the corporate world.

Nathalie Drouin, PhD (Cambridge), MBA (HEC-Montréal), LL.B., is the Associate Dean in Research and former Director of Graduate programs in Project Management, School of Management at Université du Québec à Montreal (ESG UQAM) and a full professor, Department of Management and Technology, ESG UQAM. She teaches initiation and strategic management of projects in the Graduate Project Management Programs. The results of her work have been published in major academic journals and presented at several international conferences, both research and professional. Her research has also been funded by the Social Sciences and Humanities Research Council of Canada (SSHRC), the Canadian Institute of Health Research (CIHR), the Quebec Research Council (FRSQ), and other sources such as the Project Management Institute and ESG-UQAM Research Grants (PAFARC). She is an associate researcher of the Canada Research Chair on Technology Project Management and a Member of the Scientific Committee of the Project Management Research Chair, ESG UQAM.

Michael Er, Dr, PhD Masters Inf.Tech Bachelor Building, studied construction management as an undergraduate and on completion worked professionally for over a decade across a variety of construction roles such as project manager and project supervisor. The interpretive case studies developed as part of the PhD research used Activity Theory as a lens of interpretation. Michael has several publications associated with the application of Activity Theory in research. He is currently a Senior Lecturer at the University of Technology Sydney, Australia in the Faculty of Design Architecture and Building. He continues to research in the area of construction and project management particularly in the field of innovation and technology adoption. Michael maintains strong industry contact which provides a platform for the application of his ongoing research.

Serghei Floricel, PhD, MBA, B. Eng., is a Professor at the University of Quebec in Montreal, where he teaches project feasibility and innovation project management. His research focuses on planning and organizing complex projects, and on innovation processes. He has published, among others, in *International Journal of Project Management, R&D Management, Research-Technology Management, International Journal of Innovation Management,* and has presented at numerous conferences, including Academy of Management. He is lead author of two monographs published by the PMI: *Increasing Project Flexibility* and *Refining the Knowledge Production Plan,* and co-author of *The Strategic Management of Large Engineering Projects* (MIT Press, 2001). He was Research Director for the Managing Innovation in the New Economy (MINE) program, and Principal Investigator for five other research projects. He has produced a website on managing innovation projects (www.gpi.uqam.ca) and co-developed a tool for assessing the risks of such projects.

Robert Joslin, BSc (Durham), PMP, PgMP, CEng, MIEEE, MBCS, is a project/program management consultant and academic researcher. He has considerable experience in designing, initiating and program management delivery of large scale business transformation, reengineering, infrastructure, strategy development including winning prizes for ideas and product innovation. Previously, he has been a consultant in a wide range of industries including telecom, banking, insurance, manufacturing and direct marketing whilst working for McKinsey & Co, Logica and his own consulting company. Robert is currently studying for a PhD in 'Strategy, Programme & Project Management' at SKEMA Business School in France. During this time he has published book chapters and is in the process of authoring a book on portfolio, program and project management success factors.

Kam Jugdev, PhD, PMP, is a Professor of Project Management and Strategy in the Faculty of Business at Athabasca University. She also served as an Adjunct Professor in the Department of Civil Engineering, Schulich School of Engineering, University of Calgary. Prior to becoming an academic, Kam worked in both the public and private sector industry as a project manager. She develops and teaches project management courses at both the undergraduate and graduate levels. Her federally funded research ($228,091) includes two Social Sciences and Humanities Research Council grants. Kam's research program spans: Project management lessons learned and communities of practice; project management tools and techniques; project success/failure; and project management as a source of competitive advantage using the Resource Based View of the Firm. Kam enjoys being able to relate theory to practice with students and through her research.

Catherine Killen, PhD (MGSM), M.Eng Mgt (UTS), BSc (Virginia) is the coordinator for innovation programs in the Faculty of Engineering and IT at the University of Technology Sydney, Australia. Catherine conducts research on innovation processes with a focus on project portfolio management and has published more than 50 journal articles and conference papers in the area. She develops and teaches courses and programs on technological innovation at both undergraduate and postgraduate levels. She employs qualitative, quantitative and mixed-methods in her research. Recent work includes 'best practice' survey-based research, qualitative analysis drawing upon strategic management theories, and industry-based and classroom-based 'experiments' where new methods are employed and evaluated. Catherine's current research themes include the alignment of project portfolios with organizational strategy, the evolution and contextualisation of project portfolio management approaches, and the use of visual data representations for the management of project interdependencies within a project portfolio.

Kristian Kreiner, PhD (DTU Denmark), MSc (CBS), is Professor in Organization at Copenhagen Business School (CBS). Kristian designed and directed the Center for Management Studies of the Building Process (www.clibyg.org) which was financed by the private foundation Realdania. In this capacity he has conducted multiple ethnographic studies of various aspects of construction, including architectural competitions and actual work practices on construction sites. His research interests are concerned with how work is accomplished in practice, and how organization, collaboration, coordination etc. are not premises for such work, but co-produced in the work process. Demonstrating empirically why such accomplishments are inherently difficult his research focuses on how people may become empowered to make work achievements possible.

Pierre-Luc Lalonde, PhD (École Polytechnique, Montreal), is a General Manager of the Dominican Sisters of Canada, and acts as a management consultant for various religious communities, where he helps identify and address key challenges. Under the supervision of Professors Mario Bourgault and Alain Findeli, he investigated various epistemological and methodological issues of project management practice and research. He has presented at numerous conferences and his work has been published in several journals, including *International Journal of Project Management* and *Project Management Journal*. Pierre-Luc has received prestigious scholarships from the Social Sciences and Humanities Research Council of Canada. He also received a grant for his postdoctoral research conducted under the Canada Research Chair on Technology Project Management.

Elyssebeth Leigh, EdD, MEd, Dip Ed, BA, has been a professional educator for over 30 years working with adult learners in business and academic contexts. As an experienced designer of simulations, games and role-play, she has worked in places as far apart as Africa, Russia, Finland, India and Romania. Her interest in complex adaptive systems began during her doctoral research and has continued in all her work in project management, adult education and simulation. Elyssebeth is on the Board of Simulation Australia, leads a Technical Committee for their annual conferences and contributes to the Professional Development program. Her research interests include the skills and knowledge required for effective use of simulation for learning and research. She has published widely on the educational use of simulation, and her most recent book,edited with Nygaard and Courtney, is *Simulations, Games and Role Play in University Education.*

Ralf Müller, DBA (Brunel), MBA (Herriot-Watt), PMP, is a Professor of project management and an associate dean at BI Norwegian Business School in Norway. His principal research interests are in project leadership, governance, PMOs and research methods. He is the author or co-author of more than 140 publications, and, among other acknowledgements, the receiver of the 2012 IPMA Research Award, the 2009 *Project Management Journal*'s Paper of the Year Award, and a number of best conference paper and best reviewer awards. He serves on the editorial board of seven academic journals and is departmental editor for the *Project Management Journal.* Before joining academia, he spent 30 years in the industry consulting with large enterprises and governments in 47 different countries for their project management and governance. He also held related line management positions, such as the worldwide director of project management at NCR Teradata.

Yvan Petit, PhD, M.Eng. MBA (Insead), PMP, has been an Associate Professor and part of the Project management research chair at the University of Quebec at Montreal (ESG-UQAM) since 2010. He defended his doctoral thesis entitled 'Project Portfolio Management in Dynamic Environments: Organizing for Uncertainty' in September 2011 which was published as a monograph in 2012. He has over 25 years of experience in project management, primarily in software development and R&D in the telecommunications industry. He is currently a member of the Canadian committee on the ISO TC-258 on Project Portfolio Management and was part of the core team for the third revision of PMI's *Standard for Portfolio Management.*

Sorin Piperca, M.Eng., B.Eng., is a PhD candidate in Business Administration at the University of Quebec in Montreal. His research focuses on structuring processes, project management and inter-organizational collaborations. He co-authored one monograph published by the Project Management Institute (PMI) and various other books, book chapters, and articles. He has also presented papers in many prestigious conferences, including those organized by the Academy of Management, European Group for Organizational Studies (EGOS), European Academy of Management (EURAM), and Administrative Sciences Association of Canada (ASAC). He also studied sociology at the University of Bucharest, Romania.

Julien Pollack, PhD (UTS), BSc (UNSW), B.A (UNSW), returned from practicing project management in industry in 2011, and is now Course Director of the UTS Master of Project Management program. His teaching focuses on developing students' communication and critical thinking skills. Julien's PhD involved action research into practical ways of combining project management with systems thinking techniques to meet the demands of organizational change in the public sector and won local and international awards. More recently, he has drawn on complexity theory to extend some of the closed-system assumptions on which project management theory is based. He has published articles on these topics, and one book, *Tools for Complex Projects*, with Kaye Remington. Julien's interest in theory is tempered by an understanding of the practical needs of industry. He is an experienced project manager, having worked in the engineering, telecommunications and health industries, implementing projects from organizational change and information systems development, to rolling stock manufacturing.

Shankar Sankaran, PhD, MEng, PMP, CEng, is an Associate Professor at the School of the Built Environment at the University of Technology Sydney, Australia. He is a member of the Centre for Management and Organization Studies (CMOS) at UTS and a Chief Investigator in two Australian Research Council Grants, one investigating Project Governance and the other Leadership of Not-for-Profit Organizations. Shankar has edited two books: *Effective Change Management Using Action Learning and Action Research* and *Enhancing Organizational Capability through Knowledge Management*. He is an Associate Editor of the *Sage Encyclopaedia of Action Research*. He teaches in the Master of Project Management Program at UTS and supervises several doctoral students. Shankar is the Vice President of Research and Publications at the International Society for the Systems Sciences and a distinguished fellow of the action research centre at the University of Cincinnati. He has published papers in ranked journals and presented at international conferences. His research interests are in project management, systems thinking and action studies.

Jingting Shao, PhD (SKEMA), PhD (Xi'an, China), is a post-doctoral researcher at the Institute for Industrial Economics at the Chinese Academy of Social Sciences and the Vice President of China's Young Crew project manager organization within the International Association of Project Management (IPMA). She has two doctoral degrees, one from SKEMA Business School (Lille, France) in Strategy, Programme and Project Management and one from Northwestern Polytechnical University (Xi'an, China) in Management Science and Engineering. Her research interests are in program management, leadership, and project governance. In 2011 she was awarded the 'IPMA Outstanding Research Contribution of a Young Researcher Award' and in 2012 the 'China Project Management Research Contribution Award'. She has participated in several international research projects sponsored by the Project Management Institute (PMI') and the Norwegian Centre for Project Management.

Jonas Söderlund, PhD, is Professor at BI Norwegian Business School and a founding member of KITE at Linköping University, Sweden. Jonas has researched and published widely on the management and organization of projects and project-based firms, time and knowledge integration in complex projects, and the evolution of project competence. He has written about the fundamental questions of project management research, the schools of project management research, the pressing challenges for business schools, and teaching project management in business schools. His work has appeared in such journals as *Advances in Strategic Management, International Journal of Management Reviews, Organization Studies, Human Resource Management, International Journal of Human Resource Management, R&D Management, International Journal of Innovation Management* and *International Business Review*. His most recent books are the *Oxford Handbook of Project Management* (Oxford University Press), *Human Resource Management in Project-based Organizations: the HR Quadriad Framework* (Palgrave), and *Knowledge Integration and Innovation* (Oxford University Press).

Kim van Oorschot, PhD (Eindhoven), MSc (Eindhoven), is an Associate Professor of project management and system dynamics in the Department of Leadership and Organizational Behaviour at the BI Norwegian Business School. Her current research concerns decision making, trade-offs, and tipping points in new product development projects. For this purpose she develops system dynamics models based on actual project data. Before her academic career, she was a consultant working for international companies including ASML, KPN, Stork Fokker, and NXP. She has published in such journals as *Academy of Management Journal, Productions and Operations Management, Journal of Management Studies, Journal of Product Innovation Management, Journal of the Operational Research Society* and *International Journal of Operations and Production Management*.

Jonathan Whitty, PhD, BEng (Hons), is currently senior lecturer in project management at the University of Southern Queensland, Australia. His role includes leading project management research, and directing postgraduate project management teaching programs for which he has been recognized for his contributions to developing postgraduate learning outcomes. Jonathan has two major themes to his research which have their roots either in evolutionary theory or philosophical empiricism and scepticism. His unique evolutionary approach to project management research considers all matters pertaining to projects and project management and examines them against the framework of evolution by natural, social, cultural, and memetic section. He also contributes to the literature on complexity in project management. This work leverages off evolutionary theory and considers project management to be complex emergent behaviour that manifests under the particular social and technological conditions of a capitalistic system. Project management is therefore considered to be a complex adaptation (a tool) employed by organizations and individuals to manage productivity in an environment which is both competitive and dynamic.

Foreword

Stewart Clegg

In the early 1970s I did a PhD at Bradford University that used data collected from a construction project, which was published as *Power, Rule and Domination* (1975). At the time there was very little explicit project management research and I had no idea that my small contribution would eventually feed into a burgeoning area. Burgeoned it has – project management, traditionally employed to implement projects, has developed into Organizational Project Management as organizations are increasingly using projects to deliver strategies. The emergence of program and portfolio management has also contributed to this move.

I reconnected with project management research in a study of the construction of Sydney 2000 Olympics infrastructure (Pitsis et al., 2003) and found that project management research had not kept pace with organization theory developments and that most PM journal articles were strangely disconnected from the most obvious intellectual resources in the applied social sciences emanating from organization theories and approaches. While conferences such as IRNOP attracted a more eclectic range of papers that often drew on these resources and used a wider array of research methods than surveys and interviews, including qualitative methods, this trend was not so visible in journals such as IJPM and PMJ. There was also a lack of discussion on research paradigms in papers published in PM journals which, given the 'paradigm wars' that had characterized the past 20 years in organization theory, seemed somewhat unreflexive.

PM researchers need to become more innovative in their research approaches. They need to connect with the broader currents of social science in relevant fields such as organization theory. Outside the specific field there is a great deal that can usefully be imported, transformed and translated so that it is fit for project management research purposes. More trans-disciplinary, translational and transformational approaches for conducting project related research are required and this book goes a long way to providing foundations for them. It encompasses reflections on fundamental questions underlying any research, such as the type of knowledge sought, its epistemological and ontological assumptions as well as those questions and issues not raised. The book broadens research methods and theory perspectives, drawing on contemporary approaches such as action research, soft systems methodology, activity theory, actor-network theory and other approaches adopted in related scientific and technological areas that are only recently being adopted. To achieve this, the editors have necessarily been eclectically inter-disciplinary in their contributor list. They have included contemporary research methods and designs from areas allied to project research, such as organization science, organizational studies, sociology, behavioral science and biology, providing innovative invitations to research design and methodological choice.

Overall, this book makes a significant contribution to the maturation and development of project management research as a specialism in the broader social sciences, one that is a less reliant handmaiden or under-laborer to purely technical issues but which appreciates that any material construction is always a social construction as well, one that implies episteme and phronesis, knowledge and wisdom, as well as techne or technique. Project managers may not realize it but the most important aspects of what they manage are the meanings, interpretations and politic of projects and not merely the technical aspects.

References

Clegg, S. R. (1975) *Power, Rule and Domination: A Critical and Empirical Understanding of Power in Sociological Theory and Organizational Life*, London and Boston, Routledge and Kegan Paul, International Library of Sociology.

Pitsis, T., Clegg, S. R, Marosszeky, M., and Rura-Polley, T. (2003) 'Constructing the Olympic Dream: Managing Innovation through the Future Perfect', *Organization Science*, 14:5, 574-590.

Introduction

Ralf Müller, Shankar Sankaran and Nathalie Drouin

The introduction to a book on novel methods for project management research should answer the obvious question of: Why did we write this book? We will start doing that by reviewing articles that look back over the last 20 years in the development of research methods in general management. Being the introduction to this chapter, such a retrospective cannot be comprehensive. We will only consider a few exemplary developments. Then we discuss the evolution of research methods in project management during the same period. A comparison of the two shows differences in pace, development, and maturity of methods used in management and project management research. This gap answers the question of why we wrote this book. The introduction continues by showing how we attempt to close this gap with the four sections of this book. By "we", we mean not only the editors, but also the authors who devoted their time, knowledge and energy to write the chapters for this book with a tight schedule. The editors are very grateful for their contributions!

By now it is common knowledge that the availability of methods and acceptance of research paradigms shape the design of research studies and through it an entire discipline. Moreover, the questions asked are often limited by the methodological starting positions and possibilities (Williams & Vogt, 2011). These research designs determine the nature of the research results. Thus a limited set of available methods delimits the variance in research designs, which leads to repetitive and narrowly designed studies with predictable results. This constitutes a major limitation and contradicts the purpose of research, where result should be driven by the type of knowledge that the researcher is looking for (i.e. the underlying research philosophy) and the research questions in order to arrive at relevant results. An increase in design choices allows a better fit of research designs with research questions and the type of knowledge sought, leading to more credible and applicable results.

The aim of this book is to expand the horizon of project management research designs in order to achieve a broader and more holistic understanding of the different phenomena investigated through research in projects and their management. This includes, but is not limited to, single and multiple project settings, temporary organizations, programs and portfolios of projects, project management offices, governance of projects, programs and portfolios, etc. Further on in this introduction we refer to this as project-related research.

Broadening the horizon for research designs is supported by the current state and Zeitgeist of the prevalent post-paradigm-war, which liberates the convergence of research results obtained from research designs based on different epistemological and ontological assumptions. Along with this comes a growing popularity of mixed methods approaches and associated triangulation techniques. There are indicators that this trend will extend from methodological triangulation to philosophical triangulation. Taking the latter as an example we can see how richer and more holistic understanding of complex managerial and organizational phenomena can be gained from the triangulation of results from studies based on alternative philosophical perspectives. Each of these perspectives sheds light on a different aspect of a phenomenon, which reveals the interdependence among various aspects of a phenomenon, and thus overcomes instability risks stemming from single perspectives (Bechara & Van de Ven, 2011).

Approaches like these question established frameworks of scientific inquiry and require careful philosophical reflection in order to keep the meanings and concepts in a scientific area "open" and transient (Tsoukas & Chia, 2011). The present book contributes to these discourses with philosophical and methodological perspectives that enrich today's state of knowledge about research methods in project management and both broadens the perspective as well as keeps the mind open for further change.

Trends in Management Research

Management research is a broad field and can be looked at from many different perspectives. A number of journals are solely or partly dedicated to research methods in this field. Among the top ten journals in Thomson-Reuters' Scholarly Publishing and Analysis (formerly known as the Social Science Index) *Organizational Research Methods* (ORM) is ranked highest among methodology journals in management. In an analysis of 193 articles published between 1998 and 2007 in ORM Aguinis, Pierce, Bosco, and Muslin (2007) found that the popularity of topics in research methods changes slowly, but surely. One example for that is the trend in articles addressing qualitative and quantitative research topics (Table I.1). Over the ten-year period, about half of the articles on quantitative research topics addressed analysis issues and about a third addressed measurement issues. An upward trend was especially seen in topics dealing with surveys and electronic/Web research. In contrast, articles on qualitative research topics were dominated by design issues, followed by analysis issues. An upward trend was found in articles on interpretive and action research. The ratio of topics within each of the quantitative and qualitative groups remained relatively stable over time. However, on balance, the number of articles on qualitative topics increased while those on quantitative topics decreased.

Table I.1. Trends in Research Methods Publications in ORM 1998 to 2007

	Quantitative topics	Qualitative topics	*Trend*
Design	15%	56%	→
Analysis	49%	35%	→
Measurement	37%	9%	→
Trend	↓	↑	

This should be seen in light of 90% of the articles were covering quantitative topics whereas only 10% covered qualitative topics. Aguinis et al. raised the question as to how well the coverage of topics in ORM allows for testing of theories. For that they benchmarked the balance of methodological topics in ORM against the needs of theory developers expressed in the 25 most-cited articles in the *Academy of Management Review* (AMR). Virtually all the quantitative design, measurement, and analysis topics were considered to be important by theory developers, thus covering the methodological needs of theory developers. This picture changes on the qualitative side. While about 50% of the design issues mentioned in AMR are qualitative in nature, only about 10% of ORM articles address qualitative issues. The analysis showed that theory developers would prefer a balanced ratio of quantitative and qualitative articles to address their design issues.

The dominance of quantitative studies is indicative of a predominantly positivistic paradigm in management research, with realist studies being well accepted, but post-modernist researchers struggle to being heard (Aguinis et al., 2007).

These paradigms refer to (based on Alvesson & Sköldberg, 2009; Bechara & Van de Ven, 2011):

- *Positivism:* assumes one mostly objective reality, searches for empirical identification of causal relationships with the aim to develop generalizable laws, assessed mainly quantitatively with little interference from the researcher.
- *Realism:* assumes a mind-independent reality exists and theory possibly captures partial aspects of it. This paradigm links an underlying objective reality with the subjectivity of individuals in a given situation. The researcher interferes with the data and results to a large extent.
- *Post-modernism:* is skeptical of the above philosophies and uses a wide spectrum of streams, e.g. critical theory, post-structuralism, discourse analysis, power studies etc. to develop a momentous understanding of an ever-changing reality. Subjective, reflective and reflexive methods are applied by the researcher.

In conclusion we can say that the above-mentioned trends are indicative of a gradual move towards a more balanced approach in management research methods which reduces the mismatch between the emphasis in methodology development and the needs of theory developers.

Trends in Project Management Research

The field of project management has grown and matured in many dimensions. The past 40 years show an increase in the range of research topics and published research studies use more rigorous methodologies. Simultaneously the citation rate has increased and the project management research journals are cited in a broader range of academic journals (Turner, Pinto, & Bredillet, 2011). At the same time the breadth of topics has expanded from single projects, to programs, portfolios, temporary organizations, PMOs, governance etc. This trend is especially visible during the past two decades (Sankaran, Drouin, & Müller, 2013).

A detailed analysis of the evolution of articles published between 1987 and 2007 in the three main research journals on project-related research was published by Turner, Pinto and Bredillet (2011) in the *Oxford Handbook of Project Management* (Morris, Pinto, & Söderlund, 2012). These are *IEEE Transactions on Engineering Management* (IEEE-TEM), *International Journal of Project Management* (IJPM), and *Project Management Journal* (PMJ). Below we briefly summarize the findings by comparing the state of affairs in 1997 and 2007.

The percentages of methodology sections in the papers published in these journals increased rapidly as shown in Figure I.1. This indicates a growing awareness and emphasis on the methods used for research on projects and their management.

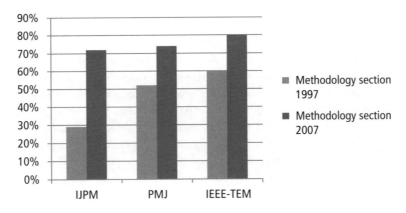

Figure I.1. Methodology Sections in Project Management Research Journals

Looking at types of papers published in 1997 and 2007 we see a change in coverage (Table I.2). Across all topics IJPM had a slight increase in literature reviews, survey and case study articles with each of them gaining up to 10 percentage points in the ratio of the journals topics, while the number of conceptual papers dropped considerably by more than 25 percentage points. PMJ increased the literature and case study articles in 2007, at the expense of conceptual papers, new technique papers, and survey studies. IEEE-TEM had a sharp increase in survey studies (more than 50 percentage points), as well as case studies and literature reviews at the expense of articles on new techniques (IEEE-TEM does not publish exclusively project management research articles).

Table I.2. Topics Coverage Change between 1997 and 2007

	IJPM	PMJ	IEEE-TEM
Literature review	+	+++	+
Surveys	+	−	++++
Case studies	+	++	++
New techniques	No change	− −	−
Conceptual papers	− − −	− −	No change

Legend: + / − = increase / decrease up to 10 percentage points
++ / − − = increase / decrease between 10 and 25 percentage points
+++ / − − − = increase /decrease between 25 and 50 percentage points
++++ / − − − − = increase /decrease of more than 50 percentage points

Overall the three journals show some common trends, such as the increase in literature reviews and case studies. Survey studies increased in two of the journals and declined in one. Conceptual papers and papers on new techniques dropped in popularity. This is, of course, just a snapshot of two years and is not necessarily representative of all developments during that period. However, the decline of conceptual work and increase in empirical studies mirrors Kuhn's (1996) observation that knowledge is first created conceptually and subsequently supported through findings from empirical research.

This complements a recent study at the Technical University in Berlin, Germany, which compared the trends within PMJ and IJPM over the period from 2000 to 2011 (Kücholl, 2012). The study showed that qualitative studies dominate (43% and 44%, respectively) over quantitative studies (35% and 34%, respectively) in the ratio of published articles in the journals. Taking both journals together, the percentage of qualitative articles increased from 28% in 2000 to 45% in 2011, while quantitative papers diminished from 32% to 29% and conceptual papers from 26% to 16% in the same period.

A slightly different picture emerges when looking at research presented at project management research conferences. By analyzing articles from 15 years of the bi-annual IRNOP (International Research Network for Organizing by Projects) conferences, Biedenbach and Müller (2009) found that between 1994 and 2007 80% to 90% of the studies took a subjective ontological stance. Epistemologically about two-thirds were based on interpretivism and about one-third on realism perspectives. Methodological trends showed an increasing use of case studies (both single and multiple cases), a slight increase in survey and interview-based studies, and a decrease in conceptual papers. Accordingly, about 80% of the studies were qualitative in nature, slightly decreasing at the expense of increasing quantitative studies.

In summary we see that published research in project management seems to be less quantitatively oriented than research in general management. Reasons for that can be found in the maturity of research in the respective fields. As Edmondson and McManus (2007) showed, the more mature a field of study, the more its research is quantitative on average. That is indicative of a high maturity in general management research and an intermediate stage in the development towards more mature research approaches in project management. The maturity of the former seems to have reached a level where theory developers would prefer more alternative views and insights to build more comprehensive theories, whereas project management theorists would prefer more studies done from different perspectives, allowing for triangulation of convergent results in order to develop theories (Jugdev, 2004). This need motivated the editors of this book to launch the present work.

The variety of methodological (and underlying philosophical) approaches nurtures the growth in knowledge and understanding of the field. Project-related research has come a long way in the past 50 years, as shown above. However, the variety in research approaches is still very limited. The analysis of IRNOP conferences shows hardly any studies using contemporary approaches, such as post-modernism or pragmatism. The reviews of published journal articles do not even mention these studies. Aguinis et al.'s (2007) conclusion that post-modernist researchers have difficulties making themselves heard in general management research publications also applies to project management research. Contemporary approaches are rarely found in project management research journals.

However, if we always do what we always did then we should not be surprised that we always find what we always found. Variety in perspectives, philosophies, and methodologies is a key for progression of the field. The way forward is difficult to predict, but there are a few milestones for orientation. A recent paper by the editors of this book reviewed 14 articles that either analyzed or commented on research that was published about project-related research (Sankaran et al., 2013). Results show, among others:

- A call for new approaches that are alternatives to rational approaches; and a growing interest in research that investigates the actuality or lived experiences of actors and their roles in projects. This is indicative of the need for more reflective and reflexive methods (such as Alvesson & Sköldberg, 2009).

- A call for organization-level research as well as project networks and complexity. This is indicative of mixed approaches using both interpretivist and, for example, quantitative social network analysis approaches.
- A call for more clarity in reports on the research paradigms, their underlying philosophy and its link with the applied methodology. This is indicative of a need for more rigorous research reporting.

This variety presents a challenge to both researchers and reviewers of reported research, as Söderlund and Bakker (2013) showed in their analysis of journal reviewers' comments in IJPM between 2007 and 2010. They found a clear trend for the increasing standard deviation of reviewer recommendations per reviewed manuscript, and thus a widening of the gap of suggested improvements of a journal submission. In times of increasing variety of methods this does not come as a surprise. Efforts are needed to help reviewers obtaining the required overview of changing and newly developed research approaches to avoid established methods, such as reflexive studies in general management, from being rejected in project management journals on the basis that "they might lead to subjective results". This happening in 2012, more than 50 years after Popper's (1959) call to emphasize the subjective involvement of the researcher, is rather embarrassing.

This suggests that project-related research should look forward to work on and with contemporary methods, but should also take into account methods that might be well established in other disciplines but new to project-related research. These include, for example, bricolage with the researcher as bricoleur (Denzin & Lincoln, 2005), systematic literature reviews (Pawson, Greenhalgh, Harvey, & Walshe, 2005) and evidence-based approaches (Pawson, 2006), reflexive methodologies (Alvesson & Kärreman, 2011; Alvesson & Sköldberg, 2009), or philosophical triangulation (Bechara & Van de Ven, 2011). Many of these are only just entering the field of project-related research.

This is why we see an urgent need for a book to guide project researchers, especially those whose unit of analysis goes beyond the single project. Such a book should include approaches used in different fields of research, such as organizational research, management research, economics, biology, education, etc. so that project researchers are able to make use of contemporary methods employed in allied fields. It should also provide guidance to the fundamental questions driving the research design, the type of knowledge being investigated and the worldview and value systems of the researcher. Therefore this book is expected to support transdisciplinary, translational and transformational approaches for conducting project-related research.

Translational research, which has become popular in medicine and health care, has two meanings. The first is to *promote multidisciplinary collaboration*, and the second is to *translate the findings* from the research more quickly and efficiently into practice. Both are needed for progressing the field of project-related research.

We have borrowed this term from the health sciences literature, where it is used to describe the entire cycle from research on a new drug to its use by the patient, thus the combination of basic and applied research to the benefit of the user. We feel that it is time to consider translational approaches in project-related research to raise the level of research in the field of projects and make it more relevant to the organizations that invest in projects. Readers interested in learning more about translational research are referred to Petronio (2012), Shapiro, Bradley and Courtney (2007), or Woolf (2008).

Transformational research promotes the taking over of an old research paradigm by a new research paradigm in the sense of Kuhn (1996). These kinds of changes are not sudden and will require time. However, there is a growing interest from funding organizations such as the European Research Council or National Science Foundation to emphasize research that has the potential for being transformational in nature.

Through this book we intend to motivate project management researchers to look at contemporary approaches such as transformational and translational research to be used in both project management and organizational research as well as to engage in trans-disciplinary and multi-disciplinary research to raise the level and variety of research approaches.

We gave the authors the greatest possible freedom to describe their approaches in order not to limit conceptualization and application of the proposed methods. Readers will find that the chapters do not reflect radical newness in thinking, but rather small but certain steps forward from the majority of research methods that we see today in our field towards wider, deeper and alternative approaches to research.

The Sections of the Book

Research methodology is a wide field and so are the dimensions for communicating it. To accomplish good theoretical foundation and applicability in practice, and thus to form a bridge from philosophy via concepts to applications, we structured the book into four sections. It starts with contemporary perspectives on the philosophical underpinnings and basic questions that should drive any research. This is followed by a section on creative and innovative contemporary research approaches. The third section looks into neighboring sciences and disciplines and a few methods that can possibly be learned from them. The fourth section deals with upcoming approaches, and promising new perspectives and methods. The book ends with an outlook by the editors.

Section 1: Philosophical Underpinnings of OPM Research

This section will explore the fundamental questions underlying any research, that is, the question of the type of knowledge sought and its contingency in context, and the worldview and values of the researcher, to provide a better understanding of these underpinnings to researchers in the field who wish to justify their research design.

The section takes the reader from contemporary research paradigms and perspectives through a discourse on the need for different research methods and different thinking about research, to the proposal for a disciplined plurality of research approaches for shaping the knowledge of the field. The section ends by modeling the process of theory development over time, which integrates the aspects of the prior chapters and sees them as building blocks of dynamic theory advancement in a longitudinal context.

Section 2: Creative and Innovative Contemporary Approaches

This section will broaden the perspective from traditional research designs, such as surveys, interviews and case studies, to contemporary approaches such as action research, soft systems methodology, activity theory, actor-network theory and other relevant contemporary approaches that are being adopted in recent years in other scientific and technological areas, but have hardly found their way into the realm of project research. The reader will see how contemporary research approaches being proposed in this section are applied and how their application transforms project management research. While doing this, the section also describes the problems and opportunities for project management researchers in using these methods.

The section starts with an example of applied actor-network theory and action research, then moves on to simulation methods, followed by an example of using systems dynamics for project-related research. The section ends with an example of a research program that integrated a variety of studies done using very different perspectives and methodologies in order to build a comprehensive and holistic view of an organizational phenomenon.

Section 3: Learning Across Disciplines

This section includes contemporary research methods and designs from areas that are allied to project research, such as organization science, sociology, behavioral science, and biology. It provides a unique and fresh set of research designs and methodological choices to learn and draw from. Readers will find guidance on integrating theories, concepts and approaches from allied fields to complement, expand and enrich their potential research.

This section shows some of the key concepts in a specific discipline (e.g. organization science, sociology, behavioral science, and biology) that could be of interest to conduct research in the field of projects. Questions of application of these methods to project-related research are addressed as well potential learning in terms of research designs.

The section moves from social sciences examples to natural sciences examples. It starts with an integration of different research streams in the field of competitive advantage and its application to project research. This is followed by an example of sociological and organizational perspectives for research on project phenomena, which is followed by examples on how to apply a behavioral science perspective to project-related research. The section ends with an example of applying the natural science perspective of genotyping and phenotyping to project-related research.

Section 4: Upcoming Approaches in OPM Research

This section extends existing project research to transformational, translational and trans-disciplinary approaches, which allows for leverage of research designs and methods across disciplines, thus increasing research quality and elevating project research to a higher level of research design.

Readers will find how project researchers think about using transformational, translational and trans-disciplinary (or interdisciplinary) approaches, their use of creativity in using research approaches across paradigms, and how researchers investigating projects and organizations can implement these approaches.

This final section starts with the description of a translational research that applied strategic management theories to organizational project management studies. This is followed by two chapters on different ways of triangulation in research studies, followed by a methodological framework to investigate the thinking processes of project managers. The section ends by using critical systems thinking as an approach to integrate research across paradigms, which links back to the first section and the fundamental philosophical questions raised therein.

The book ends with our outlook on the near future in research in our field.

We believe that the time is ripe to put more contemporary research methods on the agenda of project and project management researchers and hope that this book will stimulate many of our colleagues to take the next steps to apply them.

References

Aguinis, H., Pierce, C. a., Bosco, F. a., & Muslin, I. S. (2007). First Decade of Organizational Research Methods: Trends in Design, Measurement, and Data-Analysis Topics. *Organizational Research Methods, 12*(1), 69-112. doi:10.1177/1094428108322641

Alvesson, M., & Kärreman, D. (2011). *Qualitative Research and Theory Development* (p. 133). Thousand Oaks, CA,: SAGE Publications, Inc., USA.

Alvesson, M., & Sköldberg, K. (2009). *Reflexive Methodology* (2nd ed.). London: SAGE Publications.

Bechara, J., & Van de Ven, A. H. (2011). Triangulating Philosophies of Science to Understand Complex Organizational and Managerial Problems. In H. Tsoukas & R. Chia (Eds.), *Philosophy and Organization Theory* (pp. 312-342). Bingly, UK: Emerald Books.

Biedenbach, T., & Müller, R. (2009). Paradigms in Project Management Research: Examples from 15 Years of IRNOP Conferences. *In Proceedings of IRNOP IV Conference (International Research Network for Organizing by Projects), October 11-13, 2009, Berlin, Germany.*

Denzin, N. K., & Lincoln, Y. S. (2005). Introduction: The Discipline and Practice of Qualitative Research. In N. K. Denzin & Y. S. Lincoln (Eds.), *Handbook of Qualitative Research* (3rd ed., pp. 1-32). Thousand Oaks, CA, USA: SAGE Publications Inc.

Edmondson, A. M. Y. C., & McManus, S. E. (2007). Methodological Fit in Management. *Academy of Management Review, 32*(4), 1155-1179.

Jugdev, K. (2004). Through The Looking Glass: Examining Theory Development in Project Management. *Project Management Journal, 35*(3), 15-26.

Kuhn, T. (1996). *The structure of scientific revolutions.* London, UK: University of Chicago Press.

Kücholl, A. (2012). *Die Entwicklung der Projektmanagement-Forschung: Eine bibliographische Literaturanalyse über die letzten zwölf Jahre.* Unpublished Master's thesis, Technical University, Berlin, Germany.

Morris, P. W. G., Pinto, J. K., & Söderlund, J. (2012). *The Oxford Handbook of Project Management.* (P. Morris, J. K. Pinto, & J. Söderlund, Eds.). Oxford, UK: Oxford University Press, UK.

Pawson, R. (2006). *Evidence-based Policy: A Realist Perspective.* London, UK: SAGE Publications Ltd.

Pawson, R., Greenhalgh, T., Harvey, G., & Walshe, K. (2005). Realist review – a new method of systematic review designed for complex policy interventions. *Research Policiy, 20*(July), 21-34.

Petronio, S. (2012). Translational Research Endeavors and the Practices of Communication Privacy Management. *Journal of Applied Communication Research, 35*(3), 218-222.

Popper, K. (1959). *The Logic of Scientific Discovery.* New York, USA: Basic Books.

Sankaran, S., Drouin, N., & Müller, R. (2013). The Need for Using New Research Approaches in Project Management. *Proceedings of the PMI Research & Academic Conference. January 31 to February 2, 2013, Chennai, India.*

Shapiro, D., Bradley, L. K., & Courtney, H. G. (2007). Perceived causes and solutions of the translation problem in management research. *Academy of Management Journal, 50*(2), 249-266.

Söderlund, J., & Bakker, R. M. (2013). The case for good reviewing. *International Journal of Project Management, (in press).* doi:10.1016/j.ijproman.2012.11.007

Tsoukas, H., & Chia. (2011). Introduction: Why Philosophy Matters to Organization Theory. In H. Tsoukas & R. Chia (Eds.), *Philosophy and Organization Theory* (p. 122). Bingley, UK: Emerald Group Publishing.

Turner, J. R., Pinto, J. K., & Bredillet, C. (2011). The Evolution of Project Management Research: The Evidence from the Journals. In P. W. G. Morris, J. K. Pinto, & J. Söderlund (Eds.), *The Oxford Handbook of Project Managament*. Oxford, UK: Oxford University Press.

Williams, M., & Vogt, P. (2011). Introduction: Innovation in Social Research Methods. In M. Williams & P. Vogt (Eds.), *The SAGE Handbook of Innovation in Social Research Methods* (pp. 19-24). London, UK: SAGE Publications.

Woolf, S. H. (2008). The Meaning of Translational Research and Why it Matters. *JAMA*, *299*(2), 221-213.

Philosophical Underpinnings of OPM Research

Ralf Müller, Shankar Sankaran and Nathalie Drouin

This section contributes to the discussion about the different philosophical perspectives of research in project management. The central message of this section is the need for plurality in underlying philosophical perspectives, which give rise to different research methodologies and outcomes, and jointly contribute to socially accepted theories by way of discourse.

The section starts with Robert Chia laying the foundation of the book in Chapter 1 by looking at the research paradigms of Western thought and their underlying ontological and epistemological assumptions, as well as the limitations of single-paradigm research. Multi-paradigm research is hereby suggested as a way to overcome these limitations and an example of two complementary paradigms is given. The first paradigm combines a *being* ontology with a *representationalism* epistemology, and complements the second paradigm of a *becoming* ontology combined with a *social constructivism* epistemology, which together provide for multidimensional understanding of researched phenomena.

This view is extended in Chapter 2 by Christophe Bredillet's call for Perestroika (i.e. restructuring) in research and practice of project management. Based on Aristotle's concept of *phronesis* (i.e. practical wisdom, prudence) he suggests reconsidering the scholar-practitioner divide and joining them into the PraXitioner perspective in order to derive a new thinking and understanding of project management in practice and theory.

In Chapter 3, Jonathan Whitty builds on Plato, Aristotle, Hume and Kant to develop an example of a metaphysical and epistemological framework that can be used by researchers to scrutinize their concepts and constructs for any limitations of mainstream project management thinking in order to encourage the development of novel and transformational approaches to research.

In Chapter 4, Jonas Söderlund addresses plurality and interplay in worldviews and research approaches as a requirement for good theory development. Using the examples of processual and temporal research in project management he shows that minimum levels of integration in worldviews and approaches should be met for a productive dialogue about the evolution of project management research.

Chapter 5 widens the view and models the dynamics of theory development from a societal perspective. Ralf Müller and Jingting Shao put the *discourse* about theories in the center of a model based on Foucault, Kuhn and Lakatos. Their model shows that timeliness of appearance, choice of publication media, and aesthetics of theory must match the Zeitgeist of the society in order for a theory to be accepted, and how these criteria are synchronized and enabled through ongoing discourse.

The section departs from traditional philosophies and moves into contemporary thinking, including translational and transformational approaches. Simultaneously it develops from the level of individual researcher to that of the wider society. By doing this it addresses the following questions:

- What are the recent developments in linking philosophy and methodology?
- How do philosophical, theoretical, and methodological plurality contribute to research results?
- How do research results develop into theories?

Chapter 1

Paradigms and Perspectives in Organizational Project Management Research: Implications for Knowledge-Creation

Robert Chia

Abstract

Project Management Research is primarily concerned with the selection, formulation and production of knowledge associated with the material practices of managing and organizing within pre-defined temporal and spatial contexts. All such forms of knowledge-creation begin with the experiences and raw observations of everyday practices in organizational project management. Yet, despite sharing this common root-source, multiple and often conflicting accounts of such practices and hence their organizational consequences are possible. A variety of paradigms, perspectives and theoretical approaches can and have been adopted by academic researchers to make sense of and to justify their research findings. Paradigms are selective *modes of abstraction* that circumscribe what is thinkable and thought, so much so that the knowledge produced through each paradigm is ultimately partial, incomplete and/or contestable; a theory offers a useful if limited view of organizational life. Despite this, virtually all forms of knowledge-creation involve some combination of the fundamental processes of empirical observation, reflection, theoretical conjecturing and the verification of conceptual models developed to capture the real goings-on in organizational project management practice. This is what ultimately defines the process of research. This chapter traces the philosophical roots of Western thought and identifies the key assumptions shaping current paradigms of knowledge-creation in organizational project management and the epistemological priorities associated with each of them. It shows that all attempts at knowledge-creation are irretrievably selective; a way of knowing is also a way of not knowing. Thus, to do real justice to the practices of organizational project management, researchers must return again and again to the phenomena they investigate, to glean ever-newer insights into their inner workings. In this way, by relentlessly offering ever-novel perspectives, research helps prevent the tyranny of a dominant orthodoxy, facilitates the democratising of knowledge, and encourages the interminable search for better ways of managing and organizing to fulfil our human potentiality.

Keywords: *Being*, *becoming*, representationalism, social constructionism, methodological individualism, methodological collectivism, relationalism, practice turn

Introduction: Academic Research and the Production of Knowledge

The intellectual life of man consists almost wholly in his substitution of a conceptual order for the perceptual order in which his experience originally comes (William James, Some Problems of Philosophy, 1911/1996: 51, my emphasis).

Project Management Research is primarily concerned with the selection, formulation and production of knowledge associated with the material practices of managing and organizing within pre-defined temporal and spatial contexts. All such forms of knowledge-creation begin with the experiences and raw observations of everyday practices in organizational project management. Essentially, the production of such academic knowledge may be likened to any other manufacturing process. In producing aluminium beer cans, for instance, a thin aluminium sheet-coil is fed through a series of stamping presses where the raw material is successively cut, stamped and precision-drawn until they become the familiar cylindrical shape we instinctively recognise. These are then sent to printing/lacquering machines where they are printed externally with the necessary colours and designs and coated internally with lacquer to prevent corrosion from taking place. In each successive operation, tight and demanding specifications are set to ensure the desired outcome of a quality, reliable product. This quality-control process is similarly mirrored in the production of project management knowledge. In this latter instance, the 'raw material' is no longer an aluminium coil but the unformed, unfolding 'coil' of human life experiences; an initially undifferentiated flux of fleeting sense-impressions that 'furnishes the material to our later reflection with its conceptual categories' (James, 1912/1996: 93). Out of this brute, aboriginal 'sensible muchness' of raw experience, our attention then selectively focuses upon and labels. Thus, 'in the sky "constellations", on earth "beach", "sea", "cliff", "bushes", "grass". Out of time we cut "days" and "nights", "summers" and "winters". We say *what* each part of the sensible continuum is, and all these abstract *whats* are concepts' (James, 1911/96: 50, emphasis in original). Like the shaping and forming actions of stamping presses in a can manufacturing plant, our active attention selectively intervenes into the undifferentiated flow of lived experiences to arbitrarily cut, draw out and construct the social reality that we then subsequently find so necessary and familiar. What is conceptually left out, like the waste material in a production process, is discarded. Key aspects of this arbitrarily selected social reality are then identified, labelled and causally linked to other parts of our experiences in order to form a coherent system of explanation; they acquire legitimacy and gain significance becoming increasingly thought of as stable 'thing-like' social entities hereafter for all intents and purposes. Therefore, formalized knowledge about such entities is produced through a process of causal attribution and recombination of the various identified elements. All this implies that the project management researcher must remain alert and vigilant to the insidious tendency to reify concepts and to then mistake the abstract outputs of thought for the rich reality of lived experiences. Researchers need to be mindful about the limits and limitations of their own research and reflexively recognize that their findings are inevitably shaped by their own paradigmatic preferences. Knowledge claims are thus irretrievably dependent upon deeply embedded and often unconscious sets of metaphysical assumptions regarding the nature of reality and how we can attain formalized knowledge about it.

Research and Knowledge-Creation in Academic Inquiry

To re-search is to search again and again; to try to find new meaning to both exceptional and ordinary everyday experiences, familiar and unfamiliar happenings, and novel and taken-for-granted conceptions. Research is about re-thinking concepts, renewing observations, reliving experiences and re-enacting memories to discover ever-novel and lasting insights. Oftentimes in the process of research and inquiry such insights and understandings may come unexpectedly; shock, surprise, disbelief, fascination and wonder are often an intrinsic feature of the research process. Indeed, it is not unusual for deep insights and understandings of the phenomenon we investigate to come on the 'rebound' so to speak; sometimes full appreciation of the significance of what we have discovered only hits us after we have returned intellectually to where we first began in our journey of inquiry. Thus, paradoxically, it is often only through venturing into the unknown, away from the familiar and secure ground of what we already know that we can then return to 'where we started; And know the place for the first time' (Eliot, 1942/2001: 15). We see afresh what the phenomenon was really about and understand much better in hindsight what it was we were really searching for. Research entails assiduously mining the rich seams of human experiences and creating knowledge through this process of retrospective sense-making and systematic conceptualization. In this way, our raw sensory inputs systematically subjected to flights of disciplined imagination are increasingly given substance, form and coherence.

The flux of everyday experience, therefore, is what provides the initial source of material for our speculative conjecturing while curiosity and the forces of human will provide the motivating impulse for the conscious conceptual activity that subsequently ensues. Knowledge-creation is a process in which concepts are creatively conceived and employed to substitute for lived experience/observations; the act of conceptualization is essentially a 'secondary... and ministerial' activity (James, 1911/1996: 79). Concepts 'steer us practically' in everyday life. They 'reanimate our wills, and make our actions turn upon new points of emphasis' (James, 1911/1996: 73). Yet, despite their evident usefulness, they inevitably 'falsify as well as omit' (James, 1911/1996: 79) leaving out aspects of lived experiences that do not fit into the dominant conceptual schema. All thought, as such, is ultimately grounded in experience. Thus, even seemingly abstract notions like Plato's Ideals are conceivable only because there is first experience of the material 'imperfections' of these ideals as Aristotle noted; without experiencing ugliness, falsehood, injustice and the material effects of unfreedom, for instance, we can have no notion of the possibility of universals like beauty, truth, justice and freedom. The search for knowledge often begins with a sense of puzzlement, of something that is missing, or of a gnawing unease about the adequacy of our current forms of understanding.

Conceptualization, thus, is a kind of self-sufficient 'revelatory' activity that purports to admit us to an eternal world of universals remote from the more mundane perishable facts and passing sense-impressions of everyday life. It entails the determined substitution of a 'conceptual order' for the 'perceptual order' in which experience originates (James, 1911/1996: 51). The true method of intellectual discovery and knowledge-creation in research, therefore, is much like the 'flight of an aeroplane'. It begins on the ground of raw experience; it 'makes a flight in the thin air of imaginative generalization; and it again lands for renewed observation rendered acute by rational interpretation' (Whitehead, 1929: 5). This iterative process of imaginative rationalization produces what we call formal knowledge. Research and knowledge-creation are thus formative activities involving the determined substitution of order, structure and coherence for that 'blooming, buzzing confusion' (James, 1911/1996: 50) within which all of sensible life initially originates.

The Purpose of Research

Research is often believed to be an objective and independent means of knowledge-creation. This mostly unchallenged belief is what gives it its extensive power of persuasion. 'Our research tells us ...' is by now a popular mantra employed by researchers to persuade those less initiated into the complexities of the research process about the significance and import of their findings. The by-now widespread and common practice of commissioning 'independent' research reports have thus become a convenient means of mobilizing and persuading stakeholders on the appropriateness of particular courses of actions to be taken. It has become a definitive feature of modern democratic societies in which the legitimacy of policies formulated, the transparency and accountability of choices made, and the causal efficacy of actions taken have become the accepted *modus operandi* particularly in the world of business, politics and public affairs. Yet, as we argue here, the hidden partiality of such accounts only serve to obscure actual goings-on in the world of human affairs including especially that of the material practices of organizational project management. For, it is ultimately the capacity to get in touch with pristine reality, 'unwarped by the sophistication of

Philosophical Underpinnings of OPM Research

theory' (Whitehead, 1929: 295) that will enable us to truly appreciate the overflowing richness and profundity of lived experience and to gain genuine lasting insights into the intricate process of managing and organizing within specified temporal and spatial contexts. Hence, the ultimate end-point of project management research is not so much to arrive at a singular irrefutable and unassailable truth. Rather by providing a multiplicity of competing novel perspectives it helps prevent the tyranny of a dominant orthodoxy, facilitates the democratizing of knowledge, and encourages the search for ever-newer ways of managing and organizing to fulfil our human potentiality.

Over the past two decades, organizational project management research has emerged as an academic field specifically focused on how project, program and portfolio management practices strategically help realize organizational goals. Yet, it has often been criticized for not paying sufficient attention to the philosophical presuppositions underpinning its research methodologies and methods. This chapter contributes to the clarification of such philosophical commitments through a careful examination of the alternative theoretical traditions from which research priorities and agendas are developed and in so doing helps pave the way for the emergence of novel approaches to organizational project management research that are more ontologically-informed, epistemologically consistent and methodologically robust.

The Context and History of Western Knowledge-Creation

> *But what if empirical knowledge, at a given time and in a given culture,* did *possess a well-defined regularity? ... If errors (and truths) ... including not only genuine discoveries ... obeyed, at a given moment, the laws of a certain code of knowledge?* (Michel Foucault, The Order of Things, 1970: ix, emphasis original).

The methods and approaches involved in the creation and legitimation of knowledge within the Western world have not always been what they are. What counts as proper knowledge, as Foucault's (1970: 246-7) seminal study on the history of knowledge shows, has varied considerably from epoch to epoch. Foucault maintains that what underlay each of the Renaissance, Classical, and Modern eras in the West, was a unifying set of coded rules for forming and legitimizing knowledge. Thus, for instance, during the Renaissance period, things were ordered and hence known through the unifying principle of *resemblance*. Resemblance suggests likeness, similarity or even the regular proximity of one phenomenon to another, It provided the basis for ordering perceptions and hence knowledge-creation during this pre-scientific period. Resemblance is also found in analogies and through emulation. The human heart, for instance, is often thought of as a mechanical pump because of its similarity of function. Likewise, the seeds of the aconite plant were often used as a cure for eye diseases just because their appearance was that of 'tiny dark globes seated in white skinlike coverings whose appearance is much like that of eyelids covering an eye'

(Foucault, 1970: 142), and walnuts were used for wounds of the pericranium because the physical appearance of the walnut resembled the human brain. We can therefore see that Renaissance knowledge relied heavily on the idea of an unending spiral of linked resemblances for its system of knowledge-creation.

Foucault shows that with the beginning of the Classical age in the West the principle of ordering through resemblance was replaced by one that emphasized the breaking up and analysis of resemblances and the establishment of causal relations through the more precise principles of identity and difference. There are four key features associated with this Classical epoch. Firstly, it was now no longer sufficient to merely recognize and relate each phenomenon in terms of its resemblance to other things. Instead, each phenomenon had to be broken down into its constituent elements and systematically examined and compared. Naming, representing, classifying, and then establishing causal relations became the key activities of a knowing mind. Taxonomies, tables, and classificatory schemas replaced the idea of mere resemblance as the basis for knowledge. Linnaeus's *Systema Naturae* (1758), written in the early 18th century, provides one of the clearest examples of this taxonomic impulse evident in the Classical episteme. Secondly, accuracy of representation using precise linguistic terminology and established categories became the dominant priority in this classical ordering of things. Thirdly, every claimed resemblance must now be subjected to proof involving a comprehensive verification of the properties in terms of identity and difference. Finally, not only should similarities and differences be articulated, they must now be subjected to measurement and enumeration using some common units so that proper comparison can be made and causal relations established. Analysis, accuracy of representation, the burden of proof and the quantitative use of measurement and comparison to establish causal links thus served as the underlying formative rules of knowledge-creation within the Classical epoch. It led to the impressive achievements of science during this era.

Finally, for Foucault, within the Modern episteme, it became no longer adequate to know a thing in terms of its formal specification and location in the overarching scheme of things. Knowledge must now be sought 'outside representation, beyond its immediate visibility, in a sort of behind-the-scenes world even deeper and more dense than representation itself' (Foucault, 1970: 239). What defines the Modern episteme is a shift from the security of a single authoritative representation of things that characterized the Classical epoch to a confusing proliferation of competing accounts. Modernism thus represents the beginning of that moment of disillusionment regarding the possibility of achieving a single accurate representation (Lash, 1990). In Modernity, representations are no longer unquestioningly accepted as self-justifying starting points. Meanings are no longer stable, transparent, and self-evident. Instead, actions and intentions are now subjected to hidden motives and deeper understandings. Unconscious forces, historical embeddedness, and ulterior motives that are difficult to empirically verify have to be increasingly countenanced as legitimate causes in formulating casual explanations. Marx's notion of 'false consciousness', Freud's idea of the 'unconscious' and the notion of 'unintended consequences' (Merton, 1936), form a part of this shift in emphasis from a surface to a depth social-psychological understanding of human behavior. Pluralism and the emergence of multiple conflicting realities became the signature theme of this Modernist period. Although Foucault (1970) discussed these epistemological transformations in epochal terms and in terms of epistemes that are more or less thought to be logically incommensurable, it would be fair to say that in practice, contradictory though they appear, the organizing codes of all three epistemes nevertheless still continue to coexist as a multi-layered dimension of social and organizational reality. Each of the three cultural attitudes previously elucidated, the Renaissance, the Classical, and the Modern, are to be found in contemporary approaches in social science research including especially management and organization studies.

A heightened awareness of the importance of history, social context and situational embeddedness in the social sciences in accounting for human actions and achievements have thus become important qualifiers of more contemporary claims to knowledge. This multiplicity and plurality in the way knowledge is created, sanctioned and legitimised alerts us to an important distinction that must be made between *epistemology*, our culturally-coded knowledge of the world, and the *ontological reality* of the world in and of itself, which pre-exists knowledge and invariably 'overflows' our categories of thought (James, 1911/1996: 78-79; Whitehead, 1926/1985: 64; Bergson, 1946/1992: 161-162; Morin, 1977/1992: 393). In the quest for knowledge and the search for certainty there is therefore a need to be mindful of how dominant modes of thought irretrievably shape the way we conceptualize our human experiences. Unwittingly, therefore, we rely on an 'existing observational order' that shapes our method of discrimination and a dominant 'conceptual order' that directs our preferred mode of interpretation (Whitehead, 1933: 183). Observational discrimination, as such, is not 'dictated by impartial facts. It selects and it discards and what it retains is rearranged in a subjective order of prominence' (Whitehead, 1933: 184). These observational and conceptual orders constitutes an 'unconscious metaphysics', or paradigm of comprehension shaping our sense-making and our efforts at knowledge-creation. They direct the focus of our attention, influence what we deem significant or insignificant, mould our notions of efficacy and causality and ultimately determine our chosen method for investigating phenomena and creating knowledge through it.

Knowledge actualized in the form of theories and concept, therefore, are not universal and timelessly irrefutable truth claims as such. Instead, they are practical tools framed within specific paradigms of comprehension that are employed to interrogate reality. This is especially the case for the social sciences. The activity of knowledge-creation within the social sciences takes place within pre-specified paradigmatic premises and the knowledge produced constitutes our formalised attempt to structure, order and explain the significance and import of the plurality of observations and experiences we encounter around us. Thus, paradoxically to 'know' is also to simultaneously 'kill' (Serres, 1982: 28); to exclude from consideration (often unconsciously) aspects of experiences that do not fit into our conceptual schema precisely because they are rendered insignificant by a preferred paradigm of comprehension (Morin, 1977/1992: 16). Paradigmatic awareness entails recognition that all forms of seeing and knowing involve the simultaneous act of foregrounding and backgrounding: that there is an inevitable blindness in seeing and an unacknowledged 'owing' in our 'kn-owing'. As such, it is crucial for researchers to be acutely aware of the limits and limitations of the knowledge created through their research. This ultimately is what separates the wise from the clever and the knowledgeable. Socrates was a wise man because he was acutely aware of the limits of his own knowledge. He realized that his own pre-eminence came from his insistence on his ignorance and of how much effort it took to confront this ignorance. Socratic *learned ignorance* is what distinguishes wisdom from knowledge (Chia and Holt, 2007) for it signals an acute awareness of the apparent objectivity, delusive completeness, and air of finality that the doctrines of science convey (Whitehead, 1933: 184) in order to justify their own self-importance.

Contrasting World-Views: The Intellectual Roots of Western Thought

No science can be more secure than the unconscious metaphysics which tacitly it presupposes (Alfred North Whitehead, Adventures of Ideas, 1933: 180).

Is reality fixed and unchanging or does it flux and flow? Do the forms, patterns and regularities we notice in our observations and experiences pre-exist our focus of attention residing in an external objective realm or are they, in fact, products of our own imagination? What method of enquiry should we adopt in order to establish with the highest degree of certainty our knowledge of reality? What forms of logic, reasoning and sense-making should we employ in attempting to understand physical and social phenomena? Is human behaviour directly attributable to nature or culture? Do behaviors and actions reflect instincts, intentions or internalized social practices? These are some enduring questions that have exercised acute minds from time immemorial. The impulse to extract order and predictability from chaos and ambiguity, to wrest form from formlessness, to attribute substance, shape and simple location to social phenomena and then to fix, name, classify, and assign causal significance to them derives from a historically-cultivated Western abhorrence of flux, transience and uncertainty. It is this cultivated impulse for certainty, control and mastery over our individual and collective circumstances that fuels the insatiable need for conceptually fixing, ordering and making sense of human experiences particularly through the medium of language. This civilizing impulse to create formalized, universal knowledge derives from the ancient Greek philosophers in Athens who were, in turn, inspired by pre-Socratic thinkers before them. To truly appreciate how such an instinctive ordering impulse has come about in the West we need to recur to a historic confrontation between two competing notions of the nature of reality in pre-Socratic Greece.

Two Ontologies

The vague intuition that 'all things flow' has been an abiding yet often unacknowledged influence on the modern Western consciousness. Such a worldview first made its appearance as a key proposition of the Pre-Socratic Greek philosopher Heraclitus who insisted that the universe is in constant flux and that 'all things come to pass through compulsion of strife' (Heraclitus, in Wheelwright, 1974: 29). For Heraclitus, a native of Ephesus in ancient Greece, relentless change is an intrinsic feature of reality so much so that words (which are essentially attempts to fix, name, and stabilize meanings) are always inadequate to the task of capturing this effervescent and ever-changing reality. As a consequence a logical paradox inhere every linguistic attempt to describe reality. This is well encapsulated in a classic paradoxical utterance by Heraclitus that has been popularly translated as: 'You never step into the same river twice' (in actual fact the obscure pronouncement he made, according to Plato, was 'Upon those who step into the same rivers flow other and yet other waters' [Heraclitus, in Mansley-Robinson, 1968: 91]). For Heraclitus, therefore, nothing remains constant but change and it is through changing that things come to be; order, stability and identity are but precariously arrested moments in the relentless flux that is reality. In his view, conflict, struggles and temporary reconciliations are unavoidably the very stuff of life. Were this not the case, all of life as we experience it would not be as it is. Thus, the universe flows along of its own accord, shaping its own destiny regardless of human intentions. Human actions and interventions are therefore accorded less causal significance than our egos would have us believe. As Wheelwright observed; 'To say that the universe flows along as it is destined …or that counters are moved arbitrarily and by chance, are different ways of asserting that the major occurrences in the universe lie outside the range and power of any man' (Wheelwright, 1974: 36). In this worldview there is less room for individual heroic acts and spectacular human achievements.

On the other hand, Heraclitus's successor Parmenides insisted upon the permanent and unchangeable nature of reality. Thus: 'One way remains to be spoken of; the way how it is …(reality) must exist fully or not at all …Thus coming into being is extinguished, and destruction unknown' (Parmenides, in Mansley-Robinson, 1968: 113). For Parmenides being cannot originate from non-being, something cannot come from nothing, so much so that what IS could not have come from what IS NOT. Therefore change and transformation for Parmenides is illusory and all this talk about change is essentially misleading. As Mansley-Robinson (1968: 117) puts it plainly, 'Parmenides, then, rejects change as such, whether it takes the form of coming into being, passing away, local motion or qualitative transformation'. Thus 'motionless in the limits of mighty bonds, it is without beginning or end, since coming into being and passing away have been driven far off … Remaining the same, and in the same place, it lies in itself, and so abides firmly where it is' (Parmenides, in Mansley-Robinson, 1968: 115).

Thus, whilst Heraclitus emphasized the primacy of a perpetually fluxing, changing and emergent reality, Parmenides insisted upon its permanent, fixed and unchanging nature. One proffered a vision of reality as inclusively processual and ever-becoming, the other privileged a homeostatic and substance-based conception of reality; one in which entitative thinking takes pride of place. This intractable opposition between a Heraclitean ontology of *process* and *becoming* and a Parmenidean-inspired ontology of substantial *entities* and *being* provides us with a crucial key for understanding contemporary research paradigms in the social sciences in general and in management and organization research in particular. For it is this latter Parmenidean notion of a relatively unchanging and entitative conception of reality coupled with Plato's notion of absolute ideals, that has dominated Western thought for more than two thousand years.

Whilst it is true that Aristotle attempted to accommodate the notion of change in his revision of Platonic universals, nevertheless substance, form and stability remains primary for him. As Wilkinson (2009: 130) writes, 'Aristotelian logic and metaphysics rests on an intuition about what there is, namely that reality is in itself formed ... the real is orderly'. Aristotle postulated the existence of an enduring and unchanging substance called *hypokeimenon* (underlying material substratum) on which stability could be fixed and identity linguistically assigned. Aristotle's reality thus comprised enduring individual substances that could therefore be knowable and describable in linguistic terms. Therefore, it is 'things', substantial entities that 'change', not that change precedes the emergence of entities; *being* precedes *becoming*. This ontology of *being* in which stable, circumscribed entities are privileged over unbounded processes of change, has provided the metaphysical underpinnings for much of Western thought since the Enlightenment. It remains dominant in social scientific thinking.

According to Whitehead, Classical Enlightenment thinkers came to adopt this Parmenidean-inspired Democritean notion of reality as essentially atomistic, comprising a 'succession of instantaneous configurations of matter' (Whitehead, 1926/1985: 63) so that by the eighteenth and nineteenth century 'the world had got hold of a general idea which it could neither live with nor without' (Whitehead, 1926/1985: 64). In particular, modern science 'rested contented with this assumption as to the fundamental elements of nature ... Physicists took no more interest in philosophy' (Whitehead, 1926/1985: 63). Yet, as Whitehead argues, this tendency to view reality as comprising isolatable, stable and atomistic entities that can be simply located in space-time, has led to a 'Fallacy of Misplaced Concreteness' in which the conceptual abstractions themselves have come to be mistaken for reality in itself (Whitehead, 1926/1985: 64, 72). Whilst the physical sciences are able to progress knowledge in the way they do, because they deal with relatively stable and durable phenomena that for all intents and purposes can be construed as clearly-circumscribed entities, within the social sciences which investigates social phenomena that are far more unstable, fleeting and ephemeral, this premise becomes highly questionable. Despite this, many social scientists continue to rely on this still-dominant metaphysical outlook construing

Philosophical Underpinnings of OPM Research

social units such as 'individuals' and 'organizations' as well as 'the environment' as stable, substantial and clearly-circumscribed atomistic entities and/or agglomerations of the latter.

Nevertheless, there has been a recent resurgence of Heraclitean-type thinking in recent years that has begun to challenge the dominance of Parmenidean thought in the West. A number of important 20th century thinkers, especially Henri Bergson (1911/1998, 1946/1992), and Alfred North Whitehead (1926/1985, 1929), as well as other more contemporary 'process physicists' (Bohm, 1980; Prigogine, 1981, 1996) have unequivocally upheld the 'flux of things' as the ultimate basis of reality. Whitehead in *Process and Reality* (1929: 295) writes: 'Without doubt, if we are to go back to that ultimate integral experience, unwarped by the sophistication of theory … the flux of things is one ultimate generalization around which we must weave our philosophical system'. Similarly, the physicist David Bohm insists that, 'Not only is everything changing, but all *is* flux. That is to say, *what is* is the process of becoming … objects, events, entities, conditions, structures, etc., are forms that can be abstracted from this process' (Bohm, 1980: 48, emphasis original). It is this resurrecting of the primacy of movement and change (what Bohm calls the 'implicate order') over that of Parmenidean substantial entities and end states that enables a radically alternative *becoming* ontology for understanding social order and organization to become more *thinkable* within the social sciences in general and in management and organization studies in particular. Moreover, this metaphysical 'reversal' from *being* to *becoming* in the Western consciousness displays a surprising affinity to the rich ancient tradition of Indo-Oriental thought. As Whitehead astutely noted it is a worldview that 'seem to approximate more to some strains of Indian, or Chinese, thought than to western Asiatic, or European thought. One side makes process ultimate; the other side makes fact ultimate' (Whitehead, 1929: 9). Many other students of Oriental culture (Nishida, 1921/1990; Needham, 1962; Graham, 1989; Nishitani, 1982) have also recognized that intrinsic to Indo-Asian cultures is an instinctive proclivity to embrace change and radical impermanence as the true basis of reality in contrast to the Western preference for form, substance, stability and order.

These two competing ontologies of *being* and *becoming* have irretrievably shaped epistemological priorities and methodological predispositions in management and organization research. Whilst it is not possible to definitively relate a specific research paradigm in terms of a fixed set of ontological presuppositions in each and every instance, it is nevertheless possible to show how the direction in which a particular paradigm of research takes implicates a preferred set of underlying ontological and epistemological presuppositions that is consistent with what we have previously identified as *being* and *becoming*.

Epistemological Implications of *Being* and *Becoming* for Organizational Research

You cannot think without abstractions; accordingly it is of utmost importance to be vigilant in critically revising your modes *of abstraction. A civilization which cannot burst through its current abstractions is doomed to sterility after a very limited period of progress* (Alfred North Whitehead, Science and the Modern World, 1926/1985: 73).

Each of these two distinct and incommensurable world-views, *being* and *becoming*, carry with it specific ontological commitments that have distinct epistemological consequences and hence for research priorities in management and organization studies. On the one hand, the Parmenidean-inspired belief that reality is essentially entitative, formed, stable and hence locatable in space-time leads to a *representationalist* epistemology in which language and logic is deemed to be adequate to the task of accurately representing reality as it is in itself. For, if reality were indeed fundamentally fixed and unchanging, language would be capable of describing with precision the definitive features of a particular aspect of it. On the other, the belief that pristine reality is fluid, unformed and ever-changing leads to a view that social entities, social order, and even the everyday social structures that we find so familiar and even necessary are ultimately *socially constructed* through our selective actions and linguistic interpretations; they are temporarily-stabilized patterns of relations forged through the embedding of everyday social actions, traditions and practices into (mostly unconscious) collective habits and predispositions. Adopting either a *representationalist* or a *social constructionist* epistemological outlook brings with it wide ranging consequences as to how we view knowledge, how we go about researching social phenomena and how we interpret our research findings. In what follows, I shall develop the implications of each of these two epistemological impulses for management and organizational research.

An Ontology of Being and an Epistemology of Representationalism

According to an ontology of *being* it is substantial social 'things', i.e., 'individuals', 'organizations', 'institutions' that change. The social world is made up of stable social entities that are clearly bounded, easily locatable, and unproblematically identifiable in space-time (Whitehead, 1926/85: 61) for the purposes of linguistic representation and rigorous causal *analysis*. Analysis, as a methodological impulse which emerged during the Classical episteme as we have seen, entails the systematic separation, breaking-up and isolation of otherwise complex phenomena into discrete components for the purpose of detailed investigation. Such an approach facilitates the systematic fixing, naming and classifying of part-elements so that it is possible to then say what a thing 'IS' or what it 'IS NOT'. This paradigm of thought signals an unwavering faith in the adequacy of language to 'mirror' the key salient features of reality (Rorty, 1980).

One major consequence of such a representationalist mindset is the obsessive creation of taxonomies, tables and hierarchies for representing both the natural and social worlds. As a consequence the social sciences have also been encouraged to adopt this dominant scientific method of investigation in dealing with social phenomena. 'Individuals', 'organizations', 'environments' and 'markets' are thus conveniently construed as discrete, substantial and free-standing entities that are not dissimilar to 'rocks, trees, or houses' (Elias, 1978: 13) and hence conceptually isolatable for the purpose of social analysis. They are deemed to be bounded by a structure of 'invisible walls' and to possess definable characteristics independent of their socio-historical contexts. This widespread presumption regarding the entitative characteristics of social reality underpins much of contemporary management and organization research.

One of the most important consequences of this entitative conception of social reality, and the *representationalist* epistemology that derives from it, is that of *social atomism* and its adoption of *methodological individualism* as the basis of social analysis. Methodological individualism is first and foremost a theoretically atomistic approach to the understanding of society and social phenomena. It assumes that institutions, organizations, markets, social order and other macro-social phenomena are artefacts of deliberate purposeful actions on the part of individual actors. It maintains, following Weber (1968: 15), that what defines 'action', as opposed to 'mere' behaviour, is that it is motivated by a mental state with a propositional content. To subscribe to methodological individualism is, therefore, to privilege the assumption that actions are necessarily motivated by prior intentional states relying on mental representations.

The three key features of methodological individualism are: a) individual autonomy; b) a rejection of the primacy of social structures and relations; and c) the central role ascribed to cognition and conscious choice (Chia and Holt, 2009: 63). According to this still widespread view acts of cognition and representation precede act of doing. Rational choice and a 'consequentialist' (March, 2003) mode of thinking that espouses a means-ends logic of action are deemed to provide the sole basis for understanding human behaviour. For methodological individualists, social structures and institutions are largely symbolic artefacts of prior individual actions; only identifiable agents can be assigned causal significance in accounting for social change. In this way a *being ontology* justifies the crediting of significant event-happenings and social outcomes to the deliberate actions of identifiable individuals; an inherent *heroism* thus pervades many research accounts of organizational successes. As such causal efficacy is attributed to the high-profile actions and decisive interventions of purposeful individuals (Burgelman & Grove, 2007; Denis, Lamothe, & Langley, 2001; Siggelkow, 2001, 2002; Van de Ven, 1992). In this way, human agency is assigned an elevated status. Such a widespread world-view downplays the influence of social structures, institutions and cultural traditions in shaping human intentions and actions. It understates the possible impact of wider social, cultural and historical forces in unconsciously shaping individual and collective outlooks, tendencies and dispositions and hence the subsequent choices and decisions they might make (Bourdieu, 1990). Nor do chance circumstances and the unintended consequences of human action (Merton, 1936) feature prominently in such forms of causal explanation. But because methodological individualism elevates individual agency and intentionality it gives a sense of control over human destinies and in so doing augurs well with a positive ideology that elevates self-determination, self-interest and self-agrandization as the basis of human endeavours.

Methodological individualism is often contrasted with *methodological collectivism*, the belief that 'social phenomena can be adequately analysed and explained only by reference to facts about and features of *collections* of people … as opposed to individuals' (Schatzki, 2005: 466). This alternative methodological approach has been inspired by the sociologist Emile Durkheim who insisted that: 'Social facts must be studied as things, that is, as realities external to the individual' (Durkheim, 1982: 39). Durkheim argued that since the individual is an inherently social being, he or she is born into social structures and institutions not of his/her own making. Since such social orders pre-exist individuals they must have a significant influence on the latter's overall outlook even if the individual is, for the most part, unconscious or blissfully unaware of how these deep socio-cultural values or social structures shape his/her perceptions, 'choices', and actions. Whereas methodological individualists look to explaining social behaviour through recourse to individual intentions and decisions, methodological collectivist look to explaining social life in terms of underlying (and often unconscious) social structures, traditions and norms that exist and persist before and beyond such conscious intentions.

Yet, despite this significant difference in focus, both methodological collectivism and methodological individualism share a common ontological agenda in that *both* remain unquestionably committed to a *being* ontology and a *representationalist epistemology*. Both take as given the materiality and boundedness of the social phenomena being investigated. Both view their objects of analyses as circumscribed stable social 'entities', one micro, the other macro, possessing definable features and characteristics that can be accurately represented through precise linguistic terminologies. In this way it is possible for both methodological individualists and methodological collectivists to accord ontological primacy to their own preferred unit of analysis and to view the other as epiphenomena of the basic entities central to their approach. Thus both approaches, despite their apparent differences, share similar ontological and epistemological presuppositions; they both construe the fundamental unit of analysis in essentially static and entitative terms and consider accuracy of representation as the fundamental basis of knowledge. Social change as such is deemed to be an epiphenomenon, a transient phase of otherwise stable social entities.

Schatzki (2005: 466) puts it well when he says that methodological collectivism is 'just a more capacious form of individualism'. Likewise Archer (1995: 33) insist that the 'very terms of the confrontation between Individualists and Collectivists have to be queried before we can appreciate their growing rejection'. Both methodological individualism and methodological collectivism block an appreciation of the essentially dynamic interplay between 'structure' and 'agency' because each considers the other a

Philosophical Underpinnings of OPM Research

dependent variable leading either to an 'upwards conflation of structure' or a 'downward conflation of agency' (Chia and Holt, 2009: 65). Both succumb to a reifying way of thinking that 'greatly hampers and may even prevent one from understanding the true nature of sociological problems' (Elias, 1978: 13). This paradoxical issue of structure and agency, individualism and collectivism, has plagued the social sciences and exercised the minds of eminent sociologists for centuries. It could be argued that their inability to satisfactorily deal with this duality in explaining human action is a result of clinging on unquestioningly to an ontology of *being* and that a revise commitment to an ontology of *becoming* might offer a way out of this theoretical impasse.

An Ontology of Becoming and an Epistemology of Social Constructionism

An ontology of *becoming* begins with the assumption that change is a pervasive and ineluctable feature of reality (Bergson, 1911/1998). This idea that reality is constantly changing and in perpetual process has begun to regain prominence within theoretical physics and in philosophical circles (Bohm, 1980; Prigogine, 1989; Rescher, 1996) within the last four decades and has been taken up more recently within organizational and management research and theorizing (Chia, 1999; Tsoukas and Chia, 2002; Hernes, 2008). Process philosophical thinking does not deny 'substances' or 'entities'. Rather it sees them as 'subordinate in status and ultimately inhering in processes' (Rescher, 1996: 27). It rejects what Rescher calls the 'Process Reducibility Thesis'; that all processes are ultimately reducible to the actions of primary entities. Instead, process philosophical thinking privileges process over end-states and becoming over being. It is an intellectual orientation that accords primacy to the 'origination, flourishing, and passing of the old and the innovative emergence of ever-new existence' (Rescher, 1996: 28).

While the dominant entitative approach views change as periodic transitions taking place between otherwise stable states, a process view of reality sees change as pervasive, continuous and relentless. From a process-philosophical viewpoint, change can happen of its own volition without need for an identifiable agent of change (Bergson, 1946/1992: 147-8). As a consequence full commitment to a *becoming* ontology entails embracing a theory of process and unexpected emergence that eschews attributing success or failure solely to either the heroism or incompetence of leaders or, alternatively, to the munificence or perniciousness of a pre-existing external environment. Instead it favours crediting eventualities to the unexpected turns of circumstances brought about through ongoing interactions that ultimately influence the fortune and survival of a social unit. Hence, success or failure, survival or demise cannot be wholly attributed to individual decisions made or to pre-existing environmental forces. Rather, chance, happenstance and unintended consequences have much to say in shaping individual and organizational destinies.

Process philosophical thinking invites us to think about organizations, and other social entities as themselves relatively stabilized products of ceaseless change, emergence and self-transformation; precariously configured effects of self-sustaining process complexes. They are not primary causal agents of change as such but effects of the latter. It urges us to recognize that what really exist are 'not things made but things in the making' (James, 1909/1996: 263). The social world, in particular, is not 'ready-made'; rather, it is the material effect of ongoing enactive social processes of 'world-making' (Goodman, 1978; Chia, 2003). Social structures and entities are in effect emergent collective social orders often generated spontaneously and unintentionally through localized human coping actions and interactions. As such, social phenomena do not possess state-like qualities. Instead they are temporarily-stabilized, precariously-balanced patterns of relationships and event clusters.

Such an intellectual orientation has much to offer to the study of institutions, organizations and organizational life. Instead of focusing on organizations, their structures and their fixed attributes, attention is instead directed to the micro-practices of 'everyday practical coping actions' (Chia & Holt, 2006) and ongoing 'sensemaking' efforts (Weick, 1995; Weick, Sutcliffe, & Obstfeld, 2005) that collectively contribute towards the stabilizing of social relations and hence the possibility of organization. The study of the process of 'organizing' therefore replaces the study of 'organizations'. Instead of thinking about organizations as 'enduring totalities that resist change' (Tsoukas, 2003, p. 608), process thinking recognizes that contingency, emergence, creativity and complexity are fundamental to our understanding of organizational life. Change and *becoming* are ineluctable features of organization (Tsoukas and Chia, 2002). To understand 'organizations' processually is to recognize them as 'mediating networks' (Cooper & Law, 1995, p. 239) of social relations that are 'patterned yet indeterminate' (Tsoukas, 2003: 619), secondary effects of a scattered and heterogeneous social process.

Furthermore, and even more importantly, according to process philosophical thought, even individual persons themselves must similarly be understood as relatively stabilized effects of social relations and event clusters rather than as discrete social entities. Unlike methodological individualism, commitment to an ontology of *becoming* implies recognizing that socio-cultural practices and relationships precede individuality and personhood. The individual person, as such, is not to be understood as a bounded entity relating externally to its environment in such a way as to leave its basic, internally specified nature unaffected. Instead, each individual is essentially a socio-cultural nexus of historically shaped relationships. His/her identity and characteristics are not bestowed upon him/her in advance of his/her involvement with others but is in fact the result of a 'condensation of histories of growth and maturation within fields of social relations' (Ingold, 2000: 3). The coming-into-being of the person is part and parcel of the process of the coming-into-being of the world' (Ingold, 2000:168). Thus, instead of being an autonomous, intentional and purposeful agent, the individual is to be understood as a relatively stabilized agglomeration, or 'bundle' of culturally acquired tendencies and predispositions that Bourdieu (1990: 52) calls 'habitus'. We are first and foremost 'bundles' of relationships and event clusters, not

Philosophical Underpinnings of OPM Research

self-contained subjects. Ingold, paraphrasing the Spanish philosopher Ortega y Gasset, puts it especially well: 'We are not things but dramas; we have no nature, only history; we are not, though we live' (Ingold, 2000: 117, emphasis original). Every individual agency emerges as a locus of development within the context of a specific field of social practices.

To understand 'individuals' and 'organizations' processually, then, is to regard them as temporary 'assemblages of organizing' (Cooper & Law, 1995: 239) that are conceptually abstracted from an underlying 'sea of ceaseless change' (Chia, 2003: 131). Social entities such as individuals and organizations are in fact theoretical reifications that refer to slower-changing configurations of social relationships resulting from the sustained regularizing of human exchanges (Chia, 2003: 123; Weick, 2009: 3); no more than 'stability waves in a sea of process' (Rescher, 1996: 53). Such a process philosophical viewpoint promotes a decentred and dispersive view of 'the individual' and 'the organization' as a fluxing concatenation of event-clusters and patterned relationships that resists clear identity, simple location and static representation. It emphasizes the precariousness, artificiality and constructedness of social existence and encourages a closer, more intimate 'worm's-eye' view of individual, organizational and social life.

A *becoming* ontology associated with the process philosophical outlook is intimately related to the rise of a fundamental form of *relational thinking* (Bourdieu, 1998; Schatzki, 2005; Cooper 2005: 1693-98) as a viable alternative to methodological individualism and/or collectivism in that it puts material relations and social practices at the centre of social analysis. Several prominent social theorists and social anthropologists have attempted to develop the implications of this relational thinking for analyzing societies, organizations and individuals in terms of 'social practices' (Bourdieu, 1977, 1990; Ingold, 2000; Schatzki, 2005). Bourdieu, in particular, has developed his own 'philosophy of action', articulated in concepts such as 'field', 'habitus', 'capital' etc., that begins with everyday coping actions, social practices and interactions rather than with ready-made agents and their supposed intentions. Such a *relational* methodology seeks to explain human actions and the subsequent emergence of social entities, systems and structures in terms of the primacy of 'mindless' practical everyday coping actions and interactions (Bourdieu, 1977/2002, 1990; Dreyfus, 1991; De Certeau, 1984). It maintains that practical engagement as a basic condition in everyday life precedes mental content, conscious reflection or any form of symbolic representation. It argues that people may '"act" in every sense of the word, and yet none of all this would have to "enter our consciousness" ... The whole of life would be possible, without, as it were, seeing itself in a mirror' (Nietzsche, 1974: 354). In other words, contrary to the presumptions of a representationalist epistemology and the methodological individualism associated with it, there is no need to assume that every practical action taken must be preceded by deliberate intention and conscious cognition; actions are not always necessarily goal-driven. Although researchers may indeed observe a certain *consistency of actions* taken within a specific social context, this does not necessarily imply that deliberate purposeful intention on the part of the actor must have preceded it. Instead, it is very possible that such actions are the result of an internalized *modus operandi*; a largely unconsciously way of dealing with situations that is a result of effective acculturation and socialization. The predictability of responses thus derive, not so much from conscious intention, but from habituated social practices that have been internalized and that provide the stock background from which everyday practical coping actions are then intuitively drawn. What people do in responding to specific social situations they find themselves in is in fact 'governed by batteries of dispositions' (Schatzki, 2005: 471) rather than by deliberate and rational thought.

This background bundle of acquired social practices that make up 'the individual' possesses an elaborate phenomenological structure that Heidegger (1962) attempted to deconstruct in *Being and Time* by using unusual terms such as 'worldliness', 'readiness-to-hand' and 'for the sake of which' to create a new vocabulary of practical action that can effectively replace the overwhelmingly intentionalist vocabulary of methodological individualism with its associated vocabulary of terms like 'context', 'goal', 'intention', 'rationality' and 'purpose'. Several recent writers have attempted to articulate and expand on the implications of this relationally-based view of practical action and agency initiated by Heidegger and other similarly-minded philosophers including Friedrich Nietzsche and Ludwig Wittgenstein in what has now come to be called the 'Practice Turn' in social theory. Thus, in several seminal works, Michel Foucault (1979, 1966/1990, 1984/1992) develops his practice-based theory of individuation by showing how both discursive and non-discursive (i.e., physical) practices help produce and reproduce the individual subject who actively embeds these routines into his/her everyday practices and in so doing generates a semblance of regularity and predictability in his/her behaviour. Similarly, Pierre Bourdieu (1977/2002, 1990), Irvin Goffman (1977, 1983), Charles Taylor (1985, 1995), Hubert Dreyfus (1991) and Anthony Giddens (1984) have all help in translating the implications of a philosophy of practice into its social-theoretic consequences for the social sciences (see Rasche and Chia, 2009 for a more detailed discussion).

An ontology of *becoming* that is intimately associated with an epistemology of *social constructionism*, then focuses attention on the primacy of social relations and social practices as the basis for explaining the emergence of social phenomena such as individuals, organizations and societies. It allows for the otherwise inexplicable spontaneous and un-designed emergence of a whole range of social phenomena including language, money, cities and institutions (see Chia and Holt, 2009: 25-56). As such, it provides a significant challenge to the still-dominant paradigm of research underpinned by a *being* ontology and its epistemology of *representationalism*, and provides a viable alternative research agenda for the study of management and organization.

Conclusion

We can therefore see that the commitment to either a *being* or a *becoming* ontology brings with it radical and far-reaching consequences in the way we interrogate and make sense of social reality including especially the practices of organizational project management. This has profound implications for the development of project management study as a philosophically-informed, epistemologically-consistent and methodologically rigorous academic field of inquiry. For, the contrast in metaphysical outlook between the two worldviews of *being* and *becoming* that has been identified here as regards to the creation of knowledge and the appropriate fundamental units of analysis to be studied within organizational project management research could not be more stark. One advocates the primacy of discrete, social entities whether micro or macro, the other elevates the primacy of social relations and material practices, as the fundamental unit of analysis. One views knowledge-creation in truth-seeking representational terms, the other views knowledge as socially constructed; meaning is forged from within embedded practical coping circumstances. Workability not truth is the object of knowledge in the case of the latter. One is predisposed to assigning causal powers solely to conscious agents in the project management process, the other is inclined to view organizational outcomes as the resultant effect of the (oftentimes unexpected) interactions and relationships between multiple causal complexes. One is committed to the belief that the artefacts of our social world are the result of deliberate design and planned interventions on the part of intentional agents, the other views outcomes in the social world as oftentimes the unintended consequences of an embedded logic of practice that is essentially alien to the logic of an observer attempting to rationalize the actions of those being observed. It draws our attention to a vital distinction between the logic of 'logicians' and the logic of 'practitioners' (Bourdieu, 1990: 86-90). This point is further painstakingly made by Bourdieu when he writes: 'The shift from the practical scheme to the theoretical scheme, constructed after the event, from practical sense to the theoretical model … lets slip everything that makes the temporal reality of practice in process … The logicism in the objectivist viewpoint (i.e., from a representationalist epistemology) cannot grasp the principles of practical logic without forcibly changing their nature' (Boudieu, 1990: 81-90). Thus, with all the best will and intention, the academic researcher will not be able to grasp why project management practitioners do what they do without being acutely aware of his/her own propensity to explain what he/she observes in terms that seem sensible to him/her, but that is not so to the practitioners who are acting *in situ* and *sponte sua* (responding to the exigencies of the moment).

According to an alternative *becoming* ontology, then, the idea that individuals are the primary agents of change, that they make deliberate rational choices, set goals and act to achieve these pre-established goals, all these reflects an 'intellectuallocentricism' (Bourdieu, 1990: 29) on the part of academic researchers themselves who are thus prone to imputing to practical actors a rationality that is alien to them (Chia, 2004: 29-30). These two incommensurable ontologies, *being* and *becoming* ultimately frame research agendas and priorities in project management and organization studies. They produce different forms of knowledge that serve different purposes; one seeks validity and legitimacy through rigorous proof and justification, the other through practical expediency and effectiveness of outcome.

References

Archer, M. (1995). *Realist Social Theory: The Morphogenetic Approach*, Cambridge: Cambridge University Press.

Bergson, H. (1911/1998). *Creative Evolution*. Mineola, New York: Dover Publications.

Bergson, H. (1946/1992). *The Creative Mind*. New York: Citadel Press.

Bohm, D. (1980). *Wholeness and the implicate order*. London: Routledge & Kegan Paul.

Bourdieu, P. (1977/ 2002). *Outline of a theory of practice*, Cambridge: Cambridge University Press.

Bourdieu, P. (1990) *The Logic of Practice*. Stanford, Calif.: Stanford University Press.

Bourdieu, P. (1998). *Practical Reason: On the Theory of Action*, Oxford: Blackwell.

Burgelman, R., & Grove, A. (2007). Let chaos reign, then reign in chaos – repeatedly: Managing strategic dynamics for corporate longevity. *Strategic Management Journal*, 28: 965-79.

Cooper, R. and J. Law (1995). 'Organization: Distal and Proximal Views', in S.B. Bacharach (ed.), *Research in the Sociology of Organizations*, Greenwich, CT: JAI Press.

Cooper, R. (2005). 'Relationality', *Organization Studies* 26/11: 1689-1710.

Chia, R. (1999). 'A "rhizomic" model of organizational change and transformation: Perspective from a metaphysics of change', *British Journal of Management*, 10, 209-227.

Chia, R. (2003). 'Organization Theory as Postmodern Science', in Tsoukas. H. and C. Knudsen (eds.), The Oxford Handbook of Organization Theory, Oxford: Oxford University Press.

Chia, R. (2004) 'Strategy-as-practice: Reflections on the research agenda', *European Management Review* 1/1: 29-34.

Chia, R. and R. Holt, (2006). 'Strategy as practical coping – A Heideggerian perspective', *Organization Studies* 27/5: 635-55.

Chia, R. and R. Holt, (2007). Wisdom as Learned Ignorance: Integrating East-West Perspectives, in E.H. Kessler & J.R. Bailey (eds.) *Handbook of Organizational and Managerial Wisdom*, Thousand Oaks, CA: Sage.

Chia, R. and Holt, R. (2009) *Strategy without Design: The Silent Efficacy of Indirect Action*, Cambridge: Cambridge University Press.

De Certeau, M. (1984) *The Practice of Everyday Life*. Berkeley, Calif.: University of California Press.

Denis, J., Lamothe, L., & Langley, A. (2001). 'The dynamics of collective leadership and strategic change in pluralistic organizations', *Academy of Management Journal*, 44: 809-837.

Dreyfus, H.L. (1991). *Being-in-the-world*. Cambridge, MA: MIT Press.

Durkheim, E. (1982). *Rules of sociological method*, New York: The Free Press.

Elias, N. (1978). *What is Sociology?*, London: Hutchingson.

Eliot, T.S. (1942/2001). *Little Giddings*, London: Faber and Faber.

Foucault, M. (1970). *The order of things*, London: Tavistock.

Foucault, M. (1979). *Discipline and Punish*, London: Penguin.

Foucault, M. (1966/1990). *The history of sexuality: The care of the self*. London: Penguin.

Foucault, M. (1984/1992). *The history of sexuality: The use of pleasure*. London: Penguin.

Goodman, N. (1978). *Ways of Worldmaking*, New York: Hackett Publishing Co.

Graham, A.C. (1989). *Disputers of the Tao*, La Salle, IL: Open Court.

Gutting, G. (1989). *Michel Foucault's archaeology of scientific reason*. Cambridge, UK: Cambridge University Press.

Giddens, A. (1984). *The constitution of society*. Berkeley: University of California Press.

Goffman E. (1977). *Frame analysis: An essay on the organization of experience*. Cambridge, MA: Harvard University Press.

Goffman, E. (1983). 'The interaction order', *American Sociological Review* 48: 1-17.

Heidegger, M. (1962). *Being and Time*, Oxford: Basil Blackwell.

Hernes, T. (2008). *Understanding organization as process*, Abingdon: Routledge.

Ingold, T. (2000). *The perception of the environment*, London: Routledge.

James, W. (1890/1983) *Principles of Psychology*, Cambridge, Mass.: Harvard University Press.

James, W. (1909/1996). *A Pluralistic Universe*, Lincoln: University of Nebraska Press.

James, W. (1911/1996). *Some Problems of Philosophy*, Lincoln: University of Nebraska Press.

James, W. (1912/1996). *Essays in Radical Empiricism*, Lincoln: University of Nebraska Press.

Lash, S. (1990). *Sociology of postmodernism*. London: Routledge.

Linnaeus, C. (1758). *Systema naturae per regna tria naturae: secundum classes, ordines, genera, species, cum characteribus, differentiis, synonymis, locis* (10th edition eds.) Stockholm: Laurentius Salvius.

Mansley Robinson, J. (1968). *An Introduction to Early Greek Philosophy*, Boston: Houghton Mifflin Co.

March, J.G. (2003). 'A Scholar's Quest', *Journal of Management Inquiry*, vol. 12/3, 205-207.

Merton, R. (1936). 'The unanticipated consequences of purposive social action', *American Sociological Review*, 1: 894-904.

Morin, E. (1977/1992) *Method: Towards a Study of Humankind*, trans. J.L. Roland, Belanger, New York: Peter Lang.

Morin, E. (2008). *On Complexity*, trans Robin Postel, New Jersey: Hampton Press.

Needham, J. (1962). Science and Civilisation in China, Vol. 2, Cambridge: Cambridge University Press.

Nietzsche, F. (1974). *The gay science*, New York: Random House.

Nishida, K. (1921/1990). *An inquiry into the good* (trans. M. Abe & C. Ives). New Haven, CT: Yale University Press.

Nishitani, Keiji (1982). Religion and Nothingness, trans. Jan van Bragt, Berkeley: University of California Press.

Prigogine, I. (1981) *From Being to Becoming: Time and Complexity in the Physical Sciences*, New York: W.H. Freeman & Co.

Prigogine, I. (1996). The End of Certainty, New York and London: The Free Press.

Rasche, A. and R. Chia (2009). 'Researching Strategy Practices: A Genealogical Social Theory Perspective', *Organization Studies*, Vol. 30/7: 713-34.

Rescher, N. (1996) *Process Metaphysics*. New York: State University of New York Press.

Rorty, R. (1980). *Philosophy and the Mirror of Nature*, Princeton, NJ: Princeton University Press.

Schatzki, T.R. (2005) 'The sites of organizations', *Organization Studies* 26/3: 465-84.

Serres, M. (1982). *Hermes: Literature, Science, Philosophy*, Baltimore: Johns Hopkins Press.

Siggelkow, N. (2001). 'Change in the presence of fit: The rise, the fall, and the renaissance of Liz Claiborne', *Academy of Management Journal*, 44: 838-57.

Siggelkow, N. (2002). 'Evolution towards fit', *Administrative Science Quarterly*, 47: 125-59.

Taylor, C. (1985). *Human agency and language: Philosophical Papers I*. Cambridge: Cambridge University Press.

Taylor, C. (1995). *Philosophical arguments*. Cambridge, MA: Harvard University Press.

Tsoukas, H., and R. Chia (2002). 'On organizational becoming: Rethinking organizational change', *Organization Science* 13/5: 567-82.

Tsoukas, H. (2003). 'New Times, Fresh Challenges: Reflections on the Past and Future of Organization Theory', in H. Tsoukas and C. Knudsen (eds), *The Oxford Handbook of Organization Theory*, Oxford: Oxford University Press, pp. 607-619.

Van de Ven, A. (1992). 'Suggestions for studying strategy process: A research note', *Strategic Management Journal*, 13: 169-188.

Weber, M. (1968). *Economy and society*, G. Roth and C. Wittich (eds), Berkeley. CA: University of California Press.

Weick, K.E. (1995). *Sensemaking in organizations*, Thousand Oaks, CA: Sage.

Weick, K.E., Sutcliffe, K.M., & Obstfeld, D. (2005). 'Organizing and the process of sensemaking', *Organization Science*, 16/4, 409-21.

Weick, K.E. (2009). Making Sense of Organization: The Impermanent Organization Vol 2, New York, Wiley.

Wheelwright, P. (1974). Heraclitus, New York: Atheneum.

Whitehead, A.N. (1926/1985) *Science and the Modern World*, London: Free Association Books.

Whitehead, A.N. (1929). *Process and Reality*, Cambridge: Cambridge University Press.

Whitehead, A. N. (1933). *Adventures of ideas*, Harmondsworth: Penguin.

Wilkinson, R. (2009). *Nishida and Western Philosophy*, Farnham, Surrey: Ashgate Publishing Co.

Chapter 2

"A" Discourse on the Non-method

Christophe Bredillet

Abstract

In spite of the activism of professional bodies and researchers, empirical evidence shows that project management still does not deliver the expected benefits and promises. Hence, many have questioned the validity of the hegemonic rationalist paradigm anchored in the Enlightenment and Natural Sciences tradition supporting project management research and practice for the last 60 years and the lack of relevance to practice of the current conceptual base of project management.

In order to address these limitations many authors, taking a post-modernist stance in social sciences, build on 'pre-modern' philosophies such as the Aristotelian one, specially emphasizing the role of praxis (activity), and phronesis (practical wisdom, prudence). Indeed, 'Praxis … is the central category of the philosophy which is not merely an interpretation of the world, but is also a guide to its transformation …' (Vazquez, 1977:. 149). Therefore, praxis offers an important focus for practitioners and researchers in social sciences, one in which theory is integrated with practice at the point of intervention. Simply stated, praxis can serve as a common ground for those interested in basic and applied research by providing knowledge of the reality in which action, informed by theory, takes place.

Consequently, I suggest a 'praxeological' style of reasoning (praxeology being defined as study or science of human actions and conduct, including praxis, practices and phronesis) and to go beyond the 'Theory-Practice' divide. Moreover, I argue that we need to move away from the current dichotomy between the two classes 'scholars-experts-researchers' and 'managers/workers-practitioners-participants'. Considering one single class of 'PraXitioner', becoming a phronimos, may contribute to create new perspectives and open up new ways of thinking and acting in project situations.

Thus, I call for a Perestroika in researching and acting in project management situations. My intent is to suggest a balanced praxeological view of the apparent opposition between social and natural science approaches. I explore, in this chapter, three key questions, covering the ontological, epistemological and praxeological dimensions of project management in action.

1. Are the research approaches being currently used appropriate for generating contributions that matter to both theory and practice with regards to what a 'project' is or to what we do when we call a specific situation 'a project'?
2. On the basis of which intellectual virtues is the knowledge generated and what is the impact for theory and practice?
3. Are the modes of action of the practitioners 'prudent' and are they differentiating or reconciling formal and abstract rationality from substantive rationality and situated reasoning with regards to the mode of action they adopt in particular project situations?

The investigation of the above questions leads me to debate about 'Project Management-as-Praxis', and to suggest 'A' (not 'THE') 'praxeological' style of reasoning and mode of inquiry – acknowledging a non-paradigmatic, subjective and kaleidoscopic perspective – for 'Knowing-as-Practicing' in project management.
In short, this is about making a 'Projects Science' that matters.

A Call for Perestroika

Plato and Aristotle [...] asked: "How should one live?", and that question is as pressing now as it was in 400 BC (Putnam & Putnam, 1996: 14).

Aristotle answered this question by suggesting that individuals should achieve *eudaimonia* (well-being, happiness) (Aristotle, 1926a, Book 6). *Eudaimonia* requires activity, action, so that it is not sufficient for a person to possess a good character, a squandered ability or disposition. Philosophic wisdom (sophia) and intuitive reason (nous) do not consider the means to human happiness at all, for it does not ask how anything comes into existence. Practical wisdom (phronesis) does do this (1143b). This leads me to define the main objective of this chapter, which is:

suggesting a 'Praxis' turn, a praxeological style of reasoning in projects research, enabling practical wisdom in conjunction with philosophic wisdom and intuitive reason.

That is, one that aims at addressing one of the fundamental problems in the field: Projects still do not deliver their expected benefits and promises and therefore the socio-economical good (Hodgson & Cicmil, 2007; Bredillet, 2010, Lalonde et al., 2012). The rationalist, positivist and quantitative tradition and paradigm supporting projects research and practice for the last 60 years (Bredillet, 2010: 4) and the lack of relevance to practice of the current conceptual base of project management, despite the sum of research, development of standards, best practices and the related development project management bodies of knowledge (Packendorff, 1995: 319-323; Cicmil & Hodgson, 2006: 2-6; Hodgson & Cicmil, 2007: 436-7; Winter et al., 2006: 638).

Borrowing to both Hodgson (2002) and Giddens (1993), I could say that 'those who expect a "social-scientific Newton" to revolutionize this young field "are not only waiting for a train that will not arrive, but are in the wrong station altogether".' (Hodgson, 2002: 809; Giddens, 1993: 18).

I call for a Perestroika (Schram, 2004: 418, and email dated 17 Oct 2000 from 'Perestroika Glasnost' to the American Political Science Association (APSA) signed Mr Perestroika) in projects research and 'discipline' in the dual meaning given by Hodgson (2002: 804): 1) body of knowledge and expertise, and 2) training/education and (self-) control.

The discussion of three central questions, covering the ontological, epistemological and praxeological dimensions of the projects research in action, supports this objective, leading to suggest a praxeological inquiry before some 'opening non-concluding' comments. Paralleling Tsoukas & Cummings (1997:. 655), the three key questions can be stated as follows:

1. Are the research approaches currently being used appropriate for generating contributions that matter to both theory and practice with regards to what a 'project' is or to what we do when we call a specific situation 'a project'? (Hodgson & Cicmil, 2007: 432).
2. Which intellectual virtues is the knowledge generated from and what is the impact for theory and practice? (Aristotle, 1926a).
3. Are the actions of the practitioners 'prudent' (Aristotle, 1926a) and are they differentiating or reconciling abstract rationality from situated reasoning, espoused theory from theory-in-use with regards to the mode of action they adopt in particular project situations? (Argyris & Schön, 1974; Kondrat, 1992; Toulmin, 2002).

As a matter of clarification, I want to specify that:

- The order of the questions doesn't involve any precedence between ontology, epistemology and praxeology (Pouliot, 2007: 363; Blomquist et al., 2010: 13). There is no assumption of an a priori reality, concepts and knowledge are not reality, and lastly, in project situations and actions the problematization of what is held to be 'real' involves taking into account the constructed effects of knowledge. The situation is constructed reflexively and iteratively, based on the unstable balance that the actors attempt to maintain between the 'real' (descriptive practice) and the 'preferable' (design practice) (Hacking, 1999: 6; Lalonde et al. 2012: 428).
- Praxeology implies instilling practice with theoretical content and theoretical formulation resulting from practice (Warry, 1992: 161; Tsoukas & Papoulias, 1996: 75). The questions and the clarification comments made above reflect 'A' (not 'THE') praxeological style of reasoning (Hacking, 2002a: 159-77; Hacking, 2002b: 2; Pouliot, 2007: 361). A 'style of reasoning' is defined by '"a

new domain of objects to study" (an ontology), a new kind of "truth conditions" (an epistemology), as well as "its own criteria of proof and demonstration" (a methodology) (Hacking, 2002b: 4)' (Pouliot, 2007: 361), and this definition mirrors the three questions under investigation.

Before moving to discussion of the questions, it is appropriate to define some key concepts and to position the philosophical and theoretical stance of the chapter.

Modes of Action (Practice) and Modes of Knowledge (Theory)

Based on Aristotelian philosophy (Aristotle, 1926a; Tsoukas & Cummings, 1997: 664-5), we can highlight the relations between the different modes of action (or 'Practice') and their goals, and the relevant types of knowledge/intellectual virtues (or 'Theory') (Carr & Kemmis, 1986: 32):

1. Theoria (end goal – telos: knowledge for its own sake, Truth) involves Episteme (scientific knowledge, universal, invariable, context independent and based on general analytic and positivist rationality).
2. Poiesis (end goal: production of some artefact) involves Techne (craft/art, pragmatic, variable, context dependent, based on practical instrumental rationality governed by conscious goal).
3. Praxis (end goal: practical wisdom and knowledge, action) involves Phronesis (Ethics, Politics, deliberation about values, pragmatic, variable, context dependent, based on practical value-rationality). 'Phronesis is that intellectual activity most relevant to Praxis' (Flyvbjerg, 2004: 288).

In this work, the three concepts of praxis (Project Management-as-Praxis, activity involved in project making), practices (various tools, norms, and procedures of project work), and practitioners (actors involved in, or seeking to influence, project making) are used, following the Aristotelian tradition, and the practice tradition; I should say the praxeological tradition.

All praxis is an activity, but not all activity is praxis (Vazquez, 1977: 149).

Activity includes lively action or movement, any specific deed, pursuit, the state or quality of being active. Warry (1992) observes that the term 'praxis' is used as a synonym for 'practice'. Furthermore, 'The analytic impoverishment of praxis signals a larger problem within anthropology: The division between theory and application' (Warry, 1992: 155). We must return to the roots of the concept and explicit it. Vazquez (1977) offers a clear and simple definition of the term when he wrote:

Praxis ... is the central category of the philosophy which is not merely an interpretation of the world, but is also a guide to its transformation ... (Vazquez, 1977: 149).

Praxis is a particular form of activity, a reflexive activity underlying rational action. It is concerned with change, is present and future oriented, requires anticipation of the effect of action, rather than the interpretation of past or prior event (Vazquez, 1977: 169; Warry, 1992: 156). Praxis is 'a specific form of activity based on knowledge informed by theory and performed according to certain ethical and moral principles for political ends' (Warry, 1992: 157). Praxis offers an important focus for practitioners and researchers in social science, one in which theory is integrated with practice at the point of intervention. Praxis, as a particular form of activity, can serve as a focal point through which the discursive testing of theory is grounded through decision making and experience (Habermas, 1973: 20). Simply stated, praxis can serve as a common ground for those interested in basic and applied research by providing knowledge of the reality in which action, informed by theory, takes place (Warry, 1992: 156).

We can now see the full quality of praxis. It is not simply action based on reflection. It is action which embodies certain qualities. These include a commitment to human well-being and the search for truth, and respect for others. It is the action of people who are free, who are able to act for themselves. Moreover, praxis is always risky. It requires that a person 'makes a wise and prudent practical judgement about how to act in this situation' (Carr & Kemmis 1986: 190 quoted in Smith, 1999, 2011). Praxis as such aims at the liberation of individuals or communities from the alienating aspects of everyday practice subject to the hegemony of the rationalist forces constraining every day actions or activities (Warry, 1992: 157).

The consequence is, because praxis has a central role between theoria and poeisis (Warry, 1992: 156-7), we can generalize the notion of Practice as encompassing theoria, poeisis AND praxis.

Although there is little agreement about a definition of what a theory is (Gioia & Pitre, 1990: 587; Sutton & Staw, 1995: 372; Corley & Gioia, 2011: 12), we can use a general definition, for instance:

Theory is 'an ordered set of assertions about a generic behaviour or structure assumed to hold throughout a significantly broad range of specific instances' (Sutherland, 1975: 9; Boxenbaum & Rouleau, 2011: 274).

We can then define, as follows, the relationships between Theory, Practice and Knowledge: Knowledge 'embedded' in Practice (modes of action) – whatever it is tacit (Polanyi, 1962, 1966), implicit (Nonaka, 1994) or explicit knowledge (Gourlay, 2006) – is transformed and translated into, and is recursively and reflexively informed and transformed by, Theory – defined here as the articulation of intellectual virtues: episteme, techne AND phronesis, bearing in mind the central role of phronesis mirroring the one of praxis for Practice. This knowledge production and transfer (e.g. Kolb & Fry,

1975; Nonaka, 1994; Boisot, 1995, 1998) is processed via styles of reasoning (Hacking, 2002b: 3), epistemic scripts (Boxenbaum & Rouleau, 2011: 272), or modes of inquiry.

Praxis vs. Practice Turn

A vast amount of literature (e.g. Bourdieu, 1990; de Certeau, 1984; Foucault, 1977; Giddens, 1979) has been published since the early 1980s dealing with practice in social theory (Schatzki et al., 2001; Reckwitz, 2002), e.g. strategy-as-practice (for an overview, see Jarzabkowski et al., 2007; Carter et al., 2008; Rasche & Chia, 2009; Vaara & Whittington, 2012). These works aim at overcoming the dualism between 'individualism' and 'societism' (Schatski, 2005). 'Practice theorist aim to respect both the efforts of individual actors and the workings of the social' (Whittington, 2006: 614). The three core themes for practice theory (practices, praxis and practitioners) are forming interrelated parts of a whole (Giddens, 1984). In the project management context, the practice turn, strongly inspired by the strategy as practice stream, has gained momentum (e.g. Bredillet, 2004; Bechky, 2006; Cicmil, 2006; Cicmil et al., 2006; Hällgren & Wilson, 2008; Blomquist et al., 2010; Hällgren & Söderholm, 2011; Sanderson, 2012).

Vaara & Whittington (2012) make clear that the 'practice turn' 'defines itself in opposition to methodological individualism', how 'praxis relies on practices', and 'how social structures and human agency link together in the explanation of action' (Vaara & Whittington, 2012: 288).

My position here is exactly the reverse: practices rely on praxis, and while recognizing the link between human agency and social structures, I consider praxeology, and related praxis rooted in phronesis with an emancipatory perspective, where choice, responsibility and accountability is part of what makes a person a person, not hidden or diluted by some kind 'social' mist and fog patches.

Beyond the Gap Practice-Theory: And then Comes the "PraXitioner"!

The assumptions about the roles, behaviours and expectations of the people, as framed by the classical classes' dichotomy between scholars and managers/workers (Aram & Salipante, 2003: 1900; Van de Ven & Johnson, 2006: 806), involved in knowledge creation and transfer is at the centre of the Theory-Practice relevance and rigour debate. Some authors have pleaded for some kind of junction or integration between the 'scholars-experts-researchers' and the 'managers/workers-practitioners-participants' (e.g. Reclaiming the practical: Technical and Substantive Rationality and Discourse (Kondrat, 1992: 241); social science practitioner (Warry, 1992: 160); engaged scholars (Van de Ven & Johnson, 2006: 803; Objectivism style of reasoning (Pouliot, 2007:

360), tipping point (Rynes, 2007, 1051), practitioners in the context of project-as-practice (Blomquist et al., 2010: 13); practitioner-researcher (Jarvis, 1999), and researcher-practitioner (Lalonde et al. 2012, note 8: 429).

I suggest we need to go further in-depth to fully grasp the importance of moving to consider one single class of actors in project situations. Hacking (2002b), while reflecting about classifications posits that 'The human and the social sciences ... differ because there is a dynamical interaction between the classifications developed in the social sciences, and the individuals or behaviour classified' (Hacking, 2002b: 10). He develops the idea of 'interactive classifications' (Hacking, 2001) and 'looping effects' (Hacking, 1995) about 'how classification affect us and how we create new classes anew' (Hacking, 2002b: 12).

As a consequence, moving from the two classes dichotomy 'scholars-experts-re-searchers' and the 'managers/workers-practitioners-participants' to one single class I name 'praXitioners' is all but neutral, with regards to a praxeological (praxeology defined as study or science of human actions and conduct, praxis and practices) style of reasoning (Hacking, 2002b: 3) and to go beyond the Theory-Practice gap. I argue that this move away from the current dichotomy may contribute to create new perspectives through a new class and open up new ways of thinking and acting in project situations.

Back to the Future

The questioning of the modern rationalist tradition mirrors a similar one made within Social Sciences (Say, 1964; Koontz, 1980; Menger, 1985; Warry, 1992; Rothbard, 1997a; Tsoukas & Cummings, 1997; Flyvbjerg, 2001; Boisot & McKelvey, 2010), calling for new thinking. In order to get outside the rationalist 'box', Toulmin (1990: 11), along with Tsoukas & Cummings (1997: 655), suggests a possible path, summarizing the thoughts of many authors:

> It can cling to the discredited research program of the purely theoretical (i.e. "modern") philosophy, which will end up by driving it out of business: it can look for new and less exclusively theoretical ways of working, and develop the methods needed for a more practical ("post-modern") agenda; or it can return to its pre-17th century traditions, and try to recover the lost ("pre-modern") topics that were side-tracked by Descartes, but can be usefully taken up for the future (Toulmin, 1990: 11).

Thus, paradoxically and interestingly, in their quest for the so-called post-modernism, many authors build on 'pre-modern' philosophies such as the Aristotelian one (e.g. MacIntyre, 1985; Tsoukas & Cummings, 1997; Flyvbjerg, 2001; Blomquist et al., 2010; Lalonde et al., 2012). Maybe because the post-modern stream emphasizes a dialogic process restricted to reliance on voice and textual representation, limiting the meaning of communicative praxis, weakening for practice because it turns away attention from more fundamental issues associated with problem-definition and knowledge-for-use in action (Tedlock, 1983: 332-4; Schrag, 1986: 30, 46-7; Warry, 1992: 157).

A Difference that Makes a Difference

The problem of sciences that matter has been widely discussed e.g. in Organization Studies (Tsoukas, 1994; Tsoukas & Papoulias, 1996), Social Science (Flyvbjerg, 2001; Schram, 2004) or Management Science (Hodgkinson, 2001; Rynes et al., 2001; Van de Ven & Johnson, 2006; Kraaijenbrink, 2010). In the area of project management a stream in Critical Studies with a Foucauldian perspective has been developed by Cicmil and Hodgson (Hodgson, 2002; Cicmil & Hodgson, 2006; Hodgson & Cicmil, 2007) and through the 'Making Projects Critical' workshops and their outcomes (Cicmil &Hodgson, 2006; Cicmil et al.; 2009). A Phronetic approach stream, with a special focus on Mega Projects, has been developed and documented (Flyvbjerg et al., 2003; Flyvbjerg et al., 2012). A common ground to these approaches is the recognition of the challenge of 'power' and the influence of Foucault. And they consider a clear dichotomy between 'bottom-up' (social science) and 'top-down' (natural science) approaches (Schram, 2004: 420).

My intent is to suggest a slightly different and more balanced praxeological view of the above-mentioned dichotomy between social and natural science approaches (Knorr 1977, 1979; Latour & Woolgar 1979; Latour 1980; Knorr-Cetina, 1981a). I challenge the dominant mechanistic-cum-rationalistic assumptions and suggest alternate such as historical-cum-comparative thinking (Tsoukas & Cummings, 1997: 673; Knorr-Cerina, 1981a: 336). Addressing the above three key questions will pave the way to provide some insights into praxeological inquiry – 'inventor's paralogy' rather than 'expert's homology' only (Lyotard, 1984: xxv) and '"faulty" logic that spawns invention' (Feyerabend, 1987 quoted in Tsoukas & Cummings, 1997: 673) – as a possible meta-approach enabling level 3 acting and learning (Bateson, 1973) – to make a difference that makes a difference.

In short, this is about making a 'Project Sciences' that matter to paraphrase Flyvbjerg (2001; 2006).

Debate and Deliberations

Discussion of question 1: Are the research approaches currently being used appropriate for generating contributions that matter to both theory and practice with regards to what a "project" is? or to what do we do when we call a specific situation "a project"?

The first part of question refers to 'action' although the second part of the question refs to 'discipline' meaning both 'body of knowledge and expertise underpinning the field' and 'a system of training and (self-)control' (Hodgson, 2002: 804). Interestingly the distinction made by the two enables to clarify the link between 'project' (situation) and 'project management' (acting). However, I consider here both parts of the question as legitimate in a balanced perspective enabling to fully capture the very nature of projects, project situations and therefore their management.

Project Management-as-Praxis

'Reconnecting Means and Ends, Facts and Values' (Tsoukas & Cummings, 1997: 668). Therefore project management is both praxis – acts which shape and transform the world – AND guided by phronesis – a moral disposition to act truly and rightly (Smith, 1999, 2011). It is about human action:

> *Aristotle's emphasis on the indispensability of 'phronesis' for human action tallies with the importance now placed on practical knowledge. The formal-cum-abstract mode of reasoning which was so highly exalted by the early organization theorists (see, e.g., Thompson 1956-57: 103) is now seen as too crude to account for a multifaceted and ambiguous reality. Practical knowledge is no longer conceived in quasi-algorithmic terms, as the application of generic formulae, but in terms of acting wisely, being able to close the 'phronetic gap' (Taylor 1993: 57) that almost inevitably exists between a formula and its enactment* (Tsoukas & Cummings, 1997: 668).

People act, i.e. they have goals and they make choices of means to attain their goals. Furthermore this implies that here is a scarcity of means to attain them otherwise the goals would already have been attained. And scarcity implies costs (not necessary monetary, i.e. psychological costs) which are, in a monetary system, reflected in price (or i.e. in value(s)). Acts involve 'projection in the future' and therefore possibility of deliberation (and decision making) about the future (plan), choice of means towards and end (efficiency) oriented/informed/guided by 'phronesis' (Smith, 1999, 2011), practical wisdom, prudence (Leguérinel, 2007: 18), and 'reconnecting means and ends, facts and values' (Tsoukas & Cummings, 1997: 668). Packendorff (1997: 327) also note the relations between organized course of action, action and time, goals, consensus (to be related to 'deliberation' (Dreyfus & Dreyfus, 1998) and 'arbitrage' (Harrison, 1997; Van de Ven & Johnson, 2006), 'kind of performance evaluation criteria' (efficiency), values, roles and consciousness.

Acts involve time, irreversibility, indetermination and contingence, uncertainty (Aristotle, 1926b, 1357a; Perelman & Olbrechts-Tyteca, 2006; Perminova et al., 2008: 76) and therefore risk (Carr & Kemmis, 1986: 190; Smith, 1999, 2011: 3; Lalonde et al, 2012: 420). In relation to uncertainty and deliberation, Aristotle notes 'But we only deliberate about things which seem to admit of issuing in two ways; as for those things which cannot in the past, present, or future be otherwise, no one deliberates about them, if he supposes that they are such; for nothing would be gained by it' (Aristotle, 1926b, 1357a).

Project Management-as-Praxis reconciles means and ends, and facts and values, overcoming the dualistic way of thinking (facts must remain uncontaminated by values, if we wish to be scientific) (Tsoukas & Cummings, 1997: 668). The Aristotelian teleological understanding of the world implies to consider individuals and objects according to the purposes they have and the role they have to play. 'Individuals are not ahistorical selves, but ... defined cultural and historical circumstances ... Purposive concepts, therefore, transform evaluative judgements into factual statements (MacIntyre, 1985: 57-9) ... To call a particular action good or just or effective, is to say that this is what a good leader would do in such a situation – that is, to make a factual statement (MacIntyre, 1985: 59)' (Tsoukas & Cummings, 1997: 670).

This involves that the rationality of a science of action cannot be perfect as what happens is not the 'necessary'. It is therefore impossible to try to control action in going into the details of things (Romeyer Dherbey, 1983: 49; Leguérinel, 2007: 37-52). Knorr-Cetina (1981a), however notes that 'Philosophical evidence suggests that method in the latter [natural] sciences is based upon the same kind of cycles of interpretation commonly associated with the social sciences (Kuhn 1970; Feyerabend 1975; or the summary in Suppe 1974)' (Knorr-Cetina, 1981a: 336). This supports my plea in favour of a balanced praxeological style of reasoning.

Knowledge that matters, phronesis, practical wisdom, could be subsequently developed through praxeological inquiry where praxis guided by phronesis in situation being the focus of inquiries (Petruszewycz, 1965: 12; Smith, 1999, 2011: 3). Analogue considerations with regards to the style of reasoning, epistemic scripts or mode of inquiry can be found as well in Vico (1710) and his concept of relevance by feasibility (vs. the concept of evidence by clarity from Descartes), presented and commented by Le Moigne (2007: 117).

Discussion of Question 2: Which Intellectual Virtues is the Knowledge Generated from and What is the Impact for Theory and Practice?

Authors recognize the tensions resulting from the shock between the tyranny of the particular and practical knowledge and the decontextualized ideal of formal-cum-abstract knowledge (Toulmin, 1990: 30-35). Tsoukas & Cummings (1997) conclude:

Anybody approaching issues such as these cannot afford to ignore Aristotle. Indeed, Aristotle's Nichomachean Ethics is perhaps the text 'par excellence' for anyone concerned with the question of what exactly practical knowledge is about (Tsoukas & Cummings, 1997: 664).

The discussion of question 2 leads us to consider the three modes of action defined above (theoria, poiesis, and praxis) and the implication for different kinds of knowledge perspectives and modes of inquiry (Aristotle, 1926a; Flyvbjerg, 2004: 288; Van de Ven, 2006: 805) in association with the three intellectual virtues related to 'acting' (episteme, techne, and phronesis) as stated by Aristotle (Aristotle, 1926a; Tsoukas & Cummings, 1997: 664-5).

Mediating Theory-Practice: The Role of a Praxeological Style of Reasoning and Mode of Inquiry

Summarizing the work done by the research network 'Rethinking Project Management', Winter et al. (2006) suggest 'five directions in which the current conceptual foundations of project management need to develop in relation to the developing practice' (Winter et al., 2006: 642), structured into three main categories:

1. Theory ABOUT Practice (knowledge 'about' practice): Theory that helps us to understand practice, albeit from a particular perspective, but which does not necessarily have an immediate practical application.
2. Theory FOR Practice (knowledge 'for' practice): This is a reference to concepts and approaches that do have practical application, and here we identify three directions in which new thinking is needed.
3. Theory IN Practice (knowledge 'in' practice): Practitioners as trained technicians vs. practitioners as reflective practitioners. This is essentially a reference to how practitioners learn their craft, and how they actually practice their craft using relevant theory from the published literature on project management.

In this structuration Theory is seen mainly as relating to episteme and techne, and Practice as relating to poeisis (craft), both Theory (knowledge) and Practice being related in a passive way. Furthermore, the explicit/implicit dimension is here privileged.

While recognizing the relevance of these directions strongly rooted in a classical perspective (i.d. 'knowledge and inquiry "for" and "about" and even "in" practice' (Kondrat, 1992: 238), I argue that this work should go further and does fully build on its argument. With regard to the above discussion about the three knowledge perspectives (and to the tacit, implicit, and explicit dimensions), we can conclude the need for three more categories: Theory FROM Practice (including knowledge 'from' practice and a tacit dimension), Theorizing in Practice (active knowing 'in' practice including a tacit dimension), and Theorizing AS Practicing (knowing 'as' practicing). Extending the long-standing debate that 'research and practice produce distinct form of knowledge' (Van de Ven & Johnson, 2006: 806) and in order to enable a better understanding the relationship between 'episteme, techne AND phronesis', I would suggest considering the following complementary knowledge perspectives:

1. Theory FROM Practice (knowledge 'from' practice) (Van de Ven & Johnson, 2006: 805) – poeisis & praxis 'to' techne & phronesis: with Kondrat, (1992), reversing

the classical perspective (knowledge 'for practice') and beyond the discussion about 'knowledge and inquiry "for" and "about" and even "in" practice', recognizing that 'What has been missing from our collective conversation concerning practice knowledge is an empirical study of practice knowledge itself' (Kondrat, 1992: 238).

2. Theorizing IN Practice (knowing 'in' practice – techne & phronesis 'in' poeisis & praxis: 'our knowing is 'in' our action' (Schön, 1983: 49). Schön argues that the skilful practice shown by professionals do not consist of applying some a priori knowledge to a specific decision or action, but rather of a kind of knowing that is inherent in their action.

3. Theorizing AS Practicing (knowing 'as' practicing – techne, phronesis & episteme 'as' poeisis, praxis & theoria. Maturana & Varela (1998: 27-9) define knowing as 'effective action', and write that 'all doing is knowing, and all knowing is doing'. As commented by Orlikowski (2002), 'when we focus primarily on knowledge, we lose the centrality of action in knowledgeability' (Orlikowski, 2002: 251). Weisinger & Salipante (2000) stipulate: 'The knowing is bound with the practicing of seemingly mundane actions ... knowing as situated learning and practicing' (Weisinger & Salipante, 2000: 387). Van de Ven & Johnson (2006: 803) plea in favour of engaged scholarship is well aligned here with my view regarding to a single class of 'praXitioner' and related praxeological mode of inquiry as a way to bridge the gap between theory and practice.

As stated above in the introductive section of this chapter, and with regards to project management, some authors have taken these two directions ('from' and 'as'), explicitly or not, proposing various perspectives, e.g. 'Making Project Critical' (Hodgson, 2002; Cicmil & Hodgson, 2006; Hodgson & Cicmil, 2007; Cicmil et al., 2009), 'Phronetic Research' (Flyvbjerg et al., 2003; Flyvbjerg, 2004; Flyvbjerg et al., 2012), 'future-perfect' (Pitsis et al., 2003), 'multi-rationalities and cultures' (Van Marrewijk et al., 2008), 'Project-as-Practice' (Blomquist et al., 2010), 'PM Practice/Rethoric & Pragmatist' (Lalonde et al., 2012).

A common characteristic to these perspectives is, to a certain extent depending on the authors, the acknowledgement of the concurrent and integrative advancement of knowledge (episteme, techne and phronesis) in relation to empirical ground (theoria, poeisis and praxis). For instance, Kondrat (1992) claims that 'The roots of both science and practice are to be found in the everyday processes and achievements of human beings who seek to manage {"techne") their world and to orient their action (praxis) in relation to others in that world' (Kondrat, 1992: 243). While Van de Ven & Johnson (2006) stipulate 'We agree with Hodgkinson et al. (2001) and Pettigrew (2001) that research needs to achieve the dual objectives of applied use and advancing fundamental understanding' (Van de Ven & Johnson, 2006: 803).

Moving a step further, a logical consequence of this dual objective is to recognize that the reflexive production and transfer of knowledge (episteme, techne and phronesis) useful for the advancement of theoria, poeisis and praxis involve a balanced and pluralistic view (Knorr-Cetina, 1981b: 336; Tsoukas & Cummings, 1997: 657), 'each form of knowledge being partial – a way of seeing is a way of not seeing (Poggi, 1965)' (Van de Ven & Johnson, 2006: 808).

From the above, we can posit that connecting and mediating theory and practice requests a balanced style of reasoning, epistemic script, and mode of inquiry (e.g. Boxenbaum & Rouleau, 2011: 277). We argue that a praxeological style of reasoning, epistemic script and mode of inquiry is appropriate to project situations. Indeed:

> *practical wisdom (phronesis) which deals with both universals and particulars. More precisely, phronesis is knowing what is good for human beings in general as well as having the ability to apply such knowledge to particular situations, or, as Aristotle remarks, it is the "reasoned and true state of capacity to act with regard to human goods"* (Aristotle, 1980, 1140b 6) (Tsoukas & Cummings, 1997: 665).

Thus, considering Project Management-as-Praxis, involves recognizing a pluralistic view for knowledge (co-)production and transfer, the role of the 'praXitioner'. The mode of inquiry should be grounded on a balanced epistemo-praxeology enabling a 'kaleidoscopic' (Tsoukas & Cummings, 1997: 657), holographic (Kondrat, 1992: 242), or puzzle forms (Bruner, 1962: 93) perspective and combining Theorizing AS Practicing.

Discussion of Question 3: Are the Actions of the Practitioners 'Prudent'?

The discussion of question 3 leads us to investigate what 'praXitioners' do when they name something 'a project' (Hodgson & Cicmil, 2007: 432). As discussed above about classification (Hacking, 1995, 2002b), creating interactively a class of human activities we, as 'praXitioners', name 'project' affects us by looping effects: 'there is a dynamical interaction between the classifications developed in the social sciences, and the individuals or behaviour classified' (Hacking, 2002b: 10).

The question has to be related to another one: 'what do rigor and relevance mean in [project] management?' (Blomquist, 2010: 10) that is under conditions of uncertainty. Because action takes place over time, and because the future is unknowable, action is inherently uncertain (Von Mises, 1949). In relation to future, deliberation (judgment and decision-making) and inherent uncertainty, Aristotle noted, 'But we only deliberate about things which seem to admit of issuing in two ways; as for those things which cannot in the past, present, or future be otherwise, no one deliberates about them, if he supposes that they are such; for nothing would be gained by it' (Aristotle, 1926b, 1357a).

As developed earlier in the discussion of question 1 and about Project Management-as-Praxis, acts involve time, irreversibility, indetermination and contingence, uncertainty and therefore risk (Aristotle, 1926b, 1357a; Carr & Kemmis, 1986: 190; Alessandri et al., 1995: 752; Perelman et al., 2006; Perminova et al., 2008: 76; Atkinson et al., 2006: 688; Smith, 1999, 2011: 3; Lalonde et al., 2012: 420; Winch & Maytorena; 2011: 345; Sanderson, 2012: 433).

Therefore, far seeing in the uncertainty inherent to action tyranny of the particular, of the local, and of the timely to be escaped (Toulmin 1990: 30-35), we see rather a place for emancipation (Habermas, 1973; Gadamer, 1975) and freedom enabling to deliberate in a 'prudent' manner (phronesis) and to act to create 'a' desirable future.

Prudence: Standards or *Verstehen*?

Say (1964) mocks the naiveté of the public toward statistics:

> *Sometimes, moreover, a display of figures and calculations imposes upon them; as if numerical calculations alone could prove anything, and as if any rule could be laid down, from which an inference could be drawn without the aid of sound reasoning* (Say, 1964: xix-xx).

He argues that the mathematical method, with its seeming exactitude, can only seriously distort the analysis of qualitative human action by stretching and oversimplifying the legitimate insights of economic principles (Rothbard, 1997a: 42-3). This is acknowledged by authors such as Andriani & McKelvey (2007: 1221). Cairnes (1857: 83), another economist, demonstrates that deduced economic laws are 'tendency' or 'if-then' laws and, moreover, that they are necessarily qualitative, and cannot admit of mathematical or quantitative expression (Rothbard, 1997a: 44). Menger (1985) write an incisive critique of the idea that mathematical presentation in economics is necessarily more precise than ordinary language (Rothbard, 1997b: 63). Andriani & McKelvey (2007) provide an insightful critique of Greene's standard textbook (2002) showing how, despite some tentative to minimize the effect of varying variances, this authors ignores 'interdependent, interacting, connectionist, interconnecting, coevolutionary, mutual causal data points, events or agents' (Andriani & McKelvey, 2007: 1223).

The project management field is not to be outdone. Consider for instance Pich et al. (2002) paper, from page 1011 to page 1015 where they develop a model of project as a payoff function, and the analogy with biology the authors draw in order to validate their model completeness. Interestingly, in Section 6 of the paper, the authors use a narrative style to discuss and comments the implications of the findings based on the variables at stake and provide the meaning that the variables only cannot provide as mathematical symbols.

These few examples illustrate an important phenomenon: the dissatisfaction in face of problems, antinomies, perplexities and contradictions. 'We feel we have overcome our ancestors, when in fact we are reworking the very sources of their dissatisfaction in new ways' (Hacking, 2002b: 2). Aristotle says that right method in philosophy begin by noticing contradictions in popular belief, or conflict between general opinion and the beliefs of the wise. Dissatisfaction with the classical positivist deductive approach often results in a tendency toward inductive theorizing, 'reluctant positivist', the desire to be more 'realistic' (Earl, 1983). 'In short, defenders of the orthodox theory are often put in the awkward position of ignoring the reality' (Harrison, 1997: 183). Duhem (1956) 'expresses the firm conviction that in the sciences our fundamental explanations of phenomena are not very stable, and can be expected to go on being revised, replaced or overthrown. But our classifications of phenomena become increasingly stable with the growth of the sciences' (Hacking, 2002b: 7)

We therefore face this paradoxical situation of having:

- on the one hand classifications of phenomena governed by a tradition of 'natural sciences', rationality, universality, objective reality and value-free decision making (Cicmil & Hodgson, 2006: 11) exemplified by the development of 'Standards' and 'Bodies of Knowledge' and;
- on the other hand 'the organizational reality, which is often messy, ambiguous, fragmented and political in character' (Alvesson & Deetz, 2000: 60) leading to the quest of *Verstehen*.

Standard

Hodgson (2002) and Cicmil & Hodgson (2006) have discussed how standards, best practices and other bodies of knowledge governed by a tradition of natural science, narrow the role of the 'project manager' class making them 'implementers' and 'marginalizing their wider potential role as competent social and political actors in complex project-labelled arrangements' (Cicmil & Hodgson, 2006: 11).

In order to overcome this narrow vision, and to come back to the empirical dynamic of facts, I have mentioned, in the introduction section of this work, different stances suggested by various authors in project management: critical studies (Hodgson, 2002; Cicmil &Hodgson, 2006; Hodgson & Cicmil, 2007; Cicmil et al., 2009); phronetic approach (Flyvbjerg et al., 2003; Flyvbjerg et al., 2012), new institutional theories and theory of convention (Bredillet, 2003). One commonalty amongst these approaches is the recognition of the role of power, actors' positions, values and agendas in the construction and use of knowledge.

Verstehen

Kraaijenbrink (2010) states 'Management thought is rarely like that [certainty with managers as theory-applying rational decision-makers] and managers only really matter when there is uncertainty' (Kraaijenbrink, 2010: 2). The conclusion is that rationalist or positivist classical theories aiming at predicting and explaining management practice are only partly useful. Soft problem situations, and even the hardest of problems novelty have their soft spots, involve interweaving understanding and acting (Tsoukas & Papoulias, 1996: 74-5, see similarly Lalonde et al., 2012: 426 'even "cold hard facts" may therefore be thought of as having a degree of "plasticity"'). 'The result is that the stable regularities requisite for employing the scientific method reliably can be obtained only tentatively' (Sayer, 1984).

By contrast to the pseudo-quantitative or mathematical methods which distort and oversimplify, human action is accomplished by the use of Verstehen 'the intuitive quickness of enlightened understanding' (Schütz, 1964: 4). This can be related to the notion of relevance by feasibility (Le Moigne, 2007: 117), and Ingenium 'an "intelligent" action, "ingenium", this mental faculty which makes possible to connect in a fast, suitable and happy way the separate things' as stated by Le Moigne (2007: 118), quoting Vico (1708).

Teleological Understanding and 'Good'

Additionally, the Aristotelian teleological understanding of the world implies to consider individuals and objects according to the purposes they have and the role they have to play (MacIntyre 1985: 57-9; Tsoukas & Cummings, 1997, p. 669-70; Lalonde et al., 2012, p. 428). As Perminova et al. (2008) rightly state: 'the way uncertainty is perceived by project managers depends on personal skills, intuition and judgment … Managers' attitudes and understanding of uncertainty do not create or eliminate it' (Perminova et al., 2008: 77). Judging the contextual uncertainty is a goal-oriented and reflective intuitive process and not a rational one in a 'controlled environment'.

A consequence of the teleological understanding is that there are no abstract or ahistorical individuals, but persons defined by and interacting with historical, social, cultural context. (MacIntyre, 1985: 57-9).

This shift of perspective involves a shift from evaluative judgments *in abstracto* based on list of attributes, to factual statements *in concreto* based on what is done in a particular situation and context. Borrowing to Tsoukas & Cummings (1997), answering to the question 'What is a *good* captain' is not about providing a list of attributes '*good* captains' share, but to highlight what those recognized as *good* captains *do* (Tsoukas & Cummings, 1997: 670). In the project management context, we can illustrate this by the difference between projects managers recognized as being *good* professionals, because they own a credential supported by knowledge-based standards and list of related attributes such as years of experience, or by the recognition of the demonstrable evidence-based performance in what they *do* (performance-based standards).

Furthermore, the aspects of values and ethics are fully embedded in the teleological perspective. As Aristotle (1980, 1140b 6) put it: 'while making has an end other than itself, action cannot; for good action itself is its end'. Tsoukas & Cummings (1997) explain: 'there is an internal relationship between acting and the standards in terms of which acting is judged, which is not there when producing artifacts' (Tsoukas & Cummings, 1997: 666). For Aristotle, phronesis plays a central role because, in human actions, the moral virtues and practical knowledge go together: 'it is impossible to be practically wise without being good' (1144a 18). Prudence (phronesis, practical wisdom) involves 'knowing the right values and being able to put them into practice in concrete situations' (Tsoukas & Cummings, 1997: 666).

Prudence

Besides being value-laden by nature, prudence is required in practice for three reasons according to Nussbaum (1990: 70-75; in Tsoukas & Cummings, 1997: 666): 1) practical matters change over time; 2) practical matters are intrinsically indeterminate, ambiguous and lead to interpretation and 3) 'Aristotle suggests that the concrete ethical case may simply contain some ultimately particular and non-repeatable elements' (Nussbaum, 1990: 74).

The above discussions lead us to conclude that general belief, where prescriptive and normative knowledge (from positivist researches) and standards (general, universal laws) addressing most of the projects most of the time are an improvement and reflect a sense of being prudent, is fallacy in the area of human action: the positivist bias, the paradox to use of rationalism to bring certainty in uncertain situations by nature is both an ontological, epistemical and praxeological fault line.

In the quest for prudence (phronesis, practical wisdom) the question is whether 'praXitioners' are for instance differentiating or reconcile abstract rationality (Kondrat, 1992; Toulmin, 2002) from situated reasoning, espoused theory from theory-in-use (Argyris & Schön, 1974), with regards to values, power and uncertainty about the mode of action they adopt in particular project situations? In short are the praXitioners becoming phronimoi?

Warry (1992) offers an appropriate answer, supported by Ricoeur (1984: 20) and Tsoukas & Hatch (2001: 1005), well aligned with the balanced praxeological style of reasoning I advocate and with regards to the mediating role of praxis and phronesis:

> Gadamer's observation that understanding and interpretation must be integrated into the "moment" of application is critical (Gadamer, 1975: 273-4; see also Bernstein, 1985: 159). Praxis, as a particular form of activity, can serve as a focal point through which the discursive testing of theory is grounded through decision making and experience (Habermas, 1973: 20). Simply stated, praxis can serve as a common ground for those interested in basic and applied research by providing knowledge of the reality in which action, informed by theory takes place. (Warry, 1992: 156).

Philosophical Underpinnings of OPM Research

Kondrat (1992) add 'Indeed, the prudent person may be called on to make choices among several potentially effective (or equally ineffective) courses of action' (Kondrat, 1992: 239).

Therefore the illusion of control and the lack of understanding of time irreversibility, indetermination, and contingence are inextricably linked to purposeful human actions.

Praxeological Inquiry: A Praxeological Discourse about Praxeology!

In this section, I discuss the implication of a balanced praxeological style of reasoning, epistemic script, or mode of inquiry for knowing as practicing.

In doing so, I clearly locate the discourse in project complex and chaotic situations, in the Paretian world (Andriani & McKelvey, 2009; Andriani & McKelvey, 2007; McKelvey & Boisot, 2009; Boisot & McKelvey, 2010). The readers may be surprised and see some contradictions in my position as I refer sometimes to antagonist authors whose perspectives seem to be incommensurable. However, in a balanced and integrative perspective, I argue that the debates reflect different views, scripts, and narratives of the same action, story, and discourse of creation of a world or a reality. Moving a step further and considering the etymology of 'praxeology' we shall note that this neologism, accredited to Bourdeau in his 'Théorie des sciences' (1882, last but one chapter) comes from the Greek praxis, action, and logos, talk, speech. We could say praxeology mirrors the 'Act of Word [Logos]' creating the World! The words becoming and being the worlds …

I therefore recognize that the discourse should encompass both Gaussian and Paretian worlds. But is the Gaussian world the world of project situations?

Praxeological Inquiry and the Complexity Discourse

Project situations are complex systems in the way they involve interdependence and connections between project actors, project 'objects' and the context. This uncertainty and complexity leads to an increased variety of stimuli from the environment to the project situation, and to adaptive tension between the two. The 'praXitioner' responds in creating the necessary variety of the project management praxis – 'variety [being here] a proxy of complexity' (McKelvey & Boisot, 2009; Boisot & McKelvey, 2010: 421) – to ensure the integrity of the project situation (Ashby, 1956: 207), via deliberation, judgment and purposeful action. And reflexively the project situation increasing variety may request an adaptation of the environment. Furthermore the positioning of the particular situation under investigation in the Ashby Space helps to consider an appropriate set of research methodology supporting the inquiry.

Complexity is not only an intrinsic characteristic of a system under inquiry. It is also a matter of 'naming', of the way we think about it, of discourse. This involves a praxeological shift, a bifurcation path (Kellert, 1993), from an observer 'independent' to an observer 'dependent' mode of inquiry, from first-order to second-order complexity (Bateson, 1973, 1979a) enabling a 'dynamic understanding' (Kellert, 1993: 114). How can 'praXitioners' accommodate these paradoxical perspectives and possible contradictions? 'By generating and accommodating multiple inequivalent descriptions [an increase of "variety"] practitioners will increase the complexity of their understanding and, therefore, will be more likely, in logico-scientific terms, to match the complexity of the situation they attempt to manage (Bruner, 1996), or, in narrative terms, to enact it (Weick, 1979)' (Tsoukas & Hatch, 2001: 987).

Building on Bruner's (1986) contrast between logico-scientific and narrative modes of thinking, Tsoukas & Hatch (2001) suggest an interpretive approach to complexity (Tsoukas & Hatch, 2001: 985). Their work is in full agreement with Czarniawska (1997a: 29) when she posits that interpretive approaches, within which fits narrative approach, 'further our understanding of the complex and unpredictable – the major concern and interest of current organization studies'.

The following table proposes a summary and a synthetic mapping of several aspects discussed above.

Praxis and phronesis, in their mediating role serve as focal point (Habermas, 1973: 20), between the logico-scientific and the narrative mode, and have been recognized as 'emancipatory' (Habermas, 1971: 314; Gadamer, 1975), and offering 'a way of reflecting on disjuncture between the formal rationality and the substantive rationality' (Kondrat, 1992: 253). Project management authors such as Cicmil & Hodgson (quoting Balck, 1994: 2 in Cicmil & Hodgson, 2006: 13), Blomquist et al. (2010: 9) and Lalonde et al. (2012: 428) have acknowledged a similar view. This mediating role should especially be considered in praxeological inquiries of phase transition situations where effects are scalable (Boisoit & McKelvey, 2010: 422) located in the complex regime area of the Ashby Space, between 'edge of order' and 'edge of chaos' (Nicolis & Prigogine, 1989), in the 'melting zone' (Kauffmann, 1993) and state of 'self-organized criticality' (Bak, 1996).

The first column depicts the modes of action and related types of knowledge. The second column relates these modes of actions and types of knowledge with the place they occupy on a power-law distribution and emphasize the basic underlying ontology and logic, while the third column depicts the kind of regime with which the Ashby Space is concerned. The fourth column suggests the main mode of thought and philosophical outlook in conjunction with the mode of actions. The fifth and sixth columns suggest some methodological approaches with regards to the modes of action and their context of inquiry (world view, complexity, place of the 'observer').

Table 2.1. Mapping Complexity and Methodology

Area of Action/ Knowledge	Power-Law distribution (Boisot & McKelvey, 2010: 416)	Ashby Space area (Boisot & McKelvey, 2010: 421)	Modes of thought (Bruner, 1986: 11-43)	Social Sciences (Tsoukas & Hatch, 2001: 984)	Complexity Theory (Tsoukas & Hatch, 2001: 984)
Poeisis/Techne Theoria/Episteme Theoria/Episteme	Gaussian world (mean, standard deviation, variance) *Atomistic ontology* Deductive, inductive approaches leading to prediction	Ordered regime (edge of order)	Logico-scientific mode Modernism (Waldrop, 1992; Holland, 1995; Colander, 2006)	Objective world Variance Models (Mohr, 1982)	First-order complexity Observer 'independent' Natural and Biological Systems Models (Holland, 1995; Stacey, 1996; Pich et al., 2002; Boisot & McKelvey, 2010)
Praxis/Phronesis Praxis/Phronesis	Paretian world *Connectionist ontology* Scalable abductive approaches leading to anticipation (Boisot & McKelvey, 2010: 426-7) or 'prescience' (Corley & Gioia, 2011: 13) (See also 'future-perfect' (Pitsis et al., 2003: 574)	Complex regime (edge of chaos) Chaotic regime	Narrative mode Postmodernism (Pre-modernism) (Kuhn, 1962; Berger & Luckmann, 1966; Derrida, 1978; Lyotard, 1984; Morgan, 1997)	Social construction of the World Middle range theories (Merton, 1949) 'Petis récits' (Lyotard, 1984) Qualitative accounts • narrating organizations (e.g. case studies) • Collecting stories (storytelling) • organization as narration (interpretive organizational research rooted in literary theory) (Czarniawska, 1997a, 1997b, 1998)	Second-order complexity Observer 'dependent' Middle-level theorizing (Gell-Mann, 2002: 23) Interpretive methodology (Rorty, 1989)

Serendipity, Sagacity ... and Methodology

If I had to define in one word the essence of praxeological inquiry methodology I would say 'serendipity'. As Merton conceptualized a then little-known term in 1945, serendipity is 'the discovery, by chance or sagacity, of valid results which were not sought for' (Merton, 1945: 469). Of course, praxeological inquiry can rest on some key features, as I suggest below. However in doing so, I am not looking at being exhaustive, a vain endeavour which would ultimately contradict the inherent unlimited creative nature of human spirit.

On the basis of the previous discussion, and as a way of summary, I want to briefly underline the following tenets of the methodology.

Non (or Post) Paradigmatic

Has Anyone Found a Paradigm Out There? (Bredillet, 2010: 6).

Discussing paradigms in the Social Sciences, Dogan (2001 addresses the question: 'Is scientific progress in the social sciences achieved mostly by steady accretion or mostly by abrupt jumps?' He then summarizes Kuhn's view point: 'For Thomas Kuhn, who devised the concept "paradigm", there are no paradigmatic upheavals in the social sciences. For him the use of this term in these sciences is not justified ... In the social sciences, theoretical and methodological disagreements are beneficial to the advance of knowledge' (Dogan, 2001: 11023). Flyvbjerg (2001) suggests that social sciences should focus on what he describes a 'non-paradigmatic' phronetic social science (e.g. Van de Ven & Johnson, 2006: 805). Schram (2004), commenting on Flyvbjerg's position, puts forward the use of 'post-paradigmatic' science – 'post' meaning carry on 'but differently' – emphasizing *the aspiration to move beyond a situation where such a hegemonic approach is imposed on the discipline* (Schram, 2004: 432-3).

Empiricism

Praxeology 'rests on the fundamental axiom that individual human beings act, that is, on the primordial fact that individuals engage in conscious actions toward chosen goals' (Rothbard, 1997b: 58) and is therefore empirical in the broadest sense (Rothbard, 1997b: 64). The Aristotelian view is radically empirical. 'Concepts are not defined as abstract entities' (this is a very modem practice that took roots after the Aristotelian tradition had been discredited (Tsoukas & Cummings, 1997: 670). 'They are not separated from practices or particular contexts' (Feyerabend, 1987: 113). In this perspective, a 'historical-cum-comparative' approach is helpful (Tsoukas & Cummings, 1997: 673-4), enabling us to see 'the contingency of our dearest biases and most accepted necessities, thereby opening up a space for change' (Flynn, 1994: 32). Tsoukas

& Cummings add: 'Adopting a "kaleidoscopic", rather than a "cumulative", view of history, we can begin to appreciate the past, particularly the past outside the boundaries of our tradition, as a rich seam of ideas, the contemplation of which may enable us to think differently and innovatively about organization and management' (Tsoukas & Cummings, 1997: 673-4). Such 'historical-cum-comparative' approach leads us to search for the local, the timely, and the 'priority of the particular' (in Aristotle's thinking) (Nussbaum, 1990: 66; Tsoukas & Cummings, 1997: 674; Aram & Salipante, 2003: 190; Flyvbjerg, 2004: 288, 289; Van de Ven & Johnson, 2006: 806). A direct link can be established with the 'evidence-based' practice debate (Rousseau, 2006).

Narrative, History and Story

It is worthwhile to consider the etymology of the words 'story' and 'history'. Through their Greek and Latin origins, they conveyed a similar meaning (relation of incidents (true or false), narrative of past events, account, tale, story; a learning or knowing by inquiry; an account of one's inquiries, history, record, narrative) and the historian was 'a wise man, a judge, able to know and see'. Furthermore it is of great interest to note, with regard to power and values in project situations, that 'story' became a euphemism for 'lie' around 1690s. As says Declerck, a project is about creating and telling a 'story' rooted in 'history' (Declerck et al., 1997). Narrative thinking and approach are ideally suitable in order to integrate the general and particular, through stories and history (Taylor, 1985; Ricoeur, 1991; Griffin, 1995). More specifically, narrative thinking enables us to grasp every dimension (knowledge of regularities, patterns, scientific principles, general values) of a specific situation or of a series of events and to integrate the general and the particular in a flexible way according to multiple perspectives (Tsoukas & Cummings, 1997: 667). Narrative approach facilitates the development of second-order thinking about organizational complexity, and complex situations. In particular, it facilitates to grasp the matter of recursiveness, as well as other phenomena of complex systems such as nonlinearity, indeterminacy, unpredictability and emergence (Tsoukas & Hatch, 2001: 979).

Pluralism and Regularities

'In the absence of unambiguous foundational truth in the social sciences, the only sensible way forward can be conscious pluralism' (Pettigrew, 2001: S62). Many authors have called for a pluralistic view of science and practice (Van de Ven & Johnson, 2006: 808), a methodological pluralism in social science (Schram, 2004: 418, 431) or multiperspectivism – 'analysts are on the same footing with the participants of the situation': The cognitive and participating functions are integrated, not separated like in an interdisciplinary approach (Tsoukas & Papoulias, 1996: 77-8) (Pascal et al., 2012: 7). Besides the fundamental non-paradigmatic tenet discussed above, this pluralism facilitates the recognition of diversity of kinds of knowledge supported by different communities, each one being partial if considered separately from each other (Poggi, 1965; Van Maanen & Barley, 1986; Cook et al., 1999). Pluralism involves recognizing that past events and situations contain a number of discrete fragments – patterns shaped by contingencies, not a collective and cumulative learning process (Foucault, 1966). Moving from one period ('thought-cum-practice', one form of pattern) to another involves to 'twist the kaleidoscope' and create a new pattern (Tsoukas & Cummings, 1997: 663). If identifying patterns is a challenge (Blomquist et al., 2010: 10; Smyth & Morris, 2007: 423, 425). Andriani & McKelvey (2009), coming from a complexity science perspective propose linking patterns to scaling laws, where complexity considers whether patterns have a property of universality about them (Brock, 2000: 29; Andriani & McKelvey, 2009: 1055). Discussing Brock's work and scalability (Brock, 2000) they suggest considering what they name 'power-law' and 'scale-free' theories, moving away from reductionism, in order to look for new regularities (Andriani & McKelvey, 2007: 1213; Andriani & McKelvey, 2009: 1053; Boisot & McKelvey, 2010: 416).

Design

The field of management has been described as soft, applied, divergent and rural (Becher, 1989). A logical consequence is that management research is better served by Mode 2 research (Tranfield & Starkey, 1998; Aram & Salipante, 2003). Praxeological inquiry draws on what is described as Mode 2 research (Gibbons et al., 1994), that is transdisciplinary and problem-focused rather than Mode 1 research, traditional and discipline based. The development of middle range theories (Merton, 1949), 'petits récits' (Lyotard, 1984), or middle-level theorizing (Gell-Mann, 2002) is the privileged goal of such inquiry. However, various contexts and related relevant institutional logics of action (pure research logic, problem solving, exploitation, induction, and emancipation) – organizing principles that shape ways of viewing the world: 'Logics enable actors to make sense of their ambiguous world by prescribing and proscribing actions. Action reenacts institutional logics, making them durable.' (Suddaby & Greenwood, 2005: 38) – should be considered bearing in mind the discourses of the philosophy of science (structural realism, instrumentalism, strong paradigm, foundationalism, and critical realism) (Kilduff et al., 2011: 299).

Methodological Individualism

A consequence of the fundamental axiom of praxeology – individual beings act and engage in conscious action toward chosen goals – is the principle of methodological individualism underlying praxeological inquiry (Weber, 1957; Schatzki, 2005: 466). Moreover, 'such collectives as groups, governments, nations do not actually exist. They are metaphorical constructs for describing the similar or concerned actions of individuals' (Rothbard, 1997a: 49). And Hayek (1955) adds 'It [the objectivist view] treats social phenomena not as something of which the human mind is a part ... the existence in popular usage of such terms as "society" or "economy" is naively taken as evidence that there must be definite "objects" corresponding to them' (Hayek, 1955: 53-4, in Rothbard, 1997a: 50). However, this involves recognizing the link between human agency and social structures in the explanation of action (Vaara & Whittington, 2012: 288) (see the debate, within the 'practice turn' authors, about methodological individualism and its opposition in Vaara & Whittington, 2012).

Logics of Inquiry

The variety of contexts mirrors the variety of possible starting point and logics of inquiry. For instance Kotarbinski (1983) suggests an inductive logic, while Von Mises (1981) deducts, on the basis of the fundamental axiom of praxeology – 'only an individual has a mind; only an individual can feel, see, sense, and perceive; only an individual can adopt values or make choices; only an individual can *act*' (Rothbard, 1997b: 58) – *a priori* laws of effective and efficient actions (Leguérinel, 2007: 20). But in praxeological inquiry context 'cases in which two or more information sources come together to give information of a sort different from what was in either source separately' occurs, leading to consider the phenomena of 'double description' (Bateson, 1979b: 31) and its relation to abductive logic, meta pattern and comparisons of 'creatures' at different levels: parts with parts of the same creature, forms of different creatures with each other, and comparison between the comparisons. Bateson (1979b) calls, following Peirce (1931), abduction – 'the lateral extension of abstract components of description' (Bateson, 1979b: 157) across from one situation to another, often very different, situation (Shotter, 2009: 240). Van de Ven & Johnson (2006), referring to Schön, add to the discussion about logic of inquiry in action:

> Schön maintains that, in situations of ambiguity or novelty, "our thought turns back on the surprising phenomenon, and at the same time, back on itself" (Schön, 1987: 68), as a form of abductive reflection-in-action. Such reflection, in fact, is one way that practical knowledge becomes refined and extended into practice wisdom (Van de Ven & Johnson, 2006: 807).

Furthermore, Boisot & McKelvey (2010), defending the integration between modernist and postmodernist perspectives on organization via power-law distributed phenomena, with a focus on the study of unique or extreme phenomena, suggest an inferential strategy they label 'scalable abduction' logic (Boisot & McKelvey, 2010: 425).

Improvisation & Bricolage

Improvization and bricolage are inherent to the process of research (Garfinkel et al., 1981; Latour, 1986; Knorr-Cetina & Amann, 1990; Boxenbaum & Rouleau, 2011). As noticed by Van de Ven & Johnson (2006) 'Both practitioners and scientists engage in what Levi-Strauss (1966) termed bricolage, improvising with a mixed bag of tools and tacit knowledge to adapt to the task at hand' (Van de Ven & Johnson, 2006: 806). Improvisation is related to how thoughts and response are developed in partly novel situations. Mentioning Ryle (1979: 125), Leybourne advise that 'the vast majority of things that happen [are] unprecedented, unpredictable, and never to be repeated', and that 'the things we say and do ... cannot be completely pre-arranged' (Leybourne, 2010: 18). Bricolage refers to 'an assembly of readily available elements' (Boxenbaum & Rouleau, 2011: 278), 'to make do with those materials that area available' (Leybourne, 2010: 18). As Leybourne rightly states 'Bricolage can, of course, also occur in nonimprovisational contexts, and not all improvisation will involve bricolage' (Leybourne, 2010: 18). The praXitioner is a 'bricoleur' – a 'flexible and responsive' agent willing 'to deploy whatever research strategies, methods or empirical materials are at hand, to get the job done' (Denzin & Lincoln, 1994: 2).

Deliberation and Arbitrage

In praxeological inquiry, understanding and acting are situated and interact with ethical consideration, values and power games influences and sometimes adversarial contexts. Knowledge, 'located in the nexus between practice and contributing disciplines' (Van de Ven & Johnson, 2006: 808), is therefore created, produced, transferred and used through a 'generating mechanism of a dialectical process of inquiry' (Van de Ven & Johnson, 2006: 803) between the participants, including mutual engagement, discussion, negotiation, deliberation, arbitrage, conflict and judgment. (Warry, 1992: 156; Blomquist et al., 2010: 10). Praxeological research 'is concerned with deliberation about values and interests' (Flyvbjerg, 2004: 287; 2006: 372). As Van de Ven & Johnson add, this kind of research requires engagement (Van de Ven & Johnson, 2006: 809). Exploiting the different perspectives brought by the 'praXitioners' and participants (disciplines, experiences) require, as said above, a pluralistic approach based on intellectual arbitrage strategy (Harrison, 1997).

Methodological Guidelines

Based on the above review of some tenets on the praxeological inquiry, the following 'guidelines' may be suggested. Of course, there is no 'one best way' in this matter but rather a matter of 'ingenium' and wisdom, and many authors (e.g. Pascal et al., 2012: 7), in particular some quoted in this work, propose some invaluable approaches.

Here are the four key points to be considered, in my opinion:

1. Addressing a big question or research problem embedded in the Real World (Flyvbjerg, 2004: 295; Van de Ven & Johnson, 2006: 810). The research problem and related question is based on specific empirical situation, practice and focuses on concrete phenomena (Lalonde et al., 2012: 429).
2. Scoping of the research project as a collaborative and engaged acting and knowing community within a social site. Trust and adoption of a behaviour fostering emancipation, consciousness, active and positive praxis should be promoted (Brown & Duguid, 1991; Van de Ven, 2000; Aram & Salipante, 2003; Schatzki, 2005: 473; Van de Ven & Johnson, 2006: 811; Blomquist et al., 2010: 13; Lalonde et al., 2012: 429).
3. Designing the research in order to enable a multiple perspective inquiry process. Bottom-up research, choose an appropriate duration, select methods to obtain empirical evidence, focus on values, power, 'little things', consider practices and discourses, study cases in context, do narrative ... (Packendorff, 1995: 329; Czarniawska & Sevon, 1996; Flyvbjerg, 2004: 295; Chia & Holt, 2006: 644; Van de Ven & Johnson, 2006: 812-13; Whittington, 2006: 623-7; Pouliot, 2007: 368-74).
4. Enabling application, dissemination of the research findings and reflection (second and third level of learning, Bateson, 1973) about the roles of the participants, assumptions, models, theories, philosophical stance (Czarniawska & Sevon, 1996; Van de Ven, 2000; Aram & Salipante, 2003; Flyvbjerg, 2004: 290; Van de Ven & Johnson, 2006: 810, 814; Pouliot, 2007: 372; Lalonde et al., 2012: 429).

Limitations

Praxeological inquiry shows important strengths. It clearly demonstrates ways to improve practice and who takes the responsibility. It supports collaborative acting and knowing, and makes transparent the ethical dimension, power games and values, and what should be done to improve a situation. Furthermore, because it is grounded in the real world while being inspired by practical and philosophic wisdom and intuition, immanence in the individual praxis and transcendence in the societal field could we say, it is a credible and useful approach.

The main weakness, according to the tenants of positivism and natural sciences, is the focus of the particular, on unique or extreme events. Moreover, it doesn't address causal relationships and doesn't lead to predictions or comparisons. Lastly, the apparent lack of rigor, in a world of statistical fallacy, may lead to some defiance from the decision-makers (Leguérinel, 2007: 17; Pascal et al., 2012: 19).

To Not Conclude
A Discourse on the Non-method

In the context of project management, and on the premise that in order to enable individuals to achieve *eudaimonia* and to build a better world we need to move from the failure of the hegemonic natural sciences approaches applied to the understanding of and guiding social phenomena and from the 'deficiency in the way social sciences have developed in the second half of the twentieth century' (McGee, 2001: 12). I advocate a praxeological style of reasoning in order to grasp an efficient and effective understanding, learning and acting in the 'real world' and how human acts are shaping it.

Thus, this work is rooted deeply in Aristotelian philosophy and the praxeological tradition with, occasionally paradoxically, some concessions to post-modernism. But after all, many post-modernists are referring to pre-Enlightenment times! Furthermore, and besides its pre-modern roots, this work builds as well on the latest advancement made in Social Sciences and Complexity Science.

This is the opportunity to discuss and make sense of some key concepts such as praxis, phronesis, activity, practice, theory and practitioner and draw some important conclusions. For instance, in debating about the Theory-Practice gap, I suggest considering scholars, experts and practitioners under a single class I name 'praXitioners'. The work addresses three main questions:

Question 1: Are the research approaches currently being used appropriate for generating contributions that matter to both theory and practice with regards to what a 'project' is or to what do we do when we call a specific situation 'a project'?

Question 2: On the basis of which intellectual virtues is the knowledge generated and what is the impact for theory and practice?

Question 3: Are the actions of the practitioners 'prudent' and are they differentiating or reconciling abstract rationality from situated reasoning, espoused theory from theory-in-use with regards to the mode of action they adopt in particular project situations?

Notwithstanding the discussions, deliberations and arbitrages about each question exposed in this work, I can summarize the main conclusions as following:

To the ontological question, I advocate considering 'Project Management-as-Praxis'.

To the epistemological question, I propose contemplating 'Knowing-as-Practicing'.

To the praxeological question, I recommend prudent action (praxis guided by phronesis) linking ex ante and ex post understanding of the context and integrating deliberation and understanding into the 'moment' of action.

From these debates, I then suggest possible methodologies for praxeological inquiry raising the attention of the fact a project situation may belong to different world of diversity, variety and complexity: Gaussian or Paretian, and sometimes some aspects of a situation may lie in both sides. 'Knowing-as-Practicing' in the context of 'Project Management-as-Praxis' requires therefore phronesis, practical wisdom, or prudence and hence the PraXitioner to become a Phronimos!

By way of non-conclusion, the meaning of the title of this work should appear clear to the reader, taking a praxeological stance.

A praxeological style of reasoning involves building on interpretation and hermeneutics of living and historical discourse and narrative as a way to address the inherent complexity of any organization and society. In Aristotle's words, 'rhetoric mediates ethics and politics' (McGee, 2001: 13). Using a religious metaphor, we could say that the Word is creating the World. 'Phronesis gained from hermeneutical reflection has nothing to do with domination, but rather with willing subordination'. Hermeneutics, in the sphere of the discourse, is not knowledge as domination, but knowledge as interpretations, including application, as a form of service of what is considered as 'good' and valid (Gadamer, 1975, p. 278; McGee, 2001: 13).

But the diversity and variety of situations, and the very nature of human beings acting, involve a non-paradigmatic (other would say post-paradigmatic) perspective. There is no preferred methodology or methods supporting a praxeological inquiry; but rather a place for *ingenium*, intelligent action and moral reasoning. 'The substance of moral reasoning is an interpretation of traditional beliefs and commitments applied to concrete problems of the present' (McGee, 2001: 12).

Emancipation, that is becoming a Phronimos, comes therefore from a praxeological inquiry resting on transformative and operative hermeneutics of the Book of the World.

Ordo ab Chao? or 'the societal context that wags the tail that wags the dog that wags the tail that wags the societal context?'

References

Alessandri, T. M., Ford, D. N., Lander, D. M, Leggio, K. B., Taylor, M. (1995). Managing risk and uncertainty in complex capital projects. *The Quarterly Review of Economics and Finance*, 44: 751-67.

Alvesson, M., Deetz, S. (2000). *Doing Critical Management Research*. London: Sage.

Andriani, P., McKelvey, B. (2007). Beyond Gaussian averages: Redirecting organization science toward extreme events and power laws. *Journal of International Business Studies*, 38 (2): 1212-30.

Andriani, P., McKelvey, B. (2009). From Gaussian to Paretian thinking: Causes and implications of power laws in organizations. *Organization Science*, 20 (6): 1053-71.

Aram, J. D., Salipante, P. F., Jr. (2003). Bridging scholarship in management: Epistemological reflections. *British Journal of Management*, 14(3): 189-205.

Aristotle (1926a). *Nicomachean Ethics*, H. Rackham, Ed., (Trans. by Harris Rackham). The Perseus Project. HTML at Perseus: http://www.perseus.tufts.edu/cgi-bin/ptext?lookup=Aristot.+Nic.+Eth.+.

Aristotle (1926b). *On Rhetoric. A Theory of Civic Discourse*. J. H. Freese, Ed. HTML at Perseux: http://www.perseus.tufts.edu/hopper/text?doc=Aristot.+Rh.+1.1.1&redirect=true).

Aristotle (1980). *The Nicomachean Ethics*. Transl. D. Ross, Oxford: Oxford University Press.

Argyris, C., Schön, D. (1974). *Theory in practice: increasing professional effectiveness*. San Francisco: Jossey-Bass Publishers.

Ashby, R. W. (1956). *An introduction to cybernetics*. London: Methuen.

Atkinson, R., Crawford, L., Ward, S., (2006). Fundamental uncertainties in projects and the scope of project management. *International Journal of Project Management*, 24 (8), 687-8.

Bak, P. (1996). *How nature works: The science of self-organized criticality*. New York: Copernicus.

Balck, H. (1994). Projects as Elements of a New Industrial Pattern: A Division of Project Management. Iin D.I. Cleland and R. Gareis (eds), *Global Project Management Handbook*. New York: McGraw-Hill International Editions, 2-11.

Bateson, G. (1973). *Steps to an Ecology of Mind*. Paladin Books.

Bateson, G. (1979a). *Mind and nature*. Toronto: Bantam Books.

Bateson, G. (1979b). *Mind in Nature: a Necessary Unity*. London: Fontana/Collins.

Becher, T. (1989). *Academic Tribes and Territories: Intellectual Enquiry and the Cultures of Disciplines*. The Society for Research into Higher Education and Open University Press, Bristol.

Bechky, B. A. (2006). Gaffers, gofers, and grips: Role-based coordination in temporary organizations. *Organization Science, 17*(1), 3-21.

Berger, P. L., Luckmann, T. (1966). *The Social Construction of Reality*. Harmondsworth: Penguin.

Bernstein, R. J. ed. (1985). *Habermas and Modernity*. Cambridge, MA: MIT Press. BoK, Sissela.

Blomquist, T., Hällgren, M., Nilsson, A., Söderholm, A. (2010). Project-as-practice: in search of project management research that matters. *Project Management Journal*, 41(1): 5-16.

Boisot, M. (1995). *Information Space: A Framework for Learning in Organizations, Institutions and Culture*. Routledge, London.

Boisot, M. (1998). *Knowledge Assets: securing competitive advantage in the information economy*. New York: Oxford University Press.

Boisot, M. McKelvey, B. (2010). Integrating Modernist and Postmodernist Perspectives on Organizations: a Complexity Science Bridge. *Academy of Management Review*, 35(3): 415-33.

Bourdeau, L. (1882). Théorie des Sciences. Vol. I, XX, 490 pp.; Vol. II, 634 pp. Paris: Garnier-Baillière. Bourdieu, P. (1990). The Logic of Practice (translated by Richard Nice). Stanford: Stanford University Press.

Boxenbaum, E. and Rouleau, L. (2011). New Knowledge Products As Bricolage: Metaphors And Scripts In Organizational Theory. *Academy of Management Review*, 36(2): 272-96.

Bredillet, C. N. (2003). "Genesis and Role of Standards: theoretical foundations and socio-economic model for the construction and use of standards." International Journal of Project Management. 21(6): 463-70.

Bredillet, C. N. (2004). Understanding the very nature of Project Management: a praxeological approach. PMI Research Conference: Innovations, London, UK, 11-14 July 2004.

Bredillet, C. N. (2010). Blowing Hot and Cold on Project Management. Project Management Journal, 41(3): 4-20.

Brock, W. A. (2000). Some Santa Fe scenery. D. Colander, ed. *The Complexity Vision and the Teaching of Economics*. Edward Elgar, Cheltenham, UK, 29-49.

Brown, J. S., Duguid, P. (1991). Organizational learning and communities of practice: Toward a unified view of working, learning and innovation. *Organization Science, 2*(1), 40-57.

Bruner, J. S. (1962). *On Knowing: Essays for the Left Hand.* New York: Atheneum.

Bruner, J. S. (1986). *Actual minds, possible worlds*. Cambridge, MA: Harvard University Press.

Bruner, J. S. (1996). The narrative construal of reality. In J. Bruner (ed.), *The culture of education*. Cambridge, MA: Harvard University Press.

Cairnes, J. E. (1857). *The Character and Logical Method of Political Economy*. London: Macmillan.

Carr, W., Kemmis, S. (1986) *Becoming Critical. Education, knowledge and action research*, Lewes: Falmer.

Carter, C., Clegg, S. R., Kornberger, M. (2008). Strategy as Practice? *Strategic Organization*, 6(1): 83-99.

Chia, R., & Holt, R. (2006). Strategy as practical coping: A Heideggerian perspective, *Organization Studies, 27*, 635-55.

Cicmil, S. (2006). Understanding project management practice through interpretative and critical research perspectives. *Project Management Journal, 37*(2), 27-37.

Cicmil, S., Williams, T., Thomas, J., & Hodgson, D. (2006). Rethinking project management: Researching the actuality of projects. *International Journal of Project Management,* 24(8), 675-86.

Cicmil, S., Hodgson, D. (2006). Making Projects Critical: an Introduction. In *Making Projects Critical, Edited by Damian Hodgson and Svetlana Cicmil.* Series: Management, Work and Organisations. Palgrave Macmillan: Basingstoke, New York. 376 pp. 1-25.

Cicmil, S.; Hodgson, D., Lindgren, M., & Packendorff, J. (eds) (2009). Project Management behind the Façade. *Special issue of ephemera: theory & politics,* 9 (2): 78-194. contributions http://www.ephemeraweb.org/journal/index.htm 9 (2) May 2009.

Colander, D. (2006). *Post Walrasian macroeconomics: Beyond the dynamic stochastic general equilibrium model.* Cambridge: Cambridge University Press.

Cook, T. D., Scott, D. N., Brown, J. S. (1999). Bridging epistemologies: The generative dance between organizational knowledge and organizational knowing. *Organization Science,* 10(4): 381-400.

Corley, K. G., Gioia, D. A. (2011). Building Theory about Theory Building: What Constitutes a Theoretical Contribution? *Academy of Management Review,* 38(1): 12-32.

Czarniawska, B. (1997a). *Narrating the organization: Dramas of institutional identity.* Chicago, IL: Chicago University Press.

Czarniawska, B. (1997b). A four times told tale: Combining narrative and scientific knowledge in organization studies. *Organization, 4(1):* 7-30.

Czarniawska, B. (1998). *A narrative approach to organization studies.* Thousand Oaks, CA: Sage.

Czarniawska, B., Sevon, G. (eds). (1996). *Translating organizational change.* Berlin: De Gruyter.

De Certeau, M. (1984). *The practice of everyday life.* Berkeley: University of California Press.

Declerck, R. P., Debourse, J. P., Declerck, J. C. (1997). *Le management stratégique: contrôle de l'irréversibilité.* Lille: Les éditions ESC Lille.

Denzin, N. K., Lincoln, Y. S. (1994). *Handbook of qualitative research.* Thousand Oaks, CA, and London: Sage.

Derrida, J. (1978). *Writing and difference.* London: Routledge & Kegan Paul.

Dewey, J. (1938). *Logic. The Theory of Inquiry.* Henry Holt and Company, New York.

Dogan, M. (2001). *Paradigms in the Social Sciences. International Encyclopedia of the Social & Behavioral Sciences,* pp. 11023-11027. *http://dx.doi.org/10.1016/B0-08-043076-7/00782-8.*

Dreyfus, H. L., Dreyfus, S. E. (1998). *Frictionless forecasting is a fiction.* In N. Akerman (ed.), *The necessity of friction*: 267-289. Boulder, CO: Westview Press.

Duhem, P. (1956) *The Aim and Structure of a Physical Theory*, trans. P. P. Weiner, Princeton, NJ: Princeton University Press.

Earl, P. E. (1983). A Behavioral Theory of Economists' Behavior. In Eichner, A. S. (ed.) *Why Economics is not yet a Science*, pp. 90-125, London, Macmillan/Armonk, NY, M.E. Sharpe, Inc.

Feyerabend, P. (1975). *Against Method.* London.

Feyerabend, P. (1987). *Farewell to reason.* London: Verso.

Flynn, T. (1994). *Foucault's mapping of history.* In The Cambridge companion to Foucault. Gary Gutting (ed.), 28-46. Cambridge: Cambridge University Press.

Flyvbjerg, B. (2001). *Making Social Science Matter: Why Social Inquiry Fails and How It Can Succeed Again.* (Translated by S. Sampson.) Cambridge University Press: Cambridge.

Flyvbjerg, B., Bruzelius, N., & Rothengatter, W. (2003). *Megaprojects and Risk: An Anatomy of Ambition.* Cambridge University Press, 218 pages.

Flyvbjerg, B. (2004). Phronetic Planning Research: Theoretical and Methodological Reflections. *Planning Theory & Practices*, 5(3): 283-306.

Flyvbjerg, B. (2006). Making organization research matter: power, values and phronesis. In Clegg, S. R., Hardy, C., Lawrence, T. B., & Nord, W. R. (eds), *Handbook of organization studies* (2 ed.), pp. 370-87. London: Sage Publications, Incorporated.

Flyvbjerg, B., Landman, T., and Schram, S. (eds)(2012) *Real Social Science: Applied Phronesis.* Cambridge University Press.

Foucault, M. (1966). *The order of things: An archaeology of the humanities.* London: Tavistock/Routledge.

Foucault, M. (1977). *Discipline and punish: the birth of the prison.* London: Penguin.

Gadamer, H-G. (1975). *Truth and Method.* G. Barden and J. Cumming, trs. New York: Seabury.

Garfinkel, H., Lynch, M., & Livingston, E. (1981). The work of a discovering science construed with materials from the optically discovered pulsar. *Philosophy of the Social Sciences*, 11: 131-58.

Gell-Mann, M. (2002). What is complexity? In A. Q. Curzio & M. Fortis (eds.), *Complexity and industrial clusters:* 13-24. Heidelberg: Physica-Verlag.

Gibbons, M., Limoges, C., Nowotny, H., Schwartzman, S, Scott, P., Trow, M. (1994). *The New Production of Knowledge: The Dynamics of Science and Research in Contemporary Societies.* Sage, London.

Giddens, A. (1979). *Central problems of social theory.* London: Macmillan.

Giddens, A. (1984). *The constitution of society.* Cambridge: Polity.

Giddens, A. (1993). *New Rules of Sociological Method.* Cambridge: Polity Press.

Gioia, D. A. and Pitre, E. (1990). Multiparadigm perspectives on theory building. *Academy of Management Review,* 15(4): 584-602.

Gourlay, S. (2006). Conceptualizing Knowledge Creation: A Critique of Nonaka's Theory. *Journal of Management Studies* 43(7): 1415-36.

Griffin, L. J. (1995). How is sociology informed by history? *Social Forces* 73: 1245-54.

Greene, W. H. (2002). *Econometric Analysis*. 5th ed. New Jersey: Prentice Hall.

Habermas, J. (1971). *Knowledge and Human Interests,* trans. Jeremy J. Shapiro, Boston: Beacon.

Habermas, J. (1973). *Theory and Practice*. John Viertel, tr. Boston: Beacon Press.

Hacking, I. (1995). *The looping effects of human kinds*. In D. Sperber, D. Premack and A. Premack (eds), *Causal Cognition: an Interdisciplinary Approach*, Oxford: Oxford University Press, pp. 351-383.

Hacking, I. (1999). *The Social Construction of What?* Cambridge, MA: Harvard University Press.

Hacking, I. (2002a). *Historical Ontology*. Cambridge, MA: Harvard University Press.

Hacking, I. (2002b). Inaugural Lecture: Chair of Philosophy and History of Scientific Concepts at the College de France, 16 January 2001. *Economy and Society*, 31(1): 1-14.

Hällgren, M., Söderholm, A., (2011). *Projects-as-practice: new approach, new insights*. In: Morris, P. W. G., Pinto, J. K., Söderlund, J. (eds.) (2010). *The Oxford Handbook of Project Management*. Oxford University Press, Oxford, pp. 500-518.

Hällgren, M. and Wilson, T. (2008). The nature and management of crises in construction projects: projects-as-practice observations. *International Journal of Project Management*, 26 (8), 830-838.

Harrison, P. (1997). A history of an intellectual arbitrage: The evolution of financial economics. *History of Political Economy*, 29(4): 172-187.

Hayek, L. A. (1955). *Counter-Revolution of Science*. Glencoe, Ill.: Free Press.

Hodgkinson, G. P. (ed.). (2001). Facing the future: The nature and purpose of management research reassessed. *British Journal of Management*, 12(Special Issue): S1-S80.

Hodgson, D. (2002). Disciplining the Professional: The Case of Project Management. *Journal of Management Studies,* 39(6): 803-821.

Hodgson, D. and Cicmil, S. (2007). The Politics of Standards in Modern Management: Making 'The Project' a Reality. *Journal of Management Studies*, 44(3): 431-50.

Holland, J. (1995). *Hidden order: How adaptation builds complexity*. Reading, MA: Addison-Wesley.

Jarvis, P. (1999). *The Practitioner-Researcher: Developing Theory from Practice*. Jossey-Bass, San Francisco.

Jarzabkowski, P., Balogun, J. and Seidl, D. (2007). Strategizing — The challenges of a practice perspective. *Human Relations*, 60(1): 5-27.

Kauffman, S. A. (1993). *The origins of order*. New York: Oxford University Press.

Kellert, S. (1993). *In the wake of chaos*. Chicago, IL: University of Chicago Press.

Kilduff, M., Mehra, A. and Dunn, M. B. (2011). From Blue Sky Research to Problem Solving: A Philosophy of Science Theory of New Knowledge Production. *Academy of Management Review*, 36(2): 297-317.

Knorr, K. (1977). Producing and Reproducing Knowledge: Descriptive or Constructive? *Social Science Information,* 16, 669-96.

Knorr, K. (1979). Tinkering Toward Success: Prelude to a Theory of Scientific Practice. *Theory and Society*, 8, 347-76.

Knorr-Cetina, K. (1981a). *The Manufacture of Knowledge. An Essay on The Constructivist and Contextual Nature of Science*. Oxford.

Knorr-Cerina, K. (1981b). Social and Scientific Method or What Do We Make of the Distinction Between the Natural and the Social Sciences? *Philosophy of the Social Sciences*, 11: 335-59.

Knorr-Cetina, K., & Amann, K. (1990). Image dissection in natural scientific inquiry. *Science, Technology & Human Values,* 15(3): 259-83.

Kolb. D. A., Fry, R. (1975). Toward an applied theory of experiential learning. In C. Cooper (ed.) *Theories of Group Process,* London: John Wiley.

Kondrat, M. E. (1992). Reclaiming the practical: Formal and substantive rationality in social work practice. *Social Service Review*, 66(2): 237-55.

Koontz, H. (1980). The management theory jungle revisited. *Academy of Management Review* 5(2): 175-88.

Kotarbinski, T. (1983). *The goal of an act and the task of agent*. Praxiological Studies. Polish Contributions to the Science of Efficient Action. Gasparski, Wojciech; Pszczolowski, Tadeusz (eds). Series: Theory and Decision Library, 34, pp. 1-19, 432 p.

Kraaijenbrink, J. (2010). Rigor and Relevance under Uncertainty: Toward Frameworks as Theories FOR Practice. Working Paper. [http://www.philosophyofbusiness.org/ wordpress/wp-content/uploads/downloads/2011/05/Rigor-and-relevance-under-uncertainty-Kraaijenbrink-20-12-2010.pdf. Retrieved 14 June 2012.]

Kuhn, T. S. (1962, 1970). *The structure of scientific revolutions.* Chicago: University of Chicago Press.

Lalonde, P.-L., Bourgault, M., Findeli, A. (2012). An empirical investigation of the project situation: PM practice as an inquiry process. *International Journal of Project Management*, 30(4): 418-31.

Latour, B., and Woolgar, S. (1979). *Laboratory Life*. Beverly Hills.

Latour, B. (1980). Is It Possible to Reconstruct the Research Process? Sociology of a Brain Peptide. In K. Knorr, R. Krohn and R. Whitley (eds), *The Social Process of Scientific Investigation*. Boston, Dordrecht.

Latour, B. (1986). Visualization and cognition: Thinking with eyes and hands. *Knowledge and Society: Studies in the Sociology of Culture Past and Present*, 6(6): 1-40.

Leguérinel, L. (2007). Enjeux et Limites des Théories Contemporaines de l'Action: de la Praxéologie à la Pragmatique. Thèse de doctorat. Université Paris 8 – Vincennes-Saint Denis, U.F.R Arts, Philosophie et Esthétique.

Le Moigne, J.-L. (2007). Do the ethical aims of research and intervention in education and training not lead us to a "new discourse on the study method of our time"?. Conference Intelligence of Complexity. *Educational Sciences Journal*, 4: 115-26.

Levi-Strauss, C. (1966). *The savage mind.* Chicago: University of Chicago Press.

Leybourne, S. (2010). Project Management and High-Value Superyacht Projects: An Improvisational and Temporal Perspective. Project Management Journal, 41(1): 17-27.

Lyotard, J-F. (1984). The postmodern condition: A report on knowledge. Manchester: Manchester University Press.

MacIntyre, A. C. (1985). *After virtue.* 2nd ed. London: Duckworth.

Maturana, H. R., Varela F. J. (1998). *The Tree of Knowledge: The Biological Roots of Human Understanding,* revised ed. Shambhala Publications, Boston, MA.

McGee, M. C. (2001). Phronesis in the Habermas vs. Gadamer Debate. in John M. Sloop and James P. McDaniel (eds), *Judgment Calls: Rhetoric, Politics, and Indeterminacy,* Westview Press, 1998. Retrieved from http://mcgeefragments.net/OLD/Phronesis.in.the. Habermas.vs.Gadamer.Debate.htm. 4 July 2012.

McKelvey, B., & Boisot, M. (2009). Redefining strategic foresight. In L. Costanzo & B. MacKay (eds), *Handbook of research on strategy and foresight:* 15-47. Cheltenham, UK: Edward Elgar.

Menger, Carl (1985). *Investigations into the Method of the Social Sciences.* Translated by Francis J. Nock. New York: New York University Press.

Merton, R. K. (1945). Sociological theory. *American Journal of Sociology*, 50(6): 462-73.

Merton, R. K. (1949). *Social theory and social structure.* New York: Free Press.

Mohr, L. (1982). *Explaining organizational behavior.* San Francisco, CA: Jossey-Bass.

Morgan, G. (1997). *Images of organization* (2nd ed.). Thousand Oaks, CA: Sage.

Nicolis, G. and Prigogine, I. (1989). *Exploring complexity: An introduction.* New York: Freeman.

Nonaka, I. (1994). A Dynamic Theory of Organizational Knowledge Creation. *Organization Science*, 5(1): 14-37.

Nussbaum, M. C. (1990). *Love's knowledge: Essays on philosophy and literature.* New York: Oxford University Press.

Orlikowski, W. J. (2002). Knowing in Practice: Enacting a Collective Capability in Distributed Organizing. *Organization Science*, 13(3): 249-73.

Packendorff, J. (1995). Inquiring into the temporary organization: new directions for project management research. *Scandinavian Journal of Management*, 11 (4): 319-33.

Pascal, C. and Bertram, T. (2012). Praxeological Research Within a Learning Community: Developing Evidence Based Practice. Center for Research in Early Childhood Learning Circle, 2nd BECERA Conference February 2012. [http://www.slideshare.net/CREC_APT/praxeology-keynote-becera-2012. Retrieved: 27 April 2012].

Peirce, C. S. (1997). *Pragmatism as a Principle and Method of Right Thinking* (The 1903 Harvard Lectures on Pragmatism, edited and introduced, with a commentary by Patricia Ann Turrisi). Albany NY: State University of New York Press.

Perelman, C., Olbrechts-Tyteca, L. (2006). *The New Rhetoric: A Treatise on Argumentation*. University of Notre Dame Press, Notre Dame, Indiana.

Perminova, O., Gustafsson, M. and Wikström, K. (2008). Defining uncertainty in projects – a new perspective. *International Journal of Project Management* 26, 73-79.

Pettigrew, A. M. (2001). Management research after modernism. *British Journal of Management*, 12(Special Issue): S61-S70.

Petruszewycz, M. (1965). À propos de la praxéologie. *Mathématiques et Sciences Humaines*, 11:. 11-18.

Pich, M. T., Loch, C. H. and De Meyer, A (2002). On Uncertainty, Ambiguity, and Complexity in Project Management. *Management Science*, 48(8): 1008-1023.

Pitsis, T. S.; Clegg, S. R., Marosszeky, M. and Rura-Polley, T. (2003). Constructing the Olympic Dream: A Future Perfect Strategy of Project Management. *Organization Science*, 14(5): 574-90.

Poggi, G. (1965). A main theme of contemporary sociological analysis: Its achievements and limitations. *British Journal of Sociology*, 16(4): 283-94.

Polanyi, M. (1962). *Personal Knowledge: Towards a Post-Critical Philosophy*. Routledge & Kegan Paul: London.

Polanyi, M. (1966). *The Tacit Dimension*. Cox & Wyman Ltd: London.

Pouliot, V. (2007). "Sobjectovism": Toward a Constructivist Methodology. *International Studies Quarterly*, 51: 359-84.

Putnam, H., Putnam, R. A. (1996). What the spilled beans can spell: The difficult and deep realism of William James. *Times Literary Supplement: London*, N°. 4864, June 21, 14-15.

Rasche, A, Chia, R. (2009). Researching Strategy Practices: A Genealogical Social Theory Perspective. *Organization Studies*, 30(7): 713-34.

Reckwitz, A. (2002). Toward a theory of social practices: A development in culturalist theorizing. *European Journal of Social Theory*, 5(2): 243-63.

Ricoeur, P. (1984). *Time and narrative*. Vol. 1. Chicago, IL: University of Chicago Press.

Ricoeur, P. (1991). *From text to reality*. Vol. 2. London: Harper and Row.

Romeyer Dherbey, G. (1983). *Les choses mêmes. La pensée du réel chez Aristote*. Éd l'Age d'Homme: Lausanne, Suisse.

Rorty, R. (1980). *Philosophy and the mirror of nature*. Oxford: Blackwell.

Rorty, R. (1989). *Contingency, irony, and solidarity.* Cambridge: Cambridge University Press.

Rothbard, M. N. (1997a). Praxeology as the Method of the Social Sciences. In *Phenomenology and the Social Sciences,* Maurice Natanson (ed.) (Evanston, U.: Northwestern University Press, 1973), 2, pp. 31-61.

Rothbard, M. N. (1997b). *The Logic of Action One: Method, Money, and the Austrian School.* Cheltenham, UK: Edward Elgar, pp. 58-77.

Rousseau, D. M. (2006). 2005 Presidential Address: Is There Such a Thing as "Evidence-Based Management"? *Academy of Management Review,* 31(2): 256-69.

Ryle, G. (1979). *On thinking.* Oxford, UK: Basil Blackwell.

Rynes, S. L. (2007). Let's create a tipping point: What academics and practitioners can do, alone and together. *Academy of Management Journal,* 50(5): 1046-1054.

Rynes, S. L., Bartunek, J. M. and Daft, R. L. (2001). Across the great divide: Knowledge creation and transfer between practitioners and academics. *Academy of Management Journal,* 44: 340-355.

Sanderson, J. (2012). Risk, uncertainty and governance in megaprojects: A critical discussion of alternative explanations. *International Journal of Project Management,* 30(4): 432-43.

Say, J-B. (1964). *A Treatise on Political Economy.* C.C. Biddle, trans. New York: Augustus Kelley.

Sayer, A. (1984). *Method in Social Science.* Hutchinson, London, England.

Schatzki, T. R. (2005). The sites of organizations. *Organization Studies* 26(3): 465-84.

Schatzki, T. R., Knorr-Cetina, K. and von Savigny, E. (*eds*) (2001). *The practice turn in contemporary theory.* London: Routledge.

Schön, D. A. (1983). *The reflective practitioner: How professionals think in action.* New York: Basic Books.

Schön, D. A. (1987). *Educating the reflective practitioner.* San Francisco: Jossey-Bass.

Schrag, C. O. (1986). *Communicative Praxis and the Space of Subjectivity.* Bloomington: Indiana University Press.

Schram, S. F. (2004). Beyond Paradigm: Resisting to the Assimilation of Phronetic Social Science. *Politics & Society,* 32(3), 417-33.

Schütz, A. (1964). *Collected Papers, vol. 2, Studies in Social Theory,* A. Brodersen (ed.) The Hague: Nijhoff.

Shotter, J. (2009). Bateson, Double Description, Todes, and Embodiment: Preparing Activities and Their Relation to Abduction. *Journal for the Theory of Social Behaviour,* 39(2): 219-45.

Smith, M. K. (1999, 2011). 'What is praxis?' in *the encyclopaedia of informal education.* [http://www.infed.org/biblio/b-praxis.htm. Retrieved: 27 April 2012].

Philosophical Underpinnings of OPM Research

Smyth, H. J., Morris, P. W. G. (2007). An epistemological evaluation of research into projects and their management: Methodological issues. *International Journal of Project Management, 25(4):* 423-36.

Stacey, R. (1996). *Complexity and creativity in organizations.* San Francisco, CA: Barrett-Koehler.

Suddaby, R. and Greenwood, R. (2005). Rhetorical strategies of legitimacy. *Administrative Science Quarterly,* 50(1): 35-67.

Suppe. F. (ed.) (1974). *The Structure of Scientific Theories.* Urbana, Ill.

Sutherland. J. W. (1975). *Systems: Analysis, administration, and architecture.* New York: Van Nostrand.

Sutton, R. I. and Staw, B. M. (1995). ASQ forum: What theory is not. *Administrative Science Quarterly,* 40: 371-84.

Taylor, C. (1993). To follow a rule … In *Bourdieu: Critical perspectives.* C. Calhoun, E. LiPuma, and M. Postone (eds), 45-60. Cambridge: Polity Press.

Taylor, C. (1985). *Philosophy and the human sciences: Philosophical papers,* Vol. 2. Cambridge: Cambridge University Press.

Tedlock, D. (1983). *The Spoken Work and the Work of Interpretation.* Philadelphia: University of Pennsylvania Press.

Thompson, J. D. (1956-57). On building an administrative science. *Administrative Science Quarterly,* 1(1): 102-111.

Toulmin, S. (1990). *Cosmopolis: The hidden agenda of modernity.* Chicago: The University of Chicago Press.

Toulmin, S. (2002). *Return to Reason.* Berkeley: University of California Press.

Tranfield, D. and Starkey, K. (1998). The Nature, Social Organization and Promotion of Management Research: Towards Policy. *British Journal of Management,* 9(4): 341-53.

Tsoukas, H. (1994). Introduction: From social engineering to reflective action in organizational behaviour in *New thinking in organizational behaviour.* H. Tsoukas (ed.), 1-22. Oxford: Butterworth/Heinemann.

Tsoukas, H. and Papoulias, D. B. (1996). Creativity in OR/MS: From technique to epistemology. *Interfaces,* 26(2):73-79.

Tsoukas, H. and Cummings, S. (1997). Marginalization and Recovery: The Emergence of Aristotelian Themes in Organization Studies. *Organization Studies,* 18(4): 655-83.

Tsoukas, H. and Hatch M. J. (2001). Complex Thinking, Complex Practice: The Case for a Narrative Approach to Organizational Complexity. *Human Relations* 2001 54(8): 979-1013.

Vaara, E. and Whittington, R. (2012). Strategy-as-Practice: Taking Social Practices Seriously. *The Academy of Management Annals,* 6(1): 285-336.

Van de Ven, A. H. and Johnson, P. E. (2006). Knowledge for Theory and Practice. *Academy of Management Review*, 31(4): 802-821.

Van Maanen, J. and Barley, S. R. (1986). Occupational communities: Culture and control in organizations. *Research in Organizational Behavior*, 6: 287-365.

Van Marrewijk, A., Clegg, S. R., Pitsis, T. S. and Veenswijk. M. (2008). Managing public-private megaprojects: Paradoxes, complexity, and project design. *International Journal of Project Management*, 26(6): 591-600.

Vazquez, A. S. (1977). *The Philosophy of Praxis*, London, Merlin, NJ, Humanities Press, xii + 387 p.

Vico, G. B. (1708). *De nostri temporis studiorum ratione – La Méthode des études de notre temps* (The method of studies in our time). Présentation & traduction par PONS Alain, 1981 (texte de 1708). Paris: Grasset.

Vico, G. B. (1710). *On the Most Ancient Wisdom of the Italians: Unearthed from the Origins of the Latin Language*. L. M. Palmer (Translator). Cornell University Press, Ithaca, N.Y., 1988.

Von Mises, L. (1949). *Human action: A treatise on economics* (4th revised ed.). San Francisco: Fox & Wilkes.

Von Mises, L. (1981). *Praxeology*. The Freeman: Ideas on Liberty, 31, 515-76.

Waldrop, M.M. (1992). *Complexity*. London: Penguin.

Warry, W. (1992). The Eleventh Thesis: Applied Anthropology as Praxis. *Human Organization*, 51(2): 155-63.

Weber, M. (1957). *The Theory of Social and Economic Organization*. Glencoe, Ill.: Free Press.

Weick, K. E. (1979). The *Social Psychology of Organizing*. Menlo Park, CA: Addison-Wesley.

Weisinger, J. Y. and Salipante, P. F. (2000). Cultural Knowing As Practicing: Extending Our Conceptions of Culture. *Journal of Management Inquiry*, 9(4):376-90

Whittington, R. (2006). Completing the Practice Turn in Strategy. *Organization Studies*, 27(5): 613-34.

Winch, G. M. and Maytorena, E. (2011). Managing risk and uncertainty on projects: a cognitive approach. In: Morris, P. W. G., Pinto, J. K. and Söderlund, J. (eds), *The Oxford Handbook of Project Management*. Oxford University Press, Oxford, pp. 345-364

Winter, M., Smith, C., Morris and P. Cicmil, S. (2006). Directions for future research in project management: The main findings of a UK government-funded research network. *International Journal of Project Management*, 24(8), 638-49.

Chapter 3

Thinking in Slow Motion about Project Management

Jonathan Whitty

Abstract

Project management research takes place in an environment where many concepts and ideas are unquestioned and apparently need not be proven to be true as it is generally accepted by researchers and their subjects that they are. By way of its construction and development, this chapter provides an example of a metaphysical and epistemological framework for project management researchers to examine, critique, and re-think their own (and commonly held) concepts and ideas about the nature, relationship, and limits of what can be known about projects and project management. This particular framework is constructed from the philosophical ideas of Plato, Aristotle, John Locke, David Hume, and Immanuel Kant. Through the application of the framework, this chapter reveals the limits of mainstream project management thinking and submits that in order for project management research to move forward in truly novel and transformational ways, researchers should openly subject their concepts and constructs to such metaphysical and epistemological scrutiny.

Introduction

I am going to be bold and begin by launching into what this chapter is all about. It is about a metaphysical and epistemological approach to project management, and there are insights to be gained from both. To put this simply, if we were having a conversation about the latest bridge designs or improving the performance characteristics of an engine, we would inevitably be speaking in terms of force, tension, mass, torque, and other physical qualities we have equations for. We would be speaking in terms of physics. But if we were to speak about organisational design or improving the performance of a project team then in what terms would be speaking? What equations could we consult? Physics has its variables, such as force or mass, from which to build its equations. Physics can at least demonstrate that mass and torque exist in some measurable way. But what are the variables of the equations for organisational design and behaviour? Are there really such quantifiable and measurable things as projects or teams? Now we are speaking in terms beyond physics. We are speaking in terms of metaphysics.

Project management researchers and practitioners alike unknowingly indulge in metaphysical and epistemological questions and conversations every day. What is the best way to manage a project? What is a project? What is this project all about? How can we know and measure project management competence? In various ways each one of these questions is dealing in some way with a metaphysical formula or attempting to construct one. For example, something plus something plus some other thing equals the best way to manage a project. Of course this equation presupposes amongst many other things that a thing called a project exists and that it can be managed, whatever managed means. It also presupposes that there are measurable 'somethings' that when combined in some way are the best way to manage a project.

I have, in a way, begun to describe here the two main branches of metaphysics which are ontology and cosmology. Ontology deals with 'what is there and what is its nature?' Cosmology is the study of the totality, the overall phenomena. When combined these two pursuits consider how the particulars fit into the whole, and how the whole impacts on the particulars. We might speculate and say that good communication is one of the 'somethings' in the metaphysical equation that leads to the best way to manage a project. An ontological pursuit would deal with the nature of communication, what it is, how it takes place, how we could measure it and how it impacts on the best way to manage a project and the rest of the matters pertaining to the project. A cosmological pursuit would be to investigate how all the matters pertaining to the project and the project itself impact on communication. Metaphysics is very much a systems approach of how the parts or features influence the whole, and how the whole influences the parts.

Epistemology goes hand in glove with metaphysics. It is the study of our claims to know something. An epistemology of project management would examine our claims of how we come to know something about projects and project management. For example, is our knowledge about these topics rationalised? That is to say is our knowledge largely intuitive and abstract in some way and that observation and experience plays no part. If this is the case then perhaps our claims of knowledge are actually beliefs rather than knowledge. Perhaps our claims to knowledge are based on observation and experience and this is sufficient enough. Perhaps our claims are based on rationality and observation. If they are, then is there a right balance?

The intent of this chapter is to propose that a metaphysical and epistemological line of discourse is fundamental to the future of project management research, and researchers should pay it more attention. Project managers care about their relationships with stakeholders and their teams, and senior management, and they care about project success. Project managers care about these concepts and issues so much that they ground their understanding of their working world in them. They have a real sense that teams and stakeholders and project exist, and build their world on these constructs and ideas. Each project manager sees their day to day experience in terms

Philosophical Underpinnings of OPM Research

of such concepts and ideas, and they form the backbone of the project management body of knowledge. Project managers, and more broadly speaking everyone else in the corporate environment, behave and act as though these things are true. That is to say that even though they may know that constructs and ideas such as 'team' and 'project' are just constructs and ideas, they behave and act as though they are real.

Everything we Know is Wrong, or is It?

In order to explore and expose the limits of our understanding about projects and project management in a novel and transformational way, I am going to create a basic metaphysical and epistemological framework which in this case is constructed from the sharply honed thinking tools of some particular bygone philosophers. By thinking tools I mean the various conceptual ways of thinking about the world that includes their rational and empirical biases. By particular bygone philosophers I mean specifically Plato, Aristotle, John Locke, David Hume and Immanuel Kant. I have constructed the epistemological framework in this way for a specific reason. Plato attempted to understand the world as we experience it in terms of universals and ideals. Whereas Aristotle focused on real things that could be observed, experienced, discovered, and categorised. Both these ways of thinking continue to dominate Western thought. Locke, Hume and Kant were part of a 17th and 18th Century philosophical enlightenment movement that attempted to overturn previous ways of thinking. To a certain extent they succeeded and created a rigour of thinking about how we think about the world and how we think about our thinking that has not yet been surpassed. Sadly this enlightened way of thinking is not prevalent in the corporate and organisational environment, and project management today is almost completely analysed and conceptualised in Platonic and Aristotelian ways.

Philosophy was once described to me as thinking in slow motion. So for the purposes of this chapter I will consider philosophy to be the cognitive activity that enables us to break down, describe and assess the mental moves our minds make ordinarily at immense speed. By framing this slow motion thinking in the terms of these five great philosophers I hope to demonstrate how fresh intellectual adrenaline can be injected into research questions about projects and project management. Table 3.1 highlights the key points of the ensuing discussion. It summarises how the particular philosopher conceptualised knowledge, the pertinent thinking tool applied in the discussion, the consequential paradigm shift in thinking the tool creates, and the resultant transformational insights for project management researchers.

Table 3.1. Transformational Insights for Project Management Researchers

Philosopher	Knowledge is:	Thinking Tool	Paradigm Shift	Transformational insights
Plato	gained through contemplation of universals.	Theory of Universal Forms.	Universal concepts are incomplete and erroneous forms.	PM textbook and journal illustrations represent universal idealised principles which in and of themselves cannot function. Professional institutions are Platonic in nature. Their educational and certification programs direct the efforts of PM scholars and practitioners towards universals.
Aristotle	gained through observation and theory.	Theory of Four Causes.	PM is an efficient cause; a thinking algorithm. Its application creates and maintains the (life-cycle) form of project work.	PM knowledge is independent of individuals. It is expressed variously across a particular cohort of people.
		Impact of change on identity or essence.	The essential feature of a project is its life-cycle form. The essence of a project manager is someone who expresses project management knowledge.	Once the application of PM (the efficient cause of a project) ceases or dissipates the body of work is no longer a project.
Locke	mediated through the limits of sense-experience and organised by the function of reason.	Primary and secondary qualities.	A project is a particular series of sense-experiences brought to the mind. It is not a single entity out there in the world.	Work is only a project if it stimulates and brings about particular recognisable experiences. The essence of a project is within the mind of the individual. What is a project to some may not be to others.
Hume	personal and grounded in 'habits of the mind' and therefore unreliable and meaningless.	How we hold matters of fact and 'Habits of the Mind' such as *Cause and Effect*.	Our knowledge of projects is; limited by our own unique perspective; and whilst it arises *from* experience, it is grounded *in* particular concepts or 'habits of the mind'.	Each person will experience the same project differently. A project manager's mind has been shaped by various concepts such that a series of experiences will create the impression of a project.
Kant	sense-experience organised by perceptual and conceptual categories, and transformed into concepts and judgements.	Axioms of *a priori* perceptual categories and the four conceptual categories of quantity/quality/relation/modality.	Within a common perceptual framework, each project manager conceptualizes sense-experience differently.	Cultural and institutionally directed education and training fashions conceptual categories to be applied in a way that creates the common experience of 'project'.

Philosophical Underpinnings of OPM Research

Our Thinking is Still Pretty Old

Much of the structure of so called Western thinking can be traced back to Plato (c. 428 to 347 BCE) and Aristotle (c. 384 to 322 BCE). Their unique contribution to philosophical thought is unmatched. This is not to say that their contributions have not created problems in what today we call the physical and social sciences, and political and ethical thought. Regrettably, much of project management thinking today is grounded in Platonic and Aristotelian ways. For example, project management doctrine considers universals in the same idealistic way of Plato. And decision-making processes of today's business leaders, managers in general, and project managers in particular, are still based on Aristotle's 'develop a theory from observation' method.

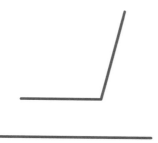

Figure 3.1. A Universal Chair

In the Grip of Platonic Thinking

Plato was a classical idealist. He believed that the idea of something, the universal principle or form that makes it what it is, is more real than the thing that embodies it. This is known as Plato's theory of forms. For Plato the things that we see in the world are mere shadows or imperfections of ideals that are not in this world. We can therefore only come to understand these universal ideals by contemplating the things in the world. For Plato this contemplation is a virtuous pursuit as it is how we come to know. I often demonstrate a problem with Plato's universal concept to student groups by placing a variety of chairs at the front of the room and I ask them to contemplate on the idea of 'chairness'. After some amusement, groups quickly come to agree on what constitutes chairness. It is usually described as a seat, with a back, all of which is elevated approximately knee height off the floor (see Figure 3.1). This example nicely illustrates the problem with universals as one could not build nor sit in the universal chair because it is suspended in mid-air. Any attempt to connect it to the grounds with a leg or legs would render it a particular chair and not a universal form.

There is much Platonic thinking in the world of project management. Most if not all drawings of project management processes in project management journals and textbooks such as the PMBOK Guide are of universal forms. These drawings are created in the same way as the universal chair. For example, the universal or ideal risk process is drawn in the form of a diagram by examining the various processes used by various organisations to manage risk. Some 'risk-managing-ness' is identified in them which then becomes the universal idealised form and the drawing in the book is made. However, these universal drawings of project management processes suffer the same fate as the universal chair in that they cannot be built or used without making them a particular. To put it another way, the features that would make such processes workable or useful or indeed comprehensible are missing from the universal drawing. Perhaps, like Plato, we feel that if we identify the universal forms that comprise projects and project management, we will in some way come to know more about the reality of project and project management. But what underpins this feeling is a belief that these universal or ideal forms are really there to be discovered. Plato would also consider incidences of poor practice in project management to be activities that obscure our experience of universal forms and necessarily mislead us in our understanding of the ideal practice.

Plato would advise that all project management literature and education should be carefully controlled and not allowed to take its own direction. This control would be achieved through some form of organised institution whose duty it was to educate project managers in universal forms which would ultimately reveal to them the true nature of projects and project management. I am sure that I do not need to further dilate on how this depicts the state of affairs of today's project management discipline, with its professional institutions and associations and their certification processes which are established on their self-published texts. What may not be so obvious is that thinking and acting in this way about universal aspects of project management is to consider its features to be eternal and unchangeable, and there is a predestined or constraining quality about this way of thinking that leaves no room for innovative or free thinking about project management. Thinking in universal terms imposes a direction on our thinking towards ideals which for Aristotle is a somewhat wasteful pursuit.

The Confidence of Aristotelian Thinking

To say that Aristotle was a student of Plato is not to say that he wholeheartedly agreed with his thinking. It was not that he was a critic of Plato, but rather he believed his mentor's teachings to be somewhat incomplete, perhaps missing something, or even overemphasising that which is not particularly important. In the context of this discussion it is important to note that he disagreed with Plato's theory of forms. Aristotle did not believe that universal forms were really 'out there' forming the eternal fabric of the universe. He believed that formal principles or universals that form things into what they are could be found 'in' the substance of the thing itself and not apart from it. For Aristotle, when we find chairness in a substance (a thing) we can say that we have found a chair. He believed that to know something one needs to know more than its universal form and he addressed this problem by applying his four causes theory.

Aristotle defines cause in terms of the 'how and the why' of the thing. To understand the cause of something Aristotles argues that four basic elements need to be accounted for, namely; the material cause (the stuff or material that makes up the thing), the formal cause (the shape or form of the thing or how the thing is formed), the efficient cause (the force that brings the material and formal together or the force that makes the thing), and the final cause (the purpose of the thing or the reason for its being). By way of example, if we apply this principle to the topic of Michelangelo's statue of David, then to account for the cause or the how and the why of the statue we must consider the marble, the shape of David, Michelangelo and his tools, and Michelangelo purpose for sculpting David from marble. This may sound logical and fill us with a sense of confidence in this way of thinking, but there are unforeseen consequences with this way of thinking about causal effects. I will address the consequences shortly.

For Aristotle the sculptor Michelangelo is only a vehicle or conduit for the expression of a specific knowledge. The statue of David is a manifestation of this knowledge. Therefore the efficient cause is a series of steps, an algorithm or rule-set so to speak about applying chisels to marble, devoid of the beliefs and intentions of the individual sculptor. However, when this knowledge is expressed in a particular sculptor, a particular form will result. The subtle theme here is that knowledge is not a thing found separately outside individuals and it is not contingent upon particular individuals, but it is something that is expressed across a group of individuals. Those conversant with today's view of how knowledge is captured across a network of agents in a complex adaptive system would find elements of this view of efficient cause very familiar.

The four cause theory is a dynamic approach which infers that things are in the world and engaged in the world; things have a purposeful role. The material, formal, and efficient cause create a concatenation or series of interconnecting events behind each event. Every event is therefore preceded by an event, and so on. This creates a great web of events connecting everything to everything else, all for a purpose or intent. The four causes are therefore used to reason, account, and explain for a thing being whatever it is. Perhaps another way of conceptualising the four causes is as the four *be*-causes. They are the four kinds of answers or responses to possible why questions. That is to say that in order to explain why a thing is what it is, we need to consider; because of what it is made, because of its form or function, because of the processes that create and hold the form, and because it moves towards its final form and fulfils a role. Aristotle's view is that everything necessarily fulfils a purpose or role.

It is an interesting exercise to apply the Aristotelian four causes thinking to traditional project management. At first glance one can see that much of project management thinking is driven by the concept of the final cause. The zeitgeist of project management advocates that projects have an aim or purpose before any planning or work commences. It is the aim or purpose of the project that appears to ignite all other causes. The material cause of a project could amount to anything from bricks and mortar to silicone, plastic and electronic charges. The essential cause (the how it is assembled management process) would in part be determined by the form of the project or what the project is to be (formal cause). Aristotle would therefore view the essential cause to comprise the management organising process or what we call project management. It is the identifiable and recognisable organising and shaping force of a project. As with the knowledge of sculptors, there is a body of knowledge that manifests in the form of practices and processes which form the essential cause of a project. It too is not found outside individuals, not contingent upon particular individuals, but it is found expressed across a cohort of individuals who we call project managers. The implications of this statement are profoundly significant. Firstly, the essential cause of a project (the practices and processes of what constitutes the body of knowledge of project management) is not to be found outside of individual project managers in some universal Platonic way. Project management textbooks therefore contain some incomplete interpretation of what the body of knowledge is. It is not the body of knowledge itself and it could never be. Secondly, the individual project manager is only a vehicle or conduit for the expression of this specific organising knowledge. Therefore the varied qualities and intentions of the individual will lead to the knowledge being variedly expressed. And thirdly, a project manager is called a project manager not because he or she manages a project (the essence or defining features of which I have not yet addressed) but because he or she articulates or expresses project management knowledge.

So what about the essence or defining features of a project? What is it or what are they? Aristotle was interested in how we go about answering 'what is it?' questions. That meant pursuing questions about substance and he approaches this in two ways which he considered were importantly coupled together. The first way concerned questions about change and the second concerned questions about identity. Coupled together these questions helped the enquiry on the impact of change on identity. Aristotle argued that everything contains an essence or an essential feature which enables it to be identified. We can therefore know what a thing is and what its natural role is. This essence of a thing must remain the same as its various attributes change over time otherwise it would be literally very hard for us to talk about it.

Even though Aristotle was an eternalist who believed that the world had been set up at some point and left to run and never change, he did consider things in themselves to be in a constant state of flux. This view raises the issue of what makes something what it is, and when does it cease to be what it is. For example, when an apple has just fallen from a tree we say it is still an apple. But as the apple decomposes (change occurs within the thing) it must at some point stop being an apple. It must at some point lose the fundamental essence that enables it to be an apple or fulfil the role of an apple. To state this point more generally, what are the essential features that something must lose in order for it to not be what it previously was? In the case of a subject such as an apple, we deal with this situation practically in our discourse by predicating

Philosophical Underpinnings of OPM Research

the subject with a word that reflect its changing state, such as rotten; a rotten apple. Aristotle would say that a new essential cause (the decomposition of organic matter) is acting on the apple. But it is still an apple until its recognisable 'essential' features have deteriorated. Here Aristotle gives primacy of form over material. For him the essence of something like an apple is not derived from its material or atomic matter as this is changing all the time. Rather the essence of something is derived from its form which means more than its shape; it refers to its functional structure, and the way it is organised to function. For example, a wooden boat may have all its parts replaced over a period of time, but as long as it retained its boat function (form) its identity would remain the same.

Applying Aristotle's essence of something to a project raises some interesting insights as to how we recognise and define a project or how we label an experience we have as project work. If we look across a range of varied projects we would see that their material and formal cause would be different. However, there would be in our mind, and through observation, a structure within which the work takes place that progressively leads to the final causes. This structure or pattern of behaviours would remain reasonably identifiable and consistent across a range of projects and it would be inextricably bound to the essential cause. That is to say that the project management processes and practices (the essential cause of a project) give the project its identifiable 'life-cycle' form. So the essence of a project, that is to say those features that make an experience a project, are inextricable from the practices and process that are recognisable as project management. A point to take from this line of reasoning is that we do not apply project management to projects, but rather a body of work is identifiable as a project *because* project management is applied to it. It is project management, the implementation of particular practices and processes that cause the form of work to be identifiable as a project.

Aristotle was a relentless observer and collector of facts and a systematic categoriser and classifier of forms into groups. He was a master of placing theory against observation in an attempt to understand and explain the world. However, there is a fundamental flaw with Aristotle's science and it is a mistake that many of us still make today. Many of his theories and assertions were just plain wrong but they were considered to be right for thousands of years, right up until the 16th and 17th centuries. This situation arose partly because Aristotle was very much a polymath and offered expertise on almost every topic imaginable. Everyone would refer to Aristotle's work in the first instance of dealing with a problem.

One simple example would be his theory that heavy objects fall faster than lighter objects, and that an object's speed would be proportional to its weight. It was Galileo who demonstrated through experiment that this apparently common-sense theory was wrong and that the rate an object falls is independent of its weight. Isaac Newton offered a more complete explanation a hundred years later. Newtown found that whilst it is true that the heavier an object is, the more strongly the earth pulls on it, it is also true that the heavier object has more inertia which makes it more resistant to acceleration, and these two effects cancel each other out, making the rate of fall independent of the mass of the object.

During the 16th and 17th centuries Aristotle slipped from the category of scientist to that of ancient philosopher. His downfall as a scientist was due to a fundamental flaw is his method; he observed and theorised but lacked an experimental structure to test his theories. The experimental or scientific method needed to be invented. This was first done by Muslim scholars of the 10th century onwards and was later enhanced by scholars of the enlightenment. Of these, Isaac Newton was possibly the most influential in refining the scientific method used today in scientific enquiry.

The scientific method is a powerfully self-correcting tool. With it we have learned to respect the facts even when they contradict our common sense, intuition, and gut feeling understanding. However, my experience is that not only is the scientific method not applied in the corporate environment, but that it is little understood. Aristotelian theorising from observation and measurement is a common occurrence in today's organisation and project environment. I very often hear from project managers that common sense, intuition, gut feeling, and years of experience are used as a basis for decision making. But as the great thinkers of the enlightenment who tackled Aristotelian ways of thinking realised, there are major problems with basing our decision making and knowledge on these things.

Things Will Never be the Same Again

I need to tell a short story before I move on, about an experience that happened to me, and continues to happen to me as I keep returning to the experience. I simply find it fascinating. It is an example of how my senses, my common sense, intuitive, and gut feelings monumentally deceive me. It is an experience that startlingly awakens me to the philosophical thinking I am about to draw on. The Museum in my home town of Brisbane has a hands-on science display. One exhibit called 'the Vortex' consists of a long rotating tunnel which rocks back and forth, through which there is a fix gantry or bridge along which one can walk. To experience the exhibit is to walk along the fixed gantry through the rocking tunnel. Before entering the tunnel it is clear that it is the tunnel that moves and the gantry is firmly bolted to the ground. But, as one walks into the tunnel, one quickly becomes unsteady and grabs at the handrail, as if it were the gantry that is rocking and the tunnel that is fixed. No matter what I do, even though I know that the gantry is fixed and the tunnel is moving, it still looks and feels as though the gantry is about to tip me over. I have tried all sorts of mental and physical manoeuvres to break the illusion but I cannot. Even when I back out of the tunnel and stand slightly outside the tunnel looking in, it still feels as though the gantry is moving. I find this a most compelling example of how my senses can deceive my sense of what is real. And if I can be deceived about this, then what else could I be misled about?

Philosophical Underpinnings of OPM Research

An Introduction to Dr John Locke

John Locke (1632-1704 CE) was a friend and contemporary of Isaac Newton. Amongst many other things (his influence in moral and political theory was immense) he was an accomplished medical doctor, a biologically influenced philosopher, and with the benefit of hindsight he could be called the father of Empiricism. As opposed to rationalism, where things are innately known and logically arrived at, empiricism is about knowing through sense experience. During Locke's time, and particularly following the rationalist René Descartes, philosophy was becoming very technical. It is important not to discount the zealous rationalist, as the intellectual preciseness of rationalism was a significant epistemological innovation. Rationalism brought rigour to philosophical discourse but not experiment. To the rationalist the ideas we have in our mind are the products of reason. That is to say that all knowledge is already 'in the mind' somewhere and the key to unlocking it is the intellectual act of reason itself. But this begs questions such as, how much knowledge is there and are there limits to it?

Locke wanted to apply the same rigour of experiment to matters of the mind and moral behaviour as his friend Newton had to the physical sciences. Locke put forward the case that ideas and knowledge is 'composed of' sense experience and then it is organised or assembled by a reasoning function of the mind. For Locke the mind is a sheet of white paper, a tabular rasa with the exception that it has the innate capacity or cognitive power for reason. The body therefore receives impressions (raw sense experiences) from the powers in the world through its sense organs (eyes, ear, touch, taste, small, etc.). For Locke the mind is passive in this action and we are given to know something by the power of the impression made upon the mind. The mind therefore reflects or reasons (a cognitive process that forms patterns and associations) upon these simple impressions and this creates complex ideas that have their own particular properties. There is of course a necessary consequence of this approach. Most significantly is that if everything we know comes from sense experience, then knowledge is limited, constrained, and shaped by our senses. Also, there are some functions the mind can do without experiencing them directly. For example it can cognitively create the opposite of something.

For Locke, things in the world have primary and secondary qualities. The primary quality of a thing is in the object and in the experience in itself. An example of this could be hardness and extension (form or shape). Secondary qualities, though produced by something in the object, are not 'in the object' by way of experience. That is to say that there is something in the physics of the object which interacts with something in the physiology of the body to create an experience. The colour of something is a good example of a secondary quality because at the small or atomic level of an object we do not find smaller coloured atomic objects. Colour therefore is not 'in' the physical constituents of the object, but there is something 'about' the object that gives us the experience of colour.

It is worth pausing on this point about how the mind creates colour for further consideration. Common sense, intuition, gut feeling, and even my experience with colours tells me that a red billiard ball is of course 'red'. But in fact creating the experience of colours is what my brain and brains in general do. I could read about the science of how light energy hits the retina of my eye and how electrical signals stimulate parts of my brain to create the experience of red. But when I look at a red billiard ball, no matter how much I tell myself the colour red is not 'out there' as part of the ball, I still see a red billiard ball. Humans have no choice in the matter. Colour is but one function or illusion our brains construct of the world that enables us to interact with the world. What if a project is just another construct?

The essence of an object is what stimulates and brings about experience. It is through the essence that we come to know what type of thing a thing is. However, Locke argues that we can never know the true or real essence of anything because we are limited by our sensory perception. But we can know the nominal essence of a thing. It is the nominal essence of an object that stimulates and brings about experience, and this experience we then use to classify its properties. Classification takes the pragmatic form of conventional names which we use to cover or represent the experience such as, cars, pens, planes, shoes. So the name apple includes the experience of round red/green, juicy, crunchy, sweet, picked from trees etc. We cannot claim to know the real essence of a thing, only the nominal essence through the mediated terms of our senses. However, there is a significant problem with Locke's nominal essence, which he was aware of, and it is worth taking special notice of. The problem is that the nominal essence of a thing has more to do with our experience of it than it has to do with the thing itself. By way of illustrating the problem, consider the wooden boat mentioned earlier. Over a period of time all the wooden parts will need replacing; the keel, the thwarts, mast, boom, and so on. No part of the original boat may remain after many years, yet it is considered to be the same wooden boat because the experience it creates for us has not changed. Therefore the nominal essence of an object is not 'in' the object. For Locke, things in the world present themselves to our senses and these are in some way brought together, reasoned, or synthesised by the mind, and it is this synthesis of sensations that we pragmatically classify and name.

Locke's view presents an interesting insight for those involved in projects. In a sense it reframes where the nominal essence of a project is, and it is not outside in any external way. But rather the essence of a project is within the mind of one who experiences it. Over the past few years I have been exploring this concept with project managers and the results of a simple experiment are interesting and varied. In short, I ask project managers to draw (no words are allowed) their answer to the question – managing a project is like? We know that crude drawings can serve as a means of representing or abstracting the state of one's emotional psyche about an experience. And what project managers' drew during this experiment is both varied and telling.

Figure 3.2. Managing a Project is Like?

Figure 3.2 shows a very small sample of these drawings. It appears that the nominal essence of a project is composed of two opposing forces which I have conceptualised as more in terms of Yin-Yang than good and bad. The drawings reveal a sense of duality with thrill, excitement, and personal satisfaction on the one hand and worry, anxiety, even fear of not getting the right outcome on the other. It seems that the structure of work we call a project can be an intrinsically rewarding activity, often exhilarating and challenging. For Locke we can never come to know the real essence of a project at the fundamental ontological level, or even know if such a thing really exists. For Locke, the nominal essence of a project, what makes a project a project, is a particular synthesis of a series of experiences that are brought to the mind through our senses. Projects are literally all in the mind.

Being biologically influenced Locke was very much biased towards the material side of his analysis. With regard to how knowledge came about he placed great importance on the senses and their gathering of the data of the world than he did on the assembly, rationalisation, or synthesis of the data. Leibniz shifted the balance and argued that the mental life of ideas or concepts is not to be found anywhere 'in' the brain in any material way. Rather ideas and concepts are qualia or mentally perceptual features which have no transducible transcription factors that relate to any specific parts of the brain. Yet, the brain must be constructed in such a non-trivial way to bring about these qualia. So perhaps the brain is built in such a way that it takes our particular experiences and constructs the idea of a project. As I once put it;

> … *what we call a project and what it is to manage one is an illusion; a human construct about a collection of feelings, expectations, and sensations, cleverly conjured up, fashioned, and conveniently labelled by the human brain.* (Whitty, 2005)

Then Came David Hume

David Hume (1711-1776 CE) was an empiricist like Locke in that he agreed that our understanding of the world depends upon sense experience and reason. But he was also a sceptic like Descartes because he was not sure if reason or experience was enough to verify that our knowledge is complete. Hume was interested in how our knowledge works. Specifically how we can affirm or deny what we believe we know. For Hume, when we slow down our thinking and examine the mechanisms by which we come to truly know something we see two modalities namely, the relations of ideas (the modern term is analytic propositions) and matters of fact (the modern term is synthetic propositions).

Analytic propositions refer to the structure of the relation of things. They are things that can be known *a priori* (i.e. without depending on our experience). By them we can know something or work something out just by sitting in our armchair. Analytic propositions are basically the logic that allows ideas to have any coherence. For example, if A = B and B = C, then A = C. We do not need to know what A, B, or C is to be able to understand and explore their relationship. Analytic propositions are basic operations which the mind performs in order to establish or pull ideas together. They do not express anything new about the nature of the world. A classic example of an analytical position is – all triangles have three sides. It is a proposition whose predicate is contained in its subject. Therefore we know it to be true by virtue of its meaning or conventions of the language. We do not need information from the real world to know it is true. So 'all project managers manage projects' is an analytic proposition because we can intuitively grasp the relationship and say it is true. If we unpack the concept 'project manager' we reveal the concept 'to manage a project'. Analytical propositions allow us to manipulate our current knowledge; they do not add new knowledge.

Synthetic propositions are concerned with things we observe. They cannot be known *a priori* so an experience is required to determine their truth. To know something from them we need to get out of our armchairs. They can be concerned with propositions of morality (how we understand or value behaviour) or probability (how we understand what we observe). So a synthetic proposition would be for me to say 'as a *matter of fact* Jon is a competent project manager', and I know this to be true because I have recently had the experience of assessing Jon's project management competence.

However, what about the *matters of facts* that I do not directly perceive nor do I remember perceiving. How can I possibly really know anything about those? Jane might say, 'Well as a *matter of fact* Jon is a very competent project manager'. What I suppose or infer from this proposition is that Jane has had the experience of assessing Jon's project management competence, but I do not *know* that she has or that he is. Hume would point out that what I have done at some level is relied on a causal or connecting relationship. I have inferred that at some point in time that Jon has performed in such a way as to cause Jane to assess him as a competent project manager.

Philosophical Underpinnings of OPM Research

Hume would also point out that this situation raises problems. The first concerns how we hold matters of fact in the mind, while the second concerns the use of cause and effect or connecting relationships.

Hume points out that there is a problem with how we hold matters of fact because we all assemble these ideas differently. There are perhaps limitless ways and possibilities that the mind can assemble or synthesize an impression to make an assessment or judgement about the world. These ways are influenced by our current perspectives, our history and background, the different intensity of the senses, our cultural and personal experiences. We develop our own very particular point of view from our limited perspective. We develop our own matters of fact and use these to establish what we know about the world. What this problem comes down to is – what we know, our knowing something, has been profoundly shaped and limited by our own point of view or perspective. Therefore we cannot be sure that our assessment of the world is correct because we only have *our* assessment. We are placed in a situation that makes us question whether we actually know anything about the world at all!

One of the things to notice in the drawings in Figure 3.2 is that each project manager has come to their project with their very own unique perspective. They reflect on their experiences of the project and assemble them in some way (analytical propositions or relations of ideas) and then they make a judgement of those ideas (synthetic propositions or matters of fact) and represent that in their drawing. For example, as a matter of fact managing a project is 'like playing the board game snakes 'n' ladders. On good days you land on a square and shoot up a ladder. On bad days you might get bitten and slide down a snake' (Whitty, 2010). But once again we are left wanting and still know nothing about the thing this person calls a project. We only know something about the consequences of the impressions a series of experiences has had on an individual.

Hume's penetrating examination of knowing shifts up a gear as he turns his critical analysis in the direction of cause and effect. He argues that the idea of cause and effect is a 'habit of the mind', and that it says more about how our brains assemble and asses the impressions we receive from the world than it says about the function of the world itself. In an attempt to condense his argument, imagine two stationary billiard balls on a billiard table; one red, one white. If I knock the white ball into the red ball, the red ball moves and we say that the white ball has *caused* the red ball to move. As we grow up, our world is filled with such causal relationships such as; my running caused the toys to fall over; my hand caused the cup to spill; my punch caused my Sister to cry. Hume argues that not only do we build up the habit of seeing casual relationships, but our minds are built in some innate way to assemble our experiences in terms of causal relationships. The cause and effect principle is important to our knowing something about the world because it presumes we have or can have knowledge about the cause of some phenomena.

In short, for Hume we habitually see cause or infer cause everywhere, even when we have little or no knowledge about the phenomena we are observing. This does not mean that we know what the specific cause of something is, but rather that we assume that there must be 'a' cause. Consequentially there has to be a cause preceding every phenomenon. For example, when we observe a storm, a natural disaster, a flower growing, birds flocking, a relationship breaking down, a mental illness, a war, a project succeeding, a project failing, our minds are lead to think 'I wonder what caused that?'. Using modern terms, the cause and effect principle could be considered to be a mental algorithm or subroutine that the brain automatically runs as it assembles sensory inputs into an idea, an opinion or judgement (matter of fact) about the world.

Hume is saying that just as our minds have structures that create the experience of colour and the very real feeling that the gantry is moving for me in the Vortex exhibit, so minds generally have structures that shape the thinking, reasoning, or synthesising processes. These structures are not necessarily innate (Kant adds later that they are built on innate structures) but can be habitually learned. Cause and effect therefore is a habit of mind. It is a mental subroutine that we habitually run and we are insensible of running it. That is not to say that cause and effect does not take place in the world, but rather as we observe, participate, or receive input from a phenomena our minds cannot help looking for and attributing cause.

The experience of a project manager is that they are presented with one event followed by another event, followed by another event. But the 'cause and effect habit of mind' interprets the experience of 'followed' in some ways as caused or connected. It is this habit of mind that assembles a series of experiences into what we call a project. The consequences of the cause and effect subroutines appear frequently and variously in other aspects of project management. For example, many opening chapters of project management textbooks have a section on project success factors which is another way of saying that something is needed to cause a successful project. Alternatively one might find a book section or paper on the top 10 reasons why projects fail. Again this is a product of a cause and effect subroutine. Project success factors have also been a valid research theme with many conference and journal papers dedicated to the topic. Cause and effect also manifest in the modern Gantt chart which graphically illustrates a concatenation of causal events. It is a visual manifestation of the connecting of one event followed by another. Furthermore, project management process diagrams for risk, procurement, or stakeholder management show causally connected relationships implying that for stage/phase 3 to be realised then (meaning a logical implication of) stage/phase 2 must be complete.

For Hume we humans favour consistency. We cannot do anything without making the assumption that the future will conform to the past. That is to say that we assume that the behaviour of things is a guide to their behaviour in the future. What caused something previously will cause something again. This is the assumption that enables a project manager to get up in the morning and create a project plan. Tools such as the Gantt chart, budget, and risk register etc. must necessarily contain matters of fact (synthetic propositions) that have not been directly perceived or tested by the project manager. Therefore the project manager makes causal inferences for them to be known or regarded as true. That is to say that the project manager supposes that someone knows through direct experience that a particular task has its rightful place in this particular project. Furthermore, PERT or CPM methods that are now embedded in modern Gantt charts infer causal or connected relationships. If task A is a predecessor of task B, and task B is a predecessor of task C, then this is an analytic proposition. One can make statements about task C in terms of tasks A and B without knowing what A, B or C are. However, this supposes that the tasks are actually connected in a causal relationship and that task C cannot happen or take place unless task A and B are resolved. But this proposition might be false. For Hume such plans, chart, and budgets are fundamentally based on assumptions of uniformity, rather than insights into the real nature of things. It is not just that we cannot be sure if any of it is based on any truth. His point is more radical than that. What Hume is saying is that it is not just that we cannot know, but that whatever we do know is always something that is created or generated based on the structure of our mind, on our habits of thinking. For Hume, what we see in project plans and charts etc. is not how projects really are, it is just how our minds come to structure and present the experience.

Hume's insightful question on epistemology could be stated as – how do we come to know that a specific phenomenon has a specific cause? He argued that we cannot know in any general sense because our observations of a phenomenon are highly personal and subjective. The cause and effect habit of mind creates a feeling that we know, but we as individuals cannot have enough information in the moment to truly know.

And So to Kant

It was Immanuel Kant (1724-1804 CE) who said that Hume awoke him from his dogmatic slumber. Firstly Kant was concerned that if the Metaphysical world of living, being, behaving, loving, learning, and so on were subject to the same formulaic and mechanical laws of Newton's physical world, then how could we account for the deviation from the causally connected chain of events. How can we account for free will? That is to say if our social and mental world is structured such that every event or behaviour has a cause, and that the cause would necessarily bring about that event or behaviour, how do we factor into this equation that we can choose to act differently, that we have choice and free will. And secondly, and not to go too far to the end of the free will scale, Kant shunned the relativist view that everyone experiences everything completely differently and felt that there must be some commonality or common grounding of experiences.

Let me attempt to put the basics of the thinking tools that arise from the Enlightenment period thus far into modern parlance. Locke introduced the idea that our knowledge of the world comes to us through our senses. Sense experience is presented to our mind through our sense devices and we somehow assemble these sense experiences together to form an idea and make a judgement. The more powerful the various impressions are, the stronger the signal, the more they shape our ideas. But our knowledge of the world is therefore limited by what these devices can sense. Then Hume comes along and adds that not only are we limited by the hardware of our sensing devices, but that the operating system our brains run to assemble these sense experiences has been written not only with the limitations of our individual experience but also with the limitations of how the operating system can possibly work. Our organic central processing unit, our brain, has a basic architecture which impacts on how the sense assembling operating system software (with functions like cause and effect) is constructed and can run. In a most significant way, Hume has uncovered that whilst our knowledge 'arises' from our experience it is not grounded 'in' experience. Our knowledge is grounded in basic concepts such as cause and effect. For Hume then, the whole situation of knowing is hopeless as one can never get to truly know something about the world because our hardware and software is simply not capable, nor can it ever be capable.

For Kant this situation begged the question: Before the mind can begin to come to know something, what are the necessary conditions for the possibility of experiencing anything at all? To put it another way; Hume says our knowledge is grounded in basic mental concepts such as causation, but Kant asks – what are *these* basic mental concepts grounded in? What provides a structure for concepts such as cause and effect to be implemented? In computing terms Hume has discovered that we have an operating system that provides a platform for all the other mental software to run on. But Kant is asking: what is it that enables us to proceed with running this mental operating system? There must be a mental BIOS that needs to be run in order for the mind to proceed to come to know something. This was to be one of Immanuel Kant's major contributions to epistemology and metaphysics.

Kant puts forward the case that we build our most basic mental concepts on fundamental axioms which we hold as unquestionably true. They intuitively feel right. All other possibilities of the mind proceed based on these axioms. We build our ideas and concepts on them. The first axiom is that we distinguish 'between' things, between one object and another in the mind. We recognise this capacity as our ability to think spatially. So there is a condition where we can distinguish between things, and this condition gives rise to what we come to understand as space. That is not to say that we *know* what space is, but there is a condition out there in the world that gives rise to what we call space. This is the same concept of how colour is not in the physical constituents of anything in the world, but that there are necessary conditions for the possibility to bring about a phenomenon that gives rise to the experience of colour. Kant is not saying that there is no such thing as space because it is all in the mind. He is saying that what we experience and call spatiality is not necessarily what space is, or what brings about the experience of spatiality. For us, spatiality is a basic principle or framework for our thinking and talking about things spatially in the world, and we hold it to be self-evident.

The spatial axiom of distinguishing 'between' things is not just about identifying things 'in' space out there in front of us somewhere. It means that we come to be able to consider something in the mind by its relationship to other things in the mind. So we are able to come to know the musical note Middle C because the mind can distinguish it in musical space, say *between* B and D. Or we come to know shoes because the mind distinguishes it in footwear space, in the mind perhaps *between* sandals and boots! Aristotle distinguishes man in 'being' space *between* women and angels. We come to distinguish projects in 'work' space perhaps *between* highly operationalised work and chaotic work. A spatial axiom in project management is how we come to know and talk about weak or strong matrix organisations. We even draw this organisational space with high functional organisation on the one end of the continuum and the project organisation on the other. The spatial axiom is therefore not about the space or gap between one project manager and another. It is a most fundamental conceptual construct that enables the mind to distinguish and therefore begin to come to know something. We know courage because it is a quality of mind we conceptualize in the mind *between* our ideas of cowardice and rashness. We know modesty because it is a state or quality *between* shamelessness and bashfulness. As Kant argues, the mind cannot come to know any other concepts without the spatial axiom.

An awareness of the spatial axiom presents us with new insight into the drawings of project managers in Figure 3.2. The drawings on the top of the figure clearly have a spatial dimension to them. For these project managers the experience of managing a project is about moving the clients or stakeholders or project team or themselves from one conceptual or emotional space to another, with all sorts of conceptual and emotional stops and bumps in-between. The spatial axiom also reveals that we come to know about project work because we distinguish it from other work, and we see work and describe tasks in terms of their relationship to other work and tasks.

The second basic axiom is the mental capacity to make distinctions 'within' things. So within the ideas we hold in our mind there are certain dynamics which we call changes or motions or actions, and the experience of observing this is what we call temporality or time. The drawings at the bottom of Figure 3.2 could be said to have a temporal 'change within things' axiom to them. For these project managers the experience of managing a project is about observing and experiencing a changing or dynamic state of some kind.

For Kant spatiality and temporality are fundamental to our conceptualisation of everything. Traditional project management literature cannot go beyond these fundamentals. All conventional project management language is couched in terms of space and time. Traditionally we perceive projects taking place in a physical space, like a construction project or some new service delivery. But software projects occupy a different space, a digital space. Duplicating software and duplicating a building is not the same. A building 95% complete is almost usable. But software that is 95% complete – well I am not really sure I know what that means. Temporality is experienced differently in software projects too. The dynamics and rates of change in a physical space are very different to the dynamics and rates of change in a digital or conceptual space. It could be said that change takes place in a linear fashion for construction type projects, though I am not even sure if that is true. Alternatively change may have a non-linear or chaotic dimension in software development or change management projects.

It was Hume that argued that knowledge arises out of experience but is not grounded in experience. Firstly, as I have explained, Kant argues that every experience that we will ever have will be within the receptive framework of spatial and temporal dimensions. We are completely unable to make a claim of knowledge without referring to these axioms. Secondly, and I will touch on this briefly, Kant argues that all our knowledge claims involve a judgement which is formed within a universal categorical framework. Kant calls this mental or intellectual organising framework the four 'pure categories of the understanding' which are; quality (unity, plurality, and totality), quantity (reality, negation, and limitation), modality (possibility, existence, and necessity), and relation (inherence, causality, community, and correlation). For Hume these categories are conditions of the mind and limitations and habits through which the mind acts. But Kant argues that it is impossible for us to think outside this framework, because this framework is the thinking mind itself. The application of these categories *is* thinking.

For Kant the pure categories of understanding including spatiality and temporality are part of our intellectual apparatus through which we can experience the world. They are so to speak an innate pair of spectacles through which we look at reality. Things can only appear (not how they are in themselves) to us in this way through these innate intellectual spectacles. The pure categories are how we view and organise reality, rather than part of reality itself. What is particularly powerful about this line of reasoning is that we come to realise that we cannot take this pair of spectacles off. For, in a way, my mind, and your mind, is the pair of spectacles.

In Kant's view, we only have knowledge of something when we have an intuition (an immediate representation of the external world to the senses) and a concept. Notice how this is a very different concept to Aristotle's four causes. Kant reasoned that our intuitions (the raw impressions we receive) need concepts (rules), and the mental or cognitive power of using these concepts he calls understanding. That is not to say that using these cognitive powers leads to understanding, but rather that using these cognitive powers is literally what understanding is. Various concepts therefore work together to create a unified perspective of the world, and Kant calls this conceptual unification – synthesis. The mind therefore synthesises the external world received through our senses. How these concepts unify is affected by our judgement. And we make judgements by applying the four pure categories of understanding to objects that we hold spatially and temporally in the mind. Rather than saying that through

Philosophical Underpinnings of OPM Research

our judgements we make up our mind, we should say that our judgements make our mind.

Kant's thinking has some major implications for our knowledge of projects and project management. For Kant, the reality of things is not accessible to us. What is accessible to us is knowledge of our perceptual and conceptual apparatus. Project management researchers and practitioners wear the same innate pair of intellectual spectacles as everyone else, but their spectacles are tinted with a particular shade of project management. In the way that everyone appears to see colours 'out there', project management researchers and practitioners also see projects 'out there', and they infer that these projects in some way require project management. However, contradictory to typical project management thinking, it is the project management tinting that imposes a project structure onto the messiness of reality in order to try and make sense of it. In the same way that one might infer or impose shapes or images in a Jackson Pollock picture, so the researcher and practitioner infers or imposes particular structures or rules on their individual experiences of work and act upon it as though it were true. Like everyone else project managers cannot take off the innate spectacles, but they can make efforts to discover them and to compensate for the tinting.

Some Concluding Remarks

So what are the implications of constructing and applying this particular metaphysical and epistemological framework for project management researchers? Significant I would say if properly inculcated. If one is to truly 're-think' project management in novel ways, then one must begin by thinking again about projects and project management and the things that think about them – our human brains. Whilst others might say that novel approaches to project management research require new or refined methodologies, I would say that we require completely new and insightful research questions, and these can only come from significant paradigm shifts in our thinking about projects and project management.

The particular framework or collective of 'dug from the past' (because none of them are new) thinking tools I have constructed and applied to project management in this chapter is simply an example of how one can examine, critique, and re-structure ones thinking of project management. I challenge researchers to critique or expand on this framework, or develop their own in a similar way.

Developing this chapter has impacted on my own development as a researcher in this field and the research questions I endeavour to pose and answer. I now conceptualise projects as a form of group experiential phenomena that appears to be emergent in a particular culture due to the idiosyncratic nature of the work performed and that of the particular cohort who attempt to manage it. Projects and their management can therefore be considered to be a form of built-in (not in-built or innate) metaphysics;

a set of culturally 'put on' spectacles that gives work its particular and recognisable project form.

References

Cohen, J. B. 1994. *Revolution in Science*. Harvard.

Hume, D. 1999. "An Enquiry Concerning Human Understanding," in *Essential Works of David Hume*. R. Cohen, ed. Oxford University Press

Kant, I. 1965. *Critique of Pure Reason*. N. K. Smith, trans. St. Martin's.

Kant, I. 1997. *Critique of Practical Reason*. Cambridge.

Locke, J. 1995. *An Essay Concerning Human Understanding*. Prometheus Books

Plato. 1937. *Meno, in The Dialogues of Plato*, 2 vols., B. Jowett, trans. Random House.

Robinson, D. N. 1989. *Aristotle's Psychology*. Columbia.

Whitty, S.J. 2005. 'A memetic paradigm of project management'. *International Journal of Project Management*, 23 (8) 575-83.

Whitty, S.J. 2010. 'Project management artefacts and the affective emotions they evoke'. *International Journal of Managing Projects in Business*, 3 (1) 22-45.

Chapter 4

Pluralistic and Processual Understandings of Projects and Project Organizing: Towards Theories of Project Temporality[1]

Jonas Söderlund

Abstract

This chapter tells the story about the evolution and current state of project management research. The overall aim is to trigger a debate about the role of theory and particularly the complementarity of theories. The main thrust of the chapter is built around a conviction that theory is best developed through an interplay between different theoretical attempts and contrasting world-views – however these contrasting world-views need to be integrated enough to allow for a productive dialogue and debate about the nature, quality and evolution of research on project organizing and project management. The chapter presents a preliminary framework for improved process theorizing in project management. At the center stage for such theorizing stands the notion of project temporality as critical for understanding managing projects in time, which might offer a novel approach to the study of project organizing.

Introduction

For many years, there was a remarkable silence about the nature and conduct of research within the domain of project management. Things have indeed changed in the past two decades. Spurred by the success of the IRNOP conferences over the last 20

---

1. This work draws on previously published work, including: Söderlund and Maylor (2012) on the hard and soft side of project management, Hernes et al (2013) on managing in time and organizational temporality, and Dille and Söderlund (2013) on temporal misfits in project organizing. I am grateful for comments by my collaborators and support from the editors of this volume. Any remaining errors rest with the author.

years – triggered by the launch of the Project Management Institute's Research and Education Conference, the strong presence that project management has had at the European Academy of Management conference over the last ten years and the recent success of project management demonstrated at the EGOS conference in Helsinki, project management research is at present certainly a vibrant community. In that respect – project management seems to be attracting new scholars and continues building a platform and arenas for the exchange of research findings and ideas within the domain of project management.

Around the world, we also note that there are actually quite a few strong research groups currently doing research and teaching in project management: in Manchester, in Cranfield, in London, in Berlin, in Helsinki, in Åbo, in Umeå, in Oslo, in Linköping, in Quebec, in Melbourne, in Sydney – I could go on. We also observe the success of publications focusing on project management, most notably a number of books published by top-ranked publishers, such as Cambridge University Press and Oxford University Press, to name a few. These are all good news and the progress has been rapid in a field where progress historically has been somewhat modest (Packendorff, 1995). We are certainly still in the era of ferment, of building capabilities, of collecting strength, of building networks, of building research teams, and we are slowly moving into a stage of maturity. In this chapter I would like to draw the attention to a few critical issues in the further development of project management as a scientific knowledge domain. The main idea will be to argue that project management research needs to be better equipped to answer a set of fundamental questions and that there are two fundamentally different views on what project management is, what a project is, and these views will also offer quite different answers to the fundamental questions discussed in the present chapter. In that respect, I am calling for a pluralistic, yet focused, development of theories in and on projects and project management.

What is a Project?

As scholars in project management – what is a project? – is a question that we have heard over and over again and to some extent it might it might be tiring to answer it again and again. On the other hand, it is indeed a recurrent source of inspiration to be thinking about the project phenomenon in novel ways – similar to thinking about 'what is a firm' we need to think about 'what is a project' – not only in practical terms, but more so in theoretical terms (Söderlund, 2004a). In that respect, there is a need to enhance our understanding of why projects exist. The 'why projects-question' is consequently critical and should engage most scholars in the domain of project management. It is indeed a fundamental question for those interested in developing a theory, or theories, of projects and project management. This simple, yet important, question can be answered in multiple ways. A simple answer would be to say that projects exist because there is a need to control the production of a set of activities, because there is a need to gather people to come up with something creative that otherwise would not be possible to bring about, because the coordination of the linkages between activities needed to complete a certain task is so complex that it requires a particular kind of temporary organizational mechanism, because, because... All these possible and probable answers are interesting. However, the point here is that – so far – even though project management scholars have been fully occupied with offering rather mechanistic and simplistic definitions of projects and project management – the intellectual rigor and flavor of these answers have been surprisingly dry. And so have the explanations to why projects exist. How come we do not see any provocative statements of what a project is? How come we do not elaborate further on the reasons why projects exist? How come we do not see completely alternative definitions of projects other than a temporary organization, a unique task, a one-off endeavor, and so on? And how come we do not see more sophisticated attempts to answer the question of why projects exist?

Consider the major developments within management studies in general, the firm is analyzed from a range of perspectives, offering numerous definitions of the firm – ranging from a governance structure, a knowledge-integration mechanism, a contractual form, a social melting pot, a culture, to name a few (see for instance Grant, 1996). And with projects, a similar list of definitions and perspectives can indeed be offered. However, a project is not a firm, although some projects can indeed also have several characteristics that overlap with that of the firm; a project is a governance structure, a contractual form, a knowledge-integration mechanism, but a project is temporary whereas the conventional idea of the firm is that of going-concern. A project is meant to last for short, whereas a firm is meant to last for long – although both are built to last during their intended lifetime. The issue of lifetime – of the dynamics of projects – of birth and death is indeed at the core of projects and project organizing; something I will discuss further in this chapter.

Project Dynamics

The unique and perhaps most interesting thing with projects is that they normally follow a kind of dynamic – from birth to death, from beginning to end. At least that is what the majority would say is true for projects – the intentional dismantling of an organization at a particular point in time. This is also what makes projects so special compared to many other kinds of organizational alternatives. The latter are normally set out to live forever – based on the logic of going-concern. Projects are not. They are meant to change the going-concern (Obstfeld, 2012). What seems to be particularly interesting in that respect is that projects are true entrepreneurial activities and pure occasions of sensemaking (Weick, 1996). This has historically been underplayed by project management practitioners and theorists alike. Projects exist. Projects are. However, what has become more and more true, especially since projects have entered more creative fields and projects have been launched in high-velocity sectors – projects become, they are constructed, reconstructed – continuously. In that respect, research needs to pay much more attention to the shaping of projects (Cova and Salle, 2011) and project entrepreneurship (Lindgren and Packendorff, 2003). Continuing on this line of thought, there would also be different kinds of births, different pre-histories of projects, different kinds of becomings. So far, we have failed to address the many ways that projects come about and that projects come to become.

If projects are born, projects – at least this is the intention – then projects also die. In that respect, projects differ from many other kinds of organizations – death is a sign of success. And so far, the death of projects has actually attracted only limited attention. Instead, most studies thus far have insightfully shed light on light on the eternal life of projects, the escalated commitment, and other such energy-infusing forces of projects. Exemplary studies include the study of Expo86 by Ross and Staw (1986). Considering the death of projects, few studies emerge, although a number of studies have documented the implications of deadlines on organizational processes. For instance, Gersick (1988) highlighted the mid-life transition operating in projects under time pressure, and Okhuysen and Eisenhardt (2002) studied the collaborative effects of teams working under time conditions. In that respect, the awareness of death seems to be important to infuse life into the project – an observation that quite interestingly corresponds to the Horndal effect (close down) in organization studies in which organizations facing close down increased their productivity considerably in a last sigh before death. Projects repeatedly struggle with such effects – but their forces seem to be driving projects in opposite directions; one force working against death in a wish for continuation, one force working towards death in an attempt to reduce the lifetime of the project.

Indeed, projects are dynamic enterprises, efforts and integration activities. But they are dynamic in quite a number of dimensions. This is one of the reasons why there is a need for multiple perspectives to possibly grasp some of the complexity, nature and life of projects (Söderlund, 2011; Turner et al., 2010; Winter and Szczepanek, 2009). Multiple perspectives capture different parts of the reality of projects – of the emerging reality of projects. This is also the reason why scholars have asked for a better understanding of project dynamics; the behavior and evolution of projects – the life of projects, the things in-between birth and death (Lundin and Söderholm, 1995; Lindkvist and Söderlund, 2002). So far, extant literature has suggested a number of process models grounded in the mechanistic, task-oriented models so common in textbooks in the area of project management (see Andersen, 2008), for a detailed analysis of the 'task perspective' of project management). Others have argued for the need to develop an alternative ontology of projects – a view that zeroes in on projects as temporary organizations – the 'organization perspective' of project management (see for instance Lundin and Söderholm, 1995; Packendorff, 1995; Andersen, 2008). However, more elaborate analysis of the life of projects, the development stages of projects, the life paths of projects, the temporality of projects, and so on, are needed to capture the reality and actuality of projects – as living and dynamic phenomena.

Philosophical Underpinnings of OPM Research

The Levels of Analysis in Project Management Research

So far, I have primarily called for research at the project level. However, understanding projects is more than that. In a previous paper, I discussed the expanding scope of project management research (Söderlund, 2004b). One of the principle arguments in that paper was that project management research is no longer only research about projects – it is also research about the context of projects, about the teams, the people in projects, and about the firms that govern and drive projects. To pursue this research, it is time to clearly explicate the different levels of analysis in project management research. This is what Sydow et al. (2004) called for in their much-cited editorial to the special issue on projects in *Organization Studies* almost a decade ago. Looking at the current literature within the area of project management, we discern: the individual level, the team level, the project level, the program/portfolio level, the firm level, the sector level. The latter may refer to collaborations across industries, to project ecologies, to industries and even nations.

Of course, there are many ways of elaborating on the levels of analysis. I suggest a simple distinction of project management as, on the one hand, being oriented towards the macro issues – meaning societal aspects of projects, antecedents and consequences of projectification, and firm-level issues. The latter would then include the reasons for turning to project-based organizational structures (Whittington et al., 1999), the problems of project-based organizational forms (Whitley, 2006), and the combination of projects, synergies between projects, and so on, most often addressed in the management of project portfolios. In addition to the macro issues – *macro project management* – we have, on the other hand, the micro issues and what might be referred to as *micro project management*. With this I am not referring to the micro-managing aspects in a negative way, rather the small things that are also important to investigate, such as the various activities, the rituals, the everyday routines, the individuals, the relationships between people, personal chemistry, and meetings in projects. In that respect, the domain of project management today embraces both macro project management and micro project management – most top managers also need to think about micro project management – for instance to detect bottlenecks in the company's project operations – and even sub-project managers might need to think about macro project management in the sense that the activities need to link with the strategy of the firm, that motivation and challenges occurring in a project might very well be explained by industry cycles, overload in the project portfolio, or problems with partners in the project ecology. Thus, practitioners in the world of project management need to think both in terms of macro and micro project management – so far we have held the belief that it is sufficient to only focus on the project level and the micro activities in the single project. However strategic project management, project portfolio management and, program management are definitely attracting our attention on things beyond the individual project.

The Hard and the Soft Side of Project Management

In line with Söderlund and Maylor (2012), I argue for the need to address the two sides of project management – the hard and the soft sides of project management. The hard side of project management is focused on the administrative tasks, in particular the use of the toolsets within PM, and associated with a hard-systems worldview. As a contrast, soft skills enable working through and with people and groups, and with that, handling the associated human factors. In some aspects and to some extent, soft skills fall closer to leadership issues and hard skills fall closer to management. In general, educators within the area of project management have been accused of educating project managers with sharp analytical skills but little understanding of social problems and the requirements of leadership. The problem is common when it comes to case-based teaching and MBA programs where students think that management is easy – they know the theories, they know the analysis, and they have all the answers. A series of papers in the *Academy of Management Learning & Education* offer concrete evidence for such a viewpoint (e.g. Benjamin and O'Reilly, 2011). Indeed, Henry Mintzberg's (2004) argument that education has only managed to address the left hand side of the brain is nicely summarized by Bennis and O'Toole (2005: 3) who stated that 'the things routinely ignored by academics on the grounds that they cannot be measured – most human factors and all matters relating to judgment, ethics, and morality – are exactly what make the difference between good business decisions and bad ones' (Bennis and O'Toole, 2005: 3) – the same is true for project management. In that respect, the criticism is highly relevant for project management. In the field of project management, there is a relatively strong tradition rooted in operations research seen in a wide application of optimization tools and techniques. Some scholars refer to this as the 'optimization school' of project management. Crawford et al. (2006) summarized the main insights from a multi-year research collaboration involving many project management scholars from a number of different countries. Their paper underlined the importance that project management as a subject area at universities and business schools needs to ensure that education and training programs are focused on making project managers become reflective leaders – rather than trained technicians. The authors' key message was that historically too much attention had been given to learning the techniques, planning methods, and formalities of project management, and little time on the more advanced and more difficult aspects, such as leadership, soft skills of project managers, and the reflective abilities of leaders. The authors claimed that there is need for reflective practitioners who are 'able to learn, operate and adapt effectively in complex project environments' (p. 722). The authors pointed out that: 'Project management practitioner development to date may therefore be seen as both narrow and shallow' (Crawford et al., 2006: 722).

The skills of the trained technician in project management are not rejected by this work, they are treated as necessary, but not sufficient, with sufficiency declining with increasing complexity of the project. An obvious conclusion is that more attention should be directed towards the soft side of project management. This introduces new skill requirements, including cultural awareness, political skills, public relations, and so on. In general it underscores the criticality of a broad view on project processes taken from developments within other areas of social science. To address the complexities of real projects, it is necessary to view them from different angles, since it is only through these multiple angles that the viewer can actually get some idea of the many features inherent in the work. Accordingly, I argue for the need of combining the hard and soft issues of management. Tools and techniques including earned value techniques, work breakdown structures, critical path planning – are necessary, but they need to be supplemented with leadership and soft skills. The latter instead require us to speak about expectations, feelings, emotions, optimism, biases, power conflicts, trust, and learning. In that respect, we need both hard and soft skills to implement projects successfully.

The opportunity associated with this challenge is that project management potentially offers an important context where the abilities of future leaders can be nurtured. It is time to make projects the school for future leaders (Bowen et al., 1994), since this is the context where a leader can learn to master the many dilemmas of management – and that this school is a school where both hard and soft skills are nurtured.

Towards a Process-oriented Understanding of Project Organizing

In most writings on project management, research within the area is considered to be highly rationalistic subscribing to a strong task perspective. This is apparent in the definitions of project management typically adhering to the version of projects as plan, projects as task, and project management as a particular problem-solving approach guided by the 'language of planning' (Andersen, 2008). At the same time it should be noted that all organizations, be they projects or non-projects, are occupied with some kind of task, with some kind of problem-solving involved. The process of the project could thus be looked upon as a process of problem-solving, of problem creation, problem definition and so on. Such process has in the team literature been referred to as the problem-solving perspective. It also works for explaining the development of a project viewed from a task perspective – the fact that the problem changes in character, that the problem moves from one stage to another and that the problem is different at the end compared to when the problem-solving process began. However, this perspective does not say much about the evolution of the social conditions or the evolution of the temporary organization. To gain an understanding of these conditions and this process, a different set of concepts are needed – concepts that capture the evolution from a loosely knit group or group of groups to a multi-team structure with established social relationships, with friendships being developed, with conflicts emerging, with conflicts solved, with frustrations, and visions swinging back and forth like a pendulum within the temporary organization. This is indeed a different perspective than the conventional task perspective.

Somewhat simplified we might then say that, on the one hand, we have the perspective that cherishes the nature of the task, the evolution of the task at hand, the problem-solving and the technical aspects of project work. A project in this perspective would be defined as a particular kind of complex task, a temporary endeavor, and project management is the solution to solving that task. The project could then be broken down into a series of activities, work packages, subprojects, and milestones. Project management as such is very much oriented towards these activities, including conceptual design, feasibility study, detailed design, detailed planning, etc.

On the other hand, we have the social perspective, the perspective which is more concerned with the social condition, with people, with relationships, and so on. We thus have two primary perspectives – which is a distinction discussed in much of the organization-theory oriented literature within the field (see for instance Andersen, 2008; Packendorff, 1995). The first one emphasizes the task, whereas the second one underlines the social dimensions and the personal relationships of project organizing. This simple distinction is very common in the team literature and in classic organizational behavior research, but has so far only been briefly touched upon in research on projects – although it is very clear that this distinction overlaps with the classic distinction between the hard and soft side of project management. Readers might recall similar distinctions made by Blake and Mouton (1964) in relational and task-oriented focus by managers, and Trist's (1981) review of the socio-technical systems literature.

Let us continue with a second distinction – namely that between content and process. This is also a relatively well-known focus of management and has been singled out as essential for understanding change processes. Pettigrew (1990) might be one of the most influential authors relying on a similar distinction. In principle, content and process refer to two interlinked but separate sides of project organizing. The former deals with the what-questions – what to produce, what to carry out in order to solve a particular problem, what to do to build a strong team, what to do to move the project forward – management and control included. For the latter, the process issues are more concerned with questions concerning when to do things, when to initiate, when to meet, and when to terminate activities and processes. In other words, here the when-questions are emphasized rather than the what-questions. Such issues would include the delivery date, the deadline, and the milestones along the way (see for instance Lindkvist et al., 1998). However, it would also include matters of timing and rhythm in project organizing. Based on these two distinctions – task and organization, on the one hand, and content and process, on the other – we might elicit four areas of project management practice and accordingly foci of project management research.

- Task and content
- Organization and content
- Task and process
- Organization and process

The basic argument here is that research has historically been occupied with either the content of the project, most notably captured by practices such as scope management, work breakdown structures and the like. Project management research has also to some extent addressed the task-oriented processes, which is apparent in the typical Gantt charts, network planning techniques, and so on where the specific activities are singled out along a timeline to determine when activities should be performed. Equally, project management research has also zeroed in on the linkages between organization and content, this is for instance documented in the responsibility distribution, division of labor, interdependencies between individual actors, relationships between teams, cross-functional teams, and so forth. However – which is the point here – little attention has been paid to the organization and process area of project management research. This is indeed troublesome, especially in these times when practitioners are talking about the need for speed, the difficulties of timing, the challenges of synchronizing cross-functional teams, and the development of absorptive capacity as a dynamic phenomenon. Thus, what would be needed is a more developed and elaborate process agenda in project management research. Such an agenda would pay more attention to terms such as deadlines, timing, time-boxing, lagomizing, temporary relationships, birth, death, grief, dynamics, pacing, timing norms, temporal misfits, etc. Below I will discuss in further detail the possibilities and problems of doing process research on projects and what it takes to develop process theories for projects.

Process Theories for Projects

The essential idea about process theorizing in organization and management studies is to reflect the world, and obviously organizations and management (or rather organizing and managing), as being in perpetual motion and in a constant process of becoming (Hernes, 2007). Consequently, process theorists pay attention to verbs, activity, change, novelty, and expression, typically recognizing that everything that is becoming has no existence apart from its relation to other things. In that respect, one might argue that process theory is engaged in ecological thinking in that it seeks to address complexity and acknowledge the significance of the particular, the local, and the timely. Thus, process theory is 'sensitive to context, interactivity experience, and time; and it acknowledges non-linearity, emergence, and recursivity' (Langley and Tsoukas, 2010: 5-6). Given a project's continuous evolution and movement, process theory seems particularly relevant to capture the involved dynamics and evolution.

Process theory also seems particularly relevant to project research since its intimate relationship to time and timing. Indeed, time and timing have definitely emerged as major topics in organizational practice and organizational research – not only in process-oriented studies, but also in other areas of organization and management studies. No doubt, project organizing is no exception. For instance, it has emerged as essential in the project management literature to be able to complete projects as quickly as possible. Fine's (1998) analysis is particularly demonstrating the linkages between project management and competition based on temporary advantages. Keywords such as time-to-market, time-based strategies, just-in-time, window of opportunity, temporary organizations – are all singled out by consultants and strategy thinkers alike to describe not only what companies are doing, but more so what they should be doing to be able to compete successfully. They are also positioned at the center for the analysis of the projectification of society. However, to advance our understanding of managing projects in time and the knowledge about project organizing in time, there is a need to go beyond conventional conceptions and concepts of time, which are primarily rooted in a simplistic clock time ontology. In other words, there is a need to make use of process theorizing to illustrate how managing happens in time, how managers transcend the past to create the future. Langley and Tsoukas (2010) suggest that a first critical step in conducting process-oriented studies is to find out how to capture time empirically:

> ... *process scholars may study their phenomenon by tracing it backward into the past (historical, retrospective studies), by following it backward into the past (historical, retrospective studies), by following it forward into the future (ethnography, longitudinal case studies), by examining how it is constituted, or by doing all of these at the same time* (Langley and Tsoukas, 2010: 11).

The study of project temporality would need all of these at the same time. If not, the theories and understanding produced will be severely constrained with regard to the experience of the present as simultaneously shaped by history and future. In that respect, there is a need not only to empirically capture the past and the future but also capture other kinds of temporalities involved in the organizing of projects. The reader who recalls Lawrence and Lorsch's (1967) classic study of integration and differentiation might remember their discussions about the difficulties of organizing for multiple time orientations in projects – simultaneously. In such settings, one might ask whether there are differences between project managers and projects concerning the weaving together of past, present and future (Schultz and Hernes, 2013), whether some managers are more capable of such weaving than others, what capabilities are needed to be able to engage in the skillful weaving of past, present and future – and, thinking about context, in what contexts the weaving is particularly important and/ or difficult.

Philosophical Underpinnings of OPM Research

Addressing Project Temporality

What kind of research methods and approaches would be particularly interesting for the study of managing projects in time? As suggested earlier, qualitative approaches are generally needed to engage in process theorizing and, as highlighted by other process theorists, particular kinds of data gathering techniques might be especially suitable to develop grounded process theories. This generally highlights the importance of conducting research that addresses and analyzes the actuality (actualities) and potentiality (potentialities) of projects, for instance through observations of project management meetings, and of observing and understanding these meetings over the project lifecycle and being able to understand the contexts in which they occur.

Research on time in projects in empirical research has historically been shallow and overly instrumental. The problem has, to a large extent, been the lack of sensitizing concepts – a temporal vocabulary – that can bring the philosophical writings into the actuality of managing and organizing, yet are still grounded in the social analysis of time – not restricted to a simplified view of time as a clock, a measure, so often relied upon in conventional studies of lead-time reduction and coordination (cf. Clark and Fujimoto, 1991). This would call for research, writings, and narratives that better address multiple ideas about time, the issue of the experience of time, and the many faces of temporality and temporariness. In-depth project narratives in that respect have the capacity to preserve multiple, experiential temporalities and thereby capture the multiple meanings that people assign to events (Tsoukas and Hatch, 2001):

> … *narratives preserve multiple temporalities, especially kairological (experiential, humanly relevant) time: its significance is not derived from the clock but from the meanings assigned to events by actors.*

Even though speed has been a typical concern for project scholars, there are many more facets of time that would be of scholarly interest. Indeed, speed stands out as critical, including the perception of time, the experience of time, the culture of time, timing, synching, and polychronicity. One important starting point would be to improve the analysis of different types of time (Hernes et al., 2013). Extant literature on time has made the distinction between a number of different dichotomies or types of time, such as objective and subjective time, kairos and chronos, A series and B series, monochronicity and polychronicity, slow and fast, global and local, and diachronic and synchronic time (cf. Hall, 1983; Söderlund, 2002). These are undoubtedly important distinctions and they offer good starting points to offer alternatives to conventional objective, clock time thinking. However, what is needed is not only better distinctions, overlapping distinctions – we also need to further these distinctions – of speaking about different kinds of subjective time and looking at the linkages between different kinds of times. The latter would, for instance, involve the relationship between objective time and subjective time – how reduced time to perform a particular task would impact the perception of time pressure.

To allow for such broad spectrum of time in projects, we need more concepts – to expand our reality and to see some of the many faces of managing projects in time. Historically, researchers have introduced a series of notions to describe what happens in organizations with regards to time. For instance, the idea of 'railway time' is an interesting example that might have continuing explanatory value also for documenting the difficulties occurring in inter-organizational projects or projects across national boundaries (Tsuij, 2006). Railway time is a term used to describe the creation of time zones to be able to improve the accuracy of departure and arrival times of trains, and to improve safety (Zerubavel, 1982). It was indeed a first example where time and timing had fundamental effects on efficiency in interdependent activities. Another example is that of 'banana time' introduced by Roy in (1959) to explain how people handle extremely monotonous work situations.

In the project management community, a number of concepts have opened new doors to an expanding understanding of projects. Perlow (1999) introduced the idea of 'interaction time' to describe certain periods during the day when people are supposed to talk to each other, compared to quiet time when people are working without interruptions from their colleagues. Shih (2004) introduced the notion of 'project time' to point out that the entire social life is captured by a dominant pacer set by the deadlines in significant projects. Evans et al. (2004) elaborated on the idea of 'beach time' to analyze how technical contractors made use of their temporal flexibility in project-intensive work. Obviously, there are many more notions and concepts of time. The point here is that, we have quite a number of concepts and notions that are rooted in the traditional clock time ontology, but rather few concepts to lead the way for a more elaborate discussion and fine-grained discussions about project temporality.

Contextualizing Project Temporality

A deeper understanding of temporality and different kinds of time is also of significance to the practitioner – from the practitioner's viewpoint one might indeed claim that some firms are better at timing activities and understanding how clients and partners experience time and organize their projects accordingly. These firms might be better at understanding the cycles of the market, the seasonal changes of demand, and the rhythmical behavior of clients and partners to launch projects at the right moment, to terminate projects whose time have passed, or to speed up projects in need of momentum. Thus, speed is more multifaceted than typically thought of in the context of projects, and being too fast can definitely cause problems to people outside the individual organization. It might be worth considering whether project-oriented companies would need to be more concerned with time and temporality than many other companies.

An argument presented in Lawrence and Lorsch's (1967) study is that the division of labor creates a differentiation which leads to a compartmentalization of the environment producing different organizational radar screens which has significant effects on how people within the organization experience and perceive time. In particular, people will tend to view different parts of the environment, which operate at different rates of time, at different speed. As a consequence, the firm – and indeed also some of its projects – would need to juggle with a number of different time orientations – with R&D typically adhering to the long-term cycles of technology development, manufacturing with the short loops of daily delivery and investments with a longer time perspective, and marketing with continuous and daily dialogues with client orders and requests. Correspondingly, project scholars would need new research instruments and mixed methods research approaches to be able to capture the multiple temporalities among actors in organizational contexts, which might require the combination of interviews, observations, documents, and perhaps even experiments to understand how actors envision the future.

As mentioned earlier, the idea of speed definitely illustrates the coming of when-questions driving other organizational questions, including those of what and why. The when-questions determine what is possible and why it should be done. An illustrative case is that of deadlines. Originally a line around a prison that the prisoner could cross only at the risk of being shot by the guard – first spoken about during the American Civil War when the lack of prison camps was acute (Gersick, 1995). Deadlines in their current version however do not signal death – rather the opposite. It is the awareness of death and of running out of time that makes people live, that makes people realize that they actually have time – time to live. Gersick (1995) has discussed this issue as a matter of 'breaking the spell' – that deadlines – and in particular mid-life crisis transitions in group development – make people think more strategically about what they are doing and why they are doing it. The awareness of a deadline introduces a profound reflection that is critical for people to be able to complete assignments on time with reasonable quality. The deadline then not only signals the light like the lighthouse that could be used for purposes of navigation, it also signals the power of a common enemy that creates the outside pressure which might stimulate a crisis-oriented kind of behavior that is so significant for setting out a common organizational endeavor. Thus, in some cases speed is indeed good, a certainly preferred choice for both individuals and organizations – but in all cases it is merely one factor. Other factors play more important roles; acceleration, ambidexterity of time orientations, and isochronism seem to be factors that are not only more important but also better destined for organizational analysis and research into the landscape of projects.

Having too much time is certainly an organizational problem that has been dealt with in project management contexts. For instance, a number of business writers have claimed that a key problem in development work is that available resources – available time – is always consumed. A natural response of such insight would be to hold back on resources – to give people less time than they actually need. It is better to give people too little time than too much time. A case in point would be engineers with too much time who might come up with all kinds of things that create problems for other people in the project, creating bugs in other parts of the system (Berggren, Järkvik, and Söderlund, 2008).

Along this line is the problem where speed becomes a problem because it violates people's perception of what is good and how long activities should take. If too quick then too bad. In that respect all social settings are surrounded by certain timing norms (Dille and Söderlund, 2011), certain ideas on preferred pace and phase – and the failure to respond to those timing norms might have detrimental consequences. This has led researchers to speak about the idea of isochronism – same time, instead of isomorphism – same structure (ibid). This stands out as particularly relevant in organizational settings where the problem of coordination is especially pressing among actors facing different institutional expectations to gain legitimacy. What might be good for the common collaborative process, for the coordination of activities between partners, might violate what is considered to be appropriate behavior by peers in the same institutional environment. The consequence is institutional temporal misfits and conflicting timing norms that may prove organizing to be impossible to bring about (ibid.).

Organizations as we know them are typically designed to live forever, responding to the principle of going-concern. Permanence is at the essence. However, an increasing amount of organizations are not designed for permanence. Instead they follow the logic of ephemera – being short-lived, being disposable (March, 1995). Pop-up organizations are used in a wide range of sectors including advertising, fashion, tourism, and entertainment. As a consequence, organizations lose important elements of permanence where transition and amnesia become heralded qualities. Organizations become fast – fast, but stupid – at least this is what we typically learn from conventional research. Empirical research gives a slightly different view on the nature of the problem. Consider work on group longevity which has indicated that the main problem with group performance is not the transition, or the temporariness (Katz, 1982). Here, the problem is one of permanence where people have actually stayed too long and thereby become too occupied with the internal harmony of the group instead of being externally aware of its wider role, its reason to exist, and its place in the external environment. Another factor then enters the scene of learning. Indeed, many would argue that the problem of temporariness is amnesia. A counterview would be to argue that the problem of organizing is that of remembering – that the memory actually becomes the problem but for a completely different reason. When unlearning is at the essence, then permanence contributes to the challenges of forgetting.

Organizations might implement a host of mechanisms and structures to solve the organizational challenges of speed and timing, of acceleration, of the dynamics of time, and of the institutional timing requirements. Empirical research is however scant in this area and despite some really interesting and insightful studies of temporality (such as Hall, 1959), we still have a long way to travel before we have uncovered the essence of temporality in project organizing. The problem, it seems, is not that extant research has failed to contribute to our understanding of matters within this area, but rather that it seems to be associated with such difficulties and risks – to design a study accurately, to link theory with empirics, are especially challenging in the area of managing and organizing in time. Difficulty should, however, not stand in the way of importance and relevance.

Conclusions and Implications

This chapter has argued for the need for better clarifying the foci of project management research, of creating a broader spectrum of dimensions to trace the development and progress of theorization within the field project management. The chapter argued in favor of a pluralistic understanding of project management, but at the same time emphasized the importance of researching with a focus. In order to contribute to the development towards the latter end, the chapter presented a few ideas on better ways to compare and clarify the foci in project management research. In particular, the chapter pointed out the importance of investigating the unique features of project organization – the birth and death of temporary organizations – to better address the particular dynamics involved in projects. Attempts have been made towards this end, but there is more to do to reflect the actuality, challenges, and hurdles of project organizing. This would also better mirror the real challenges facing project managers of what it takes to raise a project and to kill a project.

This chapter tried to make a few additional points. Firstly, research needs to be more aware of the levels of analysis covered in project management research. A first step might be to make a distinction between macro project management and micro project management.

Secondly, the chapter pointed out the importance for project management in practice and thus also to some extent project management in research to capture the dual aspects of project management, namely the hard and soft sides of project management.

Thirdly, there is a need for a better understanding of process in projects. The chapter discussed how project management can make more use of process theorizing to improve the understanding of the actuality and potentiality of project organizing. The idea of project temporalities was introduced to lead the way for a process-oriented agenda in project management research. One important gap was discussed, namely the organization-process area of project management research. In that gap a set of notions around time and timing seem critical and accordingly research would need to engage more in research on rhythm, timing, and temporality.

References

Andersen, E. S. (2008). Rethinking project management: towards an organizational perspective. Harlow: Pearson.

Benjamin, B., O'Reilly, C., 2011. Becoming a leader: early career challenges faced by MBA graduates. The Academy of Management Learning and Education 10 (3), 452-473.

Bennis, W., O'Toole, J., 2005. How business schools lost their way. Harvard Business Review 1-9 (May).

Berggren, C., J. Järkvik & J. Söderlund (2008). Lagomizing, organic integration, and systems emergency wards: Innovative practices in managing complex systems development projects, *Project Management Journal*, Vol. 39, No. 2: 111-122.

Blake, R. R., & Mouton, J. S. (1964); The managerial grid. Houston, Texas: Gulf Publishing.

Clark, K. & T. Fujimoto (1991). *Product development performance: strategy, organization and management in the world auto industry*, Boston: Harvard Business School.

Cova, B. & R. Salle (2011). Shaping projects, building networks, In P. Morris, J. Pinto & J. Söderlund (Eds.), *Oxford Handbook of Project Management*, Oxford. Oxford University Press.

Crawford, L., P. Morris, J. Thomas & M. Winter (2006). Practitioner development: from trained technicians to reflective practitioners, *International Journal of Project Management*, Vol. 24: 722-33.

Dille, T. & J. Söderlund (2011). Managing inter-institutional projects: The significance of isochronism, timing norms and temporal misfits, *International Journal of Project Management*, Vol. 29: 480-490.

Dille, T. & J. Söderlund (2013). Inter-institutional projects in time: A framework and an empirical investigation. Paper under review.

Evans, J., G. Kunda & S. Barley (2004). Beach time, bridge time, and billable hours, Administrative Science Quarterly, Vol. 49, No. 1: 1-38.

Gersick, C. (1988). Time and transition in work teams: toward a new model of group development, *Academy of Management Journal*, Vol. 31, No. 1: 9-41.

Gersick, C. J. G. (1995). "Everything new under the gun: creativity and deadlines." In C. Ford & D. Gioia (Eds.), *Creative action in organizations* (pp. 142-148). Thousand Oaks, CA: Sage.

Grabher, G. (2004). Temporary Architectures of Learning: Knowledge Governance in Project Ecologies, *Organization Studies*, 25(9), 1491-1514.

Grant, R. M. (1996). Toward a knowledge-based theory of the firm, *Strategic Management Journal*, Vol. 17, Special Issue: 109-122.

Fine, C. (1998). *Clockspeed: Winning industry control in the age of temprorary advantage.* Reading: Perseus Books. Hall, R. F. (1959). "Banana time", Job satisfaction and informal interaction, Human Organizations, Vol. 18, No. 4: 158-168.

Hall, E. (1983). The dance of life: the other dimension of time, Garden City: Doubleday.

Hernes, T. (2007). *Understanding organization as process,* London: Routledge.

Hernes, T., B. Simpson & J. Söderlund (2013). Theorizing temporality: Setting an agenda for the future while drawing upon the past, *Scandinavian Journal of Management,* Vol. 29, no. 1: 1-6.

Iansiti, M. & A. MacCormack (1997). Developing products on internet time, *Harvard Business Review,* September-October: 108-117.

Janis, I. L. (1972). *Victims of groupthink: a psychological study of foreign policy decisions and fiascoes,* Boston: Houghton Mifflin.

Katz, R. (1982). The effects of group longevity on project communication and performance, *Administrative Science Quarterly,* Vol. 27, No. 1: 81-104.

Langley, A. & H. Tsoukas (2010). Introducing "Perspectives on Process Organization Studies", In Hernes T & S. Maitlis (Eds.) *Process, Sensemaking, and Organizing.* New York: Oxford University Press, pp. 4-26.

Lawrence, P. & J. Lorsch (1967). *Organization and environment: managing differentiation and integration,* Boston: Harvard University Press.

Lindgren, Monica & Packendorff, Johann (2003) A project-based view of entrepreneurship: Towards action-orientation, seriality and collectivity. In C. Steyaert & D. Hjorth (Eds.) *New movements in entrepreneurship.* Cheltenham: Edward Elgar, pp. 86-102.

Lindkvist, L. & J. Söderlund (2002). What goes on in projects? On goal-directed learning processes, in K. Sahlin-Andersson & A. Söderholm (Eds), *Beyond Project Management,* Malmö: Liber Abstrakt.

Lindkvist, L., J. Söderlund & F. Tell (1998). Managing product development projects: on the significance of fountains and deadlines, *Organization Studies,* Vol. 19, No. 6: 931-51.

Lundin, R. A., & Söderholm, A. (1995). A theory of the temporary organization. *Scandinavian Journal of Management,* Vol. 11, No. 4: 437-55.

March, J. G. (1991). Exploration and exploitation in organizational learning, *Organization Science,* Vol. 2, No. 2: 71-87.

March, J. G. (1995). The future, disposable organizations and the rigidities of imagination, *Organization,* Vol. 2, No. 3-4: 427-40.

McDonald, P. (1988). The Los Angeles Olympic organizing committee: developing organizational culture in the short run, in M. Jones, M. Moore & R. Snyder (Eds), *Inside organizations: understanding the human dimension,* Newbury Park: Sage Publications.

McGrath, J. (1988) (Ed.). *The social psychology of time: new perspectives,* Newbury Park: Sage.

McGrath, J. (1988). Time and social psychology, in J. McGrath (Ed.), *The social psychology of time: new perspectives*, Newbury Park: Sage.

Meyerson, D., K. E. Weick & R. M. Kramer (1996). Swift trust and temporary groups, in R. H. Kramer and T. R. Tyler (Eds), *Trust in organizations*, Thousand Oaks: Sage.

Mintzberg, H., 2004. Managers not MBAs: A Hard Look at the Soft Practice of Managing and Management Development. Berrett-Koehler Publishers, San Francisco.

Morris, P., J. Pinto & J. Söderlund (2011) (Eds). *Oxford Handbook of Project Management*, Oxford: Oxford University Press.

Obstfeld, D. (2012). "Creative projects: a less routine approach towards getting things done". *Organization Science*, Vol. 23, No. 6: 1571-1592.

Okhuysen, G.A. & K. M. Eisenhardt (2002). Integrating knowledge in groups: how formal interventions enable flexibility. Organization Science, Vol. 13, No. l 4: 370-386.

Packendorff, J. (1995). Inquiring into the temporary organization: new directions for project management research, *Scandinavian Journal of Management*, Vol. 11, No. 4: 319-334.

Perlow, L. (1999). The time famine: Toward a sociology of work time, *Administrative Science Quarterly*, Vol. 44, No. 1: 57-81.

Pettigrew, A. (1990). Conducting longitudinal field research, *Organization Science*. Vol. 3: 267-292.

Whittington, R., Pettigrew, A., Peck, S., Fenton, E., & Conyon, M. (1999). "Change and complementarities in the new competitive landscape: a European Panel Study, 1992-1996." *Organization Science*, Vol. 10, No. 5: 583-600.

Ross, J. & B. Staw (1986). Expo 86: an escalation prototype, *Administrative Science Quarterly*, Vol. 31: 274-97.

Roy, D. F. (1959). 'Banana time': Job satisfaction and informal interaction, *Human Organization*, Vol. 18, No. 4. 158-168.

Sayles, L. & M. K. Chandler (1971). *Managing Large Systems*, New York: Free Press.

Schultz, M. & Hernes, T. (2013) Temporal perspectives on organizational identity, *Organization Science*, Vol. 24, 1-21.

Shih, J. (2004). Project time in Silicon Valley, *Qualitative Sociology*, 27 (2): 223-45.

Sydow, J, Lindkvist, L & DeFillippi, R. (2004). Project-based organizations, embeddedness and repositories of knowledge: Editorial, *Organization Studies*, 25 (9): 1475121489.

Söderlund, J. (2002). Managing complex development projects: arenas, knowledge processes and time, R&D Management, Vol. 32, No. 5: 419-430.

Söderlund, J. (2004a). Building theories of project management: past research, questions for the future, *International Journal of Project Management*. Vol. 22: 183-191.

Söderlund, J. (2004b). On the broadening scope of the research on projects: a review and a model for analysis, *International Journal of Project Management*, Vol. 22: 655-667.

Söderlund, J. (2005). What project management really is about: Alternative perspectives on the role and practice of project management, *International Journal of Technology Management*, Vol. 32, No. 3/4: 371-387.

Söderlund, J. (2011). Pluralism in project management: Research at the crossroad of specialization and fragmentation, *International Journal of Management Reviews*, Vol. 13: 153-176.

Söderlund, J. & H. Maylor (2012). Project management scholarship: relevance, impact and five integrative challenges for business and management schools, International *Journal of Project Management*. Vol. 30: 686-96.

Trist, E. (1981). The evolution of socio-technical systems, Occasional Paper, Toronto: Ontario Ministry of Labor.

Tsoukas, H. and M. J. Hatch (2001). Complex thinking, complex practice: The case for a narrative approach to organizational complexity, *Human Relations*, Vol. 54, No. 8: 979-1013.

Tsuji, Y. (2006). Railway time and rubber time: The paradox in the Japanese conception of time, *Time & Society*, Vol. 15, No. 2/3: 177-195.

Turner, J. R., M. Huemann, F. Anbari, & C. Bredillet (2010). *Perspectives on projects*, New York. Routledge.

Weick, K. (1996). Enactment and the boundaryless career. In M. B. Arthur & D. M. Rousseau (Eds.), *The boundaryless career: a new employment principle for a new organizational era*. New York: Oxford University Press, pp. 40-57.

Weiner, S. (1976). Participation, deadlines and choice, in J. March & J. Olsen (Eds) *Ambiguity and choice in organizations*, Oslo: Scandinavian University Press.

Whitley, R. (2006). "Project-based firms: new organizational form or variations on a theme." *Industrial and Corporate Change*, Vol. 15, No. 1: 77-99.

Winter, M., C. Smith, P. Morris & S. Cicmil (2006). Directions for future research in project management: the main findings of a UK government-funded research network, *International Journal of Project Management*, Vol. 24: 638-49.

Winter, M. & T. Szczepanek (2009). Images of projects, London: Gower Publishing.

Zerubavel, E. (1982). The standardization of time: a sociohistorical perspective, *American Journal of Sociology*, Vol. 88, No. 1: 1-23.

Chapter 5

A Model of the Dynamics in Theory Development

Ralf Müller and Jingting Shao

Abstract

This chapter models the dynamic processes that lead to the formation of new theories and their stabilization over time until their replacement by better theories. A conceptual model integrating the popular conjectures about theory dynamics by Kuhn, Foucault and Lakatos is developed and subsequently applied for the assessment of three major theories in project management.

The model puts the discourse among the members of the research community (and often also practitioner) at the center of the dynamics in the theory formation processes. Discourse starts new theory development by fostering the awareness that better theories are needed. This motivates researchers to shift their existing research paradigms to new approaches for the accomplishment of better theories. The researchers' results are assessed through discourse within the academic and practitioner community, which decides on the social acceptability of new theories. Once accepted, more research is done using the new research paradigm, leading to a program of research projects, which strengthens and shapes some core elements of the theory for its stabilization. Over time the limitations of the existing theory will surface and the discourse on the need for a better theory emerges, thus the circle is starting anew.

The present chapter uses Foucault's work on discourse as described in *The Architecture of Knowledge* as a point of departure. Through similarities between Kuhn's and Foucault's conjectures about academic discourse the Kuhnian model for new theory formation through paradigm shift is linked to Foucault's work, which is subsequently expanded with Lakatos' concept of research programs for the temporary stabilization of theories and their long-term discontinuation by better theories.

The model is applied to three popular theories from the Nine Schools of Project Management Research. These are two empirically developed theories about project success factors and project categorization systems and one conceptually developed theory on projects as temporary organizations. Results from this assessment show that timeliness of theory appearance, choice of publication media, and aesthetics of the theory must match the Zeitgeist for the acceptance of new theories through ongoing discourse. The chapter ends by relating the model and findings from the assessment of project management theories to developments in contemporary research methods, such as abductive and reflexive approaches, as a way forward towards discourse-enacted translational research.

The chapter adds to the understanding of robust theory development in a dynamic field like project management. The findings herein have implications for research design, as it allows designing, setting-up and executing studies in a way that maximizes the likelihood of developing accepted and long-lasting theories.

Introduction

The previous chapters in this book have addressed some philosophical aspects of contemporary research and research design: from the need for plurality in research, via renewed Aristotelian perspectives on practice-relevance in project management research to the link between different philosophical stances and their related methodologies. These chapters help in setting up and designing research projects that yield credible results. Given that, it is yet unclear how the results of these research studies are used by the research community to become accepted theories. This will be addressed in the present chapter.

We address the question of how theories develop and change over time from the perspective of Growth of Knowledge. The literature in this field is concerned with the ways new theories are developed from existing theories and new research results, how these theories get accepted within communities, and how they change or stabilize over time, before they are replaced by other theories. This stream of literature is dominated by three authors, namely, Kuhn, Foucault and Lakatos. Their individual works in understanding knowledge growth are often compared against each other in order to find commonalities and differences, as well as strengths and weaknesses of the different approaches. However, little effort has been put into the integration of these approaches. This is attempted with the present chapter.

Taking the perspective of Knowledge Growth allows us to refer some exemplary studies in project management to the more general literature on research philosophy and to some well established conjectures about the dynamics in theory development and knowledge growth. This, in turn, allows identifying some particularities of the dynamics of theories in project management research.

The works by Kuhn, Lakatos and Foucault derived from very different epistemological stances. Kuhn and Lakatos take predominantly post-positivistic perspectives (May & Sellers, 1988; Kulka, 1977 resp.), whereas Foucault sees himself as a modernist, and others as post-modernist. To that end we see the suggested model from a Bhaskarian realism perspective where the works by Kuhn and Lakatos are associated with Bhaskar's ontological domains of the real and the actual and Foucault's work with the domain of the empirical (Bhaskar, 1975). Accordingly we assume that the underlying mechanisms and events (as described by Kuhn and Lakatos) give raise to humans subjective experiences, discharged in form of discourse (as described by Foucault), which, in turn, reflects back and influences the underlying mechanisms and events. The related Unit of Analysis in this chapter is the dynamic of the process leading from research results to accepted theories.

The chapter continues by providing the background information that allows linking the work of Foucault, Kuhn and Lakatos into a model. This is followed by a section on the details of the elements of the model and how they are supported by other philosophers in management. In a subsequent section the model is applied to three major project management theories. The chapter finishes with a conclusion on the findings in respect of contemporary management research.

Background

Probably the most often cited writer in the field of theory dynamics is Thomas Kuhn and his classic work on *The Structure of Scientific Revolutions* (Kuhn, 1996). In this work he uses the concept of research paradigms (i.e. particular combinations of underlying assumptions in terms of ontologies, epistemologies and methodologies) as intellectual domains within which researchers design, setup and execute their studies. Paradigms are established because they once led to the development of theories with a higher predictability (in the natural sciences) or better explanations (in social science) than theories developed in other ways. However, once established these paradigms limit the further development of the theory developed through them, because one single theory, developed under one research paradigm, cannot explain a phenomenon completely. This leads to a *crisis* in terms of further theory development and researchers address this crisis by turning *to philosophical analysis as a device for unlocking the riddles of their field* (p. 88). The development of new theories, or as Kuhn terms it, breakthrough theories, is accomplished through a slight shift in paradigms in order to develop theory that covers the predictability or explanatory power already provided by existing theory plus some explanation of some new and yet unexplained part of a phenomenon. Related examples in the natural sciences include the shift from Newtonian physics to Einsteinian relativism (Kuhn, 1996) and the *cognitive revolution* in the social sciences, which is the move from merely behaviorist approaches in psychology to those including mind, expectation, perception and memory (Miller, 2003).

The work by Kuhn covers the entire cycle from theory development to social acceptance. Notably he asserts that the social acceptance of theories is not a rational but a rather irrational process, which is influenced by many aspects, such as the generation of the researcher, his or her nationality, the researcher's reputation, in other words the *Zeitgeist* (the spirit of times) and other contextual factors. To that end Kuhn refers to the theory development process as being governed by the academic community ruled by its body of citizens. This resembles a community concept from ancient Greece known as *polis*, a city-state community (in ancient Greece) which determines their own governance and rules, as opposed to rules and regulation imposed onto them, for example by their state government (McGee, 2012). The model described in this chapter refers to the *polis* community of researchers, publishers, and other stakeholder as those who are contributors to the discourse about a theory, its social acceptance, and ultimately to its replacement by a better theory.

Even though Kuhn's work covers theory generation and acceptance, the emphasis is on paradigms and their impact on research design and theory building. Aspects like social acceptance of theories and selection of theories within the community of researchers are dealt with at a less detailed and more general level.

Kuhn's work is criticized from several perspectives. One of the most often raised criticisms is the ambiguity in using the term paradigm. We address this in the next section. A further frequently found criticism is Kuhn's concept of *normal science* as being *really normal within science* (Popper, 1970), as well as the type of change that triggers the occurrence of scientific revolutions (Wray, 2005). The present chapter addresses the latter criticism by elaborating a model that represents one possible way of triggering paradigm shifts which lead to subsequent scientific revolutions, which is discourse within the stakeholder community.

Aspects of social acceptance are addressed in more detail by Michel Foucault than by Kuhn, especially in his classic work *The Architecture of Knowledge* (Foucault, 2002). In his archeological model he proposes that individual theories are individual monuments, which should be looked at like in an archeological project. The combinations of individual monuments are interpreted in various ways, and evaluated in light of a number of (partly conflicting) objectives in their contribution to the explanation of a phenomenon. More theory monuments emerge over time and researchers try to link the monuments and interpret their relationships in new ways, thereby disregarding the time of their appearance, to develop a narrative of a new theory. This development occurs through *discourse*, which is the totality of history-informed written and spoken communication about a phenomenon (such as a theory), which leads to a socially constructed understanding of a phenomenon. Foucault (2002, p. 131) defines discourse as:

> ... *a group of statements in so far as they belong to the same discursive formation; it does not form a rhetorical or formal unity, endlessly repeatable, whose appearance or use in history might be indicated (and, if necessary, explained); it is made up of a limited number of statements for which a group of conditions of existence can be defined. Discourse in this sense is not an ideal, timeless form that also possesses a history; the problem is not therefore to ask one-self how and why it was able to emerge and become embodied at this point in time; it is, from beginning to end, historical – a fragment of history, a unity and discontinuity in history itself, posing the problem of its own limits, its division, its transformations, the specific modes of its temporality rather than its sudden irruption in the midst of the complicities of time.*

Discourse widens the perspectives towards a subject into a *kaleidoscopic* view, which allows us to see and think differently about a subject or to inform subsequent developments (Tsoukas & Cummings, 1997), thus partly resembling Socrates' approach to information gathering through dialog.

Social acceptance of theories through discourse is seen as a result of a wide number of factors, such as history and current thinking in terms of society and phenomenon under study, *Zeitgeist*, prior theories and knowledge, power of individuals and institutions and/or individuals (Foucault, 2002; Kuhn, 1996). To that end Kuhn and Foucault concur on the irrationality of theory selection and acceptance. However, both are lesser concerned with the stabilization of a theory after its initial acceptance.

A major point of critique about Foucault's work is the underlying assumption of dominance of social power over the autonomy of individuals. Foucault perceives individuals as socially constructed, as a product of social forces like power, where individuals define themselves by adjusting to the power structures and not necessarily by adjusting to other individuals (Bevir, 1999). This perspective aligns with the present chapter. Here we also see the individual researcher as being anonymized, as in the double-blind review process, and forced to align to social powers such those (sometimes felt arbitrarily) given by journal reviewers and not necessarily given by individual authorities in the subject area. This congruency of perspectives strengthen the appropriateness of Foucault's work for the present chapter, but also defines one of the limitations of it, as it does exclude other forms of theory acceptance sometimes found in other scientific areas, especially those not based on double-blind review processes.

Back to stabilization of theories. This is addressed by Imre Lakatos (Lakatos, 1970, 1980), who found that stable theories derive from a number of studies on a phenomenon, which together can be interpreted as a program of research projects. Projects in such a program share a (often metaphysical) core hypothesis. Metaphorically speaking, this core hypothesis is guarded by the sequence of theories relative to them. Studies in the program that lead to refuted hypotheses are hereby seen as positive contributions, as they allow to identify the boundaries for the core elements of the theory (conditions under which they hold or not hold), which is done by further investigating refuted hypotheses as to the underlying reasons for their refutation in respect of the core elements. The sum of accepted and rejected hypotheses surrounding the core hypothesis forms a protective belt around the core hypotheses. Within this belt the core hypothesis only adjusts gradually over time through the stream of studies, which increases its robustness and ensures its long-term survival (Lakatos, 1970).

This perspective is of interest for several reasons, one being its integration of positive and the negative heuristics in theory development and the growth of knowledge, which constitutes a major step forward in the sense of Poppers verisimilitude (Popper, 1963). The other is the shift in focus from an *external* history of empirical results (i.e. causal relationships) to an *internal* history of epistemological relationships between

Philosophical Underpinnings of OPM Research

the thought-contents of research projects and their relationships within the program (Kulka, 1977).

Criticism of Lakatos' concept often addresses the lack of prescriptive criteria on when to drop a research program in favor of another (Sankey, 2011). This is to some extend addressed in the present chapter by shifting this decision into the realm of discourse in the context of a scientific crisis. The discourse is hereby seen as leading over time to a dominance in the perception of the stakeholders as to which theory to drop and which one to retain.

Even the most robust theories do not explain a phenomenon in all its aspects (Kuhn, 1996) and over time more and more of the limitations in a theory's predictive power surface, leading to what Kuhn calls a *crisis*, a point where further studies using the existing research paradigm will only marginally contribute to the existing theory. That is the time for a paradigm shift, where underlying assumptions are questioned and new research models and research designs emerge, eventually leading to new and breakthrough theories.

The discussion above indicates a circular relationship, with the three conjectures described above as its elements. The related model is shown in Figure 5.1.

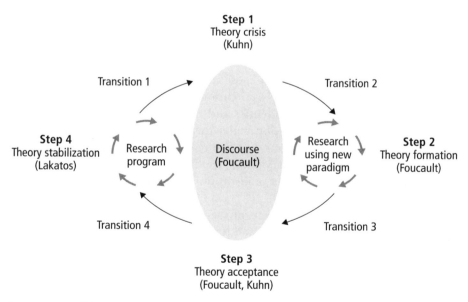

Figure 5.1. Model for Theory Dynamics

The model resembles the research and theory development process by putting discourse at the center of the process. Discourse represents the discussions that lead to original research and theory formation, thus leading to new insights and potentially new theory. Discourse on the results of this original research, which takes place for example at conferences, during the review process prior to publication, leads to social acceptance of results and selection of theories. This triggers the use of these new theories in further research, which leads to the stabilization of the core elements of the theory through further studies, thus a temporarily robust theory. However, further studies also bring up the limitations of the explanatory power of the theory, stemming from the use of the research paradigm that led to the current theory and the impossibility to develop theories that predict a wider set of characteristics of the phenomenon by use of the existing research paradigm. This brings about a crisis, which is resolved through a paradigm shift in research, leading back to new theory formation.

The Model

The following section describes the elements of the model and their interaction, starting with the *discourse* at the time of a crisis in theory (Step 1), followed by *theory formation* (Step 2), *theory acceptance* (Step 3) and *theory stabilization* (Step 4).

Step 1 and 3: Ex-ante Discourse during Crisis and Ex-post Discourse for Social Acceptance of Theories

Discourse constitutes the central element of the model. Discourse about theory relates to the other two steps in a complex set of relationships. The model can only provide a simplified picture.

For Kuhn (Kuhn, 1996) discourse is most active before a paradigm shift (i.e. at Step 1 in Figure 5.1), because of the crisis situation, which brings about an increased interaction among and between academics and practitioners in terms of ways to overcome the crisis and ways to develop better theories. This includes discourse on paradigms and ways to shift paradigms, but also research funding, interests of funding institutions, their power, monetary issues, legitimacy, Zeitgeist, ethical and even legal aspects of new studies. A number of institutions and individuals, sometimes the public, are involved in this discourse.

Once studies are under way the focus of the discourse moves gradually towards design issues, methodological questions and, in Step 3, interpretation of results, by not giving up on the aforementioned aspects. In addition to the obvious discourse of researchers with their project stakeholders and colleagues (e.g. at conferences) discourse takes place between institutions and public. When research results become available (i.e. Step 3) the discourse shifts from teams to conferences, publication media, and review processes. The discourse continues after publication through literature reviews, application, selection and proof of exiting results and theories through the research community. Steps 1 and 3 are not separate from each other; they are interconnected through continuity in discourse.

Foucault (Foucault, 2002) defines four conditions for discourse to emerge:

Philosophical Underpinnings of OPM Research

1. The object of discourse exist in a complex set of relationships with other objects.
2. These relations are external to the object of discourse and established between institutions, economic and social processes, behaviors, norms, techniques, classifications and characterizations. This network of relations allows the object of discourse to position itself relative to other objects.
3. These relations can be distinguished as a system of primary relations which are in place independent of the emergence of the object of discourse, a system of reflexive or secondary relations which emerge through the presence of the object of discourse, and a system of discursive relations which allow to speak about the object of discourse.
4. The discursive relations are external to object but internal to the discourse and characterize not the language or circumstances of discourse, but discourse itself in practice.

For its formation discourse must pass through a number of thresholds. It starts with the emergence of individual and autonomous discursive practice in form of statements. This is referred to by Foucault as reaching the threshold of *positivity* (i.e. acceptance, not in general, but as an object of discourse). These statements are then validated and verified and assessed for coherence in order to develop dominating knowledge in form of models, critiques or other about the object, hereby reaching the threshold of *epistemologization*. This knowledge is then tested for its acceptance within the realm of science and its possibility to be phrased as propositions in order to reach the threshold of *scientificity*. Finally the identification of the knowledge's axioms and elements that allow formulating propositions marks accomplishment of the threshold of *formalization* (Foucault, 2002: 205-206).

The ethics of this discourse are described by Foucault as being influenced by the power of the individual actors. Flyvbjerg (Flyvbjerg, 1998, 2001) contrasts this with discourse ethics described by Habermas who emphasizes the balance in power between discursive partners. Discourse is for Habermas one of four social action types, which are instrumental, communicative, strategic and discursive. His *Theory of Communicative Action* (Habermas, 1987) proposes that acceptance of statements brought forward by communicative partners is subject to 'critical reflection, that is, assessing one or more validity claims pertaining to what the speaker or writer expressed' (Ngwenyama & Lee, 1997: 156). The type of assessment depends on the type of social action the sender of the statement intended to execute. In discursive action communicative partners try to achieve or restore agreement for joint action or issue handling. The receiver validates the claims put forward by senders for clarity, comprehensibility, as well as contextuality and appropriateness, and may validate them for truthfulness and sincerity. Failure in validation may lead receivers to not accept statements at face value. Thus receivers can but must not accept statements (Habermas, 1987).

Contrarily, Foucault sees power as omnipresent in social interactions. He is less concerned with definition of power than with ways to analyze it. He does not see power as something acquired or shared, but as a force emerging from a cluster of relations changing from moment to moment. Power is hereby seen inherent to relations, such as those of knowledge with rationality, or individuals with state. It is always met with resistance, and this shapes and determines the execution of power in a given moment. Power is thereby context and situational dependently exercised. Discourse can in itself exercise power or be influenced by power (Flyvbjerg, 2001).

That allows modeling discursive ethics on a continuum from Habermasian balance to Foucaultian exercise of power. The former resembles a balanced communicative action between, for example, researchers in informal talks or at conferences, whereas the latter resembles situations like the peer-review process with the reviewers and journal editors exercising their power over a submitted contribution to knowledge. The totality of discourse is therefore a mix of different discourse ethics applied at different times by different institutions and individuals.

While 'everything is never said' about an object in a discourse (Foucault, 2002: 134), 'things do not have quite the same mode of existence, the same system of relationships with their environment, the same schemata of use, the same possibilities of transformation once they have been said' (ibid.: 139-40). An example of the latter can be found later in this chapter with the publications on project success factors. Pinto and Slevin's (Pinto & Slevin, 1988a, 1988b) work on the ten success factors for projects was published in 1988 in *Project Management Journal* and became a classic model in project management. In the same year Pinto and Prescott (Pinto & Prescott, 1988) published a revised version in *Journal of Management*, where they used a more rigorous methodology, which rendered three of the originally ten success factors as insignificant. In a rational World one would expect the latter paper to make the former obsolete. However, having contributed to the discourse on project success factors in one of the most read journals in the project management community and 'having the message out there' allowed the Pinto and Slevin ten factor model still to advance to one of the most often cited papers on project success factors, ranked right after the Pinto and Prescott paper (Müller & Jugdev, 2012).

In the introduction we said that discourse is shaped by context, such as history, Zeitgeist, and existing knowledge. In the section above we showed how discourse in research moves from individual statements to social acceptance of theories in an irrational manner (Foucault, 2002; Kuhn, 1996) to bring about acceptance of new knowledge. Karl Weick (Weick, 1989) suggests that these established theories are then tested in new circumstances against underlying assumptions, which makes theories obvious, irrelevant, absurd or interesting. He suggests that only the latter will stand the test of time and survive in the long run. His observation supports the model presented here, as these selections require a form of discourse to take place.

Step 2: Theory Formation – New or Breakthrough Theory through Paradigm Shift

At this stage research studies are designed and executed by individual researchers or teams. Kuhn (1996) asserts that breakthroughs in theories are accomplished only after a series of research studies have been conduced within the limitations of an existing research paradigm, and the possibilities to gain new insights with that particular paradigm have been exhausted. At this stage a crisis is reached, requiring a new way of thinking about the phenomenon under study. This leads to questioning the underlying assumptions of the existing paradigm and the shift towards new assumptions, epistemological stances, and/or methods to develop new theories with broader explanatory power than the existing theory. Thus explaining what the old theory explained plus some further, until now not understood aspect of the phenomenon. Using examples from natural science Kuhn argues that these shifts in paradigms are often relatively small, leading to new insights through changes in deductive positivistic research designs. For the paradigm shifts in social sciences he argues in favor of inductive research as an equivalent to design changes in the natural sciences.

Kuhn asserts that paradigm shifts are often brought about by relatively young researchers, who design their studies using changed underlying assumptions or approaches. This tactic, or new paradigm, is often difficult to accept by older researchers with a track record of studies within a particular paradigm.

When it comes to the definition of the term paradigm ambiguity prevails in Kuhn's work. Masterman (Masterman, 1970) identified no less than 21 different uses of this term in Kuhn's work. At a general level Morgan (Morgan, 2007) identified four levels of paradigm usage: as *worldviews*, including values, morals and aesthetics; as *epistemological stances*, such as positivism or constructivism; as *shared beliefs* among a community of researchers; and as *models or examples* of the ways to conduct research. Kuhn's use of the term spans all four levels. Most of his critics have referred to the worldview or metaphysical use of paradigms, others see in his work mostly a resemblance of the third and fourth level (Masterman, 1970). Writers in the social science frequently question the appropriateness of paradigms for their field of research by outlining the differences between natural sciences and social sciences in terms of context and situational dependency of the phenomena in social sciences as well as different aims in theory development, whereby the natural scientists aims for predictive models, whereas social scientists aim for understanding or identification of trends (Dogan, 2001; Flyvbjerg, 2001; Schram, 2004). In so doing, they mainly refer to the first and second classification of paradigms, that is, the more philosophical classification of Morgan's paradigms. Fewer disputes prevail at Morgan's more methodological levels three and four, where researchers agree on shared beliefs in their particular community of practice and the associated ways of designing and executing their research. Examples for the latter include the community of mixed-methods researchers in the social sciences who frequently associate themselves with either the pragmatism paradigm (Greene, 2008; Morgan, 2007) or the critical realism paradigm (Downward & Mearman, 2006; Maxwell & Mittapalli, 2010).

The use of different paradigms derives from differences in questions and procedures and leads to different measures and results, which can be traced back to different epistemological stances and even different ontologies or worldviews. Thus, Kuhn asserts that all research is done within a particular paradigm and deliberately leaving one paradigm means accepting a different paradigm. That means all research is done within a particular paradigm, with each of them leading to 'proofs' which reflect the paradigm specific research design. Thus *proofs* of, for example hypotheses, are an insufficient argument for judging one paradigm better than another paradigm as different paradigms link to different ontologies and epistemologies and thereby generate different types of knowledge (Kuhn, 1996). Moreover, research designs are influenced by their paradigms, which lead to merely a test of the researchers ingenuity in research design, than to a test of a particular hypothesis (Kuhn, 1970). This shifts the responsibility for theory selection into the realm of social discourse. Here research results and theories should only be interpreted within the boundaries of their underlying paradigm (Hart, 1998). This strongly emphasizes the argument by Biedenbach and Müller (Biedenbach & Müller, 2011) that no research should be reported without a clear statement about the underlying paradigm. Otherwise the results may not be interpreted in their proper context, thus leading for example to rejections of publications or ignorance within the research community.

Both Popper and Kuhn, as the most prominent representatives of this area, agree that deductive theory development goes beyond simple hypothesis testing. Theories can have high predictive power without lots of empirical evidence, just as empirically tested hypotheses might not reflect the truth to the extent that they do not lead to theories with predictive power. Popper (Popper, 1959) sees individual hypothesis testing as less important than corroboration of theories by other scientific findings. While this is done to strengthen a theory's predictability for the moment, they remain *tentative forever* and '[o]nly in our subjective experiences of conviction, in our subjective faith, we can be 'absolutely certain" (p. 280).

Despite these commonalities between Kuhn and Popper, there are also differences. Kuhn sees research merely as a puzzle solving activity, where the aggregation of study results leads to increased knowledge. He is more concerned with hypothesis testing. Popper looks at research as deductive testing of higher level theories through crucial experiments, so that each experiment advances knowledge in a quasi-inductive evolution of science (Popper, 1963; Watkins, 1970). A theory must hereby be falsifiable, refutable and testable in the first place, and to advance knowledge it should be (Popper, 1963):

- A simple, new, powerful and unifying (cross disciplinary) idea.
- Independently testable for predictability of the phenomenon.
- Passing some new and severe tests, in order to explain the reasons for refutation.

Having developed a new theory, independent of its level – in a Kuhnian or Popperian sense – marks the end of theory formation (Step 2) in the model in Figure 5.1. Now the theory is developed and subject to scrutiny through discourse. Once this discourse is passed in the sense described above (under Step 1 and 3), the theory is either rejected or becomes socially accepted and enters the stage of stabilization.

Step 4: Stabilization – Refining Theories into Crisis

Imre Lakatos' (Lakatos, 1970, 1980) model of research programs is based on the observation that theories are not rejected just because they fail to explain certain parts of a phenomenon and the hypotheses put forward to explain this particular part of the phenomenon are not supported. Rather than abandoning the theory other hypotheses will be developed and tested to explain the missing part in a theory's predictability. Non-support of these hypotheses does still not lead to abandoning of the theory. The theory will remain until it is replaced by a better one. That leads to a system of competing theories, of which the stronger (and socially more acceptable) one survives.

With that model Lakatos builds on and extends the work of Popper (Popper, 1959), a Realist who argued for a move away from *naive falsificationism* to *methodological falsificationism*. The former 'requires specifying, in advance, an experiment such that if the result contradicts the theory, the theory has to be given up' (Lakatos, 1980: 96). The latter recognizes that the former may involve fallible theories within which the experiment's results are interpreted. Methodological falsificationism therefore requires taking into account the most successful theories in a field as 'an extension to our senses' (p. 107) for the interpretation of results, thus widening the spectrum of theories far beyond those related to the strictly observational part of the theory.

Lakatos extends Popper's work to *sophisticated methodological falsificationism* in the following way (p. 116):

> *For the sophisticated falsificationist a theory T is falsified if and only if another theory T' has been proposed with the following characteristics: (1) T' has excess empirical content over T: that is, it predicts novel facts, that is, facts improbable in the light of, or even forbidden, by T; (2) T' explains the previous success of T, that is, all the unrefuted content of T is included (within the limits of observational error) in the content of T'; and (3) some of the excess content of T' is corroborated.*

Through that Lakatos requires new theories to explain new facts of a given phenomenon, not only support or linguistically refine the contents of an existing theory.

Based on this he developed criteria to distinguish between those research programs that are progressive and should be continued and those that are degenerating and should be abandoned. For a theory in a research program to be progressive it must be both:

- Theoretically progressive, that is, each new theory has excess empirical contents over its predecessor by predicting some novel, hitherto unexpected fact.
- Empirically progressive, that is, each new theory leads to discovery of a *new* fact.

Only if both conditions are met a theory (and its related research program) is regarded as progressive and to be continued. Otherwise the theory is categorized as degenerating and becomes a candidate for replacement. This replacement, however, does not take place until a theory with better predictability is found. Thus (p. 119):

> *No experiment, experimental report, observation statement or well-corroborated low level falsifying hypothesis alone can lead to falsification. There is no falsification before emergence of a better theory.*

Through that we have identified the underlying assumptions and criteria to judge on research programs' continuation or discontinuation in terms of replacement over time. This is the entry point for Lakatos' methodology for research programs, which is described in the introduction to this chapter: a series of research projects, each one contributing to the better understanding of the phenomenon (be it through supported or unsupported hypotheses), thereby shaping and strengthening some of the theory's core elements. As long as the criteria for sophisticated methodological falsifiability are met (i.e. theoretical and empirical progression) the program and its theory is continued, maybe as one of a set of competing theories. If the program becomes degenerative it indicates the need for a paradigm shift in research (i.e. a crisis in the sense of Kuhn) and therefore the need for another research program, which could be a new program to be launched, or an existing progressive program whose theory replaces the theory from the degenerating program. This decision is made in the context of discourse, which is described above.

This marks the move from Step 4 to Step 1 in the model in Figure 5.1, where the discourse on a theory in crisis led to a paradigm shift, which supported the formation of new theory. This new theory is then subject to discourse and social acceptance. Further studies under this paradigm (i.e. the same research program) lead to progressive theories, which strengthen the core elements and continuously add new insights to the existing theory, up until the capabilities of the paradigm to develop new insights are exhausted and the theory becomes degenerative and *in crisis*, and stays in this mode until a further paradigm shift leads to a new and better theory.

Applying the Model

Foucault (2002) recommends that theory, like the model above, needs to be related to practice in order to be acceptable. For that we related the model to three well established theories in the field of project management.

Philosophical Underpinnings of OPM Research

These theories were selected from the Nine Schools of Project Management Research (Turner, Huemann, Anbari & Bredillet, 2010). This set of schools traces back to the work of Anbari (Anbari, 1985) who categorized project management research publications into four different schools of thought. Later Söderlund (Söderlund, 2002) and Bredillet (Bredillet, 2004) expanded this perspective to the broader domain of management literature and identified seven schools of thought in project management research. Further work by Turner, Anbari and Bredillet expanded this to nine schools of thought in project management research, which were published first as a series of editorials in *Project Management Journal* (e.g. Bredillet, 2007). The latest and current status of this discourse is a refinement of the schools into the book *Perspectives on Projects* (Turner et al., 2010). The nine perspectives towards projects (or schools of project management research, for that matter) are: optimization, modeling, success, governance, behavior, marketing, process, decision and contingency. For ease of reading we continue to use the term schools, when we mean school and/or perspective.

Each of these schools defines a particular ontology which underpins the respective research done in a particular school. For example the success school, where a robust theory was developed by Pinto and colleagues. Through a post-positivistic research design they developed a practitioner tool, the Project Implementation Profile (PIP) and the seven, respective ten project success factors which still pervade today's thinking and research in this field (Pinto & Prescott, 1988; Pinto & Slevin, 1988b).

As a general pattern we see that project management related research programs use different combinations of qualitative, quantitative and conceptual studies to shape and bring about core elements which become dominant theories in their field. To exemplify this and to apply the above mentioned model, we chose three theories, each of them developed differently over time:

- The theory of project success factors, initially qualitatively developed by Pinto and Slevin (Pinto & Slevin, 1987), and then quantitatively tested by them in 1988, with the latter paper becoming one of the most often cited paper in the subject. This theory was developed through a combination of qualitative and quantitative methods.
- The theory on project categorization system, which started off through a paradigm shift at the conceptual level, published by Turner and Cochrane (Turner & Cochrane, 1993). This paper developed into the most often cited paper on this subject. The theory was developed conceptually and later studies operationalized it quantitatively and qualitatively.
- The theory on temporary organizations, which was triggered by applying organization theory to research on projects (Lundin & Söderholm, 1995). The theory was developed conceptually and remained at this stage until today.

We selected the most influential theories based on the google.scholar citation rates in their particular area. To assess the development of the theories we address them with four questions. These questions are associated with the transitions between the four steps of the model above:

- Transition 1 (from Step 4 to Step 1): Which weaknesses were identified in existing theory, leading to opportunities for new theory development? (based on both Kuhn and Lakatos)
- Transition 2 (from Step 1 to Step 2): What is the nature of the *crisis* with an existing theory and how was it overcome by a new theory? (based on Kuhn)
- Transition 3 (from Step 2 to Step 3): How was the new theory tested, shaped and accepted through discourse in the scientific community? (based on Foucault)
- Transition 4 (from Step 3 to Step 4): How was the new theory re-used and its core elements supported and thereby *protected* over time? (based on Lakatos)

The results are summarized in Table 5.1.

Project Success Factor Theory

Pinto and his colleagues' classical work on project success factors appeared at a time when the definition of project success criteria (i.e. the measures used to judge on the success or failure of a project) where stabilizing and the natural question of 'how can we influence the accomplishment of success criteria in a project' became immanent of the discourse of that time, thus constituting the crisis in theory. This marks Transition 1 in Figure 5.1.

Building mainly on case-based research Morris and Hough (Morris & Hough, 1987) were among the first to develop a more comprehensive framework on the pre-conditions for project success, involving the elements of attitudes, project definition, external factors, finance, organization and contract strategy, schedule, communications and control, human qualities, and resources management. They addressed success as involving both subjective and objective dimensions, success as varying across the project and product life cycle, and success as being based on different stakeholder perspectives. This grew the awareness that knowledge is needed on how to influence project success on a broader, more general scale, thus Transition 2 in Figure 5.1 and Table 5.1. Pinto and Slevin (Pinto & Slevin, 1988a) addressed this crisis through a paradigm shift which involved the reconciliation of the implementation literature on organizational change with that of project management in order to develop a measurement construct for project success, and subsequently used this construct to test their earlier developed set of ten critical success factors (Pinto & Slevin, 1987) quantitatively. This identified a significant impact of each factor on project success (Pinto & Slevin, 1988b). Also in 1988 Pinto and Prescott (Pinto & Prescott, 1988) published a refinement of the ten factor model, which used a more rigorous quantitative method in order to exclude the impact of multi-colinearity between independent variables. The results showed that only seven of the originally ten factors now correlated significantly with project success. However, the ten factor model became very popular among practitioners. Examples include the mentioning of the ten success factors in the Body of Knowledge of the UK-based Association for Project Management (APM), which defines them as 'those measurable factors that, when present in the project's environment, are most conducive to the achievement of a successful project' (APM, 2000: 18). Alongside their research studies Pinto and Slevin also developed a tool for practitioners to assess the potential success of their projects, thus provided contributions to the discourse of both academics and practitioners. This marks the transition from research results to discourse among the practitioner and academic communities (Transition 3).

Pinto and colleagues addressed the question of success factors at a time when the project management community (academics as well as practitioners) were ready for the answer. The answer to the question on how to influence project success was awaited, appreciated and absorbed quickly by the community. The publication of scientific articles together with a tool for practitioners made it a perfect fit for the application oriented community of project management. The citations for their 1987 and 1988 papers range from 350 to 500 in google.scholar thus rank among the most cited papers in project management research.

The work by Pinto, Slevin and Prescott triggered a wave of studies on project success and success factors (i.e. a research program in the sense of Lakatos), which is still going on today. For a review see (Jugdev & Müller, 2005; Müller & Jugdev, 2012). Many more success factors were identified over time, including team related factors, leadership etc. However, the factors developed by Pinto and colleagues were never seriously questioned, thus became the core elements of the theory on project success factors (Transition 4). So far a new crisis, requiring a new research paradigm, has not been articulated through the discourse within the project management community. However, this might change in the face of agile project management, open source development projects and other contemporary developments, which challenge some of the underlying assumptions of the more traditional ways of project management.

An interesting observation is the popularity of the ten factor model despite its partial disapproval through the more rigorously tested seven-factor model. One would expect the model derived from a stricter methodology to render the other model unpopular. That was not the case. One reason may be the choice of media. By using the main publication outlets of the project management community, their Bodies of Knowledge and the research journals of their professional organizations, information enters the discourse within the community easier and seems to be more 'sticky', longer lasting than information published in the more general management literature. This is a further indication of the significant role of discourse in theory acceptance.

Project Categorization Systems

The weakness of traditional definitions of the term 'project' was found in the assumption that project goals and the associated methods to achieve those goals are well understood at the start of the project. However, on some projects, the objectives and/or the methods cannot be clearly defined, leading to unrealistic plans for the subsequent design freeze and execution stage, thus a risk for project failure (Transition 1). By looking at the changes in the nature of projects by that time, Turner and Cochrane (Turner & Cochrane, 1993) identified the need for more detailed planning dimensions which allow for a more granulate planning and design of projects, in order to increase the chances for projects to be delivered successfully. By distinguishing between the clearness of project goals and the clearness of project methods, they implemented a new paradigm, which provided for a better understanding of differences among projects and the related differences in planning these projects. This allowed planning for incremental development of either goals and/or methods during the course of project execution (Transition 2).

The number of citations of the Turner and Cochrane paper increased exponentially, from 18 citations in the first five years after publication of the original paper to 56 in the second five-year term, and 119 in the third five-year term. Compared with a citation ratio of 22 and 92 within similar timeframes achieved by the second most-often cited categorization system (Dvir, Lipovetsky, Shenhar, & Tishler, 1998), it is indicated that Turner and Cochrane's model dominates the discourse on project categorization systems (source: google.scholar). This dominance was and is fuelled by more global changes, such as the rising awareness of the importance of project management methodologies for project success, and the rise of substantially new project management methodologies, such as agile. The content of the paper and the global developments complement each other for the ongoing discourse on the subject (Transition 3).

As a result of the increasing use of the model by other researchers, a research program in the sense of Lakatos (1980) developed over time, which proved and supported the core elements of Turner and Cochrane's model, that is, clearness of goals and clearness of methods, numerous times. By the time of publication it contributed to the growing awareness of projects and project management being contingent on a number of internal and external factors. To that end it contributed to the growing use of contingency theory in project management research, which is exemplified in the popular work on *One Size does not Fit All Projects* by Shenhar (Shenhar, 2001), as well as Turner and Müller's work on *Choosing Appropriate Project Managers* (Turner & Müller, 2006).

Over time the program related discourse migrated into a more general discussion on the diversity of methodological approaches and project types for project planning and execution. An example for this can be found in Crawford, Hobbs and Turner's (Crawford, Hobbs, & Turner, 2005) project categorization systems, which provides for an unlimited number of project classifications, using the dimensions of project attributes and types (Transition 4).

Philosophical Underpinnings of OPM Research

The Theory of the Temporary Organization

The look at projects as temporary organizations emerged in the 1990s in Scandinavia. At that time the popularity in developing project management methodologies (which started in the late 1980s) reached saturation and other, less uniform or process oriented ways to understand projects were asked for. Together with the stabilization of the first set of theories on project success, its factors and criteria, the quest for a deeper understanding of *what is done in projects* and *why do we need projects* emerged (Transition 1).

Lundin and Söderholm (Lundin & Söderholm, 1995) were among the first to address the question of *what is done in projects* as temporary organizations. They took an organization theory perspective and conceptually identified time, task, team and transition as the core elements of a theory on projects as temporary organizations. Simultaneously Packendorff (Packendorff, 1995) published an essay on the importance of research on projects as temporary organizations and a possible research agenda for the future (Transition 2). This entered the discourse within the project management community and made projects as temporary organizations an attractive subject, for example as theme for one of the IRNOP conferences (International Research Network for Managing by Projects), or as a special issue of the *Scandinavian Journal of Management*. The popularity of the subject triggered a series of related studies, which could be defined as part of an (unintended) overall research program in the sense of Lakatos (Transition 3). Within this program four major themes developed:

- an internal view of projects, by taking an organization theory perspective, as advocated by Lundin and Söderholm (Lundin & Söderholm, 1995);
- projects as agencies in corporate governance, taking an organization theory perspective, as advocated by (Turner & Müller, 2003);
- projects as economic transactions, taking a Transaction Costs Economics and Agency Theory perspective, as advocated by Müller, Turner, Winch (e.g. in Müller & Turner, 2005; Winch, 2001);
- projects as social interaction, taking a merely sociological perspective, such as advocated by Grabher (Grabher, 2002) and Bechky (Bechky, 2006).

Some of these themes contributed to the development of project governance models. These models address project governance at several levels in the organization, such as the project level, the middle management and the top management level (Turner, 2009), which resembles the different perspectives shown in the list above. To that end the discourse migrated the research on projects as temporary organizations partly into research on project governance and organizational project management (Transition 4). The multitude of perspectives and the diversity of project governance models calls for further research and may constitute a form of current crisis of theory in this field, which may be resolved through a paradigm shift in the future.

Table 5.1. Three Examples of Theory Development through Discourse

Stage in dynamics	Transition 1	Transition 2	Transition 3	Transition 4
Underlying concept	Kuhn and Lakatos	Kuhn	Foucault	Lakatos
Questions	Which weaknesses were identified in existing theory, leading to opportunities for new theory development?	What is the nature of the 'crisis' with an existing theory and how was it overcome by a new theory?	How was the new theory tested, shaped and accepted through discourse in the scientific community?	How was the new theory re-used and its core elements supported and thereby 'protected' over time?
Project success factors by Pinto, Slevin and Prescott	Knowledge on success criteria matured, but knowledge on how to influence the achievement of success criteria was lacking.	Lack of generalizable knowledge on success factors. Paradigm shift by integrating organizational change and project management literature to develop success measures and then test the empirically derived success factors on their impact on project success.	High acceptance by academia and practitioners. The theory came timely and filled an essential knowledge gap. Popularity was also supported by publishing tools for practitioners, contributions to the APM Body of Knowledge, as well as academic research journals of the profession.	Further research of increasingly detailed application of the success factor model, in parallel with tools for practitioners, led to many applications in academia and practice. This was complemented by numerous studies which identified further success factors, but did not seriously question those developed by Pinto et al, (1988).
Project categorization system (Turner & Cochrane, 2003)	Traditional definitions of the term 'project' were built on the weak assumption that project goals and the associated methods are well understood at the start of the project.	Ill defined project goals and methods at the beginning of the project lead to unrealistic plans for the subsequent design freeze and execution stage, thus a risk for project failure. Distinguishing between the clearness of project goals and the clearness of project methods provided for a higher granulate in the understanding of projects and their needs for planning, which allowed planning for incremental development of either goals and/or methods during the course of project execution.	The theory is highly accepted by academics and practitioners with the highest citation rate in its field. It is among the first to classify projects, and inspired subsequent studies to classify projects from various dimensions/ attributes. As one of the first categorization systems, it contributed the use of contingency theory in future research in the field of project management.	Further research continued the discussion on project categorization system from more diverse perspectives, i.e. unlimited number of project attributes and types. The categorization of projects provided for identifying the fit between projects and their context in order to achieve better project results.

Stage in dynamics	Transition 1	Transition 2	Transition 3	Transition 4
Underlying concept	Kuhn and Lakatos	Kuhn	Foucault	Lakatos
Projects as temporary organizations	Knowledge on project success criteria matured together with stabilization in the development of project management methodologies. This created the need for a deeper understanding of what is going on in projects, as well as raising the question of how projects are used in organizations.	Thinking was dominated by normative *how to* publications (e.g. methodologies), a more theoretical understanding was lacking. The paradigm shift involved integration of concepts from organization theory and project management literature. From an organizational perspective the streams for research on theory within projects and theory of projects developed in organizations.	The theory came timely and filled the gap in theoretical understanding, for both internal as well as external theorizing on projects. This stimulated discourse using further theoretical perspectives, such as those from governance theory, transaction costs economics, or sociology.	Further research used a multitude of perspectives and contributed, among others, to the development of generic models of project governance and the concept of organizational project management.

By comparing the answers to the four questions in Table 5.1 and the analysis above, we see indicators that long term survival of project management theories may be influenced by the:

- Timeliness of their occurrence (i.e. is there a discourse that asks for the theory?)
- Aesthetics of the theory (i.e. can members of the discourse, such as practitioners or academics, relate to the theory and make sense and use of it?)
- Media (i.e. is the publication media accessed by those who should make use of the theory?)
- Fit to Zeitgeist (i.e. does the theory fit to wider social and other trends, events and phenomena at that time?)

This should not be misunderstood to mean that future research should only investigate popular topics. Research on new phenomena, or as yet unknown aspects, in project management often pave the way for a new discourse to emerge, which leads to the need for new theory in the long term. This exploratory type of research is certainly needed, even if it may take longer to establish a robust and socially accepted theory.

Conclusions

This chapter has focused on the dynamics in theory development. Four stages were identified:

- An ex-ante stage of discourse, associated with a crisis in the predictive power of exiting theories.
- New theory formation, based on research results accomplished by a shift in research paradigm.
- An ex-post stage of discourse of the research results for academics, and general social acceptance of the new theory.
- Theory stabilization through research programs, which strengthen the core elements of the theory, but also show the limitations of research results accomplished through an existing paradigm.

We showed that research results are not an end in themselves, but merely contributions to a discourse on the continuously evolving understanding of a phenomenon. The acceptance of a theory is multi-dimensional and includes the history of the understanding of a phenomenon, the aesthetics and timeliness of the new theory, the level of congruency with the Zeitgeist and other social streams. Thus theory acceptance is not a rational straight forward process, but often impacted by factors unrelated to the research study *per se*.

Looking at these findings from the perspective of developments in contemporary research methods we see that the findings emphasize discourse even within the theory formulation stage by building reflection within the research paradigm and its methodology. Moreover, historically researchers have been trying to be objective by limiting the influence of personal experiences on research results, even when using social science methodologies. Methodology developments in recent years show a trend towards integration of the researcher's own experience in the research process, done, for example, through abductive methods, which allow the researcher to reflect within the triangle of empirical observations, existing theories, and own experience (Alvesson & Kärreman, 2011; Alvesson & Sköldberg, 2009; Flyvbjerg, 2001). Thus, freeing the researcher from merely mechanistic roles, such as data mining in quantitative studies and coding in qualitative studies. Therefore, allowing for the use of intelligence and existing insights to deepen the understanding of a phenomenon. This is indicative of a possible approximation of the theory formation and ex-post discourse stages in the long term. Social streams, such as the discourse through social media or crowdsourcing maybe supportive of such a closer link between these two stages.

This opens the path for 'bricolage', a concept advocated for years, for example by Denzin and Lincoln (Denzin & Lincoln, 2005) which attempts to fill holes in existing theories by use of theories (or parts thereof) developed in other sciences. This is in line with Weick's suggestion of theory development as a 'disciplined imagination' (Weick, 1989) and Popper's strive for verisimilitude (Popper, 1963), that is, to gradually

Philosophical Underpinnings of OPM Research

approach the truth using tested and accepted theories which were developed outside the researcher's home sphere, rather than accumulating knowledge over time by testing batteries of hypotheses, which might or might not be refuted merely through their particular research design and the design's impact on the collection of empirical data.

In the chapter above we have provided a model that may explain some of the dynamics in theory development. We have put the discourse in the center of these dynamics. It is the discourse that determines the survival of theories to a large extent. This discourse has the power to integrate basic and applied research by bringing together the researchers, practitioners, publishers and other stakeholders in theory development. Thus, discourse enables translational research. It links various stakeholder groups, each with its particular set of expectations and requirements for accepting a theory. This link provides for a kaleidoscopic view towards new theories and contributes to the social acceptance or non-acceptance of a new theory. By linking the various stakeholder groups we provide for the required media and communication. By working with engaged practitioners, academics and other stakeholders we provide for reflective members who want to 'push the envelope' towards better theories. Discourse for translational research allows closing the gap between academic research and practitioner needs to the benefit of all parties.

References

Alvesson, M., & Kärreman, D. (2011). *Qualitative Research and Theory Development* (p. 133). Thousand Oaks, CA,: SAGE Publications, Inc., USA.

Alvesson, M., & Sköldberg, K. (2009). *Reflexive Methodology* (2nd ed.). London: SAGE Publications.

Anbari, F. (1985). A systems approach to project evaluation. *Project Management Journal*, *16*(3), 21-26.

Apm. (2000). *APM Body of Knowledge*. London, UK: British Standards Institution.

Bechky, B. A (2006). Gaffers, Gofers, and Grips: Role-Based Coordination in Temporary Organizations. *Organization Science*, *17*(1), 3-21. doi:10.1287/orsc.1050.0149

Bevir, N. (1999). FOUCAULT AND CRITIQUE Deploying Agency against Autonomy. *Political Theory*, *27*(1), 65-84.

Bhaskar, R. (1975). *A Realist Theory of Science*. Leeds, UK: Leeds Books Ltd.

Biedenbach, T., & Müller, R. (2011). Paradigms in project management research: examples from 15 years of IRNOP conferences. *International Journal of Managing Projects in Business*, *4*(1), 82-104.

Bredillet, C. (2004). Theories and Research in Project Management: Critical review and return to the future. PhD thesis, Lille Graduate School of Management (ESC Lille), France.

Bredillet, C. (2007). Exploring Research in Project Management: Nine Schools of Project Management Research (Part 4). *Project Management Journal, 39*(1), 2-6.

Crawford, L., Hobbs, B., & Turner, J. R. (2005). *Project Categorization Systems*. Newton Square, PA, USA: PMI.

Denzin, N. K., & Lincoln, Y. S. (2005). Introduction: The Discipline and Practice of Qualitative Research. In N. K. Denzin & Y. S. Lincoln (Eds.), *Handbook of Qualitative Research* (3rd ed., pp. 1-32). Thousand Oaks, CA, USA: SAGE Publications Inc.

Dogan, M. (2001). Paradigms in the Social Sciences. *International Encyclopedia of the Social & Behavioral Sciences*. http://dx.doi.org/10.1016/B0-08-043076-7/00782-8, accessed 2010-10-09. Retrieved from http://dx.doi.org/10.1016/B0-08-043076-7/00782-8.

Downward, P., & Mearman, A. (2006). Retroduction as mixed-methods triangulation in economic research: reorienting economics into social science. *Cambridge Journal of Economics, 31*(1), 77-99. doi:10.1093/cje/bel009

Dvir, D., Lipovetsky, S., Shenhar, A., & Tishler, A. (1998). In search of project classification: a non-universal approach to project success factors. *Research Policy, 27*(1998), 915-35.

Flyvbjerg, B. (1998). Habermas and Foucault: thinkers for civil society. *British Journal of Sociology, 49*(2), 210-233.

Flyvbjerg, B. (2001). *Making Social Science Matter*. Cambridge, UK: Cambridge University Press.

Foucault, M. (2002). *The Architecture of Knowledge*. Abingdon, Oxon, UK: Routledge Classics.

Grabher, G. (2002). Cool Projects, Boring Institutions: Temporary Collaboration in Social Context. *Regional Studies, 36*(3), 205-214. doi:10.1080/00343400220122025

Greene, J. C. (2008). Is Mixed Methods Social Inquiry a Distinctive Methodology? *Journal of Mixed Methods Research, 2*(1), 7-22. doi:10.1177/1558689807309969

Habermas, J. (1987). *Theorie des Kommunikativen Handelns*. Frankfurt am Main, Germany: Suhrkamp Verlag.

Hart, C. (1998). *Doing a Literature Review*. London, UK: SAGE Publications Ltd.

Jugdev, K., & Müller, R. (2005). A Retrospective Look at Our Evolving Understanding of Project Success. *Project Management Journal, 36*(4), 19-31.

Kuhn, T. (1970). Logic of Discovery or Psychology of Research? In I. Lakatos & A. Musgrave (Eds.), *Criticism and the Grpwth of Knowledge*. Cambridge, UK: Cambridge University Press.

Kuhn, T. (1996). *The structure of scientific revolutions*. London, UK: University of Chicago Press.

Kulka, T. (1977). Some problems Concerning Rational Reconstruction: Comments on Elkana and Lakatos. *British Journal for the Philosophy of Science, 28*(4), 325-344.

Lakatos, I. (1970). Falsification and the Methodology of Scientific Research Programmes. In I. Lakatos & A. Musgrave (eds), *Criticism and the Growth of Knowledge*. Cambridge, UK: Cambridge University Press.

Lakatos, I. (1980). *The methodology of scientific research programmes*. Cambridge, UK: Cambridge University Press.

Lundin, R. A., & Söderholm, A. (1995). A theory of the temporary organization. *Scandinavian Journal of Management, 11*(4), 437-455.

Masterman, M. (1970). The Nature of a Paradigm. In I. Lakatos & A. Musgrave (eds), *Criticism and the Growth of Knowledge*. Cambridge, UK: Cambridge University Press.

Maxwell, J. A., & Mittapalli, K. (2010). Realism as a Stance for Mixed Methods Research. In A. Tashakkori & C. Teddlie (eds), *SAGE Handbook of Mixed Methods in Social & Behavioral Research* (pp. 145-168). Thousand Oaks, CA, USA: SAGE Publications, Inc., USA.

May, A. M., & Sellers, J. R. (1988). Contemporary Philosophy of Science and Neoinstitutional Thought. *Journal of Economic Issues, 22*(2), 397-405.

McGee, M. C. (2012). Phronesis in the Habermas vs. Gadamer Debate. *Fragments*. Retrieved July 4, 2012, from http://mcgeefragments.net/OLD/Phronesis.in.the.Habermas.vs.Gadamer.Debate.htm

Miller, G. A. (2003). The cognitive revolution : a historical perspective, *7*(3), 141-144.

Morgan, D. L. (2007). Paradigms Lost and Pragmatism Regained: Methodological Implications of Combining Qualitative and Quantitative Methods. *Journal of Mixed Methods Research, 1*(1), 48-76. doi:10.1177/2345678906292462

Morris, P. W. G., & Hough, G. H. (1987). *The anatomy of major projects: A study of the reality of project management*. Chichester, UK: Hohn Wiley & Sons, Ltd.

Müller, R. (2009). *Project Governance*. Aldershot, UK: Gower Publishing.

Müller, R., & Jugdev, K. (2012). Critical Success Factors in Projects: Pinto, Slevin, and Prescott – the elucidation of project success. *International Journal of Managing Projects in Business, 5*(4), 757-775.

Müller, R., & Turner, J. R. (2005). The Impact of Principal-Agent Relationship and Contract Type on Communication between Project Owner and Manager. *International Journal of Project Management, 23*(5), 398-403.

Ngwenyama, O. K., & Lee, A. S. (1997). Communication Richness in Electronic Mail: Critical Social Theory and the Contextuality of Meaning. *MIS Quarterly, 1997*(June), 145-167.

Packendorff, J. (1995). Inquiring into the temporary organization: New directions for project management research. *Scandinavian Journal of Management, 11*(4), 319-333. doi:10.1016/0956-5221(95)00018-Q

Pinto, J. K., & Prescott, J. (1988). Variations in Critical Success Factors Over the Stages in the Project Life Cyde. *Journal of Management, 14*(1), 5-18. doi:10.1177/014920638801400102

Pinto, J. K., & Slevin, D. P. (1987). Critical factors in successful project implementation. *IEEE Transactions on Engineering Management, 34*(1), 22-28.

Pinto, J. K., & Slevin, D. P. (1988a). Project Success: Definitions and Measurement Techniques. *Project Management Journal, 19*(1), 67-72.

Pinto, J. K., & Slevin, D. P. (1988b). Critical success factors across the project life cycle. *Project Management Journal, 19*(3), 67-75.

Popper, K. (1959). *The Logic of Scientific Discovery.* New York, USA: Basic Books.

Popper, K. (1963). *Conjectures and Refutations.* Abingdon, Oxon, UK: Routledge Classics.

Popper, K. (1970). Normal Science and its Dangers. In I. Lakatos & A. Musgrave (eds), *Criticism and the Growth of Knowledge* (pp. 51-58). Cambridge, UK: Cambridge University Press.

Sankey, H. (2011). Philosophical fairytales from Feyerabend. *Metascience, 21*(2), 471-476. doi:10.1007/s11016-011-9559-8

Schram, S. F. (2004). Beyond Paradigm: Resisting the Assimilation of Phronetic Social Science. *Politics & Society, 32*(3), 417-433. doi:10.1177/0032329204267292

Shenhar, A. (2001). One Size does Not Fit All Projects: Exploring Classical Contingeny Domains. *Management Science, 47*(3), 394-414.

Söderlund, J. (2002). On the development of project management research: Schools of thought and critique. *International Project Management Journal, 8*(1), 20-31.

Tsoukas, H., & Cummings, S. (1997). Marginalization and Recovery: The Emergence of Aristotelian Themes in Organization Studies. *Organization Studies, 18*(4), 655-683. doi:10.1177/017084069701800405

Turner, J. R. (2009). *The handbook of project-based management* (3rd ed.). USA: McGraw-Hill.

Turner, J. R., & Cochrane, R. A. (1993). Goals-and-methods matrix: coping with projects with ill defined goals and/or methods of achieving them. *International Journal of Project Management, 11*(2), 93-102.

Turner, J. R., Huemann, M., Anbari, F., & Bredillet, C. (2010). *Perspectives on Projects.* Milton Park, UK: Routledge.

Turner, J. R., & Müller, R. (2003). On The Nature of The Project As A Temporary Organization. *International Journal of Project Management, 21*(1), 1-7.

Turner, J. R., & Müller, R. (2006). *Choosing Appropriate Project Managers: Matching their leadership style to the type of project.* Newtown Square; USA: Project Management Institute.

Philosophical Underpinnings of OPM Research

Watkins, W. N. (1970). Against "Normal Science". *Criticism and the Growth of Knowledge*. Cambridge, UK: Cambridge University Press.

Weick, K. E. (1989). Theory Construction as Disciplined Imagination. *Academy of Management Review, 14*(4), 516-531.

Winch, G. M. (2001). Governing the project process: a conceptual framework. *Construction Management and Economics, 19*, 799-808.

Wray, K. B. (2005). Rethinking Scientific Specialization. *Social Studies of Science, 35*(1), 151-164. doi:10.1177/0306312705045811

Creative and Innovative Contemporary Approaches

Shankar Sankaran, Ralf Müller and Nathalie Drouin

The aim of this section was to motivate project management researchers to consider using innovative and contemporary approaches to conduct their research. Project management researchers have traditionally relied on surveys, interviews or case studies to conduct their research. The chapters in this section are expected to broaden the perspective of project management researchers to consider new research designs that are being used in other scientific and technology areas but are not often being used in project management.

In Chapter 6, Michael Er, Julien Pollack and Shankar Sankaran provide three novel approaches which can help in studying project activities, investigating how relationships between human and non-human aspects of projects are created and transformed during projects and studying change processes associated with projects. First, they discuss *actor-network theory*, which can be used to study various relationships that occur in projects – both internally and externally – and how these are mediated and transformed during the course of a project. Second, they elaborate on *activity theory* that is useful in studying human actions in a project management work context. Finally, they illustrate how *action research* and allied *action-oriented approaches* can be used to understand the change that often accompanies projects. The application of each approach is explained using real examples of research carried out by the authors themselves.

In Chapter 7, Elyssebeth Leigh explains how *simulation* can be used to investigate the ill-structured problems faced in projects. The work on which this chapter is based guides researchers to use simulations to conduct research to understand the effects of complexity in both project management and organizational contexts. While project managers may be familiar with the application of simulation in education and training, this chapter helps to extend the application of simulation to carry out research in projects. Examples of use of simulation in management and project management research are provided.

In Chapter 8, Kim van Oorschot encourages project management researchers to borrow from the field of *system dynamics* for studying the structure and dynamics of complex systems encountered in projects. Project management researchers interested in researching complexity in projects would find this notion very useful. Van Oorschot illustrates how system dynamics can be applied to model situations in projects that cause complexity due to interactions, delays, accumulations and nonlinear effects by using causal loop diagrams and stock-and-flow diagrams. The chapter also provides tips for deciding when system dynamics is useful and when it is not.

This section concludes with Chapter 9 by Monique Aubry, who urges project management researchers to develop *research programs* in their topic of interest through a series of research projects aimed at investigating a specific aspect of interest in projects. Aubry uses the extensive research carried out by her and her co-researchers on project management offices. She elaborates on the five phases of her research regarding project management offices, illustrating how a research program can be set up through a series of research projects and using a diverse range of approaches to expand our understanding of a specific area of research.

Together, the authors in this section try to answer the following questions of importance to project management research:

- How will contemporary research approaches being proposed in this section transform project management research?
- How can these methods be applied by project management (or organizational researchers in the project management) field?
- What are the problems and opportunities for project management researchers (or organizational researchers in project management) in using these methods?

Chapter 6

Actor-Network Theory, Activity Theory and Action Research and their Application in Project Management Research

Michael Er, Julien Pollack and Shankar Sankaran

Abstract

Projects pay attention to activities, deal with relationships and involve change. Hence research approaches that are useful to examine activities or work practices (e.g. *Activity Theory*), investigate relationships (e.g. *Actor-Network Theory*) and facilitate change (e.g. *Action Research*) could be very useful for project management researchers. While some papers in project management (PM) journals report using these approaches we expect that they will become more prevalent in the future due to the recent demand for more emphasis on detailed investigation of what is occurring in real practice and the management of complexity in projects by describing interconnections. Further, realizing intended benefits from projects requires more attention to the change process that is often left out of the scope of managing a project.

Actor-Network Theory (ANT), also known as the sociology of translation (Law 1992: 380), is a branch of sociology with roots in the study of science. ANT has been identified as '… most closely associated with the work of Bruno Latour …' (Mutch 2002: 481), with early influences to its development also including the work of Michel Callon and John Law (Law & Hassard 1999: 248), and it has now become a useful methodology in organizational research. According to Czarniawaska & Hernes (2005, back cover), ANT is rapidly making its mark as a practical, challenging and intriguing tool for studying organizations. Its unique approach to connecting people, artefacts, institutions and organizations enables it to shed light on complex ties that so far have escaped organization theory.

ANT has been used to study the relationship between project managers, project management (PM) processes and stakeholders (Blackburn, 2002). Other studies using ANT of interest to PM is the research on project management offices (Aubry et al., 2007), IT projects (Linde & Linderoth, 2006) and communities of practice (Fox, 2002).

Activity Theory (AT) has its roots in classical German philosophy, the works of Karl Marx, the cultural historical school of Russian psychology through the works of Vygotsky and Leont'ev and later enhancements by Scandinavian researchers like Yrjö Engeström.

AT is becoming very useful in the study of human action that has become 'endlessly multifaceted, mobile and rich in variations of content and form' (Engeström & Miettinen, 1999: 8). AT has been used to study information systems design (Nardi & O'Day, 1999), innovative learning in work teams (Engeström, 1999a), mobile workers in construction management (Er & Lawrence 2011) and project-specific work contexts (Kaptelinin, 2003).

Action Research (AR), which was founded by Kurt Lewin, has become very useful in studying and implementing change. AR has spread from its origin in social systems to its application by Tavistock researchers in the study of socio-technical systems, to improving teaching practices in education and to organizational research. It is based on the premise that implementing change effectively requires a cyclical process between action and reflection and involvement of people who would be affected by the change. AR has been used in PM research to implement organizational change (Sankaran & Kumar, 2010), knowledge management systems (Mau, 2005; Orr, 2007; Walker, 2007) and in the study of aid/relief projects (Steinfort & Walker, 2011).

This chapter will briefly discuss the historical origins of the three approaches with examples of how they are applied in general and in PM research. It will also discuss issues associated with these approaches and describe the commonalities and differences between them that originated from different fields and locations around the world.

Although these approaches have been used in other fields, they could be considered novel from a project management research perspective as they have only recently been reported in the PM literature. They are also translational as they inform PM researchers about how these approaches have been applied to study practices in other fields.

Actor-Network Theory

Actor-Network Theory (ANT) is an approach to research that has not been widely used in PM, but one which offers significant potential in exploring how projects are managed. Other researchers (e.g. Cicmil et al, 2006) have called for an increase in research which enquires into the '… "actuality" of project based working and management' (p. 675) rather than focusing on how PM is traditionally described. ANT is a research methodology that could act as a vehicle to contribute to this goal.

There is no unified body of literature for ANT (Cho et al., 2008: 616). It is a '… complex theoretical formation with many variations …' (Nimmo, 2011: 109), and the use of ANT in research '… assumes a familiarity with bodies of literature and ideas that are formidable in their range and scope' (Mutch, 2002: 480). As such, in reading the research literature that makes use of ANT, it is possible to find significant variation in both the areas to which ANT has been applied, and the way it has been used. However, it is possible to draw out some consistent themes within the literature that are of relevance to PM research.

A Way of Avoiding Predefinition

Latour has commented that the name 'Actor-Network Theory' has led to some misunderstanding, including about the methodological status of the approach, as it is less a theory than a way to learn from actors without imposing external concepts upon them; a way that is comparable to ethnomethodology (Latour, 1999: 20). It can be better thought of as an ontological perspective, rather than a theory (Harty, 2010: 301). This ontology is typically used as a way of enquiring into the way in which actors come together to form heterogeneous and stable networks, which can then behave as individual actors in their own right (Law, 1992: 386).

McGrath (2002: 264) identifies that a great deal of the project literature explains phenomena in terms of its relation to best practice. However, this places limits on research to those topics that can be directly related to established best practice, restricting any opportunity to venture into new territory. For ANT, '... it is important not to start out assuming whatever we wish to explain' (Law, 1992: 380). One of the significant ways in which ANT can be of benefit to PM research is the desire in ANT to avoid imposing external constructs, and instead using the constructs of the people in the situation being studied. In a PM setting, this could be used as a way of constructing accounts of how people are managing their work, without imposing reference to any of the popular PM standards or guides.

ANT was partly developed as a reaction to the way that sociological research separated social factors from other kinds of influences in a situation, granting the social a special status. From an ANT perspective, social forces should be as open to question and examination as any other phenomena, instead of being considered an assumed property of the world. Resistance in ANT to assuming pre-established distinctions without critical examination can also be seen in the rejection of classification of factors as macro or micro (Fox, 2002: 858; Mutch, 2002: 483). Similarly, from '... the ANT perspective, there is no difference as such between external and internal networks' (Aubry, 2011: 440). The subject-object dualism has also come under question (Nimmo, 2011: 109). Similarly, ANT '... incorporates a move away from dichotomization between, for instance, economic versus social determinants or stability versus change, to look at how these are interlinked and mutually constituted' (Harty, 2010: 300).

However, the anti-dualistic perspective that has become most clearly identified with ANT is resistance to the differentiation between humans and non-humans. ANT takes the agency of non-humans seriously, and endeavours to examine how humans and non-humans influence their worlds, using the same methodological terms. ANT '... adopts an analytical position of symmetry between humans and nonhumans...' (McGrath, 2002:, 252). Non-humans are considered to be more than the passive holders of symbolic projection (Latour, 2005: 10). The social and technical worlds

Creative and Innovative Contemporary Approaches

are thought of as intertwined and entangled, defining each other, and ANT allows for a free movement between these sometimes seemingly separate worlds. It is both desirable and possible to examine the human and non-human through the same analytical terms (Law, 1986: 258).

While sociological research has favored the social as a focus of research, traditional PM research has favored the technical. Aubry (2011) has noted that this is changing; that there '… is a widespread movement among project management researchers who explore how project management can be extricated from the technical barriers, which have been holding it back …' (p. 438). There is potential for ANT to contribute to PM research in providing a vehicle to bridge this socio-technical divide.

Characteristics of ANT

For an ANT enquiry, an actor, or *actant*, is an '… element which bends space around itself, makes other elements depend upon itself and translates their will into a language of its own' (Callon & Latour, 1981: 286). An actor can be a human, but is not necessarily so. For instance, Blackburn (2002: 202) notes that project deliverables can be seen as actors. Many non-human actors can be seen to influence and impact upon projects: budgets may provide opportunities, limit action, or hint at changes in the political climate; project plans may inform a situation, communicate information, or distract from more urgent issues; and available materials may impress a stakeholder, or break during production, all of which can change the course of a project.

Actors do not exist in isolation. They exist in a network of association with other actors. An '… actor is also, always, a network' (Law, 1992: 384), which may exist in stable association with other actors in such a way as to act as a unified group. On starting an ANT study, the way in which actors are connected may not be clear, but the default position is that the actors will be connected in a way that makes other actors act through the way they transform the world (Latour, 2005: 107). One of the purposes of an ANT study should then be to trace the network of associations between different actors, to uncover the ways in which they influence each other.

Actors are in constant flux and reconfiguration, based on the network of interactions of which they form a part (Callon, 1998: 253). Given the mutual influence of networks of actors upon each other, action is also not seen as an isolated and independent choice. Instead, action is viewed as the outcome of a diffuse network of association.

Action is not done under the full control of the consciousness; action should rather be felt as a node, a knot, and a conglomerate of many surprising sets of agencies that have to be slowly disentangled. It is this venerable source of uncertainty that we wish to render vivid again in the odd expression of actor-network (Latour, 2005: 44).

Enquiry using ANT

One way in which ANT has been used is in developing an understanding of the network of transformation in a situation. A network is a series of associations between actors, taking action, and prompting other actors to take action. Enquiry may '... consider network consolidation, and in particular how it is that networks may come to look like single point actors: how it is, in other words, we are sometimes able to talk of "the British Government" rather than all the bits and pieces that make it up' (Law, 1992: 380). Networks of associations between actors provide both identity and agency for actors. 'Agency and identity are not pre-existing or fundamental, essential attributes, but are generated through and by interactions within these networks' (Harty, 2010: 301). Networks in ANT do not refer to the structure of an organization (Aubry, 2011: 440), or to an organization's information system, although ANT has been used in enquiries into both of these phenomena. Instead, networks of association can cross institutional, technical, and social categories, linking actors of seemingly incompatible groups. For instance, in one seminal ANT study, Callon (1986) demonstrated how three scientists formed a temporarily stable network, and were able to act as the representatives of this network. In this study:

> *Three men have become influential and are listened to because they have become the 'head' of several populations. They have mixed together learned experts, unpolished fishermen, and savoury crustaceans* (Callon, 1986: 216).

Actors and networks are in a constant process of creation, reformation, stabilization and dissolution. The literature on ANT comments that the best time to investigate this process is during the process of creation of new associations. Porsander (2005: 17) notes that connections are most visible when they are being created. 'It is by means of studying the construction of the connections between the actions that the process of organizing can be grasped' (p. 18). ANT '... focuses on the networks construction where issues, tensions and conflicts can be observed while they unfold' (Aubry, 2011: 436). This feature of ANT also suits enquiry into PM, as projects, because of their temporary, unique and novel nature involve the creation of new associations, and the short-term stabilization of new networks. Applying ANT to these situations is simpler than to situations that have achieved a steady-state, when important associations have become assumed, stabilized and invisible, due to their regularity.

ANT in PM Research

Some evidence of ANT can be seen in the PM literature. Aubry (2011: 436) used ANT '... to capture networks construction around project management offices (PMO) deliverables that cross multiple organisational boundaries'. Blackburn's (2002) study is also of note, using ANT to interpret project managers' stories about their practice, while Linde and Linderoth (2006) used ANT to examine two organizational change projects. Linderoth and Pellegrino (2005) also reviewed two IT projects using ANT, finding the need to supplement the approach with the Social Construction of Technology theory to develop lessons for IT-dependent change projects. Harty (2008, 2010) reviewed the innovation in construction projects using ANT, while Parkin (1996) used aspects of ANT to examine decision making in project management. Aubry et al. (2007) also support the use of ANT in PM research.

ANT has had some impact in the study of IS/IT projects (Doolin & Lowe: 2002; Hanseth et al., 2004; Linderoth & Pellegrino, 2005; Cho et al., 2008; Mutch, 2002). For instance, McGrath (2002) used ANT to analyze how the London Ambulance Service recovered from a failed dispatch system. Cho et al. (2008) used ANT to examine contradictory interests and changing agency during a Swedish healthcare information system implementation. Porsander (2000, 2005) also used ANT, to study a specific project as a whole, and then to examine an aspect of the supporting IT system for that project. Heeks and Stanforth (2007: 175) found that ANT provided the opportunity to address multiple levels of analysis of an e-government information technology. Greenhalgh and Stones (2010) and Mutch (2002) used ANT to study IT within the UK National Health Service; however, both studies found the need to supplement the ANT study by drawing on structuration theory, as did Linde and Linderoth (2006) in a PM context.

ANT in Application

In a recent ANT study involving two of this chapter's authors – Pollack and Sankaran – ANT was used to reconstruct a network of interaction that spanned three different project sites. The study looked into the way in which a community of practice used a project management information system (PMIS) to develop PM capability in different organizations. Multiple actors were revealed to be acting in the environment, as individuals, as groups, and as stable networks of association that included non-human actors, such as the information system.

Comparative examination of the different ways in which the PMIS was used, through the social-constructivist lens of ANT, revealed the way in which new practice was introduced into each site, and stabilized as business as usual, eventually becoming an essentially invisible and assumed aspect of standard organizational practice. It was shown that it was not the PMIS, or the community of practice, but the stable network of relationships between the PMIS and the community of practice that was the key element for developing PM capability within these organizations. This was contrary to superficial examination of the situation, which could have suggested that it was the introduction of the PMIS that resulted in organizational capability improvement.

This case summary provides one example of how ANT has been used to delve deeper into PM. More generally, Linde and Linderoth (2006: 156) have argued that ANT '… can be applied to the analysis of a project process and can expand project management theory. This approach has some useful implications for practitioners'. ANT offers a way to extend PM research from a focus on the technical to the social aspects of PM (Leybourne, 2007: 69). However, this does not represent a rejection of the technical in favour of the social, but rather advocacy for an approach that integrates social and technical actors. ANT is not a methodology for hypothesis testing, or confirmation of predefined categorization systems. Instead, it provides an opportunity to empirically investigate the ways in which actors come together and stabilize networks of association to transform their worlds.

Activity Theory

Activity Theory (AT) was initiated by a group of revolutionary Russian psychologists in the 1920s and 1930s, and the theory is specifically credited to Lev Vygotsky, A. N. Leont'ev and A. R. Luria. The underpinning philosophy of this theory aimed to explain human consciousness and behavior. Verenikina and Gould (1998: 8) have noted that 'Vygotsky's life goal was to create a psychology adequate for the investigation of consciousness'.

AT is the study of what humans 'do'. The Russian word 'dyeyatelnost' which translates to 'activity' is a better representation of the term by referring to humans 'doing' or 'performing or operating both physically and mentally' (Hasan, 1998: 25). Further, Activity Theorists believe that what we do (an individual's activity) defines our consciousness and mediates the way we 'do' things. Within the theory, therefore, the analysis of human practice is done on the basis of 'doing' or activity.

Subject-Object and Activity

A 'Subject' is an individual or group of individuals involved in a common Activity. Whether the Activity is to be considered from an individual or group perspective is determined by the analyst or researcher.

The Subject undertakes some activity in order to achieve an 'Object' as shown in Figure 6.1. The arrow in Figure 6.1 represents the Activity, i.e. the element symbolizing work. The Activity is the point of interest in a research context as it is the 'black box' detailing how the work is done.

Figure 6.1. Subject, Object and Activity (from Kaptelinin & Nardi, 2006: 30)

In AT, reference to the object alludes to the desire (theoretical result) that the subject is trying to fulfil, or the underlying motive for the activity. The object is what drives an activity. The result of an activity is the Outcome. The outcome may differ from an object as often what one desires is not exactly what one gets.

The object is dynamic and can change or develop over the lifetime of an activity.

Creative and Innovative Contemporary Approaches

'It is possible that the object and motive themselves will undergo changes during the process of an activity' (Kuutti, 2001: 6). Therefore, in undertaking the activity, the anticipated object and the actual outcome may differ. An example used by Kaptelinin and Nardi (2006) describes how a house being built by a family may change over time and, when complete, may be substantially different to that initially envisaged.

One other consideration with relation to the object is that at any one time an individual may have more than one motive. The decision about which motive to act on is, according to Kaptelinin and Nardi (2006: 149) a function of the social context, and the conditions and means available to the individual.

Tools and Mediation

The way a worker will approach or carry out their work is mediated by their tools. According to AT, the development and use of existing tools must be viewed from a cultural-historic point of view, as such tools and associated processes were developed by earlier participating workers. The intimate knowledge that these workers possessed served to influence and shape existing tools and their use. The tools therefore have embodied knowledge that mediate work and offer signs to the subject, which assist in directing them towards a particular action.

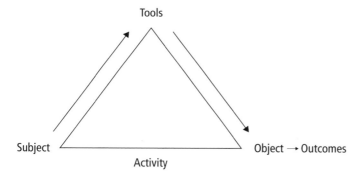

Figure 6.2. Basic Model of Activity

Tools can take various forms depending upon the context of the study; they may range from instruments, signs, procedures or machines, to language, methods, laws and forms of work organization (Hasan, 1998: 27).

Irrespective of whether a tool is physical or mental in nature, the key feature is that it provides signs (prompts or clues) that mediate the way an activity is undertaken by the subject.

Community of Practice and Divisions of Labor

Another influence that mediates an activity is the Community of Practice. The effect that the Community of Practice has upon an activity is applied through Rules to which the subject adheres. These rules are implicit and explicit governance, which direct the subject. Explicit rules are easily identified as documented codes of practice or standards that govern the requirements of workers. Implicit rules are the norms that the subject accepts as requirements (informal procedures as well as the social relationships between the subject and the community), often derived from other, more experienced workers. Kuutti (2001) noted that rules are often developed as a part of the general working culture or developed as the team works together.

A model proposed by Engström (1999a) incorporates the concept of the community and its influence. The model proposes three main elements in an activity, the subject, object and community, with a relationship that is mediated between each of these elements. The relationship between a subject and an object is mediated by tools; the subject and community are mediated by rules; and the community and object are mediated by divisions of labor.

The community has previously been described as the organization in which the subject operates (Barab et al., 2002; Engström, 2008), with the divisions of labor representing collaboration with other stakeholders (both internal and external), who collaborate in an outcome. Figure 6.3 shows Engström's model of activity.

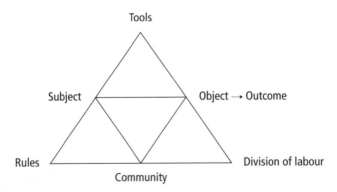

Figure 6.3. Engestrom's Model of Activity

The line of division between the subject, community of practice and division of labor is determined by the analyst or researcher. Engeström and Miettinen (1999) noted that the analyst constructs a holistic view of an activity by initially selecting a subject and then interpreting the system from that subject's point of view.

Creative and Innovative Contemporary Approaches

Applications in Research

AT has previously been applied in research in a variety of fields concerning human behavior. Examples of the areas of research include education, social studies, medical, organization studies and human computer interaction (HCI).

Although AT is essentially a theory of learning (Engeström, 2001) many researchers, such as Nardi (1998), Engeström (2000) and Bannon (1997), have previously applied it to their research, with Bannon noting that AT provides 'a general conceptual framework for understanding and analysing human activity' (Bannon, 1997). Further, Kuutti (2001) advocates AT as a potential framework for research in the area of HCI. 'Activity Theory is a philosophical and cross-disciplinary framework for studying different forms of human practices as developed processes, with both individual and social levels interlinked at the same time' (Kuutti, 2001: 5).

For example, Engeström (2008) used AT as an analytical tool to examine existing systems of work. In using AT, Engeström noted that it offered a framework that targeted the social aspects often overlooked in systems development.

To analyse a reasonably complete process of work, one typically needs to cover a lengthy chain of actions, a trajectory from the initial 'raw material' to the finished product (Strauss, Fagerhaugh, Suczek & Wiener, 1985). This is attempted by various methods of business process reengineering (Hammer & Champy, 1993). The weakness of such attempts is that they typically miss much of the 'invisible work' (Nardi & Engeström, 1998; Star, 1991) of small everyday contingencies, trouble, innovations and sideways interactions, often giving an idealistically streamlined picture of what is going on (Engeström, 1999b).

On the other hand, to capture in detail the rich texture of communicative events and interactions, one typically needs to focus on small chunks of the process and to look at them as if through a magnifying glass. A common weakness of these attempts is that they tend to focus on relatively arbitrary segments of work and communication, with no interest or ability to connect the analysis of local interactions to broader institutional, cultural and historic forces. A conceptual model of the activity system is particularly useful when one wants to make sense of systemic factors behind seemingly individual and accidental disturbances, deviations and innovations occurring in the daily practice of workplaces (Engeström, 2008: 23-7).

Researchers in the HCI field are concerned with the development of technology, and in particular in developing systems that the user wants. Knowledge workers make use of information systems to support their decision making. The information system is difficult to analyze, with many traditional researchers only accounting for 'formal work' in systems development (e.g. digitizing documents). 'Informal work' also needs to be accounted for in the analysis of work.

Davis (1991) noted that the use of an information system by an organization is aimed at providing an improved information system and therefore better performance on the job. If users reject the use of an innovation (such as mobile technology), however, then the performance impacts are lost along with the resources expended to introduce it. That is, a system that has the ability to deliver information to a user will be rendered useless if the user is unwilling to use it. It should be noted that a system that does not deliver useful or pertinent information is also unacceptable.

The information system of workers is not easily mapped. It was clear to one of the authors (Er) in the early stages of his research that a broader approach to analyzing the mobile workers' information system was required. As noted, researchers such as Gobbin (1998), Suchman (1995) and Engeström and Nardi (1999) have emphasized that traditional methods of systems analysis are limited, only taking into account 'visible work'.

Traditional tool analysis and design still use the systemic adaptive model where humans and computers are treated as objects quite divorced from the cultural environment. This paradigm does not take into account the social and cultural context in which humans use tools to achieve determined goals. It also does not take into account intentional motives behind the use of some information systems and the individual level of user cultural adaptation to particular software tool functionality (Gobbin, 1998: 116-17).

AT is a lens through which a researcher is able to interpret data that examines information systems, as it manages to encapsulate a broader view of work. Randall, Harper and Rouncefield (2007) note that:

> *activity theory moves us towards real-world contexts of use, a context that is social through and through (or cultural-historic) ... rather than the information-process models of humans and computers, an approach to the behaviour of both in a wider environment is required* (p. 91).

Example of AT Use
Based on the author Michael Er's doctoral research

It is well known that the methodology applied to a specific research project is dependent upon the research question. In my research (which applied AT) I examined the information system of Mobile Knowledge Workers (MKWs) and created a common framework that described this information system. In particular, I explored the sources of information and how this information was used by various MKWs. The research methodology selected for this research was interpretive case studies methodology (Avison & Myers, 2005).

The interpretive case study methodology, according to Walsham (2002: 104), uses theory as an 'initial guide to design and data collection; use of theory as part of an iterative process of data collection and analysis; and as a final product of the research'. AT provides a theoretical perspective through which the case studies will be examined.

Engeström (2008) undertook research that considered disturbances in the form of deviations from the planned course of events in the work process from the point of view of the production team (Producer, Director, Senior Audio Technician and others). To assist in the interpretation of this case study, Engeström used a conceptual

Creative and Innovative Contemporary Approaches

model of AT as a lens through which data was translated. Consistent with this model, I selected AT as a platform through which I investigated my case studies, assisting in the interpretation of the MKWs and their identification of, and interaction with, their information system.

The case study developed through the lens of AT encapsulates a model of the decision-making process as a component of the work activity of an MKW in the field, and the subject is the mobile worker operating away from a formal office situation as shown in Figure 6.4. The information system that the MKW interacts with is viewed as the tools, while the interaction with this information system is mediated by rules – the social norms and standards that are the influences exerted by the community of practice.

In utilising AT as an interpretive tool to provide a holistic view of the interaction by the MKWs with their information system, the role of Collaborators cannot be ignored (divisions of labor). Collaborators are considered as a potential source of information and mediating force on an activity.

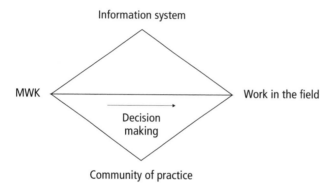

Figure 6.4. Activity Theory and the MKW

To allow for a broad view of this system, the model was created through studies of different MKWs, specifically, reporters in the field, doctors on ward rounds, and workers operating over different areas of a construction site or across a number of building sites.

The interpretive case study method is iterative in nature and requires at least two rounds of data collection, in which the theories that emerge from the first round are tested in the second. An example of this approach is that taken by Orlikowski (1996) where data collection was conducted in two phases.

Iteration in qualitative research is supported by Gorman and Clayton (2005) and allowed for refinement of my research through informed modification to the model being developed. Gorman and Clayton (2005) suggest a three-phase research process, which I followed. These are as follows:

The Initial Phase is 'Preliminary Preparation'

This stage, as described by Gorman and Clayton (2005), considers the focus and selection of a topic, literature review and formulation of the research question. These processes were undertaken prior to the start of my research.

The Second Phase is Described as 'Broad Explanation'

Typically, this phase includes such processes as conducting pilot case studies, and includes the search and selection of suitable subjects. The pilot case studies selected in my research consider the mobile knowledge work conducted by doctors examining patients on ward rounds and newspaper reporters as they develop and deliver stories from the field.

The Final Phase of this Iterative Research is the 'Focused Activity'

This phase of the research is an iteration of the previous phase once the research has been amended and refined, taking into account the findings of the pilot studies. In my research, this constitutes the main case study, which is the examination of construction site workers. Following the analysis of the pilot studies of doctors and reporters, a comparison of the identified themes was made against the evidence provided by the second case study, refining the mobile information system model (Pare & Elam, 1997).

Outcomes

Findings from the case studies were made salient with the application of AT as a lens of interpretation. AT was used as the original structure in which data was categorized and when themes appeared in the data that fell outside these areas, a contemporary model was developed and tested.

An example of a significant outcome produced by this research was the identification of 'hierarchy of consideration' in which the MKW would place information from one source over another.

The research found that information sources mediated the way the subjects of the different case studies approached an activity. This is consistent with the concepts of AT.

A theme that appeared was that information was provided to the MKW on a variety of levels, these being Data, Information and Knowledge sources. The difference between these is that on the lowest level, raw data (a data source) was provided that had to be interpreted by the MKWs. Information sources had an element of processing of data, making the information source more relevant to the work of the MKW. Knowledge sources supplied processed information, which was applied to the current context in which the MKW was operating.

The hierarchy placed information provided by a knowledge source over that which originated from an information or data source.

To illustrate the above hierarchy of information, consider a construction project. In some projects there could be hundreds of drawings supplied to the Contractor, which provide information illustrating the various elements of a build that would be considered a data source. A daily routine which is applied by a group of MKWs (foremen) is that they would access data sources such as drawings or emails and select information pertinent to the area of work in which they will be operating that day. This information is used by the Foreman, Sub-Contractors, Site Engineers and Consultants. I classified these artefacts as an information source as it had taken the original data source and applied an initial level of contextualization to it. Discussions at the point of work between the various participants further contextualized the information source to specific problems, and the application by individuals and the group can be considered a knowledge source.

Another finding of significance was that the rules identified are applied in the decision-making process of the MKW; however; the application of a particular rule is dependent upon the environmental context. The MKW would take into account both physical and social environments as criteria. The selection of the appropriate rule would be applied to the way an activity was undertaken.

Action Research

The social psychologist Kurt Lewin (1946: 34) is often cited as the originator of the term *action research* (AR) for 'research that will help the practitioner' (p. 34) to generate knowledge 'about a social system while, at the same time, attempting to change it' (Eden & Chisholm, 1993: 121). Lewin described AR as social research proceeding 'in a spiral of steps, each of which is composed of planning, action and fact-finding about the result of the action' (Lewin, 1946 in Kemmis & McTaggart, 1984: 41).

Reason and Bradbury (2008, p. 4) define AR as:

> *… a participatory, democratic process concerned with developing practical knowing in the pursuit of worthwhile human purposes, grounded in a participatory worldview which we believe is emerging at this historical moment. It seeks to bring together action and reflection, theory and practice, in participation with others, in the pursuit of practical solutions of pressing concern to people and more generally the flourishing of individual persons and their communities.*

Greenwood and Levin (2006: 3) add that AR leads to a 'more just and sustainable or satisfying situation for the stakeholders'. A more practical definition of AR by Dick (2002: 1) states:

> *Action research is a flexible spiral process which allows action (change, improvement) and research (understanding, knowledge) to be achieved at the same time. The understanding allows more informed change and at the same time is informed by that change. People affected by the change are usually involved in the action research. This allows the understanding to be widely shared and the change to be pursued with commitment.*

Figure 6.5 shows this simple representation of action research as a dialectical process.

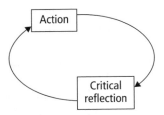

Figure 6.5. Action Research Cycle (Dick, 2001: 21)

Brief History

Although Kurt Lewin is often considered as the social scientist who coined the term 'action research', some scholars have stated that AR began much earlier. McTaggart (1992) points out that a physician named Jacob Moreno used group participation in the early 1900s several years before Lewin's work. Lewin's work in group dynamics had an influence in the setting up of the Tavistock Institute for Social Research in London by Eric Trist and his co-researchers (http://www.tavinstitute.org/about/our_history.php.).

The Tavistock movement, which started in the United Kingdom to improve coal-mining practices, was adopted in Scandinavia to start the Norwegian Industrial Democracy Project to improve working conditions in factories. A prominent example was its introduction at the Volvo factories in Sweden (Lindholm & Norstedt, 1975), moving away from the mass production systems set up in Ford following the principles of Taylorsitic thinking. The socio-technical movement spread to other parts of the world to study the social effects of introducing new technology in the form of automation to help people affected by the change (Trist, 1981). AR also has its roots in the scientific educational movement as reported by Masters (1995 quoting Mckernan, 1991). AR has a strong presence in educational research and is often used by teachers and school administrators in curriculum development and to improve their own practice (Stenhouse, 1975; McKernan, 1991; Ross-Fisher, 2008). Another variety of AR, focusing on empowerment of the poor and oppressed (Selener, 1998) and called Participatory Action Research (PAR), evolved from the development work carried out by sociologists and anthropologists such as Orlando Fals-Borda who sought to redress injustices found in Latin American societies through his research (Fals-Borda, 1987). AR still plays a strong role in community development (http://cdp-ny.org/what-we-do/participatory-action-research-and-policy/). AR has also had a long history in organization development. One prominent example is the introduction of T-Group training (Drye, 1964) set up by Lewin and his associates (http://www.infed.org/thinkers/et-lewin.htm) that resulted in the establishment of the National Training Laboratories Institute (http://www.ntl.org/inner.asp?id=178&category=2).

Creative and Innovative Contemporary Approaches

Another important application of AR is in managing organizational change effectively (Sankaran et al., 2001; Mirvis et al., 2003). Although scepticism was initially expressed by management scholars such as Eden and Huxham (1996) about the value of AR in management studies, it has since gained prominence and now finds a place in several research books written for business and management researchers (Easterby-Smith, 2012; Slater et al., 2011). Bradbury et al. (2008: 77) trace the progress of AR from Lewin's work through 'socio-technical work design, organization development programs and appreciative inquiry, to its latest applications to sustainability and redefining the role of business and society'.

AR in PM

AR could be useful in investigating PM where there is a need to seek a better understanding of processes in projects that have social implications; in working collaboratively to find practical solutions to problems arising in a project and in situations where there is a need to implement major changes in a project with the stakeholders.

Variety in AR

AR is not a specific method but refers to a family of research approaches that developed over time and have some core principles in common. AR is action-oriented, participatory and often carried out with people who are keen to solve a problem or issue affecting them. People participating in AR are often called 'co-researchers' as opposed to 'informants' in traditional research. As AR was applied across a number of fields (sociology, education, anthropology, healthcare and management) several varieties of AR developed (Reason & Bradbury, 2008; Chandler & Torbert, 2003). AR is often used with other approaches that have similar aims but one of the authors of this chapter (Sankaran) has found that combining AR with action learning and action science could be useful in carrying out management research.

AR Classifications

While AR is often participatory, it could also be used to reflect on one's own practice. Reason and Bradbury [2008, p. 6] discuss three modes of AR — first person, second person and third person:

First-person research/practice skills and methods address the ability of the researcher to foster an inquiring approach to his or her own life, to act choicefully and with awareness, and to assess effects in the outside world while acting.

Second person action research/practice addresses our ability to inquire face-to-face with others into issues of mutual concern – for example in the service of improving our personal and professional practice both individually and separately ...

... third person strategies aim to create a wider community of inquiry involving persons who, because they cannot be known to each other face-to-face (say, in a large, geographically dispersed corporation), have an impersonal quality.

The most common use of AR in a PM situation is second-person AR where a group of researchers address a problem of mutual concern. The authors expect that first-person action research will also blossom as PM researchers are trying to understand and reflect on their own practice (Paton et al., 2010). Third-person AR would be more useful to create generalizable knowledge when a larger community of researchers join together to carry extensive research despite not being collocated (see Chapter 9 of this book by Monique Aubry).

Another classification of AR useful to consider for conducting research in PM is: technical-scientific and positivist; mutual-collaborative and interpretivist and critical and emancipatory (Koshy et al., 2011). Kemmis and McTaggart (2003) relate this original classification of AR as technical, practical and emancipatory (Carr & Kemmis, 1986) to the study a practice. 'In technical reasoning about practice, the researcher adopts an objectifying stance towards others involved in the practice setting' (p. 364). Technical AR could be used when a PM researcher acts as an external researcher intervening in a problem situation to act as a 'consultant or expert' to investigate the problem but still using the general characteristics of AR. 'In practical reasoning about practice, the researcher adopts a more 'subjective' stance to the practice setting, treating the practitioners and others involved as members of the shared-life world' (p. 365). This would suit a PM researcher acting as an 'insider action researcher' (Coghlan & Brannick, 2005), striving to establish change from within. This is similar to the notion of second-person research discussed earlier. 'In critical reasoning about practice, the researcher adopts a more dialectical stance with respect to the "objective" and "subjective" and the individual and social aspects of the setting' (p. 365). Koshy (et al. 2011: 29) adds that in this mode the research can be an 'explicit vehicle for political and critical expression'. This mode of AR would suit research aimed at changing policies or professional practices within organizations, or even influencing the PM practice in general.

Action Learning

Reg Revans (1982) developed the concept of action learning in England after World War II to find new ways to develop managers to solve their everyday problems. McGill and Brockbank (2004) define action learning as a:

... continuous process of learning and reflection that happens with the support of a group or 'set' of colleagues, working on real issues, with the intention of getting things done. The voluntary participants in the group or 'set' learn with and from each other and take forward an important issue with the support of the other members of the set (p.11).

Action learning emphasizes *learning by doing* and *learning as a collaborative and social process.*

Action Science

Action science grew out of the work of Argyris and Schön (1974) and is based on the idea that 'people can improve their interpersonal organizational effectiveness by exploring the hidden beliefs that drive their actions' (Raelin, 1997: 21). Friedman and Rogers (2008: 253) clarify this further by stating that it is 'a form of social practice which integrates both the production and use of knowledge for the purpose of promoting learning with and among individuals and systems whose work is characterized by uniqueness, uncertainty and instability'.

Action Research, Action Learning and Action Science

Brooks and Watkins (1994: 11-12) combine action research, action learning and action science under the umbrella of 'action technologies' and explain their similarities under four dimensions:

1. They create new knowledge that is action based.
2. The members who work in the context of the research are central to the research process.
3. The data from the research come from the experience of the participants.
4. The focus is on action to improve professional practice.

Raelin and Coghlan (2006) describe action learning as an 'educative process helping managers to learn through primarily second-person experience (i.e., inquiring and working with others on issues of mutual concern)' while action research 'aims at contributing to dialectical knowledge, especially using second and third person (i.e., takes a broader picture to enable extrapolation and dissemination to an impersonal audience' (p. 685). Although not specifically mentioned by Raelin and Coghlan (2006), action science, with its emphasis on increasing the awareness of learners to the assumptions behind their actions, seems to focus on first-person skills of learners (i.e., reflecting on their own values and assumptions). Table 6.1 summarizes some key characteristics of action research, action learning and action science that helps to differentiate them despite their similarities in approach.

While action research, action learning, and action science have been promoted as useful in managing change, they also carry some risks (Raelin, 1999). An action science intervention can often give rise to defensive behavior as participants' innermost feelings are exposed through the psychological aspects of the intervention. In action learning, although participants may learn from the project, the project itself may fail and managers are often concerned that failure may be looked upon as incompetence. Action research in organizations often requires the insider researcher to have some influence over the situation that is undergoing change, posing ethical and moral dilem-

Table 6.1. Comparing Action Research, Action Learning, and Action Science (Based on Brooks & Watkins, 1994: 104-105; Raelin, 1999: 120-121; Raelin & Coghlan, 2006: 682)

Characteristic	Action Research	Action Learning	Action Science
Philosophical basis	Gestalt psychology, pragmatism, democracy.	Learning from experience, action research, and other eclectic views.	Lewinian action research, Dewey's theory of inquiry.
Purpose	Organizational and social change through involvement and improvement.	Understanding and changing of self and/or system through action and reflection on action, management development.	Change in reasoning and behavior leading to increased competence, justice, and capacity for learning and human development, individual and organizational change.
Epistemology	Knowing through doing and applying discoveries.	Problem solving and also problem framing.	Reflecting-in-action, making explicit tacit theories-in-use.
Methodology	Interactive cycles of problem defining, data collection, taking action or implementing a solution, followed by further testing.	Cycles of framing, action, reflection, concluding, and reframing.	Reflection on there-and-then and here-and-now reasoning, with an emphasis on online interactions.

mas of the use of power and influence in a situation that is expected to be democratic and empowering (Coghlan & Brannick, 2005).

When to Use AR

Some reasons why action research could be attractive to PM researchers are (Sankaran et al., 2005):

1. It can facilitate the integration of thought and action to improve practice.
2. Help PM researchers in self-development by critically examining their own beliefs and practices.
3. It could be used to investigate how changes occurring during projects can be implemented effectively.
4. It allows the use a variety of data collection methods that is often present in a project management environment.
5. It could provide strategies for getting critical input from stakeholders with different perspectives.

Creative and Innovative Contemporary Approaches

Example of AR Use
Based on the author Sankaran's doctoral research

My AR investigation took place in a large engineering centre of a Japanese multinational company in Singapore, which wanted to reduce its cost of operations significantly for it to stay profitable (in fact, survive) while at the same time not sacrificing the quality of its products and services. I was appointed as the head of this new centre and felt that an innovative approach to achieve the challenging goals set by the management was required. I also had to involve young managers who were reporting to me. They had been recruited and trained by the principal of the organization in Japan after a large-scale recruitment of fresh engineering graduates to carry out engineering in Singapore a few years earlier. At this time I had also enrolled in a PhD program and wanted to use what I was doing at work to contribute to my research.

With my background in engineering and predominantly technical work I was used to rational ways of solving problems using predominantly positivistic approaches. Therefore AR was a new challenge for me when the university at which I was doing my doctoral research promoted it as a methodology to be used by practising managers. After studying about AR approaches I found the concept of action learning appealing. The Planning-Doing-Reflecting-Consolidating learning cycle used in action learning (Weinstein, 2002: 11) was similar to the cyclic nature of AR. I also realized that the Plan-Do-Check-Act (PDCA), or Deming cycle, (Deming 2000: 8), used in my company for *kaizen* (continuous improvement) resonated with the principles of action learning and AR. Moreover, it used the formula $L = P + Q$ which appealed to my scientific mind. L stands for learning, P for programmed instruction (or knowledge gained through books, courses or seminars) and Q for questioning insight. Revans considered 'questioning' by peers to be more important than P.

As part of the organizational change to achieve the goals set by our management, we decided to trial 'outsourcing' as a strategy to reduce our costs drastically. This necessitated a change in the way we performed out work. The work model we were using had to be modified to suit our outsourcing strategy. Thus changing our work model became the focus of my study as it was likely to yield both management and research outcomes. I then recruited six young managers from my operation who became interested in working with me as an 'action learning set' to help changing our work model. The development of these managers through addressing a common concern at work became the 'thematic concern' for my doctoral research.

At the start we had a very fuzzy idea about how we could achieve our goals. The problem also needed our immediate attention. We were not sure what results our actions would have, but we felt it was good to adopt the PDCA cycle used by quality control circles in Japanese companies to gain political support with the Japanese management. While this model seemed adequate for ensuring continuous improvement in the organization, it lacked the 'reflection' component that would support innovative approaches.

Most of the training in the company focused on the technical aspects of our work. Non-technical training was limited to skills training by sending staff to external workshops. The organization also used on-the-job training, but this was related to specific tasks and was not broad enough. Workplace collaboration was limited to quality control circles, which were heavily influenced by the manufacturing division and did not appeal to the sales or engineering divisions. This gave me an opportunity to investigate new ways to promote management learning at my workplace.

Why AR?

There were two reasons why I chose AR as my research methodology.

First, the phenomenon I was studying did not seem to fit traditional research methods as I was studying my managers in their natural setting. Second, I was interested in doing something that I had not done before both for personal knowledge as well as for professional development.

The constraints that I faced were:

1. I had to use a small sample of engineering managers within my operation for the study.
2. It was difficult to isolate the sample in a controlled setting, as we could not afford to take the managers away from their work environment due to the immediacy of the task at hand.
3. I had to actively participate in the processes and could not be isolated from the managers while the research was being conducted as it was carried out alongside our normal work.

AR Model

Initially I started with an AR model suggested by Perry and Zuber-Skerritt (1992), which recommended setting up multiple AR projects that informed each other. The plan was to use a 'thesis AR' project to complete my doctoral study informed by the 'core AR projects' that I would set up 'real' projects to introduce change in my organization. However I modified this model to suit my particular circumstances.

My modified AR model, including the interaction between my research set and the two external sets, is shown in Figure 6.6.

The 'individual cycle' was my doctoral research. The 'participatory cycle' was with my managers or co-researchers. The 'external cycle' was the discussion I had with my peers during the process. This included three other PhD students supervised by my supervisors in Singapore as well as members of a 'learning set' I formed while doing an online AR course. They became my 'critical friends' to bounce off ideas to improve my research my findings.

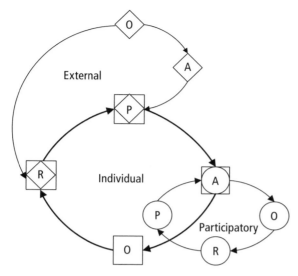

Figure 6.6. Final Action Research Model (Sankaran, 1999: 95)
(Note: P = Plan, A = Act, O = Observe, R = Reflect)

The planning phase of the individual cycle drove the action phase of the participatory cycle. The reflection phase of the individual cycle was carried out with members of the PhD set and Elogue (a learning set formed with Australian action researchers whom I came to know through my supervisor Bob Dick). This led to changes in the planning phase of the individual cycle that then acted on the action phase of the participatory cycle.

Sample

I used a purposeful or criterion-based sampling for this study. I was introducing Western methods in a Japanese company. So when I started my AR and set up a learning set, I used managers who had either completed or were in the process of completing MBA programs offered through Western universities. I needed these managers to initiate and reduce resistance to the program. As the research progressed, we added three more managers to the set who had not enrolled in MBA programs but were core members of the new work model implementation committee. In the end, the learning set was evenly balanced between these two categories of managers.

Data Collection

I collected data in various ways including minutes of discussions recorded during the AR meetings, personal reflective memos written up in a journal, secondary data from the organization, communication with members of my external cycle, feedback from my co-researchers and interview data collected from a focus group meeting conducted with my co-researchers by a third party.

All the data collected was systematically coded under specific headings using techniques applied to build grounded theory.

Data Analysis

For quite some time I was puzzled about how to analyze my data. I did not have a large amount of data and I had worked mainly with one group of managers in my organization on a single core AR project. While thinking about this dilemma I came across a book titled *Doing Exemplary Research* (Frost & Stablein, 1992).

In this book, Professor Richard Hackman (1992: 5) commenting on the exemplary research conducted by his doctoral student Connie Gersick, states that:

> ... *one lesson we learn from this research is about the value of staying very close to the phenomenon one is studying, rather than do scholarly work at arm's length ... the research question should drive the methodology... Connie invented a unique research methodology specifically tailored to her particular research question.*

I decided that I would analyze my data in different ways to make sense of them. Therefore, I used multiple methods of analysis, but in each instance I carried out the analysis to a sufficient depth to bring to the surface the answers relevant to my research questions. Thus, like Gersick, I stayed close to my phenomenon and designed a data analysis process tailored to answer my particular research questions.

My idea was to analyze the data from a 'helicopter view' and delve deeper and deeper to uncover more findings through iterations. Each of the iterations drove the next, like the AR spiral itself.

Initially, I divided my AR project into three major cycles. However, when I analyzed my data using an event listing, I found that I could separate it into five distinct cycles. I then carried out my data analysis using five cycles. Next, I coded the minutes of the AR group meetings, and wrote theoretical notes and reflective memos on the key variables of my study. I followed this up with an 'event listing' (Miles & Huberman, 1994) to study the effects of external events on my research. I then prepared a 'role-ordered matrix' (Miles & Huberman, 1994) to study the background of each researcher – where they were in the organization when the study started and where they moved to at the end of the study – to trace their growth in the organization. The matrix also summarized their learning from the research, which was obtained through their feedback one year after the research was conducted. I then carried out a comparison between what I found with similar cases reported in the literature, to confirm/disconfirm my findings. This helped strengthen my findings by triangulating it with the literature.

Figure 6.7 shows the different levels of data analysis that I carried out.

Creative and Innovative Contemporary Approaches

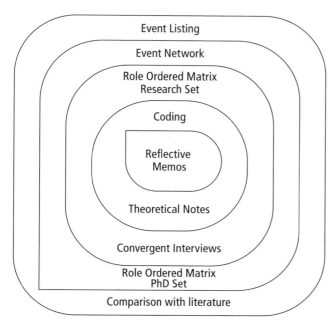

Figure 6.7. Data Analysis Levels (Sankaran, 1999: 101)

Outcomes

The study contributed to both management and research outcomes. The organization expected management outcomes and the university wanted to see research outcomes. The direct management outcome of the research was the effective establishment of the new work model in the organization. The direct research outcome of this study was the establishment of a management learning model at the workplace. All the managers of the PhD set often had difficulty in differentiating between management and research outcomes as we were focused on the former. But our supervisor helped us differentiate between them and to realize that the management outcomes came out of our actions and research outcomes from our reflections.

I also learnt the value of 'surprise' as a trigger for management learning, which matches Schön's (1983: 68) concept about learning from surprises when reflecting-in-action and Foote-Whyte et al.'s (1991, p. 97) notion of learning from 'creative surprises' in participatory AR.

My research has also personally transformed me as a manager, an observation that was echoed by the other members of the PhD set. From being someone who used to be direct in his approach to managing people, I became a more reflective practitioner.

Issues to Consider while using Action Research

While AR sounds like an attractive method, some issues need to be taken into account as there is a general concern about AR producing credible outcomes. One needs to pay particular attention in conducting AR. Action researchers tend to use techniques to establish the validity in qualitative research (Guba & Lincoln, 1985) – credibility; transferability; dependability and conformability. Other scholars such as Dick (1999) recommend a process of confirmation and disconfirmation to increase rigour. McTaggart (1997: 13) suggests establishing credibility among participants and informants, testing the coherence of arguments being presented in a 'critical community' or a community of 'critical friends' as techniques to be adopted when the research is participatory. Another issue often pointed out is the lack of generalizability from AR as it often addresses a local issue in its context.

Parkin (2009) also points out some limitations often ascribed to AR: it lacks precision; is time consuming and could face organizational and social constraints as it is often used to implement change and ethical issues that need to be carefully managed. While action researchers are advised to follow ethical guidelines used in other forms of research there are some specific issues that need to be considered. As AR is contextualized in a local problem, and usually conducted with a small group of co-researchers, it is often difficult to keep the identity of the participants confidential. Also, during an AR intervention, methods used could be changed to respond to the situation and this could cause difficulties in securing additional ethics approvals.

Often AR dissertations or theses do not follow the conventional style or form (Fisher & Phelps, 2006) and this means extra effort on the part of the researcher to adopt a suitable style that makes it easy for readers to follow. Brydon-Miller (2008) suggests that action researchers should keep social justice and democratic practices in mind to conduct ethical AR. She (p. 209) suggests:

> … our common goal is to find ways to insure that the key ethical principles of respect for persons, beneficence, and justice, as embodied in the shared values of action research – participation in democratic processes, the improvement of human life, and engagement in morally committed action – remain at the core of our practice.

Action researchers need to pay particular attention to issues of validity and ethics to produce good quality research as well as deflect any criticism about their research. These issues need to be clearly discussed in the reports or dissertations with a clear explanation on how they have been addressed.

Discussion

We have discussed three strategies for conducting research using approaches that are useful to investigate and/or improve PM practice. While the three strategies have their beginnings in different fields and locations there are some relationships between them. They can also be used together. Miettinen (1999) points out that 'the concept of nature and society production in the ANT and the concept of activity in AT have much in common as attempts to transcend the dualism between the subject and object, nature and society' (p. 170). Lewis (2007) reports a more proactive use of an AR project in a bank when he and his co-researchers used ANT to investigate the sociological phenomenon surrounding the use of information systems. His research found a way to provide a practical role to ANT in the research. He argues that while their use of ANT may not be appreciated by an ANT purist:

> *In action research, they [ANT concepts] can provide a lens through which to review the research setting and a language for discussing the turbulent events in which the research is located. We can then go beyond the management of budgets and time-scheduling that is conventionally labelled as project management; choosing to not ignore, but find ways to deal with the awkward realities and politics of real-world settings, which would facilitate the desired greater use of action research* (p. 596).

Kajaama (2012) reports on how enriching AR with AT and narrative research helped in the transformation of a Finnish public sector hospital (2012). Thus there is some evidence from the literature that ANT, AT and AR can be used to complement each other.

Conclusions

The research approaches described in this chapter could help in conducting PM research in innovative ways to increase the understanding of projects-in-practice, by 'researching the actuality of projects' (Cicimil et al., 2006). It is also in line with practice-based studies being reported recently in the PM literature (Blomquist et al., 2010) and in the special issue of the *International Journal of Managing Projects in Practice* recently (Hällgen & Lindahl, 2012).

ANT can help in considering both people and material aspects in PM research and in understanding the political and cultural issues that often arise in projects. The tendency in ANT to avoid predefinition can help to ensure that research findings more accurately mirror the experience of practitioners than external classifications researchers may wish to verify. Applying AT by focusing on activities could help in gaining an understanding of projects and reconceptualizing them from a practice viewpoint. The link between AR and transformational research is a simple one, as AR contributes to this aim in several ways, by: investigating one's own practice (first person); using the collective wisdom of participants in the research (second person); and providing a means for conducting research across virtual project teams and also initiating changes at the policy level (third person). All three approaches, whether used on their own or in combination have the potential to transform PM research in its desire to link theory and practice. Both AT and AR would require long-term commitment from the people and organizations participating in the research, which could be problematic. On the flip side they could also produce outcomes that could also have long-term benefits due to the joint ownership of the issues investigated collaboratively.

References

Argyris, C. & Schön, D.A. (1974). *Theory in practice: Increasing professional effectiveness*, San Francisco, CA: Jossey Bass.

Aubry, M. (2011). The social reality of organisational project management at the interface between networks and hierarchy, *International Journal of Managing Projects in Business*, 4, 3: 436-57.

Aubry, M., Hobbs, B., & Thuillier, D. (2007). A new framework for understanding organisational project management through the PMO. *International Journal of Project Management*, 25: 328-36.

Avison, D. & Myers, M. (2005). Qualitative research, in D. Avison, & J. Pries-Heje, (Eds) *Research in information systems: a handbook for research supervisors and their students.* Oxford: Elsevier Butterworth-Heinemann.

Bannon, L. (1997). *Activity Theory*, University of Limerick, accessed 12/5/2006, http://www.irit.fr/ACTIVITES/GRIC/cotcos/pjs/TheoreticalApproaches/Actvity/ActivitypaperBannon.htm

Barab, S., Barnett, M., Yamagata-Lynch, L., Squire, K. & Keating, T. (2002). Using activity theory to understand systemic tensions characterizing a technology-rich introductory astronomy course. *Mind, Culture and Activity*, 9, 2: 76-107

Blackburn, S. (2002). The project manager and the project-network, *International Journal of Project Management*, 20, 3: 199-204.

Blomquist, T., Hällgren, M., Nilsson, A., & Söderholm, A. (2010). Project-as-practice: In search of project management research that matters. *Project Management Journal*, 41, 1: 5-16.

Bradbury, H., Mirvis, P., Neilse, E. & Pasmore, W. 2008. Action research at work: Creating the future following the path from Lewin, in P. Reason & H. Bradbury (Eds) *The SAGE handbook of action research*, 2nd Edn., London: Sage: 77-92.

Bradbury, H., Mirvis, P., Neilse, E. & Pasmore, W. (2008). Action research at work: Creating the future following the path from Lewin, in P. Reason & H. Bradbury (Eds) *The SAGE handbook of action research*, 2nd Edn., London: Sage: 77-92.

Creative and Innovative Contemporary Approaches

Brooks, A. & Watkins, R. (1994). (Eds) *The emerging power of action inquiry technologies*, New directions n adult and continuing education series, San Francisco: Jossey-Bass.

Brydon-Miller, M. (2008). Ethics and action research: Deepening our commitment to principles of social justice and redefining systems of democratic practice, in P. Reason & H. Bradbury (Eds), The SAGE *Handbook of action research*, 2nd edn. London: SAGE Publications: 199-210.

Callon, M. (1986). Some elements of a sociology of translation: domestication of the scallops and the fisherman of St Brieuc Bay. In J. Law (Ed.), *Power, action, and belief: a new sociology of knowledge*, London: Routledge & Kegan Paul: 196-233.

Callon, M. (1998). An essay on framing and overflowing: economic externalities revisited by sociology. In M. Callon (Ed.), *The laws of the markets*, Oxford: Blackwell Publishers, 244-69.

Callon, M., & Latour, B. (1981). Unscrewing the big Leviathan: how actors macro-structure reality and how sociologists help them to do so. In K. Knorr-Cetina & V. Cicourel (Eds), *Advances in social theory and methodology: towards an integration of micro- and macro-sociologies*, Boston: Routledge & Kegan Paul: 277-303.

Carr, W. & Kemmis, S. (1986). *Becoming Critical: education, knowledge and action research*. Lewes, Falmer.

Chandler, D. & Torbert, W., 2003. Transforming inquiry and action: Interweaving 27 flavors of action research, *Action Research*, 1, 2: 133-152.

Cho, S., Mathiassen, L., & Nilsson, A. (2008). Contextual dynamics during health information systems implementation: an event-based actor-network approach. *European Journal of Information Systems*, 17: 614-30.

Cicmil, S., Williams, T., Thomas, J. and Hodgson, D. (2006). Rethinking project management: Researching the actuality of projects, *International Journal of Project Management*, 24: 675-86.

Coghlan, D. & Brannick, T. (2005). *Doing action research in your own organization*, London: Sage.

Czarniawska, B. & Hernes, T. (Eds), 2005. *Actor-network theory and organizing*, Malmo: Sweden, Liber and Copenhagen Business School Press.

Davis, F. (1991). User acceptance of information technology: systems characteristics, user perceptions and behavioral impacts. *International Journal of Man-Machine Studies*, 38: 475-87.

Deming, W.E. (2000). *Out of the crisis*, Boston: MIT Press.

Dick, B. (1999). *Rigour without numbers: The potential of dialectical processes and qualitative research tools*, 3rd Edn. Brisbane, Australia: Interchange.

Dick, B. (2001). Action research: Action *and* research, in S. Sankaran, B. Dick, R. Passfield and P. Swepson, *Effective change management using action learning and action research:*

Concepts, frameworks, processes and applications, Lismore, Australia: Southern Cross University Press.

Dick, B. (2002) *Action research: action and research* [On line]. Available at http://www.uq.net.au/action_research/arp/aandr.html

Doolin, B. & Lowe, A. (2002). To reveal is to critique: actor-network theory and critical information systems research. *Journal of Information Technology,* 17: 69-78.

Drye, R.C. (1964). T-Group theory and laboratory method, *Archives of General Psychiatry,* 11, 4, 452-3.

Easterby-Smith, M. & Thorpe, R. (2012). *Management research,* London: Sage.

Easterby-Smith, M., Thorpe, R. & Jackson, P. (2012). *Management Research,* 4th edn., London: Sage.

Eden, M. & Chisholm, R.F. (1993). Emerging varieties of action research: Introduction to the special issue, *Human Relations* 46, 121-142

Eden, C. & Huxham, C. (1996). Action research for management research, *British Journal of Management,* 7: 75-86.

Engeström, Y. (1999a). Innovative learning in work teams: Analysing cycles of knowledge creation in practice in Y. Engeström, R. Miettinen and R-L. Punamäki (eds),*Perspectives on Activity Theory.* Cambridge: CambridgeUniversity Press: 377-406.

Engeström, Y. (1999b). Activity theory and individual and social transformation, in Y Engeström, R.Miettinen & R.L. Punamaki, (Eds) *Perspectives on Activity Theory,* Cambridge: Cambridge University Press: 19-38.

Engeström, Y. (2000). Activity Theory as a framework for analyzing and re-designing work. *Ergonomics,* 43: 960-74.

Engeström, Y. (2001). Expansive learning at work: towards an Activity Theory reconceptualization. *Journal of Education and Work,* 14: 133-56.

Engeström M, Y. (2008). *From teams to knots,* Cambridge: Cambridge University Press.

Engeström M. & Miettinen, R. (1999). Activity Theory: a well kept secret, in Y. Engeström, R. Miettinen & R.L. Punamaki, (Eds) *Perspectives on Activity Theory.* Cambridge: Cambridge University Press: 1-15.

Engeström, Y. & Nardi, B., 1999. A web on the wind: the structure of invisible work. *Computer Supported Cooperative Work,* 8: 1-8.

Er, M. & Lawrence, E.M. (2011). Using activity theory to examine information systems for supporting mobile work, *eFuture: Creating Solutions for the Individual, Organisations and Society,* 24th Bled eConference, Slovenia: 517-29.

Fals-Borda, O. (1987). The application of participatory action research in Latin America, *International Sociology,* 2, 4: 329-47.

Fisher, K. & Phelps, R. (2006). Recipe or performing art? Challenging conventions for writing action research theses, *Action Research,* 4, 2: 143-64.

Foote-Whyte, W., Greenwood, D.J. & Lazes, P. (1991). Participatory action research: Through practice to science in social research in Foote-Whyte. W. (ed.) *Participatory action research*, Newbury Park, Sage: 19-55.

Fox, S. (2002). Communities of practice, Foucault and actor-network theory, *Journal of Management Studies*, 37, 6: 853-68.

Friedman, V.J. & Rogers, T. (2008). Action science: Linking causal theory and meaning making in action research, in P. Reason & H. Bradbury (Eds) *The SAGE handbook of action research*, 2nd Edn., London: Sage: 252-65.

Frost, P. and Stablein, R. (Eds). (1992). *Doing exemplary research*, Newbury Park: Sage.

Gobbin, R., 1998. Adoption or rejection: information systems and their cultural fitness, in H. Hasan, E. Gould & P. Hyland (Eds). *Information systems and Activity Theory: tools in context*. Wollongong: University of Wollongong Press: 109-124.

Gorman, G., & Clayton, P. (2005). *Qualitative research for the information professional*, 2nd edn., London: Facet Printing.

Greenhalgh, T., & Stones, R. (2010). Theorising big IT programmes in healthcare: Strong structuration theory meets actor-network theory. *Social Science & Medicine, 70*: 1285-1294.

Greenwood, D.J., & Levin, M. (2006). *Introduction to action research: Social research for social change*, 2nd edn.,Thousand Oaks, CA: Sage.

Guba, E.G. & Lincoln, Y.S. (1985). *Naturalistic inquiry*, Thousand Oaks, CA: Sage.

Hackman, J.R. (1992). Time and transitions in B. Frost, & P. Stabelin, P. (Eds), *Doing exemplary research*, Newbury Park: Sage, 73-8.

Hälgren, M. & Lindhal, M. (2012). How do you do? On situating old project sites through practice-based studies, *International Journal of Managing Projects in Business*, 5, 3: 335-44.

Hammer, M. and Champy, J.A., 1993. *Reengineering the corporation: A manifesto for business revolution*, New York, Harper Business Books.

Hanseth, O., Aanestad, M., & Berg, M. (2004). Actor-network theory and information systems. What's so special? *Information Technology & People*, 17, 2: 116-23.

Harty, C. (2008). Implementing innovation in construction: contexts, relative boundedness and actor-network theory. *Construction Management and Economics, 26*: 1029-1041.

Harty, C. (2010). Implementing innovation: designers, users and actor-networks. *Technology Analysis & Strategic Management, 22*, 3: 297-315.

Hasan, H. (1998). Activity Theory: A basis for the contextual study of information systems in organizations, in H. Hasan, E. Gould, & P. Hyland, P. (Eds) *Information systems and activity theory*. Wollongong, *University* of Wollongong Press: 19-38.

Heeks, R., & Stanforth, C. (2007). Understanding e-Government project trajectories from an actor-network perspective. *European Journal of Information Systems*, 16: 165-77.

Kajamaa, A. (2012). Enriching action research with the narrative approach and activity theory: Analyzing the consequences of an intervention in a public sector hospital in Finland, *Educational Action Research*, 20, 1: 75-93.

Kaptelinin, V. (2003). UMEA: Translating interaction histories into project contexts, *CHI 2003*: 353-60.

Kaptelinin, V. & Nardi, B., 2006. *Acting with technology: activity theory and interaction design, Cambridge, MA:* MIT Press.

Kemmis, S. & McTaggart, R. (1984). The action research reader, 3rd edn., Geelong, Australia, Deakin University Press.

Kemmis, S. & McTaggart, R. (2003). Participatory action research, in N. K. Denzin & Y.S. Lincoln (Eds) *Strategies for qualitative inquiry*, 2nd Edn., Thousand Oaks, CA: Sage: 336-96.

Koshy, E., Koshy, V. & Waterman, H. (2011). *Action research in healthcare*, London. Sage.

Kuutti, K. (2001). Activity Theory as a potential framework for human-computer interaction research, in B. Nardi (ed.) *Context and consciousness: Activity theory and human-computer interaction*, Cambridge, MA*:* MIT Press: 9-22.

Latour, B. (1999). On recalling ANT. In J. Law & J. Hassard (Eds), *Actor Network Theory and after*, Oxford: Blackwell Publishing: 15-25.

Latour, B. (2005). *Reassembling the Social.* Oxford: Oxford University Press.

Law, J. (1986). On the methods of long-distance control: vessels, navigation and the Portuguese route to India. In J. Law (Ed.), *Power, action, and belief: a new sociology of knowledge.* London: Routledge & Kegan Paul: 234-63.

Law, J. (1992). Notes on the Theory of the Actor-Network: Ordering, Strategy and Hetrogeneity. *Systems Practice*, 5: 379-93.

Law, J., & Hassard, J. (1999). *Actor Network Theory and after.* Oxford: Blackwell Publishing.

Lewin, K. (1946). Action research and minority problems, *Journal of Social Issues*, 2, 4: 34-46.

Lewis, P. (2007). Using ANT ideas in managing of systemic action research, Systems Research and Behavioral Science, 24: 589-98.

Leybourne, S. (2007). The changing bias of project management research: A consideration of the literatures and an application of extant theory. *Project Management Journal*, 38, 1: 61-73.

Linde, A. & Linderoth, H. C. J. (2006). An actor-network theory perspective on IT-projects. In S. Cicmil and D. Hodgson, D. (Eds), *Making projects critical*, Houndmills: Palgrave Macmillan: 155-70.

Linderoth, H., & Pellegrino, G. (2005). Frames and inscriptions: tracing a way to understand IT-dependent change projects. *International Journal of Project Management*, 23: 415-20.

Lindholm, R. & Norstedt, J.P. (1975). *The Volvo Report*. Stockholm: Swedish Employers Confederation.

Masters, J. (1995). The history of action research, in T. Hughes (Ed.) *Action Research Electronic Reader*, The University of Sydney. http://www.behs.cchs.usyd.edu.au/arow/Reader/rmasters.htm.

Mau, M. (2005). Action Research: Connecting Knowledge in the Australian Public Sector, DBA thesis, Lismore, Australia: Southern Cross University.

McGill, I. & Broadbank, A. (2004). *The action learning handbook: Powerful techniques for education, professional development and training*, London, Routledge-Farmer.

McGrath, K. (2002). The Golden Circle: a way of arguing and acting about technology in the London Ambulance Service. *European Journal of Information Systems, 11*: 251-66.

McKernan, J. (1991). *Curriculum action research: A handbook of methods and resources for the reflective practitioner*, London: Kogan page.

McTaggart, R. (1992). Action research: Issues in theory and practice, Keynote address to the methodological issues in qualitative health research conference, November, Geelong, Australia, Deakin University.

McTaggart, R. (1997). Reading the collection, in R. McTaggart (Ed.) *Participatory action research: International contexts and consequences*, Albany: State University of New York Press: 1-24.

Miettinen, R. (1999). The riddle of things: Activity theory and actor-network theory as approaches to studying interventions, *Mind, Culture and Activity*, 6,3: 170-95.

Miles, M. B., & Huberman, A. M. (1994). *An expanded sourcebook: Qualitative data analysis* (2nd edn.). Thousand Oaks, CA: Sage.

Mirvis, P.H., Ayas, K. & Roth, G. (2003). Too desert and back: The story of one of the most dramatic business transformations on record, San Francisco, CA: Jossey Bass.

Mutch, A. (2002). Actors and Networks or Agents and Structures: Towards a Realist View of Information Systems. *Organization, 9*(3): 477-96.

Nardi, B. (1998). Concepts of cognition and consciousness: Four voices, *Journal of Computer Documentation, 22*: 31-48.

Nardi, B. and Engeström, Y. (1998). A web on the wind: The structure of invisible work. A special issue of *The Journal of Computer-supported Cooperative Work* 8: 1-2.

Nardi, B. and O'Day, V. (1999). Information ecologies: Using technology with heart. Cambridge, MA: MIT Press.

Nimmo, R. (2011). Actor-network theory and methodology: social research in a more-than-human world, *Methodological Innovations Online*, 6, 3: 108-119.

Orlikowski, W. (1996). Improvising organizational transformation over time: a situated change perspective. *Information Systems Research, 7*: 63-92.

Orr, M. (2007). The Implementation of Electronic Health Knowledge Management Systems in Waitemata District Health Board, DBA Thesis, Lismore, Australia, Southern Cross University.

Pare, G. & Elam, M, J. (1997). Using case study research to build theories of IT implementation, in A. Lee, J. Liebenau & J. DeGross (eds) *Proceedings of the IFIP TC8 WG8.2 International Conference on Information Systems and Qualitative Research*, Philadelphia, PA, Chapman & Hall.

Parkin, J. (1996). Organizational decision making and the project manager. *International Journal of Project Management*, 14, 5: 257-63.

Parkin, P. (2009). *Managing change in healthcare: Using action research*, London: Sage.

Paton, S., Hodgson, Damian and Cicmil, S. (2010). Who am I and what am I doing here? Becoming and being a project manager. *Journal of Management Development*, 29, 2: 157-166.

Perry, C., & Zuber-Skerritt, O. (1992). Action research in graduate management research programs. *Higher Education* 23: 195-208.

Porsander, L. (2000). Translating a dream of immortality in a (con)temporary order. *Journal of Organizational Change Management*, 13, 1: 14-29.

Porsander, L. (2005). 'My name is Lifebuoy'. An actor-network emerging from an action-net. In B. Czarniawska. & T. Hernes (Eds), *Actor-Network Theory and Organizing*. Malmo: Liber & Copenhagen Business School Press: 14-30.

Raelin, J.A. (1997). Action learning and action science: are they different? *Organizational Dynamics*, 26, 1: 21-34.

Raelin, J. (1999). Preface, *Management Learning*, 30, 2: 115-26.

Raelin, J.A. & Coghlan, D. (2006). Developing managers as learners and researchers: Using action learning and action research, *Journal of Management Education*, 30,5: 670-89.

Randall, D., Harper, R. & Rouncefield, M. (2007). *Fieldwork for design: theory and practice; Participative inquiry in practice*, London: Springer-Verlag.

Reason, P. & Bradbury, H. (2008). Introduction in P. Reason & H. Bradbury (Eds). *The SAGE handbook of action research*, 2nd Edn., London: Sage: 1-10.

Reason, P. & Bradbury, H. (2008). *The SAGE handbook of action research*, 2nd Edn., London: Sage

Revans, R. (1982). *The origins and growth of action learning*, Bromley Kent: Chartwell-Bratt.

Ross-Fisher, R. (2008). Action research to improve teaching and learning, *Kappa Delta* Phi, 44, 4: 160-64.

Sankaran S. (1999). An action research study of management learning: Developing local engineering managers of a Japanese multinational company in Singapore. PhD Thesis. Adelaide: University of South Australia.

Creative and Innovative Contemporary Approaches

Sankaran, S., Dick, B., Passfield, R. and Swepson. P. (2001). *Effective change management using action learning and action research: Concepts, frameworks, processes and applications*, Lismore, Australia: Southern Cross University Press.

Sankaran, S., James, P., Orr, M. & Walker, S. (2005). Real experiences in knowledge management implementation: using action research, *International Journal of Knowledge, Culture and Change Management*, vol. 5, no. 2005/2006: 99-106.

Sankaran, S. & Kumar, M. (2010). Implementing organizational change using action research in two Asian cultures. Proceedings of the Project Management Institute's Education and Research Conference, Washington, July 7-10, 8 pages.

Schön, D. (1983). *The reflective practitioner: How professionals think in action*. New York: Basic Books.

Selener D.S., 1998. *Participatory action research and social change*. 3. Ithaca, NY: Cornell Participatory Action Research Network.

Slater, T., Alana James, E. & Bucknam, A. (2011). *Action research for business, non-profit and public administration*: A tool for complex times, Thousand Oaks, CA: Sage.

Star, S.L. (1991). The Sociology of the invisible: The primacy of work in the writings of Anselm Strauss. In D. Maines (Ed.), *Social organization and social process: Essays in honor of Anselm Strauss,* Hawthorne, NY: Aldine de Gruyter: 265-83.

Steinfort, P. and Walker, D.H.T. (2011). *What enables project success: Lessons from aid-relief projects*, Newtown Square, PA: Project Management Institute.

Stenhouse, L. (1975). *An Introduction to Curriculum Research and Development*. London, Heinemann.

Strauss, A., Fagerhaugh, S., Suczek, B. & Wiener, C. (1985). The social organization of medical work. Chicago: University of Chicago Press.

Suchman, L. (1995). Making work visible, *Communications of the ACM,* 38: 56-64.

Trist, E. (1981). The evolution of socio-technical systems: A conceptual framework and an action research program, *Occasional Paper No.2*, Ontario Quality of Life Working Centre, Ontario.

Verenikina, I., & Gould, E. (1998). Cultural-historical psychology and Activity Theory, in H. Hasan, E. Gould & P. Hyland (eds). *Information systems and Activity Theory: tools in context*. Wollongong: University of Wollongong Press: 1-18.

Walker, S. (2007). What are the major barriers to the successful implementation of knowledge management projects in the Telecommunication industry: An action research study, DBA thesis, Lismore: Southern Cross University.

Walsham, G. (2002). Interpretive case studies in IS research: nature and method, in M. Myers & D. Avison (Eds) *Qualitative research in information system,* London: Sage Publications: 101-113.

Weinstein, K. (2002). Action learning: The classic approach, in Y. Boshyk, (ed.) *Action learning worldwide: Experiences of leadership and organizational development*, Basingstoke, UK, Palgrave MacMillan: 3-18.

Chapter 7

Simulations for Project Management Research

Elyssebeth Leigh

Abstract

Operational contexts for contemporary organisations are becoming increasingly complex, uncertain and turbulent, creating unfamiliar research challenges for which familiar methodologies do not offer appropriate support. This chapter explores how various forms of simulation can be designed and used to explore ill-defined problem contexts, of interest to Project Management as a discipline and a practice. Simulation has a wide range of forms and applications, and no single definition encompasses all of these, so the chapter begins with the question 'What is simulation?' Then it locates a space for simulation in the research domain, with special reference to the nature of complexity as it is understood in project management and organisational contexts. The final section of the chapter explores how a range of simulation forms can be applied to Project Management research.

This chapter and Chapter 8 share several concepts of interest to Project Management research given that the development of system dynamics grew out of specific uses of simulation by Forrester and others to explore the emerging concepts that have now become a recognisable discipline. They knew that certain structural and conceptual features informing the construction and use of simulations remain the same, whether the end product is a paper and pen exercise or a sophisticated form of computer-aided technology. These structural and conceptual features are introduced at the beginning of the chapter, and we suggest readers explore chapters 7 and 8 in tandem.

Introduction

Organisations, and the projects, and portfolios of projects, embedded in them, are value-laden, ambiguous, ill defined, and pluralistic – containing multiple competing perspectives on reality. At present technical issues seem to dominate research activity, however the growing importance of associated 'non-technical' issues clearly requires greater attention. Simulation provides a highly suitable, robust and flexible platform with which researchers can combine analysis of technical and non-technical factors in ways that will replicate current conditions and also provide indicators of emergent trends.

Despite its potential as a multi-dimensional analysis tool for Project Management research there is not yet a fully satisfactory response to the questions of '*What is simulation?*' and '*How to use it for research?*' – in regard to the broad field of Project Management research. Unless there is already a commitment to use translational, transformational and transdisciplinary research this gap makes it hard for researchers to step into a relatively new research domain. This chapter addresses both questions and suggests a framework for simulation-based Project Management research, demonstrating along the way, how simulation readily fits into approaches seeking to integrate divergent perspectives.

The chapter therefore begins with matters of definition and scope, to establish parameters for researchers to use in considering the use of simulations for their own particular purposes. It then uses a transdisciplinary approach to combining concepts from a model of Project Management types with a Knowledge Management typology of contexts suggesting what kind of explanations/solutions may apply in particular settings. In doing so the aim is to illustrate the specific benefits of simulation for research in contexts where – for example – relationships between technical and non-technical factors are not clearly understood. Finally the chapter offers specific ideas for using simulation to explore questions of interest to Project Management researchers.

What is Simulation?

At its core, simulation is 'the abstraction of reality for a purpose' (McGarity, 2011). As such it is an immensely rich and diverse form of human activity with a long history of use. The diversity of forms includes activities as disparate as 'soft modelling' of complex problems, use of flight simulators for skill development, and face-to-face role play-based activity to improve human communication skills. There are single player simulations to teach (and test for) decision making capability and extended multi-player activities designed to assist in understanding concepts like the 'tragedy of the commons' (see for example Fish Banks, Meadows et al., 1993) and mental processes underlying the use of force (Napper, 2001). This diversity conceals the fact that all of these activities share a remarkably small set of core characteristics that define and shape their production and mode of operation. Unlike conventional strategies, which seek to impose order and limit complications, simulations create initial conditions of complexity that can be disconcerting to an untutored observer, and focus attention on consequences and outcomes that may never have been encountered before. Simulation is often considered too overwhelming for the kind of conventional research that expects to achieve stable results through a sequential process of analysis; however it can be immensely valuable to researchers prepared to ride out initial conditions of uncertainty and dis-continuity. Such complexity is seldom a comfortable place for conducting research, and before exploring how simulation can help researchers in these kinds of domains, it is helpful to understand something about them.

Why Use Simulation for Complex Research?

In the 1940s Weaver proposed a distinction between two forms of complexity. Understanding this distinction must precede any exploration of simulation as a tool for researching complexity. 'Disorganised complexity', in Weaver's view, refers to systems with a very large number of parts/elements that appear to operate mostly randomly. Today this is also labelled 'chaos' and there is awareness that the appearance of randomness may actually be caused by patterns of behaviour so large as to be inaccessible to normal modes of analysis. 'Organised complexity', on the other hand refers to systems with a smaller number of correlated 'interactions between the parts [creating] a differentiated structure that can, as a system, interact with other systems. [Such a] coordinated system manifests properties not carried or dictated by individual parts' (Weaver, 1948). This latter form of complexity is more likely to be the type attracting the attention of readers of this book. It is worth noting that 'disorganised complexity' can be simulated in specific circumstances, but are less likely to be of interest to Project Managers – or those researching this field. Recently Remington and Pollack (2008) defined complex projects as having four dimensions, of which, fortunately few projects exhibit more than one aspect of 'organised complexity' at a time. They identified the four kinds of complex projects as follows:

- *Structurally* complex projects – the physical scale of the reality is too large and complex to be understood from any single perspective.
- *Technically* complex projects – relationships among components of the project are such they cannot be fully anticipated prior to commencement of the project.
- *Directionally* complex projects – the eventual outcomes of the project are unclear, even impossible to pre-determine, and may alter within the life of the project.
- *Temporally* complex projects – the time scale for such projects is moving too fast (or slow) to allow for confident predictive analysis of the activity.

Remington and Pollack provide an excellent introduction to the concepts of complexity in projects and one purpose of this chapter is to build on their approach by exploring how simulation provides a research strategy for methodically reducing such 'organised complexity'– sometimes experienced as 'one great blooming, buzzing confusion' (James, 1890) – to the essential variables, while authentically replicating the essentials.

The Core Components of Simulation

As might be expected, each of the three key terms in McGarity's definition of simulation – i.e. 'abstraction', 'reality' and 'purpose' – requires careful examination. The first – and most vital – factor to remember, is that simulation is *always* an 'abstraction'. As such it is both reduced in scale, and created through the media of components other than those present in the real context. Secondly, simulation is never 'real'. This requires users to remain vigilant against becoming confused by the necessary distinctions between the condition of the 'real' and the representative active elements of the 'not-real' simulator built to represent – but not 'be' – the real. It is this very capacity to accurately depict miniaturised versions of relationships and interconnectedness that makes simulation ideal for researching the 'living moments' of projects. In contrast with this constructed unreality, 'reality' refers to the totality of all experiences, entities and contexts within an actual project and all that exists beyond it.

As a central component in what defines simulation, 'reality' locates all simulation activities *in relation to* what exists and is possible. Where other research methodologies position their activity alongside reality and 'look into it' to explore for answers, simulation begins with detailed analysis of the 'reality' to be examined, and then invites participants to 'step into' a miniaturised version of the whole. The extended process of prior analysis enables simulation to reduce key variables to valid and verifiable miniature replications, enabling the researcher to conduct 'as if real' explorations of those variables and their relationships.

Thirdly, the 'purposes' for simulation are usually highly specific and inevitably very varied, requiring development of suitably diverse forms of activity to meet specific goals. The resulting 'realistic' abstractions of the real are enacted, with the goal of achieving specific intended purposes. It is worth noting here, that since simulation is a means of replicating the 'real', specific iterations can take on a life of their own (much like real life), and thus outcomes other than those intended are also possible. Where a research project has settled on achieving narrowly defined and clearly delineated outcomes, simulation is not a suitable option. However, given the manner in which it creates movement and interaction, enables exploration of the patterns and habitual behaviours and assumptions alive in dynamic contexts, simulation does meet Einser's need (1994) when he lamented that:

We have been concerned too much with steady states, too little with dynamics, too much with the resting places of the human mind, too little with its rhythms.

Figure 7.1 – below – is a visual representation of relationships among the key elements in the definition of simulation, and the next section of this chapter introduces the importance of understanding the construction elements that combine to make simulations 'work' – for teaching or research.

However, before moving to an overview of how 'simulation' works, it is important to note that simulation makes use of tools frequently called 'simulators' which include such things as the models underlying system dynamics. Readers need to understand that 'simulation' is a process, intended to reproduce living, actively engaged interactiv-

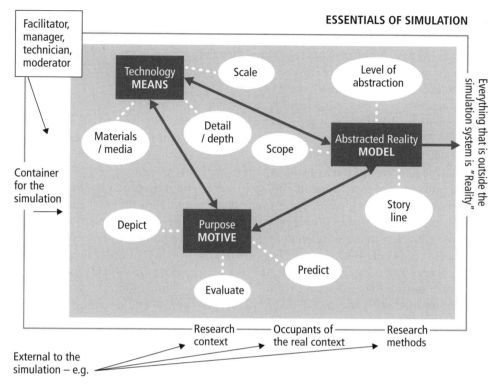

Figure 7.1. A Systems Map Representation of Key Elements Involved in Creating a Simulation

ity, much as these would/will work in real time, and 'simulators' or models are static items used to bring the simulation experience to life.

Models underlying the use, for example, of '*Monte Carlo* simulations' come to life when put into motion to explore options, alternatives and possibilities. They represent a static, immobile image of events and conditions at a moment in time, becoming a 'simulation' only when the underlying, abstracted 'model' is activated in some way. All forms of 'model' – from computer-based simulator to face to face role-play – undergo an alteration in condition – from inert to active – once brought to 'life' by a researcher wanting to explore such questions as 'what if'; 'how to'; 'when might' etc.

How do Simulations Work?

Simulations reduce complexity to manageable proportions for defined, time-limited periods. As noted above, constructing a simulation requires the designer to identify all key features of the totality of the 'system' to be replicated. A limited number of elements are then selected from this body of data and re-arranged so as to represent the 'whole' accurately. These elements are shaped into a plausible scenario with an opening gambit, to provide a viable and valid working representation of the 'real'. They are especially ideal for working with issues described by C. West Churchman, (1967) as 'wicked problem' situations since they reduce to a manageable scale – for a temporary period – the mix of incomplete, contradictory, and changing characteristics of the reality that may confront the researcher.

For research purposes, time required to analyse the whole and choose representative elements can – at times – seem to be a misdirection in regard to the immediate purpose of an investigation. And, indeed, an early decision point for a researcher occurs when considering whether there is time to conduct the analysis needed to build/adapt a 'model' of the real with which to study the presenting issue. However, a similar problem also faces those intending to use a system dynamics research strategy or, indeed, any approach requiring intimate engagement with the total environment for the purpose of studying problems within the confines of a particular context.

Those who elect to use simulation as their research method have previously decided that there is a specific value in spending time on the 'totality' in order to understand the 'particular' as a subset of the whole. If this is all sounding too difficult and abstract, it is worth noting that a frequent reason for choosing simulation as a research and/ or learning method is the wonderful sense of 'playfulness' and openness to variety and complexity that informs the carefully staged process of creating an abstraction of reality to meet a designer/user's specific purposes.

Abstracting the Details from Reality

After over-arching decisions are made about the scale of the abstraction, and its purpose and scope the researcher is ready for the final step, before beginning the research. This second stage analysis involves playing with the chosen elements in relation to four key aspects – these are the rules, roles, scenario and recording processes. The 'rules' circumscribe how sub-components of the simulation operate and interact. Rules usually define such issues as:

- How relationships develop.
- What is forbidden. Allowed.
- What are the 'givens'.
- What is 'understood' but not normally 'named'.
- What factors activate specific reactions within the simulation.
- What actions or elements lead to new options, or close down the action, etc.

Key rules will be stated explicitly via statements such as 'schools/factories/offices only operate during certain hours of the day'; 'cars are not allowed on footpaths, but, if one does intrude into that space, penalties and reactions occur according to set rules', 'managers do not make things'. However, sometimes the 'rules' imply that 'whatever

Creative and Innovative Contemporary Approaches

is not expressly forbidden is allowed'. This allows those engaged in the simulation to act in ways that surface hidden assumptions and belief systems which informing the 'real' context, yet may be unknown until unearthed by the flow of the action.

The 'roles' delineate all elements (animate and inanimate) in the reality being replicated. 'Roles' set the framework of allowable/unallowable behaviours guiding all activity. Where participants are human they may be allocated archetypes such as 'Senior Construction Engineer' or 'The major spare parts supplier' and so on. Where the simulation is computer-based, the rules may be coded instructions allowing – or forbidding – specific elements to complete or avoid certain tasks. Regardless of the detail in a role description, it is only ever a generic outline of the named functional responsibility. Some of the complexity-driven uncertainty of a simulation emerges as specific individuals occupy these functional roles and enact them in their own unique manner. In fully computer-based simulations, interactions among pre-programmed components will similarly create diversity rather than cohesion because of the large number of potential responses that can be incorporated. Where a researcher is seeking to understand how certain conditions impact on human interaction, creating 'roles' with a wide range of possible interpretations ensures a quick emergence of diversity for later analysis.

The third element of a completed miniaturization of reality is the 'scenario'. This serves to delineate the scope of the 'container' (see Figure 7.1 above) within which all activity occurs, for example 'vehicle manufacturing in Australia', 'geological exploration in Africa' etc. The scenario statement draws a boundary around the whole and enables researchers and participants to comprehend the borders of the action – in both the real and the simulation. It can be described in great detail or only sketched briefly allowing participants to bring their own assumptions, values and creativity to bear on the action as it unfolds. As is the case in Project Management the initiation phase – involving creation of rules, roles and scenario – is vital, and effective attention to detail at this time ensures successful outcomes later on.

Finally, plans for recording what happens and how interactions and reactions affect the whole must be established before action commences. For researchers this is especially important since the ebb and flow of events intimately affect the outcomes and need to be tracked with specific research questions/issues in mind. Computer-based simulations may have elaborate tracking mechanisms producing extensive data for post-event analysis. Face-to-face simulations, relying on human interactions, may include written items, activity-tracking tasks (e.g. 'note when you contact X; and what you talk about' etc.) as well as observations and subsequent recall of events and experiences. Video and audio recordings may contribute extended documentation of the sequencing and interconnectedness of events.

Once a design is completed and tested, it is ready to be enacted using a sequence of three stages. The first stage is the '*briefing*' and introduces everyone to the scenario, establishes the 'rules of engagement' and stipulates such matters as timing, task allocation and distribution of roles. The second stage is the '*action*' wherein what is to be created and explored is enacted. Regardless of the context, this stage requires the researcher to be positioned as a 'vigilant observer' (Leigh and Spindler, 1997) dis-engaged from all action. Any effort on the part of a researcher, as manager of the process, to influence events will reduce the verisimilitude of the process, and limit the chances of arriving at viable (untainted) outcomes. Although researchers must avoid influencing the action they are free to observe the flow of events, the nature of interactions and unfolding relationships. Once the action is complete, or a pre-set time limit is reached, attention moves to the final stage – called the '*debriefing*' or '*after action review*'. During this period what has been experienced and observed is analysed and recorded, and lessons learned are identified, categorised and documented. The focus then moves to further detailed analysis and reporting.

The (apparent) rigidity of this design and construction process includes a requirement that the structure does not vary once it has been fully developed and tested. This paradoxical use of an overtly rigid skeletal framework, with apparently clear delineation of events and allowable actions, leaves the 'actors' – be they human participants or computer-generated avatars – to interpret everything else according to the dictates of their own perceptions. This 'tight-loose' arrangement enables repetitions of a simulation. That is, the structure of the 'simulator' once established, remain essentially the same, while each iteration provides a unique elaboration of participants' actions and interactions – human or computerised, thus enabling testing of a range of variables to observe whether (for example) differing sets of interactions produce measurably different outcomes. The emergent flexibility within an apparently rigidly structured 'simulator' derives from the unique variability of the human participants when engaged in creating the 'simulation'. In a computer-based simulation a similar flexibility derives from alterations to initiating assumptions about specific possible interactions and reactions.

In his preface to Michael Schrage's 'Serious Play' (1999) Tom Peters celebrates the value of the unexpected paradigm of 'Ready. Fire! Aim' to promote 'rapid prototyping' enabling quick revisions to approaches to innovation, through turning upside down conventional practices. Schrage promotes simulation as a form of 'rapid prototyping' that opens all interactions to the unexpected and unanticipated and proposes that:

> ... *because organisations are communities of people and not aggregations of data the real power of prototypes comes less from the prototypes' acknowledged abilities to model reality, than their implicit threats to change behaviour. To become truly engaged in a prototype is to create a new relationship with the self and with others* (p. 156).

Summary

Simulations, for research purposes, begin with identification of the reality to be explored, establish the purpose of the specific simulation to be created, and selects the elements to be included in (and excluded from) the abstraction of that reality. These elements are categorised as the rules, the roles and the scenario which – once identified, abstracted and constructed into a viable whole – are enacted in the sequence of

Creative and Innovative Contemporary Approaches

briefing, action and debriefing. The complexity that these simple elements can create continues to defy the apparent simplicity of such a description, so the next section of this chapter addresses the question of *'why use simulation?'* before introducing a selection of the amazing variety of forms which simulation can take. The final section considers how to apply these to research in the field of Project Management.

Why Use Simulation?

Engineers use 'simulation' for such things as testing concepts like structural tensions and load bearing options; health services use simulation for training and rehearsal; educators use simulation for skill development; and aviation uses simulation for pilot and cabin crew training. Simulation is used as a research method in science, engineering, psychology and medicine and many other disciplines. A key factor uniting all these uses is that what is being researched usually cannot be interfered with, or touched, in any of the usual ways, or exists in conditions where it is not cost effective or viable to engage directly with the real conditions – or it does not yet exist. While much of the activity of Project Management is generally accessible, it is frequently difficult to engage with some specific contexts in real time, in a manner that enables normal activities to proceed unimpeded while research is conducted.

Use of simulation is not suitable for all Project Management research goals. The following is a list of conditions for which a simulation-based research strategy in Project Management contexts may be relevant:

- The time scale of the reality under examination extends beyond the life span of the research project.
  - Thus use of a simulation-based research strategy allows the researcher to telescope the time element allowing for analysis of 'what if?' questions and 'what might?' analyses of future possibilities.
- Relationships among components are unclear beyond a certain point – e.g. how will contractor and sub-contractors collaborate on solving an unanticipated 'wicked problem' facing a construction site?
  - Simulation draws together known relationship factors and allows them to be played out, to suggest more than one possible conclusion – thus allowing for advance notice and preparation for *emerging* alternatives.
  - *Remington and Pollack's 'structurally complex' projects are relevant here.*
- Projects of the type being considered have never been attempted before. There are no known – or readily accessible – precedents. Tools have not yet been developed for the work proposed, or conditions for completion are entirely new.
  - A simulation strategy allows for repeated trials of alternate options without affecting the actual context.
  - *Relevant to Remington and Pollack's 'technically complex' projects.*

- The component parts of the reality are moving too fast/slow to allow for useful examination.
  - Using simulation strategies to alter key time components can speed up, or slow down, the process allowing for more detailed identification and analysis of factors that cannot otherwise be captured in real time.
  - *Relevant to Remington and Pollack's 'temporally complex' projects.*
- The range of possible outcomes of a given project is unknown, their various consequences are unclear, there is a lack of agreement about how to proceed, or even what to talk about.
  - Simulation-based designs can provide researchers with highly flexible, repeatable, and robust research platforms with which to explore competing options for action.
  - *Remington and Pollack's 'directionally complex' projects.*
- The physical scale of the reality is impossible to scan in any viable manner – thus miniaturising the scale allows a realistic perspective on the operation of the whole.

Remington and Pollack's analysis leads to the development of tools for use *within* projects. Simulations provide realistically accessible – although hypothetical – conditions for relatively objective examination from the *outside.* Together – and separately – they demonstrate that conditions of uncertainty and complexity are amenable to reasoned action, although in quite different ways. For this reason simulation is usually more relevant for research where all – or any – of Remington and Pollack's complexity-driven conditions apply, while not being as relevant to conditions where more is known about what the initial conditions and driving factors.

Case Studies
Simulation for Emergent Research Goals
A memorable – and well known – use of a simulation/simulator strategy to research an urgent, emerging project-type problem occurred in 1970 when the Apollo 13 manned spacecraft was struck by multiple emergencies. NASA was a highly sophisticated user of simulations, and had made extensive use of an Apollo 13 Command Module simulator prior to the launch of the Mission. Once the spacecraft was crippled this simulator was used as a research platform to explore, adapt and design procedures for safely returning the astronauts to earth. All this is depicted in the movie *Apollo 13* – a graphic example of a technically complex, emergent dilemma requiring urgent research to divert a disaster. A similar use was made of the F111 aircraft simulator at Amberley Air Force base in Australia in 2006, when an aircraft lost a wing wheel on take off and the simulator there was used to calibrate all the options for returning the aircraft to earth 'safely', which was accomplished.

Creative and Innovative Contemporary Approaches

Simulation for Academic Research

Sengupta, Kishore et al. (2008) used a 'simulated game' to track the decisions of experienced project managers. They noted that the real world has, 'delays between causes and effects, and it may become difficult to link them, let alone specify the relationship between them'. They wanted to see 'how experienced project managers cope with this issue' and found that most performed no better than a naive amateur, indicating an inability to incorporate the effects of time lags into planning decisions.

Shamim Bodhanya and some of his students at the university of Kwazula Natal, use simulation to research the characteristics of complex adaptive systems and their impact on a range of social systems. This work focuses on the benefits of applying multiple perspectives and a systemic approach to developing solutions to problems in the complex domain.

During 2012-2014 Saeed Shalbafan and his supervisors at the University of Technology Sydney will use role play based simulations to explore the process of developing skills for project portfolio management. This research project will map the outcomes of individual and group participation to report on how the complex array of skills required of an effective project portfolio manager may be acquired.

In different ways all these research projects emphasise the value of simulation for exploring problems and questions for which there is no know prior answer. It is the capacity for 'playing with' the multivariate aspects of complex problems that makes simulation an effective option, although not a simple one. This is explored further in the following section.

Suitable Contexts for use of Simulation in Project Management Research

To explore the nature of suitable contexts for using simulations for research this chapter draws on two models of knowledge and practice. These were developed independently but share some intriguing consanguinities that make them a useful combination for deciding on a choice of simulation form. The first is Turner and Cochrane's well-known arrangement of projects in relation to goals and methods. Figure 7.2 is based on their original 1993 matrix as adapted for use in designing and developing simulations for learning and research (Leigh, 2005). Here projects are delineated in accordance with how well their goals and methods are defined. This focus on goals and methods has assisted the discipline of Project Management to identify, for example, that 'both goals and methods in projects in the Business Services sector tend to be less well defined than in either the Engineering and Construction or IS/IT and Telecommunications sectors' (Crawford, 2000).

Analysing interactions among particular sets of goals and methods in different project contexts enables the researcher to identify and track how the interactivity creates the unfolding sequence of events that becomes the ongoing story and eventual results of any project based undertaking. As Hussein (2007) has noted in reference to Type 1 projects: 'Simulation[s] are not about the direct application of skills to solve a particular case or a problem. This characteristic makes the use of simulation [for] solving or simulating well defined problems – such as network calculations, resource leveling or cost estimation – superfluous.' In his opinion 'a continuing problem [of conventional research methods] is the insensitivity to the dynamics of actual project contexts' (p. 6).

That is, conventional research forms do not incorporate adequate means to address the complexity of human interactions found in projects where either goals or methods are not well defined and where the potential for uncertainty and instability thus increases – as in Type 2, 3 and 4 projects.

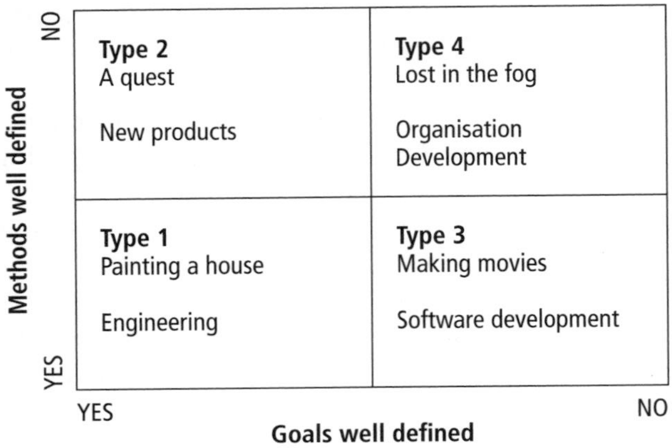

Figure 7.2. Based on Turner and Cochrane's Arrangement of Project Types (Leigh, 2005)

The 'Cynefin Domains of Knowledge' matrix was developed by Snowden et al., while working in Knowledge Management at IBM during the 1990s. Their purpose in developing the matrix was to assist comprehension of the impact of understanding that 'all human interactions are strongly influenced, and frequently determined, by the patterns of our multiple experiences, stories and anecdotes' (Lytton-Hitchins, 2005). Such patterns are unique to each of us, and our individual actions and reactions in overtly similar conditions may be strikingly different, and unexpected.

Key insights arising from this comprehension include recognition that human behaviour and intelligence i) is pattern-based rather than rule-based, ii) shifts seamlessly within and between multiple identities, iii) imputes intentionality to our own/other's actions on the basis of retrospective coherence, iv) learns through failure not success, and v) is able to create and maintain order in the face of perceived disarray (ibid). To reveal the complexity implicit in these deceptively unpretentious observations about human intelligence and behaviour the matrix adopts the unusual feature of including five 'domains' rather than the more familiar four sections. These domains enable a clearer representation of how human fallibility influences comprehension of – and responses to – cause and effect relationships created in 'ordered' and 'un-

Creative and Innovative Contemporary Approaches

ordered' systems. Figure 7.3 illustrates the Cynefin Domains in brief, while Figure 7.4 indicates recommended modes of response.

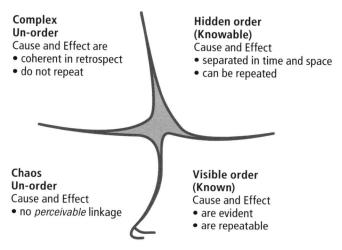

Complex
Un-order
Cause and Effect are
• coherent in retrospect
• do not repeat

Hidden order
(Knowable)
Cause and Effect
• separated in time and space
• can be repeated

Chaos
Un-order
Cause and Effect
• no *perceivable* linkage

Visible order
(Known)
Cause and Effect
• are evident
• are repeatable

Figure 7.3. Cynefin Domains of Knowledge

In an 'ordered' system we are able to design the outcome we want because we understand the nature of the set of relationships between 'cause' and 'effect'. This holds true in both the Simple domain, where order is known and visible to all, and the Complicated domain where order (while not yet known) can be discovered and is knowable. Both of these domains of 'order' operate on sets of cause and effect relationships that are predisposed to management by human effort and intelligence. However, encounters with 'un-ordered' systems require prior acknowledgement that there are no immediately observable repetitions among relationships between 'cause' and 'effect' and that all further actions involve some kind of manipulation of boundaries among evolving factors. Such contexts require recognition of, and response to, emergent patterns – *as they are emerging*. In the Complex domain the means for doing this are called (for convenience) 'probes' and do not assume that outcomes are known ahead of time (see Figure 7.4). In the Chaotic domain there are no known cues to provide prior guidance and the only possible response is to take action and later analyse the resulting responses and outcomes.

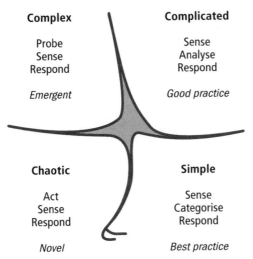

Complex

Probe
Sense
Respond

Emergent

Complicated

Sense
Analyse
Respond

Good practice

Chaotic

Act
Sense
Respond

Novel

Simple

Sense
Categorise
Respond

Best practice

Figure 7.4. Appropriate Responses for Operating Effectively in each Cynefin Domain

The irregular shape in the centre of the image represents the fifth Cynefin 'domain' of 'Dis-order' a situation in which relationships between cause and effect are *believed* to be unknowable and consequently unmanageable. The absence of apparent 'cause/effect' linkages makes this domain 'frightening' and therefore something to be avoided 'at all costs'. The very human problem represented by this domain is that the 'uncertainty' generated by 'Un-order' can reduce otherwise sensible people to a state of 'terror' creating a drive to return – immediately – to 'Order' even when known behaviours will not be effective in the 'Un-ordered' domain being experienced.

If a research project is going to plunge into Dis-order it is most likely to happen when cause and effect relationships that were being tracked disappear from sight. This might occur when a research project, thought to be operating in the Complicated domain, begins to exhibit characteristics of operating in conditions of previously un-recognised Complexity. Recovering from Dis-order requires recognition of the need to seek out relevant cause and effect relationships that will be found to be 'coherent in retrospect; not to be repeated'. Any decisions to take action towards resolution of the problem or situation – as it is currently being experienced – must focus on this. While it is unlikely that a formally established project will enter the Chaotic domain, the emotional quotient of a researcher may lead them to the belief that this is what is happening. Sudden external disasters may, however, cast a project into chaos, requiring urgent action. In such contexts sense is only achievable retrospectively.

Creative and Innovative Contemporary Approaches

Case Study – Surviving a Sudden Shift in the Operational Context

The following case study of a very recent event, illustrates how understanding and behaviour must adapt – sometimes at lightning speed – to changes in the environment. It also helps explain how cause and effect relationships are often not well understood between one Cynefin/Knowledge Management domain and another. The events in the moment were chaotic – requiring action. The after action review will be in the complicated domain, involving expert analysis. Eventually the site will return to or-dered and well-known procedures – and each has its own needs.

Work began as usual one recent morning on a major building site in the Sydney CBD. Not far into the day the site was subjected to a sudden and unexpected switch from the Ordered/Simple domain to the Chaotic/Un-ordered domain, when a fire began in the control cabin of a luffing jib tower crane. The fire began slowly then escalated into a major incident ending in breakage of the jib cables causing it to crash. The crane driver initially acted in accord with well-known 'cause and effect' behav-iours, using available fire fighting equipment in an attempt to quell the fire. When this did not work, he realised he had a very short time indeed to make the crane, the building site and nearby peak hour traffic routes safe. That he did so is a tribute to his capacity to recognise the shift in his condition from Simple to Chaotic – and *act* accordingly (*The Australian*, 2012).

In the time immediately after the fire the construction site worked in the Complex domain, probing for ways to dismantle a severely damaged crane stranded above a crowded construction site, while maintaining safety standards for the site and allow-ing some flow of traffic on the surrounding roads and limited occupancy of nearby premises. It was some time before workers on the site began to re-experience life in the Simple domain. There will be ongoing research into the 'cause and effect' rela-tionships for each element leading up and beyond the fire, and much of this research will be conducted in the Complicated domain – drawing on expert analysis in an environment far removed from the urgency experienced during the Chaotic phase of the event.

Project Management research may not often offer such a neat sequence of steps through the Domains, so a key factor for researchers to consider is what it takes to recognise the domain their work is in now, where it might move to – given a range of possible unknown events – and the kind of research they want to conduct before deciding on their method/s. If this case study was to become the subject of a research project, what perspective would be best to use for each component of the story? And how would a thoughtful researcher position each stage of the research, and design their approach accordingly.

Forms of Simulation Relevant to Project Management Research

To decide what form of simulation might best suit a Project Management research venture requires consideration both of what Type of Project it is – that is 1, 2, 3 or 4 according to Turner and Cochrane's typology (see Figure 7.2) – *as well as* which kind of domain of knowledge the activity of the research project will – or is expected to – occupy. To add to the complexity, it is possible to be conducting a research project within the parameters of one Type of project and in one particular domain of knowledge, while actually researching experience and events in a quite different domain.

For example, the Sydney crane incident, as the subject of a research project, having moved through the sequence outlined above, will be examined by subsequent researchers who will operate almost entirely in the Ordered domain. Among other things this will ensure they are unlikely to have direct access to the emotional dynamics of the seconds and minutes as the emergency unfolded. A researcher using conventional – non-simulation – methods from within the Ordered domain to analyse the confusing rush of events and reactions happening in a very short time span, may only be able to gain very distantly objective comprehension of the interactions among the motives and actions of those involved.

However one or more simulations can be created to replicate the essence of those events for three quite different purposes. One purpose could be for future training of other drivers to help them learn from the actions of the particular individuals involved on the day. A second purpose could be to establish the sequence of events for the purposes of evaluating the efficacy, speed and suitability of various responses. And a third purpose could be to conduct longitudinal research on the impact (financial, emotional and lost-time) on this site – and others like it – of the events and responses. And one well-designed simulation giving appropriate attention to the degree of abstraction and the total reality – could also address one or more of these three purposes.

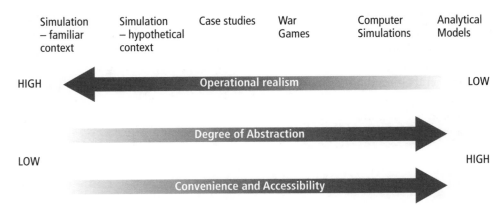

Figure 7.5. Spectrum of Reality and Emotional Engagement in Simulation (adapted from Leigh, 2003)

Creative and Innovative Contemporary Approaches

The following is therefore only a brief description of three of the more complex forms of simulation, which are considered to be the most likely choices relevant to researching the complexity of Project Management. Figure 7.5 presents a way of thinking about simulation in relation to reliance on technology, closeness to reality and degree of emotional engagement. Figure 7.6 presents relevant forms of simulation in relation to realism, abstraction, convenience and accessibility. Both Figures are simplified versions of a much more complex reality but illustrate how simulation can be selected and adapted to meet specific research and/or learning goals.

Figure 7.6. Spectrum of Simulations Showing Relationships among Factors of Realism, Abstraction, Convenience and Accessibility. Adapted from Allen (1997)

Reality and emotional Engagement	Examples	Characteristics
MOST 'REAL' *Least emotionally involving* ↑ ↓ LEAST 'REAL' *Most emotional and highly involving*	Case Study	Observations of the real world. *No requirement to become involved.*
	'In-basket' / 'in-tray' Incident process (also – 'action maze')	Non-interacting, one-to-one representation. *Some emotional attachment to quality of decision-making.*
	Hypothetical	Interacting one-to-one representation. *Emotional engagement as 'panel member'.*
	Role play	Formally structured group portrayal using one-to-one interactions. *Interactions have potential to be highly engaging.*
	Gaming simulation or Game-simulation	Informally structured group or one-to-one interactions. *May evoke strong emotions because of intersection between prior events and current experiences.*
	Machine simulation/ computer simulation	Data and decisions embedded in mathematical representations. May have group interactions about decisions. *No expectation of emotional engagement with the 'machine'. Likelihood of strong reactions to decisions/actions required.*

Some items listed in Figure 7.5 are clearly to be applied only to the Ordered domain and while they do fit within the spectrum of simulation are less likely to be useful for Project Management research, unless the intention is very limited. This is particularly true of 'case studies' and 'in-baskets' since they rely on concrete information with limited scope for exploring the unknown or unexpected.

Hypotheticals and Role Play

However Hypotheticals and Role Play introduce a requisite degree of complexity, in that human participants bring their own perspective to the structure of the activity and ensure that nothing will ever happen in exactly the same way twice.

These forms of simulation allow a researcher to construct a scenario with attendant rules and roles closely representing a current – or anticipated – set of circumstances. Then by inserting people into the action the 'game is open for play' and whatever happens next becomes the data for subsequent analysis. Thus a Hypothetical can be developed to explore a 'temporally complex' project by telescoped months or even years of slow emergence into minutes or hours of fast paced dialogue. Hypothetical individuals – usually subject matter experts (SMEs) or possessing related information – contribute to identification of possible outcomes by pitting their expertise against each other's knowledge and the hidden agenda of the scenario's creator – or facilitator – who has the task of moderating the dialogue. Using different SMEs a single hypothetical scenario can be run numerous times to generate a generous amount of data for analysis of emerging trends, conflicting perspectives and likely barriers to plans. And all this can be happening while the real project itself is slowly moving towards actuality, drawing on the benefits of the 'future-scoping' ideas emerging from the Hypotheticals.

Role Play invites participants to extend the scope of a hypothetical context by relocating the focus away from the moderator's scenario and onto their own interactions free of pre-determined intentions others than those creating the general scope of the action. Role Play emphases the emotional element in human interaction and helps researchers uncover more about how the psycho-social side of human organisation contributes to outcomes – both anticipated and unexpected. Thus a 'directionally complex' project troubled by numerous communication problems can be replicated in a Role Play format with the goals of uncovering hidden agendas, revealing political drivers and encouraging movement towards more open and honest appraisal of the real blockages hidden behind these invisible forces.

War Games

War Games are a particular form of Role Play with two special characteristics that make them especially helpful where the project is in a marketing or business development setting. The first characteristic is that players are assigned to opposing teams (usually two, but more are possible depending on the real situation) – there will be fierce competition and win/lose relationships are an inexorable outcome. The second characteristic is that War Games are turn based, allowing participants to assess the efficacy of their decision-making, negotiating skills – or whatever is being explored.

Returning to Figures 7.5 and 7.6 at this point, provides two interestingly different

Creative and Innovative Contemporary Approaches

perspectives on 'fully formed' simulation. Figure 7.5 considers all technically-based simulation as 'more abstract' while Figure 7.6 locates some forms of simulation as 'less abstract' than 'war games', and identifies computer-based simulation as 'more abstract'. This highlights the complexity of the field of simulation itself, in that both locations can be equally true depending on the scope and amount of time and money spent on the verisimilitude of the activity. What we understand to be 'real' itself becomes contestable, and this is nowhere more true than in war games.

In a military context one of the largest and most expensive simulations about which we have public knowledge was 'Millennium Challenge'. Lasting three weeks and costing an estimated $[USD] 250 million, it was intended to be a test-bed for emerging American military technologies and strategies, at the beginning of the new century. It involved 'network-centric warfare' – combining computer-based activity and actual battle equipment (ships, plans and ground forces). Opinion about its success – or otherwise – is sharply divided. In a strictly simulation-based sense the role of the facilitator as 'vigilant observer' was violated when those overseeing the action interfered to ensure achievement of anticipated outcomes thus favouring one 'side' in the battle. This meant that contextually valid actions on the part of the opposing side were overturned and results that challenged the underlying model were annulled.

Thus, while the verisimilitude of the simulation was extremely high, its very complexity concealed underlying tensions inherent in the goals driving its construction and use. As it morphed into a 'directionally complex' project it lost the opportunity to become a useful abstraction of reality providing long-lasting honest and verifiable results of the action. Thus over the time of the simulation it was both 'more' and 'less' real than what it intended to replicate.

The lesson of 'Millennium Challenge' for those considering using simulation for research in Project Management has long-term implications. For the field of simulation 'Millennium Challenge' warns against inappropriate interference after the action has begun. For Project Management it serves as a reminder that projects which fail to account for undercurrents of communication tension become ever more 'directionally complex' and less amenable to solution. Remington and Pollack (2008) note in this regard that directional complexity is often not properly acknowledged by conventional project management approaches, and that many decisions apparently based on logical, objective reasoning may equally emerge from unacknowledged cultural and interpersonal factors.

Schrage (1999) also notes in relation to business (war) games that a 'model decoupled from its reality – the passion and politics it can arouse – is little more that an intellectual exercise' (p. 136). While such exercises can be valuable, the effective use of simulation for research involves close coupling of model and passion, clearly delineated abstraction of key contextual elements and careful avoidance of unwarranted interference. When these are present the researcher has a powerful tool to command. It can provide both future oriented analysis of potential outcomes of actions not yet taken, as well as enabling reconstruction of past actions for the purpose of determining how certain things happened, and how to ensure they are not replicated in future.

Simulation is – to some extent – symbiotic with system dynamics and, as such, its less abstract forms are excellent for learning purposes but less suited for research into contexts where cause and effect can be readily identified or discovered through expert analysis. It is however unsurpassed in aiding research into contexts and conditions that are unclear, indefinite and emergent.

References

Allen, T. (1997). *War Games*, Mandarin Paperbacks, London.

Bodhanya, Shamim (2003). see http://www.youtube.com/watch?v=tCdIdq5YI-M for an introduction to his work.

Churchman, C. West. (1967). 'Guest Editorial' in *Management Science* (Vol. 14, No. 4).

Crawford, L. (2000). Project management competence for the new millennium. In: *Proceedings of 15th World Congress on Project Management, London, England.*

Duke, R. D. (1974). Gaming: the Futures Language. New York, USA, Halsted Press.

Eisner, J.R. (1994). Attitudes, Chaos and the Connectionist Mind, Blackwell, Oxford Gladwell, M. (2005). *Blink – the Power of Thinking without Thinking,* Penguin/Allen Lane, Camberwell.

Hussein, B.A (2007). On using simulation games as a research tool in project management, in Mayer, I. Mastik M, (2007). Organizing and Learning Through Gaming and Simulation: Proceedings of ISAGA Uitgeverij Eburon, Delft edited by Igor Mayer, Hanneke Mastik.

James, W. (1890). *The Principles of Psychology,* accessed on 5/12/1012, at http://plato.stanford.edu/entries/james/

Kishore, Sengupta, Tarek, K. Abdel-Hamid, Luk and N. Van Wassenhove (2008). The Experience Trap, *Havard Business Review,* the Magazine, Feb 2008.

Leigh, E. (2005). Playing Beyond the Pale, conference paper – ISAGA conference, Georgia Tech, Atlanta.

Leigh, E. (2003). A Practitioner Researcher Perspective On Facilitating An Open, Infinite, Chaordic Simulation, doctoral dissertation available at http://epress.lib.uts.edu.au/scholarly-works/handle/2100/308

Leigh, E. and L. Spindler (1998). 'Vigilant Observer': A Role for Facilitators of Games/Simulations in *Gaming/Simulation for Policy Development and Organisational Change,* Geurt, J., Joldersma, C. and Roelofs, E. Tilburg University Press, Tilburg.

Lytton-Hitchins, James (2005). Materials for a half-day Introduction to The Cynefin Method, Sydney, on behalf of the Cynefin Centre.

Mayer, I., Mastik, H (eds). Organising and learning through Gaming and simulation – proceedings of ISAGA 2007, Eburon, Delft.

McGarrity, M. (2011). Unpublished notes from Simulation Australia meeting, Sydney Meadows, D., Fiddaman, T. and Shannon, D. (1993). Fish Banks, LTD. *Game Administrator's Manual*, Laboratory for Interactive Learning, Institute for Policy and Social Science Research Hood House, University of New Hampshire, Durham, USA.

Millennium Challenge http://en.wikipedia.org/wiki/Millennium_Challenge_2002

Napper, B. Reasonable Force in Leigh, E. and J. Kinder (2001). *Fun and Games for Workplace Learning*, Sydney, McGraw Hill.

Remington, K. and Pollack, J. (2008). *Tools for Complex Projects*, Gower, Hampshire.

Schrage, M. (1999). *Serious Play: how the worlds' best companies simulate to innovate*, Harvard Business School Press, Boston.

The Australian (2012). http://www.theaustralian.com.au/news/breaking-news/sydney-crane-workers-get-hero-awards/story-fn3dxiwe-1226536914285

Turner, R. and Cochrane, R. (1993). Goals-and-methods matrix: coping with projects with ill defined goals and/or methods of achieving them, *International Journal of Project Management*, Vol. 11, No. 2.

Weaver (1948). at http://en.wikipedia.org/wiki/Complexity

Chapter 8

System Dynamics for Project Management Research

Kim van Oorschot

Something old, something new
something borrowed, something blue
and a silver sixpence in her shoe

Abstract

In a book on novel approaches to organizational project management research it seems strange to have a chapter on system dynamics. System dynamics was developed by Jay Forrester in the 1950s. System dynamics is a method, a perspective, and a set of conceptual tools, to enhance learning in complex systems. This method is interdisciplinary. It is grounded in the theory of nonlinear dynamics and feedback control developed in mathematics, physics, and engineering. But because the method is applied to the behavior of human systems, it also draws on cognitive and social psychology, economies, and other social sciences (Sterman, 2000). Project management is considered to be one of the most successful areas for the application of system dynamics (Lyneis & Ford, 2007). From this perspective, system dynamics for project management is surely 'something old'. Surprisingly though, it is very hard to find references to the use of system dynamics in two well-known scientific journals on project management (the *International Journal of Project Management*, and the *Project Management Journal*). Assuming that the majority of the project management researchers are reading these journals, we can deduct that system dynamics is relatively unknown for these researchers, or in other words 'something new'.

This offers a great opportunity for future research in project management using the system dynamics approach. Since the 1950s a large body of knowledge on so-called project dynamics has been developed. As a result, future research can stand on the shoulder of giants, use existing, well-documented and well-tested project model structures and build improved models from there. 'Something borrowed' from previous research saves time and allows researchers to focus on the new challenges in project management, like outsourcing and offshoring (globalization of project management), project team design, knowledge management, and agile project management. By using building blocks from previous models, the amount of newness of future system dynamics models in project management can be kept relatively small, simple and trustworthy (in ancient Rome, 'something blue' symbolized modesty and fidelity). This will make future models easier to understand, especially for an audience that has not much experience with these kinds of models, like the readers of the project management journals described earlier. In the end, this will result in a 'silver sixpence in her shoe' for both researchers, who can find a new audience for their work, and the project management community, who can find a new approach to understanding the dynamic complexities inherent in current project management challenges in order to improve its practices.

In this chapter I will give a short introduction about system dynamics, discuss what is old, and what can be borrowed from previous work, and provide recommendations on how to find the silver sixpence.

Something Old – The Origins of System Dynamics

System dynamics is a perspective and a set of conceptual tools that enable us to understand the structure and dynamics of complex systems. System dynamics is also a rigorous modeling method that enables us to build formal computer simulations of complex systems and use them to design more effective policies and organizations (Sterman, 2000: vii). Dynamic complex systems are characterized by interdependence, mutual interaction, information feedback, and circular causality.

The field developed initially from the work of J.W. Forrester at the Sloan School of Management. This school was founded in 1952 with a grant of 10 million dollars from Alfred Sloan, the man who built the General Motors Corporation (Forrester, 2007). It was expected that a management school in a technical environment like MIT would probably develop differently, compared to e.g. Harvard in its liberal arts environment. When Forrester, with an electrical engineering background, joined the school in 1956, he was interested to find out what an engineering background could mean to management. Forrester (2007) describes his discovery as follows:

Chance intervened when I found myself at times in conversation with people from General Electric. They were puzzled by why their household appliance plants in Kentucky were sometimes working three and four shifts and then, a few years later, half the people would be laid off. It was easy enough to say that business cycles caused fluctuating demand, but that explanation was not convincing as the entire reason. After talking with them about how they made hiring and inventory decisions, I started to do some simulation. This was simulation using pencil and paper. (…) Even with constant incoming orders, one would get employment instability as a consequence of commonly used decision-making policies within the supply chain. That first inventory-control system with pencil and paper simulation was the beginning of the system dynamics field (p. 347).

In 1961, Forrester wrote his seminal book *Industrial Dynamics*. Within ten years, his ideas were applied to corporate and industrial problems, but it also became a general systems theory to serve as a framework to analyze and organize behavior and relationships in areas as diverse as engineering, medicine, management, psychology, and economics (Forrester, 1968). Project management and management of R&D processes were among these diverse areas. Because of the breadth of the field, the name industrial dynamics was generalized to system dynamics (Richardson, 1991).

Roberts' doctoral dissertation, 'The Dynamics of Research and Development', completed in 1962, was the first scholarly effort to apply system dynamics to project management within an R&D environment (Abdel-Hamid & Madnick, 1991). His system dynamics model of R&D project management includes the full life cycle of a single R&D project. It incorporates the interactions between the R&D product, the firm, the customer, and the processes relating to the nature of the work itself (Abdel-Hamid & Madnick, 1991; Roberts, 1962). Many researchers have extended Roberts' work. A summary of the system dynamics body of knowledge in project management will be discussed in the section 'Something borrowed'. But first I will provide readers unfamiliar to system dynamics a short introduction to the approach and discuss its basic elements.

Something New – The Basic Elements of System Dynamics

To learn system dynamics, Sterman's text book *Business Dynamics* (2000) is highly recommended. In this book, Sterman provides the reader with the background of the method, describes the mathematics, gives many examples, and shows how to build computer simulations. For the purpose of this chapter, a detailed explanation of system dynamics is not necessary, but a brief discussion of its basic elements is required to understand previous work and to discover new areas of application. In the next subsection, first the two main parts of system dynamics modeling are discussed, namely, the qualitative and the quantitative part. This section ends with explaining when, or to what kind of problems, system dynamics models can be applied.

Qualitative Approach – Causal Loops

The dynamic behavior of a system, that is, the system's behavior over time, is driven by feedback processes, along with stocks and flows, time delays and nonlinearities. Feedback exists whenever 'the environment causes a decision which in turn affects the original environment' (Forrester, 1958: 39). Feedback processes explain *how* decisions can lead to either good control or a dramatic out-of-control situation. All dynamics arise from the interaction of just two types of feedback loops: negative (or self-correcting) and positive (or self-reinforcing) loops (Sterman, 2000). Negative or balancing feedback loops counteract or oppose whatever is happening to the system in an attempt to bring the system back to its equilibrium. If you are the manager of a project that is falling behind schedule, you can ask your team to work harder to catch up on the delay and bring the project back on track. This negative feedback loop is depicted as a causal loop diagram in the left-hand side of Figure 8.1.

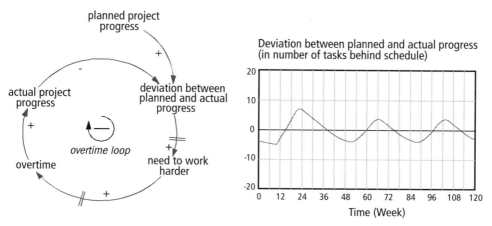

Figure 8.1. Structure and Behavior of a Negative or Balancing Feedback Loop

Causal loop diagrams (CLDs) are tools for diagramming the feedback structure of systems in any domain. CLDs are simply maps showing the causal links among variables with arrows from a cause to an effect (Sterman, 2000). On top of the CLD in Figure 8.1 the variable 'planned project progress' is shown. In this example, there is no arrow pointing to this variable, which means that this is an *exogenous* variable, which is constant and not influenced by other variables in the model. This exogenous variable determines, together with the *endogenous* (and thus influenced by at least one other variable in the model) variable 'actual project progress', the deviation between planned and actual progress. The links in CLDs also have a polarity. A positive link (+) means that if the cause *in*creases (decreases), the effect also *in*creases (decreases) above what it would otherwise have been. If the deviation between planned and actual progress increases, the need to work harder increases (positive link), and as a result, the team will work more overtime (positive link), which will increase the actual project progress (positive link) and reduce the deviation from the planned progress (negative link). This last link is a negative link (-) because here, when the cause *in*creases (decreases), the effect *de*creases (increases) below what it would otherwise have been. The CLD also shows when there is a delay between the cause and the effect. Delays are critical in creating dynamics. Delays give systems inertia, can create oscillations, and are often responsible for trade-offs between the short- and long-run effects of policies (Sterman, 2000). Delays in a CLD are denoted with a short double line perpendicular to the arrow. In the example, there is a delay between the occurrence of the deviation between planned and actual progress and the discovery of the need to work harder. Also, there is a delay between the discovery of the need to work harder and the actual occurrence of working overtime. Note that this CLD still holds if the situation is reversed and the team is getting ahead of plan. In this case the deviation between planned and actual progress is decreasing (it can even be negative), leading to a reduced need to work harder. This will reduce the amount of overtime which will reduce the actual project progress, thereby increasing the deviation from planned progress again.

The CLD provides information about the behavior over time of the variables in the system. If the CLD in Figure 8.1 shows the entire system, and there are no other variables to consider, the behavior over time of this system can be predicted simply by looking at the loop polarity (in this case a negative loop) and the delays. Because of the delays, the deviation will probably oscillate somewhat between positive and negative (and the team will work over- and undertime), but the system is more or less in balance (see right-hand side of Figure 8.1).

Of course project management is not as simple as Figure 8.1 shows, and there are many more variables and loops to consider. To keep it simple here, we will only consider one more loop, a positive or reinforcing feedback loop. Positive loops re-inforce what is happening to the system. Positive loops bring the system out of its equilibrium. An example of a reinforcing loop is shown in Figure 8.2, which is an extension of Figure 8.1.

This extended CLD shows an adverse side-effect of working overtime for too long: exhaustion. Team members that are exhausted can get sick or decide to take a day off. This leads to absenteeism, which reduces the number of productive team members. When the number of productive team members decreases, the actual project progress also decreases, thereby increasing the deviation from planned progress. As a result, the need to work harder increases even more and the remaining team members need to work even harder and longer hours (more overtime). This positive loop describes how the performance of this team, once it starts to get exhausted, keeps deteriorating. It is a vicious cycle. Also in this case, this positive loop holds when the situation is reversed. A reduction of the amount of overtime, leads to a reduced exhaustion and absenteeism and an increase of the number of productive team members. As a result, the actual progress increases and the amount of overtime can decrease even further. In this situation the positive loop is a virtuous cycle. Note that the number of negative links in a loop determines whether the loop is negative or positive. An even number of negative links results in a positive loop, whereas an uneven number of negative links results in a negative loop.

Also a positive loop provides information about the behavior over time of its un-derlying variables. When there are no other loops in a system, a positive loop shows exponential growth or decline. In Figure 8.2, where there is a combination of one negative loop and one positive loop, it is already difficult to predict what the behavior over time will be, because of the combination of the two loops. It depends on the strength of the two loops (the mathematics behind them) whether this system will

Creative and Innovative Contemporary Approaches

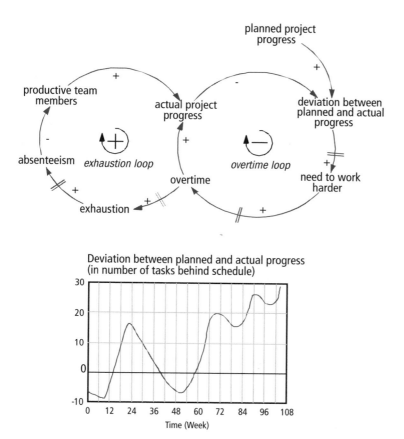

Figure 8.2. Structure and Behavior of a Combination of Negative and Positive Feedback Loop

get out of control or not. As an example, the right-hand side of Figure 8.2 shows that the project team first manages to get back on track after working overtime, but then starts to suffer from exhaustion which steadily causes an increased deviation from plan. In this case, the positive loop is stronger than the negative loop (because the graph shows that the exponential behavior dominates the oscillatory behavior).

In some cases, the qualitative part of the system dynamics approach, the CLD, is already sufficient to understand the drivers of a dynamic complex system, see for example the work of Perlow, Okhuysen, and Repenning (2002), and Van Oorschot, Akkermans, Sengupta, and Van Wassenhove (2013). But, when the goal is to test different decision making policies (what-if scenarios) to improve decision making, the quantitative part of the system dynamics approach is also required.

Quantitative Approach – Stocks and Flows

As stated in the previous paragraph, without understanding the mathematics behind all causal loops in a system, it will be difficult to predict the behavior of a system that consists of multiple balancing and reinforcing loops and time delays. Therefore we need a model containing stocks and flows. Causal loop diagrams depict the feedback structure of a system. Stock and flow diagrams show their underlying physical structure (Sterman, 2000). Stocks and flows track accumulations of material, money, and information as they move through a system. Stocks include inventories of a product, water in a bathtub, workload in a project, people in a team, or money in the project budgets. Flows are the rates of increase or decrease in stocks, such as production and shipments, inflow of water from the tap and outflow of water through the sink, rates of discovery and completion of project tasks, hiring and firing of team members, rates of acquisition and depletion of project funds. Stocks give systems inertia and provide them with memory. Stocks create delays by accumulating the difference between the inflow to a process and its outflow. Stocks characterize the state of the system and generate the information upon which decisions are based. The decisions then alter the rates of flow, which in turn alter the stocks again, thereby closing the feedback loops in the system. When drawing a stock and flow diagram, the following rules apply (see also Sterman, 2000: 192):

- Stocks are represented by rectangles (suggesting a container holding the contents of the stock).
- Inflows are represented by a pipe (arrow) pointing into (adding to) the stock.
- Outflows are represented by pipes pointing out of (subtracting from) the stock.
- Valves control the flows.
- Clouds represent the sources and sinks for the flows.
- A source represents the stock from which a flow originating outside the boundary of the model arises; a sink represents the stocks into which flows leaving the model boundary drain. Sources and sinks are assumed to have infinite capacity and can never constrain the flows they support.

Figure 8.3 provides an example of a stocks and flows diagram. The diagram contains two stocks: one that accumulates all project tasks that are still remaining, and one that accumulates all project tasks that are already completed. These two stocks determine the perceived project progress (note that this is not the *actual* project progress, because new tasks that were not part of the initial project plan can still be discovered). In this example, higher perceived project progress will result in a lower productivity of team members, leading to a lower completion rate of tasks. The lower this outflow, the higher the number of project tasks remaining, which closes the balancing loop of this example.

Mathematically, the basic structure of a formal system dynamics computer simulation model is a system of coupled, nonlinear, first-order differential (or integral)

Creative and Innovative Contemporary Approaches

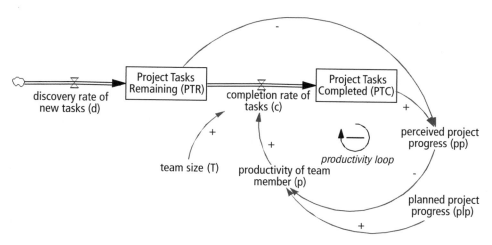

Figure 8.3. Stocks and Flows Diagram

equations. At any point in time, the number of project tasks remaining (*PTR*) is the sum of the initial number of project tasks remaining (at t = 0) and the accumulation or integration of all newly discovered tasks (*d*) from the start until that particular time minus all completed project tasks (*c*) from the start until that particular time. This is defined by the following integral equation:

$$PTR_t = \int_{t_0}^{t} (d_s - c_s)\,ds + PTR_0$$

This equation can also be written as a differential equation:

$$\frac{dPTR}{dt} = d_t - c_t$$

This last equation states that the change of the stock of project tasks remaining at a certain point in time is equal to the difference between the newly discovered tasks and the completed tasks at precisely that point in time. All variables in a stocks and flows diagram can be expressed in an equation. For example, the completion rate of tasks is a factor of team size (*T*) and productivity of team member (*p*):

$$c_t = T \mathbf{C} \, p_t$$

When the variable is exogenous, this equation is just one number. In the example depicted in Figure 8.3, team size is exogenous, so the equation for team size could be:

$$T = 10$$

Together, these equations create a system dynamics simulation model that can be used for further analysis. With the simulation model space and time can be compressed and slowed so the long-term side-effects of decisions is experienced, the understanding of complex systems is developed, and design structures and strategies for greater success can be developed (Sterman, 2000). These simulation models are also referred to as management flight simulators. Using these flight simulators different scenarios can be tested to improve learning and understanding of the effects of changing the values of variables or of changing policies.

When to use System Dynamics?

System dynamics is a suitable method when situations need to be analyzed that involve multiple and interacting processes, delays, accumulations, and other nonlinear effects, such as feedback loops and thresholds (e.g. how many days can a team work overtime before exhaustion kicks in). Simulation is effective for theory development when the research question involves a fundamental tension or trade-off, because these trade-offs often result in nonlinear relationships, like thresholds. These trade-offs may be temporal (short- versus long-run implications), structural (too much structure versus too little), or spatial (near versus far away) (Davis, Eisenhardt, and Bingham, 2007). Nonlinear relationships are difficult to discover using, for example, inductive case methods and difficult to explore with traditional statistical techniques (Davis, et al., 2007). Furthermore, methods that aim to find correlation between possible causal factors and performance outcomes, like surveys, are unsafe if any accumulating stock exists between that cause and outcome (Warren, 2008). Finally, system dynamics is capable of including human decisions and human behavior. Soft, and hard-to-quantify factors can be included in system dynamics models, like work pressure, motivation, trust, collaboration, fairness perceptions (see for example Van Burg and Van Oorschot, 2012). In operations research models, these variables are often omitted, simply because they are hard to quantify. 'To omit such variables is equivalent to saying they have zero effect – probably the only value that is known to be wrong!' (Forrester, 1961: 57).

Something Borrowed – System Dynamics Applied to Project Management

In the first section it was already mentioned that the first scholarly effort to apply system dynamics to project management within an R&D environment was Roberts' doctoral dissertation, 'The Dynamics of Research and Development', completed in 1962. Since then, Roberts has played an important role in advancing the field through studies of R&D projects. Abdel-Hamid and Madnick (1991) extended his work by applying it to a software development project. In 2007, Lyneis and Ford wrote a review paper on project management applications of system dynamics. To categorize the literature, the authors provide a meta-structure of four project model structures (note that I will not repeat all references used by Lyneis and Ford (2007), I will only add relevant references that have appeared in the literature since 2007):

1. Project features: This structure contains system dynamics models that focus on modeling features found in actual projects. These features include development processes (like the stocks of Project Tasks Remaining and Project Tasks Completed in the example in Figure 8.3), resources, managerial mental models, and decision making. Also Roberts' work falls into this category (see also Xu, Sun, Skibniewski, Chan, Yeung & Cheng, 2012).
2. Rework cycle: The canonical structure of system dynamics project models is the rework cycle. This cycle describes that when project tasks are performed, mistakes are made that require rework. This rework is usually undiscovered at first, which leads the project manager to think that progress is better or more advanced than it actually is. When the rework is discovered, the total remaining workload increases, which could lead to more work pressure (see also Lin, Chai, Wong & Brombacher, 2008; Love, Edwards & Irani, 2008).
3. Project control: Project managers need to deliver their project within typical project constraints in terms of time, budget, and quality. Project control aims to reduce deviations between planned or targeted performance and actual performance. Generally, there are two types of project control: goal-seeking (e.g. hiring more people, work harder, or work faster) and goal-adjustment (e.g. postponing a deadline) (see also Godlewski, Lee & Cooper, 2012; Abdel-Hamid, 2011; Van Oorschot, Langerak & Sengupta, 2011; White, 2011).
4. Ripple and knock-on effects: 'Ripple effects' are the primary side-effects of well-intentioned project control efforts. Ripple effects of the decision to hire extra team members are for example experience dilution or communication difficulties. The decision to work harder can lead to exhaustion (remember Figure 8.2), whereas working faster can lead to more mistakes. The ripple effect of postponing a deadline is for example disappointed customers. 'Knock-on effects' refer to the secondary impact of project control efforts, that is, the impact of ripple effects. A knock-on effect of making mistakes is that as long as mistakes remain undetected, they can create more mistakes when downstream tasks inherit these mistakes. Exhaustion can knock on to increased turnover. (see also Yaghootkar & Gil, 2012; Van Oorschot, Sengupta, Akkermans & Van Wassenhove, 2010; Lane & Husemann, 2008).

These four project model structures contribute to the understanding of the most typical project behavior: the failure to meet project targets (Lyneis & Ford, 2007). In most cases, the failure to meet project targets is caused by an asymmetric uncertainty (Van Oorschot, et al., 2010): on the one hand the project workload is underestimated (new unexpected tasks are discovered during project execution, mistakes require unexpected rework, customers desire unexpected changes of the initial design), while on the other hand the project workforce is overestimated (team members are still tied up to other projects that are delayed, it takes time to assemble a team and to train newcomers). With system dynamics modeling it can be analyzed just how substantial the total effect (that is, including all ripple and knock-on effects) is of, for example, working faster and making more mistakes or adding an extra customer change request to compensate for late delivery.

The lessons learned from system dynamics modeling can also be grouped into four categories (Lyneis & Ford, 2007). First, models can involve a post-mortem assessment of what happened in the project and of the root causes for the project's failure or success (see for example Robertson & Williams, 2006). Second, models can be used to improve project estimating and risk assessment, in other words: how can project plans and budgets take into account the asymmetric uncertainties and become more realistic and robust. The third category focuses on response or control mechanisms that can be used when problems occur (change and risk management policies fall into this category). Finally, system dynamics models of projects can help in management training and education. These project models can help to teach the system dynamics approach to both students and practitioners. Furthermore, these models, when used in a management flight simulator, can help project managers to learn about feedback loops and become better project managers. By forcing a feedback perspective on project management problems (as opposed to a linear perspective), system dynamics increases the project team's (or the researcher's) knowledge of potential counterintuitive side-effects of their decisions, both on the short – and the long term. Without simulation, mental models about these side-effects can only be tested and improved by relying on the information feedback received from the real world. However, this is not only very slow but also very ineffective because this information is often distorted, ambiguous, erroneous, and delayed. As a result, this learning in the real world, through trial-and-error is also very risky and expensive. In these circumstances, simulating scenarios with a management flight simulator is a reliable, relatively cheap and risk-free way to test project management decisions and evaluate their (side-) effects.

Something Blue – Building on Previous Work

Although the models that were mentioned in the previous section differ in their level of detail with regard to the phases of work represented, the complexity of the rework cycle, and the feedback effects that are represented, formulations of these processes have been developed and are documented for others to use (Lyneis & Ford, 2007). Using the building blocks that previous researchers have produced saves time and allows future researchers to focus on the new challenges in project management. By using elements from previous models, the amount of newness of new system dynamics models in project management can be kept relatively small, simple and trustworthy. But when so many system dynamics applications in the project management field already exist, what are the next challenges?

One of the biggest challenges in system dynamics applied to project management is the decision what to put in and what to leave out of the model, or in other words: 'challenging the clouds' (Sterman, 2000). A number of variables that were left out of previous models or were only included as an exogenous, constant value, should be either included in future models or should be made endogenous (i.e. part of a feedback loop). The reason for this is that project management has changed and is facing new challenges, and as a result, the project management models should change as well. Four challenges in future applications of system dynamics to project management can be identified.

The first is the global challenge. An increasing number of project managers have team members that are spread around the globe, working in different cultures, in different time zones, using different languages. Making sure a team member at a different part of the globe uses the same standards and delivers the right quality of work is an extremely difficult task. Different control and coordination mechanisms have been described in the literature, each with its own (nonlinear) benefits and drawbacks. Of course these mechanisms are part of a feedback loop that influences the performance of the project, which in turn influences the need for control and coordination. For example, the direct supervision of team members located at a different site, far away from the core team helps sharing ideas and best practices, which benefits the productivity of the distant team. However, too much supervision can have a negative effect on the trust that this distant team has in the core team, which could harm this productivity. In a forthcoming paper by Smets, Van Oorschot and Langerak (2013), control mechanisms and their effects on trust and project performance will be described and modeled. This model is however based on projects performed in a setting of one manufacturer and one supplier, so there is a strong need for replication in other outsourcing and offshoring settings.

The next challenge is closely related to the previous one. This second challenge is to include knowledge sharing and knowledge management in project models. As projects are being executed at different sites around the globe, and as projects involve more and more intangible skills and experiences from project team members, knowledge management becomes more important. But in order to manage knowledge team members must be allowed to share knowledge (which can be difficult if knowledge is protected by intellectual property rights). Second, team members must be willing to both share and adopt knowledge. Knowledge management costs time, and time is usually not on the side of a project team. Although probably everyone will admit that knowledge management is beneficial to project teams, these benefits will usually manifest themselves in the long run, whereas the costs (investing time) are right here and now, on the very short term. With system dynamics models, these long term effects of knowledge management (including protection, sharing and adoption) can be made clear on the short term (see for example Tukel, Kremic, Rom & Miller, 2011). This can increase the willingness of project teams to invest time in knowledge management processes.

The third challenge is the design and development of the right team. Even when a project is developed by one team located at one site, in one country, the 21st century comes with its own obstacles. First, because of the financial crisis, many organizations are downsizing, which could make it difficult to sufficiently staff a project, leading to more workload and stress for the team. Furthermore, the retirement age in many countries is increased, which not only influences the average age of a team, but also the difference in experience level (or number of years of experience) between newcomers and oldtimers. Although it is not a system dynamics research, the paper of Perretti and Negro (2006) is an interesting starting point for interested model developers. These authors discuss two dimensions of team composition: the newness of members, and the newness of member combinations. They discover nonlinear relationships between team member status and the success of mixing and matching team members, and also between the number of hierarchical layers in organizational structures and the mixing and matching success. These nonlinearities should deserve further examination, especially with regard to the ripple and knock-on effects of mixing, matching and team learning on the project and even the project portfolio.

The last challenge is agile project management. In a world of constantly shrinking product development times, and demanding customers that keep changing their minds, even during project execution, a project manager hardly has the time to sit down and think about project planning, let alone update this plan every time a change occurs. In software development, agile methods have been implemented. These agile methods prescribe short iterative cycles, actively involve users to establish, prioritize, and verify requirements, and rely on tacit knowledge within a team as opposed to documentation (Highsmith & Cockburn, 2001; Ramesh, Mohan & Cao, 2012). As such, the project team should only plan about one month ahead, after which the output is presented to the customer. Together with the customer, it decided what to work on in the next month. Although the results of these agile methods seem promising, more research is needed on for example, the effects of monthly deadlines on team stress and motivation and customer behavior. Furthermore, although many projects involve software development, most projects also have a strong hardware component (like construction projects). It remains to be seen how these agile methods can be applied to other types of projects as well. With a system dynamics model, analyses can be executed of, for example, the effect of more frequent in-between due dates (milestones) on the performance of the team, the satisfaction of the customer, and the final quality of the project result.

And a Silver Sixpence in her Shoe – From a Challenge to Successful Application

The challenges listed above, have in common that they include the so-called soft, or hard-to-quantify factors, like trust, willingness to share knowledge, experience, learning, satisfaction, and quality. In order to model these factors adequately, close collaboration with project management professionals and project teams is required. The intangible factors need to be captured in a number that relates to the mental models of these professionals. The early system dynamics analyses were mostly performed in 'consultant' mode 'in which a system dynamicist would study a corporation, go away and build a model, and come back with recommendations' (Lyneis & Ford, 2007: 354). The challenges from the previous section require that the mental models of project managers need to be understood, modeled, simulated, and probably changed to improve management processes and project performance. To achieve this, practitioners must become involved in the modeling process to learn about dynamic feedback behavior. Methods like group model building (Vennix, Akkermans & Rouwette, 1996) and the Renga approach (Akkermans, 2001) facilitate the involvement of practitioners in the modeling process.

Finally, as a special note to researchers, the system dynamics model and the new findings that are the result of the modeling process should find their way to a scientific publication. To make this kind of research more accessible, four general rules of thumb apply (Repenning, 2003):

1. Do your homework. The language and literature used for building a model with practitioners is probably not the language that is used by fellow researchers. Keep the audience in mind when labeling model variables.
2. Appropriate model size. Models can easily become too large and complicated. Although there is no rule of thumb for model size, modelers should keep in mind that they have to explain the contents of the model, and usually, its equations, in just one section of a scientific paper. Obviously, the smaller and simpler the model, the easier it is to explain it to others in just a few pages.
3. Build intuition. Standard modes of presenting system dynamics models (like causal loop and stocks and flows diagrams) can be ineffective when presenting to non-system dynamics audiences. According to Repenning (2003) a phase plot is helpful for audiences to understand the model. A phase plot shows the value of a variable at the current time (e.g. year 3), as a function of the value of that variable in the previous time unit (year 2).
4. Choose your audience wisely. System dynamicists 'share the language of mathematics and the use of formal models as inquiry tools with our colleagues in economics and operations research, but our worldview is more consistent with those in psychology, sociology and anthropology. We should not abandon our efforts to become better connected with our colleagues in economics or operations research, but there are other points of connection. In my own work, I have found it easier to sell my work to those scholars whose primary interest lies in understanding real world phenomena' (Repenning, 2003: 320).

Summary

In this chapter system dynamics applied to project management is discussed. The origins of the approach have been described and the elements of the approach were introduced. Although the approach originated in the 1950s, and its applications to project management are wide-spread, there are still many opportunities for further use of the approach to tackle the future challenges in project management. These challenges include: globalization, knowledge management, project team design, and agile project management methods. As project management is evolving from a more mechanistic, deterministic and predictable task to a more organic, complex and uncertain task, the project manager needs to deal with complex dynamic characteristics of projects, like nonlinearities, feedback loops, delays, trade-offs, and thresholds. System dynamics is an interesting approach for understanding these complex dynamic characteristics, for improving decision-making and policy design, and consequently, for contributing to the field of project management research. System dynamics applications to project management can be made even more successful when project management practitioners are actively involved in the modeling process. Not only because researchers need to understand the practitioners' mental models and the root causes of their decisions, but also because practitioners need to gain trust and understanding in the system dynamics approach and use the management flight simulators to improve their project management knowledge and decision making processes.

References

Abdel-Hamid, T.K., & Madnick, S.E. (1991). *Software project dynamics – An integrated approach*. Englewood Cliffs, NJ: Prentice-Hall.

Abdel-Hamid, T.K. (2011). Single-loop project controls: reigning paradigms or straitjackets. *Project Management Journal*, 42: 17-30.

Akkermans, H. (2001). Renga: A systems approach to facilitating inter-organizational network development. *System Dynamics Review*, 17: 179-93.

Davis, J.P., Eisenhardt, K.M., & Bingham, C.B. (2007). Developing theory through simulation methods. *Academy of Management Review*, 32: 480-99.

Forrester, J.W. (1958). Industrial dynamics – a major breakthrough for decision makers. *Harvard Business Review*, 36: 37-66.

Forrester, J.W. (1961). *Industrial Dynamics*. Pegasus Communications: Waltham, MA.

Forrester, J.W. 1968. Industrial dynamics – after the 1st decade. *Management Science*, 14: 398-415.

Forrester, J.W. (2007). System dynamics – a personal view of the first 50 years. *System Dynamics Review*, 23: 345-58.

Godlewski, E., Lee, G. & Cooper, K. (2012). System Dynamics Transforms Fluor Project and Change Management. *Interfaces* 42: 17-32.

Highsmith, J. & A. Cockburn. (2001). Agile software development: The business of innovation. *IEEE Computer*, 9: 120-122.

Lane, D.C. & Husemann, E. (2008). Steering without Circe: Attending to reinforcing loops in social systems. *System Dynamics Review*, 24: 37-61.

Lin, J., Chai, K.H., Wong, Y.S. & Brombacher, A.C. (2008). A dynamic model for managing overlapped iterative product development. *European Journal of Operational Research*, 185: 378-92.

Love, P.E.D., Edwards, D.J. & Irani, Z. (2008). Forensic project management: An exploratory examination of the causal behavior of design-induced rework. *IEEE Transactions on Engineering Management*, 55: 234-47.

Lyneis, J.M. and Ford, D.N. (2007). System Dynamics Applied to Project Management: A Survey, Assessment, and Directions for Future Research. *System Dynamics Review*, 23: 157-89.

Perlow, L.A., Okhuysen, G.A. & Repenning, N.P. (2002). The speed trap: Exploring the relationship between decision making and temporal context. *Academy of Management Journal*, 45: 931-55.

Perretti, F. & Negro, G. (2006). Filling empty seats: How status and organizational hierarchies affect exploration versus exploitation in team design. *Academy of Management Journal*, 49: 759-77.

Ramesh, B., Mohan, K. & Cao, L. (2012). Ambidexterity in agile distributed development: An empirical investigation. *Information Systems Research*, 23: 323-39.

Repenning, N.P. 2003. Selling system dynamics to (other) social scientists. *System Dynamics Review*, 19: 303-327.

Richardson, G.P. (1991/1999). *Feedback thought in social science and systems theory*. Philadelphia: University of Pennsylvania Press; reprinted by Pegasus Communications, Waltham, MA.

Roberts, E.B. (1962). *The dynamics of research and development*. Published Ph.D. dissertation, M.I.T., Cambridge, MA.

Robertson, S. & Williams, T. (2006). Understanding project failure: using cognitive mapping in an insurance project, *Project Management Journal*, 37: 55-71.

Smets, L.P.M., Van Oorschot, K.E. & Langerak, F. (2013). Don't trust trust – A dynamic approach to controlling supplier involvement in new product development, *Journal of Product Innovation Management*, (forthcoming).

Sterman, J.D. (2000). *Business Dynamics –Systems Thinking and Modeling for a Complex World*. Boston: McGraw-Hill.

Tukel, O.I., Kremic, T., Rom, W.O. & Miller, R.J. (2011). Knowledge-salvage practices for dormant R&D projects, *Project Management Journal*, 42: 59-72.

Van Burg, E. & Van Oorschot, K.E. (2013). Cooperating to commercialize technology: A dynamic model of fairness perceptions, experience, and cooperation, *Production and Operations Management*, (forthcoming).

Van Oorschot, K.E., Sengupta, K., Akkermans, H. & Van Wassenhove, L. (2010). Get Fat Fast: Surviving Stage-Gate in NPD. *Journal of Product Innovation Management*, 27: 828-39.

Van Oorschot, K.E., Langerak, F. & Sengupta, K. (2011). Escalation, de-escalation, or reformulation: Effective interventions in delayed NPD projects. *Journal of Product Innovation Management*, 28: 848-67.

Van Oorschot, K.E., Akkermans, H., Sengupta, K. & Van Wassenhove, L. (2013). Anatomy of a decision trap in complex new product development projects. *Academy of Management Journal*, 56: 285-307.

Vennix, J.A.M., Akkermans, H.A. & Rouwette, E.A.J.A. (1996). Group model-building to facilitate organizational change: An exploratory study. *System Dynamics Review*, 12: 39-58.

Warren, K. 2008. *Strategic Management Dynamics*. West Sussex: John Wiley & Sons.

White, A.S. (2011). A control system project development model derived from System Dynamics. *International Journal of Project Management*, 29: 696-705.

Xu, Y.L., Sun, C.S., Skibniewski, M.J., Chan, A.P.C., Yeung, J.F.Y. & Cheng, H. (2012). System Dynamics (SD)-based concession pricing model for PPP highway projects. *International Journal of Project Management*, 30: 240-51.

Yaghootkar, K., & Gil, N. (2012). The effects of schedule-driven project management in multi-project environments. *International Journal of Project Management*, 30: 127-40.

Chapter 9

The Design of Research Programs: Example from a PMO Research Program

Monique Aubry

Abstract

Organizations are becoming more complex. The study of phenomena in organizations managing multiple projects often requires combining multiple perspectives in the theoretical foundations and methodologies approach. This chapter provides insights to guide the design of future research programs and offers an example from the Project Management Office (PMO) research program undertaken by the Project Management Research Chair, School of Business, Université du Québec à Montréal. In this chapter, we will first define what a research program is by identifying its five major characteristics: sense making, interaction and negotiation, emergence, change process, and resource allocation based on Pellegrinelli's definition of a program (Pellegrinelli, 2011). This chapter describes the five phases of the research program with the objective of illustrating the diversity in research approaches and the sequence of how phases unfolded to form the research program. In doing so, it also explains how the PMO research program contributed to the translational and transformational approaches highlighted in this book. The framework developed by Van de Ven and Poole (2005) to classify the alternative approaches for studying organizational change under their ontological and epistemological positions has been used to situate the five phases of the research program. Their framework covers the simple sequential articulation of the phases and provides a framework that shows the underlying logic explaining the move from one phase to the other. In this way, different facets of the same phenomenon were highlighted resulting in a global, but still partial, understanding of the phenomenon. The progression of the research is revealed, phase by phase, with each phase answering a question while, at the same time, letting new ones emerge. An integrative view then shows how plurality within a research program provides good coverage of the phenomenon, which would not have been possible otherwise. Finally, the chapter ends with some research program management strengths and weaknesses for future research.

The study of project-based organizations and of organizing for projects is not a simple task. There are two major reasons for this. First, projects are temporary organizations (Lundin & Söderholm, 1995; Turner & Müller, 2003) and the management of such activities leads to challenges regarding project-based learning, project embeddedness and project capabilities (Cattani, Ferriani, Frederiksen & Täube, 2011). Second, the difficulty of studying project-based organizations relates to the spatial distribution of the coordination mechanisms among entities within organizations. A lot is known about project management structure with differentiation between functional and project structures giving rise to a variety of matrix organizations (Hobday, 2000; Larson, 2004). The design of project-based organizations is still currently monopolized by this matrix approach. However, in terms of organizational design, project-based organizations should include multiple project management activities that deal with strategic alignment, portfolio and program management, governance, etc. This approach is what is known as organizational project management (Aubry, Hobbs & Thuillier, 2007), or more simply, the project function (Aubry, Sicotte, Drouin, Vidot-Delerue & Besner, 2012; Crawford, 2010).

This chapter provides some insights to guide the design of future research programs and offers an example from a Project Management Office (PMO) research program undertaken between 2006 and 2011 by the Project Management Chair, School of Management, Université du Québec à Montréal. This research program was undertaken to provide a theorization of the project management function at the organizational level by looking at one of its mechanisms, the PMO. It was initiated to tackle this immense work, phase by phase, with the answers from one phase often leading to new questions for the next one. The intention is not to focus on the research results themselves but rather on the research process that led to this type of result.

What is a Research Program?

According to Pellegrinelli (2011), a research program such as this one is better defined within a *becoming* or a social constructivist ontology:

> *A programme is an organizational construct brought into existence to become a nexus of sense-making, evaluative, and political processes and resource allocation decisions associated with the realization of a change that may be vaguely defined, ambiguous and/or contested. A programme is essentially emergent in nature, inspired by a vision or outcome, yet sustained and shaped through on-going interaction and negotiation within its community of interest* (p. 236).

This definition fits perfectly well in the context of a research program. Five characteristics of major importance in the context of a research program can be identified from this definition. First, sense-making is the major task of the researcher's work throughout the research process: what is the problem, what do we already know from previous research and to what degree has this previous research shed light on the problematic and if it did not, how should the pertinent research question be defined, which methodological methods will better contribute to answering the research question, how should the data be assessed to really make sense of it, and so on. In short, sense-making is crucial in any research project. The same is true at the program level as critical reflection on one project serves to create impetus for the next question to be answered. It requires the researcher and the team to critically assess the satisfactory and unsatisfactory answers obtained in any given research.

Second, this reflection may bring together a number of stakeholders in and around the research, such as project management professionals and managers, employees of normative institutions, other researchers inside the project management field and outside this community, etc. This is in line with the concept of engaged scholarship as suggested by Ven de Ven (2007) where the research not only involves academics, but has the power to bring together a variety of persons who will contribute to knowledge creation and dissemination. This forms a nexus of sense-making for a longer period than just for a single project. The program provides some continuity during the quest to understand a particular phenomenon.

Third, the research program emerges. At the beginning of the program, there is usually an inspiring vision of what the phenomenon is and the basic approaches expected to be able to provide understanding or answers. This vision evolves as results from individual projects deliver partial results and are discussed in different communities, as mentioned earlier in an engaged scholarship approach. It sometimes leads to deviations from the initial plan in order to address a specific issue that was not identified initially but that still fits with the overall vision or goal of the research program.

Fourth, in general, research contributes to changes in the research community and in the professional world (this is the ultimate goal). The change process first happens through the research program process itself. The changes start to happen when stakeholders are engaged in the research program, as explained by Van de Ven (2007). It likely occurs through a community of practice learning from sharing various points of view (Lave & Wenger, 1991). In this way, change from a research program reaches a larger audience than the participants in the program itself. However, it does not follow the same process as in a business project (e.g., Gareis & Huemann, 2008). For research programs, changes are influential depending on the dissemination strategy for the research results. In a research program context, changes are more likely to influence the professional community as it addresses a major issue or a phenomenon and the results would be presented in a practical approach.

Conversely, influence within the academic community would require solid conceptual foundations to provide theoretical contributions on which future research could be built. A research program is more likely to keep the ultimate objective focused on a specific phenomenon, thereby avoiding dispersion and lack of convergence, as identified by Söderlund (2011) in his formalization of pluralism in project management research. A research program can also influence research methods as such. A research program is more likely to adopt a variety of approaches to offer different lenses on a phenomenon. Combined, the diversity of approaches constitutes a unique creative bricolage by which to understand a phenomenon that would be impossible to investigate one aspect at the time.

Fifth and last are the resource allocation decisions. Again, in a research program, resource allocation decisions do not have the same interpretation as in business. However, it is still a key issue. As the research program progresses, new resources may become available to initiate a new research or individual research project simply terminate (quite similar to any program management). As individuals are considered, new collaborations may take form spontaneously when researchers find a common ground exploring a particular perspective in the program vision. These collaborations may terminated at the end of a project or continue on through new opportunities. In research, monetary resources are an important issue. The search for funding takes considerable time. The availability of funds makes collaboration between international researchers easier. Working virtually has its limits when it comes time to discuss conceptual ideas. Funds can also facilitate the collaboration of students, which is part of our teaching work as university professors.

Examining complex phenomena in organizations calls for creativity through multiple approaches. This takes time and resources. A good example of such a research program is the Innovative Forms of Organizing (INNFORM) project that took place between 1992 and 1997 and where an international research team (Pettigrew & Massini, 2003) sought to gain knowledge on innovative forms of organizing. Through this research, Pettigrew (2003b) identified the qualities required by scholars who undertake such a research program:

Modesty and care are important attributes for any scholar, but they are particularly crucial for scholars of change. Most big questions of innovation and change require the perspective of the comparative historian to even begin to find proximate answers. And yet as scholars of contemporary innovation, we are impatient to find answers to questions which, in the haze of the present, are as difficult to pose as they are to answer (p. 331).

In this context, each research phase constituted a project with its own structure, methodology, and team working towards the delivery of specific deliverables. Those deliverables were more likely intangible such as concepts, propositions, or theories. Knowledge from each individual research project combines to form a coherent (still partial) answer to the program objective. Research programs are developed for the study of complex phenomena over several years where a diversity of theories/empirical data/methodologies is required to explain such phenomena (e.g., Fenton & Pettigrew, 2000).

Creative and Innovative Contemporary Approaches

Description of the PMO Research Program
History of the PMO Research Program

The PMO research program consisted of five major phases and lasted formally for more than six years; this program lasted for about 10 years when the initial thoughts process before the formalization of the research is included (see Table 9.1). It came about as a result of opportunities and the profound desire to provide theoretical foundations and to contribute to the well-being of people working in a multiple projects context. A detailed description of the PMO research program can be found in the Appendix before References.

Table 9.1. PMO Research Program Phases

Phase	Period	Title	Grant
Pre-research	2002-2005	Initial thoughts	
1	2005-2006	Describing the reality of PMOs	PMI research program 2006
2	2006-2007	Understanding of PMOs and their contribution to the organizational performance	
3	2008-2010	Identifying the forces driving the frequent changes in PMOs	PMI Research program 2008 Per & Eivor Wikströms Foundation, Sweden
4	2009-2011	Governance and communities of PMOs	PMI Research program 2009
5	2010-2011	The PMO's contribution to implementing a major organizational transformation in the health care field	Canada LEAD program 2009-2011

Under the term 'initial thoughts', there are several activities that contributed to an initial formalization of the issue. For example, during project management courses, students (project management professionals) were describing their reality in managing projects. In 2002, it became clear that the PMO as an organizational entity was emerging in large organizations and that a wide variety existed among them. This situation was also discussed in a recently created local PMO community of practice. This diversity strongly contrasted with the models suggested in the literature at that time. It provided the impetus to undertake an initial research project. This pre-research phase should not be overlooked since it provided the foundation from which the research program emerged and served as preparation for obtaining the involvement of several stakeholders in the research.

Phase 1: Describing the Reality of PMOs

The research program was initially defined with only two research phases (Hobbs & Aubry, 2007). The purpose of the first phase was to describe the reality of PMOs and provide an explanation for their diversity. The assumption was that explanations existed. Two successive questionnaires were developed with the collaboration of members of the local PMO community of practice and sent out to the international project management community. From this phase, 500 valid responses were received. It provided a rich description of the diversity of PMOs found in the reality of organizations and drew attention to the difficulty in explaining this diversity (Hobbs & Aubry, 2007). This challenged the usual simple PMO models found in the current literature and the underlying assumption that these models could apply to all contexts. The major outcome was a PMO descriptive model grounded in empirical data, which distinguished it from a conceptual model. The model included four components: organizational context, PMO structural characteristics, PMO functions, and performance.

Explanations for the variety of PMOs were not found in the usual variables of contingency theory such as size of the organization, region or industry (Donaldson, 2001). The descriptive model is more useful as a toolkit that reflective practitioners can use to make sense of their context and to construct the PMO best suited to their context (Schön, 1983).

Another important finding of this research pertains to PMO performance. The first attempt to find which variables explained performance was undertaken using the PMO's characteristics and functions. This approach explained 28% of PMO performance. More importantly, however, four variables outside the technical description of PMOs explained 48% of it (Hobbs & Aubry, 2010). These variables, which we refer to as embeddedness, are: collaboration with other project participants, recognition of PMO expertise, a well-understood PMO mission and the support of upper management. This finding should guide the PMO's priorities in terms of values and communication – less focus on technical characteristics and more on embeddedness.

Other statistical analyses were performed using this PMO database to develop a PMO typology. Conceptual typology for four types of PMOs was identified based on the results of correlation analysis (Hobbs & Aubry, 2008). Cluster analysis validated and refined this typology producing six PMO types identified by their structural characteristics (Hobbs & Aubry, 2011). The six types show differing levels of performance. Regression analysis on performance for the entire sample and within each type revealed, first, that the organizational context is not a good predictor of PMO performance; second, that the functions filled by PMOs are good predictors of PMO performance; and third, the functions that are the best predictors vary from one type of PMO to another. These results bring into question the search for universal best practices, which is behind much of the discussion on PMOs.

The contribution of this research phase lies in its critical approach to challenging what was once taken for granted, namely, a limited number of PMO models. The major limitation of this phase relates to the quantitative approach of using a questionnaire and the lack of contextual information on the PMO. It was expected that this phase would provide an explanation of the variation in the context (see Phase 2).

Phase 2: Understanding PMOs and their Contribution to Organizational Performance

Based on the first phase, it was not possible to explain the diversity among PMOs. With the same assumption in mind, the second phase was undertaken, this time using a qualitative approach with four in-depth case studies. This phase adopted a case study approach to overcome the limitations of the previous phase, and to provide rich contextual information (Aubry et al., 2007). The research question was: How to understand the PMO contribution to organizational performance. The research was based on three complementary fields of theory: innovation social system (Hughes, 1987; Schumpeter, 1950; Van de Ven & Garud, 1994), actor network theory (Callon & Law, 1989; Latour, 2005) and the competing values framework (Quinn & Rohrbaugh, 1983). Four in-depth case studies were undertaken to provide retrospective knowledge on PMOs and their external and internal environments. The major outcome of this research was to conceptualize the transformation process. It emerges as a concept rooted in the PMO history of each organization (Aubry, Hobbs & Thuillier, 2008). A partial explanation of the variations among PMOs was also been explored through the evolutionary pattern of variation-selection-retention, where the PMO, as a phenomenon, has been identified during a fermentation period, preceding the selection period (Hobbs, Aubry & Thuillier, 2008). This finding has a major impact on understanding and explaining why PMOs change so frequently.

A second outcome of this phase was the understanding it generated about the political system in which PMOs are embedded. Issues, tensions, and conflicts are part of the PMO's existence. More than 70 different deliverables produced by PMO personnel have been identified, one being the project status report. The itinerary of one project status report was tracked in each organization using color codes. Based on the actor network theory, the research showed how networks are constructed around controversies emerging from the color code (Aubry, 2011).

The third outcome related to performance. Based on the competing values framework, the performance of a PMO was approached as a contribution to organizational performance. This raises the idea that performance is a subjective construct anchored in the values and preferences of stakeholders. The research revealed differences in those values and preferences (Aubry & Hobbs, 2011). It also highlighted PMO performance as a process of dialogue.

This research phase led us into the internal life of PMOs, including what they really do (functions, deliverables, etc.) and with whom; it also shed light on internal dynamics along with tensions or conflicts. The researcher had to give the interviewees the freedom to talk and then listen carefully to what was being said, as in a grounded approach (Strauss & Corbin, 1990). This approach not only considered the PMO as unit of analysis, but revealed a second unit of analysis, i.e., the PMO transformation.

The results of Phases 1 and 2 revealed that the form and/or functions of the majority of PMOs are transformed every few years. Results were intriguing regarding the explanation of the diversity, but they strongly contradicted the initial assumption, which was a major result. Diversity was found not only in the description of each PMO but in the evolution of each PMO. This phase marked a turning point in the focus of this research program from one of desperately searching for regularity or linearity to one of preparing for unique settings and transformations. Phase 3 was initiated to study this transformation process. In organizations with multiple PMOs, limiting the research to one PMO at a time would not provide an overarching conceptualization of what was happening in these organizations. This limitation gave rise to research questions on governance and multiple PMOs (see Phase 4).

Phase 3: Identifying the Forces Driving the Frequent Changes in PMOs

The third phase definitely turned to the dynamics surrounding PMOs with the exploration of the PMO transformation process. The unit of analysis was not the PMO, but the transformation. This phase was partly conducted in collaboration with Umeå University in Sweden. It adopted a mixed method with the first part being qualitative with 17 case studies in Sweden and in Canada. In the second part, a quantitative approach was adopted with the aim of generalizing the results from the first one. A total of 184 valid responses were received. Again, very few strong conclusions could be drawn from the quantitative part of the research.

The objective of this phase was to obtain a generalization of the PMO transformation process. The theoretical foundations of this research phase were chosen for their capacity to explain organizational change. They were mainly based on contingency theory (Donaldson, 1996), evolutionary perspective (Massini, Lewin, Numagami & Pettigrew, 2002; Miner, 1994) and organizational dynamics (Pettigrew, 2003b; Rajagopalan & Spreitzer, 1997; Van de Ven & Poole, 1995). Wide-spread generalization of findings can be obtained using a quantitative approach. However, we were aware of the difficulty of validating a process using a questionnaire. In order to ensure the utmost quality of the questionnaire, we decided first to follow a qualitative approach before launching the questionnaire. In addition to the seven cases of PMO transformations examined in the thesis, ten case studies were conducted, half of them in Sweden and half in Canada, in order to prepare the questionnaire. Apart from the questionnaire, one major outcome of this research step was the development of a model of the forces driving PMO changes originating from events in the external environment or internal environment or from internal issues or tensions (Aubry, Müller, Hobbs & Blomquist, 2010).

The questionnaire was sent out in November 2008 through research networks. A total of 184 valid responses were received, sufficient for multiple statistical analyses. Generalization of the PMO transformation process was confirmed: findings showed that impacts after the PMO transformation resolved the initial issues (Aubry, Hobbs, Müller, & Blomquist, 2010). Curiously, however, no pattern of change was identified.

The progressive life-cycle evolution of a PMO was not confirmed in either the qualitative or quantitative studies. Variations in the reasons for change, in the characteristics or functions that changed, and in the impacts of change remained unexplained, along with the description of the PMOs obtained in the first phase of the research program.

The most important value of this research phase was the fact that it entered the field of organizational change. More remains to be done, but significant progress between organization theory and project management research has been realized. Future research should invest more work in integrating the field of organizational change.

Phase 4: Governance and Community of PMOs

Unlike all other phases, this one focused on multiple PMOs. It was a natural step in the process toward gaining a more comprehensive understanding of how organizations manage multiple projects. At the time that this phase began, the term 'community of PMOs' existed in certain large public administrations to create some sort of sharing mechanism among PMOs in order to avoid duplication. The idea of communities of PMOs seemed helpful for exploring a multi-PMO reality in large organizations (Aubry, Müller & Glückler, 2011). The objective of this phase was to understand what communities of PMOs are, whether they actually exist, and what they do. The research also aimed to explore the relationships between PMOs in particular governance situations. It was assumed that PMOs form internal knowledge networks within organizations and that studying their relationships would provide new understanding of the internal dynamics by which they share (or do not share) knowledge. Relationships between PMOs led to the proposal of a triangle framework including the three PMO roles: serving, controlling and partnering. Theoretical foundations were based on governance (Brown & Eisenhardt, 1997; Müller, 2009), network theory (Granovetter, 2005; Nohria, 1992; Powell, 1990), and communities of practice theory (Lave & Wenger, 1991). The adopted research design was based on two complementary approaches, the first one being a qualitative approach followed by a quantitative approach, and social network analysis (SNA). Case studies were from a variety of industries and regions (Müller, Glückler, Aubry & Shao, 2013).

Overall, the major finding was that very few PMOs in our sample truly form a community. Rather, they assume a controlling role and to a lesser degree, a serving role. The controlling role of PMOs follows the organizational hierarchy. The partnering role is rare. PMOs are often isolated islands; they may form networks but not communities of PMOs. A fundamental question arises as to how PMOs contribute to project management knowledge and innovation. How would they contribute to the necessary organizational transformation if confined to a controlling or serving role? (Müller, Glückler & Aubry, 2013).

The SNA approach reinforced this finding (Aubry, Müller & Glückler, 2012). The SNA empirical data came from a single organization. The results showed that PMO members do not play a strong communications role in sharing information about project management. Most exchanges happen between project managers. PMOs in a controlling role are especially isolated. The bagel metaphor applies to them: they have no relationships with other PMOs, thus creating an empty hole where knowledge flows around not between other PMOs.

This phase constituted a first attempt to understand the multiple PMOs phenomenon in large organizations. Overall, this phase provided a conceptualization of the relationships between PMOs, but more importantly, it shed light on the overall control culture that may inhibit knowledge-sharing and, ultimately, innovation.

Phase 5: The PMO's Contribution to Implementing a Major Organizational Transformation in the Health Care Field

This phase was a natural extension of Phase 2 regarding the PMO's contribution to organizational performance. The theoretical foundation is based on the competing values framework (Quinn & Rohrbaugh, 1983), organizational change (Mintzberg & Waters, 1982; Pettigrew & Whipp, 1991) and strategy-as-practice literature. In short, its purpose was to experiment with the competing values framework in the context of a PMO dedicated to a major transformation project. The research design is based on a single case where research uses a qualitative approach but with two intricate methods, one based on interviews and the other on action research. The framework rests on the assumption that multiple concurrent values form the basis of any performance evaluation. The case is set in a university hospital where a major service redevelopment project is in progress. In this case, two groups were selected for interviews on their perception of PMO performance: members of the steering committee and employees of the PMO. Interviews were conducted in two rounds – the first, a few months after PMO implementation and the second, one year later. The first findings showed strong opposition between the two groups that persisted over the period, but also, the clear emergence of common values (Aubry, Richer, Lavoie-Tremblay & Cyr, 2011).

The action research was possible because the PMO director was directly involved in the research as a member of the research team. This is quite usual for research funded by health care research institutes in Canada: it is mandatory to include a 'practitioner' on the research team to apply for a national grant. Ethical considerations were managed and empirical data were not available to this director. Analysis of the first round of interviews led to different types of changes in and around the PMO such as new functions to be undertaken by the PMO, new governance mechanisms and new communication channels. The second round of interviews confirmed differences in performance values to acknowledge the changes (Aubry, Richer, Lavoie-Tremblay, & Cyr, 2012). This part of the research not only highlighted the value differences between the two groups, but also the need for dialogue. The objective was not to reach equilibrium or unanimity in values, but to view the PMO's contribution to organizational performance as a process of dialogue. The design of this research allowed us to observe changes as they unfolded. In this particular case, working on the PMO contribution to organizational performance elicited a clear distinction between product performance and performance management.

Creative and Innovative Contemporary Approaches

In this phase, the team embarked on a 'research-as-practice' approach (Golsorkhi, Rouleau, Seidl & Vaara, 2010) to gain a grounded understanding of what was happening. Results from this case study must now be validated through several other case studies, including some outside the health care sector.

These are the five main phases of the research program. Other collaborations happened during the program which focused on more specific issues related to organizational project management, such as portfolio management (Unger, Gemünden & Aubry, 2012).

Characteristics of the PMO Research Program

Now turning to the research program characteristics, we can see how the five main characteristics took form in this PMO research program (see Table 9.2).

Sense-making. Research on PMOs has been quite challenging given the fact that results from virtually every phase were not what was expected (which is not unusual in academic research). Independent of the methodology, a critical assessment of the results has to take place when making sense of a research program, at the project level and at the program level. This is key since researchers have to move away from their initial assumptions. This is part of a research process in a critical realism paradigm (Bhaskar, 2008). Within a critical realism paradigm, research only captures a partial view of the reality, which is the case even in a program. An example of this can be found in the first phase: the variety of PMOs was an expected result, but not being able to explain the wide variety was quite challenging. Usual contingency variables were not explaining the variation (ex. size, region), and this became more evident after the second phase. As mentioned earlier, this was a turning point in the research program. It was a case of reflections and critical assessment of what happened in reality versus constructs.

Interaction and negotiation within its community of interest. There were a few communities of interest in and around this research program, including at the local and international levels, professionals and academics. At the local level, a community of practice was formed at the time this research program was initiated. The relationship took different forms such as monthly workshops on preparing a research phase, discussing challenging results or the participation of our students in debates on the issues around PMOs. The Project Management Chair served as a liaison with business partners and academics. At the international level, participation in many workshops at professional congresses or private events on PMOs provided a means of interacting with a larger audience. In the academic community, results from all phases of this research program were regularly presented at research conferences. In the context of a research program, negotiation is not the same process as in the business sector. Here it takes the form of critical comments, most of them from a constructive approach, and which are taken into account by the researcher in the research process. Criticism

Table 9.2. Characteristics of the PMO Research Program

Generic characteristics of a research program	Specific characteristics in the PMO research program	Examples from the PMO research program
1 Sense-making within individual research project and at the program level	Reflections on results and critical assessment of results. Reality versus constructs.	No explanation of the wide variety in PMOs (Hobbs & Aubry, 2007).
2 Interaction and negotiation within its community of interest	Local and international communities of interest; professionals and academics.	Gap between expectations of professional and the research results; academics' contribution to the construction of PMO model (Hobbs & Aubry, 2010)
3 The emerging research program	Each phase of the PMO research program contributes to the continuity of the vision and provides opportunities for new research projects to emerge: opportunity – unsatisfactory result – new question – opportunity	A single PMO as unit of analysis moves to multiple PMOs as unit of analysis (Aubry, Müller & Glückler, 2011)
4 Change process	Changes happen in the course of the research program, in keeping with the engaged scholarship approach. Dissemination strategy to professionals and academics influences the state of knowledge	Variety of PMOs and PMO transformation process (Aubry, Müller, Hobbs & Blomquist, 2010)
5 Resource allocation decisions	Multiple researcher profiles and availability of funds. List of researchers associated with the program (alphabetic order): Aubry, Monique, Project management, UQAM, Canada Tomas Blomquist, Project management, USBE, Sweden Johannes Glückler, Economic geography, University of Heidelberg, Germany Brian Hobbs, Project management, UQAM, Canada Mélanie Lavoie-Tremblay, Nursing, McGill University, Canada Ralf Müller, Project management, BI University, Norway Marie-Claire Richer, Nursing, CUSM, Canada Denis Thuillier, Project management, UQAM, Canada Barbara Unger, Management, BIT, Germany	Publications in different fields such as in health care (Lavoie-Tremblay, Bonneville-Roussy, Aubry, Richer & Cyr, 2012) and in different regions such as Asia (Müller, Glückler, et al., 2013).

Creative and Innovative Contemporary Approaches

from the professionals is more likely to focus on the gap between their need for a clear PMO model for efficiency and performance and our results where we offer nuances and no clear recipe. Our results are more likely to offer descriptive ingredients and process where reflective decision-makers create their own solutions for managing multiple projects in a specific context. On the academic side, one of the criticisms leveled at this research program was that it contributed to the construction of the PMO model (Crawford, 2010) but challenged the relevance of this entity in terms of the functions related to managing multiple projects. This characteristic is central to sense-making and the change process.

An emerging research program. Initially, the PMO research program was a two-phase research project (Hobbs & Aubry, 2007). It was the interplay between multiple factors that led to the emergence of this PMO research program. First of all, there was the interest of individual researchers to pursue the question for better understanding the PMO phenomenon. The intriguing results from the first phase led to the second phase, and so on. This provided continuity in the program vision, which is essential to a program's existence. Second, this continuity provided opportunities for new questions to emerge and new research projects to be undertaken to answer these new questions. As described above, the five phases can be integrated to this schema of opportunity: intriguing result – new question – opportunity. This overall approach on the emergence of a research program can also be interpreted within Lakatos' philosophical view on scientific progress (Lakatos, 1978). Following this view, a research program goes through different stages of answers and gaps or inconstancies. Focusing on business models research program, Lecocq, Demil and Ventura (2010) noted that: 'This permanent game of new empirical investigations or new hypotheses generation creates an internal dynamic, causing new questions to rise, new problems to appear for which solutions must be found, and anomalies which must be taken into account'. The PMO research program adopted this view as it has progressed.

Change process. In this PMO research program, change happened within the communities of interest while the research projects were ongoing. It was not unusual for participants in the interviews or workshops to explicitly mention that reflecting with the researcher provided a change in their perception of a certain issue and opened up new types of solutions. Other mechanisms for dissemination of the results to different audiences surely contributed to changes in the professional community. It is difficult to measure the real impact of a particular research program on an organizational behavior toward PMOs. However, two results from this research program seem to have pervaded the PMO community: the variety of PMOs and the PMO transformation process. The variety of PMOs raised the question about the myth of simple PMO models that could apply to all situations. Our results showed the importance of the context and the need for decision-makers to make sense of their own context when designing a PMO. The PMO transformation process challenged the myth of having a *wrong* or *right* PMO. Our results showed that PMOs, like other organizational entities, evolve in environments where unexpected events occur constantly and where tensions and conflicts arise, regardless of the configuration of a given PMO.

Resource allocation decisions. Overall, nine researchers participated in one or more phases of this PMO research program. The main decision was not so much around the allocation in terms of the individual agendas of these researchers, but rather around the common interests of developing knowledge in the specific field of PMOs. The hiring of nine researchers with a variety of profiles provided rich input into understanding the phenomenon. Their profiles included backgrounds in engineering, information technology, management, geography, and nursing. The team also came from a variety of regions in North America and Europe. In terms of money, this research program received five grants. The dynamism at each phase of this research program facilitated access to funding. The ability to attend conferences or working sessions was facilitated whenever necessary.

Translational and Transformational Research Concepts Applied to this PMO Research Program

This chapter on the PMO research program contributes to the overall positioning of this book on translational and transformational research. Translating research findings into practice has been examined for several years in the management field. Callon (1986), among others, did work on translation as a social process of creating networks around a technological innovation. Similarly, Pettigrew (2003a) called for a social production of knowledge and more recently, Van de Ven (2007) suggested the concept of engaged scholarship with a co-construction of research with the dynamic involvement of stakeholders in research.

Coming from a medical perspective, the translational approach has been viewed as an answer to the need 'to go beyond the knowledge discovery of the basic research enterprise to interpret and apply research outcomes in an effort to develop effective practices for the betterment of everyday life' (Petronio, 2007: 215). In the management field, the research-practice gap has been conceptualized as a two-fold issue, one of knowledge translation (lost in translation) and one of knowledge production (lost before translation) (Shapiro, Kirkman & Courtney, 2007). Some recent research approaches tend to lessen the problems of translations such as the 'as practice' (Golsorkhi, Rouleau, Seidl & Vaara, 2010; Hällgren & Wilson, 2008) and evidence-based (Rousseau & McCarthy, 2007) approaches.

This research program on PMOs deliberated adopted translational research concepts. As described above, knowledge production engaged professionals at the local and international levels as the phases of this program unfolded. The results were then shared throughout the program, not only at the end of the phases. Moreover, in the last phase, the design of this particular project used participative action research involving the head of a PMO in the research team. This provided clear direction to the practice translation of our research results. However, a lot of work still remains to be done. Personal conversations with professionals show that there is still a profound gap between research and practice in relation to PMOs.

Transformational research calls for multidisciplinary collaboration that is reflected in this research program by the diversity of the profiles of the researchers who participated in one phase or another, and their provenance regions. Having North American and European researchers led to a dynamic dialogue between two competing paradigms, the NATO (North Atlantic Treaty Organization) and the Scandinavian school of thoughts (Czarniawska, 2008). From the interplay between them, it is probable that a new integrated understanding has emerged through the research program. In this sense, a research program with this diversity of profiles and provenances is more likely to avoid the danger of being fragmented by seeking a common trend (Söderlund, 2011).

Combination of Multiple Perspectives

This research program helped to move the research in project management along new paths, such as in the field of organizational research in general: stretching boundaries, a multi-paradigmatic profile, and methodology inventiveness (Buchanan & Bryman, 2009). One key element is that choice of methods is part of the research context: 'choice of methods is shaped not only by research aims, norms of practice, and epistemological concerns, but also by a combination of organizational, historical, political, ethical, evidential, and personally significant characteristics of this field of research' (p. 2).

Stretching boundaries: This research program explored organizations facing challenges when dealing with multiple and concurrent investments and projects, a situation referred to as enterprise project management (Cooke-Davies, Schlichter & Bredillet, 2001; Dinsmore, 1999, 2001), project business (Artto & Wikstrom, 2005) or organizational project management (Aubry et al., 2007), a reality since the 1980s with multiple elements from the economic context that push organizations to innovate at a rapid pace. Many scholars have looked at this from an innovation perspective (Van de Ven, 1999).

However, it is not the project that is central here; rather, it is the organization and the mechanisms that are in place to deal with these multiple projects. Organizations have often put in place entities to deal with these projects, namely, a project management office. The popularity of this entity grew (Dai & Wells, 2004) and the related literature was produced mainly by consultants or experienced professionals (Kendall & Rollins, 2003). It is difficult to assess the current evolution of PMOs, but what is of interest for us, is that it is a good place to observe what happens in the organization regarding the management of projects at the organization level.

Multi-paradigmatic profile: Interestingly, moving research from an approach based on a single paradigm to one using a pluralistic profile is the trend in organizational research as well. Pluralism is required on theoretical side of research as organizations become more complex (Chen & Miller, 2011; Denis, Langley & Rouleau, 2007). As noted by Chen and Miller (2011), the important point is to keep coherence within the combination of different theories. The same may apply when considering the methodology aspect of research. A mixed methods approach is appropriate in this situation (Bryman, 2009; Teddlie & Tashakkori, 2010) using different epistemology to study a phenomenon: 'Such a mixed methods approach potentially provides opportunities for greater insight than can be achieved by one approach alone' (p. 5).

Methodology inventiveness: In this particular research program, no visual, photographic, video or internet-based material was used. Creativity and innovativeness came rather from the emergent recursive dynamics between the findings and the inherent limitations as the research unfolded. Two elements played a role in the methodology inventiveness. First, there was close collaboration between researchers and professionals in a continuous relationship in the approach suggested by Van de Ven known as engaged scholarship (Van de Ven, 2007). How does this work? My personal profile, with many years of experience in the field, is not unusual for this approach, but the key element was my involvement within the local PMO community of practice. This is a place where ideas were tested, challenged and reinforced or abandoned. Teaching a course on this subject also offer a source of dialogue with professionals dealing with the reality. More recently, engaging in action research with the direct participation of decision-makers and an advisory committee influenced the research process as it unfolded. The combination of these activities in and around the research process provides a means for collaborators to play a direct role in the research as co-interpreters of the findings (Buchanan & Bryman, 2009; Denis & Lomas, 2003).

The second element of inventiveness was the critical thinking of the team, which did not take the findings as the ultimate and definitive results. The ability of the research team to question the limitations of the findings led to the next stage of the research.

The PMO as a Thing and as a Process

Making sense of an emerging research program is facilitated when the overall approach can be situated within a structure. As mentioned earlier, this research program on organizational project management, and more precisely on PMOs, focused to a dynamic phenomenon of strategy implementation (Aubry, Sicotte, et al., 2012; Morris

& Jamieson, 2005), in other words, on the development of organizations. We propose in this section to turn to Van de Ven and Poole (2005) for the structure they offer for the study of organizational development and change. In this section, we will see how their framework helps to make sense of the overall research program.

The framework addresses the philosophical positioning of research in the development of and change in organizations along the two dimensions of ontology and epistemology (Van de Ven & Poole, 2005). The ontology dimension seeks clarification as to whether change is viewed as a thing or as an organizing process (Tsoukas & Chia, 2002). For the epistemology dimension, the question focuses on the methodology for conducting research and whether it is studied within a variance theory or based on an event-driven approach, or process theory. Combining these two dimensions provides four specific approaches to the study of organizational change.

Approach 1: Organization as a thing studied by a variance method
Approach 2: Organization as a thing studied by process narratives
Approach 3: The process of organizing studied by process narratives
Approach 4: The process of organizing studied by a variance method

However, these approaches are complementary:

> *Each approach focuses on different questions and provides a different – but partial – understanding of organizational change. We argue [...] that coordinating the pluralistic insights from the four approaches provides a richer understanding of organization change than any one approach provides by itself* (Van de Ven & Poole, 2005: 1394).

Table 9.3 presents the classification of the five research program phases based on the approaches proposed by Van de Ven and Poole (2005). The results show the complementarity between the four approaches, with each one revealing an aspect of PMOs that the other three could not.

The PMO as a 'Thing'

In most of the literature, PMOs are studied as a 'thing', an entity with certain characteristics and performing functions in relation to the management of multiple projects (e.g., Hill, 2004). When considered as a 'thing' in organizational change, the PMO is described at different stages, before and after the change. This ontological approach provides good understanding of what this entity is in reality and what functions it performs.

Table 9.3. Classification of Research Phases after Van de Ven & Poole (2005)

		Ontology An organization is represented as being:	
		A noun, a social actor, a real entity ('thing')	A verb, a process of organizing, emergent flux
Epistemology (method for studying change)	Variance method	**Approach I** ***Phase 1: Describing the reality of PMOs*** • PMO descriptive model • Search for a typology of PMOs • Explaining PMO performance ***Phase 2: Understanding PMOs and their contribution to organizational performance*** Competing values as a one-time assessment and in relation to the model ***Phase 4: Governance and communities of PMOs*** • Unit of analysis: Network of PMOs • Typology of relationships between PMOs	**Approach IV** ***Phase 3: Identifying forces driving the frequent changes in PMOs*** • Explanation of changes
	Process narratives	**Approach II** ***Phase 2: Understanding PMOs and their contribution to organizational performance*** • PMO transformation process: Narrative of sequence of events taking into consideration the innovation social system	**Approach III** ***Phase 2: Understanding PMOs and their contribution to organizational performance*** • Actor network theory: Construction and reconstruction of networks around the PMO's activities ***Phase 5: Contribution of a PMO to implementing a major transformation in the health care field*** • Competing values as a process of ongoing co-construction of performance assessment

Creative and Innovative Contemporary Approaches

Approach 1: PMO as a thing studied by variance method

Three phases participated in this approach.

- The first phase of the research program was undertaken using this approach. This is quite normal as, at that time, very little knowledge from academic research on PMO was available (with the exception of Dai & Wells, 2004). The research consisted of a survey in which 500 valid responses were received. From a theoretical perspective, the main outcome was the proposal of a descriptive PMO model. This research also revealed the wide variety of PMOs but had difficulty explaining this variety by the usual contingency variables (e.g. size, region, industry). This phase also included research on typology using different statistical methods. At this stage, no strong PMO typology emerged. From a professional perspective, the major finding of PMO variety and the lack of an explanation for it suggested that practitioners have the ability to create a unique PMO configuration depending on the particular context of the organization.

  Further examination of the data allowed for an alternative explanation of PMO performance. Instead of only considering the technical characteristics of a PMO as influencing the PMO's performance, results showed that the embeddeddness of the PMO within the organization was more likely to contribute to the PMO's performance.
- Four case studies were conducted in the second phase using both the variance method and process narratives. The variance approach included the search for a relation between PMO configuration (as an independent variable) and the importance of performance criteria (as a dependant variable). No such relationship was found, emphasizing the difficulty of finding any performance predictor for PMOs. In this research, the competing values framework was used as the conceptual model. However, PMO performance was seen as an organizational construct that acknowledges the diversity of values.
- Lastly, Phase 4 also applied this approach. The unit of analysis of this phase was a PMO network (and not a single PMO as in the other phases). Qualitative and quantitative approaches were used and both were oriented towards the description of the network and the governance mechanisms and the search for an explanation to enhance the quality of the relationship.

Globally, this approach served to describe the entity and its wide variety. It also provided some evidence of a common state independent of the industry or the country to which it pertains. Two studies delivered results on PMO performance. First, PMO performance is better explained as an embedded entity within its host organization than on the basis of technical characteristics. Second, there is no direct relationship between a particular PMO configuration (set of characteristics and functions) and the resulting performance.

Approach II: The PMO as a thing studied by process narratives

There is one phase that falls into this approach.

- Phase 2 was introduced above in the variance method. Four in-depth case studies were undertaken. Under this approach, the PMO is still considered as a thing but in a dynamic context of change. It could also be described as an entity, but what is important here are the events that happen over a period of time as well as the tensions and conflicts that arise. The PMO is seen not as a static entity but rather as moving from one state to another through a transformation process.

The PMO as a Process of Organizing

Approach III: Organizing PMO studied by a process narrative

There are two phases from the PMO research program that are included in this approach:

- Part of Phase 2 can be included in this approach under the actor network theory. This theory is interested at the construction and reconstruction of networks. Using the itinerary of a monthly project status report within an organization, this research showed how a network gets constructed around project issues in which the PMO is involved.
- Phase 5 was dedicated to exploring the contribution of a PMO in implementing a major transformation in the health care field. Based on the competing values framework (Quinn & Rohrbaugh, 1983), this research explored the PMO's performance in terms of its contribution to organizational performance. It showed that the PMO's performance would be better considered as a process than as a static, ad hoc set of criteria.

Approach IV: Organizing PMO studied by a variance method

- Phase 3 of the research program fits well with this approach. This phase had a qualitative component with 17 case studies followed by quantitative survey-based research with 183 responses. In both, the objective was to explain changes in dynamic external and internal environments and to provide generalization of the results. The main finding is that PMOs adjust to their environment, which is in line with contingency theory (as do organizations) (e.g., Donaldson, 2001).

Overall, these four approaches combined to provide knowledge on PMOs either as a thing or as a process. None of these phases would have individually had the potential to answer all of the wide variety of questions.

Contributions, Limitations and Opportunities

This research program on PMOs provides an example of continuity in the research vision while, at the same time, promoting creativity and innovation in order to deepen

Creative and Innovative Contemporary Approaches

the knowledge and understanding of PMOs. Many academics nowadays call for a pluralistic approach to the study of complex phenomena in organizations (Denis et al., 2007; Söderlund, 2011). One challenge was to keep the focus on a vision in order to avoid the problem of fragmented research (Söderlund, 2011) or 'paradigm soup' (Buchanan & Bryman, 2009: 5).

This chapter provided a definition of what a research program is, and its main characteristics. We focused on the methodology aspects of the research program, explaining how each of the five phases was combined in a structured approach using the Van de Ven and Poole (2005) framework. This framework provided the opportunity to show how the four research approaches combined to better offer an understanding of the PMO as a thing and as a process.

This research program is still ongoing, following two different threads: one more in-depth and the other broader. The broader thread is looking at questions in relation to what is known as the project function within the organization, or organizational project management. From this perspective, the PMO is seen as an entity within the overall mechanisms put in place to manage multiple projects in order to deliver business value. In the in-depth thread, research projects will address questions to scrutinized PMOs and the project function in specific sectors.

Overall, this research program contributed to novel approaches to organizational project management through translational and transformational approaches. In terms of the former, the research program strongly engaged professionals and academics in discussions through local and international workshops and conferences. In terms of the later, the approach mainly took the form of collaboration d between researchers with different profiles and provenances.

Acknowledgements

I cannot close this chapter without acknowledging the exceptional contribution of researchers who have put their creativity and energy to enlighten the PMO phenomenon. Particularly, thanks to Brian Hobbs who, on top of being an intense researcher in this program, was a coach for me and has continuously assessed the progression of our work in the quest for greater research quality. Special thanks go also to Ralf Müller who has provided rich impulse in anchoring research in scientific philosophical foundations while at the same time providing practical contributions. Thanks to the rich contribution of the following researchers involved at different stages of this research program: Denis Thuillier, my doctoral director, Mélanie Lavoie-Tremblay, Marie-Claire Richer, Johannes Glückler, Barbara Unger, and Thomas Blomquist. Thanks to PMI, Per and Aivor Wikströms Foundation and to the Canada LEAD program for their financial contribution. Thanks to reviewers for their helpful comments.

Appendix

Table 9.4. PMO Research Program Summary

Ph.	Title	Basic Question	Theoretical Foundation
1	Describing the reality of PMOs	To get a realistic picture of the PMO population	Wide descriptive exploration based on what people really do Contingency theory does not suffice to explain the diversity (Donaldson, 2001)
2	Understanding PMOs and their contribution to organizational performance	To understand the dynamics surrounding PMOs in their organizational context	Innovation social system (Hughes, 1987; Schumpeter, 1950; Van de Ven & Garud, 1994), actor network theory (Callon & Law, 1989; Latour, 2005) and competing values framework (Quinn & Rohrbaugh, 1983)
3	Identifying the forces driving the frequent changes in PMOs	Generalization of the PMO transformation process	Capacity to explain organizational change: contingency theory (Donaldson, 1996), evolutionary perspective (Massini, Lewin, Numagami & Pettigrew, 2002; Miner, 1994) and organizational dynamics (e.g., Pettigrew, 2003b; Rajagopalan & Spreitzer, 1997; Van de Ven & Poole, 1995)
4	Governance and communities of PMOs	Understand what communities of PMOs are, do they really exist in organizations and what do they do?	Governance (Brown & Eisenhardt, 1997), network theory (Granovetter, 2005; Nohria, 1992; Powell, 1990), and communities of practice theory (Lave & Wenger, 1991)
5	Contribution of a PMO to implementing a major organizational transformation in the health care field	How to assess the PMO's contribution to organizational performance – in the specific case of a major organizational transformation	Competing values framework (Quinn & Rohrbaugh, 1983); organizational change (Mintzberg & Waters, 1982; Pettigrew & Whipp, 1991)

Creative and Innovative Contemporary Approaches

Methodology	Outcomes	
	Theoretical	Professional
Two descriptive surveys of 500 PMOs aimed at providing a realistic portrait of the population of PMOs	PMO descriptive model grounded in empirical data; Limitation to usual contingency variables (size, region, industry) as explanation of PMO variety; No easy PMO typology; Performance is better explained using the concept of embeddedness	Reflexive practitioner (Schön, 1983) to 'create' a unique PMO configuration; Pay more attention to PMO embeddedness within the organization
Four in-depth case studies Strategy for data analysis based on grounded theory (Strauss & Corbin, 1990)	Formalization of the PMO transformation process; PMO as part of the organizational political system; Values underlying the PMO contribution to the organizational performance	Question the myth of PMO transformation to evolve from a *wrong* to a *right* PMO; Preparing for change; Establishing a process to engage in a dialogue to assess the PMO's contribution to organizational performance.
Mixed method: • 10 more case studies from Europe and North-America to develop and test a questionnaire on changes in PMO • A survey of 184 PMO changes providing rich descriptions of the conditions leading to PMO change, the nature of the change and its consequences	Confirmation of the PMO transformation process and its positive impacts; Model of drivers of PMO change: external and internal events and development of tensions; Progressive life-cycle pattern was not found in sample	PMO change is normal to ensure alignment with the external and internal environments
Mixed-method: • Four case studies in four different economic sectors of activity (banking, telecommunications, healthcare and manufacturing) and from three different regions: Europe, North America and Asia • Social network analysis (SNA) in one organization	Communities of PMOs rarely exist; Knowledge-sharing is often restricted to project control following the hierarchical design of the organization; PMOs in controlling roles are in the particular situation of an isolated island.	More attention should be paid to knowledge sharing on project management between PMOs. This is a must to avoid the issue of reinventing the wheel and to better support innovation
Global qualitative approach: • Interviews at two different times to assess the PMO contribution to organizational performance. Two groups of interviewees participated: steering committee and PMO employees • Action research with the PMO director as part of the research team (strategy-as-practice)	Confirmation of the usefulness of the competing values framework as a means but also as a process for establishing and assessing the PMO contribution to the organizational performance	Greater clarity in what performance means when considering *product* versus *management;* Establish mechanisms to share the PMO contribution to organizational performance. This can be done through governance mechanisms

The Design of Research Programs

References

Artto, K. A., & Wikstrom, K. (2005). What is project business? *International Journal of Project Management, 23*(5), 343-53.

Aubry, M. (2011). The social reality of organisational project management at the interface between networks and hierarchy. *International Journal of Managing Projects in Business, 4*(3, Emerald Highly Commended Paper Award 2012), 436-57.

Aubry, M. & Hobbs, B. (2011). A fresh look at the contribution of project management to organizational performance. *Project Management Journal, 42*(1), 3-16.

Aubry, M., Hobbs, B., Müller, R. & Blomquist, T. (2010). Identifying forces driving PMO changes. *Project Management Journal,* 41(4, Best Papers Special Issue at 2010 PMI Education and Research Conference), 30-45.

Aubry, M., Hobbs, B. & Thuillier, D. (2007). A New Framework for Understanding Organisational Project Management through PMO. *International Journal of Project Management, 25*(4), 328-36.

Aubry, M., Hobbs, B. & Thuillier, D. (2008). Organisational Project Management: An Historical Approach to the Study of PMOs. *International Journal of Project Management, 26*(1), 38-43.

Aubry, M., Müller, R. & Glückler, J. (2011). Exploring PMOs through community of practice theory. *Project Management Journal, 42*(5), 42-56.

Aubry, M., Müller, R. & Glückler, J. (2012). *Governance and Communities of PMOs.* Newtown Square, PA: Project Management Institute.

Aubry, M., Müller, R., Hobbs, B. & Blomquist, T. (2010). Project management offices in transition. *International Journal of Project Management, 28*(8), 766-78.

Aubry, M., Richer, M.-C., Lavoie-Tremblay, M. & Cyr, G. (2011). Pluralism in PMO performance: The case of a PMO dedicated to a major organizational transformation. *Project Management Journal, 42*(6), 60-77.

Aubry, M., Richer, M.-C., Lavoie-Tremblay, M. & Cyr, G. (2012). Strategic Implementation: Pluralism in Assessing Performance of a Transition Office. Paper presented at the Academy of Management 2012 Annual Meeting, Boston.

Aubry, M., Sicotte, H., Drouin, N., Vidot-Delerue, H. & Besner, C. (2012). Organisational Project Management as a Function within the Organisation. *International Journal of Managing Projects in Business, 5*(2), 180-194.

Bhaskar, R. (2008). *A Realist Theory of Science.* London: Verso.

Brown, S. L. & Eisenhardt, K. M. (1997). The art of continuous change: Linking complexity theory and time-paced evolution in relentlessly shifting organizations. *Administrative Science Quarterly, 42*(1), 1-34.

Bryman, A. (2009). Mixed methods in organizational research. In D. A. Buchanan & A. Bryman (Eds.), *The Sage Handbook of Organizational Research Methods* (pp. 516-31). London, UK: Sage.

Buchanan, D. A. & Bryman, A. (2009). The organizational research context: properties and implications. In D. A. Buchanan & A. Bryman (Eds), *The Sage Handbook of Organizational Research Methods* (pp. 1-18). London, UK: Sage.

Callon, M. (1986). Some elements of a sociology of translation: Domestication of the scallops and fisherman in St-Brieuc Bay. In J. Law (Ed.), *Power, action and belief: A new sociology of knowledge* (pp. 196-229). London: Routledge.

Callon, M. & Law, J. (1989). *La proto-histoire d'un laboratoire ou le difficile mariage de la science et de l'économie*. Paris: Presses universitaires de France.

Cattani, G., Ferriani, S., Frederiksen, L. & Täube, F. (2011). Project-based organizing and strategic management: A long-term research agenda on temporary organizational forms. In G. Cattani, S. Ferriani, L. Frederiksen & F. Täube (Eds.), *Project-based organizing and strategic management* (Vol. 28, pp. xv-xxxix). Bingley (UK): Emerald.

Chen, M.-J. & Miller, D. (2011). The Relational Perspective as a Business Mindset: Managerial Implications for East and West. [Article]. *Academy of Management Perspectives, 25*(3), 6-18.

Cooke-Davies, T. J., Schlichter, J.,& Bredillet, C. N. (2001, 1-10 novembre). *Beyond the PMBOK Guide*. Paper presented at the PMI 2001 First to the Future, Nashville.

Crawford, L. (2010, 2010/05/19-22). *Deconstructing the PMO*. Paper presented at the EURAM, Rome.

Czarniawska, B. (2008). *A Theory of organizing*. Cheltenham, UK: Edward Elgar.

Dai, C. X. Y. & Wells, W. G. (2004). An Exploration of Project Management Office Features and their Relationship to Project Performance. *International Journal of Project Management, 22*(7), 523-32.

Denis, J.-L., Langley, A. & Rouleau, L. (2007). Strategizing in pluralistic contexts: Rethinking theoretical frames. *Human Relations, 60*(1), 179-215.

Denis, J.-L. & Lomas, J. (2003). Convergent evolution: the academic and policy roots of collaborative research. *Journal of Health Services Research and Policy, 8* (Supplement 2 (October, 02, 2003)), 1-6.

Dinsmore, P. C. (1999). *Winning in Business with Enterprise Project Management*. New York: AMACOM.

Dinsmore, P. C. (2001). Enterprise Project Management: Flavor of the Day or Here to Stay? *PM Network*(Février), 24-5.

Donaldson, L. (1996). The Normal Science of Structural Contingency Theory. In S. Clegg, C. Hardy & W. R. Nord (Eds), *Handbook of Organization Studies* (pp. 57-76). London: Sage.

Donaldson, L. (2001). *The Contingency Theory of Organizations* London: Sage.

Fenton, E. & Pettigrew, A. (2000). Theoretical Perspectives in New Forms of Organizing In A. Pettigrew & E. Fenton (Eds), *The Innovating Organization* (pp. 1-46). London: SAGE.

Gareis, R. & Huemann, M. (2008). Change management and projects. *International Journal of Project Management, 26*(8), 771-2.

Golsorkhi, D., Rouleau, L., Seidl, D. & Vaara, E. (Eds). (2010). *Strategy as practice.* Cambridge, UK: Cambridge University Press.

Granovetter, M. (2005). The Impact of Social Structure on Economic Outcomes. *The Journal of Economic Perspectives, 19*(1), 33-50.

Hällgren, M., & Wilson, T. L. (2008). The nature and management of crises in construction projects: Projects-as-practice observations. *International Journal of Project Management, 26*(8), 830-838.

Hill, G. M. (2004). *The Complete Project Management Office Handbook.* Boca Raton, Florida: CRC Press LLC.

Hobbs, B. & Aubry, M. (2007). A multi-phase research program investigating project management offices (PMOs): the results of phase 1. *Project Management Journal, 38*(1), 74-86.

Hobbs, B., & Aubry, M. (2008). An empirically grounded search for a typology of project management offices. *Project Management Journal, 39*(S1), S69-S82, Best Papers Special Issue at 2008 PMI Education and Research Conference.

Hobbs, B. & Aubry, M. (2010). *The Project Management Office: A Quest for Understanding.* Newtown Square, PA Project Management Institute.

Hobbs, B. & Aubry, M. (2011, 2011/06/19-22). *A typology of PMOs derived using cluster analysis and the relationship with performance.* Paper presented at the IRNOP, Montreal, Canada.

Hobbs, B., Aubry, M., & Thuillier, D. (2008). The Project Management Office as an Organisational Innovation. *International Journal of Project Management,* 26(5), 547-555.

Hobday, M. (2000). The Project-Based Organisation: An Ideal Form for Managing Complex Products and Systems? *Research Policy, 29*(7-8), 871-893.

Hughes, P. T. (1987). The Evolution of Large Technological Systems. In W. E. Bijker, T. P. Hughes & T. J. Pinch (Eds.), *The Social Construction of Technological Systems: New Directions in the Sociology and History of Technology* (pp. 51-81). Cambridge: MIT Press.

Kendall, G. I. & Rollins, S. C. (2003). *Advanced Project Portfolio Management and the PMO: Multiplying ROI at Warp Speed.* Boca Raton, Flor.: J. Ross Publishing.

Lakatos, I. (1978). The methodology of scientific research programme. Cambridge (UK): Cambridge University Press.

Larson, E. (2004). Project Management Structures. In P. W. G. Morris & J. K. Pinto (Eds), *The Wiley Guide to Managing Projects* (pp. 48-66). Hoboken, New Jersey: John Wiley & Sons, Inc.

Latour, B. (2005). *Reassembling the Social: An Introduction to Actor-Network-Theory.* Oxford: Oxford University Press.

Lave, J. & Wenger, E. (1991). *Situated learning: Legitimate peripheral participation.* New York: Cambridge University Press.

Lavoie-Tremblay, M., Bonneville-Roussy, A., Aubry, M., Richer, M.-C., & Cyr, G. (2012). Project Management Office in Health Care: A key strategy for evidence-based change and practices. *Health Care Manager, 31*(2), 154-65.

Lecocq, X., Demil, B. & Ventura, J. (2010). Business Models as a Research Program in Strategic Management: An Appraisal based on Lakatos. [Article]. M@n@gement, 13(4), 214-25.

Lundin, R. A. & Söderholm, A. (1995). A theory of the temporary organization. *Scandinavian Journal of Management, 11*(4), 437-55.

Massini, S., Lewin, A. Y., Numagami, T. & Pettigrew, A. M. (2002). The evolution of organizational routines among large Western and Japanese firms. *Research Policy, 31*(8-9), 1333-48.

Miner, A. S. (1994). Seeking Adaptive Advantage: Evolutionary Theory and Managerial Action. In J. A. C. Baum & J. V. Singh (Eds), *Evolutionary Dynamics of Organizations* (pp. 76-89). New York: Oxford University Press.

Mintzberg, H. & Waters, J. (1982). Tracking strategy in the entrepreneurial firm. *Academy of Management Journal, 25*, 465-99.

Morris, P. W. G. & Jamieson, A. (2005). Moving from Corporate Strategy to Project Strategy. *Project Management Journal, 36*(4), 5.

Müller, R. (2009). *Governance in Projects.* Aldershot, UK: Gower Publishing.

Müller, R., Glückler, J., & Aubry, M. (2013). A Relational Typology of Project Management Offices. *Project Management Journal, 44*(1), 59-76.

Müller, R., Glückler, J., Aubry, M., & Shao, J. (2013). Project Management Knowledge Flows in Networks of Project Managers and Project Management Offices: A Case Study in the Pharmaceutical Industry. *Project Management Journal, 44*(2), 4-19.

Nohria, N. (1992). Is a Network Perspective a Useful Way of Studying Organizations? In N. Nohria & R. G. Eccles (Eds), *Networks and Organizations: Structure, Form and Action* (pp. 1-22). Boston: Harvard Business Scholl Press.

Pellegrinelli, S. (2011). What's in a name: Project or programme? *International Journal of Project Management, 29*(2), 232-40.

Petronio, S. (2007). JACR Commentaries on translation of research into practice: Introduction. *Journal of Applied Communication Research, 35*(3), 215-17.

Pettigrew, A. M. (2003a). Co-producing knowledge and the challenges of international collaborative research. In A. M. Pettigrew, R. Whittington, L. Melin, C. Sanchez-Runde, F. A. J. Van den Bosch, W. Ruigrok & T. Numagami (Eds), *Innovative Forms of Organizing* (pp. 352-74). London, UK: Sage.

Pettigrew, A. M. (2003b). Innovative Forms of Organizing: Progress, Performance and Process. In A. M. Pettigrew, R. Whittington, L. Melin, C. Sanchez-Runde, F. A. J. Van den Bosch, W. Ruigrok & T. Numagami (Eds.), *Innovative Forms of Organizing* (pp. 331-51). London, UK: SAGE Publications.

Pettigrew, A. M. & Massini, S. (2003). Innovative Forms of Organizing: Trends in Europe, Japan and the USA in the 1990s. In A. M. Pettigrew, R. Whittington, L. Melin, C. Sanchez-Runde, F. A. J. Van den Bosch, W. Ruigrok & T. Numagami (Eds), *Innovative Forms of Organizing* (pp. 1-33). London, UK: Sage.

Pettigrew, A. M. & Whipp, R. (1991). *Managing Change for Competitive Success*. Oxford, UK: Blackwell Publishers Ltd.

Powell, W. W. (1990). Neither Market nor Hierarchy: Networks Forms of Organizations. *Research in Organizational Behavior, 12*, 295-336.

Quinn, R. E. & Rohrbaugh, J. (1983). A Spatial Model of Effectiveness Criteria: Towards a Competing Values Approach to Organizational Analysis. *Management Science, 29*(3), 363.

Rajagopalan, N. & Spreitzer, G. M. (1997). Torward a theory of strategic change: A multi-lens perspective and integrative framework. *Academy of Management Review, 22*(1), 48.

Rousseau, D. M. & McCarthy, S. (2007). Educating Managers From an Evidence-Based Perspective. [Article]. *Academy of Management Learning & Education, 6*(1), 84-101.

Schön, D. A. (1983). *The Reflexive Practitioner: How Professionals Thinks in Action*. USA: Basic Books.

Schumpeter, J. (1950). *Capitalism, Socialism, and Democracy* (3rd ed.). New York: Harper & Row Publishers.

Shapiro, D. L., Kirkman, B. L., & Courtney, H. G. (2007). Perceived causes and solutions of the translation problem in management research. *Academy of Management Journal, 50*(2), 249-66.

Söderlund, J. (2011). Pluralism in Project Management: Navigating the Crossroads of Specialization and Fragmentation. *International Journal of Management Reviews, 13*(2), 153-76.

Strauss, A. L.,& Corbin, J. (1990). *Basics of Qualitative Research Grounded Theory Procedures and Techniques*. Newbury Park, Calif.: Sage.

Teddlie, C. & Tashakkori, A. (2010). Overview of Contemporary Issues in Mixed Methods Research. In C. Teddlie & A. Tashakkori (Eds), *Handbook of Mixed Methods in Soxial & Behavioral Research* (2nd ed.). Thousand Oaks,CA: SAGE Publications.

Tsoukas, H.,& Chia, R. (2002). On organizational becoming: Rethinking organizational change. *Organization Science, 13*(5), 567-82.

Turner, R. J. & Müller, R. (2003). On the Nature of the Project as a Temporary Organization. *International Journal of Project Management, 21*(1), 1-8.

Unger, B., Gemünden, H. G. & Aubry, M. (2012). The Three Roles of a Project Portfolio Management Office: The Impact on Portfolio Management Execution and Success. *International Journal of Project Management, 30*(5, IRNOP Special issue on project portfolio management), 608-620.

Van de Ven, A. H. (1999). *The Innovation Journey.* New York: Oxford University Press.

Van de Ven, A. H. (2007). *Engaged Scholarship: Creating Knowledge for Science and Practice.* Oxford: Oxford University Press.

Van de Ven, A. H. & Garud, R. (1994). The Coevolution of Technical and Institutional Events in the Development of an Innovation. In J. A. C. Baum & J. V. Singh (Eds), *Evolutionary Dynamics of Organizations* (pp. 425-43). New-York: Oxford University Press.

Van de Ven, A. H. & Poole, M. S. (1995). Explaining Development and Change in Organizations. *Academy of Management Review, 20*(3), 520.

Van de Ven, A. H. & Poole, M. S. (2005). Alternative Approaches for Studying Organizational Change. [Article]. *Organization Studies, 26*, 1377-1404.

Learning Across Disciplines

Nathalie Drouin, Ralf Müller and Shankar Sankaran

This section includes discussions on understanding and adopting various theoretical perspectives, contemporary research methods and designs from areas that are allied to organizational project management (OPM), such as social science (power and politics), behavioral science and cognitive mapping, and natural science molecular biology (genomics). It provides a unique set of concepts, research design and methodological choices to learn and draw from the literature from giants in allied fields to challenge theories and approaches used in OPM. It provides guidance on integrating such theories, concepts and approaches from allied fields to complement, expand and enrich potential to OPM research.

This section starts with Chapter 10 by Stewart Clegg and Kristian Kreiner. As the authors state, "power is similar to oxygen". No natural scientists could ignore the analysis of atmosphere in searching for signs of life; similarly power relations could not be ignored in social sciences of management and in project management. This chapter sketches the most important forms of power relations, namely, power over, power to, power with, and power/knowledge. It offers ideas and inspiration for future research in project management in proposing and adopting central concepts from the field of power studies.

This analysis of power and politics is widened in Chapter 11 by Hemanta Doloi's application of behavioral science and cognitive mapping. Among several relevant theoretical developments in exploring complex human interactions, the chapter discusses three key research methods (*social network analysis, soft systems methodology* and *artificial neural network*), and raises the importance of using these approaches given the complexity of projects and the involvement of many stakeholders. It draws on the strengths, weaknesses, opportunities and applications of these methods, and highlights their usefulness through examples from a project management context.

Chapter 12, the last in this section, is by Robert Joslin and Ralf Müller. It uses the concept of genotyping and phenotyping to exemplify the use of natural science perspectives to social science phenomena. Universal Darwinism is introduced to provide new insights in project management research. The comparative used in this chapter demonstrates fresh and innovative thinking that can help researchers to develop new research areas in projects, challenge existing research approaches and go against traditional well-established views in OPM.

Thus, this section proposes to learn across established and innovative perspectives in addressing the following questions:

- What are the key concepts in these specific disciplines (e.g. power and politics etc.) that could be of interest to conduct research in the field of project management?
- What are the lessons learned to research design aspects from these respective disciplines?
- How can knowledge on research design from these fields complement and enrich project management research?

Chapter 10

Power and Politics in Construction Projects[1]

Stewart Clegg and Kristian Kreiner

Abstract

In this chapter we have sought, as good contributors must, to be guided by the wisdom of our editors. We were asked to provide advice on what the key concepts in the power literature are that might be of interest to project management scholars; what lessons are to be learnt from bringing power back in to the analysis of project management (although it was there at the outset in Clegg's [1975] early work) in terms of research design and how can power concepts be used to improve research designs that complement and enrich project management research? We have sought to address this agenda in what follows, defining our field, broadly, as social science, especially those areas of convergence between sociology, organization theory and the specific empirical analysis of projects, sprinkled with a little philosophical understanding that we have learnt over the past 40 that we have been involved in researching project management.

Introduction

The literature on power is voluminous, just as is the literature on projects. However, the intersection between the two sets of literature is almost void. Power is a rare subject in project management research and projects have seldom figured as an interesting scene for the exploration of power and politics. As a start, this chapter will explain why project management concerns, on the one hand, and power and politics concerns on the other hand, seldom interact or blend. However, it is our main ambition to offer ideas and inspiration for future research that will fill this void. We adopt the perspective of project management and speculate how central concepts in the field of power studies may inspire us to see new aspects of the project phenomenon and how

---

1. We would like to thank the editors, as well as Liisa Naar, for their comments on this draft. They were very helpful.

a modified conception of projects may afford a clearer understanding of the relevance of power and politics to project management research.

Why is Project Management Research Largely Foreign to Power Issues?

It could be claimed that projects oftentimes represent an embodiment of power and politics. Large projects spend huge sums of money in a fairly short time and in ways that will have a significant impact on the distribution of future entitlements, obligations and benefits. For example, investment in new motorways and urban projects and the planning of their specific routes and locations will not only map and project important power relations in society but also serve to structure, constrain and enable them in various ways, as the career of *The Power Broker, Robert Moses* demonstrates in the case of New York (Caro, 1974). Projects are often mechanisms of institutional and technological change, which will ordinarily mobilize a host of stakeholders, stir public interest and debate, and engage users and sponsors in collective sense-making and strategizing as well as having significant structurational effects on the fabric of society.

Given this background, it is surprising that power and politics are apparently ignored as if they were irrelevant issues for project management research. There is acceptance that power and politics may be pronounced features of the social processes prior to the project and (to a lesser extent) subsequent to the completion of the project, as well as around the project (Flyvbjerg, 1998). The project phase itself is treated as if it were concerned only with fulfilling a well-structured objective and implementing detailed plans. Projects are conceived as 'organizational entities used to integrate activities and people across different organizational and disciplinary domains' (Morris et al., 2011: 3).

The concept of the project as an object for research allows a focus on the '... project as the unit of analysis rather than project management processes ... *per se*' (op.cit.: 3). The focus on the project as the unit of analysis represents it as an entity embedded in a context of sponsors that foster and finance it and stakeholders that interact with it.

The knowledge interest of project management research is, according to the 'normal' focus, to understand how to design and enact such a project identity so that it will survive, perform and achieve its outcomes under contextually defined conditions. Project management practice as it is actually occurring is not irrelevant but it is assumed that such practices will be studied and understood in terms of their functional contributions to factors such as the survival, performance, and achievement of the project. Normatively, projects become conceived as carefully designed organizational technologies and tools that will only function if we somehow neutralize or ignore issues of power and politics, despite these always being a part of the fabric that constitutes projects (Forrester, 1989). These are seen as inimical to efficient and effective project completion. The very conceptualization of the project renders issues of power politics almost irrelevant and if such issues are encountered in practice they will be taken to testify to the imperfection of either the design of the project or its implementation. Power and politics are epiphenomena, if phenomena at all. A general Panglossian functionalism reigns supreme in the imagining of most project relations.

Let us temper this rosy and abstracted account with a little realism. Projects are organizational entities that must build on relations of power. 'All organizations are relations of power – even the most egalitarian' (Brown et al., 2010: 525). By implication, projects are also relations of power. We will be concerned to show how such relations of power can arise and what they consist of. Fundamentally, an awareness of power and politics will serve to remind us that conflicts abound, manifestly or latently. Such conflicts are based on conflicting interests, understandings, strategies, visions, and perspectives. Moreover, the very structuring of projects, their language and language games, is itself saturated with power relations, sometimes positive, sometimes negative (Clegg, 1975)

Power is, above all a relational effect, not a property that can be held by someone or something. We do not experience power as a thing but as a relation. We cannot easily deny those relations we experience everyday, if only for the ontological reason that most actors would become chronically insecure if they were, to any great extent, to confront critically the knowledge that they hold in their practical consciousness. The relational quality of power is a potentially great source of systemic stability in everyday life and experience.

Of course, for many people, not least those at the bottom end of organizational and supply chain hierarchies these everyday conditions may be unremittingly bleak and miserable, and barely endurable, but endured they must be if no better alternative presents itself. Normally, of course, we live in hope of the future, that the next job, the next promotion, that something or other will come into being that transforms present day mundane reality. We dream of escapes, and these escape attempts are sometimes fuelled by fantasy, sometimes by resentment, sometimes both blended together. Projects offer many opportunities for hope of great outcomes achieved on time, on budget, innovatively and harmoniously as well as conditions for despair at the recalcitrance of labour, the unreliability of contractors, the faults of men and machines as well as the frailties of supply chains. However, as we shall go on to argue, there are less contingent and more constitutive grounds for seeing projects as organizational entities that are relations of power, and project management, much the same as all management, as a way of exercising power:

Management is a process of social control, in which power is likely to be distributed unevenly around the networks of all those with an interest in influencing that control. Management theory, as a body of knowledge, is thus a political discourse par excellence. It is not only knowledge pertaining to power in terms of complex relationships between individuals and corporate agencies, between one organization and another organization, those relations that frame the everyday intrigues, disclosures and dramas of working life. It is also political knowledge in the ways that its theory legitimates some practices while it marginalizes others, in the ways that its rhetoric provides not just a legitimation but the raison d'être for what it is that some people are able to do to some other people (Clegg and Palmer, 1996: 3*)*.

We will exemplify how such discourses marginalize some practices and legitimate others. However, as Latour stresses, we also want to show that while power and politics is a tempting explanatory variable – but a poor one at that (March, 1988) – we must explain what 'makes' power in the first place and what distributes it unevenly. Power is not what explains other things but what needs to be explained. Latour insists that it is important:

> ... *to maintain that power, like society, is the final result of a process and not a reservoir, a stock, or a capital that will automatically provide an explanation. Power and domination have to be produced, made up, composed. Asymmetries exist, yes, but where do they come from and what are they made out of?* (Latour, 2005: 64)

We will claim that the first step towards understanding power and politics in projects is to appreciate the conventional commitment to a conception of projects as organizational entities that hinders power and politics from becoming relevant. To circumvent this roadblock, let us first propose conceiving of projects as a cognitive style.

Projects, Projections and Projecting

Projects are not merely a form of organization. They are also a way of thinking, a cognitive style. When we project we propel potential possibilities into an imagined future. We project ourselves and our organizations into the future by thinking in the future perfect tense (Schutz, 1973). Imagining the act already accomplished we can 'look back' on the present, directing and motivating ongoing action and making sense retrospectively (Weick, 1995).

The projected future, the imagined desirable aim or purpose, forms a 'course of action' (Ryle, 2000). Such a course allows many different things to be done, but it equips such action with a specific meaning and significance. The same situation will afford different action depending on which 'course of action' is invoked, and the reaction by others will depend on their attribution of one out of many alternative 'courses of action' to the actor (Kreiner, 2013).

The intersection between the phenomena of project organization and mental projections has been noticed in the literature (Clegg et al., 2006; Winch and Kreiner, 2011; Kreiner, 2011). The ways that such ambitions on behalf of the future, the tasks committed to, the supra-policy adopted (Ryle, 2000), or umbrella plan chosen (Charles Keller quoted in Ingold, 2012: 54) relate to current ongoing action are variable and complex – if for no other reason than the history-dependent progression of any project and the dynamic conditions of its undertaking. Thus, it is important to stress that the relation between the imagination of an already accomplished act (the projection) and the ongoing current action is one of guidance. Such guidance occurs through the construction of in-order-to motives whose meaning is given by that which they seek to bring into being; hence, not only sensemaking in the here-and-now but also the production of future states through action is a process of filling in empty horizons (Schutz, 1973), with all the uncertainty and unpredictability that this implies (Winch and Kreiner, 2011). In an important sense, the actions motivated by the projected accomplishment are not particular actions so much as ways of conducting actions that might be undertaken for any number of other reasons. Projects understood as a cognitive style lead also to a particular *style of action*, rather than a particular set of necessary and sufficient actions.

Thinking in projects appears to be both a challenge and an opportunity in contexts under merely partial control. The fact that we may not always be allowed to carry out planed actions does not challenge the existence of the project. On the contrary, the planned action may be interrupted by situational contingencies and force the actor to attend to other matters of concern. However, the unpredictability of the situational constraints and requirements only puts a premium on the skillfulness of the projecting actor in the sense of being able to do things otherwise required in such a manner that it promotes (or at lease does not harm) the achievement of the projected act. Perceiving some unforeseen situation as a set of affordances, the ability to carry out action in such a way that such affordances are exploited constitutes a skilful and learned practice. We may see the power of the actor in his or her ability to produce desired outcomes and favour desired acts under conditions of limited control.

Power in the sense described above, has a clear productive and constructive character – in line with Sage and Dainty (2012). To accept that power has positive elements as a starting point does not reject the possibility of power also having effects of a more constraining, controlling, and disciplining character. To most of us, power, in this latter sense is 'patently real' (March, 1988: 147). But as March makes clear, the realness of power as a phenomenon relies on a fairly simple force model of social choices, one that is hardly relevant for most projects, as we will explain below.

Projects as Promises

It is when *projection* into the future becomes formalized that projects as organizational entities emerge. The formalization is prompted by the need to distribute work and responsibilities across multiple actors and multiple hierarchical levels. To facilitate such distribution of work and responsibility, the imagined future, as well as the multiple intermediate steps towards this future, need not only to be subject to forethought but also to planning, negotiation, and contracting. While the cognitive style of projecting allows actors to flexibly adapt and exploit the specifics of the current situation in filling in the open horizons of action, formalized projects rely on an efficient, negotiated but rigid process of implementing the project goal with the planned means and through prescribed processes.

The facilitative conception of 'power to' starts from a complex conception of power playing a specific role as a positive system property in social systems, in comparison to mechanical views that start with more reductionist conceptions of power being exercised when people and things are either made to do something that they would not otherwise do or their preferences, dispositions or nature to do some thing is arrested or stopped in some way. The facilitative *power to* conception builds, initially, from the work of Talcott Parsons, who represented power as a system property of the political system, analogous to money in the economy, functioning as a promissory note might, although today the facilitative conception of power is more often associated with Michel Foucault (1977). Their views of power see it in overwhelmingly positive terms. Power conceived in this way is creative, it accomplishes acts, and it changes the nature of things and relations.

Power is similar to money, says Parsons (1964), because both are circulatory media. Just as money functions as a generalized mechanism or means for securing satisfaction of desires within the economy – without money you may want things but one cannot buy them because one lacks 'effective demand' – so does power in political systems. Both power and money are anchored in popular confidence in their currency; it is this that provides them with their legitimacy. Given this legitimacy, power can be deployed in the expectation that others will respect it and follow its injunctions, because the obligations that it places on those over whom its remit will run, will regard them as binding because of the perception of legitimacy. Symbolic legitimacy is the orderly background within which Parsons' view of power to is embedded. Indeed, he theorizes power as the medium of order for social systems, including organizations. Hence, in projects, power functions as a generalized capacity to influence the allocation of resources for attaining collective goals. Members share institutionalized obligations by virtue of being members and within the context of membership certain sanctions are legitimized through those obligations and institutionalized roles involved in the power system. Power is the legitimate mechanism regulating commitments. Authority, on the other hand, comprises the general rules that govern the making of specific binding decisions: in projects, this authority is always a mixture of disciplinary competence, trade or professional certification, together with contractual relations between organizations and, within them, between employers and employees.

'Power is exercised within the context of norms', as Clegg (1989: 132) suggests. Thus, when power is exercised organizationally it is always within the context of binding obligations shared both by the power yielder and the power subject, and the sanctions that are threatened for non-compliance are always normatively constrained. One may not agree to consent but one does so in the knowledge of what one can expect the authorities to do in consequence. Deviance and resistance to power, because it calls forth the appropriate sanctions, actually strengthens the organizational order of the project.

Individual project actors are conceived as moral agents acting within a normative context; they are effectively socialized to be so. Where they are not, then socialization must be amiss – which is where 'power over' comes into play when actors routinely use power as a way of ensuring the reproduction of authority as a positive force, as a capacity to produce an effect. The fundamental difference between the two conceptions of the project has much to do with an understanding of 'power'. The cognitive style of projection can better be understood in terms of empowerment of the actor, in the form of offering meaning, direction and motivation but also encouraging a skilled way of perceiving the affordances of the situations, the resourcefulness of moments, the translatability of interests. It entails turning actions (planned or improvised) into resources for moving towards the projected future. It provides the actor with the *power to* pragmatically move in some desired direction. The concept of power to is what the French term *puissance*, in reference to Foucault's suggestion that attention be paid to the '… shifting arrangement of materials, relations, dispositions and techniques that are simultaneously the medium and effects of power, and which enable and constrain particular patterns of action' (Marshall, 2006: 208).

Normatively, in the prescriptive literature projects as designed organizational entities have little need for empowerment, meaning, and motivation. Action is prescribed and its compliance with plans and contracts is regarded as the only legitimate way of evaluating and interpreting it. Whatever sense and meaning such implementation may have for the actors, it doesn't really matter as long as the action is compliant. Somehow these plans and contracts exercise 'power over' the project members and, in doing so, form the basis for the exercise of power within the social hierarchy that also embodies a project.

The 'somehow' whereby plans and contracts 'exercise' 'power over' needs unpacking. First, one should note that one person's 'power to' may involve asserting 'power over' many other people; the capabilities of an organization to have the power to do something, such as achieve project outcomes, will invariably mean that its delegated agents have to assert power over others and have it asserted over them. The relevant point is that the effects of power as productive or negative are strictly contingent, so for some people the effect may be positive while for others it will be negative. Power itself isn't 'over' or 'to' in a transcendent way; it is 'over' or 'to' depending on the specific situation and the contingent position of the agents involved in the relation. You have the power to access certain areas on the corporate web site that are closed to the public in pursuit of the project's accomplishment while your employer has power over your life chances: they can assign you to another project when this one is completed or not; they can remove you while it is underway, they can countermand some decisions that you have made. Offend or upset the employer and you can be retrenched, or if the employer fails to develop successful strategies, their capital and that which they access, as well as your labour, will be wasted. Power will always exist

Learning Across Disciplines

in a complex contingent tension between a capacity to extend the freedom of some to achieve something or other and an ability to restrict the freedoms of others in doing something or other.

In the context of project management the contract and its associated documents are the central framework constituting the issues and non-issues for political discourse, inscribing its limits and its possibilities. These documents form the local normative universe of binding obligations. Contestation concerning these is patterned through the skilful professional searching for indexicality in the meaning of the documents. Indexicality was a key concept of Garfinkel (1967), a term that he borrowed from linguistics, where an indexical term would be defined as one that could only be understood in context. Classically indexical terms would be 'it' and 'this'. Without a context being provided the meaning of the terms is utterly inscrutable. What relates indexicality to power is context. In the context of projects the contract and its associated documents are the central framework shaping project discourse. Despite recommendations in the procedural handbooks of the industry, contracts are never unindexical: that is, they cannot simply be read as a precise and unequivocal set of instructions for building a building. Professionals have their different ways of acting that are, within the situated action context, rational. These frame diverse modes of rationality – discursive and interpretative work in which the rationality of the action draws on deep professional coding.

Typically, where a project is premised on a hard money contract – where the construction being undertaken is bid for on the basis of the specifications in the contract, for a definite price, and where the most competitive tender wins the contract, a constitutive framework is established in which the *meaning* of the contract plays an essential role. There are at least two reasons for this (Clegg, 1975). Both are questions of context – one immanently material to the conditions in which the specific contract is enacted and the other transcendentally constitutive of all contracts.

The immanent reasons are simple. Contractual specifications are typically large and complex bodies of documentation: Not only are there the documents on which the work is bid but there is also an associated 'bill of works' – comprising detailed consultants reports and associated documents. In an ideal world these would exist in an absolute and seamless correspondence of all detail from one document to another such that no document ever contradicted another or was in conflict with it. Given the vast amount of paper – comprising detailed specifications, reports, and projections – associated with relatively complex construction projects, that there actually is such correspondence is a large assumption to make. Many hands, at many times, using many distinct skills, produce the papers. More often than not there will be points of ambiguity or even disagreement between them. The precise meaning of them is not stipulated in the documents themselves – in Wittgenstein's (1972) terms there is no meta-rule that provides the rules for how the meaning embedded in the documents should be interpreted. It is this that provides the immanent grounds for indexicality and substantial opportunity for extensive 'language games' to be conducted between project managers and other significant actors on construction sites, in which the precise meaning of what is often imprecise documentation, is translated into contested action.

In projects action plays out in specific arenas. Project meetings are one of the main arenas. These meetings are held to discuss issues. Sometimes they have fairly formal agendas, other times they are impromptu. What is important is that they are sites in which issues and non-issues for the project are determined. The issues invariably related some actions, or absence of actions, to the contractual documents contained in the bill of works. Thus, much of what is said in meetings and discussions is said in relation to some putative but contested state of affairs in terms of the alignment of that state of affairs with the state that should have pertained in terms of the contractual specifications. The gap between these states becomes the matter at issue. Hence, the discourses involve attributions of responsibility for variance. What is said is spoken from different positions of material interest in the contract; for the head contractor the main issue will be to find indexical particulars in the contract that could be exploited in order to win some contribution to the profitability of the site through processing variation orders for which additional payments could be demanded. The architect and client team will seek to see that what they thought they had designed and were paying for actually being constructed for the price contracted. That is the point of hard money contracts – they are supposed to provide for a 'what you contracted for is what you get at the price agreed' outcome – at least in theory. In practice, industry people know that skilled and shrewd contractor project managers will find ways of creating significant – and costly – variance that client project managers will seek to minimize. That is power at work. Smart contractor project managers and their teams systematically seek to exploit any indexicality in the contract in order to maximize profitability while the architect and the client team seek to resist this at every turn.

To make it more concrete, the matter under discussion in a project meeting might be something apparently simple such as the meaning of clay. But while the meaning of clay may appear simple it soon becomes apparent that the meaning is, precisely, a matter of power. In an early case study of power in projects Clegg (1975) used actually recorded material – what people said in situated action – as textual data. The contested matter was the depth of clay that should have been excavated to prepare the site for foundation pillars that were to be constructed out of poured concrete. The issue was simple. The Consultant Engineers' drawings instructed excavation to a minimum of 600 mm. into 'sandy, stony clay'. They did not specify the depth at which such clay could be found. Accompanying the drawings were a series of reports from drilled test bore holes done as a site survey of the ground that had to be built on. These recommended excavation to a depth of two meters into clay. The Project Manager argued that there were different qualities of clay across the site, running at variable depths. There was 'puddle clay' and 'sandy, stony clay'. He defined 'normal clay' as 'sandy, stony clay'. The resulting depth of the excavations done became the subject of an acrimonious letter from the Clients' Architect to the Construction

Company. The points at issue resulted from investigation of the claimed excavation levels, which, as the letter put it, revealed little or no consistency. The counter claim from the Project Manager was that the normal clay sub-strata varied in level across the site – hence the need for additional – and unauthorized – excavation. It was a complicated dispute (Clegg, 1975: see especially Appendices 2 and 4). Power is thus exercised in the projects by securing one interpretation of indexicality with regard to the sense made of the contractual documents over that of another competing claim, framed differently. And if sense cannot be made there is ample opportunity for recourse to legal mechanisms and institutions for arbitrating on the merits of competing claims through diverse legal framing devices.

The case demonstrates that in everyday project life language games are inherently political. First, the contestation that occurs – the discourse of the project meetings – is not random. It is formed professionally, discursively. As Castells (2009: 3) says 'the most fundamental form of power lies in the ability to shape the human mind … Because it is through communication that the human mind interacts with its social and natural environment'. Castells draws on recent developments in neuroscience (Damasio, 2005; Lakoff and Johnson, 2003) to specify the role that metaphors play in, literally, etching representations of the normalcy of power relations into our brains. Metaphors are the building blocks of narrative. Narratives are composed of frames. Frames are neural networks of association accessible from language through metaphorical connections. In project management it is no exaggeration to say that project managers must interpellate many diverse disciplinary frames: design, architecture, engineering of many types, as well as the dark arts of accounting, public and community relations, and so on. Each of these disciplinary neural pathways will be framing the strategies and language games of other interested stakeholders, framing each professional representative of a disciplinary discourse in possible dissonance with those of other stakeholder relevancies.

> Framing results from the sets of correspondences between roles organized in narratives, narratives structures in frames, simple frames combined in complex narratives, semantic fields (related words) in the language connected to conceptual frames, and the mapping of frames in the brain by the action of neural networks constructed on the basis of experience (evolutionary and personal, past and present) (Castells, 2009: 143).

These networks in the mind are connected to broader networks of communication and power being fixed in part through professional practice, creating the identity of the professional self that is presented and represented in project meetings, briefings and discussions. Drawing on contemporary embodied philosophy of mind and neuroscience one can argue that such a self is a network composition connected to a world of networks embedded in practices. Neural networks constitute our professional selves and these function as structurational pathways through which familiar metaphors, constructing socially available narrative frames, are literally fused in the brain. The brain, however, is a social instrument, forged in and through practice. Such practice reinforces the identity of the professional self.

Identities and Projections

The identity of the project as an organizational technology for task achievement under difficult contextual conditions is a powerful one, in ways to be explained here. We will claim that the identity of the project – and by implication of the project manager – is adopted to make what would appear to be a very questionable promise about the future achievements trustworthy.

We may engage Nietzsche's analysis of promises as a source of inspiration. Nietzsche claimed that the promise is not a function of the identity, but rather the other way around: the identity is a function of the promise:

> *For Nietzsche, the analysis of a promise does not begin with 'the individual' and thereafter see promising as the function of a particular individual faculty, for example, the capacity to develop a memory, remembering the past and anticipating the future, leading to the ability to make and to keep promises. Rather, analysis is reversed. The act of promising requires individuals to anticipate eventualities, think causally, calculate, and compute. It is the act of promising that requires this form of identity be adopted rather than the individual being responsible and reliable and thus being able to promise. The practice of the activity creates the individual or subject. The individual or subject is the 'product'. Thus with reasoning. The practice of reasoning in a particular manner structures the individual allied to the mode of reasoning. Rationality structures the individual in a particular way. This is one of its power/knowledge effects* (Townley, 2008: 12-13).

It is the specific promise about future results that is the starting point for understanding the rhetoric and practice of project management. If you should be able to promise very specific results in some more or less distant future you must be able to convince yourself and others that you can 'anticipate eventualities, think causally, calculate, and compute' (op.cit.) – that you can plan and execute the necessary and sufficient actions to accomplish the act (in the terminology of Schutz). If you cannot make such a claim convincingly, the promise would be considered false, and nobody would authorize the promise-maker to engage in the task.

The rhetoric but also the multiplicity of project management accoutrements (in terms of planning and scheduling tools, risk management models, etc.) now takes on a more symbolic significance. Looked at through a power lens it is the various rationalities that disciplinary framing brings into play in the arena of the project that shape the language games of everyday interpretive action in and around the project. As Townley suggests, after Nietzsche, it is the practice of the activity that creates the specific individual or subject: by thinking, speaking, doing being an engineer,

Learning Across Disciplines

an architect, a designer one not only produces professional disciplinary discourse but reproduces their various rationalities. It would be naïve in the extreme to expect these to cohere, overlap and frame things the same way in a fetish of functionalist, technicist, and consensual politics. On the contrary, dissonance and difference would be the norm – as indeed they are – a norm produced through professional disciplinary practises. In Foucault's terms we can think of project management as a power/knowledge apparatus.

The Power/Knowledge Apparatus of Project Management

[Project management] is the object of a huge knowledge-power apparatus comprised of a sizable academic literature, a complex set of [PM] practices, and a massive system of statistical capture and reporting. This apparatus defines [incomplete planning and control] as a problem, an impediment to [project] performance (Adler et al., 2008: 129).

Such framing of the task and role of project management prolongs an institutionalized myth (Meyer and Rowan, 1977) which forces us to resist the normative order in order to confirm it. The oppressive nature of the power/knowledge apparatus will shine through exactly in its distortion of the experiential social learning. We confirm the functionality of proper project management tools by telling false stories of their working and effects on previous occasions. '… for an object to count as a tool it must be endowed with a story, which the practitioner should know and understand in order to recognise it as such and use it appropriately' (Ingold, 2012: 56). But the official stories of smooth communications informing rational planning are often false and their successful guidance to present practice may require the project manager not to take the stories literally. If things go wrong, such informal and discrete deviance from the official story will be deemed inappropriate and symbolically sanctioned – even if it was well-intentioned and pragmatically necessary under the particular circumstances. As Fleming and Sewell (2002) suggest power and control may indeed be subject to epistemological uncertainty because we can never be sure that any specific act is intended as an act of compliance or resistance. This interpretive indexicality is the more marked the more coded the disciplinary modes of rationality are and the more inscrutable they are one to the other: inexperienced clients being clearly the most open to project political persuasion.

From the perspective of Parsons' account of power and authority, we should accept the instrumentality of power as positive, seen against a benign backdrop of legitimately imbued and kindly regarded authority relations. However, instruments allow us to use them to exert our will; whether that will is repaid by sweet music or merely discord is a separate matter. The harmony of the accompaniment cannot be taken for granted; that it was so regarded in Parsons is, of course, the major weakness of his and all other functionalist theory. To exercise power over an instrument to unlock its capabilities to produce great music requires considerable skill, discipline and practice. It is not enough to have a Stradivarius; one must be able to unleash what a Stradivarius is capable of being and doing. Often, this will require the concerted actions of many others – the orchestration of power – where it is less the power over some entity held by its possession that matters so much as the concertative power that surrounds and embeds this potential power over resources (see Bourdieu 1977: 72 on orchestration).

Orchestration implies a great deal. First, it implies a sign system that those who are being orchestrated can read and understand in common. Second, the sign system should be infinitely translatable from any one place to another. It should be capable of travel. Third, its instantiation requires a high degree of concertation across space and time. Orchestras are often found in theatres and the theatre metaphor is one of those terms that have been stretched far from its original usage; one talks, for instance, of a theatre of war, where opposing forces seek to orchestrate their sway over a physical space defined as territory. With this metaphorical switch we shift from the orchestration of effective governance with a limited and spatially confined theatre – the orchestra pit – to one that is far more diffuse but still territorially defined, a definition that fits the construction site particularly aptly.

Power does not exist apart from its constitution; it is, as Allen (2003: 9) puts it 'coextensive with its field of operation. Power is practiced before it is possessed and it is this that gives rise to the roundaboutness of power, not some facile notion that it is a shadowy force lurking in the murky recesses'. Thus, in project management, power will be what its possible limits are constituted to be, as these are contractually framed: vary the contractual framing significantly and the possibilities of power relations will vary in consequence (see Clegg et al., 2002 and Pitsis et al., 2003 for very clear examples), not in a deterministic way but in terms of the modalities through which project relations are articulated.

Power in Projects: Empirical Accounts

Despite the fact that the power phenomenon has seldom been discussed in the context of projects there is no rule without exceptions. We will highlight three such exceptions and briefly discuss their contribution and impact. We will discuss issues such as the power phenomenon (Marshall, 2006), power effects (Sage et al., 2010), and the role of materials and embodied registers (Sage and Dainty, 2012).

Nick Marshall (2006) gives an extended account of the multiple views on and conceptions of power. He adopts a position that draws on Foucault's ideas in focusing 'less on the capacity of individuals and more on the webs of relations in which they are caught up' (p. 212). He also introduces the notion of circuits of power proposed by (Clegg, 1989) which distinguishes between *episodic*, *dispositional* and *facilitative* forms of power. The episodic form of power is related to getting things done, and in its unfolding it is conditioned by the other forms of power which are embedded in norms, relations, and resources, and in the mechanisms of discipline and production, respectively. The implication is clear in terms of understanding projects. What is obvious when viewing projects, namely that power is unevenly distributed across project participants, may need to be understood on premises rather far away from the project itself. The specifics of the project, in terms of design, plans and contractual agreements, on the one hand, and the historical process that the project follows, on the other hand, are both important. Outcomes and relations are partly outcomes and effects of agency, not determined by design and pre-existing structures. Agency matters, so to speak. But the way it matters is still heavily constrained and conditioned by phenomena and structures which neither project design nor project performance have an impact on. Still, such conceptions save us from the dangers of seeing 'people being helplessly subjected to immovable systems of power' (Fairclough, quoted in Marshall 2006: 215). In a sense, the search for power as an enabler of human agency, not its neutralizer, may be the most appropriate motivation for studying power in a project setting.

Marshall gives examples of such studies of power in project setting which recognize the duality of power but which also end up giving too little attention to human agency – in form of local achievements and resistance. It is easy to recognize the self-disciplining effects on project participants and managers when the ideal and abstract forms of knowledge about project management become imprinted on the practitioners through 'collective rituals and judgements of appropriateness' (Hodgson, quoted in Marshall, 2006: 218). Similarly, governmentality – as an alternative to the overt exercise of power – reflects implantation of 'a collaborative commitment and transparency into the moral fibre of a project' (Clegg et al., quoted in Marshall, 2006: 219). Marshall's contribution is to suggest 'a modest reconciliation between the power-over and power-to perspectives' (p. 227). He does so by demonstrating in a case study of a multi-organizational civil engineering team how the interpretative flexibility characterizes all encounters in the practical world. Nothing is black or white, not even contracts. As the case study shows, it is not some pre-existing and generalized discourse of collaboration that identifies and classifies performances and thereby disciplines them. How the generalized discourse relates to action is the subject of negotiation and in the end the episodic interactions and negotiations will sediment local notions of what collaboration means and entails:

> By negotiating what it means to collaborate, and pointing to authentic and inauthentic instances of collaboration, the different parties are fashioning a normative ideal through their episodes of interaction which is intended to regulate conduct. However, this is an incomplete and contested normalization … In this sense, the productive power of collaborative discourses, referring to their ability to constitute the subjectivity of project participants as 'good collaborators', is largely truncated and ineffective, failing to displace established norms of self-seeking behaviour. Indeed, the ultimate irony is that the power-to of collaboration is actually used as a discursive strategy in the power-over struggles between the project participants (Marshall, 2006: 228).

In Marshall's view, agency finds a role in the ability to mobilize the dispositional and facilitative forms of power to self-seeking purposes. Metaphorically speaking, it is the sailor's ability to travel against the wind direction by extracting the forces of the headwind. In our interpretation, because the project setting is so clearly task-focused and because task accomplishment may be the ultimate criterion of success, nobody can assume that they employ 'docile bodies' ready for inculcation as 'cultural dopes'. They have to explore the situation for interpretive flexibility in order to make ends meet. No doubt, they will find opportunities for interpreting and negotiating the contracts in ways that will serve their own interests. On the other hand, the collective task may still hover above them, defining the viability of the project as a mediating force. There are boundaries for self-serving behaviour, but these boundaries are ambiguous and probably negotiable. However, they may nonetheless be real in the sense that, much as the mast may break and prevent further sailing, anyone party to the project may 'pull the plug', thereby hindering agency being expressed in any fashion.

In another case study, Sage and Dainty (2012) describe knowledge work in a seem-ingly non-hierarchical design practice. Yet, the study 'reveals a number of unique ways in which ... power flows within [project-based organizations]' (p. 212). One such way is the founder Peter's enactment of an ideal architect:

> *Across material and embodied, as well as verbal, registers, Peter exhibits to the junior architects his ideal of the architect ... thoughts develop with each pen stroke – creativity embodied in a specific act of drawing and engagement with material forms ... rather than the architect whose work is delineated by abstract (often verbally presented) fashions, client briefs and technical possibilities. If we had not undertaken an ethnographic study of this design practice, it would have been extremely difficult to tease out these subtle performances of power* (Sage and Dainty, 2012: 212).

'Heterarchy means separation of powers, it builds sovereignty into practice rather than the precedent of domination', state Clegg et al. (2006). But Sage and Dainty point out that there are more subtle ways for power to be exercised. They propose four lessons from their ethnographic study. First, in studying power we should be aware of the many registers potentially involved. It is not only entailed in what people do, what they say and how they are formally related. Power is also exercised, often implicitly, in the layout of offices, in the ways things are done, and what is said and unsayable. Second, these implicit ways of exercising power may be especially relevant and prevalent in modern organizations where 'there is a pressing need to carefully balance control and authority alongside creativity and collaboration' (p. 213). Third, power could be understood in a more positive and facilitating manner. It is conducive to getting work done, to coordinating it, and to developing it. And fourth, power is a multi-faceted phenomenon: 'heterarchy encourages creativity, co-learning, motivation and communication, while hierarchy enables decisions to be made, responsibilities to be taken and disputes to be settled quickly' (p. 213). Heterarchy and hierarchy co-exist in organizations and in projects.

The balance between creativity and control may be found in different places according to the specificity of projects. Heterarchy may play a smaller or larger role as the circumstances require. However, the need to be creative, to improvise, is never completely absent. A certain amount of empowerment of individual agency through some form of heterarchy may always be feasible. The ethnographic study of the design studio revealed subtle ways of exercising power and similar ethnographic studies may also reveal subtle ways of displaying resistance and separation, or boosting or sharing of power. Stories about the controllability of future accomplishments, of the tools of management, etc. are not, we suggest, the real backdrop of project management. Resistance, in the form of informal practices or what Fleming and Sewell (2002) refer to as Švejkism (after *The Good Soldier Švejk* of Hašek's 1973 novel), which would conventionally be seen as antithetical to power, is instead often the very constitution of project management power that may also rely more on a sense of moral obligation (Clegg et al., 2002).

As a final example, let us recount the study of the unpredictable power effects of the introduction of new knowledge tools in project management, with respect to the project file (Sage et al., 2010). Disciplining effects are assumed to flow from not only this knowledge tool but from the whole arrangement of knowledge and tools that make up the obligatory accoutrement of project managers. Nonetheless, to recall Hans Christian Andersen, these accoutrements, in their prescriptive nature and assumed efficiency, are challenged by observations of practice. While project managers may not be metaphorically naked the cover provided by attempts to magnify the effectiveness of their power through power/knowledge practices may be more illusory than real. Observations reveal not so much a disciplinary apparatus of tools so much as the affordance of a high degree of flexibility in action and interpretation. In fact, such flexibility is not necessarily unintended:

> *The Project File appears far from merely an imposed corporate standard; rather it is, to some extent, intentionally designed to be a locally flexible tool. ... [It] appears that this object empowers rather than oppresses practitioners. It seems a highly adaptable tool, helping practitioners to monitor and control their projects perhaps offering a knowledge toolbox of 'best practice' solutions* (Sage et al., 2010: 634).

The authors make a convincing case for the possibility of a more reflexive (rather than prescriptive) role for project management knowledge and tools. Indeed, episodic forms of power may certainly empower agency. However, the risk of giving in to a purely functional rationality is acute. The interplay between the episodic and the more dispositional and facilitative forms of power needs still to be imagined and analysed. Sage and his colleagues acknowledge this when they conclude:

However, this case study reveals that such reflexive tools far from diminishing, or at least coun-
terbalancing, control practices and social inequalities, can covertly strengthen them. Indeed if,
for example, a project fails because a highly prescriptive process is followed it is considerably more
difficult to place blame and perhaps extract longer hours from employees than if a prescriptive
process is adapted. ... While there are clearly benefits to more reflexive PM knowledge tools, the
findings suggest that it is not sufficient to extol the benefits of such knowledge practices without
fully understanding the nuanced socio-material associations they can and do form (Sage et al.,
2010: 637).

Situational circumstances and the pressure of the task environment may lure participants to exercise judgment, and thereby exploit inherent interpretive flexibility. By
doing so, while they may promote the collective achievement of the project they also
accept the risk that is an inherent factor in project work facing complexity, uncertainty
and ambiguity. What looks to be a more modern, participative, empowering and
humanistic form of project management knowledge may indeed prepare the scene
for the exercise of control by outside stakeholders. Pursuing and building the power
to accomplish things distributes the accountability for situations when things do
not go well in an unfair and unequal manner. History has taught us that humanistic
management theories can have catastrophic consequences in practice (Singer and
Wooton, 1976).

A Case Illustration: The Power of Learning

In this section we will illustrate the ways in which a focus on power may inform our
understanding of the project phenomenon. It is concerned with the kinds of question
that the project management literature aspires to understand – and our admonition
concerning these narrow framing of the problems that neglects the issue of power.

The Disability Project

The Queen of Denmark officially opened the new headquarters of the Danish Association of Disability Organizations on the 12th of December 2012 at 12 o'clock. The
four-story office building offers a total of 12,600 square meters to the more than 300
people expected to work there. Twenty membership organizations, in addition to the
management of the Association, will rent office space here. Building costs amounts
to 180 million DKK, the equivalent of EUR 24 million.

The building was commissioned in a restricted competition between three multidisciplinary teams each led by a major Danish contracting firm. The entries were
evaluated on the quality of the design as well as the price demanded. The competition,
and later on the construction itself, was financed by very large grants from various
private foundations. The success in raising such grants was probably facilitated by
the nature of the organization as well as the bold vision behind the project, namely
to create the world's most accessible office building.

We want to construct the world's most accessible office building – with equal focus on modern office spaces and equal accessibility for everyone. Only by integrating solutions that could also work in other buildings can you really speak of a house that will spread its innovative solutions like ripples on water far out in the world. (http://www.handicaporganisationerneshus.dk/ in-english; Homepage of the building project, accessed 23 January 2013).

We will focus on the competition process and illustrate the role that notions of power may play in pointing out the relevant matters of concern and necessary questions to answer. The fundamental question is how a small, resource-less and inexperienced organization was able to pull off a project that was remarkable enough to engage the Queen for the opening ceremony? Our account will highlight four episodes that in important ways influenced the course of the project. The visionary nature of the project requires brief mention as a start.

A vision of building the world's most accessible office building is a fairly open-ended commitment. In a sense, since most office buildings are, by common consent, rather inaccessible, it could be interpreted as if the bar was set rather low. However, that was not the intention, nor was it the effect. On the contrary, the fact that the association has 40 member organizations, each representing a particular form of dis-ability, was acknowledged explicitly as well as implicitly by noting that there are at least 40 different ways an office building might be less accessible or useful. Further-more, accessibility was also translated into a concern for equality. Thus, an accessible building would not be an ordinarily designed building in which special provision was made for disabled people. It would be a building designed as being equally ac-cessible to everyone, irrespective of dis/ability. The accessibility should be built into the fundamental design, not added to it as a special effort.

Needless to say, such design is an overwhelmingly complex task – if for no other reason than the fact that what makes a building accessible relative to one type of dis-ability very often make it less accessible relative to another type of disability. To give but a single example, the open space of an atrium renders unhindered movement of a wheelchair but provides few cues by which the visually impaired might navigate. The multiple and conflicting concerns formed the dilemmas for the design and neces-sitated constant experimentation and innovation. The design of the competition can be understood as a way of facilitating such experimentation and innovation in the teams that were competing for the contract.

Each team consisted of architects, engineers and contractors. Normally, team for-mation occurs prior to the application to participate in the competition – i.e., teams are prequalified as a whole. But in this case, each architect, engineer and contractor was pre-qualified on his or her own. Five of each category was selected among the many more who had applied and the organizers of the competition decided how they should collaborate. The rationale for this unusual procedure was to avoid already es-tablished groups with already well-established ways of collaborating. Whatever skills of collaboration; whatever functional rationality of repeating established work relations and role distributions were advantages to be sacrificed for the sake of avoiding group think and routinized approaches.

As a requirement for being prequalified for the competition, all participants were obliged to take a specially designed course in building accessibility. Few had much prior experience with this kind of design for accessibility and the sample of participants was not selected on such skills and experiences. Therefore, it made sense to train them to compensate for the lack of experience. The training course included a number of practical exercises, in which different types of disability were simulated for the participants. They were to physically and mentally experience the hardship of gaining access to and finding your way around already built office buildings. The final exam was based on a critical analysis of a university building and the things required to make it more accessible.

The impact on the participants was massive. Many of them referred in interviews to this experience as an eye-opener. They felt that the entire process (including the proper competition process) had been a steep learning curve. The contractor on the winning team claimed, in no uncertain terms, that they would not be building office buildings the same way as they had done prior to this competition. Personally and emotionally the course multiplied the involvement and ambitions of the teams and their members. It reframed the competition process to become seen as a learning process geared not only to finding a design solution, but increasingly also to understanding the problems.

Sustaining the Experimentation

In order to ensure the quality of the design proposals and the broad accessibility of the various projected solutions a committee was established with representatives from a number of member organizations. At discrete points in the process, the competing teams could sound out their plans and ideas with this committee. To little surprise, no plan and no solution met with the approval of the committee. The reason was clear. Since the quality of any design solution in terms of accessibility is necessarily relative to the specific disability and since the number of represented disabilities was large, on one or more counts almost all proposed solutions could be, and in fact were, criticized. The complexity of the task was reinforced again and again. Common sense proved to be of little use. For example, when some teams proposed continuous ramps for wheelchair access between different levels in the building stories were recounted about the physical strain on the arms that such ramps produce. What was thought to be a safe and sound solution for wheelchair users was discarded from all the design proposals.

Accommodating Stakeholders

We have underscored the exploratory, even experimental nature of the design efforts that went into the competition. The experimentation was continued during the construction on site. New solutions continued to be developed, for instance in relation

Learning Across Disciplines

to fire escape technology. Also experiments with, for example, the colour shading of hallways and doors continued up to the point that the paintwork was initiated.

Explorations and experiments imply uncertainty in terms of outcomes. Ongoing learning is considered an antithesis to efficiently organizational performance (Weick and Westley, 1996). Experimental risk is normally not favoured by stakeholders. In the present case, various foundations had to commit to significant grants to make the project financially viable. How were their concerns alleviated? They ended up being affiliated reputationally with a highly successful and celebrated outcome but that was an outcome that they could not have taken for granted earlier on in the process. The office building might have ended up as an ordinary office building; the budget might have exploded; the completion might have been delayed, creating a conflict with the schedule of the Queen.

In many small ways the design of the project sought to alleviate the anxieties of the foundations. One example was the choice of three large, very experienced, Danish contracting firms as leader of the respective teams. They could be counted on to possess the necessary knowledge for completing a complex design and construction task – and could be counted on to command slack resources to step up efforts should things progress in a slower manner than required. Also the choice of contract, stipulating a final price and placing the risk for cost overruns on the contractors left a sense of a less risky engagement. Normally we would expect contractors to be less inclined to experiment with new problem definitions and experiment with novel ways of doing things but, as already mentioned, the original training course changed the framing of the task for the contractor. In this particular case, the choice of a design and build fixed price contract did not prevent learning that sought to appreciate the design task in all its complexity and ambiguity. However, it did calm the anxieties of the foundations and other stakeholders.

Analysis

The whole process may be seen as an illustration of episodic power. The power relations are effects of a shared project history and roles develop in co-evolution that effects a fit with the circumstances. There is a case to be made for indexicality in the data presented here. The meaning of the design-and-build-contract cannot be deduced from the contract itself but is framed, interpreted and enforced in ways that make sense in and of the particular context. There is a case to be made for the power-to conception in the data, since the accomplishments were far in excess of what could have been predicted and expected knowing the complexity of the task. We have suggested how the participants became powerful in accomplishing a difficult and complex design task, acting in a visionary manner that seemingly sacrificed standard self-serving interests. The solutions were not deduced from a rational analysis and calculation of the design task. The final design solutions did not resolve the complexity and the multiplicity of conflicting requirements because such resolution could not be made without narrowing the design task (e.g. by making priorities between the various types of disability). The mode of rationality was not a functional one but perhaps more a substantial one, building more on commitment to the vision of the world's most accessible office building, than on a notion of self-interest and pecuniary rewards. Only in retrospect could a more functional justification be invented, for example, in terms of improved capabilities and reputation that might prove valuable in future competitions and contracts (Kreiner, 2012).

As we mentioned above, power is something that needs to be explained, rather than something that explains other phenomena and observations. Apparently, it was in the participants' power to accomplish what they did but it was also unexpected and surprising since the accomplishment was seemingly achieved against all odds. The backdrop to such surprise is the realization that the project, by the 'nature' of things, is rendered powerless in a complex, uncertain, and ambiguous world by committing to fairly definite deliverables. The 'promise' of having the most accessible office building in the world ready for the Queen to inaugurate at a specific date was basically unrealistic, in spite of all the tools and other accoutrements that served to make the promise seem trustworthy. In a sense, by issuing such a promise stakeholders were given control over the project and its participants. Such power-over was perhaps dispositional: that is, it was to be unleashed only on the occasion of failure. However, it seemed to motivate behaviour that safeguarded the project from such a situation. It built fears and incentives for the protection of specific interests into the project relations. In terms of realizing the vision of the competition and project this backdrop, metaphorically speaking, constituted a headwind with which the project could sail forward and steer. The project achieved success in terms of the expectations of its stakeholders despite the many insuperable issues faced.

What power resided in the ability of the project to make headway in the direction they had been given? The initiation-training course was largely responsible. Those who undertook it constantly learned new obstacles that they had to navigate during the design and construction of the office building. These obstacles arose when the multiplicity of mechanisms of accessibility were pointed out by the representatives of the various groups of disabilities. Settling on a design earlier, before the specifications became too complex, must have figured as an attractive alternative. It was, however, one not chosen. It appears that the participants in the training course learned to derive pleasure from the process of living, momentarily, with a different reality to that which their ability normally predicated. They were able to develop a curiosity concerning what might come to be and possibly also accepted that this training induced in them a moral obligation to the task itself and to the people benefitting from the improved accessibility and equality. What gave them the power to make progress was the resistance of the opposition to their ideas and proposals: it was this resistance that propelled the project trajectory through new existential insights and new learning. Such existential insights and learning did not reduce complexity, diminish uncertainty or resolve equivocality but increased all these phenomena. The task became increasingly complicated more by discovering the 'wickedness' of the problems (Rittel and

Webber, 1973) than by applying, increasing or fine tuning existing rationalities. In discovering more ways in which buildings are inaccessible and through learning to pose incommensurable demands on the building design they learned through confronting dilemmas rather than eliminating them. The advisory board's repeated deconstruction of common sense design ideas could be seen as obstacles and opposition but since such deconstructions were the motor for the project teams' learning process, being set back by negative feedback was also their way forward towards a better and more complete understanding of the task at hand. The opposition, rather than being resistance to their professional power/knowledge that was to be overcome was transformed into a resourceful intellectual and emotional commitment. Their initial powerlessness in terms of finding solutions turned into a power to move on, continue the exploration, ending up by creating a design for an office building that incorporated many more contradictions and paradoxes than anyone knew existed from the outset. The thrill of newly acquired insights into a world they had assumed they already knew gave the project team the power to refrain from reducing the complexity, uncertainty and ambiguity by making gross assumptions and categorizations.

The unrealistic promise underlying projects had, in this case, surprising effects. The trustworthiness of the promise that a project makes contractually is premised on an understanding of the problems and the task – how could you otherwise calculate, plan and commit to unambiguous future outcomes in terms of costs, time and quality? But it was exactly the learning about the problems and the task that changed the focus away from this promise and the fear of being caught in making false promises. In an oblique way the project team achieved their goals by focusing on what really mattered (Kay, 2010). They did so through design thinking involving experimentation and iteration as well as constraints. They were learning the brief in co-creation with their clients, as the multiple clients' needs became better articulated through this process. If it was not like this, then the brief would have been able to educate the team about all eventualities – such as ramps even before they proposed them. Focusing on all the dilemmas and the multiple mechanisms that make buildings inaccessible they were able to design the building on the basis of a generalized insight that none of the team or stakeholders individually could have provided. Without the resistance that the slow accretion of generalized insight offered, rather than focusing on what they knew, a list of more or less arbitrarily chosen design premises, they were able to focus on the 'unknown' unknowns in what they did not know. There were so many things that they did not know until the resistance of the 40 representatives enlightened them. Because each user representative assumed that what he or she understood, or implicitly knew, would somehow be known to the other user representatives and the designers, it was the multiplicity of articulations of dismay and concerns that established the complexity of the design task and that enabled them to inform what each of them saw as having been left out of the brief.

The insight they gained was hidden in the design and difficult to recognize by the competition panel but the user representatives knew what they knew, drawing on their embodied power and its limits and possibilities. The winning design for the worlds most accessible office space was intellectually inaccessible to outsiders and other experts because there were few explicit provisions for disabled people and few clearly stated premises from which the design could rationally be deduced. The decoding of the design proposal required the same insight that was used in the encoding of a highly complex and paradoxical task into a specific building design. It was the intellectual community between the designer and the client – and the user representatives involved – that provided the network that enabled the designer to act on behalf of the community as a whole. In this way, they could act in spite of the obvious fact that they had no general solutions.

There are no solutions to the complex problems faced in advance of the project teams' encountering them, learning their parameters, and being resisted in their solutions nor is there any way of rendering the requirements of disabled users in terms of a building design that is produced before embodying the facts of those disabilities. The necessary translation of architects and other team members was internally accepted as a way of addressing, not resolving, all the matters of concern that the community hosted. Had they expected and demanded resolutions, the seeming solidity of the power/knowledge that the design teams knew they had, would have melted into air. Resistance to conventional power/knowledge enhanced the team's *power to* innovate while it restricted their *power over* the design by enhancing their *power with* the stakeholders of the disability community.

Conclusion

Power is similar to oxygen in several respects: it is essential to life, to getting things done; it is difficult to observe, it is everywhere and it's being there is frequently un-observed. In one important respect it differs. No natural scientist could ignore the analysis of atmosphere in searching for signs of possible life but in the social sciences of management, with project management being no exception, its necessity is often not only un-noted but also sometimes denied as a possible condition of existence. Power is not a thing. Power is always a relation and it is a relation that can take many forms, the most important of which have been sketched in this chapter as power over, power to, power with, and power/knowledge (see Clegg and Haugaard, 2009 for systematic address of these). Each of these affords a route for exploration of actually existing power relations. It is time for researchers of project management to add a new term to their lexicon: power. Without it, the odds are that project management will remain mired in normativity as an account of what ought to happen according to custom, precedent and tradition framing knowledge that is constantly confronted by realities whose complexities confound PMBOK recipes.

References

Adler, P. S., L. C. Forbes, et al. (2008). Critical Management Studies. *The Academy of Management Annals.* J. P. Walsh and A. P. Brief. New York, Lawrence Erlbaum Associates. 1: 119-79.

Allen, J. (2003). *Lost Geographies of Power.* Oxford: Blackwell.

Bourdieu, P. (1977). *Outline of a Theory of Practice.* Cambridge: Cambridge University Press.

Brown, A. D., M. Kornberger, Clegg, S. R., and Carter, C (2010). 'Invisible walls' and 'silent hierarchies': A case study of power relations in an architectural firm. *Human Relations* 63(4): 525-49.

Caro, R. A. (1974). *The Power Broker: Robert Moses and the Fall of New York.* New York: Knopf.

Castells, M. (2009). *Communication Power.* Oxford: Oxford University Press.

Clegg, S. R., D. Courpasson and N. Phillips (2006). *Power and Organizations.* London, Sage.

Clegg, S. R., and Haugaard, M. (eds) (2009) *Handbook of Power.* London: Sage.

Clegg, S. R. Pitsis, T., Rura-Polley T., and Marosszeky, M. (2002). Governmentality Matters: Designing an Alliance Culture of Inter-organizational Collaboration for Managing Projects, *Organization Studies*, 23:3, 317-37.

Clegg, S. R. (1989). *Frameworks of Power.* London: Sage.

Clegg, S. R. (1975). *Power, Rule and Domination.* London: Routledge and Kegan Paul.

Clegg, S. R. and G. Palmer (1996). Introduction: Producing Management Knowledge. *The Politics of Management Knowledge.* S. R. Clegg and G. Palmer. London, Sage Publications: 1-18.

Clegg, S. R., T. S. Pitsis, et al. (2006). Making the future perfect: Constructing the Olympic dream. *Making Projects Critical.* D. Hodgson and S. Cicmil. New York, Palgrave MacMillan: 265-293.

Damasio, A. (2005). *Descartes' Error: Emotion, Reason, and the Human Brain.* Harmondsworth: Penguin.

Fairclough, N. (2001). *Language and Power.* London: Sage.

Fleming, P. and G. Sewell (2002). Looking for the Good Soldier, Švejk: Alternative Modalities of Resistance in the Contemporary Workplace. *Sociology* 36(4): 857-73.

Flyvbjerg, B. (1998). *Rationality and Power: Democracy in Practice.* Chicago: University of Chicago Press.

Forrester, J. (1989). *Planning in the Face of Power.* Berkeley: University of California Press.

Foucault, M. (1977). *Discipline and Power.* Harmondsworth: Penguin.

Garfinkel, H. (1967). *Studies in Ethnomethodology.* Englewood Cliffs: Prentice-Hall.

Hašek, J. (1973). *The Good Soldier Svejk and His Fortunes in the World War.* translated by Parrott, C. Harmondsworth: Penguin.

Ingold, T. (2012). *Being Alive: Essays on Movement, Knowledge and Description.* London, Routledge.

Kay, J. (2010). *Obliquity. Why Our Goals Are Best Achieved Indirectly.* London, Profile Books.

Kreiner, K. (2013). Restoring project success as phenomenon. *Advancing Research On Projects and Temporary Organizations.* R. Lundin and M. Hällgren. Copenhagen & Stockholm, CBS Press and Liber (in print)

Kreiner, K. (2012). Organizational Decision Mechanisms in an Architectural Competition. *Research in the Sociology of Organizations.* A. Lomi and J. R. Harrison. Bingley, UK, Emerald Group Publishing Limited. 36: 383-413.

Lakoff, G. and M. Johnson (2003). *Metaphors We Live By.* Chicago: University of Chicago Press.

Latour, B. (2005). *Reassembling the Social: An Introduction to Actor-Network-Theory.* Oxford, Oxford University Press.

March, J. G. (1988). The power of power. *Decisions and Organizations.* J. G. March. Oxford, Basil Blackwell Ltd: 116-49.

Marshall, N. (2006). Understanding Power in Project Settings. *Making Projects Critical.* D. Hodgson and S. Cicmil. New York, Palgrave Macmillan: 207-231.

Meyer, J. W. and B. Rowan (1977). Institutionalized Organizations: Formal Structure as Myth and Ceremony. *American Journal of Sociology* 83(2): 340-363.

Morris, P. W. G., J. K. Pinto, et al., Eds. (2011). *The Oxford Handbook of Project Management.* Oxford, Oxford University Press.

Parsons, T. (1964). *Essays in sociological theory.* New York: Free Press.

Pitsis, T., Clegg, S. R, Marosszeky, M., and Rura-Polley, T. (2003). Constructing the Olympic Dream: Managing Innovation through the Future Perfect, *Organization Science,* 14:5, 574-90.

Rittel, H. W. J. and M. M. Webber (1973). Dilemmas in a General Theory of Planning. *Policy Sciences* 4(2): 155-69.

Ryle, G. (2000). Courses of Action or the Uncatchableness of Mental Acts. *Philosophy* 75: 331-44.

Sage, D. J. and A. Dainty (2012). Understanding power within project work: the neglected role of material and embodied registers. *The Engineering Project Organization Journal* 2(4): 202-215.

Sage, D. J., A. Dainty, et al. (2010). Who reads the project file? Exploring the power effects of knowledge tools in construction project management. *Construction Management and Economics* 28(6): 629-39.

Singer, E. A. and L. M. Wooton (1976). The Triumph and Failure of Albert Speer's Administrative Genius: Implications for Current Management Theory and Practice. *Journal of Applied Behavioral Science* 12(1): 79-103.

Schutz, A. (1973). *Collected Papers I: The Problem of Social Reality*. The Hague, Martinus Nijhoff.

Townley, B. (2008). *Reason's Neglect: Rationality and Organizing*. Oxford, Oxford University Press.

Weick, K. E. (1995). *Sensemaking in Organizations*. Thousand Oaks, Sage Publications.

Weick, K. E. and F. Westley (1996). Organizational Learning: Affirming an Oxymoron. *Handbook of Organization Studies*. S. R. Clegg, C. Hardy and W. R. Nord. London, Sage: 440-458.

Winch, G. and K. Kreiner (2011). Building not Dwelling: Purposive Managerial Action in an Uncertain World. *British Academy of Management*, 2011.

Wittgenstein, L. (1972) *Philosophical Investigations* (3rd Ed.). Oxford: Blackwell.

Chapter 11

Application of Behavioural Science and Cognitive Mapping in Project Management Research

Hemanta Doloi

Abstract

While the technological advancement of the 21st century has almost revolutionised every aspect of modern projects, human component of projects is still a critical aspect of projects. Involvement of humans is one of the key characteristics of project management and thus accurate integration of human interactions in project management is an important area for investigation within project management research. The understanding of complex phenomena of human interaction within the project organisations requires multiple theoretical perspectives. Among numerous theoretical developments applicable in investigating complex human interactions, this chapter discusses three key research methods namely Social Network Analysis (SNA), Soft Systems Methodology (SSM) and Artificial Neural Network (ANN). While SSM and SNA approaches are useful for examining complex behavioural phenomenon within a group of people or between individual members within a network setting, ANN is predominately used for mimicking the highly complex human brain for pattern recognition and accurate representation of the interactive environment. While the application of these methods is predominantly confined to finance and management literature in the past, there is an observable trend of adopting these approaches in the mainstream project management (PM) research as well. Given the increasing complexity and involvement of multitude of stakeholders in modern projects, use of these approaches for improving management practices should become more prevalent in future projects. Drawing on the strengths, weaknesses, opportunities and application contexts, this chapter aims to highlight the usefulness of these approaches with relevant examples in a project management context.

Social Network Analysis (SNA)

SNA is a powerful method for collective representation of group of actors (such as individuals or organisations) and the dyadic ties between these actors. The social network perspective provides a clear way of assessing interactions of social entities for representing global patterns, locating influential actors relative to the position of the other actors and examining the overall dynamics of the network. The social network is a multidisciplinary science emerging from social psychology, sociology, statistics, and graph theory where human interactions impacting the outcome of a phenomena is quite pivotal. The first true social network concept in the field of sociology was formulated by Moreno in 1953 for conceptualising the structures of small groups of people produced through friendship patterns and information interactions (Moreno, 1953). Extending the concept, Bavelas (1948) and Festinger (1949) laid a solid foundation of 'group dynamics' which later formed the backbone of the American Social Psychology movement in 1960s. While the development of the concept was rapidly spreading out across numerous fields of scientific studies, the most powerful anthropological developments were associated with the work on African societies carried out at the University of Manchester which was published as one of the first books on Social Networks in Urban Situation (Mitchell, 1969).

In recent years, Social Network Analysis (SNA) is becoming increasingly popular as a general methodology for understanding complex patterns of interaction (Carrington, 2005). The network perspective examines actors that are connected directly or indirectly by one or more different relationships (Haythornthwaite, 1996; Wasserman and Faust, 1994). Any theoretically meaningful unit of analysis may be treated as actors such as individuals, groups, organisations, communities, states, or countries. Regardless of unit level, social network analysis describes structure and patterns of relationships, and seeks to understand both their causes and consequences (Haythornthwaite, 1996).

Application of SNA in Project Management Research

As project management involves complex interactions of people, organisation and the project, the use of SNA in project management research is highly relevant. Deriving from the SNA philosophy, numerous actors such as individuals or groups of stakeholders, multi-level organisations or organisational units are all existing in order to form a network structure within a single project environment. Extending the SNA philosophy, Doloi (2012) conducted an investigation focusing primarily on the issues of social performance assessments with respect to extended stakeholders' contributions to the social sustainability of projects. Central to the evaluation framework in this investigation was the underlying concept of companies being able to achieving social objectives in projects by integrating the stakes of extended stakeholders in their core organisational strategies and business operations.

Integration of Stakeholders

In complex projects with many stakeholders, application of Social Network Analysis (SNA) provides a platform for integrating their perceptions holistically in the project development process. Conceptually, there are three key elements required to understand social network analysis. In the network, the 'Nodes' or 'Actors' are entities, persons, organisations, or events. The 'Links' between the nodes represent the relationships of any kind such as transfer of money, communications, friendships, exchange of resources or information etc. (Galaskiewcz, 1979). One of the key characteristics of the network is 'centrality'. Networks may have one or several or even no central actor(s) with links from many actors directed to it, which represents high or low network centrality. A central position within the network indicates the amount of power obtained through the structure and capacity to access information from the other members (Wasserman and Faust, 1994). Thus, SNA is concerned with the structural positions (such as central, isolate, bridging etc.) of actors. If an actor has many links to others in the system, then it has different network characteristics as opposed to when an actor has a fewer links within the system.

SNA has been applied to analyze the needs of stakeholders and assist in decision making (Timur and Getz, 2008) in projects. In 2008, Timur and Getz (2008) demonstrated the use of SNA in examining stakeholder relationship (Timur and Getz, 2008). Advancing the theory and practice in stakeholder research by applying it in tourism destination development, their study demonstrates the use of a network analysis methodology as a potential tool for researchers and managers in examining destination stakeholder relationships. Combing the stakeholder theory and social network analysis, it was asserted that the destination marketing/management organisations (DMOs) and stakeholders with access to or possession of critical resources have the highest centrality in urban destinations. Among all three clusters of industry, government and the community, local government and DMOs are perceived to hold the greatest legitimacy and power over others in destination development. In the UK, Prell et al. (2009) presented a case study to investigate the environmental impact on the community, and formulated stakeholder management strategy based on the SNA results (Prell et al., 2009). Analysing a case study from the Peak District National Park in the United Kingdom, individuals or groups of stakeholders were categorised based on their central or peripheral roles played within the network. Their research concluded that SNA is a sophisticated technique that brings precision and a deeper understanding of social relations among stakeholders, but used in isolation from other data the results may lead to simplistic decisions about stakeholder involvement in natural resource management. Investigating the effect of organisational position and network centrality on project coordination using SNA approach, Hossain (2009) asserted that the degree of effectiveness in coordination activities is highly correlated to the highly centralised roles within the organisation. Müller et al. (2012) utilised the SNA methodology for investigating the knowledge flows among and between the project managers and Project Management

Office (PMO) members in a pharmaceutical R&D company in China. Realising the intrinsic benefits of the SNA methodology, this chapter discusses a new SNA based framework for social performance evaluation of projects applicable in the project management research. The framework facilitates the integration of stakeholders' perspective over the project lifecycle. The focus of the followings sections are on the characterisation of social performance and integration within the evaluation framework.

Social Performance Evaluation from Stakeholder's Perspective

In order to assess the social performance in projects, the underlying social needs and necessities within the broader communities involved (directly or indirectly) over the project lifecycle must be accurately understood. For instance, the idea of what really constitutes a decent life for a particular community in relation to a project is highly subjective and it depends on the perceptions of that community. Thus, if personal needs of a community, such as food, housing, health care, freedom and liberty etc. are combined with institutional needs such as education, recreation/leisure, social relationships etc. a much broader of action is required to create opportunities in the social value creation process. The major driving force behind society and socialisation in the broadest sense is the creation of opportunities to meeting one's need and for that purpose, Malinowski (1988) suggests that categorisation of societal needs across meaningful functional systems is essential for shaping and controlling the relationships within the societal structure (Malinowski, 1988).

In order to assess the needs and opportunities of stakeholders (both internal and external) in a project, the stakeholders can be grouped into the three functional systems, namely economic, political and cultural systems as shown in Figure 11.1 (Parsons, 1966; Clarkson, 1995; Littig and Griessler, 2005; Maignan and Ferrell, 2004). As seen from Figure 11.1, every group of stakeholders has a different need in relation to project development which presents a unique scenario on social performance of the project. It is worthwhile to note that the grouping of the stakeholders is solely the author's interpretation based on the emphasis evident in the published research (Malinowski, 1988; Parsons, 1966; Rowley, 1997; Galaskiewcz, 1979). As suggested by Malinowski (1988), such grouping is deemed necessary for understanding the relative influence of one group over another in the process of social performance assessment.

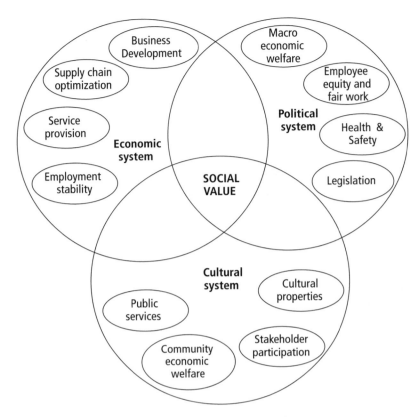

Figure 11.1. Elements Associated with Social Values in Capital Projects

As depicted in Figure 11.1, the economic group has the direct economic interests in the project; therefore their satisfaction is primarily based on the financial performance of the project. For the cultural group, the stakeholder's satisfaction is not directly associated with the financial performance of the project. However their lifestyle will be influenced by the project, such as the impact of working environment on the employees, or the level of services perceived by the end-users. The focus of the political group differs from economic and cultural group, as this group is not directly influenced by the project. The concerns from political groups are from a social justice and macroeconomic perspective, such as wealth distribution of the society and equal opportunity for minority groups.

Social performance is achieved by maximizing the satisfaction of these broad groups of stakeholders across all three functional systems. Since the requirement of social performance differs from different groups of stakeholders, the social value created from the project are multi-faceted and stakeholder specific, based on economic, political and cultural perspectives. Table 11.1 shows underlying social values from the project

Learning Across Disciplines

in terms of different functional systems as derived from the literature. These social values, in relation to stakeholders' perception in a specific project type, provide a good basis for assessing social performance in the project.

Table 11.1. Criteria for Assessing Social Values within Different Functional Systems

Social values	Description	Functional sub-system (refer to Figure 11.1)
Capital performance	Ensure the economic sustainability of the project to satisfy relevant stakeholders. Improving financial performance while reducing threats in long term socio-ecological systems.	Economic system
Internal human resources	Social responsibility towards the workforce in the project, including employment stability, OH&S for the employees, training and career development, and the assets and infrastructures to maintain a productive life.	Economic system
Service provision	The service and infrastructure provided by the project to meet the needs and maintain a satisfaction level for the users.	Economic system
Community development	The social and institutional relationships towards community. This includes cultural heritage preservation, social cohesion, protection of human rights, etc.	Cultural system
Regulation compliance	The level of conformity of the project with current regulation, including certification, public safety and fair work requirement.	Political system
Intra and Intergenerational equity	Ensure the sufficiency and effective choices pursued in a way to reduce the gap between different groups of people and preserve opportunity and capabilities for the future generation.	Political system
Information provision	The quantity and quality of information shared with stakeholders.	Political system Cultural system
Stakeholder influence	The degree to which the project actually incorporate stakeholder's opinion into operational decision making.	Cultural system
Economic welfare	The external economic impact of the project, including contribution to GDP, taxes, foreign trading opportunities, etc.	Political system Cultural system
Socio-environmental performance	The contribution of the project to the improve of environment, including reducing greenhouse gas emissions, reducing non-renewable energy use, protection of endangered species, etc.	Political system Cultural system

Application of Social Network Analysis (SNA) and Social Performance Assessment

As mentioned earlier, in order to assess social performance of a project, it is essential to cover all the stakeholders' interests in the analysis. However, participation of all stakeholders in the assessment process is a challenging task. Some stakeholders may be difficult to identify, as they are marginalized from management decisions (Daniels and Walker, 2001); pre-existing conflicts between stakeholders may lead to unwillingness to participate in assessment process (Stringer et al., 2006); and some biased stakeholders from small groups may be not be representative of the whole group (Grimble and Wellard, 1997).

In the investigation of the social relationships and analysis of social structures, SNA methodology allows modelling the social structure as a number of actors tied to one other through social relations (Carrington, 2005; Prell et al., 2009; Yang et al., 2010). Therefore, by investigating the overall pattern of the network, flow of information through the network can be examined and the position of an actor in the network can be identified.

Creation of social value in projects is usually linked to the perceived interests and satisfaction of stakeholders collectively. Thus accurate identification of the extended stakeholders and their perceptions in every aspect of project over the lifecycle is a key to the social value evaluation process. From interviewing the stakeholders in a specific project context, the social network is then established for investigating the ties and the strength of the ties between the stakeholder groups (e.g. actors). As defined by Granovetter (1973), 'the strength of a tie is a combination of the amount of time, the emotional intensity, and intimacy, and the reciprocal services which characterize the tie' (Granovetter, 1973: 1361). Strong ties between actors indicate that they have more influence on one another, share similar views, communicate more effectively and be more likely to trust each other (Prell et al., 2009; Wasserman and Faust, 1994). Figure 11.2 shows a typical network map generated from an institutional building development project. As depicted in Figure 11.2, there were 14 active stakeholders identified in the project which are represented by the circular nodes and their interconnected ties are shown by two way arrows.

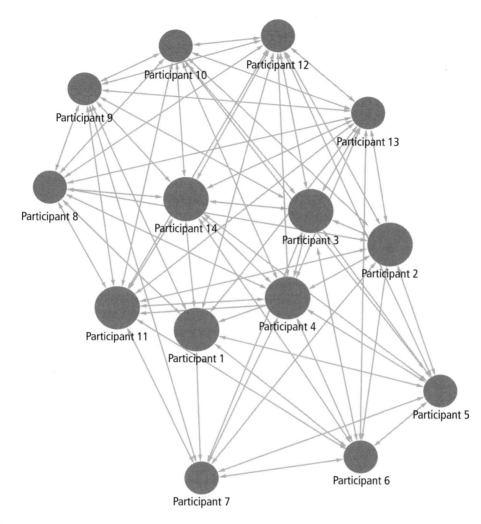

Figure 11.2. Social Network of a Building Project

With the information of how actors interconnect with each other, identifying the most influential stakeholders is essential for the stakeholder analysis. Within the SNA methodology, centrality is a measure of how a particular actor is central in relation to other actors within the project. In other words, centrality in the network identifies prominent actors who have high involvement in several relations, namely highly influential stakeholders in the network (Wasserman and Faust, 1994). Mathematically, the degree of centrality is calculated by the sum of direct ties to other actors. Strong and extensive ties to other nodes indicate that the stakeholder is more likely to influence others, thus more important (central) in the network (Knoke and Yang, 2008).

Degree of centrality is expressed in Equation 11.1 as below:

$$C_D(N_i) = \frac{\sum_{j=1}^{g} X_{ij}}{(g-1)} \quad \text{where } i \neq j$$

Where $C_D(N_i)$ denotes the degree centrality for node i; $\sum_{j=1}^{g} X_{ij}$ ums up the intensity of direct ties that node i as to the (g-1), where g being the highest number of nodes, and (g-1)(g-1) denotes the total nodes but excluding the. node (exclude node j itself).

Analysis of the interconnection between stakeholders implies the importance of stakeholders from degree centrality, whereas the satisfaction level of individual stakeholders can be derived from interviews or surveys. Thus social performance of the project can be identified from the satisfaction level of individual stakeholders and their influence in the network. Social Performance Index (SPI), as a measure of social performance of the project, is defined as the sum of social value from individual stakeholders multiplied by the influence of the stakeholder, i.e. degree centrality and the mathematical expression is shown in Equation 11.2.

$$SPI = \frac{\sum_i C_D(N_i) * S_i}{\sum_i C_D(N_i)}$$

Where, SPI s the social performance index, $C_D(N_i)$ is the degree centrality of node i, and S_i is the social value with regard to stakeholder i. Data on social value S_i is usually collected from stakeholders based on their perceived satisfaction and weightage on the criteria shown in Table 11.1.

In summary, social network analysis is found to be applicable for assessing social performance by exercising precision and deeper understanding in social relations within projects. However, success of application of social network analysis is highly reliant on the extensive collection of stakeholder's perceptions along with the accurate identification of their roles, responsibilities and relative relationships in relation to the project. In the absence of documented evidence of such data, the SNA methodology may yield suboptimal degree centrality in the network which may potentially result in a compromise in ascertaining the social performance of the project. To address the limitations of data collection process for successful application of the research using SNA in practice, it should be noted that while the accurate identification of stakeholders and capturing their interests is the key for achieving objective outcomes in the social network analysis, integration with other traditional stakeholder management approach may simplify the data collection process.

Soft System Methodology (SSM)

Soft System Methodology (SSM) is a systems approach aimed to analyse systems with complex and less clear-cut characteristics (Winter, 2006). SSM is based on systems thinking, which explores problems in the context of holistic system, and focuses on viewing the interactions between components of systems, rather than investigating the isolated components, as proposed in the philosophy of scientific reductionism. Systems theory suggested that a complex system can be appreciated and modelled by integrating the perceptions of different people involved in the system (Andrews, 2000). Later this idea was formulated further into a practical SSM methodology in order to help understanding the complex and 'messy' problems in the real world situation (Checkland, 1981).

Stages Involved in SSM Analysis

SSM involves seven distinct stages to analyse complex and organizational situations in the real world. As illustrated in Figure 11.3, the stages of applying SSM include:

1. Investigate the unstructured problem and make a proposal of the problem situation. This is the initial stage where problem owners are aware of the problem situations or space for improvement, and start the analysis.
2. Express the problem situation in the format of 'Rich pictures'. After proposing the problem situation in stage 1, the information of the problem situation is collected, including the structure of the organization, processes and transformations in the system, and issues proposed by organizational members (Checkland and Scholes, 1990). The information is then illustrated in the format of rich picture, which is a graphic representation of the manner one may think about the system.
3. The rich pictures from different organizational members is integrated together to generate a rich overall picture containing perspectives from different organizational members. A root definition can then be inferred from the overall rich picture by naming the relevant systems and identifying the input, output, as well as the transformation process. From a well formulated root definition, six key elements can be drawn out, as proposed in the mnemonic CATWOE (Table 11.2). The CATWOE represents six key processes within the SSM analysis and these are namely, Customers, Actors, Transformations, Weltanschanung, Owners and Environmental constraints. The descriptions of each of the processes are included in Table 11.3.

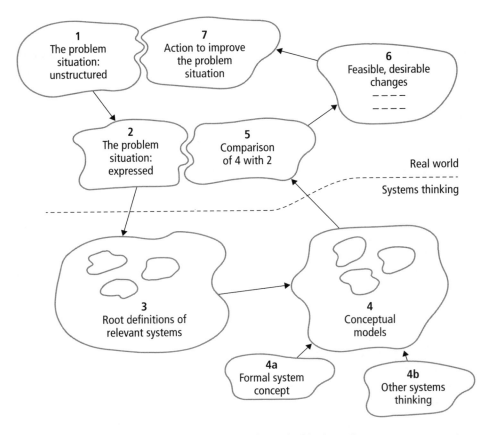

Figure 11.3. The Methodology in Summary (Adopted from Checkland, 1975)

Table 11.2. Procedures of Applying SSM

Acronym	Definition	Checkland and Scholes' description *(Checkland and Scholes, 1990)*	Agency Context
C	Customers	The victims or beneficiary of T	Public
A	Actors	Those who will do T	Staff
T	Transformation process	The conversion of input to output	Managers
W	Weltanschauung	The world's view which makes T meaning in context	Vision and values
O	Owners	Those who would stop T	Staff and managers
E	Environmental Constraints	Elements outside the systems which it takes as given	Stakeholders

4. The root definition represents the objectives that our system has to achieve. The root definition helps to develop a conceptual model of the system. A conceptual model is a model of the minimum set of activities to conform the objectives identified in the root definition. The conceptual model in this stage is only the perceptive model in our mind, therefore it does not have to include too many activities until it is analysed with respect to the real world problem.

5. At this stage, the real world situation, as shown in the rich pictures in stage 2, are compared with the conceptual model generated in stage 4. The comparison may lead to re-iterate of previous stages. By trial and error in stage 5, a conscious, coherent and defensible model can be accomplished.

6. In this stage, desirable changes and feasible activities are identified and implemented. The changes can occur in the following aspects (Couprie, 2007):
   - changes in structure, which applies to the elements of reality in the short term;
   - changes in procedure, which applies to the dynamic elements;
   - changes in attitude, which applies to the behaviour of various roles.

7. In the final stage, appropriate actions are taken to improve the real world situation and the process is modified and developed dynamically until a desirable outcome is achieved.

Issues around human related activities within the project development environment are always complex and conflicting in nature. The solution to one issue may adversely affect the other issues and thus finding optimal solutions in every situation is not quite possible without a rational approach adopted at a grass root level. Addressing these challenges, soft systems thinking seeks to explore the 'messy' problematic situations that arise predominately in human related activity. Soft systems methodology allows interpretations of the problems and to visualise the interfaces gathered in the interview process and the responses to the problems as drafted by each of the interviewees.

With increasing complexity in modern projects and complex interactions with multifaceted stakeholders across different industry sectors, there is an increasing concern about the relevance of the conventional project management theory. The conventional project management theory is predominately based on 'hard systems' characterised by a set of solid technical data. As suggested by Morris (2002), while 'hard systems' approaches of systems engineering and decision support have had a seminal impact on development of project management, 'soft systems' thinking also has an important role, particularly at the front end of projects (Morris, 2002). In order to address the soft issues in project management practice, Soft Systems Methodology (SSM) is increasingly being adopted for tackling problematical, messy situations of all kinds. Sankaran (2011) asserted that the SSM is kind of an action-oriented process of enquiry into problematic situations in which users (usually practitioners) learn their way from finding out about the situation, to taking action to improve it. SSM is particularly well suited in addressing ill structured problems faced by managers in collaboration with stakeholders using questioning and reflection (Sankaran, 2011).

While the vast majority of published research is confined to the field of information systems, the adaptation of SSM in Project Management research is not widespread. Among the handful of published research, however, most of them are found to be theoretically geared rather than based on any empirical focus (Saunders, 1992; Green, 1994; Sherman et al., 1996; Ramsay et al., 1996). Researching into the role of problem structuring methods in project management, Winter (2006) presented a case study example of SSM using empirical data from Tesco Stores Ltd. in the UK. In an attempt to address a rationalised approach into chronically ill-performing cost estimation practices in project management, Doloi (2011) investigated the role of stakeholders in the cost estimation process over the project life cycle. Based on the SSM, a number of conceptual models have been developed for improving the cost estimating practices in the real world situation. The following sections will explain the process of applying Soft Systems Methodology in project management research (Doloi, 2011).

SSM Application in Cost Estimation Practice

Cost overrun is a chronic problem across most projects and thus a comprehensive understanding of the root causes and a clear direction towards improvement is quite crucial. Investigating this chronic problem from the SSM appraoch, Doloi (2011) aimed to establish a conceptual model by identifying the underlying issues associated mainly with the perceptions of the board stakeholders involved over entire lifecycle of project.

As a first step of applying the SSM, rich pictures were developed to represent the real work situations based on the raw dataset and preliminary analysis. According to the SSM procedures depicted in Figure 11.3, semi-structured interviews with the industry experts from different perspectives of cost estimation were conducted to develop the relevant rich pictures for representing the concept maps of the stated cost estimation practice. The interviewees were selected based on their ability to respond to a complex project environment in order to capture the cognitive processes into the rich picture format. Thus, the experience and perspectives of the interviewees were drawn out through verbal response and then mapped into a graphic interpretation. From the development of individual rich pictures on the broad concept, further mapping was performed to develop the detailed rich pictures for each stage of the process from project inception through to tendering and initiation. The rich picture formed a basic model which was then developed into a basic conceptual model which in turn resulted in a broader conceptual model of the reality of the market.

From the rich pictures, the problems were then defined through a root definition by identifying CATWOE, namely the customers, actors, transformation, weltanschauung (world view), owners, and environmental constraint of the problem (refer to Table 11.2). While the numerous rich pictures were also developed over inception, tendering, initiation, implementation and handover stages of projects, due to sake of brevity, only the rich picture of the inception stage has been included in the discussion. By performing the CATWOE analysis, the root definition for cost overruns in project inception stage were highlighted.

SSM over the Project Inception Stage

Figure 11.4 depicts the resulting rich picture on the effect of cost estimating and management practices at an inception phase of the project. The images in the picture show the parties or stakeholders directly or indirectly associated in the project inception phase.

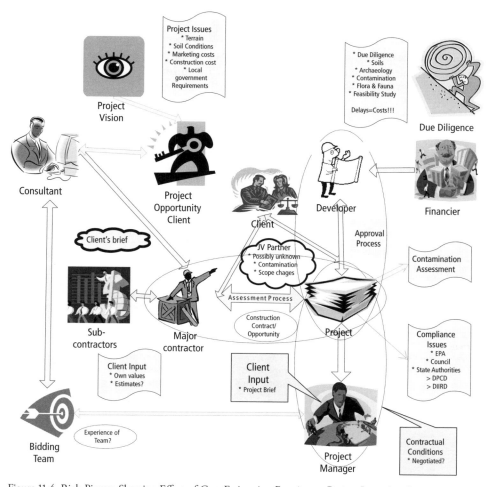

Figure 11.4. Rich Picture Showing Effect of Cost Estimation Practices at Project Inception Stage

While the dotted arrows show the weak or distant links, the solid arrows represent the strong links between the parties and underlying project attributes. Table 11.3 depicts root definition of the rich picture (Figure 11.4) in terms of CATWOE analysis. As seen, at the inception phase of a project, clients, sponsors and end-users are the key customers with highest stake on the project decisions. The list of actors includes: business development team, project manager, bidding team, land developer, consultant, financiers, contractors and sub-contractors who are perceived to have the critical roles in terms of influencing on formulation and implementation of the decision making process. The transformation is governed by relevant knowledge, processes and technology that allow identification of the underlying factors associated with cost estimations and potential causes of cost overruns. Weltanschauung refers to the phrase 'why bother' and root cause 'being bothered' is the inaccurate cost estimation and management that potentially leads to cost overrun in the execution stage of project. The environmental constraints can be represented by underlying competition, political and legislative regulations, economic climates, social and environmental variability, community perceptions and corporate objectives. Therefore, the cost estimation environment at the project inception phase can be represented using CATWOE as depicted in Table 11.3.

Table 11.3. Root Definition at Project Inception Stage using CATWOE Analysis

Element of CATWOE	Module Description
Customers	Clients, sponsors and end users.
Actors	Business Development team, Project Manager, Bidding team, Land Developer, Consultants, Financiers, Consortium, Contractors and Subcontractors.
Transformation	Knowledge, processes and technology together with identification of the potential causes of cost overruns in project inception stage.
Weltanschauung	To ensure accurate cost estimates based on accurate understanding the scope for meeting the stakeholders' expectations.
Owners	Project owners, pre-tender teams.
Environmental Constraints	Competition, Policies/legislations, economic climates, social/environmental concerns, community and corporate objectives.

Development of the Concept Models at the Project Inception Stage

The final step of the SSM is the development of conceptual models out of the rich pictures and CATWOE analysis on the measured phenomena. By developing the conceptual models, the processes articulating relational links between stakeholders and associated project related attributes are further refined. The conceptual model forms a solid base towards establishing the reference models in order for benchmarking the enhanced industry practices in real world.

Having identified the actors and the respective factors leading to cost overrun in the rich picture, Figure 11.5 depicts the conceptual model of cost overrun over project inception stage. The conceptual model reveals the following issues. For the business development team, who is the decision maker in the project, the incapability of considering the statutory compliance, lack of awareness of environmental issues, insufficient industrial knowledge, as well as inappropriate definition of project scope/duration will be the major reason of cost overruns. For land owners, they have to consider the due diligence of the tenderers, potential delays in obtaining government approvals, the financial/funding expectations, etc. The consultants of the project, have to be aware of the terrain conditions, construction costs, etc. in terms of cost estimation. Financiers are responsible for funding the project. In terms of improving the cost estimation, they have to pay special attention to details, project feasibility, market conditions, as well as the balance of project management triangles, i.e. time, cost and quality. The accuracy of cost estimation is affected by the experiences of the bidding team and project managers as well. The completeness of project brief, industrial knowledge and experience of project manager (PM) or design manager (DM) will greatly affect the quality of cost estimation.

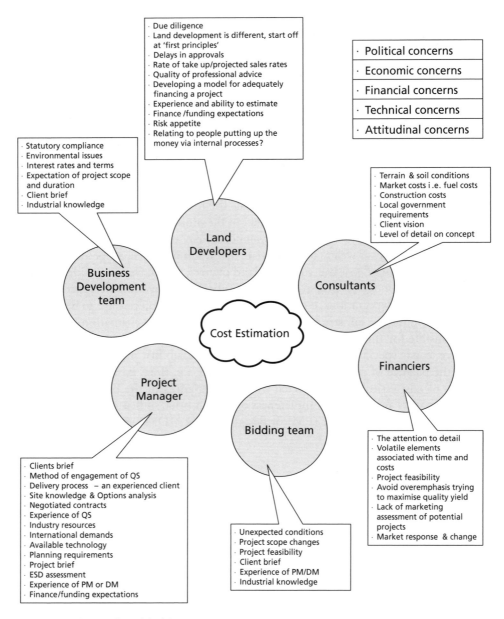

Figure 11.5. Conceptual Model of Cost Estimation in Project Inception Stage

As shown, SSM is a robust methodology for enquiring about the root causes of any messy problem situations which helps in identifying the intrinsic characteristics for improving the real world situation. However, like SNA methodology, the effectiveness of SSM application is highly dependent on gathering authentic empirical data and

Learning Across Disciplines

accurate representation of linkages between numerous actors in the rich picture. For comprehensive understanding of any messy or non-linear issues of real world practice across any industry sector, significant effort should be made in the data collection process. Once the conceptual model is generated, the key elements of the measured phenomena can be further tested using standard statistical or similar scientific methods for confirmatory analysis and validation.

While the use of SSM adds a significant contribution to the current project management body of knowledge in the context of improving cost management practice, the research is not free from shortcomings. Among the shortcomings, firstly, the model required further validation with international practices outside the Australian construction projects. Secondly, based on the concept models developed, all the underlying factors need to be tested or hypothesised on relational or structural links in order for the evaluation of the quantitative impacts of each factor on the overall cost performance in the projects. The resulting relational model can then be compared to validate with international practices which can potentially assist in standardising an international practice across the industry.

Artificial Neural Network (ANN)

The basic concept of Artificial Neural Network (ANN) or often known as Neural Network (NN) consists of an interconnected group of artificial neurons with ability for processing information using a connectionist approach. The network of such artificial neurons has the ability for pattern recognition based on past historical data which turns into adaptive systems for supporting decisions in new problem situations. As described by Zeidenberg (1990), ANN is a kind of a computer model comprising directed graph composed of nodes (sometimes referred to as units or neurons) and connections between the nodes. Each node is associated with a number, referred to as the node's activation. Similarly, a number is also assigned with each connecting node reflecting the weight in the network. The connections and the nodes to some extent depict the firing rate of a biological neuron and the strength of a synapse (connection between two neurons) in the brain. The nodes required activations by external input are called as input nodes. Similarly, the nodes representing the outputs of the learning process are known as output nodes (Zeidenberg, 1990).

Each node's activation is based on the activations of the connecting nodes and their respective weights. The rule that updates the activations is typically called the update rule. Typically, all the activations would be updated simultaneously in the network. Thus an ANN model is a parallel model and due to the lack of general availability of parallel computers, neural networks are typically simulated on conventional serial computers (Zhang and Stanley, 1997).

Learning in an ANN model typically occurs by adjustment of the weights, via a learning rule. The network is typically trained to complete an input pattern, classify an input pattern, or compute a function of its input. At the beginning of learning, with the weights all 'wrong', the network performs badly at one of these tasks. At the end, with the weights adjusted, the network performs well. Typically the update or learning rules do not change, only the weights are adjusted. After learning, the weights are usually adjusted to an optimum level (Lorterapong and Moselhi, 1996).

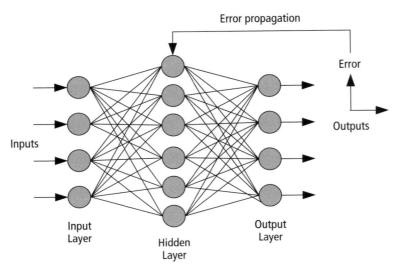

Figure 11.6. A Simple Architecture of an ANN Model

As seen in Figure 11.6, ANN is a highly interconnected network of many simple processors known as artificial neurons (Zhang and Stanley, 1997). These artificial neurons are organised into three layers in sequential order. The three layers are an input layer, a hidden layer and an output layer (Figure 11.6). The input layer receives the input values from the outside environment, to develop a pattern after a number of iterations. The information is then processed in the hidden layer before being stipulated to the future pattern of the measured phenomena through the output layer. Back prorogation is a technique where the weights of the neurons are adjusted based on feedback of the errors generated in the output layer. The weights of the neurons keep getting adjusted until the pattern is completely recognised and the output produced is capable of making decisions or predictions for unknown future situations.

Advantages and Disadvantages of ANN

Compared with traditional methods such as statistical models and expert systems, ANN has advantages in following areas:

1. ANN models can estimate a function without requiring a mathematical description of how the output functionally depends on the input. They could learn from numerical examples and represent complex nonlinear relationships of these examples. Therefore, they are very good at dealing with problems that have complex relationships among the input and output factors, such as decision making based on many complicated factors (Lorterapong and Moselhi, 1996).
2. ANN models have the *self-learning ability*. Traditional models lack the ability to learn by themselves. But an ANN model could learn through the training examples by adjusting their parameters to reduce the error of estimation. This outstanding characteristic of ANN models ensures it could improve the system performance automatically to optimize its behaviour even after it has already been established (Boussabaine, 1996; Li 1996).
3. ANN has the ability to improve the intelligence of systems working in uncertain, imprecise, and noisy environments. Thus ANN models have an advantage over traditional statistical estimation and adaptive control approaches in function estimation (Boussabaine, 1996; Li and Love, 1999).

Some of the disadvantages of ANN model are in the following areas (Lin and Lee, 1996):

1. The precision of the outputs is sometimes limited. Probably the reason for this is that the variables are effectively treated as analogue variables (even when implemented on a digital computer), and 'minimization of least squares errors' does not mean 'zero error'.
2. Training time is relatively long. Furthermore, the time required for proper training of an ANN model using one of the variations of 'back propagation' training can be substantial (sometimes hours or days).
3. The principle of how the output is produced through the input factors is not stated clearly in ANN models. They superimpose several input-output samples on a 'black-box' web of synapses. Unless we check all the input-output cases, we do not know what the neural network had learned, and we also do not know what it will forget when it superimposes new samples atop the old. This is the main reason why ANN models are not widely used.

Concept of Fuzzy Neural Network (FNN) System

Fuzzy Neural Network (FNN) or simply the fuzzy logic (FL) and neural networks are complementary methodologies. ANN usually extracts information from systems to be learned or controlled, while fuzzy logic techniques most often use verbal and linguistic information from experts (Ayub and Haldar, 1984). As far as the project management research is concerned, a promising approach is to obtain the benefits of both fuzzy systems and ANN by combining them into an integrated system to solve problems. For example, one can learn rules in a hybrid fashion and then calibrate them for a better whole-system performance. The common features and characteristics of fuzzy systems and ANN warrant their integration for a realistic representation of real world situation (Doloi, 2007; Jin and Doloi, 2009).

Application of ANN and FNN in Project Management

ANN and FNN techniques have been predominately applied in areas such as electrical engineering and automatic control to simulate the problem solving processes of a human brain and assist people in making decisions under complex situations. Some of the key application areas include solving relational equations (Blanco et al., 1995), objective recognition (Kumar and Ghoshal, 1998), linguistic processing (Bortolan, 1998), and sales forecasting (Kuo and Xue, 1999). However, over the last few decades, application of these techniques is becoming prominent in project management related research as well. Adeli and Wu (1998) formulated a regularisation neural network to estimating highway construction costs incorporating numerous attributes from construction activities. Gunaydin and Dogan (2004) investigated the utility of neural network methodology to overcome cost estimation problems in early phases of building design process. Doloi (2007) developed an integrated model combining upstream and downstream information to facilitate the project management decision making and selecting feasible project options. The model was supported by a hierarchical decision evaluation module utilising Neural Network methodology. The hierarchical module was divided into two stages to handle the project data in a progressive manner. The first stage consisted of neural network models for handling users' preferential data across range of environmental variables and underlying feasible solutions. The second stage consisted of a multi-criteria model for evaluating a trade-off decision with respect to the target outcomes of the project (Doloi, 2007). The neural network models were developed for predicting the environmental and performance variables required for formulating the criteria for soft issues by using information from previous projects and experts' knowledge. Techniques for enhancing learning and learning of the networks by introducing domain knowledge and selecting suitable representations have been discussed in previous research (Gunaratnam and Gero, 1994). Figure 11.7 shows a broad architecture of the ANN models in the integrated model. As shown, when several data points were obtained from one project, the information can be used for other projects to predict if the proposed project solution is along the lines of past similar projects. Capturing stakeholder's knowledge in this way directs project solution towards an acceptable solution.

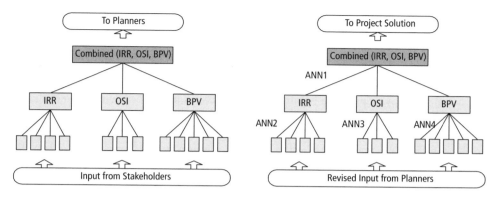

Figure 11.7. ANN Models (Source: Doloi, 2007)

Utilising the fuzzy logic methodology, Jin and Doloi (2009) developed two types of Fuzzy Interference Systems for forecasting efficient risk allocations within the privately funded public infrastructure projects. Validation of these Fuzzy Interference Systems was achieved based on empirical industry wide data collected from Australian Public-Private Partnerships (PPP) projects. In this research, it was demonstrated that fuzzy logic integrated with transaction cost economics theory can be effectively utilised to support the strategic decision making for both government and private sectors in complex PPP procurement process.

Conclusions

This chapter briefly discussed the historical origins of the two key approaches, behavioural science and cognitive mapping, applied in project management research. Under the behavioural science approach two key methodologies, social network analysis (SNA) and soft systems mythology (SSM), were discussed. Under the cognitive mapping methodology, application of artificial neural network (ANN) and Fuzzy Logic (FL) in relation to examples from project management discipline have been highlighted.

Discussing the origins, concepts and the application contexts, the effectiveness and adequacy of the research methods discussed in this chapter in investigating numerous issues in project management has been clearly demonstrated. The discussion clearly shows that these research methods are far more useful and appropriate for enquiring messy and subjective issues than traditional methods within project management discipline. Project management is fundamentally the application of knowledge, skills, tools, and techniques to project activities in order to meet project requirements and thus efficient management of stakeholders' expectations is crucial for achieving success. Thus the soft issues in project management are as critical as the technical issues and management of these is a challenging task. In order to manage the softer issues in project management, methodologies associated with behavioural science and cognitive mapping are increasingly being adopted by the researchers. Such research methods are easily extendible for developing added capacities for pattern recognitions and trend predictions in regard to tackling emerging complexities in modern projects.

In order to investigate the behaviour or soft issues associated with project development environment, the effectiveness of SNA methodology was highlighted. SNA is one of the most reliable research methodologies for incorporating extended stakeholders and their perceptions into the decision making process over project lifecycle. Referring to the use of SSM, the chronic problem of cost estimation within project management research has been discussed with empirical data collected in Australian construction projects (Doloi, 2011). The power of SSM for representing the messy real world situations and transforming into an objective reference model, especially in the cost estimating process, is clearly highlighted.

Referring to the cognitive aspect of human behaviour, the use of ANN and FNN has been discussed with relevant research examples. While ANN and FNN have great predictive power of new situations, their effectiveness is highly reliant on the historical dataset for training purposes. Thus care should be taken with the authenticity of the data source and the accuracy for achieving reliable results.

This chapter also shows that while quantitative methods are useful in looking at economic aspects of projects, new methods are required to deal with behavioural aspects in dealing with economic aspects such as costing, estimating and decision making over the project lifecycle.

References

Adeli, H. and Wu. M. (1998). Regularisation neural network for construction cost estimation, *Journal of Construction Engineering and Management*, 124(1), 18-24.

Andrews, C.L. (2000). Restoring legitimacy to the systems approach. *IEEE Technology and Society*, 19(4), 38-44.

Ayub, B.M. and Haldar, A. (1984). Project scheduling using fuzzy set concepts. *ASCE Journal of Construction Engineering and Management*, 110(2), 189-204.

Bavelas, A. (1948). A Mathematical Model for Group Structure, *Applied Anthropology*, 7, 16-30.

Blaco, A., Delgado, M. and Requena, I. (1995). Improved fuzzy neural networks for solving relational equations. *Fuzzy Sets and Systems*, 72, 311-22.

Bortolan, G. (1998). An architecture of fuzzy neural networks for linguistic processing, *Fuzzy Sets and Systems*, 100, 197-215.

Boussabaine, A.H. (1996). The use of artificial neural networks in construction management: a review. *Construction Management and Economics*, 14(3), 427-36.

Carrington, P.J. (2005). *Models and Methods in Social Network Analysis*. Cambridge University Press, Cambridge.

Checkland, P. (1981). *Systems thinking, systems practice*. Chichester: Wiley, 1981.

Checkland, P. and Scholes, J. (1990). Soft systems methodology in action. Chichester: Wiley, 1990.

Clarkson, M.B.E. (1995). A stakeholder framework for analyzing and evaluating corporate social performance. *The Academy of Management review*. 20, 92.

Couprie, D. (2007). Soft Systems Methodology. Department of Computer Science, University of Calgary, 2007, available at https://internal.shenton.wa.edu.au/ ITResources/ 12InformSys/Information%20Systems/PDFs/Rich%20Pictures.pdf (accessed in March 2010).

Daniels, S.D. and Walker, G.B. (2001). *Working Through Environmental Conflict: The Collaborative Learning Approach*, Prager Publishers, Westport, CT.

Doloi, H. (2012). Assessing stakeholders' influence on Social Performance of Infrastructure Projects. *Facilities*, 30(11), 531-50.

Doloi, H. (2011). Understanding stakeholders' perspective of cost estimation in Project Management. *International Journal of Project Management*, 29, 622-36.

Doloi, H. (2007). Developing an integrated management system for optimising project options. *Journal of Enterprise Information Management*, 20(4), 465-86.

Festinger, L. (1949). The Analysis of Sociograms Using Matrix Algebra. *Human Relations*, 2, 153-58.

Galaskiewcz, J. (1979). The structure of community organisational networks. *Social Forces*, 57, 1346-64.

Granovetter, M. (1973). The strength of weak ties. *American Journal of Sociology*, 78(6), 1360-80.

Green, S.D. (1994) Beyond value engineering: SMART value management for building projects. *International Journal of Project Management*, 12(1), pp. 49-56.

Grimble, R. and Wellard, K. (1997). Stakeholder methodologies in natural resource management – A review of principles, context, experiences and opportunities. *Agricultureal Systems Journal*. 55(2), 173-93.

Gunaratnam, D.J. and Gero, J.S. (1994). Effect of representation on the performance of neural networks in structural engineering applications. *Microcomputers in Civil Engineering*, 9, 97-108.

Günaydin, H.M. and S Zeynep Doğan, S.Z. (2004). A neural network approach for early cost estimation of structural systems of buildings *International Journal of Project Management* Volume 22(7), pp.595-602.

Haythornthwaite, C. (1996). Social network analysis: An approach and technique for the study of information exchange, part 1. *Library & information science research*. 18, 323.

Hossain, L. (2009). Effect of organisational position and network centrality on project coordination. *International Journal of Project Management*, 27, 680-89

Jin, X.H. and Doloi, H. (2009). Modeling Risk Allocation in Privately Financed Infrastructure Projects Using Fuzzy Logic. *Computer Aided Civil and Infrastructure Engineering*, 24, 509-24.

Kumar, S.R. and Ghoshal, J. (1998). Neuro-fuzzy reasoning for occluded object recognition. *Fuzzy Sets and Systems*, 94, 1-28.

Knoke and Yang (2008), Social Network Analysis, 2nd Edition, Sage Publications, London, UK.

Kuo, R.J. and Xue, K.C. (1999). Fuzzy neural networks with application to sales forecasting. *Fuzzy Sets and Systems*, 108, 123-43.

Li, H. and Love, P.E.D. (1999). Combining rule-based expert systems and artificial neural networks for mark-up estimation. *Construction Management and Economics*, 17 (2), 169-176.

Lin, C.T. and Lee, C.S.G. (1996). *Neural fuzzy systems: A neural-fuzzy synergism to intelligent systems*. Prentice-Hall, Inc. U.S.A.

Littig, B. and Griessler, E. (2005). Social sustainability: a catchword between political pragmatism and social theory. *International Journal of Sustainable Development*. 8(1/2), 65-79.

Lorterapong, P. and Moselhi, O. (1996). Project-network analysis using fuzzy sets theory. *ASCE Journal of Construction Engineering and Management*, 122(4), 308-318.

Maignan, I. and Ferrell, O. (2004). Corporate social responsibility and marketing: An integrative framework. *Journal of the Academy of Marketing Science*. 32, 3-19.

Malinowski, B. (1988). Eine wissenschaftliche Theorie der Kultur (*A Scientific Theory of Culture*). Suhrkamp Verlag, Framnkfurt.

Mitchell, J.C. (ed.) (1969). Social Networks in Urban Situations, Manchester University Press.

Morris, P. (2002). Science, objective knowledge and the theory of project management, *Civil Engg Proceedings ICE*, 150. 82-90.

Müller, R., Glückler, J., Aubry, M. & Shao, J. (forthcoming). Project Management Knowledge Flows in Networks of Project Managers and Project Management Offices: A Case Study in the Pharmaceutical Industry, *Project Management Journal* (in press).

Moreno, J.L. (1953). *Who Shall Survive?* New York: Beacon House.

Parsons, T. (1966). *Societies: Evolutionary and comparative perspectives*. Prentice-Hall, Englewood Cliffs, N.J.

Prell, C., Huback, K. and Reed, M. (2009). Stakeholder Analysis and Social Network Analysis in Natural Resource Management. *Society & Natural Resources.* 22, 501-518.

Ramsay, D., Boardman J.T. and Cole A.J. (1996). Reinforcing learning, using soft systemic frameworks, *International Journal of Project Management*, 14(1), 31-66.

Rowley, T.J. (1997). Moving beyond dyadic ties: A network theory of stakeholder influences. *The Academy of Management review.* 22(4), 887-910.

Sankaran, S. (2011). Applying Soft Systems and Action Research in Project Management Research, PMI India Research and Academic Conference, Pune, India, November 2011.

Saunders, R. (1992). Project Management: a Systems perspective. *International Journal of Project Management*, 10(3), 153-59.

Sherman, D., Cole, A.J. and Boardman, J.T. (1996). Assisting cultural reform in a projects-based company using systemigrams. *International Journal of Project Management*, 14(1), 23-30.

Stringer, L.C., Dougill, A.J., Fraser, E., Hubacek, K., Prell, C. and Reed, M.S. (2006). Unpacking participation in the adaptive management of social-ecological systems: a critical review. *Energy and Societym.* 11(2), article 39.

Timur, S. and Getz, D. (2008), A network perspective on managing stakeholders fos sustainabiel urban tourism. *International Journal of Contemporary Hospitality Management*, 20(4), 445-61.

Wasserman, S. and Faust, K. (1994). *Social Network Analysis – Methods and Application.* Cambridge University Press, Cambridge, UK.

Winter, M. (2006). Problem structuring in project management: an application of soft systems methodology (SSM), *Journal of the Operation Research Society*, 57, 802-812.

Yang, J., Shen, G.Q., Ho, M., Drew, D.S. and Xue, X. (2010). Stakeholder management in construction: An empirical study to address research gaps in previous studies. *International Journal of Project Management.* 29(7), 900-910.

Zhang, Q. and Stanley, J. (1997). Forecasting raw-water quality parameters for the North Saskatchewan River by Neural Network Modelling. *Water Resources.* 31(9), 2340-50.

Zeidenberg, M. (1990). *Neural network models in artificial intelligence.* New York: E. Horwoody.

Chapter 12

A Natural Sciences Comparative to Develop New Insights for Project Management Research: Genotyping and Phenotyping

Robert Joslin and Ralf Müller

Abstract

The methods and techniques used today in project management research provide well-established frameworks for designing and executing research studies. However, the success of these established approaches have some unforeseen consequences in terms of constraining academic thinking. The nature of a research design impacts research results and repetitive use of similar designs lead to almost predictable results. These constraints can be seen in many of the papers being submitted to academic journals, but more importantly also constrain reviewers in the peer review process by rejecting papers that actually demonstrate fresh and innovative thinking.

Contemporary methods have been developed and applied in many fields of scientific activities, which have provided for the development of new theories that challenge established theories and provide for fresh and alternate explanations of phenomena (e.g. Alvesson & Sköldberg, 2009; Flyvbjerg, 2001). This chapter introduces a natural science molecular biology (Genomics) perspective as a way to investigate social science (specifically project management) phenomena. It starts with a mapping of concepts and terminology and in doing so it explains why phenomena in genomics (study of genetics) can be compared with practices, behaviors and established thinking in project management. As a result, established thinking in the field of project management will be challenged so that many aspects of project management will be seen in a new light, that is, different. This approach includes insights such as, 'selfish projects', lessons intentionally not learned, competing project methodologies with bricolage of individual elements through use and copy across methodologies.

The chapter finishes by describing the world of the reproductive 'Survival machine' of the natural science (Darwin, 1859; Dawkins, 1974) and compares it to the world of the reproductive 'Survival project' and how the two worlds are inextricably linked.

Introduction

Discussions about the appropriateness of natural or social science approaches to research in projects and their management often refer to the context independence of natural science research. A frequently drawn conclusion from that is that all social phenomena (such as projects) are context dependent and therefore natural science research approaches are deemed inappropriate for gaining understanding of social phenomena (e.g. Flyvbjerg, 2001). This perspective may be appropriate in some research studies, but presents an oversimplification in others. A great deal of natural science research takes place in context dependent situations, just as much social science research takes place in situations of contextual independence. For example, Knorr-Cetina (1981: 358) analyzed the differences in research situations between natural and social science and concluded:

> ... that the situational logic of natural and technological science research appears similar to the situational dynamics inherent in social method, and that this similarity is strengthened by the apparent universality of interpretation in both social and natural science method. Given this similarity, it is time to reconsider customary routine distinctions between the social and the natural science which ascribe to the former what they deny to the latter. And given this similarity, it may be time to reconsider scientific method in general as just another version of, and part of, social life.

To that end this chapter uses one of the long established context-related concepts of the natural sciences and suggest its usage as a theoretical lens for research in projects and their management, thus for social phenomena such as projects. The concept of genotyping and phenotyping is used to exemplify the use of natural science perspectives to social science phenomena. Underlying is an objective ontology applied to real entities (projects as a 'thing'), using the epistemological stance of both process and/or variance methods in the sense of Van de Ven and Pool (2005). The chapter contributes to and extends a stream of project management research related literature that linked the organizational realm of projects to natural science concepts, such as the concept of ecology into project ecologies (Grabher, 2002; Söderlund, 2004).

This chapter aims to contribute to transformative research by suggesting a particular empirical natural science perspective for some social science phenomena, such as research in project management methodologies, as a comparative to existing perspectives. The National Science Foundation (NFS) describes Transformative research as involving:

> ideas, discoveries, or tools that radically change our understanding of an important existing scientific or engineering concept or educational practice or leads to the creation of a new paradigm or field of science, engineering, or education. Such research challenges current understanding or provides pathways to new frontiers.

Transformative research results often do not fit within established models or theories and may initially be unexpected or difficult to interpret; their transformative nature and utility might not be recognized until years later.

Characteristics of transformative research are that it:

- *challenges conventional wisdom,*
- *leads to unexpected insights that enable new techniques or methodologies, and/or*
- *redefines the boundaries of science, engineering, or education.*

(National Science Foundation, 2012).

Related examples are numerous and can be found, for example in Dankwa-Mullan et al. (2010). Historically seen transformative research is said to have contributed, to many of the classic theories, such as the Copernican Revolution or Einstein's theories.

The next section in this chapter describes the background and validation for the proposed comparison and the resulting new perspective for project management research. This is followed by a section on the characteristics of a natural science perspective in the social science. After that the comparative model is presented and discussed. The subsequent section exemplifies the application of the suggested perspective to a project management research question, and outlines how this perspective explains some of the project management related phenomena. Subsequently conclusions are drawn. Finally, a definition of terms is provided in the Appendix.

Background

The field of genomics, that is, the study of genetics, was selected as one of the five branches of natural sciences that lend it to be comparable with project management. Why biology rather than say physics? 'Biology is the study of complicated things that give the appearance of having been designed for a purpose. Physics is the study of simple things that do not tempt us to invoke design' (Dawkins, 1988). Project management can be inherently complex in terms of achieving desired and designed outcomes in volatile environments. There are similarities between biology and project management in terms of complexity, design, impact of a changing environment, lineage and heritage.

In this chapter the terminology of genomics and project management are mapped. From that a model is developed that provides a new perspective for addressing project management research questions. The model is validated and the perspective is exemplified using different project management research scenarios.

The initial attempts to compare phenomena (such as projects) with organisms, such as plants, or animals lead to little or no result. One of the reasons for that is that projects are temporary in nature and unique in design and outcome (Turner and Müller, 2003) whereas organisms, such as plants and animals, exhibit multiplication, heredity, and variation (Smith and Szathmary, 2000). Heredity is hereby understood

Learning Across Disciplines

as the passing on of physical or mental characteristics genetically from one generation to another. Any mutation in an organism that has survived the course of time may be seen as a potential evolution (Lynch, 2010). A more accurate social science analogy to this first comparison would be to a car production line producing identical cars as per their specification; however, any variances outside of tolerance would be seen as a *failure* compared against the original specification. A change of perspective is required if a successful comparative is to be made. This requires observing traits in the organism's phenotype, which are analogous to traits in the creation of the project's outcome. An organism is an individual form of life, such as a plant, animal, bacterium, or fungus; a body made up of organs, organelles, or other parts that work together to carry on the various processes of life. An organism's phenotype is its observable characteristics or traits, both physical and behavioral (Malcom & Goodship, 2001). The term Phenotype results from the expression of an organism's genes, the influence of environmental factors and the interactions between the two. A genotype is the genetic makeup of a cell, an organism, or an individual. When the term genotype is used it is invariably in context to study some aspect of an organism's traits of its phenotype. This specialized field of studying gene expression is called Epigenetics and has helped to understand causes of hereditary diseases by studying the responsible genes for these diseases and how to manipulate them to eradicate the diseases, or how to enhance growth and increase at the same time resilience to environmental conditions.

In a social science world, a similar concept can be applied where project traits are a consequence of the impact of a project environment on the core makeup of the project and ultimately its project outcome. Project traits are observable not only in the project outcome but also during the creation of the project outcome (like the embryonic stage of an organism). If these project traits can be traced back to responsible parts of the core project makeup then actions can be taken to either minimize or enhance the effects until project completion has been reached (project outcome).

Referring to Figure 12.1, a genotype (greek genos, race + Latin typus, type) is the genetic makeup of a cell, an organism, or an individual. One cannot see a genotype. However, a phenotype (from Greek phainein, 'to show' + typos, 'type') is the composite of an organism's observable characteristics or traits, i.e., something one can see. As an organism develops it is continually influenced by the environmental conditions which have a direct impact in its phenotype. A rose is an example of a phenotype where the rose's genotype and its environment will impact the rose's ability to develop and replicate.

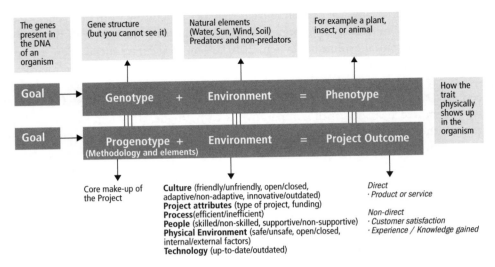

Figure 12.1. Comparative Model

The analogy in social science is that project management is the 'core makeup' of a project which can be exemplified by the *lived* project methodology with its methodology elements. During the project life cycle project traits are observed which are due to impact of the project environment on the project core makeup. The expression of a project's traits is referred to as its Key Performance Indicators (KPI's). To denote the project's core makeup in terms of project methodology and the methodology elements practically used in a project's management, the term *progenotype* is used from this point onwards. The project outcome is the equivalent to the phenotype of an organism.[2]

Every organism has a genome which is the entirety of an organism's hereditary information (Dawkins, 1974). The genome is encoded in the organism's DNA within the various types of cells. What makes a liver cell different from a skin or muscle cell is in the way each cell deploys its genome. In other words, the particular combination of genes that are turned on (expressed) or turned off (repressed) dictates cellular morphology (shape) and function. This process of gene expression is regulated by cues from both within and outside cells, and the interplay between these cues and the genome affects essentially all processes that occur during embryonic development and adult life (Ralston, 2008).

Every project has an equivalent of a genome in terms of encoded knowledge of how to initiate, plan, execute and ensure the project outcome is met. This knowledge

---

2. The term 'project outcome' is used instead of the often used term of 'project success' because the impact of the project environment on the progenotype could influence the project traits in a positive or a negative way.

is encoded in to a project's progenotype, which contains the methodology and elements of the methodology, like genes within a DNA.

A project's environment is described in terms of what impacts the progenotype and how the environment impacts the development of the project. The natural science equivalent is also an environment impacting the genotype of an organism.

Using this comparison there is a way to compare the progenotype with the genotype where the environmental factors impacts both worlds (progenotype and genotype) in terms of genes (methodology elements) being used (switched on) or, not used (switched off). Traits in the respective phenotypes can then be traced back to the respective element/genes in the progenotype/genotype.

In the social science world actions can be taken to ensure the project traits (represented by KPIs) are in-line with expectations.

A model to test the comparatives by mapping both worlds is described in detail in the next section. Before launching into the model, the topic of organisms, how they have evolved and the comparative of evolving project methodologies (progenotype) is covered. Why is evolution an important topic in this chapter? Because explaining how an environment impacts the genotype and progenotype and the corresponding impacts on the phenotype and project outcome gives *no indication* of how the organism or project outcome *evolved* or adapted to the environment over an *evolutionary* period of time.

How do organisms and project outcomes (product/service) evolve and what are the differences between them?

Organisms have evolved from bacteria, which has taken over two billion years by constant gradual evolution to what they are today (Dawkins, 1988). Project deliverables such as cars, airplanes, cities and all their infrastructure and sub-components have also evolved but over a much shorter evolutionary period. However, we can assume with reasonable confidence that both organisms and product/service based project deliverables will continue to evolve.

Darwin's theory of evolution(Darwin, 1859) states that organisms have evolved where the best-suited variants with their traits optimized for the environment successfully replicate i.e., their offspring, starting a new round of evolution. This process can be viewed as an evolutionary algorithm that creates and/or forms the fitness landscape (Wright, 1932) for the ones that are best adapted to the environment. The evolutionary process has three components:

- *variation* of a given form by mutation or recombination
- *selection* of the fittest variants, i.e. those that are best suited to survive and reproduce in their given environment
- *heredity* i.e., that the features of the best suited variants are retained and passed on to the next generation

The evolution of species happens in a glacial (snails) pace but is similar in concept to product evolution in a project environment which in comparison to natural evolution is highly accelerated. Evolution in projects is analogous to new releases of a product/service (project outcome) where problem-solving procedures in project management of trial-and-error or generate-and-test show that evolution can be seen as searching for the best solution for the problem of how to survive and reproduce by generating new trials, testing how well they perform, eliminating the failures, and retaining the successes. However, if the environmental conditions of both worlds change too quickly then there is a high risk of organisms and the project outcomes (product/service) will become extinct or obsolete. Obvious examples in the natural science world are the dinosaurs, dodo and the Tasmanian tiger, but also many of today's species that are in imminent risk of extinction is due to their inability to adapt fast enough to their rapidly changing habitat. In the project world the project outcome (product), can be designed to adapt according to the environment, but if the environment changes too quickly, then there is a risk it will become obsolete through its inability to rapidly adapt. The difference in the social science world is that a replacement product can be designed for the new environment (assuming there is a demand for it), and it may or may not contain any of the design lineage (genes) of its predecessor product.

Examples of products being replaced that are due to rapidly changing environments include: Replacement of the propeller with the jet engine, 35mm cameras with digital cameras, mechanical with digital watches and petrol cars with hybrid/electric cars. One of the important differences between natural science and social science is that humans can predict to some extent the impending environmental changes by applying intelligence in combination in using tools and techniques e.g. to combat global warming. Decisions can be taken to make something obsolete (extinct) or continuing with a product's evolution (lineage). In the natural science world an organism does not have this luxury for 'preparing itself' for adapting to a changing environment. There is no foresight or intelligence that can be applied. An organism either adapts quickly or it becomes extinct. In summary, mutations in organisms are random but evolution is not. Evolution promotes survival of species through natural selection. Product/Service evolution is also not random, there is structure and reasoning.

Characteristics of a Natural Sciences Perspective for Social Science Phenomena

In the following section we point out three specific characteristics to be kept in mind when applying the suggested perspective. These are Complexity, Replicator and Universal Darwinism.

Complexity

Everything evolves irrespective of whether it is in the field of natural or social science. Jean-Baptiste Lamarck believed that as organisms evolved, they became more and more complex. He called it 'Complexity force' or in French 'Le pouvoir de la vie' (Lamarck, 1838). In social science the management and development of project and programs can also be complex. To that end, many project influencers talk about 'reducing complexity'. This statement is easy to make without understanding the complexities and challenges to achieving a successful project outcome. If the complexity discussion was moved to the natural science field and the same people asked to build an organism, it is *unlikely* that the same comment on complexity would result. Having said this, the concern from the project influencers is really about unnecessary complexity. As Einstein so nicely put it 'Everything should be made as simple as possible, but not simpler'. Evolution in both Natural and Social Sciences is becoming more complex (Adami, Ofria & Collier, 2000; McShea, 1991) but should not be over complex, one could say a sort of practical application of Occam's Razor.

Replicator

The goal of any organism is to survive and 'replicate' so its genes have the greatest chance of survival over generations (Dawkins, 1974). The term 'replicator' first developed by Darwin and then expanded further by Dawkins is a concept of replicators in natural science. So what is the importance of a replicator in the project world? If a product or service is going to be successful then the progenotype must be resilient and have a high fidelity at the element level to ensure that it always creates a successful project outcome. To achieve this, the progenotype as well as the project outcome (product/service) needs to be *replicated* as many times as possible to build up a base for justification on future product(s)/service(s) updates. This in turn will help determine if the product(s)/service(s) start and/or continues with a lineage or not.

Universal Darwinism

Darwin's theories have been generalized over the years and called 'universal' Darwinism (Dennett, 1996) where an 'organism' has been replicated by a recognizable pattern, phenomenon, or system. To date there have been many extensions to universal Darwinism which can be grouped into two main categories: gene and non-gene based extensions. Gene based extensions cover areas including physiology, sociology, linguistics whereas non-gene based extensions cover areas including complex adaptive systems, memetics, cultural selection, and robotics. This chapter describes a gene derived extension in both natural and social sciences in terms of genotype to progenotype and organism to project outcome.

With these characteristics in mind we can now develop the comparative model.

The Comparative Model
Core Mapping

Figure 12.2 below shows the core mappings between an organism and project outcome and is used to show how project management subject areas are related to cell types.

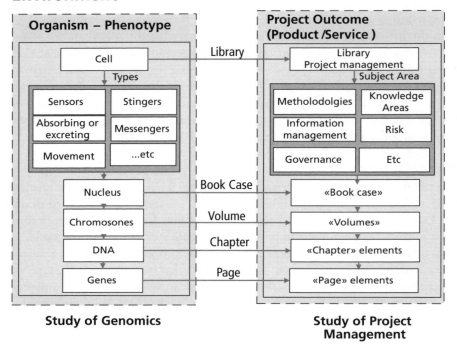

Figure 12.2. Core Mapping Table (Organism/Phenotype – Project Outcome)

To exemplify the comparison the project management subject area 'methodology' is compared within the next section with a cell type. This chapter does not go into detail of cell types; instead it just assumes a general comparative across cell types.

Comparative Model – (Genotype to Progenotype) and (Phenotype Organism to Project Outcome)

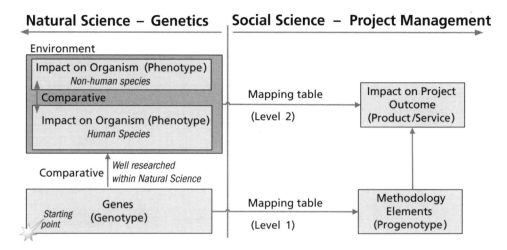

Figure 12.3. Two Level Comparative Model (Levels 1 and 2)

The comparative model in Figure 12.3 shows the basis for a two-level comparative (Levels 1 and 2) between natural science and social science, both originating from the genes (genotype). The mapping Tables are described in Figures 12.4 and 12.5 below.

Genes are the starting point because through their expression they will impact the organism's phenotype but *not* the other way around, that is a one-way causation. The first comparative is between the genes (genotype) and the methodology elements (progenotype). The second comparative (Level 2) compares an organism's (phenotype) to a project outcome (phenotype).

Figure 12.4 details the Level 1 mapping comparative between genotype and progenotype. The top half of the table depicts the world of genomics and the bottom half of project management. An organism's genes' key attributes have been taken and compared against the key attributes of a project's progenotype.

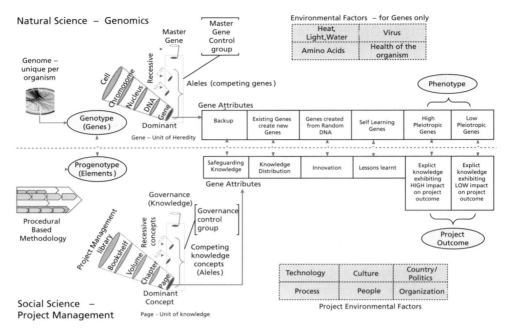

Figure 12.4. Level 1 Mapping – Genotype to Progenotype

Every organism has a unique genome, which contains through encoded DNA the entirety of an organism's hereditary information, that is, the information on how to build an organism. Comparatively, a procedural-based methodology that has been updated through lessons learned derived from a product with lineage, contains all the information on how also to build the product. The exact description of what *to build* is defined in documents that contain the information stored within a project management library. The library subject area (methodology) is analogous to a cell of a certain type. In natural sciences there are over 200 cell types in a human, and the number of cell types varies from species to species. For comparison reasons, a cell can be compared to a library and the type of cell to a subject area within that library. In illustrating the comparisons in parentheses, we can say that within each library there are book shelves (chromosomes), volumes (nucleus), chapters (DNA) and pages (genes). The comparative in this chapter is at the lowest level, the gene (unit of heredity) and the equivalent in project management is a book-page (a unit of knowledge). The analogy is derived from a model by Dawkins (Dawkins, 1974), but has been extended to include the cell type and the comparative to project management. Genes have enduring attributes that have ensured their survival over millions of years. A progenotype also has attributes that will determine if it will survive over the course of time, or, be replaced with something more adaptable. Referring to Figure 12.4, there is a similarity between the attributes of a gene and attributes of a page (unit of knowledge): backup and safeguarding knowledge, creation and distributing of knowledge, creating new genes and innovation and self-learning through lessons learned. How are genes and units of knowledge controlled to ensure that the described attributes are realized? There are several types of a gene, and one of them is the 'master gene' (Pearson, Lemons & McGinnis, 2005). A master gene controls and monitors the progress of the other genes within its domain. The control of genes is totally decentralized. Comparatively, the units of knowledge (progenotype) are controlled with something equivalent to a master gene called local governance. If we can learn from genomics then it would make sense to control progenotypes by decentralized updates like the master gene concept. Progenotypes, like genomes, contain a large amount of information. For any one person to decide on what content to update would lead to the progenotype lacking expert content and this would reflect in the projects and their traits and ultimately impact the project outcome. The Wiki concept, where Wikipedia is perhaps one of the best known Wiki, is built around the concept of decentralized updates using individuals who are experts in their knowledge domain. One person invariably takes the lead as subject matter expert coordinating other contributors. This is similar to the master gene concept. If this approach was taken to updating a progenotype, then topic experts would also decide which progenotype's elements would be the most appropriate for each project's profile.

Natural selection in genomics is where competing genes i.e., a gene that has two or more alleles (or competitors) competes to be selected and become the dominant gene where the non-selected are recessive genes (Mendel, 1865). However, in future generations it is possible that recessive genes are selected which could be due to environmental and non-environmental reasons. Recessive genes can cause problems in the organism, which may or may not be seen in the organisms traits (Dewey, Barrai, Morton & Mi, 1965). It is also possible that a unit of knowledge within a progenotype is selected which is not as applicable as its alleles (equivalent approaches) and this may cause problems which may or may not be observable as a project trait.

There are certain genes that greatly impact their phenotype's traits, which are called high pleiotropic, and genes that have less impact on their phenotype's traits (low pleiotropic). The same is true with the units of knowledge within a progenotype. Some units will have a higher impact on the project outcome (product/service) than others. The topic of project traits and what causes them that will be investigated in the 'applying the model' section.

This concludes the Level 1 comparison. We move on to Level 2 comparison between an organism's phenotype and the project outcome (product/service).

In Figure 12.5, Level 2 the mapping is shown between an organism's phenotype and the project outcome. It shows the key attributes of an organism mapped to the key attributes of a project outcome, which also includes a 'path' back to the gene (genotype) to ensure a consistency of comparison.

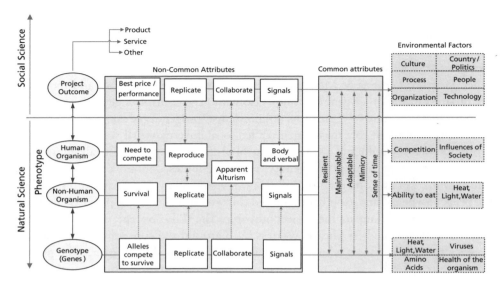

Figure 12.5. Level 2 Mapping – Phenotype to Project Outcome

The majority of a gene's attributes except for mimicry and signals (see Figure 12.5), are directly related to the gene's ability to survive and replicate. The mimicry and signals attributes (which are described later with the other attributes) have been included because they indirectly help the genes to survive via the organism.

A differentiation between human and non-human phenotypes has been shown for two reasons:

1. Human *survival* in today's world does not have the same meaning as animal survival. Humans have developed societies with human rights, government legislation and other international bodies to help humans live mostly within non-life threating environments.
2. Humans have an intelligence that allows them to predicate and to impact the future, whereas non-humans don't.

Human survival is therefore used in the context of surviving in the work place i.e., getting and keeping a paid job.

The genotype, phenotype and project outcome attributes have been categorized as non-common and common attributes. Non-common attributes are associated to a genotype, phenotype or project outcome. Common attributes are consistent across the natural to social science worlds.

Learning Across Disciplines

Non-common Attributes

A **gene competes** against its **alleles** which are competitors to becoming the dominant gene. Non-human organisms compete against each other for survival however humans compete against each other for paid jobs and fight to stay in their jobs (which often leads to territorial behavior if their territory is threatened). A project outcome, typically a product/service, competes against other similar products/services in terms of price and performance.

Replication is a prerequisite for survival in both the natural and social science worlds. When a gene replicates its fidelity which is the degree of exactness with which something is copied or reproduced: is one in a 100 million (Pray, 2008). Replication defects are normally due to environmental conditions which may cause mutations in cells. Influences like radiation, chemicals, pollution and virus can all impact an organism's cells and hence the DNA/genes contained within (Lewtas, Walsh, Williams & Dobiáš, 1997). Products are also replicated with high fidelity, and quality control checks ensure the replication process stays within pre-defined tolerances. Products like organisms suffer from defects which may be undetected by the quality control checks but are observed within the products' lifespan. This may be due to extreme environmental conditions, a product design not fit for purpose, poorly selected materials or issues associated with manufacturing.

The term 'collaborate' has been used in the context of the gene and the project outcome, however, the word 'apparent altruism' is used for organisms. Genes which don't compete (non-alleles) collaborate to produce phenotypic effects that will support their organism's survival. This could be in the form of mimicry, or other traits. The project outcome (product/service) is often designed to collaborate with other products and/or services e.g., other component parts, internet services, servers and infrastructure, or software. Whenever there is an *interface* from one product/service to another, it is a form of collaboration. Collaboration is normally associated with organisms, but there is no reason why products and services cannot be seen as collaborating by interfacing to support their collective needs within any given environment. Organisms (human and non-human) collaborate where there is mutual benefit, but they also sometimes seem to do altruistic things. This raises question as to why do altruist actions if there is not personal benefit? In evolutionary biology altruism contradicts the theory of natural selection (Dawkins, 1974). There are many explanations concerning altruism within non-human species and all of them point to an underlying self-interest. A mathematical model using game theory was created by Maynard Keens (J.M. Smith, 1982) called Evolutionary Stable Strategy (ESS) that shows that altruism does not pay off in the survival of a species. A similar model called the prisoner's dilemma also using game theory shows why two individuals might not cooperate, even if it appears that it is in their best interests to do so (Nowak & Sigmund, 1993). Humans have more complex motives than animals but the underlying acts of altruism always include aspects of self-interest for both humans and animals (Fehr & Fischbacher, 2003; Simon, 1993). Collaboration in humans with apparent altruism is really just collaboration where both parties will benefit, hence, 'apparent altruism'.

Signaling is a phenotype trait that is created by gene expression that help the organism to survive (Wickler, 1968). Signaling is the conscience act of switching on and off something that warns or attracts a recipient of the signal.

Common Attributes

Resilience is a feature that genes have built-up through using various techniques described in the Level 1 mapping. Organisms including humans are to some degree resilient to environmental conditions. Accordingly a product/service also needs to be resilient to environmental conditions.

Maintainability – if a gene or the organism cannot maintain itself it will die. Likewise with a product/service, if it is not maintainable it will fall into disrepair and soon be replaced with something that is more maintainable.

Adaptable – if a gene or organism, or accordingly a product/service cannot adapt to the environmental conditions, then it will most likely become extinct or obsolete. Some organisms have learned to become adaptable but only if the change to the environment is not too extreme and/or if it happens not too quickly (Williams, Shoo, Isaac, Hoffmann & Langham, 2008). The same is true for a product/service where environmental conditions could render them obsolete if their designed degree of adaptability is not sufficient to survive.

Mimicry is a phenotype trait that is created by gene expressions that help the organism to survive by mimicking other species (Wickler, 1968). The same happens in the product and service world where better known branded products/services are mimicked because it increases the likelihood of survival of the mimickers.

Sense of time – an organism through its genes exhibit a sense of time using a biological process called a circadian rhythm (Yerushalmi & Green, 2009). These rhythms are widely observed in plants, animals, fungi and cyanobacteria and oscillate in 24 hours cycles. Products/Services also have built in clocks that ensure at operational times do no interfere with maintenance and upgrade windows. The projects that create the products/services also work to time through their schedules to ensure deadlines are met.

With the mappings now complete between Natural and Social Science with reasonable explanations to the comparability, the authors believe that from a theoretical perspective Genotyping and Phenotyping – phenomena can be applied to project management research.

The next section describes how to apply the model.

Applying the Model

Based on the discussions so far, a natural science perspective suggests the genotype as the independent variable and phenotype as the dependent variable with the environment as the moderator variable.

To simplify the explanation below the following environmental factors (i.e. moderator variables) are described in a project and natural science (genotype) perspective

- Individual (personality of project manager)
- Organization (culture)
- External environment that the organization is in (stable or volatile).

The independent variable progenotype is subdivided into elements where each element can be considered like a 'unit of knowledge', a similar analogy to a gene being a unit of heredity.

There is no formal definition of a unit of knowledge within the field of project management; therefore the following working definition is used for this chapter 'unit of knowledge is the smallest unit of information that is able to take on the state of being true of false'. Using this definition, a methodology element can now be defined as a 'unit of knowledge' constituting an affirmation being the smallest unit that can be 'true or false'.

A progenotype (i.e. parts of a methodology in its environment) is applied to a project to achieve a desired outcome. The progenotype describes what knowledge is required and how this knowledge is to be applied to a project to achieve a successful project outcome.

A project contains processes, tools and techniques, deliverables and stakeholders, which can be referred to as project elements. The sum of the elements constitutes a project. A project element in this context is defined as 'an essential or characteristic part of a project'.

Referring to Figure 12.6, assuming project outcome traits are measurable we can state the following hypotheses:

- H1 There is a direct relationship between progenotype (project methodology) and project outcome.
- H1a The relationship between progenotype and project outcome is moderated by the project environment.

Unit of analysis is the relationship between the progenotype and project outcome.

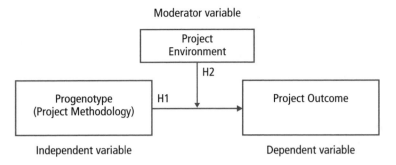

Figure 12.6. Research Model

In applying the model the following example is used (Figure 12.7): a project manager has experience, which was gained from several project implementations. Some of his or her projects created new versions of Product 1. The lessons learned from previous versions of Product 1 have been fed back into Project 1's unique progenotype. Some of this knowledge was generalized and put into the organization's generic progenotype.

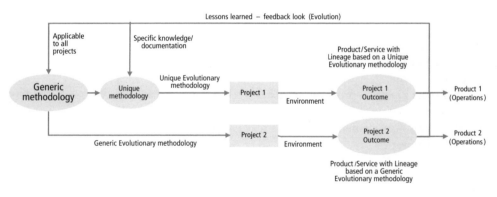

Figure 12.7. Progenotype with Evolution and Lineage

Both the generic progenotype and the unique 'project 1' progenotype are evolving like an organism's genome when it replicates. Both progenotypes are adapting through the lessons learned benefiting the next generation of projects. However, the generic progenotype does not have a lineage (unlike the unique 'project 1' progenotype). In an evolutionary sense, if an organism's genome is always based on an average mix of genes within a species then it cannot evolve (Darwin, 1859), and probably is extinct after an epoch. With this comparative there is a risk that if an organization tries to use a generic progenotype over a period of time *without* some level of customization

Learning Across Disciplines

e.g., to a product, an organization type, a project type, then the projects that use the generic progenotype are sub-optimally run. Organizations that endorse the generic progenotype approach are likely to become uncompetitive against companies that have customized their projects' progenotypes and reaped the full benefits in their resulting projects' outcomes. The conclusion is that the generic progenotype will no longer be used, and in the worst case organizations adopting a generic progenotype approach that don't adapt it will eventually go out of business.

Continuing with the project manager example; the project manager has retired, and a new project manager is assigned to project 1, which he or she has *not* worked on before. The project progenotype has evolved with every new product release.

In the Figure 12.6 the project manager is considered an environmental factor. He or she can decide whether to implement Project 1's unique progenotype or, to change the units of knowledge of the progenotype by:

- replacing them
- leaving some out
- complementing existing units of knowledge with his or her own personal units of knowledge.

The change to the unique progenotype may or may not improve the traits of the project during the project's development (embryonic stages) and at the final outcome. If the units of knowledge are excluded and not replaced with something equivalent then there is a high probability that the deficiencies in the methodology will appear as project traits during the project development and at the final project outcome (if it ever gets to this point).

The project manager now decides to substitute units of knowledge from the unique progenotype with his or her own units. Depending on how these units of knowledge are integrated into the progenotype and how applicable the units are to the project environment will influence the project traits either in a positive, neutral or negative way. There is an equivalent in natural science where the genome of a species has been modified by a virus or another organism (larva), which splices (changes) the DNA structure by introducing its own genes (Dawkins, 2004). The effect is that the change in the phenotype and behavior of the organism during its embryonic and fully grown stages are mainly to the benefit of the larva or virus and less so to the organism itself (Dawkins, 2004). The comparative is where the project manager changes the unique progenotype's (genome) to achieve the project outcome but may *also* personally benefit from the changes that would have not been the case if the progenotype was implemented without change.

A Natural Science example resulting in a *negative* outcome would be the introduction of a virus that creates havoc in the organism (see example below), or a gene mutation resulting in a heredity disease which often results in a premature death.

A Natural Science example resulting in a *positive* outcome would be seen as a gene evolution giving phenotype traits that provide an advantage over the species that don't have this mutation.

Very few gene mutations result in a positive outcome, most result in negative outcomes (Loewe, 2008). Could this be a word of warning for the project managers who are considering altering established progenotypes who *don't* have an in-depth understanding of the project environment *or don't know* how the units of knowledge in the progenotype interact with each other within that project environment?

For project managers with little or no experience who venture to change a highly evolved progenotype (derived from a product with lineage), there is a likelihood of a failed project outcome (if ever it gets to this point). In the natural science world, some viruses cause havoc in the infiltrated organism and the result is that the organism's immune system is triggered which normally kills the virus after a hard fight. The analogy in the social science world is the 'inexperienced project manager' vastly deviating from the highly evolved progenotype without understanding the implications that would trigger the organization's immune system. The trigger is its 'Governance', resulting in a similar outcome – removal of the project manager, but probably not before harm is done to the project in terms of wasted resources and damaged reputation.

There are two other environmental factors described in the model, which would also act as moderator variables: organization culture and external market environment. Depending on culture type and the state of the external market environment (stable or volatile), both can either positively or negatively impact the project during the embryonic stages and final project outcome.

The progenotype contains many units of knowledge, which relate to different parts (elements) of a project, for example, financial aspects, planning, scheduling, or risk. If a project manager leaves out one or more units of knowledge from the progenotype, then the resulting project traits should be traceable back to the cause of the problem. However, if all the environmental factors impact the project in some way, for example, through inexperienced project manager actions, closed environments, volatile markets etc., this will impact multiple project traits which will make it difficult to determine, which project traits are symptoms and which are root causes. The determination of the root cause(s) may be further complicated because each unit of the progenotype will have varying degrees of impact on the project traits (called pleiotropic effect). Projects that are out-of-control are often misdiagnosed when symptoms are addressed while root cause(s) are ignored. This happens because of a lack of understanding of cascading cause-and-effect issues in complex environments. In the project world and in the natural science world's most issues can be traced back to one or maximum two root-cause issues. The challenge is to quickly find them before irreparable damage is done to the project.

Until now, the project manager has been described as an environmental factor where the unit of analysis is the impact of the Progenotype on the project outcome. However, the project manager is also an organism driven by his or her own genes need for survival. This gives rise to a second level of comparison, Level 2 in Figure

12.3 between the human (organism) and the project outcome. The unit of analysis now becomes the impact of the project manager (and his or her team) on the project outcome.

With both levels (1 and 2) in the comparative, the real world of project management is more accurately modeled, but the downside is added complexity in applying the comparative.

Three example questions are posed here where the answers are derived by the Level 2 mapping shown in Figure 12.5:

1. The 'Lessons Learned' feedback loop is an important part of ensuring a progenotype (methodology) evolves. However, why does it seem that lessons sometimes are intentionally *not* learned?
2. Are projects designed to help other projects or are projects inherently 'selfish'?
3. Are project progenotypes (methodologies) complementary or are they really competing with bricolage of individual units of knowledge through use and copy across progenotypes?

The project management related questions are discussed in the following section using the proposed perspective.

Lessons Intentionally Not Learned

An example of lessons intentionally *not* learned is when a project manager believes he or she knows better and takes a decision not to use part(s) of the unique progenotype (project methodology) that have evolved over several project generations. This is a conscious decision *not* to learn or use knowledge gained from his or her predecessors. The question is why does a project manager believe he or she knows better when clearly a great deal of knowledge and experience has been synthetized from project learning into a continually improving progenotype?

One explanation taken from the natural science perspective is that organisms are driven by survival instincts. A human in this case (project manager), strives to survive in the world he or she knows and will use all available resources that are believed to give him or her, the maximum advantage. Taking something that has been developed by someone or group of people does not necessarily give an edge nor does it differentiate because he or she is genetically driven to succeed by competing in the same environment. Humans have intelligence and the ability to understand the implications of risks. However, achieving success in a work place (irrespective of how success is measured) often overrides the implications of the risk events *especially* if the environment is new, and the risks are not fully understood. Lessons not-learned in projects do not lead to death *unlike* in the animal world where this would inevitably lead to a fatal mistake. If the implications were the same in the project world then every lesson would *be* learnt *based on the assumption the project manager is capable of assimilating and integrating the new knowledge.*

Selfish Projects

Are projects created with a sense of altruism or are there 'selfish projects' that have little or no interest in helping other projects to succeed if there is no mutual benefit? There are two perspectives of looking at projects. Referring to Figure 12.3 one perspective is from the genotype- progenotype (level 1), and the second perspective is the phenotype of the organism to the project outcome (level 2).

Taking the first comparative (level 1): genes compete with their alleles to ensure they become a dominate trait and likewise the similar 'units of knowledge' compete to be used within the progenotype. But at a project level each project is competing with every other project in terms of resources, senior management attention and funding. Therefore, one project has little or no interest in helping another project to succeed especially knowing that if by doing so, there is a risk of it being cancelled. Its evolutional Progenotype will stop there.

Now using the level 2 comparison of human characteristics and the project outcome (see Figure 12.5), humans must be adaptable and competitive to survive. A project outcome (product/service) has equivalent characteristics to human characteristics – it needs to compete to survive first during its creation and later when it is operational. Every organism strives to survive and replicate. Therefore, everything it does, is for this purpose and to ensure it maintains fitness in its species (Dawkins, 2004). A concept called Evolutionarily Stable Strategy (J.M. Smith, 1982) shows, mathematically, the best survival options for an organism depends on what others in the same species are doing. The theory leads to testable predictions about the evolution of behavior, of sex and genetic systems, and of growth and life history patterns. Smith proved that altruistic strategies are not sustainable for a species (J.M. Smith, 1982). Acts of apparent altruism also exist within the workplace but always with a self- interest (Rotemberg, 1994). A Project Manager is only interested in his or her project and not in other projects (unless dependencies exist) especially in organizations, which incentivize success of individual projects. This can lead to behavior that promotes selfishness to the extreme with the focus around his or her project and the project outcome.

In summary, in a Genotype to Progenotype comparative (level 1); projects are fighting for survival so that they have little or no interest to help each other. In a phenotype to project outcome comparative (level 2); the project manager is concerned only about his or her project often to the detriment of other competing projects, hence the all-encompassing term 'Selfish Project'.

Bricolage of Competing Individual Methodology Elements (Units of Knowledge)

Every gene fights for survival with its allele(s) and so does every methodology element (unit of knowledge). If one looks at the individual genes within an organism's genome each gene's goal is to replicate and be present in as many organisms as possible within that species (Dawkins, 1974). The same is true for every unit of knowledge within the progenotype. Once a unit of knowledge is selected for any given project it no longer needs to compete and therefore will collaborate with all other units of knowledge within the progenotype to increase the probability of a successful project outcome. However, irrespective if a unit of knowledge is selected or not for any given project its goal is to be used (replicated) in many projects' progenotypes as possible. This will create a bricolage of individual units through use and copy across progenotypes. Will the individual units of knowledge survive the course of time? It will depend on the success of each project and hence the combination of units of knowledge for each project environment. Only the most aligned progenotypes to any given project environment will survive.

Survival Machines and Survival Projects

The chapter has described the importance of genes in organisms where the body or frame of the organism is almost secondary to the genes. Looking back from an evolutionary perspective, DNA formed in bacteria around 2.3 billion years ago (Blank, 2004) and as the bacteria evolved into the organisms of today (such as humans, animals, birds, etc.) the genes had to acquire protective bodies. As the demands on the genes bodies increased the bodies had to evolve and in doing so became more and complex (Lamarck, 1838). This change of perspective from an organism centric evolution to a gene centric evolution has helped explain concerns regarding evolutionary theory relating to altruism and selfishness (Darwin, 1859; Dawkins, 2004).

The change of perspective from organism to gene has led to the labeling of organisms as survival machines (Dawkins, 1974) where the importance is attached to the information stored within the genes and not to the organism itself.

Is it possible that the project and the project outcome (project/service) can be compared in a similar way? Projects and the outcomes are seen as 'survival projects', 'survival products' and 'survival services'. Could it be that the knowledge used to design, build and evolve the products and services is more important than the value of the products and services?

'Monetary value' versus the 'value of knowledge', is an age old dilemma as to which has a greater importance. This chapter does not intend to answer this last question, but just to show that survival machines and survival projects can, in many ways, inextricably be linked.

Conclusions

The chapter has focused on the evolutionary theme based an organism's genotype in the Natural Science world and how environmental factors influence an organism's traits which, when compared to a project's essential core (progenotype), showed similar characteristics.

Evolution and lineage go hand-in-hand when describing an organism and the same is true for a product/service (project outcome) that has survived the course of time through adaption and replication.

Darwinism was introduced showing how the concept of natural selection can be applied to the world of project management and projects. A two-level comparative was put forward, mapping first the attributes of a project's methodology the progenotype to the attributes of an organism – the genotype, then second; mapping the attributes of an organism (human) to the attributes of the product outcome (product/service). The mapping showed how projects (from conception to completion and then into operations) fight for survival just like the genes of an organism (including the organism itself). The comparative was built showing how projects have their own entities and exhibit behavior similar to an organism. Project assets like funding, resourcing and senior management attention are key survival requirements but no guarantee of actual survival to achieve successful project outcome. The comparison showed that environmental conditions have as much impact on an organism as they do on a project and it's progenotype. The embryonic stages of an organism's development are critical to ensure a healthy organism that can survive in its environment which is also true in the project world.

The chapter puts forward a new perspective on projects by considering every project to have a core essence (progenotype) that needs to be understood, leveraged and maintained so as to be able to reach the full potential of the project during the difficult stages of development until the project outcome is achieved. The chapter also highlights the dangers and opportunities of the project environment and a way for the project stakeholders to ensure the project environment enriches a project, like in nature, rather than to starve or hinder project growth (progress).

Universal Darwinism has helped provide new insight in many disciplines and the authors believe this is also true for project management. Research questions like the ones in this chapter describing a moderator variable that is environmental in nature could use a natural science comparative.

For example, a hypothesis that:

- There is a correlation between X and Y, which is moderated by an environmental variable e.g., people, culture, project attributes, physical environment, technology.

Projects should be seen in terms of their progenotypes and their knowledge as core assets. Core assets have an identity and the ability to replicate in the right environment. So every endeavor should focus on understanding and developing progenotypes. Perhaps the value of revenues generated from products and services should be complemented with the value of the knowledge contained in the progenotype?

The comparative used in this chapter could help in identifying new research areas in projects, challenged established thinking by using a natural science comparative or help explaining research results that go against established thinking which risk being discarded.

The authors believe that there are many more natural science comparatives that can be developed that will give new insights like the concept of the progenotype.

Appendix

Definition of Terms

Term	Definition	Source
Cell	Biology the smallest structural and functional unit of an organism, which is typically microscopic and consists of cytoplasm and a nucleus enclosed in a membrane.	Oxford dictionary
Chromosome	A thread-like structure of nucleic acids and protein found in the nucleus of most living cells, carrying genetic information in the form of genes.	Oxford dictionary
DNA	Deoxyribonucleic acid, a self-replicating material which is present in nearly all living organisms as the main constituent of chromosomes. It is the carrier of genetic information.	Oxford dictionary
Evolutionary Stable Strategy (ESS)	In game theory, behavioral ecology, and evolutionary psychology, an evolutionarily stable strategy (ESS) is a strategy which explains why altruism is not sustainable.	John Maynard Smith
Fidelity	The degree of exactness with which something is copied or reproduced.	Oxford dictionary
Fitness landscape	In evolutionary biology, fitness landscapes or adaptive landscapes are used to visualize the relationship between genotypes (or phenotypes) and reproductive success.	Sewall Green Wright
Gene	(in informal use) a unit of heredity which is transferred from a parent to offspring and is held to determine some characteristic of the offspring. (in technical use) a distinct sequence of nucleotides forming part of a chromosome, the order of which determines the order of monomers in a polypeptide or nucleic acid molecule which a cell (or virus) may synthesize.	Oxford dictionary
Genome	The entirety of an organism's hereditary information.	(Dawkins, 1974)
Genotype	The genetic constitution of an individual organism. Often contrasted with phenotype.	Oxford dictionary
Heredity	The passing on of physical or mental characteristics genetically from one generation to another. The relative influence of heredity and environment.	Oxford dictionary

Term	Definition	Source
Lineage	A sequence of species each of which is considered to have evolved from its predecessor: e.g. the chimpanzee and gorilla lineages. A sequence of cells in the body which developed from a common ancestral cell: e.g. the myeloid lineage.	Oxford dictionary
Methodology	A system of methods used in a particular area of study or activity.	Oxford dictionary
Methodology element	A unit of knowledge.	Authors
Mimicry	In evolutionary biology, the close external resemblance of an animal or plant (or part of one) to another animal, plant, or inanimate object.	Oxford dictionary
Nucleus	A dense organelle present in most eukaryotic cells, typically a single rounded structure bounded by a double membrane, containing the genetic material.	Oxford dictionary
Organism	An individual animal, plant, or single-celled life form.	Oxford dictionary
Phenotype	Organism's phenotype is its observable characteristics or traits both physical and behavioral.	(Malcom & Good-ship, 2001)
Pleiotropic	The production by a single gene of two or more apparently unrelated effects. Pleiotropy occurs when one gene influences multiple phenotypic traits.	Oxford dictionary
Progenotype	*Progenotype* is used to denote the project core makeup (project methodology and the methodology elements).	Authors
Project	A temporary endeavor untaken to create a product, service or result.	PMI PMBoK 5th Edition
Project Element	An essential or characteristic part of a project.	Authors
Project Outcome	The results of the project in terms of deliverables and non-deliverables irrespective of whether the original project success criteria were achieved.	Authors
Traits	A genetically determined characteristic.	Oxford dictionary
Unit of Knowledge	Unit of knowledge is the smallest unit of information that is able to take on the state of being true or false.	Authors

References

Adami, C., Ofria, C., & Collier, T. (2000). Evolution of biological complexity. *Proceedings of the National Academy of Sciences of the United States*, 2000(10). Retrieved from http://www.pnas.org/content/97/9/4463.long. Last access at 2012-10-09.

Blank, C. (2004). Evolutionary timing of the origins of mesophilic sulphate reduction and oxygenic photosynthesis: a phylogenomic dating approach. *Geobiology*, Volume 2, Issue 1, pages 1-20, January 2004, http://onlinelibrary.wiley.com.

Dankwa-Mullan, I., Rhee, K. B., Stoff, D. M., Pohlhaus, J. R., Sy, F. S., Stinson, N., & Ruffin, J. (2010). Moving toward paradigm-shifting research in health disparities through translational, transformational, and transdisciplinary approaches. *American journal of public health*, 100 Suppl, S19-24. 7.

Darwin, C. (1859). *On the Origin of Species*. John Murray, London, UK.

Dawkins, R. (1974). *The Selfish Gene*, (30th Editi.). Oxford University Press, Oxford.

Dawkins, R. (1988). *The blind watchmaker*. 1986. Harlow Logman.

Dawkins, R. (2004). Extended Phenotype – But Not Too Extended. A Reply to Laland, Turner and Jablonka. *Biology & Philosophy*, 19(3), 377-396.

Dennett, D. C. (1996). *Darwin's Dangerous Idea: Evolution and the Meanings of Life*. Simon & Schuster, New York, USA.

Dewey, W. J., Barrai, I., Morton, N. E., & Mi, M. P. (1965). Recessive Genes in Severe Mental Defect. *American journal of human genetics*, 17(3), 237-56. Retrieved from http://www.pubmedcentral.nih.gov/articlerender.fcgi?artid=1932604&tool=pmcentrez&rendertype=abstract. Last access at 2012-10-09

Fehr, E., & Fischbacher, U. (2003). The nature of human altruism. *Nature*, 425(6960), 785-91.

Flyvbjerg, B. (2001). *Making Social Science Matter*. Cambridge, UK: Cambridge University Press.

Grabher, G. (2002). Cool Projects, Boring Institutions: Temporary Collaboration in Social Context. *Regional Studies*, 36(3), 205-214.

Knorr-Cetina, K. D. (1981). Social and Scientific Method or What Do We Make of the Distinction Between the Natural and the Social Sciences? *Philosophy of the Social Sciences*, 11(3), 335-359.

Lamarck, J. B. P. A. (1838). Histoire naturelle des animaux sans vertèbres. *Histoire* (Vol. V, pp. 1-232). J.B. Baillière. Retrieved from http://www.biodiversitylibrary.org/bibliography. Last access at 2012-11-06

Lewtas, J., Walsh, D., Williams, R., & Dobiáš, L. (1997). Air pollution exposure-DNA adduct dosimetry in humans and rodents: evidence for non-linearity at high doses. *Mutation Research/Fundamental and Molecular Mechanisms of Mutagenesis*, 378(1-2), 51-63.

Loewe, L. (2008). *Genetic Mutation*. http://www.nature.com/scitable/topicpage/genetic-mutation-1127. Last access at 2012-11-11

Lynch, M. (2010). Evolution of the mutation rate. *Trends in Genetics*. Retrieved from http://www.sciencedirect.com/science/article/pii/S0168952510001034. Last access at 2012-10-02

Malcom, S., & Goodship, T. H. J. (2001). *From Genotype to Phenotype*. Bios Scientific Publishers, *Oxford, UK*

McShea, D. (1991). Complexity and evolution: what everybody knows. *Biology and Philosophy*, Issue 1969, 303-324.

Mendel, G. (1865). Experiments in plant hybridization (1865). *Cosimo Inc, New York, USA.*

National Science Foundation. (2012). What is transformative research? Retrieved from http://www.nsf.gov/about/transformative_research/faq.jsp#Q1. Last access 2012-12-13.

Nowak, M., & Sigmund, K. (1993). A strategy of win-stay, lose-shift that outperforms tit-for-tat in the Prisoner's Dilemma game. *Nature*. 364, pp. 56 – 58

Pearson, J. C., Lemons, D., & McGinnis, W. (2005). Modulating Hox gene functions during animal body patterning. *Nature reviews*. Section Genetics, 6(12), 893-904.

Pray, L. (2008). DNA replication and causes of mutation. *Nature Education*, 1(1). Retrieved from http://www.nature.com/scitable/topicpage/dna-replication-and-causes-of-mutation. Last access at 2012-10-17

Ralston, A. (2008). Gene Expression Regulates Cell Differentiation. *Nature* **1(1)**. Retrieved from http://www.nature.com/scitable/topicpage/gene-expression-regulates-cell-differentiation-931. Last access 2012-12-12.

Rotemberg, J. (1994). Human relations in the workplace. Journal of Political Economy. 102(4), 684-717.

Simon, H. (1993). Alturism and Economics. *The Americian Economic Review*. 8(2), 156-161.

Smith, J. M. (1982). *Evolution and the Theory of Games*. Cambridge University Press. UK.

Smith, J., & Szathmary, E. (2000). *The origins of life: From the birth of life to the origin of language*. Oxford University press, UK.

Söderlund, J. (2004). On the broadening scope of the research on projects: a review and a model for analysis. *International Journal of Project Manag*ement, *22*(8), 655-667.

Turner, J. R., & Müller, R. (2003). On The Nature of the Project as a Temporary Organization. *International Journal of Project Management*, 21(1), 1-7.

Van de Ven, A. H., & Poole, M. S. (2005). Alternative Approaches for Studying Organizational Change. *Organization Studies*, 26(9), 1377-1404.

Wickler, W. (1968). Mimicry in plants and animals. Retrieved from http://repositorio.fciencias.unam.mx:8080/xmlui/handle/123456789/100067. Last access at 2012-10-14.

Williams, S. E., Shoo, L. P., Isaac, J. L., Hoffmann, A. a, & Langham, G. (2008). Towards an integrated framework for assessing the vulnerability of species to climate change. *Public Library of Science, Biology*, 6(12), 2621-6.

Wright, S. (1932). The roles of Mutation, Inbreeding, Cross breading and Selection in Evolution. In (Jones, D.F., ed.) *Proceedings of 6th Int. Congress on Genetics*, Vol. 1, pp. 356-366, Brooklyn Botanic Gardens, New York, NY, USA

Yerushalmi, S., & Green, R. M. (2009). Evidence for the adaptive significance of circadian rhythms. *Ecology Letters*, Wiley, 12(9), 970-81.

Chapter 13

Translational Approaches: Applying Strategic Management Theories to OPM Research

Catherine P. Killen, Kam Jugdev, Nathalie Drouin and Yvan Petit

Abstract

This chapter illustrates the use of translational approaches in Organizational Project Management (OPM) research. The focus of this chapter is the application of strategic management theories and research approaches from the strategic management field to Project Management and Project Portfolio Management research. Four sections each illustrate a separate research example and show how the earlier research has inspired and provided examples for later research studies. Each section first provides the theoretical background through a literature review of the relevant theoretical perspectives from the field of strategic management. The theoretical perspectives are the resource-based view, dynamic capabilities, and absorptive capacity. The application of these theoretical perspectives to OPM research is then illustrated through detail of the four separate research examples.

This chapter aims to inspire future researchers to learn from and build upon these examples. This chapter not only illustrates current advances in OPM research, it provides a framework for further advances in translational research by linking the theory and approaches from two disciplines in practical research examples. In this way, this chapter is designed to contribute to the development of OPM research by providing examples and guidance for theory development and future translational research.

Introduction

This chapter focuses on the translation of theories and approaches developed and used in field of strategic management for application in Organizational Project Management (OPM) research. The particular focus of this chapter is the translation of these approaches to research on the specific practices and capabilities for project management (PM) and project portfolio management (PPM) in industry and government applications.

As researchers interested in OPM, these are exciting and challenging times. We are working in an area of increasing importance with high potential benefits to organizations and to society. OPM and its components such as PM and PPM have lofty aims. Through a suite of OPM methods and influenced by a range of factors, they aim to achieve organizational strategy and ensure the effective allocation of resources to provide the best return to investors and to society. Some researchers look to the efficiency of PM and PPM capabilities to explain the ultimate success and survival of organizations. Amid multiple perspectives and approaches to OPM research, it is clear is that the impact of OPM is high, and that this impact is growing. OPM now affects an increasingly broad range of organizations, extending well beyond traditional areas for PM such as product development, research and development, and construction projects.

The wide impact of OPM multiplies the importance of research in this area and highlights the need for rigorous and relevant research methods. In practice-based disciplines such as PM and PPM, the research aims to contribute to solving the puzzle of how best to manage OPM, and to lead to understanding that improves practice. This research is being conducted in a shifting landscape where capabilities, awareness and expectations are developing rapidly. There is no best way to study OPM organizational phenomena and, as the research in this field matures, the types of research methods in use continue to diversify. The application of a wide range of established research approaches, including the translation of approaches and perspectives from other disciplines, provides a solid base to strengthen OPM research.

While the numerous opportunities for exploration are exciting, it is also challenging for researchers looking for guidance and examples in such a young and dynamic research environment. This chapter provides needed guidance for researchers by bringing together examples of OPM research that draw upon the field of strategic management. This chapter provides examples of four translational approaches to PM and PPM research that involve the integration, adoption and development of strategic management theories.

The field of management has been evolving for centuries, with the development and application of methodologies and theories for management research gaining prominence throughout the past century (Koontz, 1980). The theories serve to strengthen the rigor of the research and provide explanatory and predictive power. Among the variety of management specialties, strategic management is a particularly well-developed discipline. The study of PM and PPM is, in contrast, a relatively recent phenomena (Kerzner, 1994). Until recent years, much of the PM and PPM research has been conducted without connection to the established body of management research and therefore has not benefited from the wealth of experience in the field.

Research in the relatively young disciplines of PM and PPM has been advancing in recent years as studies have been conducted with increased methodological rigor, such as those that develop and test conceptual models through sophisticated statistical analysis and others that employ qualitative multiple-case studies involving in-depth interviewing, observation, and analysis (Turner, 2010). However, most PM and PPM research remains largely atheoretical (Jugdev, 2008; Söderlund, 2004) presenting an opportunity to further advance PM and PPM research by drawing upon established theories from strategic management. This chapter aims to contribute to the advancement of PM and PPM research, especially translational approaches that apply theories from other disciplines.

While there are many aspects of management research that tie in with PM and PPM research, the examples in this chapter draw upon theories from the field of strategic management. Theories and frameworks from the field of strategic management were chosen for these research examples based on the roles that PM and PPM play in the implementation of organizational strategy and in informing strategy development.

Research in the strategic management field explores why some organizations are more successful than others, and aims to expose the mechanisms that help some organizations achieve and sustain a competitive advantage (Grant, 2010; Rumelt, Schendel & Teece, 1994). Competitive advantage is the ability of an organization to create more value than its rivals, and therefore achieve superior return on investment (Barney & Hesterley, 2006). Sustained competitive advantage requires capabilities that provide enduring benefits and are not easily copied by competitors or rendered obsolete (Barney & Clark, 2007; Kwak & Anbari, 2009). In fast-changing environments, capabilities that enable organizations to adapt rapidly and repeatedly can lead to strategic advantages (Eisenhardt, 1989; Teece, Pisano & Shuen, 1997). Established PM and PPM capabilities that have been developed over time and customized to an organization's environment are repeatedly associated with better outcomes, see for example (Alvarez & Busenitz, 2001; Cooper, Edgett & Kleinschmidt, 2001; Jugdev, Mathur, & Fung, 2007; Killen, Hunt & Kleinschmidt, 2008), prompting PM and PPM to be viewed as strategic organizational capabilities. Following this strategic management view of organizational capability and competitive advantage, the examples presented in this chapter illustrate the translation of strategic management theories to explore the role of PM and PPM in achieving organizational strategy.

Translational research is often described as 'bench to bedside research'. In health care, the translational continuum starts with basic scientific discovery, and leads to development, delivery, and adoption (Dankwa-Mullan et al., 2010). For example, research identifying a specific compound to treat breast cancer must be complemented with translational research that tests for efficacy and effectiveness so that the treatment can be used in the general population. In the medical world there has been a push to value and promote translational research as it is essential to enable patients to benefit from scientific discoveries (Straus, Tetroe & Graham, 2009). Translational research in the management field similarly aims to bring the benefits of knowledge to a wider audience through applied research (Shapiro, Kirkman & Courtney, 2007). According to the Organization for Economic Cooperation and Development (OECD), 'Applied research is undertaken either to determine possible uses for the findings of basic research or to determine new methods or ways of achieving specific and predetermined objectives ... applied research gives operational form to ideas' (Tijssen, 2010: 1843). Much of the research in the disciplines of PM and PPM is applied research, bringing academic enquiry into organizational settings and producing findings that have implications for industry practice. Translational research in PM and PPM is illustrated in this chapter through the application of three theories from strategic management to enhance applied PM and PPM research; these theories are the resource-based view of the Firm (RBV), dynamic capabilities (DC), and absorptive capacity (AC). In line with the bi-directional translation identified in healthcare (Dankwa-Mullan et al., 2010), the translational research illustrated in this chapter also provides knowledge flow in the opposite direction.

This chapter is designed to provide an instructive illustration of the use of translational approaches in PM and PPM research. Four sections each outline an example of PM or PPM research that draws on the RBV, DC or AC theories from the field of strategic management. Each example provides background literature and discussion on the theory and its applicability to the research problem. Methodological considerations include the rationale behind the selection of a particular theory, exploration of the advantages and disadvantages of the theory for application to the research question and a discussion of the challenges faced and approaches used. Lessons learned are emphasized and ideas and pointers for future research are summarized. By packaging this information in a cohesive framework, this chapter is designed to provide guidance for both novice and experienced researchers interested in translational approaches for PM and PPM research.

Example 1: Examining Project Management through the Resource-based View Lens

This example summarizes three related studies that applied strategic management perspectives to PM research using the RBV. These studies were initiated in the late 1990s in a doctoral study that used strategic management theory to anchor PM research. The RBV offered explanatory power for the study on how companies develop and/or sustain their competitive advantage in PM. In addition, the research was strengthened by the well-developed conceptual and empirical base provided by the RBV. This translational approach was continued in two further studies summarized in this section, and has inspired further translational research including other examples presented in this chapter.

This section starts with a review of the RBV and a discussion of its relationship to PM.

What is the RBV and what is its Relevance to Project Management?

The 'Theory of the Growth of the Firm' (Penrose, 1959) laid the foundation for the RBV, a term that was actually coined 25 years later (Wernerfelt, 1984). Penrose's classic paper spans economics and organizational theories to extend our understanding of how firms differentiate themselves from competitors to improve their competitive positions in the market.

According to the RBV of the firm, a company consists of a bundle of assets or resources. Only some of the resources can be labeled as strategic assets. The distinction between resources and strategic resources is that the strategic ones are a source of competitive advantage (Amit & Schoemaker, 1993). Over the years, researchers found that strategic assets are knowledge-based and involve explicit and tacit knowledge (Eisenhardt & Santos, 2000; Kaplan, Schenkel, von Krogh & Weber, 2001; Kogut & Zander, 1992; Nonaka, 1994). They also determined that these resources were embedded (ingrained) in a company's unique internal skills, knowledge, resources, and ways of working (Foss, 1997; Rumelt et al., 1994). Some examples of strategic assets include quality, reputation, managerial skills, brand recognition, patents, and culture (Barratt & Oke, 2007; Castanias & Helfat, 1991; Chakraborty, 1997; Hawawini, Subramanian & Verdin, 2002; Kogut, 1993).

There are several streams within strategic management that relate to the RBV, such as DC and AC. There are also different views on the distinctions between related terms such as resources, capabilities and core competencies. The research reported in this example applies the RBV and focuses on organizational resources (or assets) (Barney, 2007; Wernerfelt, 1984).

Key assumptions of the RBV are that a firm's resources are heterogeneous (differentiated resource bundles) (Penrose, 1959) and can be immobile making them costly and time consuming to copy (Selznick, 1957). The VRIO framework (valuable, rare, inimitable, organizational support) proposed by Barney (2007, 2001) is a useful way to characterize strategic assets. In the framework, strategic assets are identified as being valuable, rare, inimitable, and involving organizational support. According to the VRIO framework, there are levels of competitive advantage. A company can achieve competitive parity through resources that are valuable; temporary competitive advantage through resources that are both valuable and rare; and competitive advantage through resources that are valuable, rare, and inimitable. As a company strives for the ideal position of a sustained competitive advantage, increasing degrees of organizational support are applied to maintaining these resources – this is the final criteria for strategic resources according to the VRIO.

In the late 1990s, the RBV and VRIO framework were being used in conceptual and empirical papers in strategic management. These studies provided research examples and inspiration for the application of the RBV to PM research (Jugdev, 2003). At that time, the research in the strategic management field was developing rapidly and theories such as the RBV were taking great strides. This was not mirrored in the PM literature which stood in stark contrast with little attention to its own theoretical base (Koskela & Howell, 2002; Packendorff, 1995). Furthermore, this early PM literature review revealed few empirical studies on PM as a strategic asset. One early study in this area investigated film making as a project-based enterprise (DeFillippi & Arthur, 1998). For more recent conceptual and empirical papers on the RBV see (Arend, 2006; Barney, Ketchen, & Wright, 2011; Connor, 2002; Newbert, 2007; Priem & Butler, 2001a, 2001b; Ray, Barney & Muhanna, 2004; Wade & Hulland, 2004; Wiklund & Shepherd, 2003; Yun-tao, Run-xiao & Tao, 2010).

Despite the limited attention to PM as a strategic asset, as PM research evolved, researchers began to recognize that the field involved practices based on tangible and intangible assets (DeFillippi & Arthur, 1998; Fernie, Green, Weller & Newcombe, 2003). Tangible assets are concrete and based on codified or explicit knowledge, whereas intangible ones are based on tacit knowledge. Codified and tacit knowledge have also been labeled as 'know-what' and 'know-how' (Nonaka, 1994) in the knowledge management literature. Most of the PM literature initially focused on the tangible assets and codified knowledge as shared through PM offices, methodologies, and tools and techniques (Kloppenborg & Opfer, 2002; Ulri & Ulri, 2000).

The following sections summarize three translational studies that draw from and contribute to the RBV.

Three RBV Studies based on the VRIO Framework
RBV Study 1: The VRIO Framework

The first study in this series examined PM as a strategic asset through the first RBV-based study in the PM discipline. The study (conducted between 2000 and 2003) employed a mixed-method approach and is the basis for a doctoral dissertation (Jugdev, 2003).

Data were collected from four diverse international companies. A total of 67 interviews were analyzed along with the results of a survey of 28 responses on PM maturity (Jugdev, 2004a, 2004b). The findings indicated that these companies did not develop PM as a strategic asset. Instead, PM was a strategic enabler (as per Information Technology terms) and fit the competitive parity category (Jugdev, 2004b, 2005, 2008). The study identified groupings of tangible PM resources (such as PM methodologies) and groupings of intangible resources (such as culture-embracing PM, social networking, and knowledge sharing). The findings indicated that a superior reputation or a high PM maturity level were helpful but insufficient for a competitive advantage through PM. The study also helped identify elements of organizational support practices, such as leadership, continuous improvement, and relating PM to strategic goals.

A further conceptual examination of the tangible assets in PM indicated that while valuable, these specific resources were not rare or inimitable and therefore did not meet the VRIO criteria for sources of competitive advantage (Jugdev & Thomas, 2002).

RBV Study 2: The First VRIO Survey

The second study (conducted between 2004 and 2007) was built on the earlier work and collected empirical data through a questionnaire survey. The study used questions based on Barney's advice regarding the assessment of each element of the VRIO framework (Barney, 2007) as follows:

- Valuable: Do a firm's resources and capabilities enable the firm to respond to environmental threats or opportunities? (p. 138).
- Rare: Is a resource currently controlled by only a small number of competing firms? (p. 138).
- Inimitable: Do firms without a resource face a cost disadvantage in obtaining or developing it? (p. 138).
- Organization: Are a firm's other policies and procedures organized to support the exploitation of its valuable, rare, and costly-to-imitate resources? (p. 138).

Two hundred and two members from Project Management Institute's' (PMI') North American membership completed the survey (Jugdev & Mathur, 2006a, 2006b). The data were analyzed using exploratory factor analysis and then a structural equation model was developed. The exploratory factor analysis revealed three tangible resource factors that were labeled 'PM maturity', 'training and development', and 'sharing know-what'. One intangible resource factor, 'sharing know-how', also emerged from the data. In VRIO terms, the 'sharing know-how' factor influenced the three VRIO framework factors identified as PM process variables (Valuable, Rare, and Organizational Support characteristics) but not 'Inimitable'.

The structural equation model examined the relationships between the independent and dependent variables. The findings reveal that tangible resources ('PM maturity' and 'sharing know-what') indicate the establishment of competitive parity through valuable and organizational PM factors. However, the intangible PM resource labeled 'sharing know-how' indicates that the PM process is both valuable and rare and thus reflects temporary advantage. The findings emphasize that whereas tangible resources are valuable, they do not directly result in the PM process being rare so they are not a source of competitive advantage.

The translational research process and the creation of a survey to apply the VRIO framework to PM was both rewarding and challenging. An important lesson from this study is the need to acknowledge the challenges involved when operationalizing an unobservable construct. This study was not able to identify a factor for 'Inimitable' because only two items had been use to assess this construct in the questionnaire.

RBV Study 3: The Second VRIO Survey

The third study (conducted between 2008 and 2013) built upon the second study and refined the research instrument incorporating some of the lessons learned. For example, this second VRIO survey incorporated better ways to assess the 'Inimitable' construct. One hundred and ninety-eight North American PMI° members responded to the survey. In terms of findings, the exploratory factor analyses identified resource groupings that were labeled as:

- Valuable PM/IT resources (structured knowledge, unstructured knowledge, IT resources).
- Rare knowledge-sharing PM resources (processes, tools).
- Inimitable PM resources (codified knowledge practices, uncodified knowledge practices) (Jugdev & Mathur, 2012; White, Fortune, Jugdev & Walker, 2011).

The study followed the approach used in the RBV literature whereby an intermediate dependent variable was used to test the RBV empirically (Ray et al., 2004). This study further elucidated the PM process (as the intermediate dependent variable) and organization level performance (as the aggregate dependent variable).

The research on the application of the RBV to PM reported in these first three studies is continuing (Mathur, Jugdev & Fung, 2013). A recent analysis indicates that valuable resources consist of assets that capture and disseminate PM knowledge and IT tools (which enable the application and sharing of this knowledge). However, it is the resources consisting of knowledge sharing processes that document and share PM knowledge as the related knowledge sharing tools and techniques that are unique. The inimitable PM assets consist of proprietary tangible assets and intangible assets which are embedded in a firm's routines and relationships. The exploratory factor analysis findings indicate that the 'Organization' factor (organizational support) includes PM alignment, PM communication, and PM integration, all of which contribute to embedding PM practices into the fabric of a company's culture.

The research studies that comprise Example 1 illustrate practical examples of the translation of research from the strategic management domain for application to PM research and the evolution, growth and development of new PM research approaches. These examples show how the application of the RBV to PM research enabled the developing field of PM research to stand on the shoulders of the 'RBV theory giant'. The path was not simple due to the need to absorb the volume, depth and range of literature, research methodologies, debates and guidance on the application of the RBV. Particular challenges were faced in designing instruments to apply the theory in a PM context for the first time. However this background provides a richness of learning and illustrates the benefits of the guidance provided by past experience and extant literature on the RBV. Example 2 continues with a summary of a translational research study drawing on a related theory that focuses on competitive advantage in dynamic environments.

Example 2: Identifying Project Portfolio Management as a Dynamic Capability

The second example moves from the realm of PM research to the study of PPM capabilities. The use of strategic management theories was inspired by the early work reported in Example 1, as this study aimed to understand the relationship between PPM capabilities and competitive advantage. Whereas the RBV was found to be useful for the investigation of PM and competitive advantage in Example 1, this study found that an offshoot of the RBV, the DC framework, was more applicable. To set the scene for this research example, the basics of the DC framework are summarized first, building on the RBV overview in Example 1.

Dynamic Capability and its Relevance to PPM Research

An organization's PPM capability is responsible for the effective deployment of strategy. PPM capabilities provide a holistic perspective for ongoing strategic decision making to maintain the most effective combination of projects and to ensure that appropriate resources are allocated. This is an increasingly important area of organizational capability in an increasingly dynamic environment. A relatively new body of empirical research into PPM practices has started to generate findings related to PPM practices and outcomes. However most of this research is fragmented and does not draw on a solid theoretical perspective or base.

Strategic decisions about how best to spend or invest resources are central to organizational strategy (Teece et al., 1997) therefore the application of strategy frameworks to PPM research may be able to improve understanding. An organization's PPM capability is one of the internal organizational capabilities or resources that an organization uses to gain competitive advantage. Therefore, the RBV of strategy presents a theoretical framework that is relevant to the study of PPM practices. Classic RBV perspectives, as outlined in research Example 1, offer a model that is applicable to a fairly static environment; however many PM environments are dynamic. This is especially true in new product and service development environments studied in research Example 2. Even in slow-moving industries, new product development is unpredictable and dynamic and requires an ever-changing mix of resources (Danneels, 2002; Zollo & Winter, 2002). The DC framework is a development of the RBV that identifies and focuses on the specific class of organizational capabilities or routines that provide advantages in dynamic environments.

Teece et al. (1997: 516) initially defined DC as 'the firm's ability to integrate, build, and reconfigure internal and external competencies to address rapidly changing environments'. As the concept has evolved, other authors have used terms such as 'patterned elements' (Winter, 2003), 'routinized activities' (Zollo & Winter, 2002), 'core micro-strategies', or the relatively stable sets of routines that are involved with shaping strategy (Salvato, 2003). Some definitions focus on DCs as 'higher-order' capabilities due to their ability to change other organizational capabilities (Winter, 2003). One such definition defines a DC as a 'learned and stable pattern of collective activity through which the organization systematically generates and modifies its operating routines in pursuit of competitive advantage' (Zollo & Winter, 2002: 340). Emphasizing the relationship between DC and the resource base, Helfat (2007: 4), defines DC as 'the capacity of an organization to purposefully create, extend, or modify its resource base'.

Although DCs are considered a type of resource-based capability, they are different from the traditional resources described by the RBV. For example, while the VRIO framework proposes that resource-based competencies must be difficult to copy or imitate to provide lasting competitive advantage (Barney, 1998; Chakraborty, 1997), DCs are often easy to copy and acquire (Eisenhardt & Martin, 2000). DCs also often show strong commonalities across organizations and industries, and thus allow the identification of 'best practices' that may be transferred or acquired more easily than some resource-based capabilities. DCs cannot add value alone; they do this by reconfiguring the existing resource-base (Eisenhardt & Martin, 2000) and therefore can be considered 'enabling resources' (Smith, Vasudevan & Tanniru, 1996). The relative ease by which DCs may be copied or acquired limits their ability to independently provide lasting value. DCs also require the prior establishment of supporting capabilities through a sequential order of implementation (Eisenhardt & Martin, 2000) and play an important role in allocating resources, as well as in identifying the desired development and direction of resources and capabilities in line with strategy (Wang & Ahmed, 2007). Therefore, the presence of DC as well as underlying resource advantages that are VRIO, is required for long-term competitive advantage in dynamic environments (Teece et al., 1997).

Teece, Pisano and Shuen's 'processes, positions, and paths' (PPP) framework (Teece et al., 1997) provides a model of the mechanisms at play in the relationship between resources, DCs, learning, and performance. Through the PPP framework, DCs are shown to be organizational routines (or processes) that are path-dependent and rely strongly on the resource position of the organization (the underlying resource base) to generate sustainable competitive advantage.

The growing body of research and literature on DC includes criticisms that point out the need for more empirical research. The identification of specific organizational processes as DCs is promoted in order to generate empirical research for the continued development and validation of theoretical frameworks (Eisenhardt & Martin, 2000; Helfat, 2007). The body of empirical research on DC is enhanced by the recent identification of the longer-established 'absorptive capacity' (AC) concept as a crucial DC in knowledge-based competition (Fosfuri & Tribó, 2008; Zahra & George, 2002). The AC is discussed in the fourth research example presented in this chapter. Other literature also debates the validity of the DC concept due to definitional problems and tautologies (Priem & Butler, 2001a) prompting suggestions of better ways of defining capabilities and resources that allow empirical testing of the theories (Barney, 2001; Eisenhardt & Martin, 2000; Helfat, 2007; Peteraf & Barney, 2003; Zollo & Winter, 2002). The identification of organizational routines such as PPM as a DC provides opportunities to increase the body of empirical research to test and develop DC theory. In addition, the DC theory has the potential to provide a theoretical base to help explain PPM and its relationship with the development of organizational competitive advantage as illustrated in the research example below.

PPM as a Dynamic Capability using the Processes, Positions and Paths Framework

PPM was first identified as a DC in the PhD study outlined in this research example (Killen, 2008). The study explored the relationship between an organization's PPM capability and its ability to establish sustained competitive advantage through new product and service offerings. At the time, the atheoretical nature of the PPM literature did not provide theoretical examples for exploring the relationship between PPM capabilities and competitive advantage. The lack of accepted theories to draw upon for the research presented a challenge for the study, and therefore one of the research questions explored whether theories or frameworks could be developed or whether existing theories or frameworks could be applied to assist in this understanding.

While looking for theoretical underpinning for PPM, the research also investigated other 'what' and 'how' questions in a mixed-method two-phase study. The first phase employed a quantitative questionnaire-based survey with 60 responses that focused on the 'what' questions (what is being done now, what are the outcomes, what is the comparison with other studies, what is the comparison between new product development and new service development project environments). Among other findings, the survey findings highlighted the strategic importance of PPM capabilities. The second phase used a qualitative multiple-case study focusing on six successful innovators to explore the implementation and evolution of PPM capabilities focusing on the 'how' questions (How are PPM capabilities developed? How can theory explain the relationship between PPM and competitive advantage?).

It is important to note that this research did not immediately narrow down the search for a suitable theory to the DC framework. In fact, while exploring alignment with several existing strategic management theories such as Porter's competitive forces (Porter, 1980) or Miles and Snow's typologies (Miles & Snow, 1978), as well as the RBV and DC, the research also looked for patterns that may indicate the development of a new theory. This process of the research was exploratory and needed to be thorough and open to new insights and ideas in order to allow new connections and discoveries to be made.

During the in-depth second phase of the research, the PPP framework of the DC was found to provide useful explanatory power. Extant PPM research did not draw upon such theories, however some early work by Jugdev (2004, 2007) justified the use of the related RBV framework for PM research and this experience provided added confidence for the application of the DC to understand PPM capability. Due to the strong evolutionary component of a DC, the study targeted research participants familiar with the historical developments of PPM within their companies and some of the semi-structured interview questions were designed to gain information on the past evolutionary paths and future plans for the organizational PPM capability. All data were transcribed and analyzed using the NVivo qualitative data analysis software. The data were coded and interpreted using within-case, cross-case and embedded-case analyses (Killen et al., 2008).

The findings of the study firmly supported the use of the DC perspective and negated the need to try to propose or develop a new theory. The PPP framework developed by Teece et al. (1997) helped to illuminate the relationships between the processes used for PPM, the resource position of the organization, and the historical paths and future options available and the development of competitive advantage in a dynamic environment. The findings supported the proposition that DCs co-evolve through a combination of tacit and explicit learning mechanisms, and proposed an enhanced model to show how investments in organizational learning activities are regularly used to enhance these learning mechanisms in a PPM environment (Killen et al., 2008; Zollo & Winter, 2002). Furthermore, the application of the PPP framework helped to justify and explain the ongoing evolution of PPM capabilities as part of the functioning of a DC as the capability must change and evolve in response to environmental dynamism in order to remain effective (Eisenhardt & Martin, 2000; Teece et al., 1997).

The identification of PPM as a DC is significant for several reasons. Most importantly:

- The application of the DC framework moved the research beyond simple 'best practice' correlation-based relationships and provides an understanding of the mechanisms that enable a PPM capability to lead to competitive advantage.
- The DC framework provides a framework that helps to analyse the existing literature as well as to conduct future research on PPM capabilities.
- The study of PPM capabilities is enhanced by a growing body of literature investigating DCs, their establishment and evolution through organizational learning, and their relationship to sustainable competitive advantage. The literature is also strengthened by the addition of PPM capability as an example of a specific organizational capability that acts as a DC.

Several methodological lessons were learned during the application of DC theory to this research. The importance of capability evolution to the study of DC meant that as much longitudinal data as possible needed to be collected and future studies that set out to evaluate capability evolution should ideally develop a longitudinal data collection approach. Such an approach would provide increased depth and rigor by capturing a detailed understanding of the development of PPM capabilities and the role of investments in learning activities, their influence on the effectiveness of learning mechanisms, and the resulting changes to the PPM capabilities and outcomes.

Lessons were also learned with respect to defining and categorizing the findings in order to determine the level of alignment with DC theory. There is a tension between being too prescriptive and too flexible in defining and categorizing elements of DC in an organizational environment. Prescriptive and pre-determined definitions and research approaches that look for specific activities have the potential for missing important elements of DC that were not pre-identified. However, definitions that are too loose and explorations that are too flexible will fail to produce data that are rigorous enough to support analysis. The lesson learned is to be mindful of this tension and to tailor the approach to the situation. The approach used in this research, as it was exploratory in nature, leaned toward flexibility to ensure that emergent themes could be captured, while taking steps to ensure that definitional rigor was maintained in order to support analysis and conclusions. To this end, an iterative approach to analysis and identification of themes and activities was employed in the multiple-case study research. Follow up questioning was used with some of the early organizations, and all data were re-analyzed in full with the benefit of learning and identification of emergent themes at the end of the data collection period.

This research demonstrated that the DC framework can enhance understanding of the relationship between PPM capabilities and competitive advantage and several conceptual models were proposed; however, it was based on a limited amount of qualitative data and the proposed models have not been tested. Future research studies require careful attention to definitions and methodology in order to operationalize these models for testing and validation or adjustment.

This research experience was exploratory and represents the first translation of the DC frameworks from the strategic management domain to the study of PPM capabilities. Subsequent research along this theme includes research experience 3 in this chapter. These translational research endeavors draw from the strategic management domain and bring new perspectives and a growing body of literature on DCs that can be used to evaluate and understand PPM capabilities. In addition, the DC-based research in the PPM domain adds to the development of DC theory by providing, first, an example of a specific organizational capability acting as a DC and, second, a link to the existing research on PPM that can form evidence to further the understanding of DCs.

Therefore, the translation of knowledge goes both ways; the translational research not only takes findings from the strategic management field for applied research in PPM, it also strengthens and contributes to the strategic management field. The following research experience continues on this theme by applying a DC framework to PPM framework.

Example 3: Using Dynamic Capabilities to Study Project Portfolio Management in Dynamic Environments

The third research example builds on the theme explored in the second research example. The work seeks to understand how uncertainty affects project portfolios managed in dynamic environments. This section first introduces some additional literature on DC frameworks to complement the review provided in Example 2 before summarizing the third research example.

This research was triggered by the observation that the PPM literature had focused primarily on project selection, prioritization, and balancing the portfolios and that little research had been done on the management of portfolio changes once they had been selected. Although PMI° has introduced the notions of risk management in the Standard for Portfolio Management (Project Management Institute, 2012), there is little additional guidance or empirical evidence on how portfolio managers should handle uncertainty and changes affecting their project portfolio. The Standard mentions that, in projects, the project manager tries to keep change to a minimum while the 'portfolio manager continually monitors changes in the broad environment' (p. 6). This research studied how these changes to the environment and uncertainties are managed at the portfolio level.

The research question was 'How is uncertainty affecting project portfolios managed in dynamic environments?' The aim was to develop a framework that would facilitate the investigation. The notion that organizations have to face changing environments is not new and is now commonly accepted especially in sectors dealing with new technologies. Many theories and ideas on this topic have been published, primarily in the fields of Organization theory, System Theory, Sociology, and Strategy.

Selecting a DC Framework for the Research

The concept of uncertainty had been identified, at least 50 years ago, when proponents of the structural contingency theory (Burns & Stalker, 1961; Lawrence & Lorsch, 1967) theorized that the rate of environmental change and the level of uncertainty affected organizations. Their initial research focused on the impact on structures and management techniques while subsequent authors broadened the understanding of the impact of the changing environments to the decision process (Child, 1972; Grandori, 1984; Howell, Windahl & Seidel, 2010).

Organizations are connected to, and interact with, their environments and as such can be conceived of as *open systems* (Beishon, 1972: 18) 'capable of self-maintenance on the basis of throughput of resources from the environment' (Scott, 1998: 89). Since the *open-system* is defined as a system in interaction with its environment, the boundaries of the system must be determined. However, the position of this boundary is somewhat arbitrary and can be difficult to delineate, especially in socio-technical systems. Duncan (1972) preferred to re-define the environment as 'the totality of physical and social factors that are taken directly into consideration in the decision-making behavior of individuals in the organization' (p. 314).

Thompson (1967) uses the notion of 'domain' to determine the points at which the organization is dependent on external events. Organizations try to place a buffer between the external environment and the technical core (i.e., the key activities for the organization) and seek to place their boundaries around those activities which, if left to the task environment, would be crucial contingencies. While striving for rationality, complex organizations are faced with the impossible task of acknowledging and analyzing all options in an optimal manner. To face this uncertainty, Thompson suggests that organizations striving under norms of rationality, might take a number of actions to buffer their core technologies from environmental influences, to smooth out input and output transactions, and to anticipate and adapt to environmental changes which cannot be buffered or levelled.

According to Weick (1969), the environment does not exist out-there ready-made to be scrutinized and investigated, but can also be influenced and modified. He argues that 'organizing consists of adapting to an enacted environment, an environment which is *constituted by* the actions of interdependent human actors' (Weick, 1969: 27). Weick's organizing model is composed of three main components: *enactment, selection*, and *retention*. In the first phase (*enactment*), Weick treats the environment as information which must be processed by the organization. These informational inputs are typically ambiguous, uncertain, and equivocal. The equivocality refers to the multiple interpretations that can be given to a situation. Different categories of *sensing* mechanisms are proposed to interpret the environment based on whether environmental data is considered analyzable or not and whether the organizational intrusiveness is passive or active. *Retention* refers to the phase where the information identified in the previous phases (enactment and selection) is analyzed and rationalized. The model posits that scanning and interpretation are not solely concerned with the external environment, but also consider the experience learned through the action of enactment and selection.

Weick's organizing model (1979, 1995) proposes an interpretative approach where people in the organization are assumed to interpret events and select activities to reduce the uncertainty through interactions with each other, and to retain some of the experience gained. This interpretation system view is concerned with specialized information reception, equivocality reduction, and sensemaking. This perspective represents a move away from mechanical and biological metaphors of organizations. Organizations are more than transformation processes or control systems. To survive, organizations must have mechanisms to interpret ambiguous events and to provide meaning and direction to participants.

The notion of sensemaking is often associated with interpretation mechanisms at the individual level, for example with how managers make sense of the equivocality associated with certain events. A number of studies have indeed been carried out at this level of analysis (Balogun & Johnson, 2004; Louis, 1980; Smith, 2002; Thomas, Clark & Gioia, 1993; Thomas, 2000). 'Organizational sensemaking', the organizational processes put in place for sensemaking have also been studied (Engwall & Westling, 2004; Maitlis, 2005; Patriotta, 2003; Weick, 1993, 2009).

Although the above theories helped in the understanding of dynamic environments, it was felt that they were hard to operationalize in the specific research setting of PPM. The literature on DC was reviewed (see Example 2 for detail of the background literature); however the objective in this study was different. This research aimed to identify a model or a framework that could be applied to address the research question.

Teece (2007, 2009) proposed a new model for DC which has been employed in the study reported in this research example. The model identifies classes of relevant micro-foundations (i.e., distinct skills, processes, procedures, organizational structures, decision rules, and disciplines) and their interrelationships into three process groups:

- *Sensing* referred to structures, tools, and processes to sense, filter, and interpret changes and uncertainties.
- *Seizing* included the structures, the tools, and procedures for identifying that changes are required once a change or uncertainly has been sensed.
- *Reconfiguring* was defined as the actions taken to ensure alignment of projects and resources with the changes identified by the sensing mechanisms and decided upon in seizing.

Collis (1994) and Winter (2003) discuss the ways in which regulating mechanisms can include second-order controls such as DCs that govern the rate of change of ordinary capabilities. Following this logic, a first-order capability includes skills at performing a particular task i.e., the basic functional activities of the firm (or substantive capability). A second-order (or meta-capability) is defined as the competence to build new first-order competences or to improve the activities of the firm (1994). The third-order would include improvements to the second-order capabilities. Following this pattern, it would be possible to conceive innovations 'to innovate the innovation that innovates the innovation that innovates ... and so on ad infinitum' (Collis, 1994: 148). Such higher-order capabilities can be considered DCs as they relate to the creation and extension of the resource base. Third and fourth-order capabilities (or meta-capabilities) are related to the learning-to-learn capabilities.

In a similar vein, Schreyögg and Kliesch-Eberl (2007) propose a separate management activity and the concept of capability monitoring as 'a dual-process model of capability dynamization'. Danneels (2008) also uses the idea of second-order competence to study how firms explore new markets and new technologies in order to develop new competences which could add to their resource-base. Zahra, Sapienza, and Davidson (2006) apply similar topologies to study the key differences in the DCs between new ventures and established companies. In addition, Ambrosini, Bowman, and Collier (2009) propose a hierarchy of capabilities with different typologies of DC (incremental, renewing, and regenerative capabilities) depending on the perceived environmental state (stable, dynamic, or hyper).

Using the Updated DC Framework to Study PPM in Dynamic Environments

The research in the third example of this book chapter investigates the elements that constitute *sensing – seizing – reconfiguring/transforming* to address the research question. The lowest elements, in Teece's model (2009), are called micro-foundations, and include distinct skills, processes, procedures, organizational structures, decision rules, and disciplines. This concept is replaced by the term *organizing mechanisms* proposed by Dawidson (2006) who also studied PPM. She proposed a framework which classified these *organizing mechanisms* in three areas:

- The *organizational processes*, i.e., how the portfolio management activities were organized;
- How the *tools and methods* were used; and
- The *organizational structures* i.e., how the relevant organizational participants became involved.

Skills and *disciplines*, although included in Teece's micro-foundations model, are excluded from the scope of this research. However, the specific decision rules used for PPM, called basis for PPM decisions in this thesis, are included as part of the analysis.

Four portfolios were studied in this research example: two in an organization in the software development industry and two in the financial industry. The organizations each have well-established PPM capabilities that have been in existence for more than two years – long enough to have encountered changes and uncertainties. The portfolios are complex and include a large number of dependencies between projects. Questionnaires were developed according to the three main process groups in the framework (sensing, seizing and reconfiguring) to facilitate the subsequent coding and analysis of the interviews in Atlas.Ti° (qualitative software).

The experiences from this research show that the DC framework is well suited to the study of PPM processes in uncertain environments. The study allows for the observation of the processes through a different lens. Although the initial conceptual framework was useful to collect data and to structure the interviews, it had to be enhanced during data analysis. The terms *reconfiguring* and *transforming* were defined to refer to two different concepts to support the analysis. It became clear that there were at least two orders of changes occurring in the organizations, and that it would be useful to distinguish and treat these two concepts separately. In the context of this PPM study, the term *reconfiguring* was used to refer to the following first-order activities:

Learning Across Disciplines

- Changes in the project portfolio structure. This included any changes in the project configuration: new projects, new sub-portfolios, and termination of projects;
- Changes in the allocation of financial and human resource to the project portfolios;
- Operational changes related to a better alignment of the portfolio to the changes in the environment.

The term *transforming* was defined to refer to the second-order capability evident in the improvement and building of new first-order competences. In the context of this PPM study, the term *transforming* was used to refer to the following second-order activities:

- Modifying the *sensing-seizing-reconfiguring* mechanisms used in the first-order level of PPM described above (for example, changing the governance structure, modifying the rules used for reconfiguring, adding a new sensing mechanism).
- Introducing new structures, processes, or tools to support the PPM activities which might not directly result in changes in the first-order sensing-seizing-reconfiguring mechanisms (for example, modifications to the software development process, and new architecture to support a more flexible product structure).

The study was limited to the first two orders of DC and did not include consideration of how portfolios were selected, prioritized, and authorized. In the PPM context, a third level of DC could be identified as related to the portfolio selection. Budgets and human resources are allocated to project portfolios at the highest levels in organizations based on vision, mission, and strategies. The choice to invest in one portfolio or another is a strategic decision and dependent on the changes identified in the environment. This is often the level at which DC is discussed. This third order also includes the evaluation of the performance and improvements to the second-order capability. This research studied a number of well-established portfolios for which a budget, a vision, and a mission had been approved. The process leading to the establishment of these portfolios was not formally investigated in detail and future research that investigates such third-order mechanisms might offer additional insights.

This research experience has illustrated the application of the *sensing-seizing-reconfiguring* DC framework to help understand how uncertainty affects project portfolios managed in dynamic environments and builds upon the translational research themes initiated in Examples 1 and 2. As was also observed in Example 2, the translation of knowledge not only takes findings from the strategic management field for applied research in PPM, but the research also contributes to the theory by operationalizing and clarifying some of its concepts. The fourth and final research experience involved an examination of PM research using the AC lens.

Example 4: Applying Absorptive Capacity to Project Management Research

This final research example takes the strategic lead from Example 1 in a different direction. While Examples 2 and 3 focused on the PPM perspective and employed the relatively recent DC to explore dynamic environments, this example uses a PM perspective and employs the well-established AC concept. AC is chosen for this research to understand the translation of knowledge from an innovation to action in the school context. A brief overview of the AC is presented first to underpin the final research example.

A Framework of Absorptive Capacity for Project Management Research

Absorptive capacity (AC) consists of the capabilities to recognize the value of new knowledge, to assimilate it and to apply it to commercial ends (Cohen & Levinthal, 1990; Todorova & Durisin, 2007). AC has become one of the most significant constructs in the last twenty years as the importance of external knowledge resources has become increasingly important. Numerous theoretical and empirical studies have analyzed firm's capacity to absorb knowledge (Camisón & Forés, 2010). The concept of AC shows enough flexibility to be applied in a variety of research fields such as organizational learning (Cohen & Levinthal, 1990; Sun & Anderson, 2010), strategic management and innovation management (Zahra & George, 2002), the knowledge-based view of the firm and dynamic capabilities (Volberda, Foss & Lyles, 2010), project management (Bakker, Cambré, Korlaar, & Raab, 2011) and to be extended to the field of education and health. According to Volberda et al. (2010: 932), 'the diversity in theories and empirical methods has contributed to the rapid advance of the emerging AC field by cultivating the simultaneous development of specialized areas of inquiry that investigate different dimensions, antecedents, level of analysis, and outcomes of AC and contextual factors that affect AC'. For an extensive review of the underlying theories and empirical studies of the concept of AC, see Volberda et al. (2010).

Inspired by Zahra and George (2002), Deschesnes, Drouin, and Couturier (2013) proposed a conceptual framework adapted to a school context to understand schools' capability to absorb an innovation. The conceptual framework (see Figure 13.1) is a process model using the four dimensions used by Zahra and George (2002) to describe AC. Volberda et al. (2010: 936) recommend that 'the study of AC in a dynamic way requires the use of process models which allow investigating the pace and paths of change'.

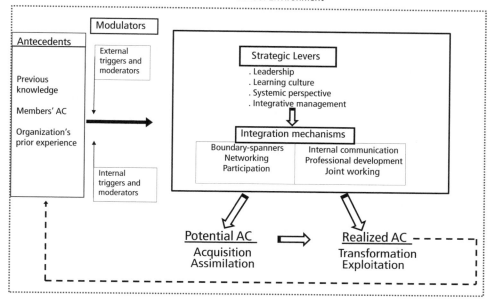

Figure 13.1. Conceptual Framework of School AC to innovate in comprehensive health promotion (Adapted from Deschesnes et al., 2013)

These dimensions; acquisition, assimilation, transformation and exploitation, are divided into two subsets in the model: potential absorptive capacity (PAC) and realized absorptive capacity (RAC). The development of schools' AC is contingent to a variety of components such as the school's environment (influence by governmental ministries for education and health and by schools' administrative boards); internal and external modulators that induce or intensify organizational efforts to seek external knowledge; antecedents that include previous experience by school staff in the implementation of innovative approaches; school staff earlier capacity to absorb an innovation which emphasizes the importance of individuals' ability to learn; and the organization's prior knowledge basis and experience (Zahra & George, 2002). In fact, the learning potential for AC is determined by prior related knowledge or what Cohen and Levinthal (1990) labeled the 'cumulativeness feature'. The model also highlights that AC are anchored in six integration mechanisms that enable individuals in the organization to absorb external knowledge: internal communication mechanisms; boundary-spanners; formal and informal networking; professional development; participation of schools members; and joint working. As illustrated in Figure 13.1, these integration mechanisms are activated by four interlocked *strategic levers* i.e., leadership, learning culture, systemic perspective, and integrative management structure. Thus, it is the interaction between the components of the whole process (i.e., the influence of strategic levers and integration mechanisms, etc.) that allows an organization to explore, acquire, reconfigure, optimize and exploit its resources to address new challenges or to produce added value for the school community.

Although AC is a well-established management theory supported by a large body of research, very few studies have been done on the notion of AC in the project context (Bakker et al., 2011; Biedenbach & Müller, 2012). Findings by Bakker et al. (2011) assert that successful project knowledge transfer is a complex process that involves a configuration of multiple factors. The study links these findings with the view of projects as complex temporary organizational forms in which successful project managers cope with complexity by simultaneously paying attention to both relational and organizational processes. Biedenbach and Müller (2012) focused on the R&D function of pharmaceutical and biotechnology organizations and explored how absorptive, innovative and adaptive capabilities within the early project phases affect project and portfolio performance. The findings reveal overall effects on the short- and long-term project success and portfolio performance. The research example below summarizes another study that applies AC to PM.

Applying Absorptive Capacity to Project Management Research

The final research experience presented in this paper shows how concepts from AC helped to illustrate the mechanisms at play in a major government organizational change project in Quebec, Canada aimed at improving student health. The concept of AC holds potential for health promotion projects in schools[1] (elementary and high schools) since it reflects the ability of these schools to respond to strategic change by building its capabilities for: 1) acquiring external knowledge; 2) assimilating the external sources of knowledge; 3) transforming the shared knowledge at a group level to the level of school's organization and; 4) exploiting the newly acquired knowledge into schools' operations. The AC framework also provides an appropriate perspective for PM research through a multidimensional approach to evaluate the concrete integration of an innovation through the lenses of the implementation of a major and complex project. It helps schools to capture the challenges they face in translating this innovation into operations by using PM, in particular the planning aspects. Few researchers have captured the richness and multidimensionality of the AC process (Volberda et al., 2010), and to our knowledge, none use the dimensions of AC to try

---

1. The 'health promoting schools' concept has been advocated by the World Health Organization (World Health Organization, 1997) as an effective approach to promote health-related behaviours and well-being among school communities and to contribute to the achievement of equity in health: Because of its multifaceted, integrated and concerted nature, it is a challenge with regard to its incorporation within the core business of schools.

to reveal why organizational settings such as those found in schools have difficulties in implementing an innovative project.

The research explored eight schools' capabilities to absorb new knowledge from a government project, the Healthy Schools Project (HS Project), to innovate health behaviors in schools. The study investigated the ability of schools to respond to strategic change by constructing capabilities to acquire external knowledge, assimilate it, transform the shared knowledge at a group level to the schools' organizational level, and exploit the newly acquired knowledge into the schools' operations. All eight schools adopted the healthy school concept for at least three years and used the following planning process to do so: creating a multidisciplinary team; developing a comprehensive vision of students' health and well-being; jointly assessing students' needs and their environment that reflect a comprehensive health approach; setting priorities based on reflexive analysis of existing actions and successful practices in health promotion; integrating actions selected in the success plan; and implementing selected actions.

The results indicate that schools demonstrate some capacity to acquire and assimilate knowledge. Key actors such as school principals played boundary-spanning roles, importing and acquiring new ideas from the healthy school concept to the HS Project, used to implement the innovative approach. Training by Professional Development (an external stakeholder of the project) allows the HS Project team members develop their capacity to acquire knowledge. The PM planning process plays a central role in the assimilation of new knowledge. It allows the integration of the construct of health promotion within the HS Project. Involvement of team members in the planning process, acts as an additional mechanism by which new knowledge was identified, acquired and assimilated. However, very few transformations and exploitations resulted from the HS Project; the schools only exhibited a few some signs of transformation (recognition of new opportunities, reframing emergent problems in line with health promotion principles).

To translate the knowledge from the health promotion concept and successfully implement it through the HS Project, schools need to develop the ability to acquire and assimilate the knowledge and apply it to their operations. This 'need to apply' reflects the schools' ability to translate the knowledge into action. Schools need to develop both potential and realized ACs to do so. Such translation of knowledge is a complex process and involves the interaction of multiple mechanisms and strategic levers. Projects such as the HS Project are best viewed as complex temporary organizational forms (Bakker et al., 2011; Turner & Müller, 2003). They are dynamic, iterative and complex processes that include AC as well as the influence of mechanisms and strategic levers to be successful. Research in PM should investigate the mechanisms and strategic levers that play a key role in the translation of new knowledge in the project context. The AC framework proposed and used in this research has the potential to structure research on the translation of knowledge through projects. Bakker et al. (2011) and Volberda et al. (2010) assert that project managers and firms managers should be geared towards a multi-dimensional framework in managing the AC to implement successful innovative projects. More research is needed to develop specific studies to deeply understand the types of knowledge that should be absorbed for innovative projects to be successful, what are the key roles of project managers and how we can refine the relationship between knowledge translation and the project processes. AC is a bridging concept between translation of knowledge and many fields such as PM. However, according to Volberda et al. (2010), this broad applicability is also a weakness of the AC construct since its applicability and managerial implications may sometimes be unclear.

Limitations to this study should also be noted. First, it was conducted with schools and interviewees based in Québec, Canada. Further specific research to school context should involve other provinces in Canada and in other countries to enhance the understanding the complex dynamic of translating knowledge in a project context. Second, only eight cases were studied limiting the generalizability of the resulting understanding of the AC, its mechanisms and strategic levers and its relationship to the translation of knowledge into action. Future research should build on the research presented in this example by conducting research in public as well as private organizational settings and expanding the use of the multi-dimensional approach in understanding the AC to various types of PM and PPM environments.

Summary

This chapter presents four research experiences based on the RBV, DC, and AC theories from strategic management as applied to PM and PPM. Commonalities between the research examples include a strong strategic focus, recognition of the importance of knowledge and learning, and research questions seeking understanding and explanation that have been addressed through translational research approaches. Each of the research experiences demonstrates the translational nature of the research and explains the paths taken by the authors in their research journeys. In the process, each of us searched for theoretical approaches to meet our needs and identified a suitable theory from the field of strategic management. However, when forging new ground, learning and adaptation is high as illustrated by these research examples. Challenges were faced, lessons were learned, and the theories were adapted for our PM and PPM research.

Table 13.1 provides an overview of the four experiences identifying the unit of analysis (PM or PPM) and the theory (RBV, DC or AC). The table provides a snapshot overview of the research experiences detailed in this chapter, highlighting the research challenges, main findings, lessons learned, and the suggested areas for future research stemming from each research experience.

Table 13.1. Summary of the Four Research Experiences (Adapted from Killen et al., 2012)

Research Experience	Unit of Analysis	Challenges	Main Findings	Lessons Learned	Future Research
1. PM as a strategic asset through the **RBV**	**PM**	Previous research did not consider PM resources as a source of competitive advantage. A translational research approach using the RBV provided this perspective.	Translational research using the RBV provides benefits for identifying and categorizing PM resources. Intangible PM resources directly contribute to competitive advantage through PM. Tangible resources do not.	Developed approaches for wording unobservable constructs such as *Inimitable*. Mixed methods studies can be applied to translational research on PM and competitive advantage with rewarding results.	Examine intangible PM resources and categorizations. Apply situated learning theory (communities of practice) to intangible PM resources. Relate intangible assets in the context of agile development.
2. PPM as a **DC** using the PPP framework	**PPM**	Lack of extant literature and research methods that use a theoretical base for PPM research limit depth of understanding.	A translational research perspective based on DC theory aligns with the learning and change observed and outlines mechanisms through which PPM can contribute to competitive advantage.	Tracking capability initiation and evolution, learning and change are beneficial for the study of PPM as a DC. To apply the DC perspective to PPM, elements of the capability must be defined in terms of DC frameworks to facilitate analysis.	Proposed conceptual models on learning and PPM drawing upon DC theory should be tested. Longitudinal studies could be used study to PPM evolution in further detail.
3. Using **DC** to study PPM in dynamic environments	**PPM**	To translate the theoretical concepts of dynamic capabilities into a framework used to collect and analyze data.	Terminology such as *reconfiguring* and *transforming* were ill-defined in the literature. DC could be decomposed into multiple orders.	DC framework is well suited for translational research on PPM processes in uncertain environments. Challenges in classifying organizing mechanisms into sensing, seizing, reconfiguring/ transforming and in expressing/ translating DC for interviewees.	Investigate the multiple orders of DC in PPM: resource re-allocation, process improvements, and portfolio selection.

| 4. Applying **AC** to PM research | **PM** | To show how concepts from AC helped to illustrate the mechanisms at play in organizational change projects. | *Potential AC* (the ability to acquire and assimilate new knowledge) was more easily achieved than *realized AC* (the ability to transform and exploit this new knowledge). Key actors, training, PM planning process and team involvement play a role in the absorption of the innovation. | AC conceptual framework helped to: i) structure the research on the translation of knowledge through projects; ii) to appreciate the mechanisms and processes with the greatest influence on the level of absorption. | Validate the AC conceptual framework in other contexts such as private organizational settings and expand the use of the multi-dimensional approach to various types of PM and PPM environments. |

The translation of strategic management theories to PM and PPM is a growing theme for PM and PPM research methodology. This set of research examples is structured to help researchers interested in such translational approaches to compare and learn from these early experiences. The research examples indicate how PM and PPM research can mature and advance as the use of translational approaches grows. The translational studies not only illustrate the benefits of drawing from and building upon research and theories from the strategic management domain, they also illustrate how these studies build upon each other. To complete the knowledge loop, the examples also show how translational PM and PPM research can contribute to the development and validation of the theories – strengthening the strategic management field while being strengthened by it. Future studies are important for the continued advance of PM and PPM research. The chapter provides illustrative examples to guide future research and demonstrates the broad potential for continued fruitful research stemming from the relatively recent translation of strategic management theories to PM and PPM research.

Acknowledgements

Some of the ideas in this chapter were developed in preparation for a panel discussion led by the authors at the IRNOP 2011 conference (International Research Network on Organizing by Projects – June 2011). A related paper on this topic has been published in the International Journal of Project Management in 2012. This chapter builds upon and draws on these previous works, in particular the journal paper:

Killen, C.P., Jugdev, K., Drouin, N., Petit, Y. (2012), Advancing project and portfolio management research: Applying strategic management theories, *International Journal of Project Management*, Vol 30, Issue 5, pages 525-538. doi:10.1016/j.ijproman.2011.12.004

The authors acknowledge the contribution of Dr. Jonas Söderlund who moderated the panel presentation. The authors would also like to acknowledge the support of the University of Technology, Sydney, Australia, Université du Québec à Montréal, Quebec, Canada, and Athabasca University, Alberta, Canada. The resource-based PM studies in this chapter are acknowledged as part of a research program funded by the Social Sciences and Humanities Research Council of Canada. Finally, the Healthy Schools Project study (applying AC to PM) is acknowledged as part of a research program sponsored by The Quebec Research Council (FRSQ) and by The Canadian Institutes of Health Research (CIHR) and was conducted in collaboration with Marthe Deschesnes, PhD, head of the research program and Yves Couturier, PhD.

References

Adams, S., & Berg, M. (2004). *The Nature of the Net: Constructing Reliability of Health Information on the Web* (Vol. 17).

Alvarez, S.A., & Busenitz, L.W. (2001). The Entrepreneurship of Resource-Based Theory. *Journal of Management*, 27(6), 755-775.

Ambrosini, V., Bowman, C. & Collier, N. (2009). Dynamic Capabilities: An Exploration of How Firms Renew their Resource Base. *British Journal of Management*, 20, S9-S24.

Amit, R., & Schoemaker, P.J.H. (1993). Strategic Assets and Organizational Rent. *Strategic Management Journal*, 14(1), 33-46.

Arend, R.J. (2006). Tests of the Resource-Based View: Do the Empirics Have Any Clothes? *Strategic Organization*, 4(4), 409-421.

Bakker, R.M., Cambré, B., Korlaar, L., & Raab, J. (2011). Managing the Project Learning Paradox: A Set-Theoretic Approach toward Project Knowledge Transfer. *International Journal of Project Management*, 29, 494-503.

Balogun, J., & Johnson, G. (2004). Organizational Restructuring and Middle Manager Sensemaking. *Academy of Management Journal*, 47(4), 523-549.

Barney, J., Ketchen, D.J., & Wright, M. (2011). The Future of Resource-Based Theory: Revitalization or Decline? *Journal of Management* 37(5), 1299-1315.

Barney, J.B. (1998). On Becoming a Strategic Partner: The Role of Human Resources in Gaining Competitive Advantage. *Human Resource Management*, 37(1), 31-46.

Barney, J.B. (2001). Is the Resource-Based 'View' a Useful Perspective for Strategic Management Research? Yes. *The Academy of Management Review*, 26(1), 41-56.

Barney, J.B. (2007). *Gaining and Sustaining Competitive Advantage*. Upper Saddle River, NJ: Person Education, Inc.

Barney, J.B. & Arikan, A.M. (2001). The Resource Based View: Origins and Implications. In M.A. Hitt, R.E. Freeman & J.S. Harrison (Eds.), *The Blackwell Handbook of Strategic Management* (1st ed., pp. 124-188). Malden, MA: Blackwell Publishers Ltd.

Barney, J.B., & Clark, D.N. (2007). *Resource-Based Theory: Creating and Sustaining Competitive Advantage*. Oxford; New York: Oxford University Press.

Barney, J.B., & Hesterley, W. (2006). Organizational Economics: Understanding the Relations between Organizations and Economics Analysis. In S. Clegg, C. Hardy & W.R. Nord (Eds.), *Handbook of Organization Studies* (pp. 111-148). London: Sage.

Barratt, M., & Oke, A. (2007). Antecedents of Supply Chain Visibility in Retail Supply Chains: A Resource-Based Theory Perspective. *Journal of Operations Management, 25*(6), 1217-1233.

Beishon, R.J. (1972). *Systems Behaviour* (Third Edition). London: Harper & Row.

Biedenbach, T., & Müller, R. (2012). Absorptive, Innovative and Adaptive Capabilities and Their Impact on Project and Project Portfolio Performance. 30(5), 621-635.

Burns, T., & Stalker, G.M. (1961). *The Management of Innovation*. London: Tavistock.

Camisón, C., & Forés, B. (2010). Knowledge Absorptive Capacity: New Insights for its Conceptualization and Measurement. *Journal of Business Research, 63*(7), 707-715.

Castanias, R.P., & Helfat, C.E. (1991). Managerial Resources Rents. *Journal of Management, 17*(1), 155-171.

Chakraborty, K. (1997). Sustained Competitive Advantage: A Resource-Based Framework. *Advances in Competitiveness Research*, 5(1), 32-63.

Child, J. (1972). Organizational Structure, Environment and Performance: the Role of Strategic Choice. *Sociology*, 6(1), 1-22.

Cohen, W.M., & Levinthal, D.A. (1990). Absorptive Capacity: A New Perspective on Learning and Innovation. *Administrative Science Quarterly*, 35(1), 128-152.

Collis, D.J. (1994). Research Note: How Valuable are Organizational Capabilities? *Strategic Management Journal*, 15, Special Issue, 143-152.

Connor, T. (2002). The Resource-Based View of Strategy and its Value to Practising Managers. *Strategic Change*, 11(6), 307-316.

Cooper, R.G., Edgett, S.J., & Kleinschmidt, E.J. (2001). Portfolio Management for New Product Development: Results of an Industry Practices Study. *R & D Management, 31*(4), 361-380.

Dankwa-Mullan, I., Rhee, K.B., Stoff, D.M., Pohlhaus, J.R., Sy, F.S., Stinson Jr, N., & Ruffin, J. (2010). Moving toward Paradigm-Shifting Research in Health Disparities Through Translational, Transformational, and Transdisciplinary Approaches. *American Journal of Public Health*, 100(S1), S19-S24.

Danneels, E. (2002). The dynamics of product innovation and firm competences. *Strategic Management Journal*, 23(12), 1095-1121.

Danneels, E. (2008). Organizational Antecedents of Second-Order Competences. *Strategic Management Journal*, 29(5), 519-543.

Dawidson, O. (2006). Project Portfolio Management: An Organising Perspective *Department of Technology Management and Economics; Operations Management and Work Organisation* (Ph.D. thesis, 151 p.). Göteborg (Sweden): Chalmers University of Technology.

DeFillippi, R.J., & Arthur, M.B. (1998). Paradox in Project-Based Enterprise: The Case of Film Making. *California Management Review*, 40(2), 125-139.

Deschesnes, M., Drouin, N., & Couturier, Y. (2013). Schools' Absorptive Capacity to Innovate in Health Promotion. *Journal of Health Organization and Management*, 27(1), 24-41.

Duncan, R.B. (1972). Characteristics of Organizational Environments and Perceived Environmental Uncertainty. *Administrative Science Quarterly*, 17(3), 313-327.

Eisenhardt, K., & Santos, F. (2000). Knowledge-Based View: A New Theory of Atrategy? In A. Pettigrew, H. Thomas & R. Whittington (Eds.), *Handbook of strategy and management* (pp. 544). London, ENG: Sage Publications.

Eisenhardt, K.M. (1989). Making Fast Strategic Decisions in High-Velocity Environment. *Academy of Management Journal*, 32(3), 543-576.

Eisenhardt, K.M., & Martin, J.A. (2000). Dynamic Capabilities: What Are They? *Strategic Management Journal*, 21(10/11), 1105-1121.

Engwall, M., & Westling, G. (2004). Peripety in an R&D Drama: Capturing a Turnaround in Project Dynamics. *Organization Studies*, 25(9), 1557-1578.

Fernie, S., Green, S.D., Weller, S.J., & Newcombe, R. (2003). Knowledge Sharing: Context, Confusion, and Controversy. *International Journal of Project Management*, 21(3), 177-187.

Fosfuri, A., & Tribó, J.A. (2008). Exploring the Antecedents of Potential Absorptive Capacity and its Impact on Innovation Performance. *Omega*, 36(2), 173-187.

Foss, N.J. (Ed.). (1997). *Resources, Firms, and Strategies: A Reader in the Resource-Based Perspective*. Oxford, UK: Oxford University Press.

Grandori, A. (1984). A Prescriptive Contingency View of Organizational Decision Making. *Administrative Science Quarterly*, 29(2), 192.

Grant, R.M. (2010). *Contemporary Strategy Analysis* (7th Ed.). Chichester; Hoboken: John Wiley & Sons.

Hawawini, G., Subramanian, V., & Verdin, P.J. (2002). Is Performance Driven by Industry – or Firm-Specific Factors? A New Look at the Evidence. *Strategic Management Journal*, 24(1), 1-16.

Helfat, C.E. (2007). *Dynamic Capabilities: Understanding Strategic Change in Organizations*. Malden (MA): Blackwell Publishing.

Howell, D., Windahl, C., & Seidel, R. (2010). A Project Contingency Framework Based on Uncertainty and its Consequences. *International Journal of Project Management*, 28(3), 256.

Jugdev, K. (2003). Developing and Sustaining Project Management as a Strategic Asset: A Multiple Case Study Using the Resource-Based View. Unpublished PhD thesis Project Management Specialization. Calgary, AB: University of Calgary.

Jugdev, K. (2004a, July 11-14). Project Management as a Strategic Asset: What Does it Look Like and How Do Companies Get There? Paper presented at the 3rd Project Management Research Conference, London, UK.

Jugdev, K. (2004b). Through the Looking Glass: Examining Theory Development in Project Management with the Resource-Based View Lens. *Project Management Journal*, 35(3), 15-26.

Jugdev, K. (2005). Project Management as a Strategic Asset: What Does It Look Like and How Do Companies Get There? In D.P. Slevin, D.I. Cleland & J.K. Pinto (Eds.), *Innovations: Project Management Research 2004* (Vol. 1, pp. 161-174). Newtown Square, PA: Project Management Institute.

Jugdev, K. (2008). Good Theory: Developing a Foundation for Project Management. *International Journal of Product Development*, 6(2), 177-189.

Jugdev, K., & Mathur, G. (2006a, July 16-19). *A Factor Analysis of Tangible and Intangible Project Management Assets.* Paper presented at the 4th Project Management Research Conference, Montreal, QC.

Jugdev, K., & Mathur, G. (2006b). Project Management Elements as Strategic Assets: Preliminary Findings. *Management Research News*, 29(10), 604-617.

Jugdev, K., & Mathur, G. (2012). Classifying Project Management Resources by Complexity and Leverage. *International Journal of Managing Projects in Business*, 5(1), 105-124.

Jugdev, K., Mathur, G., & Fung, T. S. (2007). Project Management Assets and their Relationship with the Project Management Capability of the Firm. *International Journal of Project Management*, 25(6), 560-568.

Jugdev, K., & Thomas, J. (2002). Project Management Maturity Models: The Silver Bullets of Competitive Advantage. *Project Management Journal*, 33(4), 4-14.

Kaplan, S., Schenkel, A., von Krogh, G., & Weber, C. (2001). Knowledge-Based Theories of the Firm in Strategic Management: A Review and Extension. MIT Sloan Working Paper 4216-01.

Kerzner, H. (1994). The Growth of Modern Project Management. *Project Management Journal*, 25(2), 6-9.

Killen, C.P. (2008). Project Portfolio Management for Product Innovation in Service and Manufacturing Industries (Ph.D. thesis, 464 p.). Sydney (Australia): Macquarie University.

Killen, C.P., Hunt, R. A., & Kleinschmidt, E.J. (2008). Learning Investments and Organizational Capabilities: Case Studies on the Development of Project Portfolio Management Capabilities. *International Journal of Managing Projects in Business*, 1(3), 334-351.

Killen, C.P., Jugdev, K., Drouin, N., & Petit, Y. (2012). Advancing project and portfolio management research: Applying strategic management theories, *International Journal of Project Management*, 33(5), 525-538.

Kloppenborg, T., & Opfer, W. (2002). The Current State of Project Management Research: Trends, Interpretations, and Predictions. *Project Management Journal*, 33(2), 5-18.

Kogut, B. (1993). The Nature of the Firm: Origins, Evolution, and Development. *Administrative Science Quarterly*, 38(3), 503-507.

Kogut, B., & Zander, U. (1992). Knowledge of the Firm, Combinative Capabilities, and the Replication of Technology. In N. Foss (Ed.), *Resources, Firms, and Strategies: A Reader in the Resource Based Perspective* (Vol. 1, pp. 306-325). Oxford, United Kingdom: Oxford University Press.

Koontz, H. (1980). The Management Theory Jungle Revisited. *The Academy of Management Review*, 5(2), 175-187.

Koskela, L., & Howell, G. (2002, July 2002). The Underlying Theory of Project Management is Obsolete. Paper presented at the Frontiers of project management research and application, Seattle, WA.

Kwak, Y.H., & Anbari, F.T. (2009). Analyzing Project Management Research: Perspectives from Top Management Journals. *International Journal of Project Management*, 27(5), 435.

Lawrence, P.R., & Lorsch, J.W. (1967). *Organization and Environment: Managing Differentiation and Integration*. Boston (MA): Harvard Business School Press.

Louis, M.R. (1980). Surprise and Sense Making: What Newcomers Experience in Entering Unfamiliar Organizational Settings. *Administrative Science Quarterly*, 25(2), 226-251.

Maitlis, S. (2005). The Social Processes of Organizational Sensemaking. *Academy of Management Journal, 48*(1), 21-49.

Mathur, G., Jugdev, K., & Fung, T. (2013). Project Management Assets and Project Management Performance Outcomes: Exploratory Factor Analysis. *Management Research Review* (in press), 36(2).

Miles, R.E., & Snow, C.C. (1978). *Organizational Strategy, Structure, and Process*. New York: McGraw-Hill.

Newbert, S.L. (2007). Empirical Research on the Resource-Based View of the Firm: An Assessment and Suggestions for Future Research. *Strategic Management Journal*, 28(2), 121-146.

Nonaka, I. (1994). A Dynamic Theory of Organizational Knowledge Creation. *Organization Science*, 5(1), 14.

Packendorff, J. (1995). Inquiring into the Temporary Organization: New Directions for Project Management. *Scandinavian Journal of Management*, 11(4), 319-333.

Patriotta, G. (2003). Sensemaking on the Shop Floor: Narratives of Knowledge in Organizations. *The Journal of Management Studies*, 40(2), 349-375.

Penrose, E.T. (1959). The Theory of the Growth of the Firm. In N. Foss (Ed.), *Resources, Firms, and Strategies: A Reader in the Resource-Based Perspective* (Vol. 1, pp. 27-39). Oxford, United Kingdom: Oxford University Press.

Peteraf, M.A., & Barney, J.B. (2003). Unraveling the Resource-Based Tangle. *Managerial and Decision Economics*, 24(4), 309-323.

Porter, M.E. (1980). *Competitive Strategy: Techniques for Analyzing Industries and Competitors*. New York: Free Press.

Priem, R.L., & Butler, J.E. (2001a). Is the Resource-Based 'View' a Useful Perspective for Strategic Management Research? *The Academy of Management Review*, 26(1), 22-40.

Priem, R.L., & Butler, J.E. (2001b). Tautology in the Resource-Based View and the Implications of Externally Determined Resource Value: Further Comments. *The Academy of ManagementRreview*, 57-66.

Project Management Institute. (2012). *The Standard for Portfolio Management* (Third Edition). Newtown Square (PA): Project Management Institute.

Ray, G., Barney, J.B., & Muhanna, W.A. (2004). Capabilities, Business Processes, and Competitive Advantage: Choosing the Dependent Variable in Empirical Tests of theResource-Based View. *Strategic Management Journal*, 25(1), 23-37.

Rumelt, R.P., Schendel, D.E., & Teece, D.J. (1994). Fundamental Issues in Strategy. In R.P. Rumelt, D.E. Schendel & D.J. Teece (Eds.), *Fundamental Issues in Strategy: A Research Agenda* (pp. 9-47). Boston: Harvard Business School Press.

Salvato, C. (2003). The Role of Micro-Strategies in the Engineering of Firm Evolution. *Journal of Management Studies*, 40(1), 83-108.

Schreyögg, G., & Kliesch-Eberl, M. (2007). How Dynamic Can Organizational Capabilities Be? Towards a Dual-Process Model of Capability Dynamization. *Strategic Management Journal*, 28(9), 913-933.

Scott, R.W. (1998). *Organizations: Rational, Natural, and Open System* (Fourth Edition). Upper Saddle River (NJ): Prentice-Hall.

Selznick, P. (1957). Leadership in Administration: A Sociological Interpretation. In N. Foss (Ed.), *Resources, Firms, and Sstrategies: A Reader in the Resource-Based Perspective* (Vol. 1, pp. 21-26). Oxford, United Kingdom: Oxford University Press.

Shapiro, D.L., Kirkman, B.L., & Courtney, H.G. (2007). Perceived Causes and Solutions of the Translation Problem in Management Research. *Academy of Management Journal*, 50(2), 249-266.

Smith, A.D. (2002). From Process Data to Publication: A Personal Sensemaking. *Journal of Management Inquiry*, 11(4), 383-406.

Smith, K.A., Vasudevan, S.P., & Tanniru, M.R. (1996). Organizational Learning and Resource-Based Theory: An Integrative Model. *Journal of Organizational Change Management*, 9(6), 41-53.

Söderlund, J. (2004). Building Theories of Project Management: Past Research, Questions for the Future. *International Journal of Project Management*, 22(3), 183-191.

Straus, S.E., Tetroe, J., & Graham, I. (2009). Defining Knowledge Translation. *Canadian Medical Association Journal*, 181(3-4), 165-168.

Sun, P.Y.T., & Anderson, M.H.Y.J. (2010). An Examination of the Relationship between Absorptive Capacity and Organizational Learning, and a Proposed Integration. *International Journal of Management Reviews*, 12(2), 130-150.

Teece, D.J. (2007). Explicating Dynamic Capabilities: The Nature and Microfoundations of (Sustainable) Enterprise Performance. *Strategic Management Journal*, 28(13), 1319-1350.

Teece, D.J. (2009). *Dynamic Capabilities & Strategic Management – Organizing for Innovation and Growth*. New York: Oxford University Press.

Teece, D.J., Pisano, G., & Shuen, A. (1997). Dynamic Capabilities and Strategic Management. *Strategic Management Journal*, 18(7), 509-533.

Thomas, J.B., Clark, S.M., & Gioia, D.A. (1993). Strategic Sensemaking and Organizational Performance: Linkages among Scanning, Interpretation, Action, and Outcomes. *Academy of Management Journal*, 36(2), 239-270.

Thomas, J.L. (2000). Making Sense of Project Management: Contingency and Sensemaking in Transitory Organizations (300 p.): University of Alberta (Canada).

Thompson, J.D. (1967). *Organizations in Action: Social Science Bases of Administrative Theory*. New York: McGraw-Hill.

Tijssen, R.J.W. (2010). Discarding the 'Basic Science/Applied Science' Dichotomy: A Knowledge Utilization Triangle Classification System of Research Journals. *Journal of the American Society for Information Science and Technology*, 61(9), 1842-1852.

Todorova, G., & Durisin, B. (2007). Absorptive Capacity: Valuing a Reconceptualization. *The Academy of Management Review*, 32(3), 774-786.

Turner, J. R. (2010). Evolution of Project Management Research as Evidenced by Papers Published in the International Journal of Project Management. *International Journal of Project Management*, 28(1), 1-6.

Turner, J. R., & Müller, R. (2003). On the Nature of the Project as a Temporary Organization. *International Journal of Project Management*, 21(1), 1-8.

Ulri, B., & Ulri, D. (2000). Project Management in North America: Stability of the Concepts. *Project Management Journal*, 31(3), 33-43.

Volberda, H.W., Foss, N.J., & Lyles, M.A. (2010). Absorbing the Concept of Absorptive Capacity: How to Realize Its Potential in the Organization Field. *Organization Science*. 21(4), 931-954.

Wade, M., & Hulland, J. (2004). The Resource Based View and Information Systems Research: Review, Extension, and Suggestions for Future Research. *MIS Quarterly,* 28(1), 107-142.

Wang, C.L., & Ahmed, P. (2007). Dynamic Capabilities: A Review and Research Agenda. *International Journal of Management Reviews,* 9(1), 31-51.

Weick, K.E. (1969). *The Social Psychology of Organizing.* Reading (MA): Addison-Wesley.

Weick, K.E. (1979). *The Social Psychology of Organizing* (Second Edition). Reading (MA): Addison-Wesley.

Weick, K.E. (1993). The Collapse of Sensemaking in Organizations: The Mann Gulch Disaster. *Administrative Science Quarterly,* 38(4), 628-652.

Weick, K.E. (1995). *Sensemaking in Organizations.* Thousand Oaks (CA): Sage.

Weick, K.E. (2009). *Making Sense of the Organization: The Impermanent Organization.* Chichester (UK): John Wiley & Sons.

Wernerfelt, B. (1984). A resource Based View of the Firm. *Strategic Management Journal,* 5(2), 171-180.

White, D., Fortune, J., Jugdev, K., & Walker, D. (2011). Looking Again at Current Practice in Project Management, *International Journal of Managing Projects in Business,* 4(4), 553-572.

Wiklund, J., & Shepherd, D. (2003). Knowledge-Based Resources, Entrepreneurial Orientation, and the Performance of Medium-Sized Businesses. *Strategic Management Journal,* 24(13), 1307-1314.

Winter, S.G. (2003). Understanding Dynamic Capabilities. *Strategic Management Journal,* 24(10), 991-995.

World Health Organization. (1997). Promoting Health through Schools: Report of a WHO Expert Committee on Comprehensive School Health Education and Promotion. Geneva: World Health Organization.

Yun-tao, Y., Run-xiao, W., & Tao, L. (2010). *Relations of Enterprise's IT Resources, IT Capability and Sustainable Competitive Advantage: An Empirical Study.*

Zahra, S.A., & George, G. (2002). Absorptive Capacity: A Review, Reconceptualization, and Extension. *The Academy of Management Review,* 27(2), 185-203.

Zahra, S.A., Sapienza, H.J., & Davidson, P. (2006). Entrepreneurship and Dynamic Capabilities: A Review, Model and Research Agenda. *The Journal of Management Studies,* 43(4), 917-955.

Zollo, M., & Winter, S.G. (2002). Deliberate Learning and the Evolution of Dynamic Capabilities. *Organization Science,* 13(3), 339-351.

Upcoming Approaches in OPM Research

Nathalie Drouin, Ralf Müller and Shankar Sankaran

This section extends project management research to apply transformational, translational and trans-disciplinary approaches, which allows for leverage of research designs and methods across disciplines, thus increasing research quality and elevating OPM research to a higher level of research design.

This section starts with Chapter 13 by Catherine Killen, Kam Jugdev, Nathalie Drouin and Yvan Petit. This chapter applies strategic management theories and research approaches from the strategic management field to project management (PM) and project portfolio management (PPM) research. It presents four research experiences based on the resource-based view, dynamic capabilities and absorptive capacity theories as applied to PM and PPM. It aims to inspire future researchers to learn from and build upon these examples. This chapter not only illustrates current advances in OPM research, it also provides a framework for further advances in translational research by linking the theory and approaches from these strategic disciplines in practical research examples.

Chapter 14 is by Roslyn Cameron and Shankar Sankaran. This chapter takes a detailed exploration of mixed methods research (MMR) designs as an indicator of a movement towards more complex and innovative research designs in which both qualitative and quantitative approaches are combined, integrated, fused and blended. According to the authors, the two-dimensional linear concept of triangulation so often used in pure quantitative mono-methods research or in qualitative research as a measure for validity has become a thing of the past for those utilizing MMR. The authors feel that a discussion about MMR makes a useful contribution to a book promoting translational approaches in PM research by assisting PM researchers to study complex phenomena.

Chapter 15 is from Serghei Floricel, Marc Banik and Sorin Piperca. This chapter proposes an alternative approach that combines three strands: theory development, qualitative understanding and quantitative corroboration. By reflecting on a recent research project, it suggests ways in which these strands could be explicitly interwoven in a "triple helix" in order to sustain a healthy intra-field dynamics between conceptual, empirical and practical advances. The key to success seems to reside in two abilities: 1) to embrace multiple methods and multiple theoretical paradigms, and relish in their unavoidable polyphony. It involves using triangulation as a means for creating and renewing the tensions that reenergize knowledge production; and 2) to carefully morph an evolving theory into a set of issues for qualitative understanding, then into a set of tools and analyses for quantitative corroboration and, finally, into a set of tentatively validated practical prescriptions.

Chapter 16 by Pierre-Luc Lalonde and Mario Bourgault goes beyond the dominant research approaches and addresses the need to reinvent project management by placing it on a new foundation: The "practitioner-researcher", a new actor in this paradigm who assumes short-term responsibility for project success and engages in a broader philosophical inquiry that is at once theoretical, ethical, and even aesthetic in order to attain professional insight. The chapter presents two distinct research models for characterizing project management: research "for" project management (refers to investigations of day-to-day practices as conducted by project practitioners), and research "into" project management (refers to the fundamental, well-known research protocols applied to study project management). It also points out some limitations to models and proposes the necessity for looking beyond this superficial duality.

Chapter 17, the last in this book, is by Julien Pollack. This chapter draws on the *critical systems thinking* literature, which has a long tradition of exploring how methodologies can be combined in practice, and this tradition can be used to inform the management of project management research. It highlights particular significance in developing the discussion of pluralism in project management research in clearly distinguishing the level to which a research approach belongs within a paradigm; Reed's four strategies for combining methodologies; the oblique use of methods; grafting and embedding; and the more general cases of pluralism in series or parallel.

Thus, this section proposes to address the following questions:

- How should project management researchers think about using transformational, translational and trans-disciplinary (or interdisciplinary) approaches?
- How can project management researchers be more creative in using research approaches across paradigms?
- How do project management researchers extend their research approaches to investigate how organizations can realize their strategies?

Chapter 14

Mixed Methods Research Design: Well Beyond the Notion of Triangulation

Roslyn Cameron and Shankar Sankaran

Abstract

The aim of this chapter will be to make a detailed exploration of mixed methods research (MMR) designs as an indicator of a movement towards more complex and innovative research designs in which both qualitative and quantitative approaches are combined, integrated, fused and blended. The MMR movement has now developed to a stage where there are over 40 MMR designs and even typologies of typologies. The two-dimensional linear concept of triangulation, so often used in pure quantitative mono-methods research or in qualitative research as a measure for validity, has become a thing of the past for those utilising MMR. There is also a significant amount of cross-fertilisation between the disciplines within the MMR community with the following disciplines all contributing to methodological advances in MMR design: health, nursing, medicine, business/management, education, engineering and psychology/counselling. The usefulness of conducting MMR in trans-disciplinary teams will become apparent to organisational project management researchers through the discussion of complex and novel MMR designs.

MMR is useful when a phenomenon being studied is complex and needs multiple methods to investigate it. MMR has been found useful in a variety of fields and applications including management and organisational research but does not seem to be prominent in project management (PM) research despite the need for investigating better approaches to deal with complexity in projects. The authors of this chapter feel that a discussion about MMR will make a useful contribution to a book promoting translational approaches in PM research by assisting PM researchers to study complex phenomena.

Introduction

Mixed methods research (MMR) refers to a research strategy that involves 'the collection, analysis, and integration of quantitative and qualitative data in a single or multiphase study' (Hanson et al. 2005: 224). A complex phenomenon often needs more than one method to investigate it adequately. Morse and Niehaus (2009: 13) state that such investigations required the use of more than one research project in the past but this can be time consuming and costly. While triangulation was used as a strategy to overcome this difficulty it is often insufficient for the purpose. This chapter will show how advances in MMR have made it possible to conduct research into complex phenomena by combining the methods in a single study or a series of studies and going beyond the notion of triangulation.

MMR is an approach that is gaining in popularity and prevalence across a multitude of disciplines and is most popular within the fields of education, evaluation, health and medical sciences, social and behavioural sciences, and business and management disciplines. As the body of literature and conceptual and methodological knowledge of MMR has grown rapidly over the past decade so has the number of definitions as to what constitutes mixed methods research. This led Johnson, Onwuegbuzie and Turner (2007) to undertake an analysis of mixed methods definitions and in doing so they identified nineteen different definitions. The result of their analysis led to the development of the following definition:

> Mixed methods research is the type of research in which a researcher or team of researchers combines elements of qualitative and quantitative research approaches (e.g., use of qualitative and quantitative viewpoints, data collection, analysis, inference techniques) for the purpose of breadth of understanding or corroboration (Johnson, Onwuegbuzie and Turner, 2007: 123).

Cohen and Manion (1989: 269) make the link between triangulation and mixed methods '… triangular techniques in the social sciences attempt to map out, or explain more fully, the richness and complexity of human behavior by studying it from more than one standpoint and, in so doing, by making use of both quantitative and qualitative data'. This chapter will trace the history of the concept of triangulation and its relationship to the emergence of MMR. This will be followed by a detailed discussion of MMR design typologies as testament to the extent of the conceptual development in the MMR movement. An analysis of an MMR study in project management (PM) identified in a MMR prevalence study undertaken by Sankaran, Cameron and Scales (2012) found that the use of mixed methods in PM research has increased marginally over the past five years and is not keeping pace with the trends of using of mixed methods in management research. PM research papers were also found to not explicitly acknowledge the use of mixed methods. It was difficult to find a paper that followed the guidelines to describe the use of mixed methods based on definitions found in the literature of MMR methodology.

This chapter will explore the concept of triangulation, one of the oldest metaphors used in research, which can be dated back to the work of Campbell and Fiske (1959). Different types of triangulation are discussed before a more critical discussion is taken on the over use of the term and how the development of MMR and associated foundational methodology, concepts and MMR design typologies has seen researchers travel well beyond triangulation as a linear and two-dimensional validation strategy. Different MMR design typologies are presented before evaluating a published piece of project management research that has been classified as a mixed methods study (Milosevic & Patanakul, 2005).

Triangulation and Beyond

Knowing a single landmark only locates one somewhere along a line in a direction from the landmark, whereas with two landmarks one can take bearings on both and locate oneself at their intersection (Fielding & Fielding, 1986: 23).

Bazeley and Kemp (2012) trace the history of triangulation back to the work of Campbell and Fiske (1959) and to its increasing utility in qualitative research by Denzin (1978):

Triangulation is one of the oldest metaphors in the mixed methods lexicon. It remains the most used and perhaps the most abused metaphor of all. Use of the term in the methodological literature can be traced to Campbell and Fiske's landmark article in 1959, which argued for the value of a multitrait-multimethod (correlation) matrix to assess both the validity and the discriminatory power of measures of multiple traits associated with personality. This reflected matrix embraced a series of heterotrait-heteromethod and heterotrait-monomethod triangles separated by validity diagonals and a reliability diagonal (p. 61).

Denzin (1978) used the term triangulation to argue the use of a combination of methodologies in research, and initially saw triangulation as a validation strategy (Flick 2004: 179). The term is borrowed from military and navigation strategies, and is used to explore a viewpoint from multiple perspectives (Neuman, 2006). 'The triangulation metaphor used in research was derived from construction, surveying, and navigation at sea. The premise was based on the idea of using two known points to locate the position of an unknown third point, by forming a triangle' (Thurmond, 2001: 253). The concept of triangulation as derived from naval military service is utilised by researchers as follows:

Applied to research, it meant that investigators could improve their inquiries by collecting and converging (or integrating) different kinds of data bearing on the same phenomenon. The three points to the triangle are the two sources of the data and the phenomenon. This improvement in inquiries would come from blending the strengths of one type of method and neutralising the weaknesses of the other (Creswell, 2008).

Denzin (1978) recognised four differing types of triangulation as a means for validation: triangulation of data; investigator triangulation; triangulation of theories and methodological triangulation. These are summarised in Figure 14.1.

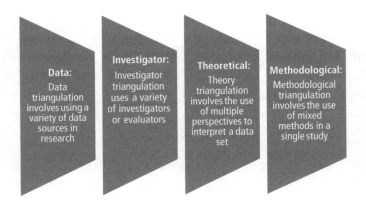

Figure 14.1. Types of Triangulation. Source: Denzin & Lincoln (2005)

In addition to these types of triangulation Cohen and Manion (1989: 272) add three additional types of triangulation to the mix including: time triangulation; space triangulation; and combined levels triangulation. Figure 14.2 summarises these three types.

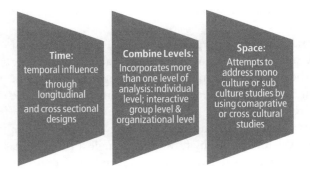

Figure 14.2. Additional Types of Triangulation. Source: Cohen & Manion (1989)

The concept of triangulation has not been without its critics, and such critiques have in some cases led to expanding the notion and its uses. Flick (2004) expands on the work of Denzin, advocating for three modes of application of triangulation: triangulation as a validation strategy; as an approach to generalisation of discoveries; and as a pathway to additional knowledge.

Upcoming Approaches in OPM Research

Tashakkori and Teddlie (2003: x) make the link between the concept of triangulation and MMR designs as follows:

> ... *mixed methods designs evolved from the notion of 'triangulating' the information from different data sources. A technique that emerged first from psychology (Campbell & Fiscke, 1959) and sociology (Denzin, 1978) but that reached its fullest application in applied research areas such as evaluation (e.g., Patton, 1990) and nursing (e.g., Morse, 1991).*

Twin (2003: 546-7) examined the status of mixed methods research in the field of nursing and noted the debate and critique on the use and misuse of triangulation that was evident in the mid 1990s in both the USA and UK. She refers to what amounted to confusion about the definition and underlying concepts of triangulation and the implementing of different types of triangulation. Sandelowski (2003) also refers to the confusion given to the interpretation of the concept of triangulation. She describes triangulation as 'the process specifically aimed toward the realist goal of establishing convergent validity' (Sandelowski 2003: 328). Nonetheless, she argues that confusion arises when authors use the term 'triangulated study' as if this is a methodology in itself. She claims triangulation has been given too much meaning and as a result 'has no meaning at all':

> *Triangulation appears as a 'near talismanic method' (Miles & Huberman, 1994: 266) for democratizing inquiry and resolving conflicts between qualitative and quantitative inquiry* (Sandelowski, 2003: 328).

Tashakkori and Teddlie (2003: 674) agree with Sandelowski and conclude:

> ... *what do we do when it [triangulation] appears to be over-used to the point where it means nothing? Can the term be rehabilitated, or does it carry too much baggage? Only time will tell .... it is unclear whether the term has any meaning when it is so broadly defined. Despite the popularity of the term, we encourage mixed methodologists to refrain from using it unless they specify how it was specifically defined in their research context.*

It would appear that the MMR movement has gone beyond the concept of triangulation despite the early development of the concept by Campbell and Fiske (1959); Denzin (1978) and; Patton (1990) and its popularisation. The development of MMR design typologies has further added to the argument that the MMR community has developed to the point where the concept of triangulation has become obsolete and relegated to possible MMR design types (e.g., Greene & Caracelli, 1997; Creswell, 2003).

Mixed Methods Research Designs

The emergence of the mixed methods movement has seen the development of an array of MMR designs. These designs are depicted by the mixed methods notation system and visual flow charts that have been adopted by the MMR community. This MMR notation system can be traced back to the work of Morse (1991) and was further developed in 2003. Table 14.1 provides a summary of Morse's MMR notation system.

Table 14.1. Morse's MMR Notation System. Source: Adapted from Morse (1991, 2003)

QUAN or quan	refers to quantitative methods
QUAL or qual	refers to qualitative methods
Use of upper case	refers to emphasis, primary or dominant method
Use of lower case	refers to lower emphasis, priority or dominance
"→"	indicates data collected sequentially
"+"	indicates data collected simultaneously or concurrently
"="	symbolises converged data collection

This basic notation system has been developed further by several authors (Plano Clark, 2005; Morse & Neihaus, 2009; Cameron 2011, 2012) to depict more complex MMR designs. The MMR notation system when combined with the visual depictions adopted by the MMR community provide a hallmark to the MMR community and the basis to presenting MMR designs. The visual depictions are procedural flowcharts that were first developed by Steckler, McLeroy, Goodman, Bird and McCormick (1992).

Tashakkori and Teddlie (2003: x) in their preface to the first edition of the *Handbook of Mixed Methods in Social and Behavioural Research* note that 'Eminent social and behavioural scientists conducted mixed methods research throughout the 20th century, but it was only during the last decade of that century that researchers began giving unique names to their designs'. One of the first and most rudimentary MMR design typologies was developed by Morgan (1998) for health research. Figure 14.3 details this typology which contains four complementary MMR designs: Qualitative preliminary; Quantitative preliminary; Qualitative follow-up; and Quantitative follow-up.

Principal Method Quantitative	Principal Method Qualitative
Qualitative Preliminary Qual → QUAN	Quantitative Preliminary Quan → QUAL
Qualitative Follow-up QUAN → qual	Quantitative Follow-up QUAL → quan

Figure 14.3. Complementary MMR Designs. Source: Morgan (1998)

Since this early work a plethora of MMR designs have been developed, the most notable being those by Creswell (2003), Creswell and Plano Clark (2007) and Tashakkori and Teddlie (2003).

Teddlie and Tashakkori (2003: 26-27) listed five reasons why typologies of MMR designs have been developed:

1. They help to provide the field with an organizing structure.
2. They help to legitimize the field by providing examples of research designs that are clearly distinct from qualitative and quantitative research designs.
3. They are useful in establishing a common language or nomenclature.
4. They assist researchers in deciding how to proceed when designing MMR.
5. They are useful pedagogical tools.

Nonetheless, as Maxwell and Loomis (2003: 244) point out, 'the actual diversity in mixed methods studies is far greater than any typology can adequately encompass'. These authors argue against the use of MMR design typologies for the reason just stated and because they assert most typologies leave out important components of research and are usually linear and do not take into account the complex whole of the study. They also claim that most MMR design typologies do not clarify the relationship between the quantitative and qualitative parts of a design. Despite these criticisms it would be fair to say that in general MMR designs are plentiful and are a generally accepted and utilised aspect of those actively utilising mixed methods in their research.

Due to the limitations imposed on this chapter it will not be possible to present all the main MMR typologies so we have chosen a sample of different MMR design typologies to demonstrate the diversity in the field. The first of these is by Greene and Caracelli (1997) in which they divided the designs into either component or integrated designs as depicted in Table 14.2. Component designs are ones in which 'the methods are implemented as discrete aspects of the overall inquiry and remain distinct throughout the inquiry', and integrated designs are those that involve 'a greater integration of the different method types' (Greene & Caracelli 1997: 22-23).

Table 14.2. Greene and Caracelli (1997) MMR Design Typology. Source: Adapted from Greene and Caracelli (1997: 22-25)

Mixed Method Component Designs	Mixed Method Integrated Designs
Triangulation: Different methods uses to research the same phenomenon toward convergence and increased validity.	Iterative: Dynamic interplay over time between different methodologies.
Complementarity: Results from one dominant method are enhanced or clarified by results from another method type E.g., QUAN +qual or QUAL +quan.	Embedded or nested: One method located within another resulting in creative tension.
Expansion: Inquiry paradigms frame the different methods used creating distinct components side by side.	Holistic: Necessary interdependence of different methods for understanding complex phenomenon.
	Transformative: Give primacy to value-based and action-orientated dimensions of different traditions of inquiry.

Creswell, Plano Clark, Gutmann and Hanson (2003) developed a typology for advanced MMR designs based on four criteria: implementation; priority; integration; and perspective. This results in six types of advanced MMR designs as summarised in Table 14.3. Implementation relates to how and when the data is collected (sequential or concurrent). Priority is concerned with which data (either QUAN or QUAL) is given the most priority or whether the priority is even. Integration refers to whether the integration of the data occurs at either the interpretation stage or the analysis phase of the study. Perspective relates to whether there is a theoretical perspective present and is explicitly stated. Creswell et al. (2003) build on the work of Greene and Caracelli (1997) and their reference to transformative designs that 'give primacy to the value-based and action-oriented dimensions of different traditions' (Greene & Caracelli 1997: 24). Creswell et al (2003: 222-223) elaborate this:

The commonality across transformative studies is ideological, such that no matter what the domain of inquiry, the ultimate goal of the study is to advocate for change. The transformative element of the research can either be experienced by the participants as they participate in the research or follow the study's completion when the research spawns changes in action, policy, or ideology ... In summary, the nature of transformative mixed research methodology is such that in both perspective and outcomes, it is dedicated to promoting change at levels ranging from personal to the political.

Hence the inclusion of 'vision, advocacy, ideology and framework' in the sequential and concurrent transformative designs in the advanced MMR designs put forward by these authors as depicted in Table 14.3.

Table 14.3. Advanced MMR Design Typology. Source: Adapted from Creswell, Plano Clark, Gutmann and Hanson (2003: 224-226)

Design Type	Description	Chart
Sequential		
Sequential explanatory	Quan followed by qual Priority: usually QUAN but can be QUAL or even Integration: at interpretation phase Theoretical perspective: may be present	QUAN → qual
Sequential exploratory	Qual followed by quan Priority: usually QUAL but can be QUAN or even Integration: at interpretation phase Theoretical perspective: may be present	QUAL → quan
Sequential transformative	Quan followed by qual Or qual followed by quan Priority: QUAN, QUAL or even Integration: at interpretation phase Theoretical perspective: definitely present (i.e. conceptual framework, advocacy, empowerment)	QUAL → quan Vision, Advocacy, Ideology, framework QUAN → qual Vision, Advocacy, Ideology, framework
Concurrent		
Concurrent triangulation	Concurrent data collection: quan and qual Priority: preferably equal but can be QUAN or QUAL Integration: interpretation or analysis phase Theoretical perspective: may be present	QUAN + QUAN
Concurrent nested	Concurrent data collection: quan and qual Priority: QUAN or QUAL Integration: analysis phase Theoretical perspective: may be present	QUAN → Analysis of findings QUAL → Analysis of findings
Concurrent transformative	Concurrent data collection: quan and qual Priority: QUAN or QUAL or even Integration: usually analysis phase Theoretical perspective: definitely present (i.e. conceptual framework, advocacy, empowerment)	QUAN + QUAL Vision, Advocacy, Ideology, framework quan QUAL Vision, Advocacy, Ideology

The last typology of MMR designs chosen is that of Tashakkori and Teddlie (2003), who distinguish between mixed methods designs and mixed model designs. The former combines the mixing of the methods stage while the latter involves mixing the qualitative and quantitative approaches in several stages of a study. A mixed model study will have two strands or phases of research. This results in six designs as summarised in Table 14.4. Concurrent designs collect data at the same time, sequential designs collect data in sequences and in conversion designs there is only one method of study and one type of data; however, they convert the data from QUAL to QUAN or QUAN to QUAL and then further analysis occurs (Tashakkori and Teddlie, 2003: 689).

Table 14.4. Tashakorri and Teddlie MMR Design Typology. Source: Tashakorri and Teddlie (2003: 686-689)

Procedure	Mixed Method Study	Mixed Model Study
Concurrent	*Concurrent missed method design*	*Concurrent missed model design*
	One kind of question is simultaneously addressed by collecting and analysing both QUAN and QUAL data. One type of inference is made on the basis of both data sources.	Two strands of research with both types of research questions (QUAN and QUAL), both types of data (QUAN and QUAL) and analysis (QUAN and QUAL) and both types of inferences (QUAN and QUAL) that are brought together at the end to reach a meta-inference.
Sequential	*Sequential mixed method design*	*Sequential mixed model design*
	One type of question, two types of data (QUAL and QUAN) that are collected in sequence with one dependent on the other and analysed accordingly with one type of inference.	Questions from the second strand emerge from the inferences of the first strand. The first strand is often an exploratory study, with the second often being confirmatory. The second strand involves new data, their analysis, and inferences in the other approach. The final meta-inference is either confirmatory or non-confirmatory.
Conversion	*Conversion mixed method design*	*Conversion mixed model design*
	One type of question, one type of data (QUAL or QUAN) that is transformed (qualitised/quantisied) and analysed accordingly again and one type of inference is made based on all the results.	Multiple approach questions are asked, one type of data (QUAL or QUAN) collected and analysed and is then transformed to another data type (qualitisied/quantitisied) and analysed accordingly again. Two types of inferences are made on the basis of each set of results and pulled together to generate a meta-inference.

Upcoming Approaches in OPM Research

An example of the Sequential Mixed Model Research Design in the field of human resource management (HRM) is provided in Figure 14.4. In this study the first phase of the research involved a quantitative survey, which was followed by focus groups (QUAN à qual). This provided an inference for the first phase or strand of the study; an inference being an outcome or 'the end result of interpretations of the findings' (Tashakkori & Teddlie, 2003: 691). In the second phase or strand of the study a model that was developed from the inferences of the first phase was tested in the field and

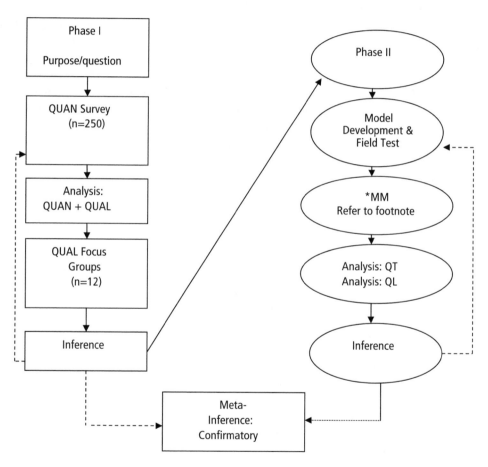

*MM

Program participants (n=19) Pre-program survey with Analysis: QT + QL
Post program survey with Analysis: QT + QL
Program trainers (n=3) Post program evaluation with Analysis: QL

Figure 14.4. Sequential Mixed Model Design. Source: Adapted from Cameron (2009)

Mixed Methods Research Design

evaluated using a combination of QUAL and QUAN methods. This again resulted in an inference from the results from the second phase. A confirmatory meta-inference was then reached. A 'meta-inference is obtained by integrating these initial inferences' (Tashakkori & Teddlie, 2003: 691). The meta-inference was confirmatory as the inference from the first phase was confirmed by the inference from the second phase. This involved a process of interpretation by integrating the results from each phase.

Use of MMR in Organisational PM

A study conducted by the authors by reviewing papers published in three ranked PM journals from 2006 to 2011 found only nine papers that could be considered to be using mixed methods well. The three journals were: *International Journal of Project Management* (IJPM); *Project Management Journal* (PMJ); and *IEEE Transactions on Engineering Management* (IEEE-TEM). Sankaran, Cameron and Scales (2012) classified the articles in these journals as per the Hurmerinta-Peltomaki and Nummela (2006) classification of MMR designs as shown in Figure 14.5. Morse and Neihaus (2009) developed an evaluative framework for mixed methods studies and this framework was used to evaluate the 25 articles identified in this study out of which nine were selected as good examples.

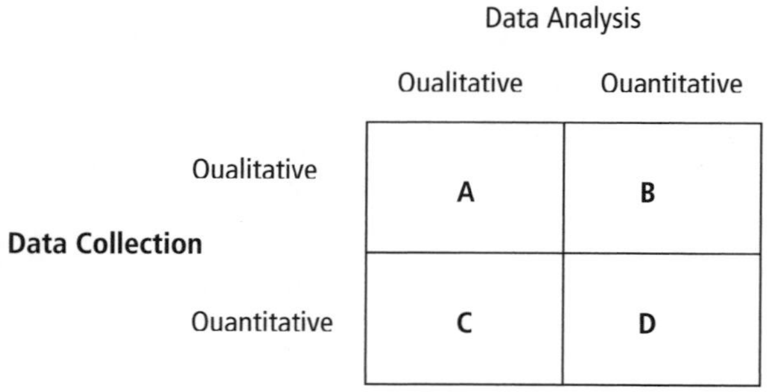

Data Analysis

		Oualitative	Ouantitative
Data Collection	Oualitative	A	B
	Ouantitative	C	D

Figure 14.5. MMR Classification. Source: Hurmeri

The nine papers that were identified as being good examples of MMR were identified as follows in like groups:

1. Chai and Xin (2006), *IEEE-TEM*,   AD
2. Luu et al. (2008), *IJPM*,   AD
3. Milosevic, D. and Patanakul, P. (2005), *IJPM*, AD
4. Morris and Jamieson (2005), *PMJ*,   AD
5. Müller and Turner 2007, *IJPM*,   AD

6. Kutsch and Hall 2009, *PMJ*,   AB
7. Lechler and Cohen 2009, *PMJ*,   AC
8. Morris, Jamieson and Shepherd (2006), *IJPM*, BD
9. Lee-Kelley, L (2006), *IJPM*   ACD

The AD classification (of which there were five articles), are MMR studies where the qualitative data is analysed qualitatively and the quantitative data is analysed quantitatively. The AB classification involves qualitative data analysed qualitatively and quantitatively. The AC classification has qualitative and quantitative data, both analysed qualitatively. The BD classification has both qualitative and quantitative data, both analysed quantitatively. The ACD MMR study involves qualitative and quantitative data, both analysed qualitatively and the quantitative data is also analysed quantitatively.

Morse and Niehaus (2009: 161) have developed a 'dissection chart' to systematically examine the adequate design of MMR in published papers. They suggest that in order to dissect a paper, one will have to read the entire paper by first making notes, highlighting the aim of the study, examining the research questions that were asked, looking at the sample used for the components of study, noting the methods and examining the pacing of the data collection and interface points. The analysis should then use the criteria listed below:

1. Identify:
   a. Theoretical drive – investigating whether the researcher approached the study inductively or deductively will allow the reader to determine the appropriateness of the theoretical drive.
   b. Core component – or the primary part of the aim(s) and research questions.
   c. Supplemental component – or the component that is not complete but supports the core component.
   d. Points(s) of interface – to note how the different datasets were combined and analysed (separately and then combined or together).
2. Identify the type of MMR design (qualitatively driven and quantitatively driven designs).
3. Evaluate the adequacy of the study by answering the following questions:
   a. What is the nature of the phenomenon under investigation?
   b. Were the QUAL/QUAN methods/strategies appropriately used? Give reasons.
   c. What is the nature of the primary sample? Was it appropriate? Was it adequate?
   d. Did the supplementary component of the project require a different sample? If so, was it adequate and appropriate?
   e. Consider the generalisability of the study. Has the author(s) over/under-generalised? Give reasons.
4. An evaluation of the rigour of the study:
   Can the core component stand alone?

Is the supplementary component adequate for the study purposes?
What violations to reliability and validity (if any) occurred?

5. Outline the design of each MMR article by drawing a flowchart.

One of the papers, Milosevic and Patanakul (2005), is now dissected using the criteria suggested by Morse and Niehaus (2009). The paper reports a study on standardised project management (SPM) in the USA and involves three sequential stages:

1a. Theoretical drive – The research intent was described as 'an exploratory study into the impact of standardized project management (SPM) in high-velocity industries' (p. 181). So we can classify the purpose of the research as 'discovery'. The paper describes a three-step approach (Qualitative $\rightarrow$ Quantitative $\rightarrow$ Qualitative). It was inductively driven.

1b. Core component – Although this was not clarified by the authors, it was concluded after reading the paper that the paper used both QUAL and QUAN with equal intensity in the first two phases of the research. The first step addressed the research question: 'What are the major factors in SPM efforts on Organizational Project Management (OPM) level?' (p. 191). The second step helped address the question: 'What SPM factors at OPM level are of interest as they impact on project success?' (p. 192).

1c. Supplementary component – This was quite clear from the methodology. It was the third-stage qualitative component to enrich the findings that was a qual.

1d. Points of interface – In Step 1 a multiple case study was used to define constructs for standardized PM. This was followed by a survey in Step 2 using hypotheses testing to report on quantitative findings. Step 3 used multiple follow-up case studies to enrich findings from hypotheses testing. The datasets in Steps 1 and 2 were analysed separately but the analysis in step 3 combined the results from Steps 1 and 2 as well.

2. MMR design – Being an inductive study it was qualitatively driven initially but the quantitative component also seemed to weigh in heavily to investigate the phenomenon. This could have been made clearer by the authors.

3. Evaluation – The phenomenon being investigated was the use of SPM at an organisational project level. The qualitative and quantitative components were used adequately. It was necessary to use a mixture of predominantly qualitative methods (interviews/secondary data/literature review) to arrive at the constructs of SPM being used at an organisational level. To test the construct the authors developed a questionnaire and conducted surveys. This was a deductive part of the research and it was appropriate to use quantitative methods. The follow-up interviews helped clarify specific points arrived at in the second step and it was appropriate to use a small number of interviews for enrichment.

The primary sample size used for Step 1 was 12 project managers across six organisations. It was a purposeful sample. Further explanation was not provided as to the nature of the sample (characteristics of project managers and types of organisation) that could have helped our analysis. The sample size for Step 2 was 55 (diverse sample). Although no justification was provided for the size of the sample, it seemed adequate for the type of analysis carried out (simple correlation coefficients and linear regression). Step 3 again used a purposeful sample of five that was deemed to be adequate. While the authors claimed their findings were significant (this could be overgeneralization based on the size of the study), they did admit that more empirical testing was needed.

To stand alone, Steps 1 and 2 would be required, as Step 2 could not have been carried out without completing Step 1. This led us to believe that the first QUAL and QUAN were both core components. This does create a dilemma for judgeing this paper according to the Morse and Niehaus (2009) chart. However, the supplementary component was adequate for the study. The authors did explain the measures used to achieve validity and reliability.

Figure 1 in the paper (p. 184) clarified the flow and could serve as a flowchart although it did not match the templates suggested by Morse and Niehaus (2009).

Overall the authors consider this paper to be a good example of MMR based on the dissection carried out by the Morse and Niehaus (2009) chart. However, better use of MMR terminology and acknowledgement of the growing body of MMR methodological concepts would have made the reporting of the study better.

The Morse and Niehaus (2009) dissection chart includes items such as an examination of theoretical drive, sampling and validity, which would be good for investigating any research project. However, certain items like the core and supplementary components and points of interface would apply specifically to an MMR study. The process will also help PM researchers who want to use MMR to set up their research appropriately.

Summary

This chapter has mapped the use of triangulation and its relationship to MMR and argues that MMR designs have developed and progressed well beyond the linear and two-dimensional concept of triangulation to the development of an array of MMR designs that have different purposes and levels of complexity. It is argued that triangulation has been overused to the point that it has no meaning (Sandelowski, 2003; Tashakkori & Teddlie, 2003; Twin, 2003). The chapter then presented a sample of some of these MMR design typologies that demonstrate an array of designs available to the PM researcher. Some of these are simple and others are advanced and complex. Nonetheless, the PM researcher now has available a growing body of MMR foundational theory, concepts and designs from which to draw when needing to use both qualitative and quantitative methods in a research inquiry.

In this chapter we have shown the increased use of MMR designs in research being reported in several fields allied to PM. Two other chapters in this book, Chapters 15 and 17, also promote combining research methods to provide deeper insights into the phenomenon being researched. We believe that the use of MMR designs in PM can assist researchers to investigate complex phenomena. It will also assist them in conducting trans-disciplinary studies with researchers in healthcare, education, social research and organisational research where MMR designs are prevalent. Knowledge of MMR designs could also encourage PM researchers to move away from traditional methods such as surveys, interviews and case studies to adopt more innovative approaches by using MMR designs not just for triangulation as a validation strategy, but also to add more in-depth investigation and a broader perspective of the phenomenon being researched.

References

Bazeley, P. & Kemp, L. (2012). Mosaics, triangles and DNA: Metaphors for integrated analysis in mixed methods research. *Journal of Mixed Methods Research*, 6, 1: 55-72.

Cameron, R. (2009). Adult learning and career transitions: Development of a lifelong learning model for engagement, recognition and transitions. PhD Thesis, Southern Cross University: Lismore, Australia.

Cameron, R. (2011). Mixed methods in business and management: A call to the 'first generation'. *Journal of Management and Organisation*. 17, 2: 245-267.

Cameron, R. (2012). Applying the newly developed extended Mixed Methods Research (MMR) notation system. *British Academy of Management 2012 Conference*, 11-13th September, Cardiff, Wales.

Campbell, D.T., & Fiske, D. (1959). Convergent and discriminant validation by the multitrait-multimethod matrix. *Psychological Bulletin*, 56: 81-105.

Chai, K-H. & Xin,Y. (2006). The application of new product development tools in industry: The case of Singapore, *IEEE Transactions on Engineering Management*, 53 (4): 435-554.

Cohen, L. & Manion, L. (1989). *Research Methods in Education* (3rd Ed.). London: Routledge.

Creswell, J.W. (2003). *Research Design: Qualitative, Quantitative, and Mixed Methods Approaches.* (2nd Ed.). Thousand Oaks, CA: Sage.

Creswell, J.W. (2008). *Educational research: Planning, conducting, and evaluating quantitative and qualitative research*, 3rd edn., Upper Saddle River, NJ: Prentice Hall.

Creswell, J.W., & Plano Clark, V.L. (2007). *Designing and Conducting Mixed Methods Research.* Thousand Oaks, CA: Sage.

Creswell, J.W., & Plano Clark, V.L. (2010). *Designing and conducting mixed methods research*, 2nd edn., Thousand Oaks, CA: SAGE.

Creswell, J.W., Plano Clark, V., Gutman, M.L., & Hanson, W.E. (2003). Advanced mixed methods research designs. In A. Tashakkori., & C. Teddlie (Eds.), *Handbook of Mixed Methods in Social & Behavioral Research*, Thousand Oakes, CA: Sage: 209-240.

Denzin, N.K. (1978). *The research act: A theoretical introduction to sociological methods*, 2nd edn., New York: McGraw Hill.

Denzin, N.K., & Lincoln, Y.S. (2005). (Eds.). *Handbook of Qualitative Research*, 3rd edn., Thousand Oaks, CA: Sage.

Fielding, N., & Fielding, J. (1986). *Linking data: The articulation of qualitative and quantitative methods in social research.* London and Beverly Hills: Sage.

Flick, U. (2004). *Introduction to qualitative research.* Thousand Oaks, CA: Sage.

Greene, J.C., & Caracelli, V.J. (1997) *Advances in mixed-method evaluations: The challenges and benefits of integrating diverse paradigms*, San Francisco, CA: Jossey-Bass.

Hanson, W.E., Creswell, J.W., Piano Clark, V.L. & Creswell, J.D. (2005). Mixed methods research design in counselling psychology. *Journal of Counselling Psychology*, 52, 2: 224-235.

Hurmerinta-Peltomaki L., & Nummela, N. (2006). 'Mixed methods in International Business Research: A Value-added Perspective', *Management International Review.* 46(4): 439-459.

Johnson, R.B., Onwuegbuzie, A. & Turner, l. (2007). Toward a definition of mixed methods research. *Journal of Mixed Methods Research.* 1: 112-133.

Kutsch, E. & Hall, M. (2009). The rational choice of not applying project risk management in information technology projects. *Project Management Journal.* 40, 3: 72-81.

Lechler, T.G. & Cohen, M. (2009). Exploring the role of steering committees in realizing the value from project management. *Project Management Journal.* 40, 10: 42-54.

Lee-Kelley, L. (2006). Locus of control and attitudes to working in virtual teams. *International Journal of Project Management.* 24: 234-243.

Luu, V.T., Kim, A.Y. & Huynh, T.A. (2008). Improving project performance of large contractors using benchmarking approach. *International Journal of Project Management.* 26: 758-769.

Maxwell, J.A. & Loomis, D.M. (2003). Mixed methods design: An alternate approach. In A. Tashakkori. & C. Teddlie, (Eds.), *Handbook of Mixed Methods in Social & Behavioral Research,* Thousand Oakes, CA: Sage: 241-272.

Miles, M. B. & Huberman, A. M. (1994). *Qualitative Data Analysis: an ExpandedSourcebook,* Thousand Oaks, CA: Sage.

Milosevic, D. & Patanakul, P. (2005). Standardized project management may increase development project success. *International Journal of Project Management*, 23:181-192.

Morris, P.W.G. & Jameison, A. (2005). Moving from corporate strategy to project strategy, *Project Management Journal*, 36, 4: 5-18.

Morris, P.W.G., Jameison, A. & Shepherd, M.M. (2006). Research updating the APM knowledge 4th edition. *International Journal of Project Management*, 24: 461-473.

Morse, J. (1991). Approaches to qualitative-quantitative methodological triangulation. *Nursing Research*, 20, 2: 120-123.

Morse, J. ((2003). Principles of mixed and multi-method research design. In A. Tashakkori., & C. Teddlie (Eds.), *Handbook of Mixed Methods in Social & Behavioral Research* Thousand Oakes, CA: Sage: 189-208.

Morse, J. & Neihaus, L. (2009). *Mixed Method Design: Principles and procedures.* Walnut Creek, CA: Left Coast Press.

Morgan, D. (1998). Practical strategies for combining qualitative and quantitative methods: Applications to health research. *Qualitative Health Research*, 8, 3: 362-376.

Müller, R. & Turner, J.R. (2007). Matching the project managers 'leadership style' to project type. *International Journal of Project Management*, 25: 21-32.

Neuman, J.W. (2006). *Basics of social research: Quantitative and qualitative approaches.* Boston: Pearson/Allyn and Bacon.

Patton, M.Q. (1990). Qualitative evaluation and research methods, 2nd edn., Newbury Park, CA: Sage.

Plano Clark, V.L. (2005). Cross-disciplinary analysis of the use of mixed methods in physics education research, counselling psychology, and primary care. Doctoral dissertation, University of Nebraska-Lincoln.

Sandelowski, M. (2003). Tables or Tableaux? The challenges of writing and reading mixed-methods studies. In A. Tashakkori., & C. Teddlie, (Eds.), *Handbook of Mixed Methods in Social & Behavioral Research*, Thousand Oakes, CA: Sage: 321-350.

Sankaran, S., Cameron, R. & Scales, J. (2012). The Utility and Quality of Mixed Methods in Project Management Research, Rotterdam: EURAM Conference 2012 June.

Steckler, A., McLeroy, K.R., Goodman, R.M., Bird, S.T. & McCormick, L. (1992). Toward integrating qualitative and quantitative methods: An introduction. *Health Education Quarterly*, 19, 1: 1-8.

Tashakkori, A., & Teddlie, C. (Eds.) (2003). *Handbook of Mixed Methods in Social & Behavioral Research.* Thousand Oakes, CA: Sage.

Teddlie, C. & Tashakkori, A. (2003). Major issues and controversies in the use of mixed methods in the social and behavioural sciences. In A. Tashakkori. & C. Teddlie, (Eds.), *Handbook of Mixed Methods in Social & Behavioral Research.* Thousand Oakes, CA, Sage: 3-50.

Thurmond, V.A. (2001). The point of triangulation. *Journal of Nursing Scholarship*, 33, 3: 253-258.

Twin, S. (2003). Status of Mixed methods research in Nursing. In A. Tashakkori & C. Teddlie, (Eds.), *Handbook of Mixed Methods in Social & Behavioral Research.* Thousand Oakes, CA: Sage: 541-556.

Chapter 15

The Triple Helix of Project Management Research: Theory Development, Qualitative Understanding and Quantitative Corroboration

Serghei Floricel, Marc Banik and Sorin Piperca

Introduction

The project management discipline is a fairly young, practice-oriented subfield of organization and management studies. In its most prominent forms, it relies upon three pillars – normative postulates of rationality, the codification of practice and generalizations from empirical data – in order to devise prescriptions for project management practice. If these pillars are to be combined, the ideal guide to practical action would be a normative recipe that enriches a rational kernel with details drawn from experience and generalized empirical patterns. Yet, scrutinizing each pillar reveals a number of problems that undermine the validity and applicability of the ensuing prescriptions. Moreover, because each pillar is advocated by a distinct 'voice' in the project management field, but their dialogue is contradictory, the outcome is unproductive polyphony (Bakhtin, 1984) rather than generative integration. In this chapter, we propose an alternative approach that combines three strands: theory development, qualitative understanding and quantitative corroboration. By reflecting on a recent research project, we suggest ways in which these strands could be explicitly interwoven in a 'triple helix' in order to sustain a healthy intra-field dynamic between conceptual, empirical and practical advances.

Conceptual Background
The Context of Project Management Practice and Research

Project management is a new field, both as a distinct profession and as an academic area. The rise in interest in project management coincided with the recognition that some human endeavors are quite complex and with the rise of systems engineering and management science, among others, as ways of addressing this complexity (Simon, 1981; Alexander, 1964; Sapolsky, 1972). Practitioners who first confronted these issues came from various engineering disciplines, such as construction, aerospace and software, which valued logical and mathematical arguments as well as practical recipes at the expense of scientific explanations, and especially social theories (Bunge, 1967; Vincenti, 1990). In turn, with few exceptions, such as Stinchcombe and Heimer (1985), social sciences did not pay a lot of attention to projects. It is not surprising that initial recipes, even for non-technical aspects of project management, relied on the mathematical and logical 'sciences of the artificial'—more specifically on decision theory and operations research.

In areas where this approach could not be applied, project management developed as a practice-oriented field, via contributions made by practitioners for practitioners in trade journals, conferences and training programs. These contributions took the form of project narratives, decision heuristics and rules learned through practical experience, as well as more elaborate prescriptive models (see for example Garvey and Lansdowne, 1998). Over time, with the coalescence of key ideas within the organizational field and the institutionalization of professional associations and communities of practice, the codification of practice became more systematic. Examples of this evolution are the emergence of PMI and PRINCE 2 standards of practice, as well as the Capability Maturity Model and, recently, the Agile Manifesto, in the software-based industries. To make sense of their experience and develop practical recipes, practitioners often relied implicitly on the same 'sciences of the artificial' and on the tenets of bureaucratic rationality that had become pervasive and taken for granted. However, most of these 'theoretical' assumptions remained implicit and, as a result, were not subject to critical scrutiny.

The first cohort of academic contributions to the field of project management were close to the codification of practice but sought to proffer more general conclusions by providing statistical evidence for the key success factors in various projects (Cooper, 1979; Boehm, 1984; Pinto and Slevin, 1987). These contributions were, however, largely atheoretical and lacked measurement and statistical sophistication (Brown and Eisenhardt, 1995). Soon after, a first generation of theory-based academic contributions emerged, inspired by economic and legal theories, which were themselves rooted in the postulates of decision and other normative theories. Typically, these models resulted in recommendations for efficient investment decision, contract design, risk management and activity scheduling (Chapman and Ward, 1994; Diekmann et al., 1996; Smith and Nau, 1995).

When a distinct academic subfield of social sciences dedicated to project management eventually emerged in the late 1990s, it quickly zeroed-in on specific issues such as projects as temporary organizations (Packendorff, 1995), unfolding processes over the life of a project (Floricel and Miller, 2001), particularities of complex systems development (Gann and Salter, 2000), inter-project synergies and transitions (Prencipe and Tell, 2001), and formalization in projects and project-based organizations (Aubry,

Hobbs and Thuillier, 2007). Because most of these themes are not fundamentally new, researchers leveraged theories emerging from the study of ongoing organizations, such as theories of strategic action, managerial cognition, social networks, structuration and institutionalization. However, the influence of these 'grand theories' was not universally appreciated. Under the umbrella of the 'practice view', some academics began to focus on what practitioners are doing concretely, in an attempt to shed the lenses imposed by established organizational theories and develop fresh insights into project processes (Sergi, 2009).

Inspired by these advances, the first steps towards a closer interaction between researchers and practitioners occurred. Professional associations, in particular the Project Management Institute, recognized the importance of a more systematic and theory-based inquiry and began supporting academic research, an example of which is the research project discussed later in this chapter. Conversely, management scholars and other social scientists became increasingly involved in the activities that produce standards of professional practice, such as the Project Management Body of Knowledge (PMBOK).

We consider this tendency towards a stronger theoretical and empirical basis, in combination with a closer attention to practice and practitioners, as a very encouraging development for the field of project management. In this chapter we suggest an approach that could reinforce this encouraging tendency to make it irreversible, as well as more intellectually productive and practically relevant. We begin by discussing the factors that have kept the three pillars of project management prescriptions – normative rationality, practice codification and empirical generalizations – apart, while subsequently we propose three alternative strands of project management research and explain how they could build upon each other to form an integrative, dynamic and practically relevant knowledge production and prescription elaboration process.

Critical Analysis of the Three Pillars that Support Project Management Prescriptions

Normative rationality, practice codification and atheoretical empirical generalizations are among the most common bases for justifying decisions and practical action in a variety of domains. They correspond to three 'voices' that can be often heard in the managerial, political, and other kinds of social discourse. We call these voices, respectively, the 'voice of reason', the 'voice of experience' and the 'voice of necessity'. As a consequence of their competition, the strengths and weaknesses of each pillar have been long scrutinized, and the arguments that emerge from the criticism of one pillar often serve as a justification for emphasizing another pillar, reinforcing the polyphony among these voices.

As mentioned in the introduction, a first source of project management prescriptions is a series of *rationality postulates* originating in decision theory, economics, and bureaucratic theories of organization and management (Von Neumann and Morgenstern, 1943; Weber, 1947; Milgrom and Roberts, 1992). These postulates provide conceptual underpinnings for project selection, organization and contact design, and activity planning (March and Shapira, 1987; Krishnan and Ulrich, 2001).

Perhaps, the most basic of all these roots is decision theory, which aims to provide a method for selecting an outcome-maximizing choice among several alternatives. Simply put, decision theory emphasizes the logical consistency of a choice in light of goals and preferences expressed in the form of values or utilities attributed to various possible decision outcomes. In the case of uncertain outcomes, the methods also take into account the probability distribution of all possible outcomes to identify the most desirable expected outcome. Utilities and probability distributions distill the totality of the decision maker's volition as well as knowledge of the project and its context to a few, highly abstract, indicators. Mathematicians (von Neumann and Morgenstern, 1943; Savage, 1954) have translated the expected utility approach into a series of postulates and calculus methods that are presented as norms ('the way things should be') of rational action. These norms are closely related to the standard methods for evaluating and selecting projects as well as technical and contractual solutions (Bierman and Smidt, 1960; Howard, 1988). Further refinements for projects include, for example, game theoretical models that take into account the possible reaction to an action from project competitors or contractors (Medda, 2007), real option models that take into account the value that stems from the flexibility of delaying or reversing parts of a project decision (Huchzermeier and Loch, 2001), and contracting models that take into account the opportunism of project participants (Shavell, 1979).

This kind of normative rationality infused what we call the 'voice of reason' in the project management field, by advocating order and coherence in decision making. As suggested in the introduction, this voice is advocated by practitioners with an engineering background, broadly speaking, who are trained to apply a series of rule-based procedures to the shaping of reality (Bunge, 1967). But a distinctive characteristic of this voice is also its emphasis on decision makers' subjectivity, that is, on the *a priori* preferences and beliefs. We see this in many facets of the decision calculus ranging from the focus on logical consistency, to procedures for 'extracting' subjective utilities and probabilities (Kadane and Winkler, 1988). Given such subjective focus, scrutinizing a method in terms of consistency appears to be, in fact, one of the few means of validation (Emirbayer and Mische, 1998). This internal focus seems particularly relevant in a project context, given that projects do not yet exist in the word, but only in the planners' imagination.

A loosely related conceptual root is the bureaucratic ideal type as a rational means of organizing (Weber, 1947), which also focuses on internal efficiency at the expense of goal adequacy, and favors hierarchical subordination based on professional skills as well as interpersonal relations guided by rules. The ideal type of bureaucracy has become one of the most widespread 'rationalized myths' of organizing, taken for granted in most areas of human activity (Meyer et al., 1984). In project management, this drive translated in a preference for hierarchical project organizations and, more importantly, in the development of project management rules and of project management offices

(PMOs) and professional associations in charge of developing and ensuring the application of rules and professional certifications.

But several arguments can be made against the possibility and usefulness of emphasizing internal coherence and efficiency. First, the roots of these norms of rationality are quite obscure, from scholastic deliberations about the existence of free will (Thomas Aquinas, Summa Theologica, Part I, Question 82 and Question 83), to commonsensical considerations about games of chance (Bernoulli, 1738), and a study of public service organization in eighteenth century Prussia (Kiser and Schneider, 1994). In practice, these postulates have been called into question by logicians, economists and researchers of human behavior (Allais, 1953; Simon, 1978; Tversky and Kahneman, 1974), who point to many 'deviations' from the norms of rationality. Within the 'voice of reason' discourse, these were labeled bounds, paradoxes, biases or heuristics, implying that everyday human behavior is not rational (Shapira, 1995). Even more fundamentally, the internal, subjective focus and the highly abstract nature of decision models have been criticized on grounds that they detract from learning, in particular, by using statistical evidence (von Mises, 1981) or by developing concrete models of the relevant aspects of the world (Bunge, 1988). In other words, the focus on internal consistency and efficiency could be the main force that pulls the first pillar away from the other two pillars of project management prescriptions.

The second source of prescription is the *codification of practice*. Narratives and discussions about the sources of success and failure help practitioners make causal attributions and identify remedial actions (Brown and Duguid, 1991). Experienced project managers, who lived through many crises, acquire beliefs about the nature of upcoming events in projects, and a repertoire of strategies for dealing with each type of event. Their everyday experience is also distilled into rules of thumb regarding resource requirements for various types of projects and tasks, as well as maxims regarding the best way to organize projects and teams (Bunge, 1967). While most of this experience is lost or passed on through apprenticeship, some is codified in the form of checklists of tasks, resources and risks, contingency plans, standard operating procedures and responsibility definitions (Prencipe and Tell, 2001). For instance, some of it has evolved into rules for designing various types of contracts, mainly with respect to risk sharing and mitigation strategies (see for example Langford, Gosoroski and Graves, 1990). From time to time, this kind of experience gets distilled into broader innovative paradigms, such as the 'agile approach' (Thomke and Reinertsen, 1998) or 'Integrated Project Delivery' (Cohen, 2010), which emerge from frustration with prevalent prescriptions, typically with those derived from rationality postulates.

The orientation towards concrete practical know-how infuses project management prescriptions with what we call the 'voice of experience'. This voice is advocated by managers who, battered by past unexpected events and odd deviations from the expected evolutions, call for attending separately to every eventuality (Shapira, 1995). Its ideal for project management prescriptions consists of mapping as many particular possibilities and developing action-to-outcome rules for each of them. These rules focus on attaining concrete useful results at the expense of abstract consistency or of identifying generic empirical patterns that cover many possible results. Focusing on internal coherence in light of a few abstract variables, or paying attention only to broader patterns or common underlying factors are seen as less important because experience teaches managers that every detail can make the difference between project success and failure. These particularities of the voice of experience pull the codification of practice apart from the other two pillars. While this voice shares with the voice of reason a focus on gleaning subjective knowledge, its aim of producing actionable and effective practical rules can interfere with the quest for overarching logical parsimony and consistency. Essentially, translating practical rules into abstract logical schemes based on a few variables leaves out the cues that provide concrete guidance to managers. Also, while the voice of experience shares with the voice of necessity an interest for learning about the outside world, its aim to produce rules for every circumstance leads to a rich, multifaceted depiction of the reality, which detracts from the quest for generic patterns or common underlying factors. In essence, precise rules derived from past experience have narrow applicability, essentially limited to very similar projects and circumstances (Gavetti and Levinthal, 2000; Fleming and Sorenson, 2004).

As a result of these obstacles, the codification of practice is forced to proceed on its own, via the development of ever more detailed repertories of events with associated action-to-outcome rules. This approach is deemed a legitimate source of prescriptions in many areas of practice (Bunge, 1967). In particular, new technology development, including in areas such as aviation and pharmaceuticals, has often given more credence to know-how acquired via trial and error than to prescriptions derived from scientific theories (Kline, 1987; Vincenti, 1990; Nightingale and Martin, 2004). Areas such as medicine and law also rely heavily on the critical interpretation, codification, discussion, classification, and tracing of past cases and remedies. The experience is preserved, diffused, updated and retrieved via a massive system of records and publications available to all those working in the respective area. Prescriptions for action (i.e., medical procedures or legal proceedings) learned from experience are taken for granted by the profession as the rules by which the profession is practiced. Because they trust the system that produces these prescriptions, practitioners rarely question their validity. While project management, through professional associations, has made inroads into creating a similar system of codification of practice, its scope and legitimacy have yet to achieve a level similar to other areas of practice (Schindler and Eppler, 2003; Williams, 2004).

The third source of prescriptions consists of *empirical generalizations* with little or no theoretical foundation. For example, statistical approaches for analyzing best practices aim to determine key success factors and relate them to project performance without resorting to explanatory mechanisms (see for instance Cooper, 1979; Henard and Szymanski, 2001). Likewise, such analyses may identify patterns of evolution in key variables such as cost (Boehm and Pappacio, 1988; Casten, 1995; Flyvbjerg et al., 2002; Stefánsson, 2002), and correlate them to other characteristics such as project capacity. Recently, data mining has been proposed as an approach for defining the characteristics and the feasibility of projects (Moyle, Bohanec and Osrowski, 2003). Attempts are also made to incorporate the detected empirical patterns in simulation models and computer assisted decision support tools used for resource allocation and risk management in projects. For example, pharmaceutical firms use statistical modeling based on data collected from past projects to indentify decision criteria for project selection or attrition in the early stages of drug development (see for example, Rogers, Gupta and Maranas, 2002; Sengoku, Yoda and Seki, 2011; Solo and Paich, 2004).

A particularity of this pillar is a preference for measurable, meaning externally oriented yet quite abstract variables. The atheoretical analysis of these variables is purported to bring in the 'voice of necessity', advocated by top managers, financial consultants, economists, and government representatives. The resulting patterns of necessary relations between key elements of a project (costs, prices, contract forms etc.) are believed to hold true regardless of context. The purported universality of such relationships enables practitioners to abstract from the details of the project and quickly zero-in on some essential conclusions in a large variety of contexts. Yet, these characteristics also pull this pillar apart from the other two. First, the universality of these relationships comes at the expense of the ability to go beyond wide-ranging but less precise indications and provide concrete practical guidance in specific project situations. Second, although the abstract variables this voice favors are quite loosely coupled with many concrete aspects of projects, they are still oriented towards correspondence with the external reality in which the project is executed. This may make difficult their translation into internally oriented, decision variables, such as Bayesian probability and, especially, utility, which are the material used in logically coherent decision models.

Figure 15.1a positions the three pillars that inform project management prescriptions in a two-dimensional space created by the internal versus external orientation of prescription elaboration procedures, and, respectively, the concrete versus abstract material used in these procedures. The figure also describes the forces that pull each of these pillars apart from the other two, and hence, create obstacles towards their combination in an integrated knowledge production and prescription elaboration process. As a consequence of these forces and of the distinct voices that are behind each of them, activities related to each pillar are likely to follow separate paths, with minimal synergies between them. Integrating these activities and their results is likely to be left to the unsystematic efforts of individual managers. In order to prevent this eventuality from slowing down and even reversing the trend towards collaborative development involving project management researchers outlined above, we propose below an alternate possible model for the elaboration of project prescriptions, which was inspired by the metaphor of a 'triple helix'.

a) The three pillars (voices) and the forces that pull each one of them apart:

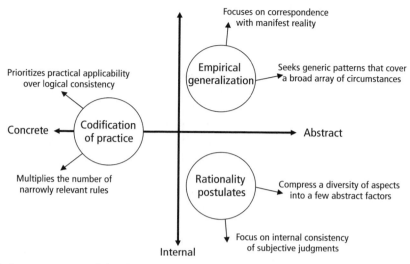

b) Triple helix components and their knowledge-production stimulating dialogue:

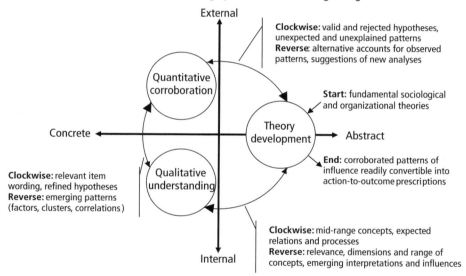

Figure 15.1. Comparison of the Three Pillars of Project Management Prescriptions with the Triple Helix Approach Proposed in this Chapter

Outline of the Triple Helix Approach

Our goal in developing this approach is not to propose a new scientific method but to suggest a process for elaborating project management prescriptions that would give a much stronger voice to researchers, unleash synergies between their contributions and those of practitioners, and increase the pace of knowledge and prescription production. The metaphor of the triple helix, one of the forms initially proposed for the spatial structure of the DNA molecule, alludes to the spiral of dialectic evolution. While involving an eternal return to similar issues, in time, internal contradictions bring the evolution to a new level of development or understanding. The three spirals of the helix evoke the three pillars discussed above, modified as described below, which now become intertwined strands. Etzkowitz and Leydesdorff (2000) have used the same triple helix metaphor to describe how three 'voices', namely industry, government and universities, join forces to produce a virtuous dynamics in the domain of innovation. Figure 15.1b depicts the triple helix approach, using the same system of coordinates as that used in Figure 15.1a.

The first difference is that the three pillars are replaced by three strands, namely theory development, qualitative understanding and quantitative corroboration. As Figure 15.1b illustrates, each strand is placed about half-way between two of the pillars discussed previously, which, in our view, helps unleash synergies rather than pull the contributing strands apart. Moreover, instead of centrifugal forces, the figure suggests a systematic dialogue between these strands, consisting of both mutual enrichment and contradictions. In our view, this dialogue is responsible for the potentially more dynamic nature of the triple helix approach, which enables the rapid exploration, mapping and elaboration of tentative prescriptions for key issues. This is more useful for a young and still rapidly developing area of practice such as project management than a process oriented towards the optimization and definitive validation of prescriptions.

The pivotal strand in the triple helix approach is *theory development*. Its importance stems from the fact that, in our view, theory is the main source for the subsequent elaboration of project management prescriptions. Project management researchers are mainly in charge of this strand, which means that they also play a central role in the triple helix process. Theory development is about half way between the pillars of rationality postulates and empirical generalization, because it attempts to maintain logical consistency as much as possible, while being oriented towards describing and accounting for the patterns of the external world. While operating primarily with abstract concepts inspired by fundamental organizational and sociological theories, the theory development brings these concepts closer to a mid-range level of abstraction (Glaser and Strauss, 1967), enabling them to capture the specifics of projects and project-based organizations, as well as actors' situated understanding of these contexts. Resulting theories would also include explicit process models (Langley, 1999) that would explain the ways in which project elements interact, and would account for the generic patterns of relations between these elements. These theoretical elements would provide the basis for the empirical strands of the triple helix, discussed below.

The second strand of the triple helix is *qualitative understanding*, which aims to make theories become increasingly relevant for practice, by using qualitative empirical research, such as case studies, to connect theoretical concepts and mechanisms with the issues, situations and actions occurring in projects, as practitioners perceive them. This strand relies on semi-grounded methods (Corbin and Strauss, 1990) applied to data resulting from semi-structured interviews, field observations, and documentary analysis. As can be seen from Figure 15.1b, in the abstract-concrete and internal-external space, this strand is situated about half-way between the locations of the postulates of rationality and the codification of practice. This is so, because the proposed methods remain focused on the internal world of project participants, namely their situated goals, perceptions and reasoning, but they are also oriented towards aspects of the external world, by capturing the actors' interpretation of contexts and actions. Also, while these methods capture practices and provide evidence of their effectiveness, the aim of qualitative understanding is not the mechanistic codification of practice that is seen in medicine and law. Instead, as will be detailed below, the elaboration of practical prescriptions relies on theory and the 'second order' interpretation of observable practices it enables. The semi-grounded method advances theory via detailed analysis, classification and comparison of instances of theoretically relevant phenomena. This helps dimensionalize concepts and encourages a more sophisticated interpretation of practices. In addition, tracing processes inside each case would suggest new ways to account for the effects of practices, while comparisons across several cases would help identify patterns that could be used for preliminary validation of theoretical expectations (Miles and Huberman, 1994).

Finally, the third strand, *quantitative corroboration*, relies primarily on psychometric approaches in order to provide additional validation of theoretical expectations. As illustrated in Figure 15.1b, this strand is positioned half way between the pillars of practice codification and empirical generalization. In the approach we propose, the items included in the psychometric instruments are connected to theoretical constructs, but are also informed by the richer and more practically relevant understanding of the project reality provided by the qualitative understanding strand. Moreover, while most data analysis focuses on corroborating hypotheses resulting from the theoretical models, exploratory analyses are also performed. Hence this method can validate or uncover quite general patterns in the external reality, but these patterns will remain close to the concrete practices and concerns that are relevant for project managers. Consequently, results could easily be transformed into relevant practical prescriptions, while empirical generalizations based on econometric indicators provide only coarser guidance. The latter could still be used, in a theory-informed manner, to provide further corroboration that would allay concerns regarding the possibility of subjective bias, but would be less direct and less practically relevant.

The most common ordering of activities and path of influence between the three strands follows a clockwise direction in Figure 15.1b (indicated by larger arrowheads). In this sequence, each strand provides an input to the subsequent activity, and one of its outcomes, perhaps the most salient, at the end of the cycle is the corroboration or refutation of hypotheses. In light of this sequence, the triple helix approach has elements in common with the standard models of scientific hypothesis development and testing (see for example Popper, 1963), as well as comparable safeguards regarding the validity of conclusions. The addition of a semi-grounded qualitative strand ensures that inductive theorizing complements deduction from fundamental theories. Besides, the combination of qualitative methods, above all the comparison of influences across cases, and quantitative methods, in particular, pattern identification from psychometric data, as well as, possibly, from panel data, amounts to a kind of triangulation, in which the use of distinct methods and independent observations provides additional validation of findings.

However, as mentioned above, validity is not the central concern of this approach. Tentative validation would suffice initially, provided that the method meets two additional goals. The first goal is the ability to support a self-sustaining process of research and theory development that could accelerate knowledge production in the young project management field. The second goal is to produce a theoretical output that is not only practically relevant but also easy to convert into action-to-outcome prescriptions. Achieving these goals creates different requirements for the triple helix process, often contrary to those stemming from knowledge validation concerns. In particular, these goals call for a stronger dialogue between the three strands, consisting not only of direct, feed forward transfers (clockwise oriented in Figure 15.1b) but also of strong reverse transfers of feedbacks (represented by the smaller counterclockwise arrowheads in Figure 15.1b).

When seeking endogenous acceleration, unexpected or unaccounted for empirical patterns, invalidated hypotheses, or contradictory findings from triangulation are not necessarily undesirable. Disappointing or unexpected results would readily trigger a new cycle in the spiral of knowledge production, starting with the elaboration of alternative theoretical accounts. Seemingly contradictory findings about the same phenomenon might provide further insights regarding its multidimensional and intricate nature. More generally, from this perspective, the aim of combining qualitative and quantitative methods is not to provide additional validation but to secure a more 'in-depth understanding of the phenomenon in question' (Denzin, 2012: 83). For example, qualitative research would enrich the theory by suggesting new interpretations and concepts, by identifying the various dimensions of a concept, by gauging the range, namely the extremes and the gradations of a variable, and by uncovering new influence paths. These could be fed back to the theory development strand but also fed forward to the development of quantitative instruments and statistical hypothesis tests. In turn, the exploration of psychometric data could suggest a different dimensionality, based on factor analyses, or different influences based on correlative analyses, and trigger new rounds of inductive qualitative analyses.

From the perspective of ensuring practically relevant and readily applicable conclusions it is less important to have totally independent methods and observations but more important to morph (Denzin and Lincoln, 2000: 6) the results of one strand into premises for the next one. This way, a theory that is logically coherent, but is also externally oriented and has a mid-range level of abstraction can be translated into a series of issues to be investigated by the qualitative understanding strand. The rich, practically relevant results of the latter can then provide language and hypotheses for the research instruments and analyses of the quantitative strand. If possible, the concepts and survey items used in the psychometric instrument would also refer to concrete practices used in projects, such as organizational and contractual forms, and include relevant measures of project success. The corroborated results of sophisticated statistical analyses could then be used to identify the most effective practices, and recommend them for practical application in clearly defined contextual conditions and with explicit accounts of their influence.

We argue that, if an adequate balance is found between stimulating the pace of knowledge production and validating results, and between scientific rigor and practical relevance, applying triple helix approach is likely to result in an iterative process with three closely intertwined and mutually reinforcing strands. The process is likely to alternate between periods of convergence, fruitful in terms of prescription output, and periods of divergence, which produce more doubts than confidence. It is important to note that the balance is difficult to find, because, like in the case of the three pillars, there are divergent forces. For example, the inductive, or grounded theorizing, as opposed to deductive, fundamental theory-informed research, as well as qualitative, as opposed to quantitative methods, draw upon different epistemic traditions which often argued against combining them, on grounds that their assumptions, objectives, criteria and methods of inquiry are intentionally different (Onwuegbuzie & Johnson, 2006: 49; Maxwell, 1992). Only recently, the mixed methods literature has started to address these 'paradigm wars' and offer solutions for reducing their consequences (Burke Johnson et al., 2007; Bazely and Kemp, 2012; Ellignson, 2009). Likewise, many authors have argued that there is a fundamental incompatibility between the aims and methods of science and those of practice, because they operate with objects having very different levels of complexity (Nightingale 1998), and because practical applications involve the human will, not just describing natural phenomena, and it is impossible to tell what ought to be by knowing what is (Polanyi, 1966).

In sum, we propose the triple helix model as a possible approach for enhancing the collaboration between academic researchers and practitioners in elaborating project management prescriptions. We believe that this approach has the potential to increase the pace with which high quality prescriptions are elaborated for a broad variety of issues. In the following section we reflect on a recent research project that applied many of the triple helix elements identified above. Our intention is not to showcase a project or to suggest how the approach should be applied, but to describe the experience of this kind of research, with all its doubts and setbacks. In doing this, we followed in the steps of other researchers, such as Smith (2002), who proposed similar personal accounts of their research journey in the hope of inspiring and reassuring other researchers.

Reflections from our Recent Research on Complex Projects

We have considered how a recent research project on the response capacity of complex project organizations (Floricel, Piperca and Banik, 2011), could be useful in illustrating how the triple helix model of theory development described above could be implemented. The study was based on the premise that the manner in which project management organizations respond (i.e., the response capacity) to unexpected events conditions the performance of the project in terms of several key measures such as completion time, the quality of the completed project structure, and cost overruns. This case research, together with its pre-history and post-history, illustrates well the triple helix approach, in particular the endogenous development of theory, and some practical challenges that can be encountered while integrating the three strands of the helix.

The research on the response capacity originates in a theoretical issue that the first author confronted during his work on his dissertation in the late 1990s and his participation in the International Research Programme on the Management of Engineering and Construction (IMEC, see Miller and Lessard, 2001). The apparent paradox observed in this research was that projects relying on prescriptions based on rational postulates, in particular those using BOT-type schemes for risk allocation between participants, had, for the most part, poor performance. One reason for this is that their contractual arrangements were rigid and precluded participants from reacting to unexpected events. Since complex projects were bound to encounter unexpected events, it was important to instill in their organizational structure a trait called governability (see Floricel and Miller, 2001), consisting of four distinct properties. Based on the dimensions of governability, the research was able to characterize projects in terms of three organizational archetypes, with some archetypes being more governable than others. Although the research was based on 60 case studies which enabled a number of qualitative comparisons, there was no quantitative analysis that would corroborate the emerging hypotheses.

In terms of the triple helix, the Floricel and Miller (2001) paper remained squarely within a single theoretical paradigm, inspired by the rationality postulates. However, by 2003, a series of readings about inter-organizational networks and ideas such as loose coupling, prompted the first author to return to the issue of governability and analyze its properties from the point of view of organization theory. The properties were reduced from four to three and labeled: cohesion, flexibility and resourcefulness. In order to become closer to concrete elements actionable by managers, each property was analyzed into three dimensions each refined by a review of the literature and a re-analysis of the dissertation cases. Results were presented at a conference (Floricel and Miller, 2003). Readers of the paper found that it contained too many concepts, which would hamper efforts to empirically trace the influence of each dimension and sub-dimension to clearly identify the drivers of project performance.

After some time, the first author initiated a research project, which caught the attention of a professional association, the Project Management Institute (PMI), and of a government research funding agency, the Social Sciences and Humanities Research Council of Canada (SSHRC), both of which supported the study. This research project is the main focus of the analysis presented here. The team that participated in the study was mainly composed of the three authors of this chapter. Therefore, in what follows, the team will often be referred as 'we'.

In the conceptual framework of the research, we replaced the term governability by the term *response capacity*, to avoid confusion with the term governance, but also to connect with the dynamic capabilities theory (Teece et al., 1997), which was becoming the dominant account of organizational dynamism. Response capacity was defined in terms of same three properties, but, as a result of an additional theorizing effort, the number of dimensions for each property was reduced to two. More notably, we added two other sets of variables and two kinds of processes to the model. In particular, because, from our prior research, response capacity properties appeared closely tied to the intended organizations and contractual structure of the project we wanted to understand how the organizational response capacity properties emerge from planning activities. To this effect, we analyzed the three archetypes described above and reviewed the project management literature to identify four dimensions of planning activities, which were eventually named knowledge production, participation, argument and risk allocation. Inspired initially by the structuration theory of Giddens (1984), we assumed that these activities sow the seeds of the mature organizational structure of the project, but do so in ways that are not necessarily intended by planners. We were also interested in the processes by which this emergent structure will react to unexpected events as well as in the specific aspects of project performance that this reaction will impact. Hence, we theorized the reaction processes and proposed four dimensions of project performance. The resulting theoretical framework (see Figure 15.2), with three sets of variables and two connecting processes as well as a series of hypotheses about the influences between the variables was later presented in a conference paper (Floricel and Piperca, 2009). In terms of the triple helix, this paper made the first steps toward bringing more fundamental theories as an input in the theory development strand, and also attempted to make the theoretical model even more relevant to project management practice.

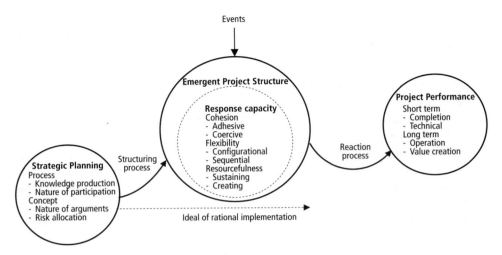

Figure 15.2. The Theoretical Framework of the Research Project on the Response Capacity of Complex Projects. Adapted from Floricel, Piperca and Banik (2011)

While preparing for the empirical research, it became apparent that structuration theory, although useful, provided an incomplete view of emergent structuring processes as they relate to project organizations. Therefore, we sought additional theoretical inputs, which led us to a review of two other theories, namely actor-network theory (Callon, 1986) and communication systems theory (Luhmann, 1995). We selected theories that assimilate organizations to, broadly speaking, 'flat' networks of actors, in order to highlight the emergent properties of organizations, and in reaction to the rational-functionalist and bureaucratic views with which practitioners seemed to approach the subject. Each theory also provided a different perspective of how project organizations evolve. Through the lens of actor-network theory the emphasis is on actors, who actively maintain and rebuild relatively fragile organizational systems. In contrast, structuration theory gives an equal weight to actors and social entities, in a process of recurrent yet quite resilient structural reproduction. Finally, communication systems theory prioritizes the social system, which by way of a top down, ecological selection processes shapes the couplings between actors.

The additional theoretical inputs enabled us to reconceptualize the nature of the organizational emergent structure and to hypothesize new mechanisms for the two structuring processes depicted in Figure 15.2. In order to integrate the three fundamental theories, which belong to different sociological paradigms, we relied on the mechanismic approach (Hedström and Swedberg, 1996; Davis and Marquis, 2005). Basically, we deemed the central processes proposed by each theory to represent alternative social mechanisms, i.e. bits of processes that are all potentially present but can be activated in certain conditions and not activated in others. This sensitized us to the way planning activities and their outputs create conditions for subsequent organizational structuring, and enabled us to anticipate the range of our theoretical variables. To summarize, the initial set of activities consisted of theory development that paid attention to actions and organizations rather than decisions while deriving insights from sociological theories in order to better understand the observed processes. The main effect of this activity was to sensitize us to many new relevant aspects in data collection and analysis.

This enabled us to work in parallel, during the summer of 2008, to develop the qualitative interview instrument. This activity was one of the two stages that would best fall under the metaphor of 'morphing'. Namely, while we were careful to use terms as neutral as possible, the interview instrument ensured that the respondents would address project practices and other aspects related to the key variables and processes in the theoretical framework. In addition, projects were selected in order to ensure, in light of the preliminary information that we gathered about them, a variance with respect key variables, such as the nature of knowledge production and the breadth of participation in planning. Qualitative data collection started in the fall of 2008. By the fall of 2009, we interviewed key participants in 17 projects, for a total of 46 interviews. The projects were from three different types of industries, eight in Europe and the rest in North America. The first step in the data analysis, which started as soon as data were collected, was to write a narrative report for each case. The first draft of the report was prepared by doctoral or master's students, based on a predefined template that followed the main lines of the theoretical framework. In addition to the interview transcripts, case writers used secondary data provided by the interviewees or obtained from other sources. The first author read these drafts and helped produce an improved version, which was then sent to interviewees requesting their feedback.

The second author joined the team for the subsequent analysis steps, to provide a fresh 'external' perspective. Together we analyzed the interviews and the case narratives using a semi-grounded theorizing approach (Corbin & Strauss, 1990). The initial coding scheme was closely related to the constructs in our prior theoretical framework, but at the same time, the analysis was quite flexible, as we wanted to understand how managers make sense and address various issues related to project planning and the emerging organization. Another concern was gauging even better the dimensions and the range of variables, which we achieved by identifying instances ('exemplars' in the grounded theorizing terminology) of variables and of gradations along each variable. For example, a planning committee composed of 10 partners with equal voting rights would be at the *pluralist* extreme of the participation variable, while a planning process in which the decision remained entirely in the hands of a single manager (with participants from other organizations working as consultants), would be at the *dominated* extreme of the same variable. The diversity of projects used for case studies was very helpful in this respect. The outcome was a qualitative semantic ladder of sorts, which could then be used to evaluate cases and compare across them in the more holistic round of the qualitative understanding strand. This holistic stage was an intermediary step in the process of gradual morphing towards quantitative corroboration. Hence, each case was evaluated with respect to each variable in a quasi-quantitative manner, using qualifiers such as 'clearly pluralist' and 'most likely pluralist'. To ensure consistency across evaluations, each case was discussed in weekly meetings of the three authors, usually in batches of three cases. Each researcher had the 'lead' on one case, by re-reading it more carefully and preparing preliminary ratings using a table that included all variables and space for a summary of evidence for the selected rating. Each project table was checked by at least one other researcher and the first author re-checked all ratings for consistency.

The qualitative research produced significant feedback towards the theory development strand. First, it reassured us with respect to the practical relevance of the theoretical framework, because all practitioners we interviewed seemed very keen to discuss the issues that we proposed. It also enabled us to consolidate our understanding of the nature and range of variables, via comparisons among cases discussed in the same meeting and with cases and situations encountered in previous meetings. After each meeting, researchers prepared and circulated theoretical memos outlining the emerging theoretical insights. One of the key insights resulting from this stage of qualitative research was the concept of influence trajectory, namely a sequence of influences beginning with a value on a planning variable, which, in turn, impacts the value of response capacity variable and ultimately affects the rating of a variable capturing project performance. Hence, an additional analysis, at the frontier of qualitative and quantitative, was devoted to identifying such influence trajectories, by relying explicitly on comparisons across all 17 cases (Eisenhardt, 1989; Miles and Huberman, 1994). Namely, ratings in the tables completed previously were cross tabulated for all projects to identify relations between project planning, response capacity, and respectively, performance variables. This offered a first corroboration to theory-derived hypotheses and allowed us to formulate more refined versions that could be tested in the quantitative phase of the research. These results were presented in their turn at a research conference (Floricel, Banik and Piperca, 2010) in order to obtain feedback from academics.

The quantitative stage began in the summer of 2010 with the development of the psychometric-type survey, which represented another stage of morphing theory to qualitative understanding and to quantitative corroboration. Survey items were intended to capture theoretical constructs directly; a few were inspired by the theory, but most were based on the findings of the qualitative stage and often used wording found in interviews. Compared to the measures that would have been available to us had we limited ourselves to econometric-type indicators, these psychometric scales more directly and reliably captured the constructs of interest. They stemmed from in-depth discussions during the semi-structured interviews around these concepts, and were selected as a result of the theory-informed, yet semi-grounded sensemaking and dimensionalization activities during qualitative analyses. But the wording also ensured that these items were relevant and understandable for project managers, and referred to the way participants constructed the context and activities of a project. In addition, their use would yield readily actionable results, because quantitative corroboration aimed to relate, in a theory-informed way, project practices and performance indicators. Detected relations could be easily translated into practical prescriptions.

The survey was pretested with practitioners in August 2010, and administered via the Survey Monkey website in the fall of 2010 resulting in 80 responses from a variety of industries (except pharmaceutical, which we eliminated because qualitative research showed that projects in this industry have a different nature from the others). All projects and respondents were different from those involved in the qualitative stage. We began the analysis stage by evaluating the reliability of scales, using Cronbach's Alpha and in some cases principal component analyses. In certain cases, a good reliability was obtained only by eliminating certain items from the scales. This provides an example of tension between qualitative understanding and quantitative corroboration, in that sometimes what is captured in qualitative research cannot necessarily be morphed into reliable quantitative measures. Namely, some wording we selected in the qualitative stage, and used in items, corresponded to the middle of the range of certain variables. Yet, unlike items that captured the extremes, these items did not contribute to increase the internal reliability of scales and did not load well on principal components. While their wording helped us understand and map the universe of phenomena related to a given variable, we eliminated most corresponding items from quantitative analyses. However, we were left wondering whether the respective items could have been used in different kinds of analyses such as capturing nonlinear effects. We could not check this, given the relatively low number of answers we obtained, in spite of a sustained effort. This may suggest another kind of practical incompatibility of the triple helix approach: while managers were keen to participate in qualitative interviews, they were not as eager to answer a survey.

In spite of such difficulties, the quantitative corroboration stage, which relied on 'measurements' that were researcher-independent (a stage missing in the IMEC program, part of the prehistory discussed above), provided important results, and led to important theoretical developments. It made us realize that some of our hypotheses were not resulting from a thorough understanding of organizational processes, as much as from what may be best described as management fads. These include overly pluralistic planning and a tendency to share risk between participants, as well as non confrontational contract administration during project execution. In fact, as we first noted during the analysis of qualitative data, what may be regarded as some of the 'worst' management practices (i.e., according to contemporary management thinking) such as concentrating decisional of power, allocating risk to participants and bureaucratic administration (i.e., managing according to literal wording of a contract) were actually more often associated with high project performance. Centralized planning, regarded in modern management circles as anti-participative or anti-democratic, gave rise to an influence trajectory that seemed to increase overall performance. But even most importantly, we realized that the impact of these practices, often associated to the rationality postulates, do not work because of the reasons supposed by the respective pillar. For example, the impact of the centralized control in planning on performance was mostly indirect. Centralized planning helped establish a project organization with high sequential flexibility, which enabled very agile responses to unexpected events by quickly referring problems to the highest levels in the organization.

The low number of quantitatively corroborated trajectories that spanned planning, response capacity and performance (which may be in part due to the low number of cases which weakened the statistical power of our results) led us to reconsider the idea that most aspects of performance result from mediated trajectories. In fact, the overall pattern of statistical results led us to the conclusion that project performance is influenced by planning directly, and indirectly, via its impact on the some response capacity properties, as well as, in an autonomous manner, by other, purely emergent response capacity properties. In order to deepen our understanding of these differences, we performed additional principal component analyses of response capacity properties and found that they can be further grouped in a 'mechanistic' class and an 'organic' class. Properties composing the mechanistic class are more easily amenable to deliberate cultivation during planning, while properties of the organic class appear more likely to emerge in less controllable manner, with little impact from planning. This is the key findings of the focal research project. All theoretical, qualitative and quantitative results of this project were published in a research monograph (Floricel, Piperca and Banik, 2011).

But subsequently, the tensions between theoretical expectations and feedback from qualitative research and especially quantitative corroboration, as well as some divergent findings between the last two strands, triggered a new round of theoretical development, whereby two themes that were secondary in the research that focused on the response capacity emerged as central and likely to generate a new spiral of the triple helix. First, we realized that, while our qualitative and quantitative research seemed to focus on variables rather than processes, a significant portion of our face-to-face discussions and email exchanges addressed change episodes, occurring throughout the project life cycle, as early as the planning stage and as late as project exploitation. We identified commonalities between these episodes, which helped the third author realize that change in project organizations takes place in relatively short but dramatic bursts, which punctuate longer periods of apparent stability. As a result, the third author refocused his ongoing dissertation work on the study of 'structuring episodes', namely the process of transition from one apparently stable project structure to another. A second theoretical development stemmed from the results of the quantitative corroboration. The fact that planning did not appear linked to organizational structures in the ways we expected, prompted us to reconsider the nature of planning activities and what determines their lasting impact on project organizations.

A significant advance in theoretical development with respect to both these emerging themes was enabled by a fortuitous encounter with the work of nineteenth century German philosopher Schopenhauer (1966). As a result, the first author realized that a parsimonious framework inspired by the concepts of will and representation could capture the relevant aspects of planning and organizational processes. Also, this framework seemed to enable us to integrate more tightly the three fundamental sociological theories that previously supported our theorizing, as some reviewers argued that the three theories were based on incompatible assumptions, and hence were nearly impossible to integrate.

The emerging theoretical insights were developed in papers presented at three conferences in the summer of 2012. The papers dealt, respectively, with the planning as a processes of combining will and representation (Floricel, Banik and Piperca, 2012), with the influence of planning on structuring (Floricel, Piperca and Banik, 2012), and with the processes that occur in structuring episodes (Piperca and Floricel, 2012). While the new basic framework allowed us to integrate more tightly various theoretical strands, the emergence of two new themes opened new horizons for empirical research. Initially, this involved a return to qualitative data gathered previously, with a focus on the practices managers used to make sense and deal with the need for change. This involved a new round of analysis, category identification, instance classification and identification of patterns in the relevant processes. In the summer of 2012 we developed a new questionnaire for semi-structured interviews and endeavored to perform new case studies of complex projects, in order to deepen our qualitative understand the new themes. One case study has been performed at the time of this writing, and this may be regarded as the latest wrapping of the strands in the triple helix model.

The entire research process is summarized in Table 15.1, which presents the various research activities and their context, their connections to the three helix strands, the impact on the development of theory, and the dissemination of ideas.

Table 15.1. The Process of Research Included in the Focal Project, its Prehistory and Subsequent Developments

Period	Context	Helix strands	Stage of idea development	Dissemination
Late 1990s-2001	First author's work on his doctoral dissertation and participation in the IMEC research program.	Theory development – mainly decision theory; one refinement: Luhmann (1993) phenomenological analysis of risk. Qualitative understanding; 60 case studies.	Governability – a property of the project structure to react to unexpected events; with four elements: cohesion, flexibility, reserves, and generativity.	Doctoral dissertation Journal publication Conference papers
2001-2003	First author's refinements of his previous ideas.	Theory development: organization theory; interorganizational networks. Qualitative understanding; the 60 case studies reanalyzed.	The 4 elements reduced to 3: cohesion, flexibility, resourcefulness, each with 3 dimensions and subdimensions.	Conference paper
2007-2009	Two research grants. The third author joins the team.	Theory development: dynamic capabilities and structuration theory added. Later, used insights from structuration theory, actor-network theory, and communication systems theory to explain the processes.	Governability renamed response capacity; the same 3 elements but each with only two dimension and no other subdimensions. Two sets of variables added (planning and performance, each with 4 dimensions) and two kinds of processes (structuring and reaction).	Conference paper
2008-2010	Same research grants. The second author joins the team. Third author's dissertation.	Qualitative understanding: semi-grounded approach; triangulation in data collection and analysis; comparison across cases; case narratives; 17 case studies.	Refine the theoretical model – ex. identified extremes and 4 gradations along each variable; elaborate or refine hypotheses to be tested in the quantitative stage. Structuring processes seem more important than initially considered.	Conference paper Journal publication

2010-2011	Same research grants. Third author's dissertation.	Quantitative corroboration: psychometric-type survey; 80 participants.	Support for hypotheses and refinenement of theoretical model: influence trajectories revised; dimensions regrouped; two themes emerged as important: planning and structuring episodes.	Conference paper Book chapter Research monograph
2011-2012	Same research grants. Third author's dissertation.	Theory development: will and representation. Qualitative understanding: 17 cases reanalyzed.	The two processes analyzed in more detail: planning process, its influence on structuring, and structuring episodes.	3 conference papers
2012-?		Qualitative stage – new case studies to be done (1 so far).	The processes to be further analyzed.	

Discussion and Conclusions

The purpose of research in project management can be defined as developing an account, or, more generally, a representation of project evolution in its social and material context. The practical goal of such research is to suggest actions that can increase the chances of superior project performance. Such practical goals are more easily attainable if the various aspects of the emerging representation are integrated or, at least, converge towards integration. However, our discussion of the three traditional pillars and of the three strands of the triple helix suggests that different paradigms are likely to provide polyphonic or largely incompatible perspectives. Moreover, by forcing integration, researchers can forego the generative benefits that stem from the tensions between various aspects of the representation.

The story of our research, with its prehistory and current developments, suggests a dynamics consisting of periods of convergence alternating with periods of divergence. Periods of convergence are the result of our deliberate effort to bring together various perspectives, based on an explicit recognition of the fact that many of the messy problems in project management that are not neatly addressed by a single theory or methodological approach. In particular we cultivated a process of morphing theory into qualitative understanding and into quantitative corroboration. Periods of divergence usually stem from newly emerging tensions between these three strands and even inside the strands themselves. Like in a hermeneutic cycle, attempts to resolve 'local' tension advance the deciphering of the puzzling phenomena on many other fronts. The divergent thrust is also stimulated by encounters with new fundamental theories and by critical observations from the readers of the research results. While such divergence blurs the neat picture of project processes and moves away the perspective of arriving at practical prescriptions, it also results eventually in significant advances in understanding.

The sum of our experience suggests that different research methods and paradigms can be intertwined in a triple helix, and reinforces our conviction that every loop of the spiral also leads to a significant advance in the understanding and mastery of relevant processes. The key to success seems to reside, first, in an ability to embrace multiple methods and multiple theoretical paradigms, and relish in their unavoidable polyphony. This ability involves using triangulation not as a process aiming for the ultimate 'fixing' of a truth, but as a means for creating and renewing the tensions that reenergize knowledge production. The second condition for success seems to be the ability to carefully morph an evolving theory into a set of issues for qualitative understanding, then into a set of tools and analyses for quantitative corroboration, and finally, into a set of tentatively validated practical prescriptions. As the narrative presented in this chapter suggest, the seemingly contradictory aims of renewing tensions and morphing as smoothly as possible can be achieved naturally in the same research project.

Because our research has not yet resulted in explicit practical procedures or recommendations, a question may remain regarding how the triple helix model produces practical prescriptions. The answer seems to reside both in the empirical orientation of the research and in the involvement of practitioners and their professional associations at all stages of research, from validating research programs, to participating in qualitative interviews and validating the results of case studies, to pretesting quantitative instruments and providing feedback on the results of statistical analyses. In these conditions, the morphing process is likely to ensure that research results are very close to being in an action-to-outcome form, which is easily convertible into practical prescriptions.

References

Alexander, C. (1964). *Notes on the Synthesis of Form.* Boston, MA: Harvard University Press.

Allais, M. (1953). Le Comportement de l'homme rationnel devant le risque: Critique des postulats et axiomes de l'école américaine. *Econometrica*, 21: 503-456.

Aubry, M., Hobbs, B. and Thuillier, D. (2007). A new framework for understanding organisational project management through the PMO. *International Journal of Project Management*, 25(4): 328-336.

Bakhtin, M.M. (1984). *Problems of Dostoevsky's Poetics.* Minneapolis: University of Minnesota Press.

Bazeley, P. & Kemp, L. (2012). Mosaics, triangles and DNA: metaphors for integrated analysis in mixed methods research. *Journal of Mixed Methods Research, 6(1), 55-72.*

Bernoulli, D. (1738). 'Specimen Theoriae Novae de Mensura Sortis' (Exposition of a New Theory on the Measurement of Risk) original in: Commentarii Academiae Scientiarum Petropolitanae, 5: 175-192; translated by L. Sommer, Econometrica, 1954, 22: 23-36.

Bierman, H. & Smidt, S. (1960). *The Capital Budgeting Decision.* New York: Macmillan.

Boehm, B.W. 1984. Software engineering economics, *IEEE Transactions on Software Engineering,* SE-10(1): 4-21.

Boehm, B.W. & Papaccio, P.N. (1988). Understanding and controlling software costs. *IEEE Transactions on Software Engineering,* 14(10): 1462-1477.

Brown, J.S. & Duguid, P. (1991). Organizational learning and communities-of-practice: Toward a unified view of working, learning, and innovation. *Organization Science,* 2(1), 40-57.

Brown, S.L. & Eisenhardt, K.M. (1995). Product development: Past research, present findings, and future directions. *Academy of Management Review,* 20, 343-378.

Bunge, M. (1967). Technology as applied science. *Technology and Culture,* 7(3), 329-347.

Bunge, M. (1988). Two faces and three masks of probability. In *Probability in the sciences,* E. Agazzi (ed.), pp. 27-49. Drodrecht, Holland: Kluwer.

Burke Johnson, R., Onwuegbuzie, A.J. & Turner, L. (2007). Towards a definition of mixed methods research. *Journal of Mixed Methods Research,* 1: 112-133.

Callon, M. (1986). Some elements of a sociology of translation: domestication of the scallops and the fishermen of St Brieuc Bay. In J. Law (ed.), *Power, Action and Belief: A New Sociology of Knowledge?* pp. 196-223. London, Routledge.

Casten, T.R. (1995). Electricity generation: Smaller is better. *Electricity Journal,* 8(10): 65-73.

Chapman, C.B. & Ward, S.C. 1994. The Efficient Allocation of Risk in Contracts. *Omega, International Journal of Management Science,* 22: 537-52.

Cohen, J. (2010). *Integrated Project Delivery: Case Studies.* AIA National, AIA California Council, AGC California and McGraw-Hill.

Cooper, R.G. (1979). Identifying industrial new product success: Project NewProd. *Industrial Marketing Management,* 8(2): 124-35.

Corbin, J. & Strauss, A. (1990). Grounded theory research: procedures, canons, and evaluative criteria. *Qualitative Sociology,* 13(1): 3-21.

Davis, G.F. and Marquis, C. (2005). Prospects for Organization Theory in the Early Twenty-First Century: Institutional Fields and Mechanisms. *Organization Science,* 16(4): 332-43.

Denzin, N.K. (2012). Triangulation 2.0. *Journal of Mixed Methods Research,* 6(2) 80-88.

Denzin, N.K. & Lincoln, Y.S. (eds). (2000). *Handbook of qualitative research (2nd ed.)*. Thousand Oaks, CA: SAGE.

Diekmann, J., Featherman, D., Moody, R., Molenaar, K. & Rodriguez-Guy, M. (1996). Project cost risk analysis using influence diagrams. *Project Management Journal*, 27(4): 23-30.

Eisenhardt, K.M. (1989). Building Theories From Case Study Research. *Academy of Management Review*, 14(4): 532-50.

Ellingson, L. (2009). *Engaging Crystallization in Qualitative Research: An Introduction*. Sage Publications.

Emirbayer, M. & Mische, A. (1998). What is agency? *American Journal of Sociology*, 103(4), 962-1023.

Etzkowitz, H. & Leydesdorff, L. (2000). The dynamics of innovation: From National Systems and 'Mode 2' to a Triple Helix of university-industry-government relations. *Research Policy*, 29(2): 109-123.

Fleming, L. & Sorenson, O. (2004). Science as a map in technological search. *Strategic Management Journal*, 25, 909-25.

Floricel, S. & Miller, R. (2001). Strategizing for anticipated risks and turbulence in large-scale engineering projects. *International Journal of Project Management*, 19: 445-55.

Floricel, S. & Miller, R. (2003). The governability of inter-organizational networks in turbulent environments. Paper presented at the *Academy of Management Conference*, Seattle.

Floricel, S. & Piperca, S. (2009). A theory of the response capacity of complex projects. Paper presented at the *Academy of Management Conference*, Chicago.

Floricel, S., Banik, M. & Piperca, S. (2010). An Empirical Study of the Response Capacity of Complex Projects. *Academy of Management Conference*, Montréal.

Floricel, S., Banik, M. & Piperca, S. (2012). Project planning as will and representation. Paper presented at the *Special Workshop Strategy-as-Practice*, Université Paris-Dauphine.

Floricel, S., Piperca, S. & Banik, M. (2011). *Increasing Project Flexibility: The Response Capacity of Complex Projects*. Newton Square, PA: Project Management Institute.

Floricel, S., Piperca, S. & Banik, M. (2012). The structuring effect of planning on project organizations. Paper presented at the conference of the *European Group for Organization Science (EGOS)*, Helsinki.

Flyvbjerg, B., Holm, M.K.S. & Buhl, S.L. (2002). Underestimating Costs in Public Works Projects: Error or Lie? *Journal of the American Planning Association*, 68(3): 279-96.

Gann, D.M. & Salter, A.J. (2000). Innovation in project-based, service-enhanced firms: The construction of complex products and systems, *Research Policy*, 29(7-8): 955-72.

Garvey, P.R. & Lansdowne Z.F. (1998). Risk matrix: An approach for identifying, assessing, and ranking program risks. *Air Force Journal of Logistics*, 25:16-19.

Gavetti, G. & Levinthal, D. (2000). Looking forward and looking backward: Cognitive and experiential search. *Administrative Science Quarterly*, 45, 113-37.

Giddens, A. 1984. *The constitution of society. Outline of the Theory of Structuration.* Berkeley and Los Angeles: University of California Press.

Glaser, B. and Strauss, A. (1967). *The Discovery of Grounded Theory.* Chicago: Aldine.

Hedström, P. & Swedberg, R. 1996. Social Mechanisms. *Acta Sociologica*, 39(3): 281-308.

Henard, D.H. & Szymanski, D.M. (2001). Why Some New Products Are More Successful Than Others. *Journal of Marketing Research*, 38(3), 362-75.

Howard, R.A. (1988). Decision Analysis: Practice and Promise. *Management Science*, 34(6): 679-95.

Huchzermeier, A. & Loch, C.H. (2001). Project management under risk: Using the real options approach to evaluate flexibility in R&D. *Management Science*, 47(1): 85-101.

Kadane, J.B. & Winkler, R.L. (1988). Separating probability elicitation from utilities. *Journal of the American Statistical Association*, 83(402): 357-63.

Kiser, E. & Schneider, J. (1994). Bureaucracy and Efficiency: An Analysis of Taxation in Early Modern Prussia. *American Sociological Review*, 59(2): 187-204.

Kline, R. (1987). Science and engineering theory in the invention and development of the induction motor, 1880-1900. *Technology and Culture*, 28(2), 283-313.

Krishnan V. & Ulrich, K.T. (2001). Product Development Decisions: A Review of the Literature. *Management Science*, 47(1): 1-21.

Langford, D.J., Gosoroski, S.J. & Graves, G.M. (1990). Turnkey Contracts: The Pitfalls and the Benefits. *Power Engineering*, 94(January): 31-34.

Langley, A. (1999). Strategies for theorizing from process data. *Academy of Management Review*, 24(4), 691-710.

Luhmann, N. (1993). *Risk: A Sociological Theory.* New York: Aldine De Gruyter.

Luhmann, N. (1995). *Social Systems.* Stanford, Ca.: Stanford University Press.

March, J.G., & Shapira, Z. (1987). Managerial perspectives on risk and risk taking. *Management Science*, 33(11): 1404-1418.

Maxwell, J.A. (1992). Understanding and validity in qualitative research. *Harvard Educational Review*, 62: 279-99.

Medda, F. (2007). A game theory approach for the allocation of risks in transport public private partnerships. *International Journal of Project Management*, 25(3): 213-218.

Meyer, J.W., Boli, J. and Thomas, G.M. (1994). Ontology and Rationalization in the Western Cultural Account. In *Institutional Environments and Organizations*, W.R. Scott, J.W. Meyer and associates (Eds), pp. 9-27. Thousands Oaks, CA: Sage.

Miles, M.B. & Huberman, A.M. (1994). *Qualitative Data Analysis (2nd ed.).* Thousands Oaks, CA: Sage.

Milgrom, P. & Roberts, J. (1992). *Economics, Organization and Management.* Englewood Cliffs, N.J.: Prentice Hall.

Miller, R.E. and Lessard, D. with S. Floricel and the IMEC Research Team (2001). *The Strategic Management of Large Engineering Projects.* Cambridge, Mass.: MIT Press.

Moyle, S., Bohanec, M. & Osrowski, E. (2003). Large and Tall Buildings. *Data Mining and Decision Support,* 745: 191-202.

Nightingale, P. 1998. A cognitive model of innovation. *Research Policy,* 27: 689-709.

Nightingale, P. & Martin, P. 2004. The myth of the biotech revolution. *Trends in Biotechnology,* 22(11), 564-69.

Onwuegbuzie, A.J. & Johnson, R.B. (2006). The validity issue in mixed research. *Research in the Schools,* 13(1), 48-63.

Packendorff, J. (1995). Inquiring into the temporary organization: New directions for project management research. *Scandinavian Journal of Management,* 11(4), 319-333.

Pinto, J.K. & Slevin, D.P. (1987) Critical factors in successful project implementation. *IEEE Transactions in Engineering Management,* EM-34: 22-27.

Piperca, S. & Floricel, S. (2012). The role of structuring episodes in the development of complex projects. Paper presented at the *EURAM Conference,* Rotterdam.

Polanyi, M. (1966). *The Tacit Dimension.* Garden City, NY: Doubleday.

Popper, K. R. (1963). *Conjectures and Refutations: The Growth of Scientific Knowledge.* London: Routledge & Kegan Paul.

Prencipe, A. and Tell, F. (2001). Inter-project learning: processes and outcomes of knowledge codification in project-based firms. *Research Policy,* 30: 1373-1394.

Rogers, M.J., Gupta A. & Maranas, C.D. (2002). Real Options Based Analysis of Optimal Pharmaceutical Research and Development Portfolios. *Industrial & Engineering Chemistry Research,* 41(25): 6607-6620.

Sapolsky, H.M. (1972). *The Polaris System Development.* Cambridge, Mass.: Harvard University Press.

Savage, L.J. (1954). *The Foundations of Statistics.* Dover Publications, New York.

Schindler, M. & Eppler, M.J. (2003). Harvesting project knowledge: A review of project learning methods and success factors. *International Journal of Project Management,* 21(3), 219-228.

Schopenhauer, A. (1966). *The World as Will and Representation. Volume I.* Translated by E.F.J. Payne. New York: Dover Publications.

Sengoku, S., Yoda, T. & Seki, A. (2011). Assessment of Pharmaceutical Research and Development Productivity with a Novel Net Present Value-based Project Database. *Drug Information Journal,* 45: 175-185.

Sergi, V. (2009). *La fabrication d'un projet technologique: Étude des pratiques collectives et de la capacité d'action des documents.* Doctoral Dissertation: HEC Montreal.

Shapira, Z. (1995). *Risk Taking: A Managerial Perspective*. New York: Russell Sage Foundation.

Shavell, S. (1979). Risk sharing and incentives in the principal and agent relationship. *The Bell Journal of Economics*, 10: 55-73.

Simon, H.A. (1978). Rationality as process and product of thought. *Journal of American Economic Association*, 68: 1-16.

Simon, H.A. (1981). *The Sciences of the Artificial (3rd ed.)*. Cambridge, Mass.: MIT Press.

Smith, A.D. (2002). From process data to publication: A personal sensemaking. *Journal of Management Inquiry*, 11(4): 383-406.

Smith, J.E. & Nau, R.F. (1995). Valuing risky projects: Option pricing theory and decision analysis. *Management Science*, 41(5): 795-816.

Solo, K. & Paich, M. (2004). Modern Simulation Approach for Pharmaceutical Portfolio Management – Multimethod Simulation Software. Presentation at the *International Conference on Health Sciences Simulation* (ICHSS'04), January 18-21, 2004, San Diego, California, USA. Available at: http://www.xjtek.com/anylogic/articles/38/

Stefánsson, V. (2002). Investment cost for geothermal power plants. *Geothermics*, 31(2): 263-272.

Stinchcombe, A.L. and Heimer, C. (eds) (1985). *Organization Theory and Project Management*. Bergen, Norway: Scandinavian University Press.

Teece, D.J., Pisano, G. & Shuen, A. (1997). Dynamic capabilities and strategic management. *Strategic Management Journal*, 18(7): 509-533.

Thomke, S. & Reinertsen, D. (1998). Agile Product Development: Managing development flexibility in uncertain environments. *California Management Review*, 41(1): 8-30.

Tversky, A. & Kahneman, D. (1974). Judgment under uncertainty: Heuristics and biases. *Science*, 185: 1124-1131.

Vincenti, W.G. (1990). *What Engineers Know and How They Know It*. Baltimore: John Hopkins University Press.

von Mises, R. (1981). *Probability, Statistics and Truth*. (2nd English edition) New York: Dover.

von Neumann, J., and Morgenstern, O. (1943). *Theory of Games and Economic Behavior*. New York: J. Wiley.

Weber, M. (1947). *The Theory of Social and Economic Organization*. New York: The Free Press.

Williams, T. (2004). Identifying the hard lessons from projects – easily. *International Journal of Project Management*, 22(4), 273-279.

Chapter 16

Project, Project Theories, and Project Research: A New Understanding of Theory, Practice, and Education for Project Management

Pierre-Luc Lalonde and Mario Bourgault

When will you begin to live virtuously, Plato asked an old man who was telling him that he was attending a series of lectures on virtue. One must not just speculate forever; one must one day also think about actual practice. But today we think that those who live as they teach are dreamers. (Immanuel Kant, The Philosophical Encyclopedia)

Abstract

This chapter sets forth the basic concepts of an epistemology-based approach to project management research. Aware that our discipline is not peopled solely by researchers, we stress the importance of integrating practical and pedagogical aspects into a framework for project management research.

We begin by presenting two distinct research models for characterizing project management: research 'for' project management, and research 'into' project management. The first model refers to investigations of day-to-day practices, as conducted by project practitioners. The second refers to the fundamental, well-known research protocols applied to study project management. Although there appears to be a need for both these models, we will point out some inherent limitations to each of them, and we will propose the necessity for looking beyond this superficial duality.

First, we must emphasize that the project is not an event that can be dealt with in the same manner as an object. The project is not a given: it lies ahead, a work in progress. We will demonstrate the need to get into the thick of things, where the action is, in order to witness project management in practice. In a departure from the two models first presented here, we will trace an alternative route: project management research 'through' project management, which we call *project research*. We will present a broad outline of this approach: briefly, project management is considered at once a scientific and a professional discipline. With this two-fold objective, to contribute to the scientific knowledge and to improve the practice of project management, we will attempt to redress the fact that the theories produced so far by the academic community have resulted in some improvements and support for professional practice, but we believe we can do better.

We will present a real-life, on-going project in order to illustrate this research approach and its methodological repercussions. Based on a study addressing judgement formation during the conduct of a project, we will underscore the key aspects of a research approach that combines theory and practice within a single framework. As a central player, the practitioner-researcher is ideally placed to jump start this research project approach, thereby revitalizing project management research. And this can be accomplished by renewing the theory-practice link and by undertaking some reflective work, that is, by reflecting *on* the project and *in* the project: in short, by theorizing in-and-on the project. We shall keep in mind that the project is not a problem to be solved, to be wrapped up. The project is inherent in all societal development, and always will be. So it must be approached afresh each day, with small gains made and minor victories won. We believe that a new type of practitioner is needed, and a new type of researcher: the reflective practitioner-researcher, who must be ready to push the limits, to expand the boundaries of current forms of thinking, speaking, and acting as a full member of society, and to set forth a real alternative.

Keywords: Project theories, project research, project practice, project pragmatics, project management education.

Introduction

To change or even ask questions about the basic tenets of a field implies more than just an intellectual act: it involves a political act (Bourdieu, 2000). Because they question the boundaries of a field, and in the words of Kuhn (1975), can also bring about a 'paradigm shift', a political act creates situations that can change even the rules for belonging to a specific field. Building on previous works (e.g., Söderlund, 2002, 2004a, 2004b; Hodgson & Cicmil, 2006; Bredillet, 2004), this chapter discusses one such political initiative.

It has long been recognized that organizations are coping with major challenges in terms of project management, and despite much progress and many developments in the field, we can still see some limitations to our approaches. Researchers have criticized the widening gap between the development of a corpus of methods and techniques and the utility of these when they are applied by practicing professionals (Morris et al., 2006; Atkinson, 1999; Williams, 1999). According to Williams (2005), the application of project management orthodoxy does not help prevent project failure, any more than it guarantees project success. Some researchers go further by suggesting that certain failures actually result from traditional project management methods (Maylor, 2001; Thomas, 2000). Overall, it appears that, despite any number of advanced methods and sophisticated tools, we must admit our limited capacity to manage the complexity of modern projects.

Against this background, the rules for belonging to the field of project management have begun to change, and through political acts, some researchers have begun to integrate the social sciences into project management research. In the early 1990s and the dawn of the 21st century, researchers in various disciplines, particularly engineering and business, began to adopt new perspectives on project management. Among others, they brought in ideas from the fields of economics, marketing, sociology, and psychology. However, although these developments had long been called for, they were unable to establish much order in the debate over the basic tenets of the discipline. On the contrary, it appears that the foundations, as well as the intellectual grounds that underlay them, were rent asunder. The basic principles therefore remain far from clear, and questioning them has become ever more salient.

Not too long ago, Söderlund (2004a) stressed the need to reflect on basic principles and discuss them, suggesting on the one hand that project management could attain the status of an academic discipline, but on the other that it has not yet obtained that status.[1] In fact, as Bourdieu (2001) rightly argues, the more autonomous the discipline, the less the basic tenets are questioned. Accordingly, the more self-constituted the field, the more it becomes autonomous from other fields. Therefore, the fact that researchers are calling for reflection on the epistemological underpinnings of the discipline (e.g., Smyth and Morris, 2007; Cicmil and Hodgson, 2006; Cicmil et al., 2006) and the fact that other disciplines occupy so much space in the project management field suggest that there is no such thing as an autonomous field of project management. Instead, it may be thought of as a work in progress, one that is not yet complete. We are still waiting for a definition of project management that is epistemologically grounded, and only history can say whether project management will become an autonomous academic discipline.

We believe that we must examine more closely what project management *is* (i.e., its identity) in order to discern its uniqueness. More specifically, it would be instructive to look at the various forms of research through which our practical and scientific knowledge of project management is being built. From this critical analysis, we hope to make a tentative contribution to the field. Generally speaking, this chapter joins the noisy debate on the epistemological standing of project management, and it raises questions about the types of research conducted in its name. For our analyses, we have drawn on ethics, rhetoric, and pragmatism as well as the applied arts and design. We propose that it is possible to undertake research projects that are consistent with the

---

1. 'The aim of the present paper is to introduce a discussion and debate about some fundamental theoretical issues related to project management research. The underlying reason is that such a discussion would contribute to the development of project management research on a general level and further its status as an academic discipline' (Söderlund, 2004a: 184).

dual identity of project management, considered as both a scientific discipline and a professional practice. Note that our intention is not to question the scientific credibility of current project management studies. It is instead to challenge their capacity to simultaneously advance our understanding of the world from a project management standpoint and to improve how professionals deal with the uncertainties of real-life project management.

Through an exploration of three different research approaches (research 'for' project management, research 'into' project management, and research 'through' project management), we will outline the contours of a proposed 'good practice' of project management research. 'Good' because it is consistent with the characteristics of the discipline and is viewed from a project management perspective (not from the perspectives of other disciplines); 'good' because it is consistent with the specificity, complexity, and dignity of human beings. We then illustrate how this good practice can be applied in a real-life, on-going project.

Research *for* Project Management and Research *Into* Project Management[2]:

Identifying Some Limitations in the Development of Project Management Research

Research for Project Management

Professional project managers have little (or no) love for theory. Their objectives are more concrete, so to speak. However, professionals who oversee projects do some research, do they not? In addition, are the project actors not continuously occupied with a 'research project', in which they must strive to define problems, inform themselves about situations, and gain a better understanding of what needs to be done? This is undeniable.

So what can we say about this particular type of research? We can say that its purpose is to benefit management, and in fact, practitioners actually carry out a type of inquiry process. According to Schön (1983), it takes the form of a conversation

---

2. This characterization of the different research approaches draws on the field of design research, including the works of Frayling (1993) and Findeli (2004). Referring to Herbert Read's (1967) model of education through art, Frayling (1993) distinguishes research *for* art and design from research *into* art and design and research *through* art and design. We have adapted this model for project management research.

between the practitioner and a situation.[3] In principle, this type of research should aim towards 'good management'.[4] It may be considered a cognitive exercise that precedes every problem-solving process. Professionals work according to heuristic principles, actions being the constituents of the processes. They do not systematically apply research hypotheses, prescribed procedures, or guidelines in order to act. Instead, even though they are not researchers in the strict sense, they embody the spirit of inquiry. They must be seen more as 'doers' than 'researchers', and they often have difficulty accounting for what they do. They respond to situations by drawing on their aptitudes, flair, and flexibility, which are generally derived from hard-won experience. The end goal is the project, or more precisely, the object of the project (we will return to this important distinction later). What happens is that although professionals make use of existing knowledge, they also create new knowledge, along with new ways of thinking about this knowledge and new ways of doing things. However, this knowledge and these innovations remain embodied within the project, and within the organization that undertakes the project. In the same way, even though the various objects, artefacts, and other project outcomes, as well as all the processes that produce these outcomes, incorporate a considerable amount of knowledge, the objects and processes of the project are not knowledge as such. The knowledge that professionals use is implicit, tacit (to borrow Polyani's [1966] term), and forms part of the practitioner's consciousness.

It is apparent that this approach includes research, or what we may call a process of inquiry (Dewey, 1938). It is also apparent that this type of research is highly relevant for project management practice: the aim is consistent with examining the parameters for a project situation intelligently and responsibly in order to take appropriate action. Insofar as this research approach relates to real management experience, it allows improving the know-how of project practitioners. Nevertheless, this know-how must be reinvented each time a new situation crops up. Certainly, the results would be advancements in tangible project management outcomes: higher profits, competitive demarcation, development of new strategies, deadlines met, cost control, and so on. However, the goal here is management, not knowledge or understanding. To use a metaphorical example, we could say that setting up a new

---

3. The designer 'shapes the situation, in accordance with his initial appreciation of it, the situation "talks back", and he responds to the situation's back-talk. In a good process of design, this conversation with the situation is reflective. In answer to the situation's back-talk, the designer reflects-in-action on the construction of the problem, the strategies of action, or the model of the phenomena, which have been implicit in his moves' (Schön, 1983: 79).

4. The adjective 'good' is deliberate. Closely related to the intellectual ambitions of this chapter, it refers to a well-known topic in pragmatism that has been little addressed in our community: the impossibility for any scientific approach to produce value judgements by drawing deductions from factual judgments. As a community of researchers, practitioners, and professors, it is our responsibility to define what the 'good practice' of project management might be.

inventory system would be 'relevant' for project management, but that writing a book chapter would not.

Therefore, even though this type of research is indispensable for practitioners, it is not scientifically acceptable, for a number of reasons. First, there is no production of new scientific or theoretical knowledge for project management. The knowledge and know-how that professionals seek and use is not meant to be transferred, published, or discussed. Thus, research 'for' project management does not aim to produce any kind of theoretical discourse, does not have as its objective to amass and establish a body of knowledge, and does not systematically organize or disseminate the knowledge it produces. In short, there is no effort to assemble a rigorous scientific corpus. Furthermore, this type of research does not employ the rigour typically required in scientific research protocols. Managers do not have the time, the training, or the detachment to concern themselves with processes that bear the stamp of scientific accuracy and impartiality, among others.

Considering the limitations of this type of research, should professional project management be considered without value for our discipline? Is the practitioner's approach to a management situation naïve compared to the scientific approach? From a resolutely pragmatist perspective, we must answer in the negative.[5] In fact, we believe exactly the opposite: notwithstanding some failed projects, managers have shown that they are capable of bringing projects to term using a plethora of effective approaches. That is, the approaches are relevant, useful, and capable of spawning new and fecund practices. However, given that these are the practices of actual project actors who carry out the projects, it is unfortunate that their practical thinking and actions cannot contribute to advance the knowledge on projects and project management. It is precisely through these actions and practices that projects are born and grow to fruition. They should be legitimized and valued for purposes of both the practice and science. It is simply that the two areas are based on different validation criteria. This research approach, which is necessary and useful for practitioners, is non-scientific, hence open to criticism, because it involves a discipline which is also a science. Project management is sitting on the fence: on the one side lies the field of practice, and on the other lies the fields of science.

Research into Project Management

The above-described research approach, research 'for' project management, may be thought of as professional solipsism, which goes against scientific orthodoxy. That is, whereas research 'for' project management requires the complete and unconditional engagement of the practitioner, the orthodox approach implies a standing back from pro-

---

5. John Dewey's philosophy of technique defends a conception of technique and technology (of the project?) that encompass both art and science. More particularly, he rejected the hierarchies of knowledge, whereby *theoria* (knowledge) was placed higher than *praxis* (action) and *poiesis* (making). For a detailed review, see Hickman (1992).

fessional practice. It seems to be either all black or all white. From the orthodox stand-point, project management practice gets left out. It gets left out so that the researcher can become familiar with scientific research, the very practice of research and the research profession, and so that the principles of objectivity that characterize the methodological canons are respected, thus conferring scientific credibility on the undertaking.

Consequently, project management researchers have abandoned the uncertain world of practice and based their research problems on more established disciplines. Instead of developing a distinctive approach to project management (a discipline that is at once scientific and project-management-oriented), studies have, not surprisingly, drawn on disciplines such as operational research (OR), economics, marketing, psychology, and sociology, to name but a few.[6,7] However, as has been previously suggested (Lalonde et al., 2010), by borrowing the basic tenets of other disciplines, project management research has not managed to develop its own identity in terms of knowledge particularities, originality, or an epistemological core. It would be most unfortunate if the discipline simply settled for making weak contributions to project management knowledge. 'Weak' because by borrowing from sociology, for example, we get 'sociological theories of project management', which are not theories of project management in the strictest sense. Thus, a major stumbling block in the discipline is that we currently do not know to what extent our research objects are either shared by other disciplines or borrowed from them. It appears that any examination of project management, in whatever manner and from whatever perspective, is enough to be considered project management research.

Because no epistemology proper to the discipline has been developed to date, project management in particular, and the management sciences in general, remain what Déry (1995) calls an exercise in epistemological poaching. This criticism compels us to suggest that we can build strong theories of project management: theories developed from the standpoint of project management. That is, the standpoint is that of a scientific discipline as well as the professional practice of conducting projects. Let us be clear: we are not questioning the scientific rigour or credibility of studies conducted from the perspectives of other sciences. Nevertheless, as confirmed pragmatists, and adopting a practice-based perspective, which is the perspective of the professionals

---

6. Not surprisingly, because this is not the first time that a discipline seeking credibility has borrowed its basic tenets from other disciplines that were not or no longer in question. Recall the classic case of sociology, a neologism made up of the Latin *socius* (society) and the Greek *logos* (knowledge), first used by Auguste Comte in 1839. However, this founder of positivism used the term unwillingly. Comte wanted to use a more powerful term: social physics, which would be more relevant for our proposal. Fascinated by the birth of industrial society and scientific rationality, Comte wanted to refer to physics, reflecting his wish to establish a 'true' science that accounted for the laws that govern the social world.

7. For a detailed review of the various disciplines involved in projects and project management, see, e.g., Söderlund (2002) and Bredillet (2008).

within our community, we are questioning the relevance of these 'weak' theories for practitioners and for the advancement of the discipline.

Projects and Project Theories: Preliminary Considerations for Project Management Research

The aim of this brief description of the two research approaches (professional solipsism versus scientific orthodoxy, or research 'for' project management versus research 'into' project management) was to provide a broad outline for a third approach with promising potential to respond to the requirements of both scientific rigour and advancements in the practice. Before delving further into this third approach, we will offer some general remarks in order to situate our proposal.

We have criticized the fact that scientific research in project management has settled for borrowing perspectives from other, established disciplines instead of creating a separate, project-management-based viewpoint. We must therefore consider what the project management viewpoint might be. Certain questions arise. What do we want to know about a world that includes projects? What are the particularities of our discipline, and how does the project management viewpoint differ from those of other disciplines? What noteworthy contributions does the project management viewpoint bring to the table, compared to the viewpoints of operational research, computer sciences, and sociology? And if this viewpoint can really be distinguished from the others, what are the repercussions on the objects of investigation and the research questions that drive our discipline?

For our purposes, the discipline of project management is concerned more about things as they should be than things as they are. This positioning is based on the distinction made by Simon (1996, 1969) between the natural sciences and the so-called artificial or 'design' sciences. Thus, 'Engineering, medicine, business, architecture, and painting are concerned not with the necessary but with the contingent – not with how things are but with how they might be – in short, with design' (Simon, 1996/1969: xii.). Simon further states that:

Everyone designs who devises courses of action aimed at changing existing situations into preferred ones. The intellectual activity that produces material artefacts is no different fundamentally from the one that prescribes remedies for a sick patient or the one that devises a new sales plan for a company or a social welfare policy for a state. [...] Schools of engineering, as well as schools of architecture, business, education, law, and medicine, are all centrally concerned with the process of design (Simon, 1996/1969: 111).

Accordingly, we consider project management from the Simonian perspective. Thus, project management is concerned with the process of transforming the technico-economic, social, environmental, and even cultural ecosystem. What concerns this discipline is the project in all its variants: political, technical, technological, innovative, architectural, design, event-based, political, and so on.[8]

Traditionally, project management focused mainly on the project execution phase, supported by the application of a variety of management tools and techniques. However, over two decades of research, increasing attention was paid to the design phase of the project. Compared to the execution phase, the design phase was more difficult to parameterize. Among other things, this is attributable to the fact that the upstream phases incorporate more political and strategic aspects, and these complex phases involve more uncertainty and ambiguity. In keeping with the project concept, we must not only revisit the upstream phases, we must also follow the project's course further downstream. This has already been done in studies on project audits. However, project audits marks only the end of the execution phase. It would be more instructive to travel even further downstream, to the reception[9] phase, or the point at which the project leaves the organizational sphere and enters the 'habitat', where it can begin to change the 'habitability' or liveability of the world. From the project standpoint, we must consider not just the organizational sphere, but societal and community spheres as well. It is here in the reception phase that the project's repercussions for the environment and the day-to-day lives of the users must be taken into consideration. Today's heightened concerns about ecological and social impacts should be driving project management researchers to investigate these consequences. In short, it is not enough to conduct research solely on organization and operational aspects of design and execution. Just as the research has explored further upstream, it must now venture further downstream. We should therefore be working with a larger image in mind, a much broader conception of the project, one that is more holistic, where the very liveability and sustainability of the world enters into the equation. Project management implies grasping all the project phases as an integrated whole, as well as taking into account the various project agendas (e.g., technical, physical, industrial, economic, symbolic, and cultural), information sharing mechanisms among the project actors throughout the phases (design, execution, and reception), project feasibility, project impacts (economic, technological, social, and environmental), and consequently the capacity of people to live and dwell in a world 'of-and-in-project'. In this view, project management is concerned less with the actual state of the world (the purview of the descriptive sciences) than the world as it could and should be. In this sense, we are using Simon's (1996/1969) term, a 'science of the artificial'. At the risk of stating the obvious, what project management is concerned with is the phenomenon of the project, right? So it comes down to this: it is a project discipline. Furthermore, this discipline has the weighty task of forging links to other project disciplines – such as

---

8. For a detailed review of the project conduct space, see Boutinet (1999, 2005).

9. 'Reception' is used here in the sense of reception theory (see, e.g., *Reception Theory: A Critical Introduction.* Holub 1984), whereby meaning does not lie in the work of art itself but rather in an interaction process between the audience and the artwork.

Upcoming Approaches in OPM Research

engineering, architecture, and design – involved in project settings, and of combining their strengths.

From this standpoint, there is a case for introducing project theories into project management.[10] These theories are attempts to understand and theorize the project. They posit that researchers are not simply interested in project 'objects' (e.g., buildings in architecture, new products in industrial design, new technology in engineering) as such, or tools (task structuring, team structuring, timeline planning, risk assessment and quantification), because these objects and tools do not say everything there is to say about the project. On the contrary, the objects are project outcomes, and the tools become meaningful only through actual project conduct. The project is a phenomenon in which the tools play a major role, and which culminates in a technological object, for example. However, as Boudon (1992) contends, to the extent that the project truly becomes an object of knowledge, the attention must move away from objects and toward the projects that have brought them into being. More precisely, attention must be paid to the type of work that produces the projects. In other words, the practice and the acts involved in project management should be the central concern, because it is through these acts that projects exist. In fact, it is hard to imagine project objects and tools unless a project is being conducted! The idea here is that the object of the project is actually a representation of the project: the project precedes it, and not the reverse. The tools, for their part, attempt to parametize the object of the project (in architecture, the building), as if this object were already in existence. The project is then perceived as a system of activities and structures that end up producing a pre-identified artefact, which is available to be efficiently examined and managed. In both cases, we note that the interest is not in the project as such.

Several years ago, Söderlund (2004a, 2004b) used the term 'project research' in an attempt to establish an alternate terminology. His aim, and with reason, was to distinguish it from the term 'project management', which was associated with quantitative and technicist approaches. Accordingly, he referred to the 'project field' and the 'project research field' rather than the project management field. This new terminology was meant to demonstrate that it was impossible for the project management field to holistically account for the diversity of studies that addressed project-related issues.[11] In this sense, Söderlund (2004b: 656) suggests 'that it might be more relevant to talk about "project research" instead of "project management research". Project research is here suggested as a concept capturing much of the recent development within the field'.

Although we believe that it is pertinent to consider the concepts of project theories,

---

10. To our knowledge, the term was first introduced into project management by Söderlund (2002), who states, 'The interpretation of what "projects" are is clearly an important question in order to develop the *"theory of projects"*' (Söderlund, 2002: 29, our emphasis).

11. 'Project management seems to be a research field with potentials of bringing different disciplines to focus on a focal phenomenon of study, i.e. projects' (Söderlund, 2004a: 184).

Project, Project Theories, and Project Research

project research, and the project field, we should not restrict their use to simply depicting recent developments, as Söderlund (2004b) does. On the contrary, these concepts, despite their as yet fuzzy contours,[12] can enable us to depart from the other research approaches described above (research 'for' and 'into' project management) and to find new ways of understanding and conducting project management research. We may now define an original position for project management research as a discipline that generates knowledge that is congruent with its distinctive foundation: the project. At the risk of repeating ourselves, we contend that the particularity of project management (considered from the perspective of project theories) is that it does not concern project object but rather the project itself. That is, the project is a projection: a social, organizational, or entrepreneurial movement with multiple dimensions (technical, social, and environmental), a stepping forward, in short, a process of transforming the world. This is the crucial difference between a project and an object: the project is not a given or something placed before us, and it is up to us to enact it.

Project Research: Toward Project Management Research 'Through' Project Management

We have said that the above-mentioned research approaches can serve as reference points for the development of an alternative approach. This approach should allow for the fact that project management is not a scientific discipline in the traditional meaning: it is at the same time a professional practice. In this sense, the objectives of project management are two-fold: first, to build a body of knowledge concerning the project, and second, to contribute to the improvement of project conduct practices. This dual objective implies two key research criteria that should guide project management research. On the one hand, scientific rigour is required so that recognized scientific standards are met. On the other hand, the research should be relevant, and it should lead to advancements and improvements in project management practice. We will now look at the impacts of these criteria on research and the development of research protocols to meet these requirements.

First, let us recall that in research 'for' project management, we underscored its critical importance for the practice and for successful projects, and we stressed the need for this type of research for project conduct itself. Although the characterization of the practice as an art form and the role that professional intuition appears to play do not pose a problem, we nevertheless argued that this research approach was insufficiently

---

12. The fuzzy contours of the concepts of the project, project theories, project disciplines, and project research should not constitute an obstacle to our approach. On the contrary, it is exactly because we have this object of research (the project), however unstable, that we wish to employ more rigour and go beyond mere reflection and research to something that is more fundamental, more philosophical in nature.

thorough to allow a precise discourse that could fully account for project management. Concerning research 'into' project management, we underscored its scientific rigour, but questioned the fact that it is insufficiently grounded or engaged in real-life project situations. We then argued that the project is not a study object like others: it is a work in the making. In certain cases, the research approach is detached from the concerns of practitioners and project end-users, leading to models and theories that are disconnected from reality. Because project management concerns projects, and because projects imply a process of transforming the world, we may criticize this research approach for its lack of engagement in the projects, whether organizational, technological, social, political, or other. Finally, we may criticize this approach for embracing the perspectives of other scientific disciplines too rapidly, of failing to create a unique project management standpoint, and consequently of contributing more to the very disciplines from which it borrows its reference points.

This brings us to what we might call research 'through' project management, or more simply, project research. Called project-grounded research by Findeli (2004), this approach is understood to take place within the project, in the thick of the action, within an actual professional project. We argue here the necessity to integrate the project (for innovation, engineering, construction, urban planning, design, computerization, etc.) into the research. The research approach is therefore grounded in the project, or, to borrow from existentialism, it is situated in the project. This grounding is taken from the pragmatist view that in order to think properly, one must think in action, or 'think on our feet'. Whereas the practitioner works 'for' project management and the researcher looks 'into' project management, the practitioner-researcher acts and reflects 'through' project management. Recalling Findeli's epistemological stance (2004: 9-10) toward design research, research 'through' project management is similar to 'action research' (without necessarily including the political dimension of his theoretical and ideological legacy), and similar to the grounded theory approach, although we are going beyond the sole theoretical contribution (complete engagement in the project, through acts, responsibility, and reflection). It is similar as well to ethnomethodology and to Merleau-Ponty's (1975) phenomenology. Despite recently renewed battles surrounding the distinct role of the human and natural sciences, or the modern *Methodenstreit*,[13] all these methods have acquired legitimacy, and have been widely disseminated, taught, and recognized in universities.

Without going into the particularities of these methods in detail, we must emphasize one distinctive feature: under the project research approach, the researcher is no longer limited to being a research expert. As posited by Findeli and Coste (2007), the researcher's accountability exceeds the strict boundaries of science and knowledge. By engaging in an actual professional project, the practitioner-researcher also becomes accountable for the good conduct of the project, and for good project

---

13. For a review of the debates concerning quantitative and qualitative methods, see, e.g., Bryman (1984).

management. We are reminded that many candidates for a master's or doctoral degree in project management have had not only professional education, in many cases they have had professional experience. For example, we note that candidates coming from professional fields such as engineering, architecture, and industrial design stand apart from social sciences researchers, who lack this hands-on background. It is therefore important for project management to recognize, valorize, and capitalize on aspects that distinguish it from the humanities, and to provide for appealing and relevant research projects in which these hands-on skills can be put to good use. Thanks to management training and experience (which researchers from the exact sciences and humanities do not normally have), the practitioner-researcher can initiate a project research process. This perspective on research and practice makes even more sense, given that master's and doctoral graduates are increasingly entering the professions.

Recalling the tripartite conception of the project (design-execution-reception), and mindful of the need to conduct research that is relevant to the practice, research questions developed under this approach should foster human and practical dimensions of the project, from upstream to downstream, from the design phase (what do we want to do?) to the execution and operational phases (how are we going to do it?) and on to project reception (how is this project impacting us?). The objects of investigation should relate mainly to the practices involved in the various project phases. The research questions should address the events and processes by which the project actors and end-users forge complex relationships with the 'artificial' world that is thought, wished, and achieved, and which in turn impacts them. In addition, because the research project is carried out in practice – in action, through acts – and because it is in practice that reflection can rightly be carried out,[14] we insist on the fact that, given our standpoint, there should be tangible results in the short term, and not just abstract findings in the longer term, as in a scientific approach.

Finally, insofar as we would like to improve the practice, and hence the judgement of practitioners, on-going attention must be paid to the reflective dimension of the process. We will briefly highlight the virtue of self-learning as part of this approach. The practitioner-researcher must strive to reflect on his or her cognitive path in practice. By being involved in the project, the practitioner-researcher must work on developing the practical know-how required to do the work. The advantage is that this compels the practitioner-researcher to 'be' in the practice rather than speculate about it (not yet knowing exactly what project management is). By coping with the

---

14. Here again, we adopt a pragmatist position: the aim is to clarify ideas and prevent confusion by relating them to practical outcomes. This two-fold nature (theory and practice) of project management suggests that we can 'pragmatize' the descriptive science approaches used in the humanities and social sciences. This would allow us to conduct more fruitful research in project management than research 'into' project management allows. Insofar as the project management issues addressed are sociological, for example, and addressed from a sociological perspective, the research settles too easily for advancing the knowledge in these other disciplines.

practice, the practitioner-researcher gains more insight, confidence, and authority in all respects. This approach does not simply allow knowing, it allows one to 'be' differently, such that the theories that are developed in project management can contribute to both science and practical life. In project research, what some may call an interpretive bias becomes a methodological advantage. The practitioner-researcher, engaged in the research object, is strongly positioned to discover the more relevant research questions for specific situations, and to develop new approaches that could improve project conduct. In addition, if the capacities are there and the efforts are made, new theoretical models can be developed.

The above discussion presents the broad outlines of project research. We will now turn to a brief description of an on-going research project that illustrates the project research approach.

An Account of an On-Going Project Research
Practical Aspects (Integrating Oneself into the Project) and Theoretical Aspects (Research Problem, Conceptual Framework, and Theoretical Framework)

Project research, as described above, may be undertaken in a number of ways, for instance, under a study as part of a master's or doctoral program in project management. In the present case, the General Manager of a long-term care centre run by a religious community is collaborating with our research centre to conduct the study. From our standpoint, he acts as a practitioner-researcher. Holder of a Ph.D., he is familiar with qualitative research methods as well as the epistemological and theoretical issues of project management.

As part of his duties, he is participating in the development of an architectural project for a new long-term care centre. The project was the initiative of two religious communities that are planning how to deal with an aging membership. The practitioner-researcher serves as the project management advisor for one of these communities. These communities not only have to find a sustainable solution to their aging problem, they also have to consider their diminishing capacity to manage their resources as time goes on. In fact, due to increasing age and increasing difficulty in recruiting new members, there is nobody left who is capable of handling the administration and management of a health care centre. The project is therefore to develop a space in which the members of these communities can continue their way of life, whether autonomously or not. In other words, the architectural project has to integrate a space for semi-autonomous and non-autonomous members with physical or cognitive incapacities and a space for members who are still autonomous. The overall complex has to accommodate about 130 members and allow them to pursue their way of life. This is the background for the project, which is still under consideration, and which served as the catalyst for our research project.

This brief presentation of the project demonstrates the practical component of the research approach. To this we must add the scientific and theoretical components, which are equally embodied in the practitioner-researcher. Of the issues that are currently hot in project management and are also of interest to us, some are inherent to project management practice. More precisely, we are interested in the judgement formation process within the project situation.[15] In this sense, we seek to gain a deeper understanding of the actions and thoughts behind the conduct of the project. We pay particular attention to the communications and discussions among the actors. In short, we look at their acts of language and the intentions of these acts. Once the project was initiated by the religious communities, it was rapidly taken up by the various groups of actors who entered the project, including real estate developers, architects, real estate agents, service care providers, administrators, and eventual purchasers. It is easy to see how the various actors' intentions might run into conflict. In this situation, we wanted not only to better understand how social judgments are formed, but also to participate in the formation of judgments 'in action'. It is noteworthy that the representatives of the community were sometimes reluctant to get involved or to express their opinions. The reason for this is simple: on the one hand they are overwhelmed by the complexity of the project, with all the knowledge and interventions it entailed, and on the other hand, because they are all over 67 years old, they are unable to keep pace with the flow of information coming from all the professionals working on the project. Although the representatives are not experts in project design and management or real estate funding and development, they would nevertheless inhabit the new living space, and they have some intuitive ideas about the design (e.g., layout, room sizes, location) as well as the management (e.g., funding, entry period at the centre, administration, methods of payment, accommodation agreement), which have to be expressed and clarified. One of the tasks of the practitioner-researcher is to integrate the voices of the communities by helping them articulate their vision and by explaining it to the other actors.

Parallel to this integration on the ground, a master's or doctoral candidate would have to familiarize himself or herself with the actual project management issues (theoretical, philosophical, epistemological, and methodological) and do the intellectual work required to develop a conceptual and theoretical framework. In the case at hand, the practitioner-researcher is pursuing this scientific project as a continuation of a doctoral research project. He is therefore aware of the overall scope of the discipline. As mentioned above, the issues of interest are mainly language, discussion, and verbal interactions, which are typically addressed in microsociology. By placing verbal interactions at the centre of the study, it is acknowledged that projects are rarely conducted by individuals working in isolation. The social dimension of project conduct necessarily implies that discussions are required for the work to get done. We consider here

---

15. For an exploratory study of this process, see Lalonde et al. (2012).

that the day-to-day project activities arise primarily from communications among the actors, and that these communications generate meanings. On the other hand, the conceptual framework defends a philosophical anthropology that accounts for the freedom of the actor, whereby the actor is not determined entirely by social norms. Although actors do not always act rationally, they may still be able to explain, talk about, and report on what they do, and why they do it (or at least attempt to do so). In other words, they may be said to embody a concept used in ethnomethodology, whereby the actor is not a 'cultural dope', a naïve being who applies models, techniques, and recipes automatically, mechanically, or involuntarily. As an illustration of the reflective capacity of the project actors, we presume that their interactions give rise to relevant and compelling rationales for their actions, demonstrating their understanding of the situations in which they participate. With respect to the practical component of this project research, we consider more particularly that the end-users of the project (in this case, the aging members of the two religious communities), that is, the 'inhabitants', are neither simple consumers nor 'users' in the functional sense. They are project actors in the strongest sense. That is, they are the bearers of the project: a project to inhabit the world, their world, by means of a living project that they have to define and achieve. They have to make judgements about the quality of the architecture, the landscape, and the day-to-day functioning of their way of life, and they want to make improvements. We therefore focus more on the upstream phase of the project than on the execution phase. Nevertheless, we never lose sight of the implications for the reception phase, for either the community members or the citizens living in the vicinity. Thus, in line with the precepts of action research, we focus more on the actors in this study than on the operational processes and tools. Finally, without going into great detail, we note that our theoretical framework draws on ethics, rhetoric, ethnomethodology, and contemporary design research.

The Research Question and Method

Once the researcher has been integrated into a project team and has begun to address the epistemological, philosophical, and theoretical issues, a preliminary version of the research question can be broached. The research question is subsequently developed, changed, and established as the project is carried out. At least, it can be stated in general terms. In the present case, the question may be stated as follows: in what way do the actors form judgements about the various concrete situations that occur during the project? This question can be answered in a myriad of ways. However, because the idea is to develop a protocol for project research, the researcher must integrate within a project team so as to be in a position to 'think in action'.

As suggested by Findeli (1998), this is not a situation whereby a social sciences researcher is parachuted into the project arena as a participant observer. Instead, from a perspective such as action research, as a competent practitioner, and therefore as a potential contributor to the project, the practitioner-researcher integrates into the project and is simultaneously guided by a scientific mandate. In our case, the practitioner-researcher has a bachelor's degree in industrial design as well as a master's and a Ph.D. degree in engineering project management. With this strong foundation in industrial design and project management, he is in a position to advise the religious communities, arrange meetings, and ask questions about decisions from the members' standpoint. In short, he is situated in such a manner that he can participate with the other actors to 'produce' the project.

The researcher's engagement is further justified in terms of the methodology. The practice of project management, and more particularly in this case, the acts of language that are inherent in the judgement formation process, cannot be induced simply by asking the actors to report them. As Argyris and Schön point out, with respect to the professional, 'We must construct his theory-in-use from *observations* of his behavior' (Argyris & Schön, 1974: 7). Argyris and Schön (1974) make a distinction between 'theories-in-use' and 'espoused theories', as follows:

> *When someone is asked how he would behave under certain circumstances, the answer he usually gives is his espoused theory of action for that situation. This is the theory of action to which he gives allegiance, and which, upon request, he communicates to others. However, the theory that actually governs his actions is his theory-in-use, which may or may not be compatible with his espoused theory* (Argyris & Schön, 1974: 7).

Because theories-in-use can account for human actions and the behaviours of actors while executing a project, these are the theories that interest us. Data collection methods using directed and semi-directed interviews and questionnaires are generally associated with espoused theories: they obtain the actors' reports, which may reflect more on what they believe they do, or would like to do, than what they actually do. Our empirical approach to the practice should therefore allow observing the 'external' world that the project affects as well as the 'internal' world of the project actors, or their intentions, thoughts, values, preferences, and so on. Through these observations, the practitioner-researcher can begin to examine how judgements are formed as the project unfolds.

In the present case, the practitioner-researcher is first and foremost a professional. In fact, he was invited by the client to participate in the project in this capacity, under a professional mandate. At the same time, he began to observe the various actors and hold open discussions with them, as a 'regular' worker. Gradually, through these discussions, trust was built, and the practitioner-researcher was able to implement the scientific component of his mandate. He engaged in many informal talks both before and after project meetings. Over time, and with increasing involvement, he developed relationships with the actors outside the workplace, listened to their stories, and familiarized himself with the nuances of their language.

Besides nurturing a climate of discussion and trust, the practitioner-researcher also took notes and made recordings (audio and visual) of some of the meetings. For reasons of confidentiality and sensitivity of content, it was not always possible to record the discussions. In this case, free notes were taken. For purposes of discourse analysis, it is usually recommended to use audio-visual recordings in order to capture the data. However, one may also use note-taking to report observations (Kerbat-Orecchioni, 2005). When the researcher is prevented from making recordings, the topics of the discussions are identified and the greatest possible number of verbatim quotes are included.[16] In addition, in his privileged capacity as a professional, the researcher can supplement his data with secondary sources, such as informal *in situ* interviews with the actors and administrative and technical documents to which he has access (e.g., financial plans, 3D models, minutes of meetings, contracts).

This approach to the project situation enables the practitioner-researcher to understand the project from in and within the action, not as a sociologist who regards the project from an academic perspective, but instead as a practitioner, who supports and participates in the project as it unfolds, while remaining consistent with the requirements of a scientific approach. This allows us to identify a fundamental project research perspective, one that invites the practitioner-researcher to conduct interpretive work out of action, but also reflective work in action. The interpretation, or qualitative analysis, should be performed in the normal manner. This part of the research, which Glaser and Strauss (1967) call the constant comparative method of qualitative analysis, consists of a widely described and recognized process of interpreting the data and identifying conceptual categories.[17] However, this is not a case of an applied theory,[18] but instead a reflective exercise combined with an attempt at grounded theorization, which may be expressed as theorization-of-and-in-the-project. To fulfil the requirements of academics and researchers in our field, this type of research could culminate in a master's or doctoral thesis or an article published in a scientific journal. And we must not forget the practitioners and professionals working in the field of project management: our practitioner-researcher should be capable of speaking their language. How can this be accomplished? By rolling up one's sleeves and getting involved in the actual running of a project, by being engaged, by acting, by getting into the thick of things. As stated by Findeli and Coste (2007), in the practitioner-researcher we find a new type of practitioner, and a new type of researcher: the enlightened practitioner-

---

16. Note that in studies on strategy, recent works by Jarzabkowski and Seidl (2008) are based on detailed notes and verbatim quotes.

17. According to Suddaby (2006), this is an organic process that determines the capacity of a particular category to express the observed reality. It is particularly applicable to understanding how meanings are constructed through intersubjective experience (Suddaby, 2006; Gephart, 1999). It is also an appropriate research method for the interpretivist paradigm (Gephart, 1999). In management, Langley (1999) advocates it as the analysis strategy of choice for understanding microscopic processes in organizations. Finally, note that grounded theory is simply a contemporary version of Plato's dialectic, from a predominantly neopositive perspective.

18. The model of a *theory applied* to professional practice has been denounced as a major epistemological incongruity for the professional disciplines (Schön, 1986, 1983).

researcher, who acts in accordance with interpretive work performed in and outside of the action, with awareness and reflection, and who helps bring the project to fruition.

Conclusion: Educating the Reflective Practitioner

We have noted that we may consider different research approaches in our discipline, and we have deplored the fact that science is estranged from practice and that practice is equally estranged from science. By characterizing project management as a discipline that is both scientific and professional, and by positioning it within the realm of the artificial sciences and project theories, we argue for a research approach that is grounded in action, leading to a theorization-of-and-in-the-project, rather than a theory applied to the project.

Accordingly, research 'through' project management has been proposed as the approach of choice in a discipline that includes researchers, of course, but also professionals and professors. Thus, although the project management discipline requires new knowledge to be produced, we must also acknowledge that this discipline is based on a practice, which must be taught as well. Because the make-up of our research community and the roles of the various actors set this discipline apart, we should revisit our ways of conducting research. Considering the range of interests of our key actors, it is clear that the approaches adopted by the exact and human social sciences are insufficient for this purpose. By grounding our research in real project management situations, we can redress the lack of human and social verisimilitude in contemporary basic research. Thus, by stating things about the project that no other discipline can so clearly state, by the originality of its propositions, and by the relevance and fecundity it brings to professional practice, and therefore for its scientific as well as its anthropological and practical content, project research can contribute to the development of the project management discipline.

In a project research setting, the practitioner-researcher must learn how to practice thinking in action, to form judgements that are free, and to discover in himself or herself the solutions to problems in each and every situation. There is an urgent need to develop a project-embedded framework and approach, in which theories are derived from the very act of project management, and where these theories can act as stimulants, guidelines, and means to renew practical life. In this way, we increase the professional responsibility of the researcher, who benefits in turn from the pedagogical contribution of the advocated pragmatic posture. We propose an individual who integrates the roles of both practitioner and researcher: the enlightened practitioner-researcher, whose scientific research approach guides and enriches the hands-on work of the practitioner. As an approach to project management research, project research is presented here as a valuable paradigm for both practice and education. It goes beyond the dominant research approaches and addresses the need to reinvent project management by placing it on a new foundation. The practitioner-researcher, as the new actor in this paradigm, must not only assume short-term responsibility for project success, he must also engage in a broader philosophical inquiry that is at once theoretical, ethical, and even aesthetic in order to attain professional insight. This is no easy task. To those who might see in this approach a utopian vision, we respond with Spinoza's concluding remarks in the *Ethics*: 'The road to these things that I have pointed out now seems very hard, but it can be found. And of course something that is found so rarely is bound to be hard. For if salvation were ready to hand and could be found without great effort, how could it come about that almost everyone neglects it? But excellence is as difficult as it is rare' (Spinoza, 2010: 137). What we hope for is nothing more nor less than to underscore the need to strive toward excellence, in response to the call for more relevant theories and for a practice that is not only more effective but also more just, and, we believe, more beautiful. In all these matters, we can only aspire to be the best that is humanly possible.

References

Argyris, C. & Schön, D. A. (1974). *Theory in practice: Increasing professional effectiveness.* San Francisco: Jossey-Bass Publishers.

Atkinson, R. (1999). Project management: Cost, time and quality, two best guesses and a phenomenon; It's time to accept other success criteria *International Journal of Project Management, 17*(6), 337-342.

Boudon, P. (1992). Projet architectural et projet architecturologique. In ROPS (éd.), *Le projet: un défi nécessaire face à une société sans projet* (pp. 17-30). Paris: L'Harmattan.

Bourdieu, P. (2001). *Science de la science et réflexivité.* Paris: Raisons d'agir.

Bourdieu, P. (2000). *Propos sur le champ politique.* Lyon: Presses Universitaires de Lyon.

Boutinet, J.-P. (2005). *L'anthropologie du projet* (1er éd.). Paris: Quadrige/Presses Universitaires de France.

Boutinet, J.-P. (1999). *Psychologie des conduites à projet* (3e éd.). Paris: PUF.

Bredillet, C. N. (2004). Beyond the positivist mirror: Towards a project management 'gnosis'. Paper presented at the IRNOP.

Bredillet, C. N. (2008). From the editor. Exploring research in project management: Nine schools of project management research. *Project management journal, 39*(3), 2-5.

Bryman A. (1984). The Debate about Quantitative or Qualitative Research: A Question of Method or Epistemology. *The British Journal of Sociology, 35*(1), 75-92.

Cicmil, S., & Hodgson, D. (2006). New possibilities for project management theory: A critical engagement. *Project Management Journal, 37*(3), 111-122.

Cicmil, S., Williams, T., Thomas, J., & Hodgson, D. (2006). Rethinking project management: Researching the actuality of projects. *International Journal of Project Management, 24*(8), 675-686.

Déry, R. (1995). L'impossible quête d'une science de la gestion. *Gestion, 20*(3), 35-46.

Dewey, J. (1938). *Logic. The Theory of Inquiry*. New York: Henry Holt and Company.

Findeli, A. (1998). La recherche en design. Questions épistémologiques et méthodologiques. *International Journal of Design and Innovation*, 1(1), 3-12.

Findeli, A. (2004). La recherche-projet: une méthode pour la recherche en design. *Communication présentée au Symposium de recherche sur le design du Swiss Design Network*. Bâle, Suisse.

Findeli, A., & Coste, A. (2007). De la recherche-création à la recherche-projet: un cadre théorique et méthodologique pour la recherche architecturale. *Lieux-communs*, 10, 139-161.

Frayling, C. (1993). Research in art and design. *RCA Research Paper*, 1(1), 1-5.

Gephart, R., P. (1999). Paradigms and research methods. *Research Methods Forum, 4* (Summer). Consulted April 29, 2010, at: http://division.aomonline.org/rm/1999_RMD_Forum_Paradigms_and_Research_Methods.htm.

Glaser, B. G., & Strauss, A. L. (1967). *The Discovery of Grounded Theory: Strategies for Qualitative Research*. Chicago: Aldine.

Read, H. (1967) *Education Through Art*. London: Faber and Faber.

Hickman, L. (1992). *John Dewey's Pragmatic Technology*. Indiana: University Press.

Hodgson, D., & Cicmil, S. (2006). *Making Projects Critical*. New York: Palgrave Macmillan.

Holub, R. C. (1984). *Reception theory: A critical introduction*. London: Methuen.

Kerbrat-Orecchioni, C. (2005). *Le discours en interaction*. Paris: A. Colin.

Kuhn, T. S. (1975). *The Structure of Scientific Revolutions* (2nd Ed.). Chicago: University of Chicago Press.

Lalonde, P-L., Bourgault, M., & Findeli, A. (2012). An empirical investigation of the project situation: PM practice as an inquiry process. *International Journal of Project Management*, 30(4), 418-431.

Lalonde, P-L., Bourgault, M., Findeli, A. (2010). Building pragmatist theories of PM practice: Theorizing the act of project management. *Project Management Journal*, 41(5), 21-36.

Langley, A. (1999). Strategies for theorizing from process data. *Academy of Management Review*, 24(4), 691-710.

Maylor, H. (2001). Beyond the Gantt chart: Project management moving on. *European Management Journal, 19*(1), 92-100.

Merleau-Ponty, M. (1975). *Les sciences de l'homme et la phénoménologie*. Paris: Centre de documentation universitaire.

Morris, P. W. G., Crawford, L., Hodgson, D., Shepherd, M. M., & Thomas, J. (2006). Exploring the role of formal bodies of knowledge in defining a profession – The case of project management. *International Journal of Project Management*, 24(8), 710-721.

Polanyi, M. (1966). *The Tacit Dimension*. New York: Doubleday & Company.

Read, Herbert (1967). *Education through Art*. London: Faber and Faber.

Russell, Bertrand (1946). *History of Western Philosophy* (2nd Ed., London: Allen and Unwin, 1961).

Schön, D. A. (1986). Toward a new epistemology of practice: A response to the crisis of professional knowledge. In A. Thomas & E. W. Ploman (Eds.), *Learning and Development: A Global Perspective* (pp. 56-79). Toronto: Ontario Institute for Studies in Education.

Schön, D. A. (1983). *The Reflective Practitioner: How Professionals Think in Action*. New York: Basic Books.

Simon, H. A. (1996/1969). *The Sciences of the Artificial* (3rd Ed.). Cambridge, Massachusetts: MIT Press.

Smyth, H. J., & Morris, P. W. G. (2007). An epistemological evaluation of research into projects and their management: Methodological issues. *International Journal of Project Management*, 25(4), 423-436.

Söderlund, J. (2004a). Building theories of project management: Past research, questions for the future. *International Journal of Project Management*, 22(3), 183-191.

Söderlund, J. (2004b). On the broadening scope of the research on projects: A review and a model for analysis. *International Journal of Project Management*, 22(8), 655-667.

Söderlund, J. (2002). On the development of project management research: Schools of thought and critique. *Project Management Journal*, 8(1), 20-31.

Spinoza, B. (2010). Ethics demonstrated in geometrical order. Translated by Jonathan Bennett. Consulted August 13, 2012, at: http://www.earlymoderntexts.com/pdf/spinethi.pdf.

Suddaby, R. (2006). What grounded theory is not. *Academy of Management Journal*, 49(4), 633-642.

Thomas, J. L. (2000). *Making sense of project management: Contingency and sensemaking in transitory organizations*. Ph.D., University of Alberta, Al., Canada.

Williams, T. M. (2005). Assessing and building on project management theory in the light of badly over-run projects. *IEEE Transactions in Engineering Management*, 52(4), 497-508.

Williams, T. M. (1999). The need for new paradigm for complex projects. *International Journal of Project Management*, 17(5), 269-273.

Chapter 17

Pluralist Project Research: Drawing on Critical Systems Thinking to Manage Research Across Paradigms

Julien Pollack

Abstract

Pluralist research has been widely acclaimed as providing benefits that research which relies on a single technique, methodology or paradigm, cannot. However, there are very few examples of project management research which attempt to bridge methodological or paradigmatic divides. This chapter draws on the field of Critical Systems Thinking, a field or research which has a long history of exploring how approaches to managing research can be combined in practice, to explore opportunities to enrich project management research. Of particular significance in developing the discussion of pluralism in project management research are: clearly distinguishing the level to which a research approach belongs within a paradigm; Reed's four strategies for combining methodologies; the oblique use of methods; Grafting and Embedding; and the more general cases of pluralism in Series or Parallel.

Introduction

This chapter explores approaches to conducting pluralist research in the field of project management. A pluralist approach to research involves using multiple approaches to exploring or answering one research question or area of enquiry. The challenge for pluralist practice involves the problem of how to combine the most appropriate parts of different approaches and how to do this in some sort of philosophically cohesive manner (Skyrme, 1997: 220). This chapter draws on the well developed field of Critical Systems Thinking (CST) a branch of Systems Thinking that explicitly addresses ways of combining tools, techniques, methods, methodologies and philosophies from different schools of thought and practice. Although the Systems Thinking field is predominantly occupied with the development of methodologies for taking action in a management context, concepts about ways of combining approaches are easily translated to address concerns about how pluralist project management research can be managed.

Pluralism is widely reported to provide benefits that reliance on a single approach cannot. Using only a single approach entails a necessarily limited view of a situation (Mingers, 1997a: 9). A single approach does not reflect the '… richness, diversity and interdependence …' (Skyrme, 1997: 219) of real life, and '… also produce silences around certain issues and themes' (Brocklesby, 1997: 198), as particular approaches focus practitioner attention on particular aspects of a problem situation. It is possible that the complexity inherent in problem situations may best be dealt with by adopting a pluralist approach (Lai, 2000: 226; Murthy, 2000: 31). Use of multiple approaches allows the practitioner to enter a '… problem situation with fewer preconceived ideas …' (Brocklesby, 1997: 190), increasing choice and flexibility (Skyrme, 1997: 217). Such an approach also provides the opportunity of '… exploiting the creative tensions among differentiated methods' (Zhu, 2000: 187). 'By thinking systemically and using a range of tools to enable us to hold in mind more than one ideology, discipline, or framework at the same time …' (McIntyre, 2002: 9) sustainable practice becomes more possible. Combining '… methodologies expressing different theoretical rationalities …' (Jackson, 1997a: 214) can allow practitioners to get the most out of pluralist practice. Furthermore, blending approaches, such as qualitative and quantitative techniques, can allow the practitioner to reach a wider audience than would otherwise be available (Wolstenholme, 1999: 422), while simultaneously increasing both rigor and relevance (p. 424). Pluralist practice also provides benefit to fields as a whole, not just the individual practitioner, allowing for traditional approaches to be buttressed with new, or different, ideas (Jackson, 1999: 13). It would be difficult to argue that the field of project management research is not richer for the wider variety of research approaches, and combinations of approaches, that are appearing in the literature.

Triangulating Research Data

Triangulation was arguably the first popular formalisation of the use of multiple techniques to explore a single research question. Denzin's (1970) principle of triangulation has had considerable impact, particularly within the field of evaluation. For Denzin (pp. 26-7), the concept of triangulation proposes that multiple methods must be used in all investigations, as no single method can reveal all the relevant features of a situation. Ianni and Orr (1979: 94) summarise Denzin's work, listing four sources of triangulation: data, including time, space, and person; theoretical, using multiple perspectives on a single set of objectives; investigator, using several investigators for the same research; and methodological. Triangulation as an approach is reported to allow the researcher to flow between inductive and deductive processes (Patton, 1990: 46), to '… cover all bases …' (Pulley, 1994: 6), and avoid '… potential analytical errors and omissions' (Kaplan & Duchon, 1988: 582). Disagreements about the nature and appropriateness of triangulation have persisted for decades in these fields, more so than is apparently indicated by cursory perusal of the literature, as there '... is, indeed, a disagreement over whether or not there is a disagreement' (Reichardt & Cook, 1979: 8). In the fields of social, educational and evaluation research, however, practice has developed faster than the theory (Mingers, 1997a: 3-4). As such, triangulation focuses on the combination of qualitative and quantitative data or data collection techniques (Patton, 1990) or '... two method-types ...' (Reichardt & Cook, 1979: 9), without typically engaging in consideration of the methodological, philosophical or paradigmatic issues associated with pluralism.

However, neglecting to consider these issues can limit consideration or research planning to a level of tool and technique application, devoid of consideration of theoretical underpinning. It can be useful to think of a continuum between research tools/techniques, methods, methodologies and philosophies. The philosophical end of the spectrum provides a greater theoretical focus, and provides a contextual context for the application of tools and techniques. By contrast, the tool and technique level of the continuum provides an increasing practical focus on action taken in a research context, and provides a practical justification for the philosophical level (Figure 17.1). Readers are referred to the author's earlier work (Pollack, 2006) for a detailed examination of these issues.

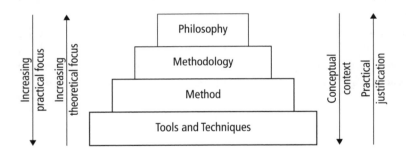

Figure 17.1. Hierarchical Relationship within a Paradigm (based on Pollack, 2006: 388)

An approach to pluralist research should address all levels of the research paradigms involved, from underpinning philosophy to the techniques researchers use to collect data. There is more to distinguish the two primary research paradigms than whether the data collected is qualitative or quantitative, and a wide variety of authors have categorised the differences between these research paradigms. This chapter does not engage with the discussion about the characteristics which identify research paradigms in any depth. Instead, readers are referred to Burrell and Morgan (1979: 3) who provided a system of four polarities for analysing philosophical assumptions about the nature of social science, and Fitzgerald and Howcroft (1998: 319) who also focus

Upcoming Approaches in OPM Research

on the philosophical differences between paradigms. In addition, Spencer, Ricthie et al. (2003: 45) examine tendencies for association with qualitative and quantitative research, while Crawford and Pollack (2004) focus on the influence of different paradigms on project management research and practice. The two primary research paradigms have alternatively been referred to as quantitative and qualitative, objectivist and subjectivist, or positivist and interpretivist. For the purposes of this chapter, these paradigms will be referred to as hard and soft, partly to avoid the implication of reference to a particular level in the hierarchy (Figure 17.1), and partly to maintain consistency with the author's prior work.

Evidence suggests that the practice of methodological or theoretical pluralism is not yet well developed within the project management literature. In July 2012 a search was conducted of the full-text electronic copies of the International Journal of Project Management (IJPM) through the Science Direct database and the Project Management Journal through the ProQuest database, with the intention of establishing the penetration of pluralist thought in the PM literature. Terms indicative of pluralism were searched for, including: pluralism, pluralist, incommensurability, incommensurable, multimethodology, critical systems thinking, and triangulation. Results have been summarised in Figure 17.2, with bar height indicating the number of journal articles that mentioned the search term. For discussion, the results have been grouped as results for the search of 'triangulation' and all other terms. From this, it is apparent that terms associated with mixing research approaches are increasingly common. It is also clear that project management research tends to engage at the level of 'triangulation' more commonly than the more methodological concerns associated with 'pluralism' or 'incommensurability'.

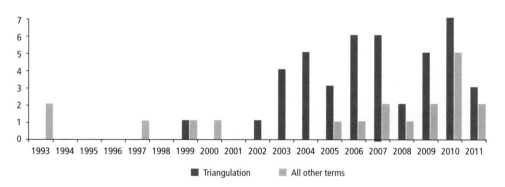

Figure 17.2. Frequency of Papers Including Terms Indicating Pluralism in Project Management Research

Other researchers have commented that Project Management tends to draw on other disciplines, and '… has been more often compared to a heterogenous toolbox than to a body of knowledge in elaboration' (Urli & Urli, 2000: 33). The field is led by practice, with a focus on practical techniques, rather than theory testing and development (Betts & Lansley, 1995: 210). Given this, it is not surprising that of all the search terms used, 'triangulation' was the most popular given the focus of triangulation on the data collection tools and techniques.

A Question of Incompatible Assumptions

At the philosophical level of the hierarchy, the issue of paradigmatic incommensurability is a significant issue to many authors when considering the viability of pluralism. The issue of paradigmatic incommensurability for the combination of different approaches lies in the incompatible assumptions that the philosophies that overarch different approaches make about the world. As their underpinning philosophical assumptions are incompatible, some consider that the associated methodologies, methods, tools and techniques are also incompatible.

The general response in the systems field has been to regard incommensurability as a problem to be resolved; as '… a hard nut to crack …' (Jackson, 1997a: 215). Midgley (1997: 256) notes that some aim towards '… a "unification" of paradigms …' through rational analysis, while it is also a common tactic in the systems field to examine '… how it is possible to stand above the paradigms and work with them in this manner' (Jackson, 2003: 82). To this end, there was a tendency in the CST literature to look for resolution at higher levels of abstraction and to add the prefix 'meta', e.g. metaphilosophy (Gao, Li et al., 2003: 18), metatheory (Midgley, 2003: 108), metamethodology (Jackson, 1999: 19), and metaparadigm (Jackson, 1997b: 370). Metamethodology is viewed as a way to protect paradigm diversity, manage the relationship between the paradigms (Jackson, 1997b: 372) and address the heterogeneity and complexity of problem situations (Jackson, 1999: 19). Due to evaluation problems inherent in the incommensurability between the paradigms, there was a perceived '… need to establish a base for judgements, so that interventionists do not enter an anything goes romp' (Flood & Romm, 1997: 310). It was thought that if practitioners wish to mix approaches '… or bring them together in a framework, we have to justify this at the level of philosophy' (Midgley, 1997: 256).

Some authors, however, choose to point out the irony of the will towards metamethodology as a way to govern pluralism, in that their response then actually involves '… a will to a singular truth …' (White & Taket, 1997: 382). This synthesis of the paradigms at a higher level could actually then be problematic as '… it excludes heterogeneity by (artificially) imposing singularity at a meta-level' (p. 384). Although at one stage it was popular to draw upon the work of philosophers from other disciplines to provide theoretical support for CST, particularly the work of Habermas (Gao, Li et al., 2003: 4), this position has substantially changed. Jackson (1999: 18) has stated that it '… is no longer tenable to believe … that paradigm incommensurability can be solved by reference to some meta-theory such as Habermas' … theories'.

Some authors question whether paradigmatic incommensurability, the lack of comparability between the paradigms, is actually a problem for pluralist practice. Yeo (1993: 116) views the hard and soft paradigms as complimentary and inseparable, emphasising their mutual compatibility rather than their difference, as does Weber (2004). The paradoxes between the different paradigms do not have to be fought, but can be accepted, understanding that both sides of the contradiction have merit (Morgan, 1990: 293-4). To Mingers (1995: 45) the philosophical incompatibility '... does not seem to be a very significant problem. All design starts as concepts and ideas which are debated and developed, but there must be a path towards greater correctness'. Although actors can only operate from within one paradigm at a time (Mingers & Brocklesby, 1997: 497), they '... can operate in different paradigms sequentially over time ...' (Burrell & Morgan, 1979: 25), assuming, of course, that they can overcome personal barriers to such practice. It is unlikely that a single 'resolution' of the paradigm debate can actually be found. More pragmatically, the differences between the paradigms must be accepted and worked with at the level of practice. Pluralists '... must learn to live with and manage a degree of paradigm incompatibility' (Jackson, 1997b: 367).

Barriers to Pluralism

This chapter regards the differing assumptions of the philosophies associated with the hard and soft paradigms as only one of many issues to be managed in combining approaches across paradigms, preferring to focus on practical strategies for surmounting barriers to taking pluralist action in research contexts. However, given the expected benefits from pluralist practice which crosses paradigms, it is relevant to ask why such practice is not more prevalent. A number of barriers to combining approaches across paradigms can be identified in the literature. Philosophically, multiparadigm pluralism faces the problem of paradigmatic incommensurability, which single paradigm pluralism avoids (Mingers, 1997a: 6). Culturally, it has been noted that disciplines tend to split into subcultures around paradigms and practices, and it can be more difficult to 'sell' pluralist research to funding bodies (Mingers, 2003b: 246), while academics might also be concerned about becoming a 'jack of all trades, but master of none' (Brocklesby, 1997: 202).

Psychologically, barriers to adoption relate, in various ways, to the '... problems of an individual agent moving easily from one paradigm to another' (Mingers, 1997a: 13). The adoption of pluralist practice is heavily influenced by a practitioner's previous experience (Brocklesby, 1997: 203; Mingers & Brocklesby, 1997: 507; Munro & Mingers, 2002: 369), and their beliefs and values (Mingers & Brocklesby, 1997: 499). Correspondences have also been identified between personality types and the approaches developed within the different paradigms (Mingers & Brocklesby, 1997: 500; Mingers, 2003b: 246). For instance, it has been identified that '... those towards the quantitative end of the spectrum are often considered more introverted ...' (Wolstenholme, 1999: 423), and that some analysts based in the hard paradigm may feel uncomfortable, if not threatened, by a soft approach (Daniel, 1990: 80-81). However, by contrast Ormerod (1997a: 53) found that no inherent paradigmatic conflict was experienced by participants when moving between states commonly associated with the hard and soft paradigms. 'Participants happily moved from thinking about and debating different points of view to discussing the "facts" and designing good (hopefully the best) strategies.'

Pluralist practice is also dependent upon the specific abilities of the practitioner (Mingers, 1997b: 416), and requires '... comfort with several styles of engagement' (Mingers, 2003b: 246). A practitioner may be required to assume different roles or guises, associated with different paradigms (White & Taket, 1997: 392) and it is a basic requirement of multiparadigm pluralism that the practitioner can '... perform effectively ...' in a particular paradigm (Brocklesby, 1997: 197). For instance, hard methods tend to require mathematical, analytical and computing skills, while soft methods tend to require facilitation and people skills (Munro & Mingers, 2002: 369). This need for skill diversity has been identified as a major feasibility issue for pluralist practice (p. 371), as '... few practitioners ... are well versed in more than one approach' (Ormerod, 1997b: 419). Interestingly, Ormerod sees a positive side to this, stating that designing an intervention is a far from trivial activity, but becomes somewhat simpler if one '... has a limited choice of approaches dictated by personal competence' (p. 424), resulting in a reduction in the number of possible combinations of approaches.

Individual's world views may also cause obstacles to operating within certain paradigms (Mingers & Brocklesby, 1997: 499). Working from within a new paradigm involves more than utilising a new set of linguistic tools (Brocklesby, 1997: 205), as paradigms can influence the fundamental way that meaning is attached to words. For instance, Kaplan and Duchon (1988: 581) found that researchers trained in different approaches regularly understood the same words differently, and that persistent effort was required to understand and uncover these differences. Insights cannot necessarily be transferred easily between approaches from different paradigms (Wolstenholme, 1999: 424). New rules for what is considered to be knowledge have to be incorporated into practice (Brocklesby, 1997: 205), learning the explicit premises of a paradigm is not enough. The beliefs of a lifetime can create a certain inertia of conceptualisation, which require considerable effort to change. Knowing and operating within a paradigm requires that the practitioner becomes bodily involved in the paradigm through experience and practice (Mingers & Brocklesby, 1997: 501), a process which '... may be said to require both a learning and an *un*learning' (Brocklesby, 1997: 209 – original italics). Changing the basic assumptions of what one considers to be knowledge and how one constructs premises concerning the status of reality is no simple feat, something which, '... although manifestly possible, is not often achieved in practice' (Burrell & Morgan, 1979: 24-5).

Frameworks for Managing Pluralist Practice

To conduct multiparadigm pluralist research, a researcher must possess the skills necessary to operationalise varying techniques and be psychologically able to change world-views, while constructing a research methodology that remains internally coherent. Combining '… both perspectives into some kind of "hard-soft" methodological framework of practical utility and consistency is certainly not a straightforward matter' (Miles, 1988: 55). Due to the complexities of this issue, this chapter has sought support from the systems thinking literature, a field which has a long history of debate about ways of combining approaches across paradigms.

Developments in the systems field, and the divide between hard and soft systems thinking, can be thought of as falling into distinct Kuhnian scientific paradigms each with their own assumptions and specialised discourses (Spaul, 1997: 326). Perception that the different paradigms were in competition for the same territory led to the systems movement being regarded as in the throes of a 'Kuhnian crisis' (Jackson, 1987: 150). During the 1980s, a confrontational posture was common between the different schools of the systems movement, which itself was seen as being in the throes of a paradigmatic bind (Spaul, 1997: 326). The different systems schools were seen as incommensurable (Schwaninger, 1997: 148). Before the development of CST, a belief pervaded the field that a practitioner '… simply had to make a choice between the paradigms …' (Brocklesby, 1997: 189).

Arguably, more significant than the debates about paradigmatic incommensurability in the CST literature were the development of strategies for combining approaches from different paradigms in practice.

Reed's Four Strategies

Reed (1985: 174) developed four strategies for combining approaches in the context of organisational studies: isolationism; pragmatism; imperialism; and pluralism. These concepts were adopted by the CST literature as possible tactics for its development (Jackson, 1999), or as strategies for resolving the debate between the hard and soft camps (Fitzgerald and Howcroft, 1998: 313).

The first strategy is isolationism. An isolationist approach involves operating from within a single paradigm, opting for paradigm closure by ignoring the possibilities inherent in other paradigms (Fitzgerald & Howcroft, 1998: 321). Isolationists see their own approaches to problems as self sufficient, believing that there is little, or nothing, to learn from the other paradigms, which may not appear to them as useful or even sensible (Jackson, 1999: 13). It has been found that isolationism is common (Cao, Clarke et al., 1999: 205), with isolationism being particularly popular in organisational cybernetics and traditional management science (Jackson, 1997b: 351). The isolationist strategy can be linked to the belief that the different paradigms are irretrievably incommensurable (Flood & Romm, 1996: 87). 'The isolationist argument has perhaps been advanced most notably by Burrell and Morgan (1979) ...' in their portrayal of different research approaches as mutually exclusive and characterised by disinterested hostility (Fitzgerald & Howcroft, 1998: 321).

Amongst those who actively mix approaches, pragmatism is possibly the most prevalent of the four identified strategies. The pragmatist approach is to bring together the most effective parts of different approaches based solely on what works in practice, without worrying about '... "artificial" theoretical distinctions ...' (Jackson, 1999: 14). In many cases, consultants and management scientists would prefer to focus on the pragmatic concerns of a situation (Brocklesby, 1997: 192), claiming that multiparadigm issues can be effectively dealt with '... in an ad hoc or intuitive manner ...' (p. 203), instead of being distracted by '... theoretical niceties ...' (Jackson, 1999: 13). Due to this unawareness of, or lack of concern for, paradigmatic grounding, people often '... happily mix methods with apparently conflicting philosophical underpinnings ...' (Ormerod, 1997b: 416). However, combining methods without regard for theory has been called '... superficial and perilous' (Lane & Oliva, 1998: 216). 'Pragmatism appears as a form of philistinism which disavows any explanation for action other than the most direct terms of the problem at hand ...' (Spaul, 1997: 327). Furthermore, the lack of attention that pragmatism pays to theory can inhibit the transfer of research findings. Theory provides a common language which can bridge disciplines and application areas, without which it can be difficult to pass on learning and experience to others (Midgley, 1997: 251).

Much like pragmatists, imperialists are willing to combine approaches from apparently conflicting paradigms. However, unlike pragmatism, which demonstrates no commitment to any particular paradigm, imperialism represents a fundamental commitment to one particular paradigm, but a willingness to incorporate methods and techniques from other paradigms when they can be of benefit to the favoured paradigm (Gregory, 2003: 125; Jackson, 1997b: 351), and do not directly contradict the central assumptions of the favoured paradigm (Jackson, 1999: 14). However, imperialism has critics within the CST literature. Imperialism is identified as ultimately failing because of the lack of a general translation scheme for the reduction of arbitrary discourses (Spaul, 1997: 327), and as denaturing approaches that are co-opted to a different paradigm, thus preventing realisation of the approaches' full potential (Jackson, 1999: 13; Jackson, 1997b: 352). However, in passing, it is questioned whether approaches used in such a way aren't *re*natured, instead of *de*natured, perhaps delivering a different, but nevertheless effective potential.

Of Reed's (1985) four strategies, pluralism is the favoured strategy within the CST literature, and '... there are several forms of extant pluralism ...' (Gregory, 1996: 58) within the CST literature. As briefly discussed above, pluralism is the '... use of different methodologies, methods and/or techniques in combination ...' (Jackson, 1997b: 347). A pluralist approach is then differentiated from an imperialist approach in that no one paradigm is assumed to be granted hegemony over an intervention. Like pragmatism, pluralism allows for '... a contingent toolbox approach where different methods with complementary strengths could be used ...' (Fitzgerald & Howcroft, 1998: 321) to suit the needs of an intervention. Similarly, Ragsdell (1998: 510) comments that complementarity '... suggests that no particular strategy is superior, but more or less appropriate for the situation at hand'. Approaches are combined in such a way that they can be adapted to the variety of management problems that arise (Fitzgerald & Howcroft, 1998: 352; Jackson, 1999: 14). However, this does not mean that 'anything goes', that pluralism is atheoretical (Midgley, 1996: 25), or that approaches are purely picked pragmatically to suit the situation, while '... compromising the idiosyncratic observations and principles' (Gao, Li et al., 2003: 5). Instead, pluralists view different approaches and paradigms as complementary, and make explicit use of theory to identify the strengths and weaknesses of different approaches, and the questions to which they are suited (Midgley, 1996: 25). Pluralism can then be thought of as extending through theory to practice: in epistemology, by acknowledging different ways of knowing the world; in ontology, by recognising different types of objects and relations; and in axiology, in recognising different ways of guiding action (Mingers, 2003a: 561).

The System of Systems Methodologies

Midgley (1997: 252) and Mingers (1997a: 5) note that the first real contribution to the developments of a theoretical framework for addressing pluralism in systems thinking was the Jackson and Keys' (2003) System of Systems Methodologies (SOSM). Prior to the development of SOSM it had appeared as if the systems field was undergoing a 'Kuhnian crisis' as hard systems thinking encountered increasing numbers of situations to which it was not suited, and was increasingly challenged by other approaches (Jackson, 2003: 79). Most combinations of approaches in the systems field were then from the perspective of a single paradigm (Jackson, 1997b: 348; Jackson, 1999: 14). SOSM changed this by categorising practice environments and illustrating that different approaches were suited to different applications (Jackson & Keys, 2003: 70). Once '... it became obvious that all systems approaches had their limitations, pursuing pluralism started to look attractive' (Jackson, 1999: 12). SOSM legitimised the existence of methodologies from different paradigms by aligning different paradigms with different areas of concern (p. 15), and represented a shift in the systems field from '... the isolationism of earlier periods to the mechanical complementarism stage' (Gregory, 1996: 298). Nevertheless, SOSM focuses on choice between approaches, not ways of combining them (Jackson, 1997b: 350; Jackson, 1999: 15).

Being Oblique

As discussed above, the connection between paradigm or methodology and the '... methods, tools and techniques usually associated with it, need not be a close one' (Jackson, 1999: 17). There '... are no compelling reasons why an agent should not apply techniques and tools in the service of different philosophical principles or in isolation of the theories that spawned them' (Brocklesby, 1997: 193). Approaches can be detached from their original paradigms and used, critically and consciously, to support different forms of logic (Midgley, 1997: 272; Mingers & Brocklesby, 1997: 498; Mingers, 1997a: 14). Flood and Romm (1997) refer to this practice as the 'oblique use' of a method.

One approach to using methods and techniques divorced from their parent methodology is by first formally decomposing the methodology. Mingers (1997b: 434) suggests a systematic approach to decomposition, based on the distinctions '... between philosophical principles (why, methodological stages (what), and techniques (how) ...' for the purposes of identifying detachable elements, their functions and their purposes. Ormerod (1997b) emphasises combining approaches based on the transformational potential of methodological stages, methods, tools and techniques. He argues that '... the transformational potential of a method is more important than its theoretical underpinnings, that the practical constraints are more important than issues of incommensurability ...' (p. 433). Techniques are often detached from a methodology (Mingers & Brocklesby, 1997: 505), and are usually then being put to the service of a different methodology from the same paradigm (p. 499). However, crossing paradigm borders is also possible, for instance a positivist tool might be incorporated into an interpretivist study (McQuinn, 2002: 385). Otherwise, an interpretivist technique could be used in a non-participative manner, with the assumption that it describes the real world.

The main issue with oblique practice has to do with legitimacy (Mingers, 1997a: 8) due to resulting changes in context and interpretation when a technique is moved between methodologies or paradigms (Mingers, 1997b: 434), requiring a new understanding of the inputs and outputs of an approach used obliquely (Mingers & Brocklesby, 1997: 505), and the new epistemological ramifications which may be associated with any paradigm change. Oblique use does not guarantee failure. However, '... it signals the loss of the intellectual coherence which was originally offered by the separate approaches and which one might well prize ...' (Lane & Oliva, 1998: 216).

Total Systems Intervention

Another significant development in the management of pluralist practice was Total Systems Intervention (TSI), a methodology originally developed by Flood and Jackson (1991a, 1991b). SOSM is at the heart of TSI (Gregory, 1996: 299). The development of TSI partly abated the search for an all encompassing systems methodology (Flood,

2000: 10), and served to legitimate the practice of '… using methodologies adhering to different paradigms in the same intervention on the same problem situation' (Jackson, 1997b: 354), a significant development on that provided by SOSM. Facilitated by the incorporation of SOSM and metaphors based around Morgan's (1986) *Images of Organization*, the process of using TSI can be summarised as iterative cycle between three stages: creativity; choice; and implementation.

TSI still focused on the '… use of "whole" methodologies …' (Jackson, 1997b: 355), instead of using parts of methodologies, but does provide insight into how methodologies can be used obliquely. Imperialism becomes something that is consciously chosen, instead of following on from unquestioned assumptions. 'One methodology, encapsulating the presuppositions of a particular paradigm, is granted "imperialistic" status – but only temporarily; its dominance is kept under continual review' (Jackson, 1999: 16). Other approaches are given a secondary status and operated under the guidance of the temporarily dominant paradigm. The imperialist status of the dominant methodology is regularly reviewed in relation to the needs of the situation at that particular time. If the needs change, then a different set of assumptions may be seen as more appropriate to the situation. The approach that is given imperialist status, and the dominant paradigm, can change, thus providing a new epistemological framework. The imperialist status and the dominant/secondary relationship between approaches changes in relation to which paradigm is held as dominant at a particular time. Imperialist status, oblique use, and the dominant/secondary relationship become aspects of an intervention that are explicitly chosen in response to situational needs.

Grafting One Method onto the Start of Another

Grafting and Embedding are two approaches to combining methodologies that were originally developed by Miles (1998) to manage pluralism in information systems development, but were adopted by the CST literature, and also have application to project management research. Grafting and Embedding have been recognised by a variety of authors (e.g. Rose & Meldrum, 1999: 3; Mathiassen & Nielsen, 2000: 244; Zhu, 2000: 187; Holwell, 2000: 790; Rose, 2002: 250; Avison, Eardley et al., 1998: 455; Calway, 2000: 123; Champion & Stowell, 2002: 273; Oura & Kijima, 2002: 79). However, despite the recognition that these authors give to the value of the distinction between Grafting and Embedding, or Miles' work in general, few make more than passing mention to these different forms of pluralist practice.

Grafting involves attaching a soft approach onto a more traditional, hard practice, allowing for a process of transforming a situation typified by social complexity into a simpler problem to which hard approaches can be applied (Miles, 1988: 56), a way of combining approaches which is also called 'front-ending' (Rose, 1997: 264). Grafting may involve using a soft approach to clarify or explore a situation, before it gives way to a hard methodology (Gammack, 1995: 162).

Although not always referred to as 'Grafting', a variety of authors acknowledge the potential for a sequential movement from soft to hard approaches in an intervention (e.g. Zhu, 2000: 199; Midgley, Gu et al., 2000: 72). Patton (1990: 46) identifies a similar tendency for a flow in research from inductive approaches to deductive hypothesis testing, while Kaplan and Duchon (1988: 574-5) note a tendency for research to flow from qualitative to quantitative techniques. Fitzgerald and Howcroft (1998: 322) identify much the same tendency, with the caution that this is '... a bit simplistic as it precludes the possibility of research endeavours which are both "hard" and exploratory or "soft" and confirmatory'.

A number of issues regarding the use of Grafting have been identified. To Jackson (1997a: 219) Grafting may distort both the soft and hard approaches used, as the soft approaches will be used in the expectation that they will supply one particular kind of result, while the hard approaches '... are operating in an hermeneutic climate and are front-ended by a soft logic'. Zhu (2000: 199) notes that many raise concerns about '... the feasibility and practicality of the perceived "paradigm shift" ...'. For instance, Ormerod (1997a: 52) questions whether a single person could do justice to, and effectively switch between, both the hard and soft paradigms in a Grafting intervention, or how learning could be transferred between the front and end sections of a Grafting intervention if the different sections are managed by experts in the different paradigms. Miles (1988: 56) also notes that Grafting is '... systematic by nature and, therefore, it falls short of a paradigm shift to "soft" systems thinking ...', which, in other words, would make Grafting an imperialist approach, governed by the hard paradigm.

Embedding one Method within Another

Unlike grafting, where different approaches are used sequentially within an intervention, as if they were separate stages in a single method, Embedding involves using hard and soft approaches in parallel (Taylor, Moynihan et al., 1998: 432). This approach involves '... two interrelated levels of methodological operation; "hard" methods are deployed at one level, but in a subordinated manner to operations at a metalevel ...' (Miles, 1988: 57), where iterations of a soft approach can take place. Hard practice becomes embedded in a soft systemic framework (Miles, 1988: 59). The central shift between Grafting and Embedding is in the paradigm that guides the intervention. In Grafting, a soft approach is used in order to bring structure or clarity to a situation so that a hard approach can be used. By contrast, in Embedding, the soft approach provides the philosophical framework for the intervention, with other tools and techniques embedded in it, or subsumed by it (Miles, 1988: 98; Gammack, 1995: 162; Ormerod, 1995: 88). This change in imperialist status illustrates how operating from within a different paradigm can produce models for action which are not simply structurally, but qualitatively, different. In Grafting, an ill structured problem is reduced to a hard one, with the former being treated as a special case of the latter. In Embedding, the hard approach becomes a special case of the soft (Miles, 1988: 56). Hard approaches are then applied when they are considered appropriate (Mingers, 1995: 29), such as when goals momentarily clarify or significant measurable variables are identified.

Embedding provides important advantages, such as engendering '... a sustained collaborative relationship ...' between participants and enabling '... the investigative thrust of a "soft" systems approach to be operated whenever and for as long as its users deem it profitable to do so ...' (Miles, 1988: 59). Unlike the grafting approach, embedding is conducive to sustained collaboration (pp. 58-9), instead of ending the focus on collaboration with the transfer from soft to hard approaches. Ormerod (1997a) notes that concerns about the practitioner's ability to swap between paradigms and transfer knowledge between paradigms '... seem to be better addressed when hard analysis or models are embedded in a soft approach' (p. 52).

Other research (Pollack, 2009) has examined the possibility that a more significant differentiation between Grafting and Embedding is not which paradigm has imperialist status, but the serial or parallel natures of Grafting and Embedding, respectively. Grafting involves using different paradigms in series, while Embedding uses them in parallel. The more general case of Pluralism in Series can involve a movement from soft to hard, or hard to soft. Similarly, the general case of Parallel Pluralism need not entail a soft imperialist status. It would be possible to use the techniques of both hard and soft paradigms within one research project with either under the overarching guidance of the hard paradigm, or while alternating imperialist status throughout the research. Parallel Pluralism also bears some similarity to TSI, but acknowledges that in practice it may be necessary to use parts of methods instead of whole predefined methods, and that multiple changes of imperialist paradigm may be needed to reach the desired research goals.

Discussion

Review of the CST literature has revealed that there are a wide variety of ways in which research involving multiple approaches can be combined. Mingers (1997a: 7) has provided a summary of the different ways in which methodologies and parts of methodologies can be combined, based on the number of methodologies and paradigms involved, on whether the methods are used in the same or different interventions, on whether whole or parts of methodologies are used, and on whether the intervention is governed by one imperialist paradigm or not. Although Table 17.1 was developed to classify different potential combinations of methodologies from different systems thinking paradigms, it can also be effectively used to classify the different potential combination of project management research.

Table 17.1. Different Possibilities for Combining Methodologies (based on Mingers, 1997a: 7)

Type of pluralism	One/more methodologies	One/more paradigms	Same/different intervention	Whole/part methodology	Imperialist or mixed
Methodological isolationism	One	One	-	-	-
Paradigmatic isolationism	More	One	Different	Whole	-
Methodology combination	More	One	Same	Whole	-
Methodology enhancement	More	One	Same	Part	Imperialist
Single paradigm multimethodology	More	One	Same	Part	Mixed
Methodology selection	More	More	Different	Whole	-
Whole methodology management	More	More	Same	Whole	-
Multiparadigm methodology enhancement	More	More	Same	Part	Imperialist
Multiparadigm multimethodology	More	More	Same	Part	Mixed

The Critical Systems Thinking literature has a long tradition of exploring how methodologies can be combined in practice, and this tradition can be used to inform the management of project management research. Of particular significance in developing the discussion of pluralism in project management research are: the distinction between the levels within the paradigm to which a research method belongs; Reed's four strategies for combining methodologies; the oblique use of methods; Grafting and Embedding; and the more general cases of pluralism in Series or Parallel.

References

Avison, D., Eardley, W. & Powell, P. (1998). Suggestions for Capturing Corporate Vision in Strategic Information Systems. *Omega, International Journal of Management Science*, 26(4): 443-59.

Betts, M. & Lansley, P. (1995). International Journal of Project Management: a review of the first ten years. *International Journal of Project Management*, 13: 207-217.

Brocklesby, J. (1997). Becoming Multimethodology Literate: an Assessment of the Cognitive Difficulties of Working Across Paradigms. In Mingers, J. & Gill, A. (Eds.), *Multimethodology: The Theory and Practice of Combining Management Science Methodologies* (pp. 189-216). Chichester, John Wiley & Sons.

Burrell, G. & Morgan, G. (1979). *Sociological Paradigms and Organisational Analysis*, Aldershot, England: Gower Publishing.

Calway, B. (2000). Systems Approach for Virtual Learning Development. *Proceedings of 1st International Conference on Systems Thinking in Management* (pp. 118-123). Technical University of Aschen.

Cao, G., Clarke, S. & Lehaney, B. (1999). Toward systemic management of diversity in organizational change. *Strategic Change* 8: 205-216.

Champion, D. & Stowell, F. (2002). Navigating the Gap Between Action and a Serving Information System. *Information Systems Frontiers*, 4(3): 273-84.

Crawford, L. & Pollack, J. (2004). Hard and soft projects: a framework for analysis. *International Journal of Project Management*, 22: 645-53.

Daniel, D. (1990). Hard problems in a soft world. *International Journal of Project Management*, 8(2): 79-83.

Denzin, N. (1970). *The research act in sociology: A theoretical introduction to sociological methods*, London: Butterworths.

Fitzgerald, B. & Howcroft, D. (1998). Towards dissolution of the IS research debate: from polarization to polarity. *Journal of Information Technology*, 13: 313-26.

Flood, R. (2000). The Relationship of 'Systems Thinking' to Action Research. In Bradbury, H. & Reason, P. (Eds.), *Handbook of Action Research*, London: Sage.

Flood, R. & Jackson, M. (1991). Overview. In Flood, R. & Jackson, M. (Eds.), *Critical Systems Thinking: Directed Readings* (pp. 1-9), Chichester: John Wiley & Sons.

Flood, R. & Romm, N. (1996). Diversity Management: Theory in Action. In Flood, R. & Romm N. (Eds.), *Critical Systems Thinking: Current Research and Practice* (pp. 81-92). New York: Plenum.

Flood, R. & Romm, N. (1997). From MetaTheory to 'Multimethodology'. In Mingers, J. & Gill, A. (Eds.), *Multimethodology: The Theory and Practice of Combining Management Science Methodologies* (pp. 291-322), Chichester: John Wiley & Sons.

Gammack, J. (1995). Modelling subjective requirements objectively. In Stowell, F. (Ed.), *Information systems provision: the contribution of soft systems methodology* (pp. 159-185), Berkshire, England: McGraw-Hill.

Gao, F., Li, M., & Nakamori, Y. (2003). Critical Systems Thinking as a Way to Manage Knowledge. *Systems Research and Behavioral Science*, 20: 3-19.

Gregory, A. (1996). The Road to Integration. Reflections on the Development of Organizational Evaluation Theory and Practice. *Omega*, 24(3): 295-307.

Gregory, W. (2003). Discordant Pluralism: A New Strategy for Critical Systems Thinking. In Midgley, G. (Ed.), *Systems Thinking, Volume 4* (pp. 123-142), London: Sage. Originally published in *Systems Practice*, 1996, 9(6): 605-625.

Holwell, S. (2000). Soft Systems Methodology: Other Voices. *Systemic Practice and Action Research*, 13: 773-98.

Ianni, F. & Orr, M. (1979). Toward a rapprochement of quantitative and qualitative methodologies. In Cook, T. & Reichardt, C. (Eds), *Qualitative and Quantitative Methods in Evaluation Research* (pp. 87-102), Sage.

Jackson, M. (1987). New Directions in Management Science. In Jackson, M. & Keys, P. (Eds), *New Directions in Management Science* (pp. 133-64), Aldershot: Gower.

Jackson, M. (1997a). Critical Systems Thinking and Information Systems Research. In Stowell, F. & Mingers, J. (Eds), *Information Systems: An Emerging Discipline?* (pp. 201-238), London: McGraw-Hill.

Jackson, M. (1997b). Pluralism in Systems Thinking and Practice. In Mingers, J. & Gill, A. (Eds), *Multimethodology: The Theory and Practice of Combining Management Science Methodologies* (pp. 347-78), Chichester: John Wiley & Sons.

Jackson, M. (1999). Towards coherent pluralism in management science. *Journal of the Operational Research Society*, 50: 12-22.

Jackson, M. (2003). The Origins and nature of Critical Systems Thinking. In Midgley, G. (Ed.), *Systems Thinking, Volume 4* (pp. 77-92), London: Sage. Originally published in *Systems Practice*, 1991, 4(2): 131-49.

Jackson, M. & Keys, P. (2003). Towards a System of Systems Methodologies. In Midgley, G. (Ed.), *Systems Thinking, Volume 4* (pp. 59-76), London: Sage. Originally published in *Journal of the Operational Research Society*, 1984, 35: 473-486.

Kaplan, B. & Duchon, D. (1988). Combining Qualitative and Quantitative Methods in Information Systems Research: A Case Study. *MIS Quarterly*, 571-86.

Lai, L. (2000). An Integration of Systems Science Methods and Object-oriented Analysis for Determining Organizational Information Requirements. *Systems Research and Behavioral Science*, 17: 205-228.

Lane, D. C. & Oliva, R. (1998). The greater whole: Towards a synthesis of system dynamics and soft systems methodology. *European Journal of Operational Research*, 107: 214-35.

Mathiassen, L. & Nielsen, P. A. (2000). Interaction and transformation in SSM. *Systems Research and Behavioral Science*, 17: 243-53.

McIntyre, J. (2002). Critical Systemic Praxis for Social and Environmental Justice: A Case Study for Management, Governance, and Policy. *Systemic Practice and Action Research*, 15(1): 3-35.

McQuinn, W. (2002). Comment on how to conduct an action research study in the domain of information systems development. In Ragsdell, G. et al. (Eds.), *Systems

Theory and Practice in the Knowledge Age, New York: Kluwer Academic/Plenum Publishers.

Midgley, G. (1996). The Ideal of Unity and the Practice of Pluralism in the Systems Science. In Flood, R. & Romm N. (Eds), *Critical Systems Thinking: Current Research and Practice* (pp. 25-36), New York: Plenum.

Midgley, G. (1997). Mixing Methods: Developing Systemic Intervention. In Mingers, J. & Gill, A. (Eds.), *Multimethodology: The Theory and Practice of Combining Management Science Methodologies* (pp. 249-290), Chichester: John Wiley & Sons.

Midgley, G. (2003). What Is This Thing Called CST? In Midgley, G. (Ed.), *Systems Thinking: Volume 4* (pp. 109-122), London: Sage. Originally published in *Critical Systems Thinking: Current Research and Practice*, 1996, Flood, R. & Romm, N. (Eds.), Plenum: New York.

Midgley, G., Gu, J. & Campbell, D. (2000). Dealing with Human Relations in Chinese Systems Practice. *Systemic Practice and Action Research*, 13: 71-96.

Miles, R. (1988). Combining 'Soft' and 'Hard' Systems Practice: Grafting or Embedding? *Journal of Applied Systems Analysis*, 15: 55-60.

Mingers, J. (1995). Using soft systems methodology in the design of information systems. In Stowell, F. (Ed.), *Information systems provision: the contribution of soft systems methodology* (pp. 19-49). Berkshire, England: McGraw-Hill.

Mingers, J. (1997a). Multi-paradigm Multimethodology. In Mingers, J. & Gill, A. (Eds), *Multimethodology: The Theory and Practice of Combining Management Science Methodologies* (pp. 1-20), Chichester: John Wiley & Sons.

Mingers, J. (1997b). Towards Critical Pluralism. In Mingers, J. & Gill, A. (Eds), *Multimethodology: The Theory and Practice of Combining Management Science Methodologies* (pp. 407-440), Chichester: John Wiley & Sons.

Mingers, J. (2003a). A classification of the philosophical assumptions of management science methods. *Journal of the Operational Research Society*, 54: 559-70.

Mingers, J. (2003b). The paucity of multimethod research: a review of the information systems literature. *Information Systems Journal*, 13: 233-49.

Mingers, J. & Brocklesby, J. (1997). Multimethodology: Towards a Framework for Mixing Methodologies. *Omega, International Journal of Management Science*, 25: 489-509.

Morgan, G. (1986). *Images of organization*, London: Sage.

Morgan, G. (1990). Paradigm diversity in organizational research. In Hassard, J. & Pym, D. (Eds), *The Theory and Philosophy of Organizations* (pp. 13-29), London: Routledge.

Munro, I. & Mingers, J. (2002). The use of multimethodology in practice – results of a survey of practitioners. *Journal of the Operational Research Society*, 53: 369-78.

Murthy, P. N. (2000). Complex Societal Problem Solving: A Possible Set of Methodological Criteria. *Systems Research and Behavioral Science*, 17: 73-101.

Ormerod, R. (1995). The role of methodologies in systems strategy development: reflections on experience. In Stowell, F. (Ed.), *Information systems provision: the contribution of soft systems methodology* (pp. 75-101), Berkshire, England: McGraw-Hill.

Ormerod, R. (1997a). Mixing Methods in Practice: a Transformation-Competence Perspective. In Mingers, J. & Gill, A. (Eds), *Multimethodology: The Theory and Practice of Combining Management Science Methodologies* (pp. 29-58), Chichester: John Wiley & Sons.

Ormerod, R. (1997b). The Design of Organisational Intervention. *International Journal of Management Science*, 25: 415-35.

Oura, J. and Kijima, K. (2002). Organization Design Initiated by Information System Development: A Methodology and its Practice in Japan. *Systems Research and Behavioral Science*, 19: 77-86.

Patton, M. Q. (1990). *Qualitative Evaluation and Research Methods*, 2 edn. London: Sage.

Pollack, J. (2006). Pyramids or Silos: Alternative Representations of the Systems Thinking Paradigms. *Systemic Practice and Action Research*, 19: 383-98.

Pollack, J. (2009). Multimethodology in series and parallel: strategic planning using hard and soft OR. *Journal of the Operational Research Society*, 60: 156-67.

Pulley, M. L. (1994). Navigating the evaluation rapids. *Training & Development*, 48: 19-24.

Ragsdell, G. (1998). Participatory Action Research and the Development of Critical Creativity: A 'Natural' Combination? *Systemic Practice and Action Research*, 11(5): 503-515.

Reed, M. (1985). *Redirections in organizational analysis*, London: Tavistok.

Reichardt, C. & Cook, T. (1979). Beyond qualitative versus quantitative methods. *Qualitative and Quantitative Methods in Evaluation Research* (pp. 7-32), London: Sage Publications.

Rose, J. (1997). Soft systems methodology as a social science research tool. *Systems Research and Behavioral Science*, 14: 249-58.

Rose, J. (2002). Information, transformation and information systems development – an extended application of Soft Systems Methodology. *Information Technology & People*, 15(3): 242-68.

Rose, J. & Meldrum, M. (1999). Requirements generation for web-site developments using SSM and the ICDT model. *Proceedings of BIT '99*. Manchester Metropolitan University: UK.

Schwaninger, M. (1997). Status and Tendencies of Management Research: a Systems Oriented Perspective. In Mingers, J. & Gill, A. (Eds.), *Multimethodology: The Theory and Practice of Combining Management Science Methodologies* (pp. 127-51), Chichester: John Wiley & Sons.

Skyrme, D. J. (1997). Multimethodologies – the Knowledge Perspective. In Mingers, J. & Gill, A. (Eds), *Multimethodology: The Theory and Practice of Combining Management Science Methodologies*, (pp. 217-240), Chichester: John Wiley & Sons.

Spaul, M. (1997). Multimethodology and Critical Theory: an Intersection of Interests? In Mingers, J. & Gill, A. (Eds.), *Multimethodology: The Theory and Practice of Combining Management Science Methodologies* (pp. 323-46), Chichester: John Wiley & Sons.

Spencer, L., Ritchie, J., Lewis, J. & Dillon, L. (2003). *Quality in Qualitative Evaluation: A framework for assessing research evidence.* Accessed Online at http://www.strategy.gov.uk/files/pdf/Quality_framework.pdf, UK Cabinet Office: Government Chief Social Researcher's Office.

Taylor, M., Moynihan, E. & Wood-Harper, A. (1998). Soft Systems Methodology and Systems Maintenance. *Systemic Practice and Action Research*, 11(4): 419-434.

Urli, B. & Urli, D. (2000). Project Management in North America, Stability of the Concepts. *Project Management Journal*, 31: 33-43.

Weber, R. (2004). Editor's Comments: The Rhetoric of Positivism Versus Interpretivism: A Personal View. *MIS Quarterly*, 28(1): iii-xii.

White, L. & Taket, A. (1997). Critiquing Multimethodology as Metamethodology: Working Towards Pragmatic Pluralism. In Mingers, J. & Gill, A. (Eds), *Multimethodology: The Theory and Practice of Combining Management Science Methodologies* (pp. 379-405), Chichester: John Wiley & Sons.

Wolstenholme, E. (1999). Qualitative vs quantitative modelling: the evolving balance. *Journal of the Operational Research Society*, 50: 422-28.

Yeo, K. T. (1993). Systems thinking and project management – time to reunite. *International Journal of Project Management*, 11: 111-117.

Zhu, Z. (2000). WSR: A systems approach for information systems development. *Systems Research and Behavioral Science*, 17(2): 183-203.

Conclusion

A *Near Future* for Doing Research in OPM

Nathalie Drouin, Ralf Müller and Shankar Sankaran

The idea for this book started in the imagination of the three editors during a coffee break in the faculty cafeteria of Umea University in Sweden. Around the coffee machine, a good idea was born, the way most projects are initiated! This idea then worked its way to the current title, *Novel Approaches to Organizational Project Management Research, using Translational and Transformational Research*. The book gradually took shape and work was continued by a geographically dispersed team (with the editors living in Montreal, Canada, Malmö, Sweden, and Sydney, Australia) mimicking a virtual project team. Getting the book ready on time for publication involved finding collaborating authors around the world from seven different countries (Australia, Canada, China, Denmark, France, Norway and Scotland), who were ready to support our idea enthusiastically. Various research perspectives, angles and methods were scrutinized by these authors with diverse profiles that promote multidisciplinary exchanges to enrich and transform our thoughts on conducting organizational project management research. Technologies supported by the internet helped us throughout this process to become more accessible and the barriers of distance disappeared. Of course, our families were wondering what we three were up to in the unearthly hours talking over Skype. Nevertheless, we should bear in mind that this great adventure began with a face-to-face meeting, where friendship between editors was initiated and expanded to collaborators.

The intent behind this book is to open the minds of project management researchers' to the necessity of transforming and translating knowledge from various sources including allied fields into OPM research to raise the level and variety of research approaches that they employed. Transformation relates to the need to change, and to change, we need to identify what we should change first and how we can translate this change into practice. To encourage the researchers to do this, we identified and approached representative thinkers who became our collaborators to share their reflections, bring variety in perspectives, philosophies and methodologies to foster progression in our project management field. To us this is just a beginning. We do not claim to have developed exhaustive approaches to translate and transform research in OPM. This book presents and discusses, what we believe, to be reasonable examples of the most representative contemporary methods that will also need to evolve over time. We should always keep in mind that:

There is nothing permanent except change
(Heraclitus, c.535BCE-.475 BCE, Greek philosopher)

A Progression of Key Learnings

Throughout the book, a progression of key learnings is offered to the reader. Section 1, for instance addresses the contemporary understanding of research philosophies and their impact on research design and theory building. The contributing chapters show a clear trend towards plurality in perspectives, multi-paradigm approaches and the integration of the results from multi-paradigm research in the form of a disciplined search for complementarities, and convergent and divergent results in order to build a holistic understanding of research phenomena. Moreover, the growing importance of various forms of discourse at different points in time has been shown, such as during research design, during sampling of informants, and when communicating results for acceptance by a wider public. These two trends are interlinked. Increasing plurality in philosophical perspectives requires more disciplined integration during research design, execution and communication of results, which is achieved through more discourse and more communities to discourse with, such as academics, practitioners and the wider public. Looking into the future, we see the increase in philosophical plurality and discourse as a clear trend for several years to come.

In Section 2, the interlinked view of plurality and discourse is extended to research designs. Due to the recent interest in managing complexity in projects and the demand by researchers and practitioners for more emphasis on detailed investigation of what is occurring in actual practice, classical project management research methodologies fail to accurately mirror the experience of practitioners. Thus, the contributing chapters in Section 2 drew upon some contemporary research approaches from allied fields that are beginning to be used by project management researchers. The chapters in this section looked at dialectical approaches to study actuality in projects, and observe and reflect on changes that occur during projects. The utility of simulations that could aid in troubleshooting as well as study research situations in projects using model-ling was explored. Section 2 concluded with how you can investigate various aspects of a phenomenon under study using a variety of methods to enrich understanding of a specific aspect by setting it up as a research program. Thus, we begin to see the increased need for research designs and methods to study human actions and activities that capture the softer side of project management (such as political and cultural issues) besides studying the hard side.

Section 3 provides guidance to more rigorously integrate, while designing, executing and communicating results, communication theories, concepts and approaches from allied fields to complement thereby enriching potential research. Again, chapters in this section challenge traditional well-established views in OPM to foster the development of new research areas in projects. Contributing chapters in Section 3 sketch important concepts from the social sciences of management and the natural sciences perspectives. OPM research cannot afford to ignore the knowledge development from these dominant fields to avoid constraining academic thinking. What this means for researchers is that they should leave their comfort zones and explore new conceptual directions that may take more time to master but are worth the effort, to improve the quality and richness in their research approaches.

Section 4 focuses on combining methods to study projects. It helps researchers to use a palette of approaches to conduct deeper and focused studies. It elevates project research to a higher level of research design in translating the knowledge so far discussed throughout the book into practice. To manage research across paradigms, the contributing chapters of this final explores how theory development and methodologies can be interwoven to inform the management of project management research. The section starts with ways to apply strategic management theories and research approaches from the strategic management field. It then takes a detailed exploration of mixed and multiple methods in research design, drawing from a long tradition of critical systems thinking literature. In sum, the section addresses the need to reinvent organizational project management research by placing it on a new and innovative foundation.

A Near Future in Research in our Field: Where to Now?

This book has been a tremendous opportunity for the editors to collaborate and bring together the experience and knowledge of prominent researchers in the field of project management and allied fields to share their willingness to change and improve the ways on how we conduct research in project management. James Baldwin (1924-1987), an African-American writer, once said: 'Not everything that is faced can be changed, but nothing can be changed until it is faced.' With this book, we face the reality that something needs to be done: to improve the rigour in conducting research in our field and, to increase its credibility to be recognized as a solid research domain. We hope that the book will allow researchers to improve the richness of their research in the field of project management by providing novel approaches to further develop organizational project management research. To give some guidance on where to go now, we developed the *equation of knowledge development* made up of three footsteps to stimulate more contemporary research methods and rigour in the discourse on organizational project management.

This equation reflects each section of the book to provide the reader with directions to develop stronger research foundations by using multi-paradigm research. It opens the door to a more scholar-practitioner perspective and places a higher level of importance on the need to develop pluralistic understanding of OPM. It proposes that we not only become more innovative and creative with regards to methodologies we use to conduct research, but also develop the capability to learn and get inspired from well-established theories. It proposes a progression of key learnings to be combined to slowly but surely transform the discourse in our project management field and translate to promising new perspectives and methods. Overall, the co-editors do not expect transformation to happen overnight but hope that this book will inspire you to start taking steps toward a sustainable change in the way we do research in OPM. If this is accomplished then the aims of the book would be fulfilled.

Enjoy!